S0-EKN-648

BUSINESS COMMUNICATION

PRINCIPLES AND APPLICATIONS

WILEY SERIES IN BUSINESS COMMUNICATION

The manuscript for this book was developed under the guidance of C. Glenn Pearce, Consulting Editor for Business and Organizational Communication. Dr. Pearce is a professor at Virginia Commonwealth University.

JOHN WILEY & SONS

WILEY

NEW YORK
CHICHESTER
BRISBANE
TORONTO
SINGAPORE

BUSINESS COMMUNICATION

PRINCIPLES AND APPLICATIONS

SECOND EDITION

C. Glenn Pearce
Virginia Commonwealth University

Ross Figgins
California State Polytechnic University

Steven P. Golen
Arizona State University

Production supervised by Laura McCormick
Cover and text design by Sheila Granda
Cover illustration by Roy Weimann

Photo Credit List

Part 1 Opener: Laimute E. Druskis/Taurus Photos. Part 2 Opener: Courtesy IBM. Part 3 Opener: Suzanne Szasz/Photo Researchers. Part 4 Opener: Ken Karp. Part 5 Opener: Bill Gallery/Stock, Boston. Part 6 Opener: Rhoda Sidney/Monkmeyer.

ISBN 0-471-84851-4

Printed in the United States of America

10 9 8 7 6 5 4 3 2 1

This book is dedicated to

My parents, in memory
—Glenn

My wife, Jacque Weiss, in memory
—Ross

My wife, Dorothy
—Steven

PREFACE

This second edition of *Business Communication: Principles and Applications* has been extensively revised. Everything from content and organization to approach has been changed.

WHAT'S NEW?

The book has been completely rewritten to make the style simpler, the pace faster, and the tone friendlier and more interesting. Intriguing and informative scenarios have been added to get each chapter started and to illustrate *every* major point made in the book. Truly, this second edition is a book of explanations! And, of course, everything has been completely updated.

A great amount of new material has been added. This includes Chapter 5 on business communication technology, Chapter 7 on routine letters and memos, a chapter on communicating in international business, one-half a chapter on proposals, an appendix on legal and ethical issues in business communication, standard grading symbols, and several long cases at the end of both Part 4 on employment and Part 5 on report writing.

Many sections have been expanded to include desirable new material. For example, there are now 15 questions instead of the original 10 at the end of every chapter, and many more exercises have been added, especially letter, memo, and report problems. Also, more examples of resumes, application letters, and computer graphics have been included, along with checklists at the end of every chapter and within many chapters. More information has been added on listening skills, oral reports, data bases, and the principles of business communication.

Several other revisions will enhance the usefulness of the book. One is that the popular chapter on communication barriers has been revised to add depth to the discussion, and the chapter has been moved to Part 1 of the book—Chapter 2. Another is that the planning and data collection phases of report writing have been merged into one chapter, giving the report writing part five chapters instead of the original six. Another is that every type of letter or memo covered in correspondence is now illustrated by using the "first draft/critique/revised draft" technique that was so well received in the first edition. Yet another change is that the discussion of interpersonal and group communication in the first edition has been rewritten to emphasize interviewing and holding successful meetings and conferences. Other changes are that the entire book is more extensively illustrated, and the chapter summaries are now in list format for easy reference.

The changes really are too numerous to mention them all in a short preface, but they do combine to make the revised edition a truly innovative, up-to-date text for your use in a business communication class. Every change was made with both the instructor and the student in mind. After all, you are our friends and colleagues and we are here to serve you just as well as we possibly can.

ORGANIZATION OF THE TEXT

You are bound to like the much, improved organization of the text. It looks like this:

Part I covers theory and principles in four chapters. Chapter 1 presents language and communication (theory); Chapter 2, overcoming communication barriers; Chapter 3, fundamental writing techniques; and Chapter 4, style and tone. Then Part 2 covers communication technology in two chapters. Chapter 5 presents and explains the technology itself, and Chapter 6 covers word processing and dictation, including how they are actually done. This is *applied* instructional material.

Letters and memos are presented in four chapters in Part 3. Chapters 7 and 8 cover good news—routine requests, favorable responses, and goodwill messages. Chapter 9 covers bad news and Chapter 10 persuasion. Part 4, a popular part in the first edition, follows with two chapters on employment—Chaper 11 on the employer's role in the process and Chapter 12 on the applicant's role. As mentioned earlier, a series of comprehensive cases on timely employment topics follows at the end of this part to round out the discussion.

Part 5, which covers written reports, is organized into five chapters that proceed step by step from the planning stage to the report writing stage. Specifically, Chapter 13 is on planning the process and data collection; Chapter 14 on organizing, interpreting, and outlining data; Chapter 15 on visual aids; Chapter 16 on the formal report; and Chapter 17 on informal reports and proposals. And as mentioned earlier, a set of comprehensive cases that draw on the student's grasp of the entire report writing process are included at the end of this part.

The last part of the text proper, Part 6, presents oral communication and several special applications in four chapters. Chapter 18 covers oral presentations and oral reports. Chapter 19 covers listening and nonverbal communication. Chapter 20 covers interviews, meetings, and conferences; and Chapter 21 covers a variety of exciting aspects of communication in international business. This part is followed by a comprehensive series of appendices on the following topics: grammar review (also available on computer software with exercises), correspondence parts and format, research reference sources, documentation methods, reading skills, and legal and ethical issues.

ACKNOWLEDGMENTS

Few books are ever written unassisted, and this one is no exception. We owe a debt of gratitude to a host of outstanding professionals, too many in fact to mention all of them by name. We are particularly grateful to the following individuals, who have played a vital role in bringing this new edition to reality.

Dr. R. Jon Ackley, Chairman of the Department of Management at Virginia Commonwealth University, wrote the new chapter on writing routine request letters and memos, Chapter 7, and the chapter on the applicant's role in finding a job, Chapter 12. Dr. David Hogge, President of The Written Word, a consulting firm in Richmond, Virginia and an adjunct business communication faculty member at Virginia Commonwealth University, revised the chapters on unfavorable news and persuasive letters and reports—Chapters 9 and 10. Also, several evening students at Virginia Commonwealth University wrote some of the letter and memo cases for Chapters 9 and 10. Each of these cases is based on an on-the-job experience. The students were Scott J. Barnes, Rodney D. Brown, Barbara A. Bush, Teresa Earles, Alice Hardy, Karen E. Holgate, Holly A. Morookian, Dennis W. Motley, Susan N. Sandland, Alison W. Smith, Michael J. Walsh, and Kenneth Wolf. Professor Virginia Steel, Business Librarian at the Arizona State University, updated and revised the appendix on business research reference sources, Appendix C.

The reviewers, who read the copy and gave us invaluable feedback, were as follows: Brenda Baity, California State University; Carolyn Beth Camp, Linn-Benton Community College, Corvallis, Oregon; Meada Gibbs, North Carolina A & T State University; Jean Gonzalez, Cypress College, Cypress, California; Gail Hotelling, SUNY/Delhi; Larry Hudson, California State University; Gail Hoffman Johnson, Delta College, University Center, Michigan; Edwina Jordan, Illinois Central College; Retha Hoove Kilpatrick, Western Carolina University; Jewel Linville, Northeastern State University, Tahlequah, Oklahoma; John Waltman, Eastern Michigan University; and Thomas Willard, University of Arizona.

Several people who provided different types of encouragement and assistance are Hugh Wilson of Richmond, Virginia, who managed production and provided editorial assistance while the text was being written; Jeanette W. Gilsdorf of Arizona State University, who gave especially valuable assistance and support; and Claire Thompson, Lynn McElroy, and Erika Levy of John Wiley, who coordinated the project and kept everything moving along smoothly and efficiently. We are are also grateful to the editorial, production, and design staff at John Wiley—Deborah Herbert, Laura McCormick, Sheila Granda, and Sally Ann Bailey, among others.

Those people who played a fundamental role in the development of the first edition of this book must be remembered too. Their influence has carried over to the second edition in a thousand ways. They are the following: Ray Beswick of Syncrude Canada Ltd.; Ed Goodin of the University of Nevada, Las Vegas; Bill G. Rainey of East Central University; Natalie R. Siegle of Providence College; Lois Bachman of the Community College of Philadelphia; Hilda Allred of Kingston, Rhode Island; Jean W. Vining of Houston Community College; Mary Ellen Adams of Indiana State University; David P. Dauwalder of California State University; Doris Engerrand of Georgia College; G. Pepper Holland of Mississippi State University; Patti Ernst of Fort Smith, Arkansas; Alfred B. Williams of the University of Southwesten Louisiana; Belford E. Carver of Southeastern Louisiana University; Pernell H. Hewing of the University of Wisconsin-Whitewater; William Neal of Utah State University; Joann Spitler of Virginia Commonwealth University, Laura B. Greer of John Tyler Community College; Annelle Bonner of the University of Southern Mississippi; Gretchen N. Vik of San Diego State University; Vanessa Dean Arnold of the University of Mississippi; Russell A. Duke of George Mason University; Bobbi Rothstein of the University of Rhode Island; Martha H. Rader of Arizona State University; C. Jeanne Lewis of Fayetteville State University; Christine Horn of Grand Prairie Regional College; Hilda M. Jones of Oregon State University; Merryl S. Penson of Columbus College; Halsey Taylor of California State Polytechnic University; Leonard Kruk of Shaw-Walker Corporation; Marietta Spring and Gaye C. Dawson, both of Virginia Commonwealth University; and Pat Fitzgerald and Cindy Zigmund, both of John Wiley & Sons.

A special thanks goes out to all the students and instructors who used the first edition of this book. Thanks to you, there is a second edition. And to those who haven't yet used the book, please consider giving us a trial. Based on what our earlier users have said about how much they enjoyed using the material, we feel confident that if you use the book you will be glad you did.

C. G. P.
R. F.
S. P. G.

CONTENTS

PART 1

COMMUNICATION THEORY AND PRINCIPLES

CHAPTER 1

LANGUAGE AND COMMUNICATION

This book is about *business communication.* The focus is on developing your ability to use sound communication principles in business situations. Effective communication depends on establishing a common understanding with others. To accomplish this, we use language—the language of our bodies and the language of written or spoken words. It is not necessary to become a language specialist to communicate effectively on the job. But some knowledge of language theory will help you to understand the processes of writing and speaking clearly. Chapter 1 reviews the general characteristics of language and meaning, showing the ways people send and process messages. It also discusses how to apply communication theory so that you may move toward effective business communication.

NATURE AND CHARACTERISTICS OF LANGUAGE

What is language? If your answer is "words," you have the right idea, for language is *words (or other symbols) communicated in a meaningful order.* For example, if you move the words around in this sentence, you would probably either alter its meaning *or* make it meaningless.

How would you define language?

When used in certain ways, words can evoke meaning for other people, but words themselves do not have meaning. They are simply symbols that people have agreed will represent certain things or thoughts. Language and people, then, are interdependent. Language cannot exist without people to assign it meaning and use it, nor can people exist in communities without using language. Yet, while language is universal in that all humans use it, it is also specific, individual. When you select words to communicate messages, and when you apply meaning to messages sent by others, you are reflecting your own personality and your own thoughts.

Language then is a system of symbols that

1. Represents meaning agreed upon by those who use it.
2. Communicates ideas using an agreed-upon structure.
3. Acts as a primary means for people to communicate with one another.
4. Passes human knowledge from one generation to the next.
5. Reflects the personalities of individuals and societies.
6. Represents a society's interests and values.
7. Changes to meet a society's needs.
8. Enables abstract thought.

By examining these qualities of language, we can begin to understand the relationship between language and meaning. Without meaning, language has no value. With meaning, or content, you can use language to communicate ideas and share knowledge.

The Five Elements of Language

Stop for a moment and try to recall what you were just thinking about. Suppose, for example, that you were thinking of your first job interview. Behind these thoughts is a series of mental pictures, for example, what the personnel manager looked like, where the interview was held, or perhaps where you were when the personnel manager called to offer you the job.

How does it help to know the elements of language?

All of us carry such pictures of reality in our minds. These images—experiences—shape our viewpoints and, therefore, can be said to influence our thoughts and actions. As new information enters our experience, altering it, so are our viewpoints also altered. Our individuality—who we are—is the sum of all these experiences. It is hardly surprising then that people often have different viewpoints about the same circumstance.

People use language to define and redefine their experiences in the world about them, including their business environment, every day. At the same time, because language is imprecise, it is the source of much misunderstanding. You can eliminate much of this misunderstanding through an awareness of the basic elements of language, that is, recognizing that language is *artificial, limited, abstract, arbitrary*, and *redundant*.

How Is Language Artificial?

Language is a creation of people. No word or other symbol has any reality outside the minds of those who use it. The symbols do not exist until speakers create them. Each symbol is attached, through usage habits, to particular thoughts or things, called *referents*.

How do referents relate to language's being artificial?

For instance, a recently invented device allowed computer users to manipulate what they saw on the screen without touching the keyboard or the screen. When the user slid this invention—a small rectangular box—around on the desk top, a little light moved on the screen.

The quick, gliding movement of the device and the light reminded the developers of a mouse. The term "mouse" now has a meaning not faintly imagined before the introduction of this device.

The process by which this particular naming occurred is easy to trace. That is not always the case. But, regardless of whether we know how a word came into common usage, the important point is that we have selected it for use—from the almost limitless choices available—in a particular way. Language is artificial because it exists only because we human beings have created it and modified it as need be.

Most of our impressions of the "real world" are determined by language habits. Even though language is an artificial creation, "invented" to describe reality, it influences our view of what reality is and how we understand it. The problem with this relationship is that we sometimes change one, the symbols (the language), and feel that we have altered the other, reality.

How Is Language Limited?

Language approximates the real world. No word or symbol can stand for the full reality of anything, or transmit that full reality from one person's mind to another's. Think of a favorite co-worker. Suppose his name is Bob.

If you are reporting to a supervisor on work you've done together, the symbol "Bob" is the only symbol available to stand for this person. The actual *thought* of Bob in your mind is a faster than light jumble of "Bob–nice–and funny–and hard working" and "I'm a little jealous because he solves problems faster than I do" and "People around here don't appreciate what Bob is worth" and "Bob got up grumpy yesterday" and dozens of other impressions, facts, and emotions that make up your mental construct of the symbol "Bob."

Is language fixed or does it change with time?

A symbol is limited, then, in the amount of meaning it can carry. In addition, reality constantly changes, while most language symbols remain fairly fixed. (Language does change—but very slowly.) "Bob" today is not quite the same as "Bob" yesterday. The "office" last week, before the new manager arrived, is not the same as the "office" will be two weeks from now.

Because we keep using the same symbols even when reality changes, we may tend not to perceive the changes quite as they are. Picture a building you worked in several years ago and have not seen since. Although it has probably changed in some ways, the words you might use to describe it would describe the old reality of your mental picture.

This example illustrates our problem: How do we use a fairly fixed set of created symbols to stand for a complex and changing reality? The limited nature of language can and does lead to communication difficulties—as in the case of the outmoded company policies that do not keep pace with what employees actually do.

Because language is limited, we frequently supplement words with other kinds of symbols. Have you ever noticed people using their hands while they talk? They do it to enliven their words or describe things that are beyond simple verbal description such as the cut of a business suit or the shape of a spiral staircase. What kind of symbols would you use to explain to someone in a letter the sound a certain copying machine makes when its almost out of paper?

For another example, assume that you have just accepted a job in another city but you've never visited the company's offices. You telephone to ask how your new office is furnished. You learn that you'll have ten pieces of office furniture: a desk, a swivel chair, a computer table, two bookcases, two side chairs, two files, and a waste-basket. Would you be able to tell the person you're talking to how you would like the furniture arranged?

How can you supplement language with other symbols?

It wouldn't be easy, but it could be done. The other person would have to describe the office exactly, so that you would understand it, and you'd have to explain exactly where you wanted each piece of furniture, so that the receiver would understand it.

The effort and time required, because language does not satisfy this purpose effectively, might lead you to decide to wait until you got there to do your office arranging.

But suppose you discovered that the company had another office in your area and that the two locations were linked by computer. Using a graphics program you could ask for a diagram of your new office and then draw the furnishings exactly where you wanted them placed.

What these examples illustrate is the finite quality of language. Language is only a sketch of the most apparent and pertinent features of anything. For this reason, communicators must remember two things:

How can you avoid problems based on the limitations of language?

1. They must avoid mistaking changed reality because of unchanged language.
2. They must be careful to use language as accurately as possible *and*, when appropriate, supplement it with a range of alternatives, from simple graphics or gestures to audio or visual recordings.

How Is Language Abstract?

Language is abstract because words always represent generalized ideas of things or thoughts. This means that an idea is never quite the same each time you use the word representing it. For example, you may use the word *building* to represent anything from a skyscraper to a cottage. Even if you are more specific and use the word *skyscraper*, you are still employing an abstraction, as skyscrapers come in innumerable sizes, shapes, and so forth. To abstract is to generalize, and to generalize is to leave out many details.

Abstraction is essential because all knowledge is based on the ability to generalize successfully. When we discover a number of similar items, for example, paper clips, staples, and thumbtacks, we group, or categorize, them through abstraction, labeling them as fasteners. This ability to categorize frees us from the need to redefine constantly all the new information we receive. Instead, we process it in terms of what we already know. If this were impossible, we would be unable to make sense of anything we had not experienced.

Does moving up the ladder of abstraction indicate gaining or losing details?

Words differ in their level of abstraction. As things or thoughts become increasingly abstract, the words that represent them lose more and more details. As a result, they are increasingly removed from the reality of everyday experience. Figure 1-1 shows a sequence of generalizations as a ladder of abstraction. Note that each word is a subcategory of the one above it. In other words, each step up the ladder represents a broader language category, a sort of language shorthand. Because we can categorize ideas through abstraction, we can use language to communicate progressively more abstract and

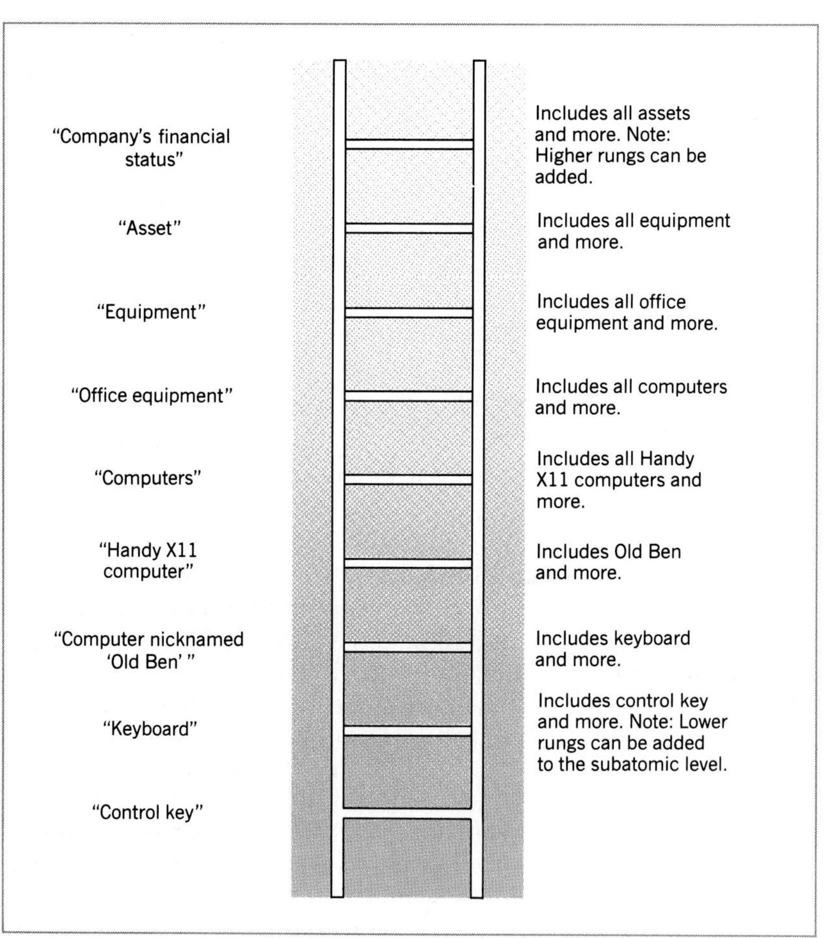

FIGURE 1-1 Ladder of abstraction.

complex ideas. In your own life, *if you know the correct words to use, you can communicate at the very specific or very general level that best fits your purpose at the time.*

How Is Language Arbitrary?

What is the relationship between a word and what it stands for?

Language is arbitrary because no inherent relationship exists between a word and the thing or thought it represents. A word represents a specific thing or thought only because people who speak a language agree that it does. All languages set up some sort of arbitrary relationship between words and things or thoughts. For example, the word *maison* in French and the word *casa* in Spanish are as arbitrary as our own word *house.*

A language, whether it is English, French, or Spanish, is a cultural system of agreements in which words represent certain things or thoughts. Learning these agreements is part of learning the language.

The arbitrary nature of language causes problems when a word undergoes a change in meaning or agreement. Sometimes the change may not be universally accepted. For example, when microcomputers were introduced into the office, *typing* or *typewriting* became, at least for some, *keyboarding.* While some people may feel that keyboarding and typing are the same, others see them as representing different activities.

This shows us that while language can change to include new concepts, words can come to have a number of specific and arbitrary meanings.

How Is Language Redundant?

Does redundancy make it easier or harder to interpret language?

Every language has the capacity for redundancy, or repetition, that may aid or impede effective communication. On the one hand, repetition may allay confusion by reinforcing a message. For example, look at this simple sentence: *A couple of realtors are driving their cars to the meeting.* How many signals do you find in it indicating the presence of more than one person? Five! The first two are the plural nouns, *realtors* and *cars.* The third is the agreement of the verbs—*are driving.* The fourth and fifth are the words *couple* and *their.* As you can easily see, here redundancy clarifies meaning.

On the other hand, redundancy may contribute to wordiness by adding to the number of symbols needed to express an idea correctly and clearly. This situation is clearly shown in the analysis of the sentence example. At the same time, however, that you might delete a word to eliminate wordiness, you would eliminate some meaning. Perhaps you might avoid this problem by asking, "How correct and how clear do I need to be to get across my desired meaning?" Redundancy becomes a problem if you add unneeded words or repeat the same idea unnecessarily. In addition, when making a decision about cutting repetitive segments, be sure to consider the receiver's familiarity with the subject as well as its complexity and ambiguity.

How Words Get Their Meaning

Meaning is the significance we attach to words. Assigning such meaning is part of the selective process people use to make sense of the world. We derive meaning through a process that involves three components: *referents, thoughts,* and *words.* A thought is a perception in a person's mind. Through thought, we are able to assign a symbol to a referent, or thing, the symbol will represent. A word is a symbol assigned to represent a referent. To illustrate how the process works, assume that you see a slip of paper currency with the head of George Washington on one side (referent), think about it (thought), and then say *dollar* (word). A simple diagram of meaning looks like this:

What three components are involved in deriving meaning from words?

The meaning of a word is accurate to the extent that the accepted relationship in the real world between it and its referent coincide. The study of the meanings of words, their relationships, is called *semantics.*

When we deal with something physical such as a dollar, the process is clear. But it is less clear when something nonphysical or abstract is involved. For example, there are no physical referents for the words *love* and *hate.* We form their referents through our experiences of these emotions or feelings rather than by direct observation of them in the physical world.

As meaning becomes more abstract, does it also become more objective?

In these instances the relationship between thoughts and words is abstract; that is, it has neither a physical base nor properties. Unlike the word *memorandum,* for example, where we can point to a type of message, we cannot test the accurate use of an abstract word such as *love* to something external. Instead, we check it by noting examples of its use by others and seeing if ours corresponds to theirs. In this way, we are able to create mental referents for abstract words.

From this you can see that as meaning becomes more abstract, it also becomes more subjective. With greater subjectivity, the opportunities for disagreement and misunderstanding also increase. Therefore, to ensure accuracy in your business communications, try to use the most concrete words possible. But be warned. Even if you do, you will never achieve complete accuracy, because meaning—since it exists only in our minds—is itself an abstraction. The meaning assigned to words can differ subtly or greatly from person to person. Often these discrepancies do not create noticeable problems on the job. But sometimes a significant miscommunication occurs.

One way you can avert such a difficulty is to recognize that many words have special meanings beyond their dictionary definitions. A word's *denotative* meaning is its literal or dictionary definition. This meaning represents the word's most widely accepted usage, the one most people agree on. In contrast, a word can have an implied or *connotative* meaning, which is not found in the dictionary, but is the individual meaning people give it. For example, the dictionary defines the word *aggressive* as "marked by combative readiness" or "forceful energy and initiative." However, *aggressive* also has a connotative meaning, and it can imply, depending on who is using it, a desirable or undesirable trait. To some people, someone who is aggressive tries to dominate others, disregarding their rights. To others, an aggressive person has bold self-confidence.

How do denotative and connotative meaning differ?

As this example shows, denotative meaning is more objective than is connotative meaning. For this reason, if you want to lessen the possibility of misunderstanding, avoid using words with connotative meanings whenever possible in your business environment. And, if you must use such words for special reasons, be very sure you know the connotation the receiver will apply.

HUMAN FACTORS THAT AFFECT COMMUNICATION

Of course, effective communication involves more than words and meaning. For example, words cannot exist without people, and human factors affect the outcome of every communication. The major factors are level of communication, internal filters, and receiver's background.

Levels of Communication

How can you categorize language from simple to complex?

A helpful way to view communication is to divide it into four categories of message processing from the simple to the complex, from individuals to groups. These divisions or levels of communication are *intrapersonal, interpersonal, organizational,* and *mass.*

Intrapersonal communication occurs within the individual. It is the electrochemical system that links all parts of the body with the brain. For example, if you begin to "feel cold" (information received by the body and sent to the brain), you may decide to "turn up the thermostat" (information sent from the brain to the hand). Intrapersonal communication also involves thinking that is the foundation of all message processing. Without first communicating internally, we cannot proceed to the other levels. In fact, even when we speak to others, we continue a simultaneous internal dialogue with ourselves—weighing, considering, planning, processing information.

Interpersonal communication is direct one-to-one engagement. Usually, it takes the form of two people speaking together on a face-to-face basis. The advantage of this form of communication is that feedback (response) is immediate. In contrast, organizational and mass communication assumes a receiver(s) who is not in the same location as the sender. These levels of communication rely on various technologies (or media) to transfer the message. Memos, letters, and reports are examples of organizational communication, whereas radio, television, and newspapers are examples of mass communication. Organizational and mass communication (which sometimes share similar technologies) have the advantage of spanning distance; they also have disadvantages, the most important of which is delayed feedback.

Why is feedback important in communication?

We can determine the effectiveness of our communication at each level by the nature of *feedback*. Feedback represents the response to a communication, and the sender of a message uses it to measure his or her effectiveness. We can most easily measure feedback at the intrapersonal level. For example, in the temperature-adjustment situation cited earlier, if your hand responds when you send it a message to turn up the thermostat, communication was successful.

Using the same criteria of measurability, feedback at the interpersonal level is second best, followed by that given at the organizational and mass level. (See the last section of this part of the chapter for a more detailed discussion of feedback.)

How People Filter Information

Twenty minutes into a meticulously prepared speech, a bank president realized she was not reaching her audience. The room was hot and stuffy; from the lectern, the president could see more than one member of the audience nod off to sleep.

This example illustrates the critical role the receiver plays in a message's success or failure. You may have aleady noticed how much a person's willingness to listen to you affects how much of your message gets across. This willingness results from *readiness,* a mental state characterized by an audience's receptiveness to communication.

If you are receiving a message, your state of readiness will be determined by how the communication meets your needs, goals, and desires. Acting as mental monitors, they regulate our readiness to receive a particular message. They do this by overseeing or *filtering* what gets through to our conscious mind.

What are the three internal message filters?

Each of us has three internal filters that govern this process: *selective exposure, selective perception,* and *selective retention.* When you choose how to spend your time and where to focus your energy, you are using your selective exposure filter. For example, suppose you want to buy something to read before boarding a plane. So you locate the airport newsstand and head for the racks where the magazines are displayed. The business magazines are on the third row. Since these are the magazines that most interest you, you quickly discover where they are and focus on them before you choose several to take on the plane. By ignoring all other information, except that which interests you, the business magazines, you are employing selective exposure. We all use this filter to some degree every day in the business environment, choosing to read or ignore a memorandum, taking time to attend a seminar on mainframe computers, and so forth. Figure 1-2 shows an example of selective exposure.

Selective exposure can work to help or hinder communication. On the positive side, it helps you be more efficient. On the negative side, it can cause you to deny information to yourself and, conse-

FIGURE 1-2 Selective exposure at work.

How do the three message filters function?

quently, to others. To apply selective exposure positively, first make sure you have all the information you need about a topic before communicating your thoughts about it to others. When you do communicate, include the relevant information so that, if necessary, others can make a valid decision based on what you have imparted.

Each of us has experienced that rush of interest when certain subjects have taken on a special meaning. For example, when you learn a new word such as *takeover,* it seems as if suddenly you are hearing and seeing it everywhere. However, *takeover* existed before you noticed it. Until now, you simply *ignored* it because you were practicing selective perception. Probably you had picked up the general meaning, but you had attached no particular significance to it.

Hearing and seeing what we want to is the simplest form of selective perception. If unchecked, it can lead to large gaps of knowledge and awareness. Figure 1-3, which shows two people's quite different attitudes about a "new job," reveals selective perception at work.

Selective retention, the third filter, causes us to remember pleasant events and forget unpleasant ones. Generally, we tend to ignore messages that evoke bad memories or retain them only briefly. Conversely, we pay particular attention to messages that evoke good memories. This filter also operates when people associated with es-

FIGURE 1-3 Selective perception at work.

FIGURE 1-4 Selective retention at work.

pecially pleasant or unpleasant memories have something to communicate to us. Figure 1-4 shows the operation of selective retention.

How to Analyze People's Backgrounds

In business, you will at one time or another send messages to individual receivers and small groups. In each of these situations you can communicate more effectively if you know something about the background of your audience. In fact, the more you know about people, the better you can communicate.

Naturally, the audience in one-on-one communication is the easiest to analyze because, besides yourself, there is only one other person to consider. For example, suppose you decided to call somebody in another company to check out a rumor that it was having trouble selling one of its new products. As usual, you do not have that much time to prepare what you are going to say. Nevertheless, before you actually pick up the phone, you might ask yourself these five questions so that when you speak, your message is as effective as possible:

1. What position does the person hold in his or her company?
2. What do I know about his or her work experience and educational background?
3. Exactly what does he or she need to know about the subject under discussion?
4. What does he or she now know about the subject?
5. How do his or her interests, values, and priorities affect the situation?

Taking the time to answer these questions will help you in any business communication. By doing so you will think of some things you may want to add to your message and decide to eliminate others.

What kinds of background information are most helpful to a communicator?

Background analysis of a group should consider specific facts and attitudes as well as what they already know. For example, suppose you are preparing a letter for prospective contributors to the United Way. First, you will need to decide which group or groups to approach. This requires a *demographic* analysis of the various groups you are considering. "Demographics" refers to the basic statistics that describe groups (or populations) of people. This objective, or "hard" data, can include information about age, sex, political preference, income and educational levels, ethnic background, and so forth.

After selecting your target group, you will next want to define its members' particular concerns to find the right approach to them. This means doing a *psychographical* analysis. Sometimes referred to as "soft" data, these include attitudes, needs, opinions, values, and perceptions. Knowing them will help you to tailor the brochure precisely to the group's concerns. For example, you may discover that its members want to use their money in such a way that it is tax deductible. Therefore, you might emphasize in the brochure that a contribution to the United Way is tax deductible.

The final step in analyzing the background of your target group is *preknowledge*, which involves determining what group members already know about the United Way. For example, your target group may be familiar with some of the organization's traditional programs. Therefore, you might decide to mention them only briefly, stressing, instead, the new programs United Way has instituted. Preknowledge analysis, then, helps you to substitute the information your audience may want to know for the information it already knows.

Using Feedback to Improve Communication

When someone comes up to you after a speech and says, "Great talk . . . I really learned a lot about mutual funds," you are receiving *feedback.* Feedback is an individual's reaction to your message that lets you know how effectively you have communicated. It may be *verbal, nonverbal,* or both, depending on the receiver's preference. If feedback is positive, you can assume that you have communicated effectively, because your receiver's interpretation corresponds to your own. When this occurs, you can either stop communicating on the subject or send another different message. If, however, feedback is negative, your receiver's interpretation diverges from your own. When this occurs, it is a signal that you may need to send a corrective message before either stopping or continuing to another topic.

Can feedback be both verbal and nonverbal?

Feedback may be either *direct* or *delayed.* Direct feedback occurs when you are in the receiver's presence or on the telephone, for example. Suppose you write a memo on a new account and show it to your boss. He or she reads it in your presence and then looks up and says, "Congratulations. You did a fine job." In this instance feedback was direct, verbal, and positive. If, in the same situation, your boss had said nothing, but had merely smiled broadly, the response would still be direct and positive, but nonverbal. And, if the boss had congratulated you, then smiled, he or she would be expressing a positive response both verbally and nonverbally.

In this context it is important to note that direct verbal and nonverbal responses may sometimes contradict each other. Thus your boss might have said, "Congratulations. You did a fine job," and frowned. When such a discrepancy occurs, it is best to await further feedback before deciding whether your boss liked your work or not.

In contrast to a direct response, delayed feedback occurs when you are not in the receiver's presence or there is no other provision for immediate feedback. Like direct feedback, it can be positive or negative, and verbal or nonverbal, or some combination of both. An example of delayed verbal positive feedback may be that a week after you write your memo on the new account, you receive it back with a note signed by your boss praising it. A similar delayed response expressed nonverbally might be that you are given several additional accounts a week after you submit the memo.

In general, is direct or delayed feedback better?

In general, it is better to receive direct rather than delayed feedback. For instance, being in the receiver's presence permits you to read response cues more accurately. Also, it permits you to ask clarifying questions and to get an immediate response, which will then help you to send out quickly any corrective message if necessary. In contrast, not being in the receiver's presence can slow you down. Since time elapses before a receiver responds, you cannot get out any corrective message as swiftly as you can with direct feedback. Also, to compensate for not having the receiver's continuous reactions to your message—as you would with direct feedback—you must take what you guess this might be into account in composing your message. In this sense, sending a message that you imagine will receive delayed feedback probably requires more skill than does sending those that are likely to get a direct response.

Many businesspeople do not bother to analyze delayed feedback because it often seems to come too late. If the decision has been made about the merger or the problem in shipment solved, why bother with something that happened earlier in the process? Some information in the delayed feedback, however, may cause you to reverse your decision or return to the problem with an alternative solution. Besides, analyzing this type of feedback is an excellent way of improving your communication skills.

SENDING, RECEIVING, AND PROCESSING MESSAGES

So far, you have seen that communication is a process involving sending and receiving messages. Next, we shall describe the structure of the communication process and the factors involved in it.

Functions of Communication Models

What is the value of a communication model?

A communication model is a diagram of how messages are *originated, transmitted,* and *received.* It explains how communication works by showing the interaction that occurs during the process as well as the people and the parts of the process involved. Diagramming this process can help you visualize the flow of communication.

The three basic elements of a communication model are the *sender,* the *receiver,* and the *message* itself. Using them, Harold Lasswell devised the first communication model (explanations added in parenthesis):[1]

Who (sender)

Says what (message)

In which channel (medium)

To whom (receiver)

With what effect (results shown by feedback)

In Lasswell's model, the sender is the person who originates the message and is, therefore, the information source or encoder. The message is the content, or what is communicated. The channel is the carrier through which or by which the message is transmitted to the receiver. The receiver is the person to whom the message is communicated and

[1] Harold D. Lasswell, "The Structure and Function of Communication in Society." In John Bryson, ed., *The Communication of Ideas.* New York: Harper & Row, 1948, pp. 37–51.

who, in turn, interprets or decodes it. The effect is the result of this communication, its effectiveness determined by the sender measuring the feedback he or she gets from the receiver.

Now how does this model explain the communication process? Suppose you meet a co-worker at the copy machine and say "Hello," to which he or she nods in acknowledgment. According to Lasswell's model, a complete communication event has occurred and works this way:

How does the Lasswell model work?

You were the sender of the message. It was just one word ("hello"). The air between the two of you acted as the channel through which the message was transmitted. Your co-worker was the receiver, who, interpreting it, responded with a nod. The nod served as your feedback, telling you that the message had been received.

In some way, however, clear as this model is, it is still incomplete. For one thing, it does not reflect the continuous, connected nature of most communication events. Thus you may have noticed that your co-worker's response initiated a second communication event, revolving around your response as you received the message or not. Using Lasswell, this second event can be traced the same way as the first. The result would be two similar, yet discrete, models. As such, they would hardly reflect the real connection between the two, which is the way they flow into each other.

Lasswell's model also leaves out how *noise* affects the communication event. Noise is any unplanned interference in the communication environment that might distort the message. Both the quantity and the quality of the message the receiver gets may be affected. In this way, noise distorts interpretation, or the decoding part of the communication process.

How do channel and semantic noise differ?

There are two types of noise: *channel* and *semantic*. Channel noise is any interference in the mechanics of the medium used to send a message. Sound itself—such as static or background voices on a telephone line—is an example of channel noise. So too are "fine print" in a legal contract, type too small to read easily, and an uncomfortable conference chair.

Whereas channel noise originates externally, semantic noise is internal, resulting from errors in the message itself. Most frequently, semantic noise occurs when the sender and the receiver assign different meanings to the same words. For example, the sender may use the word *opportunistic* in a positive way (meaning to take advantage of a situation), but the receiver interprets *opportunistic* negatively (meaning to take an unfair advantage). Other examples of semantic noise are confusing sentence structure, misspellings, and incorrect grammar or punctuation.

Figure 1-5 shows a basic model of all aspects of the communication process. From it, you can see that the communication process is a continuing one, affected by its environment. During this process a

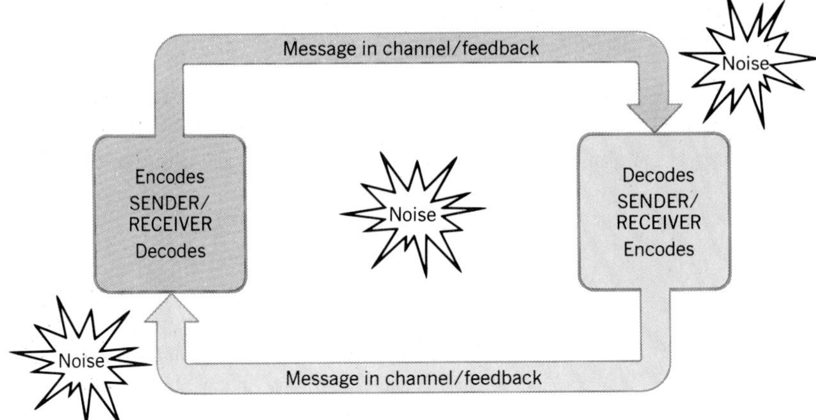

FIGURE 1-5 Basic model of continuing communication process (assume that first message is encoded by sender at left).

communicator acts as both a sender and a receiver of messages. In other words, he or she originates, transmits, and interprets them.

How Channels and Networks Operate

In communication, a channel is the medium that carries a message from the sender to the receiver. Business channels include the telephone, correspondence, reports, electronic and voice mail, newsletters, and so forth. These act as vehicles through or by which messages travel. Since each has its own characteristics with advantages and disadvantages, to communicate effectively on the job, you need to learn what these are. For example, telephones allow enormous numbers of people to communicate with each other and to receive immediate verbal feedback, but communicators are unable to see one another. And, unless recorded, conversations are intangible and short-lived. In contrast, although the new computer bulletin boards close the geographical distance between senders and receivers—and save time as well—only a limited number of people have access at this stage of the technology.

Would you use formal or informal channels to send official messages?

Communication channels are either *formal* or *informal*. Formal channels are for sending official, planned messages, those you communicate in your role as company representative. For example, if you write an article in the company newsletter about the new benefits plan, you are using a formal channel. Messages sent through formal channels are authoritative: you are responsible for what your article says and are easily identifiable as its source. In contrast, informal channels are for sending unofficial, usually unplanned messages. For example, if you and some of your co-workers meet by chance in the hallway and share information about the benefits plan, you are using an informal channel. Sometimes informal channels spring up accidentally—as in a chance meeting in the hallway. At other times, however, they are formed more deliberately—as when some employees seek out others who seem to be knowledgeable about the plan.

Communication *networks* are systems or patterns of communication channels through which information flows from senders to receivers. Like channels, networks may be *formal* or *informal.* Formal networks are organized in some prescribed way. In the business environment, they are usually based on roles or job titles, but they may also be based on status. Even so, because rules for behavior are often unwritten, employees may worry at one time or another whether their actions are appropriate within the context of the formal network. For example, an assistant to the head buyer in a department store may not know if it is all right to take the boss to lunch, or a newly hired marketing researcher may be unsure how long intraoffice memos should be.

Is the grapevine a formal or an informal network?

Commonly called *grapevines,* informal communication networks are more loosely organized and, consequently, less strict than are formal networks. Usually, they emerge to fill unrecognized needs for information. Most often, they arise, flourish, and then decline when no longer needed. Many, however, are surprisingly stable, especially when they provide reliable information that is otherwise unobtainable. "Unofficial" announcements and other types of rumors, as well as office gossip, are examples of informal communication networks. People in a grapevine usually know each other, often by name, and communicate on a continuing basis.

What happens when accessibility is restricted in networks?

Accessibility is the key to the effectiveness of both formal and informal networks. The more accessible senders and receivers are to each other, the more effectively the network operates and the easier it is to communicate. Frequently, networks are *restricted* because some members have complete access, whereas others have only limited access. For example, in most companies a stock clerk will have limited access to the president, but the president will have unlimited access to the stock clerk.

Figure 1-6 shows six common patterns of communication net-

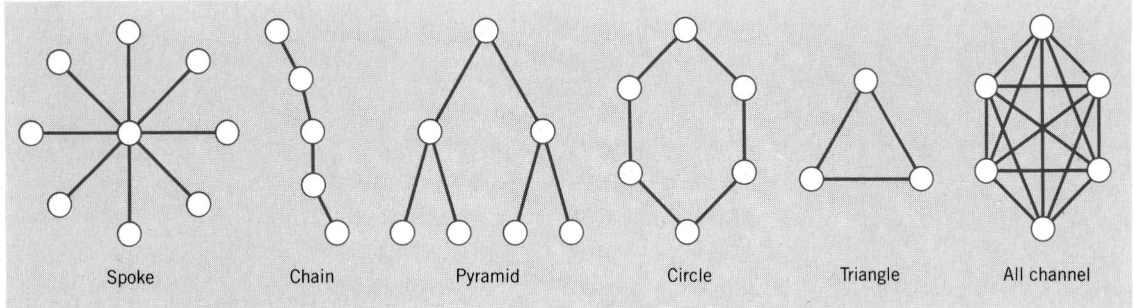

FIGURE 2 Basic network patterns.

works. Except for the all-channel and triangle patterns, each of them is restricted, because information must pass through other people or situations.

The way a network is set up determines who learns what, when he or she learns it, and from whom.

USING COMMUNICATION TO INFORM AND PERSUADE

In the business environment, you communicate for many different purposes. For example, you may communicate to build corporate loyalty, to buy and sell products and services, to train new employees, or to manage those under you. Yet whatever your specific communication goal, behind it is a larger goal: you communicate to get your job done—to reach your work objectives, whatever they may be.

Your business communication works best if you know the results you want from your message. It also means anticipating the receiver's reaction to your communication. Based on what you expect this to be, you can devise an appropriate plan for communicating.

When to Inform, When to Persuade

What are the purposes of messages?

The purpose of a message is to *inform* or *persuade* others about some subject and to improve goodwill. If you expect the receiver's first response to be favorable, then deliver the message in a straightforward, *direct* manner. But where you expect an initially unfavorable or resistant reaction, an *indirect* approach may be preferable.

For example, suppose you are the firm's marketing director. Two of your representatives are developing ways to boost sales in their territory. One of them, Martin Hammel, has an excellent sales record. In 28 months, he has tried three sales strategies. Although the first resulted in only a slight increase in his sales, the other two boosted them by 25 percent each. With such a record, Martin should expect a favorable initial response from you when he presents his latest strategy. Therefore, he should tell you directly what it is because his primary purpose is to inform.

The other representative devising a new plan is Eliza Clark. She has worked for you for three months and her record is undistinguished at best. In fact, she lost two regular accounts last month because of what you called "poor judgment." As a result, Eliza should expect an initially skeptical response to her plan on your part. She should anticipate that you will be critical and will ask many questions. Consequently, she should devise an indirect way of telling you her strategy because her primary purpose is to persuade you to accept her ideas.

Designing Messages to Inform or Persuade

Should messages to inform and messages to persuade be organized the same way?

Messages to inform are frequently designed differently from messages to persuade. For informational messages, a direct plan is advisable, whereas for persuasive messages something indirect is preferable. Before devising your plan, decide whether you want to persuade or inform. For example, suppose you need to tell several executives about the agenda for a meeting. Does this call for a persuasive or an informational communication? Clearly, you want to provide information, such as which topic will be discussed first. Once you have decided that your purpose is informational, you might write an agenda that lists topics in order of importance. In another instance, you might need to prepare a directory of company executives' telephone numbers. After deciding that your purpose seems to be to inform, you could prepare a list that is alphabetically arranged.

With experience, deciding what your purpose is should become easier. For example, you will begin to see that most of your correspondence and oral and written reports are informational because they tell others about company business. These messages will either contain good or favorable news, or routine or neutral information. Although how you will arrange this information will differ, depending on the situation, your overall plan should always be direct. (Several types of direct plans for good or routine information are presented throughout the book.)

Similarly, experience will help you to decide which communications require persuasion. Generally speaking, contract negotiations often require persuasion, as do activities where you feel the receiver would initially resist your message and thus needs to be convinced by your communication.

What three factors should you remember when composing persuasive messages?

Naturally, persuasive communications are more difficult to devise than are those designed to provide information. When you compose a persuasive message, it is important that you keep in mind these three factors: *order of presentation*, *audience needs*, and *word choice*. Persuasion relies on an indirect order of presentation based on an argument strong enough to induce a desired response in the receiver. In communication terms, an argument is a set of reasons that support a particular viewpoint or conclusion. A typical persuasive message for a report might

1. Establish that a problem exists.
2. Show why a solution is needed.
3. Define the characteristics of a good solution.
4. Encourage action to adopt the proposed solution.

In making a persuasive plan, it is also necessary to consider the receiver's needs, both personal and organizational. Needs not only differ from person to person, but also from situation to situation, so analyze both factors each time. Helping receivers to meet their needs is a powerful persuasive technique. Although you cannot always be aware of a receiver's present needs, research and experience will help you to become remarkably accurate. But remember, for a persuasive message to be successful, you must satisfy a significant need in the receiver.

Finally, your choice of words can strengthen your argument. For this reason, companies spend millions of dollars on finding exactly the right words to use in advertising their products. Remember, though, that words have denotative as well as connotative meanings. On the one hand, this allows you to choose words that fit a situation precisely; on the other, it means that you have to be careful, too. Because words are double-edged, the risk for miscommunication is also great.

Special business situations such as announcements of lay-offs or budget cuts call for persuasion. Less frequent than routine situations, they are, nevertheless, almost always more important. Sometimes they are even quite critical. Thus, they require more careful planning. (Several types of indirect plans for various persuasive situations are presented throughout the book.)

What two things do studying communication enable us to do?

Our purpose in this chapter has been to describe the process of communication, to present a *general* overview. Because communication studies attempt to account for one of the broadest and most complicated human activities, no universal principles apply to all situations. Nevertheless, studying the basics of *how* and *why* communication works is valuable. It enables us to do two things: communicate better with others and, when the situation arises, solve communication problems. These problems, called *barriers*, are the subject of the next chapter. You will find that your knowledge of the communication process will assist you in this important task of identifying, analyzing, and alleviating these difficulties whenever and wherever they arise.

SUMMARY

1. Language is words communicated in a meaningful order. People and language are interdependent, so a language is a society's voice—past, present, and future.
2. The five general elements of language are (a) language is artificial, (b) language is limited, (c) language is abstract, (d) language is arbitrary, and (e) language is redundant.
3. To work, language must mean something to people. Meaning is the significance we attach to words.
4. Meaning involves referents, thoughts, and words.
5. The two types of meaning are denotative and connotative.
6. The four basic levels of communication are intrapersonal, interpersonal, organizational, and mass.
7. People tend to filter the messages they receive through one of three person-

alized mental screens: (a) selective exposure, (b) selective perception, and (c) selective retention.

8. The more you know about receivers' backgrounds, the better you can communicate with them. When studying a group's common characteristics, consider demographics, psychographics, and preknowledge.
9. Feedback allows a communicator to evaluate the success of a message, the extent to which it was received as intended.
10. Feedback may be verbal, nonverbal, or both as well as direct or delayed.
11. Communication models help us to visualize how the parts of the communication process interact. The parts considered include senders, receivers, messages, feedback, and noise.
12. A communication channel carries a message from the sender to the receiver. Channels may be either formal or informal.
13. A system of channels is a network. Networks, too, may be formal or informal.
14. The purposes of communication are to inform, persuade, and build goodwill.
15. A knowledge of theory helps business communicators to communicate more effectively and to solve communication problems known as barriers.

Review Questions

1. Could civilization exist without language? Briefly explain your answer.
2. What do we call repetition of symbols or words in language? Explain how this works.
3. According to what you have read in this chapter, would you say meaning in words is found in people or in the dictionary? Explain your answer.
4. Is thinking a form of communication? If so, at which level does it operate? Explain your answer.
5. According to psychologists, forgetting to do a chore you don't like is called "selective ________."
6. Does moving up the ladder of abstraction make a message more specific or more general? Will this lead (most likely) to an increase or a decrease in misinterpretation?
7. We are all familiar with the homily, "One picture is worth a thousand words." What element of language does this underscore? Explain.
8. Does "feedback" have to be verbal? Explain your answer.
9. Assume that you are preparing a message for a general audience. You can't get any specific information about them, neither demographics nor psychographics. What would be your best course of action to get ready to present the message?
10. What kind of network is the company *grapevine*? Explain your answer.
11. If to *inform* is the first goal of business communication, what is the second? Briefly explain the relationship between the two goals.
12. What is the first step in developing a persuasive argument? Give an example taken from an on-the-job experience.
13. Why is feedback, most often represented by a loop, important in business communication?
14. What are *demographics*? How can they be important where a large audience is concerned?
15. When is the best time to prevent a communication problem? Why?

Exercises

1. Take a look at the scale of semantic differential presented here. To use it, take words that interest you. Words such as *college, fraternity, sorority,* and *profit* are good ones. Mark your responses to the words you choose on each end of the scale. Even if the alternatives do not seem appropriate, select the one that is closest to your attitude about each particular word.

	extremely good	very good	somewhat good	neutral	somewhat bad	very bad	extremely bad	
cruel:								: kind
curved:								: straight
masculine:								: feminine
untimely:								: timely
active:								: passive
savory:								: tasteless
unsuccessful:								: successful
hard:								: soft
wise:								: foolish
new:								: old
good:								: bad
weak:								: strong
important:								: unimportant
angular:								: rounded
calm:								: excitable
false:								: true
colorless:								: colorful
usual:								: unusual
beautiful:								: ugly
slow:								: fast

When your list of words is completed, and you have marked your responses, compare your reactions with those of others in your class. Do they differ greatly? Would you use different word pairs on the scale in any instances? What changes would you make?

2. Look at the ladder of abstraction shown in Figure 1-1. Using the word *dollar,* make a list of four or five items that could appear in the categories immediately above and below it. You also might use the words *accounts, employer, construction, stock analyst, deficit.* Be prepared to discuss in class how the principle involved can be used to form a definition for a word or an outline for a report.
3. Look over the sample network patterns shown in Figure 1-6. Consider the flow of messages between the parts of each pattern. What do you think is the major strength and weakness of each pattern? Can you give an example to support your analysis?
4. Make a list of the copyright dates in the latest edition of a dictionary, *Webster's Unabridged,* for example. Why are there so many? Explain what this tells us about the nature of language?
5. Referring to the office arrangement problem described in the discussion of limitations of language, seat two people facing each other at a table. Place a barrier of some sort between them so they can see

each other but cannot see the area immediately in front of each other. (A large piece of cardboard works well.) Have one person arrange six or seven dominoes in a simple pattern and then explain it to the other using only words. Give each group 3 or 4 minutes to complete the exercise. Evaluate the results in terms of effective communication. What were the problems? How could they be solved?

6. Using the network patterns in Figure 1-6, list examples from real life that illustrate each one.
7. Select a speech topic, such as "Individual Retirement Accounts for Young People" or "Careers in Civil Service." Assume that the students in your class are your audience. Conduct an audience analysis survey, including demographics, psychographics, and preknowledge. Were any of the data discovered surprising? How would your survey information affect the way you would design the presentation?
8. Explain what "effectiveness" means in business communication. Based on your own work experience, describe a problem caused by ineffective communication.
9. Match a communication network pattern from Figure 1-6 to any organization with which you are familiar. What would be the effect on the group if another pattern were present? Use specific details to illustrate your response.
10. A broken typewriter or printer key that makes "o's" look like "c's" is an example of "noise" in the communication process. Use your imagination to list 10 other examples.

CHAPTER 2

OVERCOMING COMMUNICATION BARRIERS

Solving Communication Problems

The Nature of Barriers

Identifying Communication Barriers

Intrapersonal Communication Barriers

- Differences in Background and Language
- Differences in Perception
- Fact-Inference Confusion
- Rigid Categories
- Categorical Thinking

Interpersonal Communication Barriers

- Emotional Reactions
- Negative Emotional Behavior
- Negative Attitudes about a Message or Its Source
- Ineffective Information Gathering
- Inappropriate Timing of Messages

Organizational Communication Barriers

- Organizational Characteristics
- Fear of Superior's Perception
- Negative Attitudes in Organizations
- Misunderstood Application of Media
- Information Overload

It had been a busy afternoon in the large department store so the clerk in the Will Call area was tired when the customer approached him. Looking up wearily, he asked, "What can I do for you?" In reply, the customer passed him a call ticket for an inexpensive sale item. The clerk glanced at it and said, "I don't have any more of these in stock. A bunch of vultures cleaned me out. You'll have to go to the Customer Service Desk to get a rain check. Be sure to fill out a postcard with your address, too. Here, take this ticket with you. It's the wrong color. You should have gotten the green copy, not the pink one. Go back to the department where you got this and exchange it for the right color ticket. And don't lose it or the rain check. How does anyone expect me to fill orders if I don't have the right paperwork?"

The customer, who hadn't said a word, slowly picked up the pink ticket, tore it down the middle, and walked away.

What went on in this encounter? Was there any communication? If so, what kind? How many of the clerk's instructions do you think the customer will follow? What was the purpose of the clerk's message? What message did the customer actually hear? Who, if anyone, was at fault? What do you think will happen next?

All business communications fall into one of two categories: either they are successful or they are not. When a communicator achieves his or her goal—whether it is to inform, persuade, or improve goodwill—he or she is communicating successfully. But when, as in the example of the customer and the clerk, communication fails, it is necessary to identify the problem and then to remove whatever communication barriers exist.

SOLVING COMMUNICATION PROBLEMS

Communicating in business is no easier than is communicating anyplace else. In business, as in the private sector, there are good, bad, and indifferent communicators. For example, some people never listen at meetings; others write incomprehensible memos; and still others take forever to tell you that they think the departmental reorganizational plan has faults. The range of communication and related problems is vast. It's potentially as large as all the writing and speaking everyone does in a day on the job.

What causes most communication problems?

Most problems arise because people make erroneous assumptions about the person to whom they are sending a message, about the medium being used, and even about themselves. To a great extent, these may be headed off if the sender of the message thoroughly analyzes the situation before communicating, thereby anticipating any problems that may occur.

Even the most thoroughly prepared communicator will still make mistakes—even though such errors are rarely as frequent or as severe as the ones made by a careless communicator.

If you do, however, discover a communication error in a message of yours, what should you do? First, you should ask yourself, "What shall I do to solve this immediate difficulty?" Second, you should ask, "What shall I do to avoid a repetition?" Answering both questions involves the same activity, namely, identifying the cause of the problem and choosing an appropriate way to alleviate it.

Briefly, here are the steps you should take when faced with such a communication problem:

What are the steps in solving a communication problem?

1. Identify the problem.
2. Discover its cause(s).
3. Evaluate alternative solutions.
4. Select and apply the best solution.
5. Follow through.

Perhaps, surprisingly, accomplishing Step 1 is not always as easy as it looks. Of course, if a retailer you are supplying yells at you because the shipment is late, you know immediately that you have a problem. But more frequently, people are unaware of a communication problem—and so either don't correct it or do so only after the situation has reached crisis proportions. Nevertheless, both obvious and hidden problems in communication are signaled by the same cue: the response we receive is not what we expected. In other words, something about the feedback is wrong or off.

Thus the key to identifying and solving both types of communication problems is the same: first, we analyze the feedback we get, or in some cases, note the absence of any feedback at all. For example, you know that generally your boss is very generous in praising an idea she likes. So, if you present her with a detailed cost estimate for a new building project and she returns it with a scrawled "OK" on top, then you might guess that your message or cost estimate somehow failed to communicate what you wanted, which in this case, was to persuade your boss of the correctness of your estimate.

Now that you are aware that there is a problem, you can go on to the next step and ask yourself where the difficulty lies. Looking over the estimate, you see that you have organized it in such a way that the essential facts are hard to find because they are lost in a welter of insignificant details. Having established what the barrier to good communication is, you can continue to the third step, exploring possible solutions, and select the best of these. As a result, you decide to put your most important information in tabular form and to add a brief summary at the end.

At this point, you may think your work is over for the immediate problem has been corrected. However, good communicators always continue to the final step and complete their follow-up activities. This involves first checking to see that the solution not only solved the problem but also did not create any new difficulties. For example, in putting costs in tabular form, did you manage to play down the less important details? Yes, they do seem less jarring, but are they now lost? After all, you still want your boss to digest these facts, or you would not have included them. If they are indeed "lost," then you have solved your problem at the cost of creating another.

Why is follow-through especially important in solving communication problems?

If, however, you have not created any new problems, you can complete the second part of your follow-up, which consists of taking steps to avoid any recurrence of the original problem. This action may be formal, for example, establishing, with your boss's approval, a format for estimates to be used by the entire department, or informal, for example, simply filing the experience away for reference when preparing written reports.

THE NATURE OF BARRIERS

Can you describe a communication barrier?

What are communication barriers and where are they found? The communication model presented in Chapter 1, Figure 1-5, assumes a free flow of information. The only negative element in it is "noise." Actually, the study of barriers, or the many separate factors that inhibit or distort a message, is an expansion of the notion of "noise" or interference. By examining such obstacles, we shall see how both people and organizations inhibit the communication process.

A barrier may be compared to a screen or sieve; it allows some information to pass through, but not all of it. Barriers are hard to detect and to isolate because we do not necessarily know if we have received the entire message or a distorted one. This is particularly true when more than one barrier is present at the same time.

Nevertheless, becoming familiar with possible barriers will prepare you to solve real problems, not simply to react to symptoms. For example, suppose the director of a charitable organization tells everyone that they will have to work next Sunday on telephone solicitation. A volunteer who has been with the organization 10 years objects loudly. If the director rebukes him sharply for protesting and he says nothing more, then an apparent problem has been solved—interference with a message. Yet, clearly, the director may by this action be ignoring a more significant problem: the possibility of staff discontent. For example, members of the organization may feel overworked and underappreciated. That an experienced worker reacted so emotionally may be a symptom that the director is communicating just such a message. Moreover, if unattended to, this perception could lead to decreased morale and to the loss of competent volunteers. Thus, someplace in the director's mind, a bell should start to ring during this exchange or soon afterward when reviewing it. Among the first questions to ask is, "Why did this incident occur?"

To communicate effectively in business—whether as an entrepreneur or a top-level company executive—you need to understand how barriers operate, why they interfere with communication, and how you can decrease their negative effect. And, most important, you need to recognize the cues that signal miscommunication.

IDENTIFYING COMMUNICATION BARRIERS

How many times have you said, "What I meant to say was . . . "? Probably you have murmured this more times than you can remember. For, despite the best intentions, our written and spoken messages are frequently misunderstood.

At this point it would be tempting simply to list and define the major barriers that exist and warn you about them. But a mere list won't help you: there are far too many such impediments.

Because they are so numerous, it may be more useful to group them into three clusters related to the processes of message formation and delivery in business. Thus, you will commonly find barriers at the *intrapersonal*, the *interpersonal*, and the *organizational* (or systems) levels in business communication.

INTRAPERSONAL COMMUNICATION BARRIERS

Intrapersonal barriers are unique to the individual sender or receiver. In other words, they arise from a person's individuality. No two of us have the same education or experience. Nor do we have similar personalities, goals, values, or ways of perceiving the world. This is why people often draw different conclusions from the same information.

How do intrapersonal barriers differ from the other types?

Still, the potential barriers that exist within us usually do not stem from our differences, but from the *assumption* that we are the *same*. For example, have you ever been in a class where your instructor accidentally gave a lecture intended for a more advanced class, or built his or her remarks around a concept that the entire class did not know? In both these instances, the barrier to communication was the lack of common knowledge—the sender sent a message that you were unable to decode. The instructor assumed you knew something you did not. Because of this, he or she mistakenly felt you would be able to follow the lecture. Only when the problem was identified was your instructor able to select and initiate the best solution to correct the error. In business too many miscommunications occur because people assume that others have more in common with them than they actually do.

Such miscommunications also originate from a second type of intrapersonal barrier: the misapplication of reasoning, which is discussed further under the separate headings "Fact-Inference Confusion," "Rigid Categories," and "Categorical Thinking."

Differences in Background and Language

As we mentioned earlier, no two people are alike. Each of us is a product of our genetic inheritance and our learning through formal education and experience. This background determines how we receive or interpret messages. Once we become aware of this variety, we cannot then expect anyone else to have exactly the same perception of the world. In fact, the degree to which we are aware of differences will affect any attempts to communicate successfully. For example, suppose you are a stockbroker explaining to a client the unsuccessful takeover bid a company has just weathered.

Then, in the midst of explaining why you don't think the company's securities are a good investment at this time, you use the term "junk bond," which you've already used a number of times in the discussion. The client asks, "What's a junk bond?" Suddenly, you realize that your client is probably unfamiliar with a number of words and concepts you've introduced. In fact, he or she probably doesn't know what you're talking about.

Having identified the problem as unfamiliar terms, the solution is easy: you explain the concept of junk bonds as high-yield securities that are below investment grade, illustrating the concept by using words whose meanings you both understand.

A skilled communicator keeps differences of perception constantly in mind—differences in knowledge, language skills, training, and values—to prevent them from becoming barriers. To strengthen your own communication skills, first consider what your audience might not know or understand. Second, build that information into your message. Then, construct a bridge for the audience between familiar and unfamiliar information.

What is the key to awareness of differences in background and language?

The key to becoming aware of differences is empathy. *Empathy* involves the effort to understand someone else well enough to predict where he or she may have difficulty understanding your message because of the difference between you both. Only if you empathetically know the receiver's frame of reference can you speak or write within it, thus diminishing ambiguity and decreasing the number of multiple meanings in your communication.

One essential characteristic of language discussed in Chapter 1 was that the receiver's interpretation of a word sometimes differs from the sender's intention. Remember that a word's meaning does not reside in it, but rather in the mind of the receiver. The greater the disparity between them, the more formidable the communication barrier.

The multiple definitions of words also compounds the communication problem. For example, the 500 most used words in the English language have on the average 28 different definitions apiece. Add to this that many of the words we use are abstract—and, consequently, more vulnerable to misunderstanding—and the magnitude of the problem begins to emerge. Aware of this, good communicators are careful to explain their ideas in context and to repeat or rephrase certain difficult words.

If you are writing your communication, you may want to ask yourself, "Am I likely to use words or refer to concepts that are unfamiliar to my receiver?" If so, be considerate: either define the words as they appear or use more familiar words.

If your communication is spoken, be attentive to feedback as a way of testing whether you are getting your message across. One technique is to ask your receivers to paraphrase what you've said; another is to encourage them to ask you questions based on what they heard.

But what if you are a receiver, not a sender? Applying the same principles will help you to improve communication by diminishing the possibility of language barriers. One technique you can try is anticipating another person's message and thereby preparing yourself to receive it.

For example, if you know that a budget meeting is scheduled for next week, do some homework beforehand: (1) Read the documents that will be discussed. (2) Make sure you know the meaning of the terms the budget director and his or her assistants will probably use. (3) Also, during the meeting itself, ask questions to clarify what you still do not understand. In business, it is never wrong to request more information about a subject.

A more subtle aspect of the language barrier directly relates to a person's image. Thus an inappropriate choice of words can disclose more about a speaker's or writer's attitudes than he or she intends. For example, what would your opinion be of someone who used vulgar language throughout a panel discussion on the international monetary situation? Or, how would you view a corporate president who spoke only in academic jargon? It is unlikely that these individuals' choice of words would positively affect your image of them.

Differences in Perception

Why don't all people process information the same way?

Everyone sees the same situation through his or her own eyes. This means that no two people process information the same way, because no two people perceive reality the same way. Remember the concept of selective perception discussed in Chapter 1? We all tend to see things as we believe—or would like—them to be.

Suppose a dispute breaks out between a worker and his super-

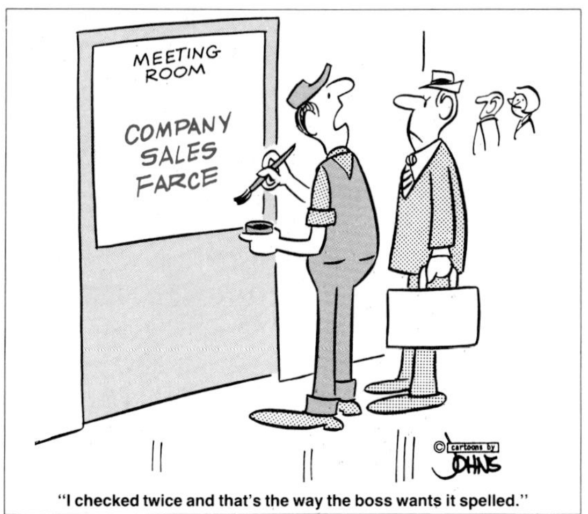

"I checked twice and that's the way the boss wants it spelled."

visor, and you are asked to find out what happened. Naturally, you will have to interview the two people involved. Do you expect that they will recall the incident in the same way? More likely, each will see the other as the one at fault. Now suppose that two other workers witnessed the incident and you decide to interview them also. The first witness you speak to is strongly prolabor and tends to view all management as oppressive. Do you think his attitude will affect his perception of who initiated the argument? As for the second witness, she is clearly no friend of the worker. Do you think her dislike of him will affect her judgment of what happened?

The answer to each of these questions is, yes. In fact, not only do people's backgrounds influence their perception of reality, but different backgrounds can lead them to give entirely different accounts of it. A clear, objective statement of what actually occurred during the dispute may be impossible to obtain from these witnesses.

How can we avoid perceptual barriers?

The best way for you to avoid these perceptual barriers is first to recognize that they exist. Therefore, never immediately commit yourself to a conclusion. Consider an event or a communication from a variety of perspectives. Then look at it empathetically—as in a situation involving language barriers—through the perspective of each person. Weigh all the information and try to verify it. A technique good communicators use in situations such as this is to interview the participants one by one. Next, paraphrase what each has said, asking him or her to correct any mistakes. Not only does this allow you to check the facts, it also provides insight into the differences in perception.

Fact-Inference Confusion

You are returning from lunch and you see a fellow employee dash out of the building, apparently very upset. Looking at her face, and also knowing that she had been recently reprimanded by your boss, you assume she had been reprimanded once again. But this would be conjecture on your part. Actually, the only factual statement you can make on the basis of what you have seen is that this employee left the office in a hurry. Your notion that she was upset because of a reprimand is speculation, not fact.

How does a fact differ from an inference?

What has occurred here is an example of fact-inference confusion. This occurs when people fail to distinguish between what actually exists—a fact—and what they assume to exist—an inference.

The racing employee might have several explanations: she might be removing herself from a bad experience in the employer's office, *or* she might be catching a ride home, *or* making an important telephone call, *or* making a bank deposit before closing time. The fact is that you saw her rushing. No inference about the cause is safe without additional information.

Inferences themselves are not necessarily illogical. Even so, we make them so frequently that it would be absurd to try to verify each of them. Besides, many of them are relatively unimportant and carry very little risk. For example, suppose you assume that blue is your assistant's favorite color or that the supply of copy paper will not run out today. It is highly probable that neither of these inferences will seriously affect your work life.

Some inferences, however, require more sensitivity on our part because they may have more serious consequences. Thus, in the previous example of the employee who ran out of the office, if you had not only believed your assumption that she had been reprimanded but also passed it on to other workers, you might have caused trouble for her and, ultimately, for yourself as well.

Another kind of inference, which may also be risky but which we often make, occurs when the facts are simply unavailable. For example, proposal writers must use carefully projected figures because the events they are describing have not yet occurred. The language of a proposal—such as, "Based on our experience, we can reasonably assume a 100 percent return on venture capital in 18 months"—usually reflects this caution.

What is the most important thing to remember about fact-inference confusion?

In general, it is best to be similarly careful about inferences that may affect your work life. *Remember, once you confuse an inference with a fact, any conclusion you draw from it is likely to be incorrect.* To avoid this problem, make it a practice to sort through information, labeling facts as facts and inferences as inferences. Then, if you feel an inference is worthy of investigation, try to find sufficient supporting evidence to justify your conjecture. Even if you uncover support for your inference, do not relabel it as a fact. Instead, use qualifiers, such as "evidence suggests" or "in my opinion" to remind yourself and the receiver that this is not established as fact.

Another way to identify inferences involves the use of synonyms for *inference* to test for its presence. Among these are *assumption, speculation, forecast, projection, conjecture, hypothesis,* and *intuition.* For example, suppose you are writing a report on the future of the steel industry. You want to write this sentence, "Changes are inevitable within the industry." You are aware that the use of the word *are* makes this a statement of fact. But is it really a fact or is it an inference? If any of the synonyms for inference applies to your sentence, then it is not factual. As you review the list of them, you can see that the word *forecast* applies to the statement because you are talking about a future development. Therefore, you are dealing with an inference, not a fact. To reflect this, you decide to change your sentence to "Changes *seem* inevitable within the industry."

We have been talking about inferences as intrapersonal barriers to communication and how to become more aware of them. In this context, we have also discussed some strategies for their removal from messages you send or receive. In contrast, it should also be noted that inferences are usually more dramatic than facts, and for this reason they are frequently the primary source of gossip and rumor in organizations.

Rigid Categories

Without the ability to generalize, or group similar information into categories, our lives would be a mess. Quite literally, we would be unable to learn anything—for learning requires that we take information gathered in one situation and apply it to a new situation we view as similar. For example, we would forever be sticking our hands in a flame if we had not generalized that fire burns.

Yet, although categorizing is essential to learning, carried to extremes, it can also act as a barrier to learning. This occurs when people develop rigid thought patterns that prevent communication. In business, such a mentality causes many problems. For example, the real estate broker who refuses to sell an apartment for under $50,000, although comparable apartments are going for far less, because "this particular apartment is worth more," is standing not only in his or her own way but also in that of the company as well. So too is the sales manager who stays with an unsuccessful marketing strategy because "it always takes a year to see if a plan works."

How can you recognize rigid category barriers?

People with rigid thought categories like the real estate broker and the sales manager

1. Cannot learn from new information.
2. Reject any view that contradicts their own.
3. Fail to discriminate between things that only seem to be the same.
4. Tend to perceive similarities between things and to overlook differences.

Three common types of rigid categorizing are *frozen evaluation, polarization,* and *blindering.*

Frozen Evaluation

People whose evaluations are frozen disregard new information, acting instead as if situations, events, and people are unchanging, fixed and frozen forever. Another name for frozen evaluation is bias or prejudice. Because categorizers assume that evaluations they have already made will always be appropriate, these predetermine their reaction to ideas, people, or the environment around them. Consequently, by ignoring variations and differences, they are led to unreliable conclusions. For these reasons, such a mind set causes trouble in private life and in business.

What is another name for frozen evaluation?

Take the case of Mr. Shattock, the supervisor of the stationery supplies department of a large corporation. One day in the company cafeteria he is greeted by a young woman who had previously worked for him for a short time before being reassigned to purchasing. After two years there, she has just been transferred back to stationery supplies and informs her old boss of this. At first, he does not remember her, but then it comes back to him and he says, "Yes, you were always asking for time off, missed a lot of work, and left things for others to finish up. I had to speak to you about the quality of your work." The woman sighed and explained that her father had been very ill at the time and she had the entire responsibility for his care. "But after he got better," she said, "I was able to concentrate on my job. Mrs. Packard in purchasing has been very pleased with my work. I've had two superior performance evaluations and been put in for a productivity bonus." "I'm very happy to hear that," Mr. Shattock replied. "However, once you're in my department, I expect you to shape up. No reporting late, no leaving others to finish what you started." Hearing these words, the young woman looked at him in bewilderment. Apparently, he had not heard a word she had said.

Clearly, Mr. Shattock had not heard in the sense of taking in the new information he had just received. And, no matter what she might do, this employee is stuck with a frozen evaluation, a "poor attendance/poor work habits" label.

When can something be done to challenge frozen evaluations?

Sometimes prejudices such as Mr. Shattock's are so deeply rooted within a person's psyche that they cannot be challenged. But when they are less ingrained, something can be done about them. Most of us have certain blind spots, or areas where our categories may be frozen. One worker may believe that women do not bring the same intensity to their work as men do; another might think that executives over 50 are old-fashioned. Good communicators are aware of this tendency in themselves. Thus, they are constantly reevaluating their assumptions. To them, every person and event is unique, and their generalizations about them are simply conveniences, valid as long as new information continues to support them.

Polarization

Can you explain how polarization is a common, logical fallacy?

When people polarize things, they tend to view them as if only two alternatives existed. This common, logical fallacy is referred to variously as "either/or," "yes/no," "them/us," "black/white," that is, binary thinking.

Of course, in many situations only two choices *do* exist—as in questions of fact. For example, either a stock rose five points during trading today or it did not. But sometimes people assume there are only two alternatives when others do exist.

In doing so, they create barriers to communication and, ultimately, to the solution to their problem. Often these barriers are relatively minor. For example, suppose the word processor you are using to write a letter of inquiry to a drug company breaks down. Annoyed, you say to yourself, "My machine's down again. I guess I'll have to do this letter on the typewriter." If we examine this statement to see if it contains any possible barriers to communication, we say that the first part—"my machine's down again"—conveys an accurate message, in this case, to yourself. Word processors are either/or machines: they either work or they do not work. Moreover, either your machine has previously broken down or it has not. In the second part, however—"I'll have to do this letter on the typewriter"—you mistakenly assume an either/or situation: either my word processor works or I have to use the typewriter. But is the typewriter your only alternative to the word processor? Perhaps you could use someone else's machine. Or maybe the letter does not have to be written immediately and you can wait until your own machine is repaired. By assuming an either/or extreme, you have narrowed your options.

Other examples of polarization can cause greater problems. For example, suppose your company is considering a merger with a larger company. The president of your company, who strongly favors the idea, holds a meeting with you and several other top executives to discuss the matter. During the discussion, the boss turns to each of you and asks rather heatedly, "Are you with us or not?" Everyone is aware that the remark is more of an implied demand than a real question. Moreover, it has the effect of shifting the legitimate question of whether to merge into the illegitimate either/or issue of company loyalty or disloyalty. The likely result of this remark will be to cut off further communication from the others present. Even if any of you had serious reservations, you would probably hesitate to voice them since that would be seen as disloyal.

What if you are in a situation like the one described, where only two alternatives seem possible? Before deciding between them, stop and ask yourself if your choice is really so narrow: recognizing that other ways exist is often the first step toward finding a better solution to your problem. Perhaps even in the situation just described, the executives in the room had responses other than to either sit quietly or question the merger.

Blindering

When does blindering occur in communication?

Blindering is a third kind of rigid categorizing that people employ that can act as an intrapersonal communication barrier. It occurs when people are puzzled about a problem and as a result adopt a "one-size-fits-all" solution. Their reasoning is "if my solution solved one problem, why won't it solve another?" For example, the retailer who began with one store and has since expanded to six in a large metropolitan area thinks that her personal supervision of each detail, which worked when her operation was small, will also be effective in the new situation. However, what happens is exactly the opposite: because she cannot do it all, business begins to suffer.

By limiting herself to what worked previously, the retailer has misapplied that original experience. Blindering is a barrier because it skips an important step in problem solving: seeking innovations. You may recall that earlier in the chapter the third step in problem solving required evaluating alternative solutions. Good problem solvers never rely solely on old solutions to new problems. They know that sometimes they might work but not always. Unlike people who wear blinders, they realize that each problem must be looked at freshly and that each solution has just been born.

Categorical Thinking

Besides the three types of rigid thinking, another kind of thinking in categories acts as a communication barrier, namely, the *allness* syndrome. More informally, subjects of this syndrome are often called "know-it-alls." In receivers, the syndrome takes the form of an attitude that seems to say, "I already know everything important about this subject, so I'm not listening to you." Naturally, the usual response to such behavior is that the sender thinks the receiver is inflexibly dogmatic.

The business environment has its share of individuals who refuse to listen because they see themselves as the expert. They range from the editor who resents having to attend a meeting on editorial budgeting because, "I've been doing this for ten years and I have better things to do with my time," to the employee in accounting who dismisses some new procedure because the person introducing it "knows less about accounting than I did in third grade." In both instances, receivers refuse information because they feel they know everything and hence need to be taught nothing.

Naturally, the "allness" syndrome afflicts senders as well as receivers. For instance, after sales in the Midwest had declined for the second straight month, the sales manager of the auto parts company told the staff, "Everyone in this territory is doing poorly." Although this was an accurate assessment of the group's performance within the territory, individual performances varied widely. Nevertheless, the manager presented a nondiscriminating perception as if it neatly described the situation. In such circumstances, the salespersons who met or exceeded their quotas would surely resent being seen in the same light as poor performers.

What words give clues that you're thinking categorically?

Often, certain words are a clue to the presence of this barrier. These include *all, always, everybody, everything, everytime,* and *everyplace* and their opposites, such as *none, never, nobody, nothing,* and so forth. It is a good practice to listen for these words as you receive messages. If a sender's message is sprinkled with such terms, then he or she is probably a categorical thinker who will distort the communication between you.

What if you detect some tendencies toward categorical thinking in yourself? How might you correct them? For example, suppose you are the sales manager who lumped all the salespersons together, saying they had performed poorly. Afterward, in thinking about the meeting, you become aware that you used the phrase, "everyone in this territory." This tips you off that you may have been thinking categorically. The more you consider the matter, the more convinced you are of your mistake. But how can you correct it?

One way is to use the ladder of abstraction discussed in Chapter 1. It is clear from it that you, the sender, were abstracting on higher levels (seeing your salespeople as a group, not as individuals, and seeing what they have in common—group sales—and ignoring what they do not—individual sales). In turn, your salespeople, the receivers, are listening on a lower level (as individuals). To eliminate the communication barrier, you might revise your message: omitting abstractions such as gross sales and thereby descending the ladder to the individual level. You could do this by meeting individually with each person to discuss his or her performance. Or you might meet only with the group that did not make its quota.

Finally, you might avoid this difficulty to a great extent by qualifying abstract or categorical statements with words or phrases, such as "in most cases" or "probably." Similarly, try to label opinions with phrases like, "it seems to me" or "the evidence I have indicates." And when you have too little data, you might simply say, "I don't know," instead of hiding things with an obtuse abstraction.

INTERPERSONAL COMMUNICATION BARRIERS

Which two kinds of interpersonal barriers are discussed in this section?

We have seen how communication barriers originate from intrapersonal problems. Now let us turn to another source of barriers: interpersonal relationships, or any individually-based transaction occurring *between* people. Here we will examine two kinds of barriers: obstructions stemming from (1) a negative communication climate and (2) ineffective communication habits. (See Chapters 19 and 20 for further discussion of applications of interpersonal communication.)

When two or more people meet and begin to interact, the very characteristics that distinguish them can cause communication problems. In a business situation, we can neither change another person's personality nor would we want to; however, we can learn to understand how our differences affect communication.

Emotional Reactions

Nearing his retirement, the senior partner of a nationally prestigious law firm received many sincere tributes during a special dinner given in his honor. When finally asked to speak, he rose from his seat, began to say a few words, and was unable to continue. In spite of his years of public speaking, he was choked with emotion.

Virtually every situation we encounter evokes some kind of feelings within us. Normally, these do not cause any change in our behavior, but sometimes they do. Depending on the emotions involved and their intensity, our response may create a barrier to communication. Probably the most troublesome emotions in this respect are our most basic: anger, love, hate, jealousy, joy, embarrassment, and fear. Usually—although this was not so for the senior law partner—positive emotions, such as joy, interfere less with our ability to communicate than do negative emotions, such as fear of authority or of punishment.

Since they are an essential part of us, we have to recognize that emotions will always be present in business encounters. By increasing self-awareness, permitting ourselves to feel, and building empathy toward others, we can learn to deal with the emotional currents of the work environment.

Negative Emotional Behavior

Your boss calls you into her office and asks why you are late with filing a report on department store sales during December. You answer that it was impossible to get any work done during the holidays, and she should have known that before assigning this task to you. Later, in analyzing the encounter, you realize that you reacted defensively.

In what two ways do people react negatively to communication?

Depending on their personalities and the situation, people often react negatively by either being *defensive*—as you were—or *hostile*. Both responses have the same origin: each occurs when the receiver of a message feels threatened by either a real or a perceived danger. Whereas hostility or aggression—usually shown by anger—is a counterattack to the threat, defensiveness is a resistance to it.

Both these responses have an extremely negative effect on communication. People exhibiting them tend to misinterpret, ignore, or overact to messages. In turn, those witnessing such behavior tend to lower their opinion of the senders of such messages.

One way to avoid triggering hostile or defensive reactions is to anticipate what may set them off in you. Everyone sees certain situations as threatening; the question is which ones cause you distress: Is it job interviews? performance reviews? project evaluations? Any ordinary business day is crowded with such potentially threatening events.

How can you prevent a reoccurrence of your own hostile or defensive behavior?

Suppose you have identified which situations evoke hostile or defensive behavior on your part. Now what do you do when faced with one of them? For example, job interviews may frighten you terribly. At the end of the week, you have an appointment with the marketing manager of a textbook publisher to discuss a sales position. Already, you can feel the tension mounting. In the past, job interviews have brought out a streak of hostility in you. To prevent a reoccurrence, you might try practicing the interview in your mind, much as an actor or actress rehearses a part. In practicing, run through the scene as you would like it to go. This, however, does not mean that you should avoid rehearsing your answers to any potentially touchy questions, such as "Why are you leaving your present job after only eight months?" In fact, the more trouble spots you cover, the better your chances are of substituting nondefensive behavior for hostility during the actual interview. After you have thoroughly rehearsed, you should take steps to prevent yourself from getting into an emotional "state" before the interview. Therefore, during the intervening time, do as many pleasurable things as you can such as going to a movie. Perhaps even more important, try to keep things in perspective. Sure, you want the job, but it will not be your last opportunity for work in this field. Besides, there are other good publishers that might need your services. Finally, during the interview itself, if you do feel yourself becoming hostile, simply pause and regain your control before continuing.

What if, instead of sending a hostile or defensive message, you are its receiver? Often, managers and administrators find themselves in this uncomfortable position. Are there some ways to avoid or soften these responses? For example, suppose two division supervisors are competing for the same spot—vice president for overseas operations—in your shipping company. One way to diminish the possibility of hostility or defensiveness on either of their parts is to focus on the job description in talking to the applicants, and not on their qualifications. Then, after you have made your final decision, and, preferably, before announcing it, you should talk privately with the losing candidate. The focus of this discussion should be explicit praise of his or her contributions to the company and a frank estimate of the possibilities for advancement.

Even with the best preventive tactics, you may still be confronted with extreme behavior. What can you do to limit the effects of a destructive response? The first thing to remember is that in almost any occurrence of an emotional outburst, the communicator would prefer not to be acting this way. However, his or her emotions are preventing effective communication.

To assist someone in this state, first find a quiet place—if you are not already in one—away from other employees. Try to calm the person down; one way is to remain calm yourself. Then see if he or she wants to talk about the strong feelings that caused the problem. Throughout, listen carefully and try to understand why this person acted so emotionally. The clues and insights you gain may, in turn, help you to move him or her away from the emotional edge. Moreover, as you appear less threatening, you will be more reassuring yourself. This will usually result in less hostile or defensive messages from the agitated sender.

What common signal tells you an emotional outburst is happening or is about to happen?

For either senders or receivers of such messages, a common signal that an emotional outburst is either about to occur or is occurring is a *change in vocal modulation* on the sender's part. Sometimes his or her voice becomes sharp, or it might crack or rise to a shout. When this happens, the other person often responds similarly. The result is that focus often shifts from message content to decibel count. At this point, the people involved have become combatants, not communicators. If you find yourself in such a situation, lower your voice and urge the others to lower theirs too. Only when this is achieved can real communication resume.

Another reason to control such behavior is that communication studies indicate that receivers are generally uncomfortable around people who shout or speak very loudly. Not only do receivers judge such communicators adversely, but they also frequently discount their messages as well.

Negative Attitudes about a Message or Its Source

The faces around the conference table looked bored or lost in thought when the representative from the Easter Seal Association stopped talking. She had been very clear in her presentation, but about halfway through it, everyone had stopped paying any attention. What had gone wrong?

What role does lack of interest play in creating negative attitudes?

Sometimes, as here, *lack of interest* causes receivers not to pay attention to a message. But why are they uninterested: Is it because of something in themselves? in what the sender does? in the message itself? Perhaps the English essayist G. K. Chesterton was right to say that "in all the world there is no such thing as an uninteresting subject. There are only uninterested people." If, however, no subject is inherently boring, does the sender or the receiver bear more responsibility for the way in which a message is received?

Again, we turn to Chesterton's statement, which seems to imply that it is the sender's responsibility to present information in such a way that its value is obvious to the receiver. One of the best ways to do this is to show how your message concerns or affects the receiver. For example, have you ever noticed that you may be paying scant attention to some conversation going on around you until you hear your name mentioned? In fact, the problem with the talk by the representative from the Easter Seal Association was just this: she had forgotten to make her listeners feel that the matter concerned them directly.

What happens when the receiver of a message thinks the sender isn't credible?

Another barrier to reception of a message may lie in the perception by the receiver that the sender lacks credibility. *Lack of credibility* may not be caused by the same things as lack of interest, but its outcomes—the receiver's inattention or indifference—are the same.

Credibility arises from predictability, or the positive assumptions we make about someone's future behavior based on our experience with him or her. When a sender's words (or actions) conflict with these perceptions, credibility is weakened. For example, if your boss promised you a raise a year ago and failed to give you one, it may be difficult to believe a similar promise that you will receive it next month.

To combat lack of credibility, the sender must gain the trust of others. Gaining a reputation of being reliable takes time; enough positive experiences must occur that the receiver is aware of a pattern of consistency in the sender.

Building or rebuilding confidence also takes caution. If, for example, you give a client an estimate for a job and he or she questions it, you should avoid saying anything like, "Don't worry. You can trust me." Most probably, the result of such a remark will be to raise doubts about you rather than to inspire confidence. Instead of declaring your credibility, you can show it by creating an atmosphere that promotes open communication, by conveying a feeling of confidence in others, and by encouraging their participation in the communication process. Once this trust is established, deeds must follow words if it is to continue.

How can resistance to change create communication barriers?

Another related problem that senders of messages must face is *resistance to change.* At first, this may seem an unusual attitude for modern businesspeople to have in a world where technological and managerial innovations occur at an often breathtaking pace in small as well as large companies. However, in every workplace, a countercurrent—a tendency to resist the new—coexists in both employers and employees. Because communicators' messages frequently are related to change of one kind or another, this attitude is particularly important for communicators to understand.

People resist change because it is human nature to establish a known and comfortable way of doing things and then to defend it. By definition, this tendency toward inertia, or preserving the status quo, subverts new ideas and new ways of doing things. A classic example of this kind of thinking occurred when the railroads decided to replace steam engines with diesel. The railroad workers union, afraid of what this change might mean, insisted that train crews remain as they were previously. Therefore, to meet this demand, the companies had to agree to "featherbedding," to have a fireman on each train even though the diesel made the shoveling of coal obsolete.

This reaction may seem extreme, one that today's workers would not be capable of, yet it happens continually. How many times have you heard someone say, "But we've always done it this way"? If you want to be an effective communicator, try to keep in mind that people tend to feel threatened by what is unknown, untried, and unpredictable.

In addition, learn to appreciate the reasons for opposition to a suggested change. Generally, the primary obstacle for you to overcome in proposing a new way of doing things—whether it is a new method of filing documents or moving the company outside the city—is the receiver's fear of strangeness. So your initial messages should educate and familiarize everyone with the advantages of the proposed change. Moreover, these benefits should be explained in terms of listeners' lives, not profitability. Does this sound familiar? It should, since you are simply applying the empathetic approach to message design. Another way of familiarizing receivers to the new is to encourage their participation. In this way, they can "join the team," help "keep us competitive," and be involved in "our progress."

Ineffective Information Gathering

Probably your single most important communication activity on the job will be to obtain current and accurate business information. Without such data, you will neither be able to identify problems nor to solve them.

To their detriment, and that of others, some people never use the basic skills required to gather good information, choosing either to subvert or ignore the data. They do not listen to fellow employees. They glance at letters and skim reports. They disregard nonverbal information. They neglect to seek feedback. In short, they simply assume that if anything important happens, they will find out about it . . . somehow.

Many others, however, do understand the value of information, especially in making decisions and solving problems. To gather it, they have learned how to surmount certain common communication barriers.

Is listening an active communication skill?

One of these obstacles is *poor listening habits.* Listening is not the same as hearing. Hearing, which is the ability to distinguish sounds, is passive. In contrast, listening, or being attuned to the speaker's words and nonverbal messages is active—indeed, *inter*active. Thus, if a person doesn't listen, even though he or she may have heard every word spoken, a formidable barrier exists.

How can you know you are a good listener?

Who is a good listener? If you answer yes to the following three questions, then *you* are a good listener. But if you answer no to any of them, you can improve your listening skills. The questions are

1. Do you listen with understanding, acceptance, and empathy for the speaker?
2. Do you listen attentively and carefully to his or her message?
3. Do you think of each listening situation as a learning situation?

As you work on these skills, you will begin to see that you are receiving messages more accurately. You may also notice some secondary gains. For example, if you listen empathetically to a coworker's suggestions about overtime pay, he or she might turn more receptive to your idea for budgetary reform. (See Chapter 19 for a more detailed discussion of listening skills.)

What problems in the work environment affect listening?

In addition to psychological factors, good listening is affected by physical conditions. No matter how hard you concentrate, you cannot listen attentively if there are too many distractions around you. Large offices and workstations are often filled with the sounds of activity. Typewriters clatter, telephones ring, air conditioners or fans whir, fluorescent lighting buzzes, people chat and laugh. None of these sounds is conducive to good listening. If you feel these sounds that accompany your office life are interfering with your listening, try either to eliminate the source or move to a quieter area like an empty conference room or to an office where the door may be shut.

Some of the same advice that applies to listening follows for being a good receiver of written messages. For although the medium is different, attentive reading requires many of the skills necessary for good listening. The major difference is that a written message may be reread and kept for reference. In reading, as in listening, it is important to "read" the message's context as well as its surface facts. By this, we mean the communicator's underlying meaning, what he or she is really trying to say. For example, if you read a report on the costs of adding more staff, try to understand the author's point of view, whether he or she uses facts convincingly, and so forth. (For more on improving your own reading techniques and skills, see Appendix E.)

A second kind of barrier to gathering information is *misunderstood nonverbal communication*. Nonverbal cues or actions, which include facial expressions, posture, body movement, eye contact, and gestures, may be intentional or unintentional. Whichever, all our words are accompanied by nonverbal communication. Normally, these underscore what we are saying, as when we smile in thanking supervisors for the effort they put into a three-day sales meeting.

How does misunderstood nonverbal communication relate to gathering information?

Sometimes, however, nonverbal messages may contradict the verbal communication. For example, suppose you are instructing an employee on how to finance a corporate venture. Throughout the last part of your explanation, you notice a puzzled look on this person's face. Yet, when you are finished, the employee claims to have understood you completely. Are those words feedback enough? Probably not. Since the nonverbal communication—the puzzled expression—contradicts them, you should probably ask him or her to repeat or paraphrase your instructions. In this way, you can check to see if this person really understood you.

As for yourself, be aware of your own use of nonverbal behaviors. Try to avoid any that may be easily misinterpreted. For example, you may doodle constantly when seated and talking to another person. After a while, you might observe that some of your co-workers misinterpret this as a sign that you are bored. Therefore, you may decide to simply extinguish the habit.

Conversely, we should be cautious when interpreting nonverbal behavior in others, for it is hardly a rigorous component of language. In fact, all we can ever say is that "this behavior may mean . . . ". Any more specific assignment of meaning would constitute an inference—unless additional clues, such as words and a wealth of other nonverbal behaviors, form a clear pattern that affirms our interpretation.

Despite the risk of possible misinterpretations, never ignore nonverbal communication. It may be the first indication of a communication problem, as when a departmental director discovered that the reason why one of her workers always nodded in the wrong place when listening was because he had begun to have a hearing problem. By becoming attuned to nonverbal cues, identifying their patterns, and seeking to document your interpretation of them, you will enhance your ability to understand verbal messages.

How can assumptions about physical appearance and dress create communication barriers?

A third barrier to information gathering arises from generalizations based on *assumptions about physical appearance or dress.* Both the way we dress and look and the way we perceive how others dress and look strongly affects communication. In fact, many experts consider physical appearance to be one of the most important forms of nonverbal communication. Both our first impressions of people, and thereafter, our openness to receive their messages are colored by how we perceive them physically. Among the elements we take into consideration in making such assessments are height, weight, body formation, skin, hair and eye color, hair style, personal hygiene, and mode of dress. In general, the more closely the sender's appearance conforms to the receiver's notions of appropriateness, the higher the potential for positive communication between them. Conversely, people tend to discount and, even to avoid, individuals whom they judge by their appearance to differ radically from themselves.

Sometimes our assumptions about a person based on the physical impression they make on us turns out to be inaccurate. For example, one executive almost did not hire the most efficient office manager she ever had because the person was overweight. Another nearly missed out on an extremely effective production supervisor because the man's hair seemed too long.

In general, experienced business communicators strive to be fair and open-minded about other people's appearance. Nevertheless, one criterion of judgment they will apply is dress, especially in employment interviews. Quite simply, an applicant is expected to dress appropriately for the occasion. If, for example, a candidate for a managerial position in a printing company comes to an interview wearing jeans or "kids' clothes," such as bib overalls, getting the job will be unlikely.

Such expectations on the interviewer's part do not mean that he or she is biased. In business, dress is simply one of the ways by which people evaluate one another. If you want to be properly valued, it may be useful to analyze your own dress to see whether it gets in the way of how you and your messages are perceived. A similar awareness of other elements of your physical appearance may also yield dividends. For example, although you may be unable to change your eye color, you can decide on a new hair style to make your business image either more or less conservative.

How does inadequate feedback affect the quality of information you gather?

A fourth barrier to information is *inadequate feedback.* Suppose you overcome some of the barriers we have discussed and gather the information you need for an important project. You transmit this information in the form of a memo to your supervisor and wait impatiently for a response. Several weeks later, you still have gotten no reply. Without the additional information contained in your supervisor's response—such as the identification of areas of need and an evaluation of how successfully you communicated your message—you cannot move ahead on the project. Here, as in most business situations, the old adage "no news is good news" simply does not apply.

The consequence of nonresponse behavior is the development of an information vacuum. *Clear and swift feedback is the first step in preventing costly time-consuming mistakes.*

Suppose, for example, the managers in your company have delayed sending in their personnel evaluations. As a result, the top management has not fired several employees who are incompetent, nor has it promoted a number of others to key spots on the basis of superior performance. Already the problems caused by the original postponement are showing: one of the excellent but ignored workers is looking for another job, "where my talents will be appreciated and my skills used"; another is coming into work later and leaving earlier; and still another is spending a lot of time complaining about office politics. Meanwhile, because of some mistake one of the incompetent workers made, an entire job has to be redone.

If feedback in your business environment seems inadequate, work to develop a climate that encourages it as well as information sharing. By asking questions, seeking clarification, reading and listening carefully, and looking for nonverbal cues, you can finally complete the communication cycle.

Inappropriate Timing of Messages

What three kinds of "time" create communication barriers?

Depending on when a message is delivered, it too may assist communication or become a barrier to it. In this context, we need to distinguish among (1) *on time,* meaning a message is delivered when promised or expected; (2) *timeliness,* meaning the message is appropriate to the current situation; and (3) *timing,* meaning the sender selects the best psychological moment to deliver the message.

Sending messages so that they arrive *on time* is essential to the conduct of any business. The quality of many daily decisions is directly affected by the right information being in the right place at the right time. Suppose your supervisor, Ralph Bench, has to decide whether to accept a construction bid by 3 o'clock in the afternoon. In the morning he asks you to find out more about a job the construction firm did two years ago. After frantic searching you finally locate the one person able to supply you with the necessary information. On the phone that person tells you something that casts serious doubts about the company's ability to do the job. Hanging up, you rush into your supervisor's office to convey this information. "I'm sorry that we didn't have this when we needed it," Ralph says when you tell him what you know. "I accepted the bid 15 minutes ago."

Why must some messages be on time to be useful?

Similar interactions occur frequently in offices: a message is delayed—no matter what the reason—and the decision is made without it. The message, then, is rendered useless. Not surprisingly, senders who consistently miss deadlines begin to have a certain lack of credibility.

Timely messages arrive at the appropriate time and contain the appropriate information. For example, suppose you work for a hospital supplier that wants to bid on a contract with a large university medical center. Your supervisor has been too busy lately to deal with the subject. So, on your own, you work up current inventory figures and price updates. One day, when the boss mentions the bid to you, you respond by showing what you have done. In all likelihood, you have just earned high marks for being timely.

Is a timely message always well timed?

Sometimes a message has the best chance of being effective only at a certain time. Part of being a good communication planner consists of recognizing this fact. But how you plan the *timing* of your message depends on the situation. For example, sometimes a rapidly sent message has great effect because of its immediacy. At other times, however, a slightly delayed message may make the receiver anticipate its receipt and hence be more receptive when it does arrive.

As a rule, the best psychological moment to deliver a message is when you have the receiver's complete attention. Ideally, you might try in advance to discover whether the receiver has some budget meeting later in the afternoon or is distracted because an assistant is sick for the second day in a row. If you detect no such concerns, now might be an excellent time to present your message.

If, however, you sense too much interference, try to find a better time to deliver the message. Suppose you had set up an appointment to discuss your idea with your supervisor on the same day as the budget meeting. When you walk into the office, you immediately see that the boss is tense and preoccupied. In these circumstances, you should first recognize that your message will get a lower priority at this time. Then either reschedule the appointment or write your message as a memo to allow more choice of when to read it.

ORGANIZATIONAL COMMUNICATION BARRIERS

In one giant corporation, every employee—from the highest to the lowest—can complain about company policy directly to the president. The policy of another large company is distinctly different—employees must put any complaint in writing to their immediate supervisor. A third relies solely on the old-fashioned suggestion box.

As such alternatives show, each organization—from the local mom and pop store to a multinational corporation—creates its own communication climates, which are as varied as the people who are responsible for the organizations themselves. Large corporations and governmental agencies develop complex organizational charts based on levels of responsibility. These charts, in most cases, also define communication networks, sketched in Chapter 1. In a typical pyramid (hierarchical) structure, the flow of information is from the top down; feedback, upward information, is not guaranteed. And, thus, a typical communication barrier, inaccessability, is created. Nevertheless, all organizations share two characteristics: (1) they have written or unwritten communication policies describing the acceptable ways to do things, and (2) their structure and complexity tend to create communication barriers.

What two communication characteristics are shared by all organizations?

Although such barriers are also interpersonal—after all, organizations are composed of people communicating with one another—they are also by-products of the system itself. For example, if two neighbors meet in the street and have a conversation, it would differ noticeably from one they might have as the vice president of production and the first-line factory supervisor inside a manufacturing firm. For one thing, the meeting inside the factory would be less casual. For another, the supervisor may not be able to communicate as freely about plant operations to the vice-president as to the neighbor.

Every workday every employee repeatedly sends and receives messages—and, as the size and complexity of the organization increases, so do the number of messages and the possibilities for communication-related problems. One of the business communicator's primary tasks is to recognize and alleviate such difficulties. The importance of this activity cannot be understated. Communication barriers are barriers to the smooth coordination of various activities carried out to reach a company's goals; they can impair the entire organization's success.

Organizational Characteristics

The larger an organization is, the more people it will employ and the more specialized their jobs will be. A typical hierarchical organizational chart illustrates how size increases complexity. For example, such a chart shows that upward messages ascend one step at a time from the employee to his or her immediate supervisor. In contrast, downward messages usually are either individually directed or are sent to all subordinates. Upward messages, then, not only travel more slowly than do downward ones, but they may also have to pass across a dozen or more desks.

In organizations, does size increase complexity?

This cumbersome process helps us to understand why corporate communications frequently seem impersonal and why superiors are often slow or are unable to react to the concerns of employees below them. In this traditional climate of communication, many employees, becoming frustrated with normal channels, turn to an informal system—the grapevine—for information. Such secondary channels are often prime vehicles of rumors and inaccurate information.

Many large, modern corporations are finding that the traditional hierarchical structure restricts efficient two-way communication so they have tried to improve upward message flow. For example, some have established a senior executive position—director or vice president of communication or information—with the responsibility of improving communication policies and procedures. Other organizations have modified the standard pyramid structure, basing their innovations on the principle of the "all-channel network" illustrated in Chapter 1, Figure 6. Some signs of these changes are quality circles and management by walking around.

Although many organizations are altering policies and structures to improve communication, you do not have to wait for these changes to improve quality on a personal level. For example, the number of times a message has to be repeated clearly slows its progress. As the

What is a transfer station?

typical organizational chart shows, the more people who have to process a message, that is, the more *transfer stations* it must pass through, the more slowly it moves *and* the greater the risk of misinterpretation, or garbling of information, before the message reaches its destination.

Depending on the situation, you may avoid the major problems of too many transfer stations—distortion, delay, or loss—by putting your message in the form of a memo. Then, instead of distributing it to "everybody," decide just who should receive a copy. Implement your strategy with a selected routing list, indicating it on the "cc" line of your memo. A second alternative may be to present your message orally, carrying it up the line from person to person. Although more time consuming, this approach permits you to solicit feedback and on the basis of these responses to adjust the message before continuing to the next receiver. One word of caution: If you do adopt this plan, follow regular channels; that is, do not go over anyone's head.

TOO MANY TRANSFER STATIONS?

A Corporate President Once Told a Vice President,
Next Thursday at 8:30 P.M., the first television commercial advertising our newest product, an inexpensive, battery-operated razor, will be aired on Channel 17. The commercial shows a man, dressed in a tuxedo, shaving himself—without water—in the middle of the Mojave Desert. Since this is our first excursion into this medium, I would be interested in our employees' reactions. Could your arrange to have an opinion survey on my desk before lunch on Monday?

The Vice President Told a Regional Manager,
The President wants everyone to watch 17 television commercials next Thursday at 8:30. He also wants written employee reactions to our newest excursion in the survey medium, a parched man, dressed in an airy tuxedo, shaving a battery-operated cactus in the middle of the Sahara Desert, submitted Monday morning. We will all eat an inexpensive lunch on our desks that day.

The Regional Manager Told a Division Manager,
The President wants 17 of our newest employees to act in a television commercial at 8:30 A.M. on Thursday in the desert. All employees can help our media excursion by watering the cactus. For those without opinions, a pencil and parchment will be provided. A free lunch will be eaten at the same time, provided there is desk space. Airy tuxedos will be required. Men, though, are reminded to shave.

The Division Manager Told a Department Supervisor,
The 17 volunteers (see attached list of newest employees) for our waterless cactus commercial will be required to order formal attire by 8:30 next Thursday at the Desert Inn. There will be no dessert after the free lunch on Monday, but pencils will be provided.

The Department Supervisor Told the Employees,
Bus #830 for all those attending the free company excursion will leave for the Desert Inn in Palm Beach Monday morning. Those not properly dressed or who haven't shaved will have to watch Cactus Jack on Thursday on television. Lunch will consist of 17 desserts.

Fear of Superior's Perception

Suppose you are a junior accountant in a fast-growing drug chain. Because of your work, you are in line for a merit salary increase that has to be approved by your boss. One day you discover an irregularity in the general ledger that might make your superior look bad. Should you reveal the information?

Certainly, when making this kind of decision, people worry about retaliation. Will your boss prevent your promotion, transfer you to another department, or, even worse, have you fired? Whether such fears are justified, the fact that many employees in similar situations would be tempted to suppress or alter the information indicates how fear may create a significant communication barrier. The common advice given new employees, "Just do your job and don't make waves," certainly underscores the reluctance of many workers to communicate bad news.

How can a supervisor encourage subordinates to communicate more freely?

As a supervisor, how might you encourage the people under you to communicate more freely? First, you need to recognize that every one, yourself included, wants to make a good impression. Second, you should try to create an open and supportive atmosphere. One way to do this is to show the members of your department that you respect them. Such an attitude will reduce their fear of you and of saying the wrong thing; at the same time, it builds their own self-confidence and goodwill. In the end, this should lead everyone in the department to communicate more easily. Increased job satisfaction and productivity also flourish in such a climate.

Whereas "What will the boss think?" may prompt some employees to withhold unpleasant messages, the same fear may cause others to do exactly the opposite: to send everything forward. More specifically, they may be afraid that their boss will somehow judge them as careless because they have left out some important information. The result is long, thick reports bulging with every possible chart and fact, no matter how remotely they relate to the subject. Unfocused messages of this sort waste everyone's time. By eliminating them, a good supervisor applies the same remedy as when messages are withheld.

Negative Attitudes in Organizations

Any time a group of people gathers together, members will eventually divide themselves into smaller groups according to common interests. This socialization process also occurs in the business environment.

For example, in any large company you can find an amazing number of formal and informal groups engaged in a wide variety of recreational, social, and community activities. Usually, these groups tend to reinforce their members' values, attitudes, opinions, and behaviors. Sometimes a communication barrier can surface when such a group's views conflict with those of nonmembers and an insider/outsider relationship develops. For example, this may occur when members of a union in a clothing factory are angry with nonmembers who refuse to support their demands for employee wage scales to be made public by the company.

How can managers benefit from the tendency of people in organizations to form groups?

By understanding how this socialization process works in their company, good managers can benefit from a number of these groups as reinforcers of organizational values. For example, by introducing new employees to members of such groups, a supervisor may encourage productive orientation sessions and also strengthen the corporate image.

Misunderstood Application of Media

When you speak to someone, sound waves carry your words through the air. When you write a memo, the medium is words on paper. As groups of people increase in size, the media they use to transfer messages change too. Computer networks, for example, can send communications to vast numbers of people quickly and over great distances.

Modern business enlists a variety of media: graphs and charts, bulletin boards, telephones, films and slides, electronic mail, and teleconferencing, among others. Letters, for example, because they are a written record, offer senders and receivers a greater chance to be accurate than do messages delivered on the telephone. However, telephone messages can be sent and received more rapidly than can letter messages. Whenever we must make a choice among the various media, we need to assess each of their assets, liabilities, and potential barriers to see how they will affect our message.

When might a multimedia approach to communications be beneficial?

In some situations, you may decide on a multimedia approach. Doing this may reinforce your message and help to prevent misunderstanding. For example, a salesperson may first speak to a customer on the telephone and then send a follow-up letter. The phone call may have permitted the deal to be closed swiftly, whereas the letter sent later may have confirmed what was agreed on in writing. Sometimes too, one kind of medium calls for the support of another. For example, when you are preparing a report—and especially if it includes a lot of numerical data—you probably need visual aids such as charts and graphs.

Information Overload

Information overload occurs when a receiver is no longer able to deal effectively with incoming information. We have all experienced this at one time or another, not being able to read the print before our eyes on the night before an exam or nodding off in the second hour of a lecture on some tedious subject. The primary causes of overload are fatigue, the difficulty and quantity of messages, and boredom. Once we reach this saturation point, further communication is either impeded or goes right by us.

This problem does not originate only in organizations. But organizations do generate a staggering amount of data, which is often "copied" to virtually everyone.

Much of what is sent is either irrelevant or too detailed. It falls on the receiver, then, to decide what things to save and what to throw out. This takes time, which might be more usefully spent elsewhere. A related problem concerns the time pressures and other constraints employees must face to produce and report still more information. In business, the prevailing idea often seems to be that the more information employees communicate, the more productive they are.

What should be the real criteria for judging performance?

But is this so? Obviously, a 10-page report on international monetary priorities is not necessarily superior to a 2-page summary of the same subject. *The real criteria for judging performance should be the quality of the information and its usefulness to understanding the problem or situation.*

To diminish the possibilities of information overload in your office, try not to add to the problem. One way is to screen any message you plan to send by (1) directing it only to people who will benefit from the information and (2) emphasizing major ideas and deleting useless details. Your fellow workers will send messages of thanks.

SUMMARY

1. Business communication does not always achieve its purpose. Errors and misunderstandings are frequent. The first step in solving them is understanding what went wrong. This chapter is devoted to the description and analysis of the most common communication barriers.
2. The steps in solving a communication problem are (a) identifying the problem, (b) discovering the cause(s) of the problem, (c) evaluating alternative solutions, (d) selecting and applying the best solution available, and (e) following through.
3. A communication barrier is a form of communication "noise." It is anything that interferes with a free flow of information in the workplace.
4. Communication barriers can be grouped into these classifications: (a) intrapersonal (within the individual), (b) interpersonal (between individuals), and (c) organizational (within the particular organization).
5. Intrapersonal communication barriers involve (a) differences in background and language; (b) differences in perception; (c) fact-inference confusion; and (d) rigid categories, for example, frozen evaluations, polarization, and blindering; and (e) categorical thinking.
6. Interpersonal communication barriers involve (a) emotional reactions; (b) negative emotional behavior; (c) negative attitudes about message or source, for example, lack of credibility and resistance to change; (d) ineffective information gathering, for example, poor listening habits, misunderstood nonverbal communication, erroneous assumptions about appearance or dress, and lack of adequate feedback; and (e) inappropriate timing of messages.
7. Organizational communication barriers involve (a) characteristics such as size and structure, (b) fear of supervisor's perception, (c) negative attitudes in the organization, (d) misunderstood application of media, and (e) information overload.
8. Understanding communication barriers, their symptoms, and causes is just the first step in alleviating miscommunication. Once you identify the type of barrier that exists, you can apply the most effective cure.

Review Questions

1. What is a communication barrier?
2. At what three communication levels are barriers found?
3. What do we call the confusion between what actually exists and what people assume exists?
4. What is "allness"? How can you guard against it in your communication?
5. Defensiveness and hostility are examples of which communication barrier?
6. According to the chapter, "credibility grows" from what?
7. Is nonverbal communication a credible source of information? Explain your response using specific examples.
8. Why is an applicant's attire important in a job interview? Give an example of appropriate and inappropriate dress for such an interview.
9. What are the major causes of information overload? How can a communicator decrease message overload?
10. How many different messages were communicated in the case of the Will Call clerk at the beginning of this chapter? List each.

11. What concept related to understanding is a key to avoiding barriers arising from different backgrounds, education, and experience?
12. Is the assumption that "we are all the same" helpful in combating communication barriers? Explain your response.
13. Is the avoidance of generalizations a good way to eliminate communication barriers? Explain your response.
14. What is "blindering"? Explain your response by adapting an incident from your own experience.
15. Why do people resist change so strongly? As a business communicator, what could you do to overcome this barrier?

Exercises

1. Identify the intrapersonal communication barrier that best describes each of the following situations:
   a. "Every time I have a meeting with Bill, I end up disagreeing with him about a particular issue."
   b. "John, did you notice the letter from the home office on Mary's desk? I'll bet she is going to get a promotion."
   c. "Have you ever tried to follow Sam's activity briefings? It seems as though he gets mixed up too often."
   d. Question: "Sandy, where is the report that I asked you to do on the Foster account?" Reply: "I don't remember your asking me to do a report."
2. Identify the interpersonal communication barrier that best describes each of the following situations:
   a. "If you need any information from me, be sure that you ask specific questions and don't waste my time!"
   b. "Mr. Perkins just gave me a job assignment, but I'm not really sure what I'm supposed to do."
   c. "Tim Evans, the district sales manager, is calling a meeting this afternoon. I hope there's a lot of coffee in the meeting room—I'll need it!"
   d. "I don't care how much time it might save; I still like the old system!"
3. Identify the organizational barrier that best describes each of the following situations:
   a. "I'm not telling my boss anything that happened in the plant. She'll go through the roof!"
   b. "As soon as I'm just about finished with one project, I get six more to complete."
   c. "Bill, have you ever tried to get some cost estimates from the production department? It's as tough as anything you can imagine!"
   d. "This room is awful to work in. I can hear everything everybody says, and there's no privacy."
4. Form a group with six or seven members. Give the first member a written message and ask that person to read it over and then whisper the message to the next person. Follow this sequence until each member of the group has participated. Then compare the written message with the message that the last member of the group received. What observations can you make regarding the process? What barriers does the exercise illustrate? How does this exercise relate to an actual business situation?
5. Look at the communication model in Chapter 1 (Figure 1-5). Choose one barrier from each classification (intrapersonal, interpersonal, and organizational), and identify where each barrier may arise in the model.
6. From your own experience, describe a situation that illustrates one barrier from

each classification (intrapersonal, interpersonal, and organizational).

7. Assume you're the employee in the meeting with Mr. Shattock that was described in the section on frozen evaluation. What would you do to break the barrier?
8. Practice your listening skills by turning oral messages into written ones. Bring a set of notes you've taken in another class. Summarize these notes. Prepare an essay test question that would cover 2 to 3 weeks of information about the subject. Now, what relationship does this exercise reveal to exist between oral and written messages?
9. Reread the incident described in the introduction to this chapter. Assume you are the customer service manager and you receive a blistering letter with a torn receipt attached from the customer who walked out on the Will Call clerk. Analyze the problem. Identify the barriers. Devise a plan to alleviate them. What kind of response are you going to send to the customer?
10. Watch an afternoon soap opera on television—preferable one involving a business situation. Make a list of the communication barriers you observe. Be ready to describe and evaluate them at your next class meeting.

CHAPTER 3

FUNDAMENTAL WRITING TECHNIQUES

Ann Johnson works for a company that monitors mutual fund performance. She needs to get the message to her boss that during 1987, equity mutual funds registered an average gain of 27.17 percent, which, although failing to match the 31.79 percent average of the Standard & Poor's 500-stock index for the period, represents a 17 percent increase over the fund's 1986 performance. Should Ann send this message orally or put it in writing? Concerned that her boss might forget these percentages or remember them inaccurately if she told them to her, she decides to write a memo.

Sometimes written business messages help process certain kinds of information better than spoken messages do. Generally, written messages are preferable in situations where (1) information is complex or detailed, (2) receivers need time to consider the information before giving feedback, and (3) senders and receivers would like a permanent record for reference.

In each of these instances, the effectiveness of your communication depends on two basic skills: how well you analyze the situation to discover the appropriate action and how well the message you write meets the objectives you have set for it.

PLANNING AND ACHIEVING WRITING OBJECTIVES

Suppose you need to prepare a letter to potential clients about a new tour your travel agency has organized to the Far East. How would you go about preparing this letter? First, you need to identify both your general and specific goals. Consider your purpose. Will you need to

What are the basic goals of business communication?

1. *Inform,* or transfer information from one person to another—in this case, from you to your clients.
2. *Persuade,* or influence the receiver's actions or attitudes—in this case, to have clients decide to take the tour.
3. *Build goodwill,* or create and maintain a positive communication climate between sender and receiver—in this case, to affirm the attractive prices of your agency's tours, the quality of accommodations it reserves for clients, and so forth.

Once you have established your goals, set clear objectives. Planning helps you to define these objectives and offers you a system for monitoring your progress toward them. Through planning, you clarify your purpose and identify what to say and how to say it.

Planning gives order to the writing process. Here is a five-step method for organizing a writing plan:

Step 1 *Identify the purpose for writing.*

The purpose is your primary reason for writing. In other words, it is your objective or the desired result. For example, the purpose of a memo may be to schedule a meeting on plant safety rules for handling toxic gases.

Step 2 *Determine the message content.*

To get your purpose across, you need to determine the contents of your message. That is, you need to decide which points to make and which details will support them. For example, your memo on scheduling a meeting on safety rules may include the following content:

Time and date of meeting

Meeting place

Agenda

Type and amount of preparation people need to do

Materials for people to bring to meeting

Names of those attending

Name(s) of person(s) conducting meeting

Can you list the steps in organizing a writing plan?

A good way of checking to see if your message is complete is to ask yourself what you would want to know if you were the receiver. Or you might apply the checklist journalists use and ask if it answers the questions *who, what, why, when, where,* and *how.*

Step 3 *Organize the content by priority.*

After determining the contents of your message, you should decide which information to state first, second, and so on. Base your sequence on such factors as order of importance, time and budget constraints, and the reader's needs.

Step 4 *Set a time schedule.*

You will probably be able to complete a simple written message such as a routine letter of inquiry about a new portable computer's availability within a short time. In contrast, a long report on the budget for the family care unit of a hospital may require days or even weeks to complete. For such messages, set a reasonable time schedule based on the situation in advance and then follow it.

Step 5 *Devise a system for monitoring progress.*

If a writing project requires several or more hours to complete, set up a system to monitor the process to ensure that everything is progressing smoothly. Thus you should check to see that you are on schedule, that time constraints are not affecting the quality of your work, and that whatever procedures you have chosen are efficient.

PLANNING CHECKLIST

Asking yourself the following questions should speed up the planning process for any business writing you do:

1. What is my purpose for writing? (Jot down key words that define the primary reason.)
2. What content should I include? (Jot down key words that list every point you need to make, keeping in mind who your reader is and what his or her information needs are.)
3. In what order should I present my information? (Jot down a sequence to present your information logically.)

How can this checklist help you plan messages well?

However, if your audience is not already aware of the problem or your purpose for writing, you may need to introduce a purpose or provide background.

4. What time schedule is best for me? (Jot down a schedule you can realistically meet.)
5. Which monitoring system shall I use? (Jot down times and procedures for checking your schedule, work quality and methods of work.)

WRITING FOR THE READER: ANALYSIS

John Prieto, an attorney, is head of the legal department of a large airline carrier. Currently, he is negotiating with the pilot's union over salary increases. As part of his job, he has to write a daily memo to the president of the company keeping him informed of developments. Knowing the receiver's impatient personality, the lawyer makes it a rule never to write more than a one-page update.

Every message you write should be adapted to its reader. Often—like John Prieto—you may know your reader well. Sometimes, however, you may need to do some research about your reader, especially if your message is important. In general, the more you know about your reader, the more effective your message will be. Asking yourself the following questions should help you to increase your knowledge about your readership:

1. *What is my relationship with the reader?* Is the reader a customer or client? a colleague or peer? a superior? a subordinate? Answering

this question will help you choose the appropriate tone. For example, you might express your opinion of the advertising plan for the company's new perfume more informally to a colleague than to your supervisor.

What questions need answering to analyze a reader?

2. *What position does the reader hold?* Is the reader an engineer, a sales manager, a production supervisor? Is his or her position managerial or nonmanagerial? What basic interests and objectives might a person have who holds that position? For example, if your reader is the head engineer of a chemical company, you might be especially careful to present technical material in a sufficiently sophisticated manner.
3. *What is the reader's reading level?* If you don't know, you might make a good guess by noting his or her position within the company. Some jobs require a high school education, others a college degree, and still others, more advanced work. Usually, education is a good indicator of someone's reading level. For example, if you are writing a memo to the head of the mail room, who you know has only a high school education, keep your sentences fairly short and uncomplicated and avoid overusing abstract words.
4. *What are the reader's interests?* Knowing your reader's job-related and social interests can help you to personalize a message. For example, suppose you want to persuade your boss to choose one book developer over another for a wildlife series. You just happen to know that one developer, Mrs. Dent, has a special interest in the design elements of a book. In your memo to her, then, you emphasize the superior design of the developer you prefer.
5. *What knowledge of the subject matter does the reader have?* Is your reader a novice or an experienced professional? Is he or she up to date on the field's recent technical developments? In knowing this, you will also know if you need to explain technical terms and concepts and how much detail to include to make your message clear.
6. *What is the reader's background?* Is your reader in sales, finance, production? Does he or she live on the East or the West Coast? in France or Japan? Initially, you will be able to answer such questions about almost any reader. Later, if you are alert, you will learn more about his or her background. For example, you might discover that the sales manager you have been dealing with is a former college sports director. Using this knowledge, you may decide to sprinkle your messages to him with appropriate sports language or analogies.
7. *Does the reader have any strong feeling about certain subjects?* As you write a message, try to see it through your reader's eyes. This means you need to be sensitive about provoking him or her by

using biased or prejudiced language. Although you may not always know your reader's specific biases, you can certainly avoid generally irritating labels such as "nerd," "redneck," "workaholic," and so forth. Referring to controversial life-styles and political and religious issues is also risky.

8. *What are the reader's unspoken needs?* Sometimes readers do not directly state their needs. For example, one reader may prefer to receive frequent updates even when you have no new information to report, but he or she may never tell you this explicitly. By learning, however, "to read between the lines" of *his or her* messages, you can become more sensitive to such unspoken needs and thereby be able to reach this person more effectively with your message.

9. *Does the reader need information quickly?* Suppose your reader requests that you write a report on whether to recommend a loan to a Third World country by Friday. Your efforts to meet your reader's needs, particularly time deadlines, may result in your reader being more responsive to the message itself.

Using Appropriate Words

Just how important is it to use appropriate words?

You have analyzed your reader and so can begin the main task—writing the message itself. You sit before the typewriter or the word processor and nothing comes. What do you do? First, remember that good writing is sometimes defined as using the best words in the best order. This is as true of business writing as of any other form. So begin with the words themselves.

Try to select those that will not only convey your meaning but will also make your message easier to read.

Denotative and Connotative Meanings

As we explained in Chapter 1, all words have denotative, or "dictionary" meanings. Many also have connotative, or implied, meanings. When a word is used only denotatively, its meaning is normally clear. For example, most of us can agree on the meaning of such words as *automobile, window, cat, day,* and *pencil.* Thus, a reader will have no trouble interpreting them if they appear in a business message.

Do all words have connotative meanings?

In contrast, readers may have varied interpretations of words with connotative meanings. For example, one reader may interpret "duty" or "obligation" or "responsibility" somewhat or entirely differently from another. When you use such abstract words with connotative meanings in a message, you can never be certain how a reader will "filter" them. You can, however, try to choose words or phrases without negative connotations. Thus, in describing a colleague who took the opposite side in a debate with you over whether to extend a loan to a troubled car manufacturer, you might avoid the word "opponent." For some readers, it may imply you regard the other person as an enemy.

Concrete Nouns and Pronouns

The subject of a sentence is usually either a noun or a pronoun. The more precisely you choose your subjects, the more easily the reader will understand your message. Make your nouns as concrete and specific as you can. For example, the sentence, "Call our office if you have any questions," is far less clear than is, "Call Jane Baldwin, the program analyst in our office, if you have any questions."

If asked, could you find concrete substitutes for abstract nouns and pronouns?

The ladder of abstraction described in Chapter 1 may be helpful in this context. Whenever you find yourself using an abstract word, try to see if you can substitute one that is more concrete or lower down the ladder. For example, suppose you are writing a statement about the net worth of a thousand-head herd of livestock. You decide that it would be more impressive to substitute the more abstract word "asset" for "livestock." In doing so, however, you would probably cause your reader to be more confused than if you had stayed with your first and more concrete choice.

Precise Verbs

How precise should a verb be?

At the heart of any sentence is the verb, the word or set of words that identifies the action. Like nouns and pronouns, verbs have to be selected carefully to make your messages more precise. For example, suppose you want a colleague to review a report on credit markets before you submit the report to a supervisor. So you scrawl a note to her, asking that she please "read" it. But is this what you really want her to do? Perhaps you would have conveyed your need for her to read it carefully if you had used a more precise verb such as "review," or "screen," or "critique," instead.

Descriptive Adjectives and Adverbs

Adjectives and adverbs describe things in sentences. An adjective modifies a noun or a pronoun by telling us more about it. An adverb performs the same function for a verb, an adjective, or another adverb. Choosing precise adjectives and adverbs is another way of improving the clarity of your messages. Let's see how they work to do this in a simple sentence, such as the following:

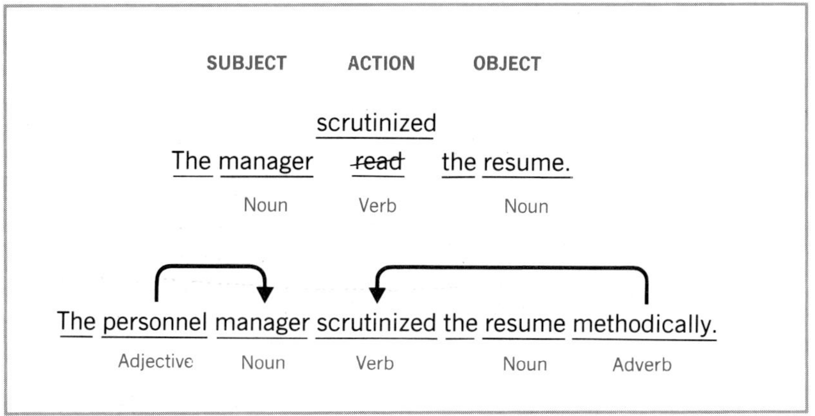

In this sentence, the addition of both the adjective and the adverb tells exactly who scrutinized the resume and how attentively he or she read it.

Just as precise adjectives and adverbs can improve your writing, so may imprecise ones confuse it. For example, such descriptive words as *fine, very, nice, real* or *really,* and *fair* or *fairly,* among others, add to a message's length but may not add to its clarity. Thus, if you write a note to your assistant saying that you will be busy for *most* of tomorrow, your message is less precise than if you say you will be busy between 10 A.M. and 3:30 P.M.

Do you use lots of superlatives when you write?

Strong, emphatic descriptive words may also be imprecise. Often, superlatives like *fantastic, fabulous, amazing, great,* and *terrific* fall into this category by overstating reality. For example, suppose you want to write a memo telling your staff that sales for the company's sports magazine were *fantastic* in January. Certainly, this is stronger than saying they were good. But will your staff believe you? They might not because, like everyone else, they know people tend to apply such words to quite ordinary performances. Therefore, before you use *fantastic* in your memo, make sure the situation is appropriate—that is, January's sales really were extraordinary.

Suppose that you do decide to use *fantastic* because it does accurately describe the magazine's sales performance. Then follow with an explanation of how sales are fantastic. By doing this, you will make your entire message more precise. Otherwise, you will erode both your message's and your own credibility.

Constructing Effective Sentences

A sentence is composed of word and word groups, such as phrases and clauses, that make up a complete thought. How we combine these elements determines the effectiveness of our written messages. To make your sentences coherent, effective, and interesting, you should try to (1) vary their type, (2) vary their length, (3) use connectives, and (4) vary the format.

1. *Vary sentence types.* Use a variety of sentence types to make your message more interesting or to change its emphasis or tone. In business, any written message a page or more in length should probably contain simple, compound, and complex sentences. Because, however, they are often long and difficult to read, use compound-complex sentences sparingly. When you do include such sentences, reread them to make sure they are clear. Any combination of sentence types, though, should also be used to express the most appropriate message for your reader. Basic sentence patterns are used for these purposes:

   Simple = presents information at the simplest level.

   Compound = combines information, but also suggests relationships through connectives ("and" = equality, "but" = contradiction); thus this pattern begins analysis.

   Complex = combines information, important for understanding conditions that qualify the primary idea; also a basic pattern to show subordination of ideas.

   Why vary sentence type and length?

   Isn't consistency better?

   By understanding the use of these basic sentence patterns, you can make your writing more purposeful and more interesting to read. (Appendix A contains more information on sentence types.)

2. *Vary sentence length.* Sentences should average 15 to 20 words. Whereas too many short sentences make a message choppy and disjointed, too many long ones obscure it as well as slow the reader down. Also, if you include too many sentences of the same length, the effect will be monotonous. Varying the length of your sentences for clarity and emphasis helps your reader understand your message.
3. *Use connectives.* Connectives are the bridges of a sentence. They connect its parts, showing the progression of ideas and the ways in which they relate to one another. For example, in the sentence, "We will finish revising the Morris contract this week, and all other work is also on schedule," the connective *and* binds the two thoughts together, giving them unity. The following is a list of some useful connectives:

   Time Connectives

   after, afterward
   first, second, etc.

   for example
   further

Time Connectives (cont'd)

meanwhile
next
still
until
when, whenever
while

Likeness Connectives

accordingly
also
and
as, as if
for example
just as
likewise
similarly

Why bother to classify connectives?

Comparison/Contrast Connectives

after all
although
briefly
but
generally
however
if, then
instead, rather
nevertheless
nor, or
specifically
though
yet

Cause and Effect or Association Connectives

because
consequently
for
if, then
not only, but also
since
so
therefore
thus

Be careful how you use connectives. If the thought flow between parts of a sentence or between sentences is already clear, you may not need one.

What does sentence structure refer to?

4. *Vary sentence structure.* When Henry Stone, the spokesperson for a medium-sized oil company, writes a memo, it seems to be composed only of simple declarative sentences such as, "Business in the last quarter was excellent." Certainly, there is nothing wrong with this sentence; it is both clear and short. Yet, when newspaper reporters receive Henry's memos, they tend to shake their heads, as if they were trying to clear them. For Henry Stone pays a price for his coherence and that is a loss of reader interest.

Good business writers vary the structure of their sentences. Sometimes they begin with clauses or phrases. Or they present some of their ideas as questions. They try, however, to avoid rhetorical questions (statements in question form) because readers may misinterpret them.

For example, suppose you write a simple declarative sentence such as the following:

> We must discontinue this procedure because it is ineffective.

Looking over your message, you decide that it already contains too many sentences of this type, so you restructure the sentence.

> Because the procedure is ineffective, we must discontinue it.

Such attention to style as well as to content has an important payoff: your reader will look over what you write with greater interest.

Developing Organized Paragraphs

Just as well-constructed sentences help to form effective paragraphs, well-organized paragraphs can help to form effective messages. Such paragraphs have a certain structure, length, and thought flow.

Paragraph Structure

The secret behind every good paragraph is the same: all sentences are tightly organized to form a central or whole idea. A paragraph's whole idea consists of a main thought, which is called a *topic sentence,* and *supporting details.*

Are deductive and inductive paragraphs mirror images of each other?

Most of the time business writers organize their paragraphs either deductively (directly) or inductively (indirectly). Both methods of structuring use a main thought and supporting details to convey a central thought. *Deductively* organized paragraphs begin with the main thought, followed by supporting details. *Inductively* organized paragraphs reverse the process and begin with supporting details, followed by the main thought (see Figure 3-1). Here are examples of each method:

> **Deductive (main thought in italics)**
> *Because sick leave in the office set a record yesterday, we will have to hire temporary help to complete the Aspen Project.* Sarah used a day of sick leave to take her children to the dentist. James was hospitalized after an accident while driving to work. Mary Ann had to fly to the bedside of her mother. Eduardo and Renée were bedridden with influenza, which has reached epidemic proportions here in Chicago.

> **Inductive (main thought in italics)**
> Sarah used a day of sick leave to take her children to the dentist. James was hospitalized after an accident while driving to work. Mary Ann had to fly to the bedside of her mother. Eduardo and Renée were bedridden with influenza, which has reached epidemic proportions in Chicago. *Therefore, since sick leave in the office set a record yesterday, we will have to hire temporary help to complete the Aspen Project.*

Suppose you had to decide whether to describe the situation in the Chicago office inductively or deductively. No matter which method you choose, the good way to begin is to jot down the main thought and then use it as a framework for listing the supporting details. After you have done this, think about what you want to accomplish. If your most important goal is to be understood, organize the paragraph deductively. If, however, you want to persuade your

Why do the triangles or pyramids in Figure 3 point in opposite directions?

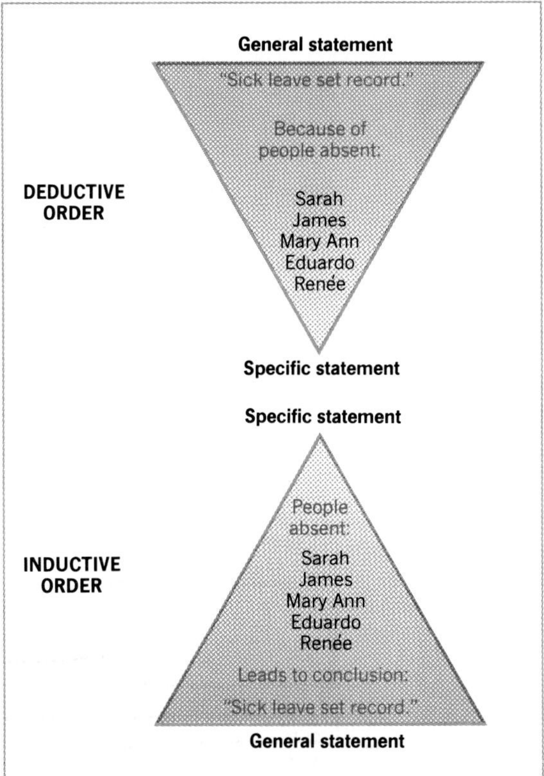

FIGURE 3–1 Deductive and Inductive Reasoning

boss to hire some temporary help even though the company has a limited budget, organize it inductively to persuade your reader by restating the problem before presenting the solution. In general, structure paragraphs deductively except where you need to persuade the reader to agree with your ideas. In that situation, use an inductive organization that will lead your reader to arrive at the same conclusion as you did.

Paragraph Length and Thought Flow

Some effective paragraphs may contain only a few words. Others may be composed of several hundred. Letter and memo paragraphs tend to be short. Report writers also try to be concise and to vary paragraph length to aid readers. Even technical writers, who often must present complex information, know that short paragraphs are usually easier to read and to understand. The purpose of "good" business communication is to present your ideas clearly so your reader can understand and respond appropriately.

A smooth thought flow within and between paragraphs also makes reading easier by giving a message unity. The following are three guides to improving this aspect of your written communication:

What good does it do to organize the details within paragraphs?

1. *Organize the supporting details within paragraphs.* The content of the message itself provides the best clues about how to organize details. Several possibilities are:

   a. From least to most important, or the reverse.
   b. Through comparison and contrast.
   c. In a time or date sequence.
   d. By defining the main thought.
   e. Through classification.

   To illustrate how this may work for you, try a time sequence. Assume that you need to write a paragraph summarizing what happened today at work. To arrange details chronologically, you would naturally begin with the first event of the day—receiving a call from a worried customer—and continue to the last event—stuffing a 100-page sales analysis into your already bulging briefcase just before you switch off the light in your office.

2. *Use connectives.* Connectives are just what their name implies: they connect parts of sentences as well as ideas with one another. Within paragraphs, use them to smooth the thought flow from sentence to sentence. For the same reason, use them between paragraphs as well. For example, the insertion of words such as *however* and *therefore* at the beginning of a paragraph act as a signal to the reader that the ideas that follow will relate to those in the preceding paragraph. (See page 72 for a list of connectives.)

3. *Repeat key ideas.* Repeating a key idea cues the reader to its importance. In a memo, for example, the major idea might be found three (or more) times: on the subject line, in the introduction, and as part of the conclusion of the message. This process is called structuring for emphasis, which should not be confused with *unnecessary* repetition or redundancy, and is a common device used to add emphasis and to focus the reader's attention.

Using Parallel Construction

Parallel construction occurs when two or more parts of a sentence are assigned an equivalent structure. In this way writers balance ideas that have equal weight or significance. When you write any business communication, you should express such thoughts in parallel grammatical form.

Parallel construction is like a series of building blocks you can use to make your writing clear and unified. That is, you can employ it right up the scale from word to word, phrase to phrase, clause to clause, sentence to sentence, and paragraph to paragraph. The following shows some of these uses:

Word level (all adjectives):
The comptroller's office agreed to send duplicates of the *May, June,* and *July* reports.

Phrase level (all noun phrases):
The assistant comptroller, the production manager, and *the inventory control chief* agreed to furnish reports for comparison.

Clause level (all dependent clauses).
Please fill out Form 1 if you work under 20 hours a week, Form 2 if you work 20–39 hours a week, and Form 3 if you work 40 hours a week or more.

Clause level (all independent clauses).
The executive assistant worked out the comparisons, his supervisor wrote the report, and *the director of transportation released the disputed shipment.*

What happens when parallel ideas aren't written in parallel language?

Another, and very common, form of parallel construction occurs when you use coordinating or correlative conjunctions to connect elements within a sentence. (Some commonly used coordinating conjunctions are *but, or, and, so, for, yet,* and *nor. Both-and, either-or, neither-nor, if-then,* and *not only-but also* are some frequently used correlative conjunctions.) The following are several examples of how to revise for a more logical use of parallel construction:

Initial Jane's stockbroker advised her to sell Abcar shares and buy Inovar shares.
Revised Jane's stockbroker advised her to sell Abcar shares and to buy Inovar shares.

Inital Not only must we balance the books, but also taking the inventory is necessary.
Revised Not only must we balance the books, but also we must take the inventory.

Initial (headings in a report)
A. Production Needs
B. Sales Needs
C. Needs in Inventory

Revised A. Production Needs
B. Sales Needs
C. Inventory Needs

Initial (headings in a report)
I. Diseases in Peach Trees
II. Diseases in Apple Trees
III. Diseases in Orange Trees

IV. Diseases in Winesap Trees
V. Diseases in Golden Delicious Trees

Revised (Note: Winesap and Golden Delicious are apple varieties.)

I. Diseases in Peach Trees
II. Diseases in Apple Trees
  A. Winesap
  B. Golden Delicious
III. Diseases in Orange Trees

As you can see from the examples, deviating from parallel form can mislead a reader about the meaning of a message. This happens most often when the subject matter is unfamiliar or the ideas are complex.

GAINING CREDIBILITY

What does it matter whether language is credible?

The first thing Susan Rosetti does after she has settled into her seat on the commuter train that takes her to work each morning is to open the financial section of the newspaper to her favorite columnist. Asked why she thinks so highly of this writer, Susan says quite simply, "I can always trust him to be fair and objective."

What Susan is talking about is credibility. Whereas good messages are coherent, they are also believable; that is, they seem fair and objective. Sometimes, however, although what you are saying is truthful, it may not sound so. Much depends on how you say it. In this section we will show you some ways to improve your writing credibility.

Being Objective

Suppose you are writing a report on a chain of midpriced apparel stores. You decide to include two statements. The first is, "Since 1980 the number of outlets has grown to 300." The second is, "During the next several years, the number of stores will continue to grow." Which statement do you think a reader would find easier to believe—the first, which seems to be objective and factual, or the second, which is your opinion?

Should you ever offer opinions in writing?

Probably, most readers would choose the first because they have more faith in objective statements than in opinions. Yet this does not mean that you should avoid stating opinions in your business messages. In fact, you can express them quite credibly by simply calling them what they are—your views. The following are three ways in which to make such views seem more objective.

1. *Cite sources.* Always give the sources of your information, especially when you are presenting key ideas. For example, did you

acquire the data from a survey, from talking with superiors, or from company records? Cite the source. For example,

> The results of tests run July 20 by Philip Goldman, chief engineer at Dubont's Sprackling Division in Philadelphia, show that . . .

2. *Quote sources.* Many writers prefer to paraphrase because they can fit such material into the text more easily than something that is directly quoted. Yet direct quotes can add weight to an argument, as in the following:

> Louis DuBois, president of the French Lines, said in a speech before the National Association of Business that "If the industry is to survive, international tax laws must be changed in the next two years . . . "

3. *Use figures and graphic aids.* By citing figures, you can show readers why you have made certain statements. Graphics aids such as diagrams and charts also help by illustrating ideas or showing relations between complex data.

Assume that you were working for a government agency devoted to meeting the housing needs for the elderly. You discover that the standard application form is both cumbersome and confusing. You would surely get stronger support for your proposal to introduce a new, easier-to-read application form if you included a few well-chosen statistics to support your suggestion. For example, "Only 10 percent of the applicants are able to complete Form AA-2 correctly" or "Assisting applicants to complete their application forms properly takes, on the average, two hours out of every staff member's day." A chart showing how much time a new form could save would probably make this argument for change even more apparent.

Being Fair

How does fairness make writing more credible?

Certainly, the quality of fairness is a virtue in our society. In praise, we say a judge's decision is fair-minded, that a labor mediator deals fairly with both sides, that a college professor gives fair grades, and so forth. In writing, too, a sense of fairness on the author's part is viewed by most readers as an asset. Fairness gives balance to writing, and balance in turn implies thought and planning. Also fairness suggests objectivity and thus makes a message credible. The following guidelines should help you to give an impression of fairness in any message you write.

Show Different Viewpoints

Showing differing viewpoints makes your writing seem balanced. Here are two examples of how to accomplish this:

> Although the majority of employees favored extending insurance coverage to include dental expenses, 25 percent were unwilling to pay the higher rates required for the additional coverage.

> Groton's citizens believe that the Dynamics Company should receive the defense contract. They favored Dynamics over the Aerospace Company by a 450-to-60 vote. In contrast, Portsmouth's citizens indicated by a 232-to-72 vote their belief that Aerospace should receive the contract.

Readers of these two messages may assume that there is nothing to hide because the writers made an effort to present information in a balanced manner. In your own messages, you should feel equally self-confident, openly disclosing views that are not only similar but different from yours.

Give Complete Information

While awaiting the judge's decision in a case that would determine his company's future, the president of the mining firm in question paced up and down the length of his office, mopping his brow. When informed that the decision had gone in the company's favor, he sighed in relief and confided to his lawyer that today had been the most tense of his entire business career. Pausing, he added, "No, that's not quite true. Two months ago when we had that merger scare, things were pretty bad too."

No matter where you are in the business hierarchy, much of what you will do involves dealing with emotional issues. Some of these will have serious consequences for both you and your company. That is why it is critical for you to give complete information, for only in this way can good decisions be made. For example, suppose you have been sent to New England by the Dynamics Company to research local public opinion about who should receive the defense contract, your company or the Aerospace Company. After watching the citizens vote on the issue in three towns, you write the following report to Dynamics' executive board:

> Groton's citizens believe that Dynamics Company should receive the defense contract. They favored Dynamics over the Aerospace Company by a 450-to-60 vote. Although the vote was not considered representative because it was taken on a Sunday morning when many people were unavailable, Newport's citizens favored Dynamics by a 23-to-10 vote. Portsmouth citizens, however, voted 232 to 72 that Aerospace should receive the contract.

In writing your report, and in your desire to give your company good news, you might have left out that the Newport vote was unrepresentative. Yet deleting such information would ulitmately hurt your company because then the executive board would have incomplete information.

Avoiding Unrelated Matters

What types of matters might be "unrelated" where written messages are concerned?

For a long time your family has been friends with Jason Berlin, the president of a company that manufactures office copiers. Now your own firm wants to purchase 20 of these machines, and you ask to negotiate for them. Perhaps you may be able to get a discount because you know the president personally. So you write a note to him, asking whether he might be able to lower the price "for an old friend." In reply, you get a brief, impersonal letter giving the manufacturer's usual list prices. A little later you hear from mutual acquaintances that he resented your use of the friendship as a way of getting a business favor.

Good business writers know that their messages must never seem coercive. The reader must always feel that any decision is his or her free choice to make—based on the situation itself.

USING EMPHASIS

It is almost redundant that businesspeople are always in a hurry. During an average business day, an executive may read a number of documents ranging from one-paragraph memos to book-length reports. What these documents have in common is information and some point to make—whether it is a request for more yellow pads for the staff or a recommendation that the company try to sell off its radio and TV stations.

Because readers have to analyze so much information, they want to know quickly what the major thrust of a message is and why it is important to them. The techniques of highlighting information range from simple repetition of key words to knowing exactly what amount of space to devote to a specific topic. Also, the words you choose and the visual or graphic elements that accompany your written message will help to focus the reader's attention.

Structuring for Emphasis

Why do we pay attention to some things in a message and not to others? The following are some techniques to use to emphasize the important points in any message of yours:

1. *Open and close with key ideas.* All business readers pay special attention to two parts of a message: the beginning and the end. At the start, they want to know what the subject is; at the end, they are interested in the conclusion presented. Therefore, always open and close with your key ideas. If you put them someplace else, you risk losing your reader's attention.

2. *Use repetition.* Suppose you want to emphasize the importance of deciding whether to close a paper plant in the next month before contract negotiations with the workers begin. In your memo on the subject, you should repeat the importance of the time factor because this will reinforce the reader's perception that a decision will have to be made quickly.

Could you distort a message through undue structuring for emphasis? If so, how?

3. *Use proportion.* The amount of your message that is devoted to a specific item—in relation to the message's length—will underscore its importance or unimportance. For example, if more than half your memo on speculating in gold discusses the negative consequences of jumping into the market, then you may be advising against speculating, even if you do not say so outright.
4. *Write short sentences and short paragraphs.* Short sentences and short paragraphs catch the reader's attention. If you want to emphasize that family rivalries are often the cause of changes in the wine industry, then say it as briefly as you can. Stripped of modifiers, sentences can be as short as one or two words. If you really want your reader's attention, limit your short paragraphs to one sentence or perhaps two.
5. *Choose the best words and use the active voice.* In essence, writing is always about words. If you choose concrete and precise nouns, pronouns, and verbs as well as adjectives and adverbs that accurately describe them, you will be able to emphasize, not obscure, your important points. In addition, the active voice ("The president needs your help" rather than "Your help is needed by the president") always makes a messade stronger and more vivid.

Designing for Emphasis

The glossy magazine ad shows a man in a crisp cotton suit beside a well-dressed woman in the glittering lobby of a luxury hotel. Underneath, printed in large letters, is the message: "For those who want to be suitable anyplace."

Articles and advertisements in magazines are perhaps the most obvious examples of how design may enhance a message. Yet, even in simple business communication, you can use design techniques to emphasize important points. The following are some ways to do this:

1. *Use headings.* Headings break up a text and make it easier to read. Although experienced writers use them most often in reports, headings can quite effectively emphasize key sections of memos and letters.
2. *List items.* If you have 10 points to discuss in your report on how the current antitrust law affects your company, you might think of beginning with your most important point, and proceeding to

what you think is least important. By doing this, you lead your reader to think of your points in exactly the same way; that is, he or she will naturally feel, at least initially, that your first point is also most important. Here are four ways to list ideas:

a. Line spacing, such as single, double, or triple spacing
b. Numbering, or enumerating, such as 1, 2, 3 or I, II, III
c. Alphabetizing, such as a, b, c or A, B, C
d. Bullets, asterisks, dashes, such as • • •, **, - -

3. *Use capitalization and underlining.* Suppose you want to emphasize that the sale items in your clothing store are not refundable. You can emphasize this in the message you tape to the sales desk: "ITEMS NOT REFUNDABLE" or "Items not refundable." If you do use capitalization or underlining to emphasize a word, phrase, clause, sentence, or paragraph, limit this to six or fewer consecutive lines. If you do more, the effect is reversed and your points are harder to read.

How can you design for emphasis when writing a message?

4. *Leave white space.* Surrounding parts of a message with additional white space—more blank lines or wider margins—will emphasize the message for the reader. Some writers call this strategy "framing the message."

5. *Use boldface, italic, and alternate type styles.* If you have a word processor, you can change the size and typeface of different parts of your message. If you decide to add italics for emphasis, however—or any of these other techniques—use them with moderation. For example, if you use Gothic type in one place, Helvetica in another, and Times Roman in still another, you may distract your reader.

6. *Color.* In the past, business messages have been written in black lettering on white paper. Recently though, we have seen much more use of color. One advantage of color is that it attracts a reader's eye. For example, you may choose to write your resume on biege paper so that it stands out from other resumes a company has received. If you decide to use colored paper or lettering, make sure the colors you select are appropriate to your audience. Most bank managers would not approve of a balance sheet on hot pink paper, but a sales manager might appreciate such creativity and risk taking.

7. *Use figures and other graphic aids.* Suppose you need to specify the rising costs of an airline company in relation to its employees. You could explain this point in a number of sentences, which would probably be difficult for your reader to follow. Or more neatly and succinctly, you could show these rising costs with a bar graph like one of those in Chapter 15.

No matter how many of these techniques you employ, after you have completed your message, recheck it to see that is indeed easy to read. For that is, after all, the goal of all these techniques.

CHECKING YOUR MESSAGE'S READABILITY

The Fog Index

Many formulas exist to compute readability. Of these, Robert Gunning's Fog Index is most often used in business and industry. Follow these four steps to compute the reading level of a message using the Fog Index[1]:

Step 1 *Find the average sentence length.*

Choose a passage of continuous sentences containing at least 100 words; the passage may be a complete message or part of one. Count the number of words in the passage and then the number of sentences. (Count independent clauses as separate sentences. For example, "We read. We learned. We improved." This should be counted as three sentences, even if semicolons or dashes are used instead of periods.) Divide the number of words in the passage by the number of sentences to get the average number of words in a sentence.

What does the Gunning Fog Index measure?

What steps are involved in computing an Index?

Step 2 *Find the percentage of "difficult"* words.

"Difficult" words are those containing three or more syllables *except*

a. Words that are capitalized.
b. Words formed by combining short words (*nonetheless* and *hereafter,* for example).
c. Verbs made into three syllables by adding *ed* or *es* (*confounded* or *disposes,* for example).

Now count the number of difficult words, counting each one each time it appears in the passage. Divide the number of difficult words by the total number of words in the passage and multiply the result by 100. The answer is the percentage of difficult words.

Step 3 *Add the answers in steps 1 and 2.*

Add the average sentence length to the percentage of difficult words.

Step 4 *Multiply by 0.4.*

Multiply the answer in step 3 by 0.4 to obtain the reading grade level (Fog Index) of the passage.

[1] Adapted from Robert Gunning, *The Technique of Clear Writing,* rev. ed. (New York, McGraw-Hill, 1968), pp. 38–39. Used by permission.

If you prefer to use a mathematical approach for computing a reading grade level, apply this formula:

$$\text{Fog Index} = \left[\frac{B}{C} + \left(\frac{A}{B} \times 100\right)\right] \times 0.4$$

where

A = number of "difficult" words in the passage
B = number of words in the passage
C = number of sentences in the passage

Note: In dates, count each word separately; for example, *January 10, 1987* is three words. In numbers and symbols, count each word separately when spelled out or when spaces are left between: for example, *$250* is one word but *two hundred fifty dollars* is four words; *six and two thirds* is four words, but *6 2/3* is two words.

Applying the Fog Index

The "difficult" words in the following paragraph from a sales letter are underlined, and the Fog Index computation follows:

Could you measure the readability of something you've written?

> The booklet has been received warmly. For example, the Information Service Institute has adopted it as a text for use in a statewide teacher training program for city organizations; these groups have included fire, police, and parks departments. The institute trains members of the departments to serve as teachers. Then the teachers conduct workshops within their own organizations. Many of these departments have purchased multiple copies of the booklet. Also, the booklet has been ordered by hundreds of private companies across the nation. In some cases, a copy was ordered for each person who conducted a workshop. In other cases, a single copy was bought for use as a reference manual for the company's training division.

Step 1	Number of words	116	
	Number of sentences	9	
	Average sentence length (116 ÷ 9)		13
Step 2	Number of "difficult" words	13	
	Percentage of "difficult" words (13 ÷ 116 × 100)		11
Step 3	Steps 1 and 2 answers added		24
Step 4	Reading grade level of passage (24 × .4)		10

The tenth-grade reading level means that a person who reads in the tenth-grade range can read the passage easily. Business messages usually are written between grade levels 8 and 12. If you consistently write messages within this range, most readers will find them easy to read. Remember that long sentences and words of more than two syllables raise the reading grade level. Adjusting the Fog Index grade-level to your reader's needs and preferences will improve your message's readability.

Using a readability formula that is based mainly on word and sentence length is only part of what you need to do to make sure your writing is readable. You can also imagine that you are the reader. Then ask, "What types of messages do I like reading?" Probably you like the words in them to be precise, the sentences and paragraphs well organized, and the meaning clear enough so that you don't have to reread a sentence or a passage three times to understand it.

These factors, along with many others, affect a message's readability. There is no simple formula for making your own writing readable. But by applying the advice in this chapter and the next, you can make it more readable than might otherwise be the case.

PROOFREADING MESSAGES

Once you have written your message and have tested its readability, your job is still incomplete—for now you need to proofread it. Proofreading is your last opportunity to check that everything is in order. It permits you to catch errors that in the heat of creation you may have overlooked. Therefore, make it a practice always to proofread your work, whether it is a brief letter of thanks to a local auto parts distributor for the excellent sales of your products or a 50-page report that is going to be read by your supervisor. When perfect copy is especially important, ask someone else to proofread your message as well.

Types and Methods of Proofreading

In proofreading, you need to ask yourself the following three questions:

What kinds of proofreading are there?

1. *Context:* Did I say what I meant to say in the way I meant to say it?
2. *Accuracy:* Did I make any mechanical errors—spelling, punctuation, capitalization, grammar?
3. *Form and appearance:* Is my layout correct—are all parts in place and is the spacing correct? Does the entire document look balanced?

Proofreading for everything at once is hard and will usually result in your overlooking some mistakes. So it may be better if you proofread separately for context, accuracy and appearance and form.

Four methods of proofreading are

1. Read forward. (from the beginning to the end)
2. Read backward. (from the end to the beginning)
3. Ask another person who writes well to read it.
4. Read it with another person simultaneously.

Are all proofreading methods of equal value? If not, why not?

Each of these methods has its own advantages. If you read your message forward, you will be most likely to find any errors in context and accuracy. If you read it backward, you will be more likely to discover typographical errors. Having someone else read it will act as a double-check against context and accuracy errors because sometimes in proofing we can overlook our own mistakes. Proofreading along with someone else accomplishes the same task. When doing this, each person should read from a separate copy. Because proofing with another person takes additional time and effort, use it only for especially important writing or when much mathematical data are included.

The Three P's System

How many times should you proof a message? The easy answer is: until it is error free. But how often do you have time to reread something until this state of perfection is achieved? Naturally, the answer depends in part on how carefully you proofread. If you proof carefully, one reading is usually enough for informal notes and brief memos. But if you have written a long report or speech, try to recheck it at each stage of development.

Why is a system helpful in proofreading?

Proofreading long works such as reports is complex, and therefore overlooking errors is easy to do even when two or more people read the material. Using a *system* when proofreading can solve the problem. The *Three P's System* that follows is a practical and flexible method for finding errors in long documents. Either you or another person can use it independently, or you can use it when proofreading with another person. The three P's stand for *preconditions, procedure,* and *postconditions.* Here is how it works:

P1: Preconditions

1. *Allow at least 3 hours to lapse before proofreading a message.* For even better results, allow about 24 hours to lapse, but do not wait longer than three days. Ideally, you should wait until you can approach it with a fresh perspective, but with your original goals still clear.
2. *Proofread at the rough draft stage when possible.* The sooner you make changes, the more time you save. Since you can most easily change things at the draft stage, try to proof then as well as later.

3. *Learn to use standard proofreading symbols to mark changes.* Using standard symbols makes it easy to interpret changes. Check a dictionary such as *Webster's Ninth Collegiate,* or perhaps your instructor will provide a list of these symbols.

P2: Procedure

First, *proofread for overall effect.* Reflect on the message as the reader will do. Does it say what you wish to say, only what you wish to say, and in the way you wish to say it? Then, proofread for the *Seven C's* of writing:

What are the Seven C's?

1. *Is it clear?* Are all points clearly stated using familiar, direct language? Are complex points simplified? Are points stated in proper relationship with one another?
2. *Is it complete?* Are all important points included? Has everything been said that should be said?
3. *Is it concise?* Are only relevant points included? Is the message succinct? Is it worded precisely?
4. *Is it concrete?* Are facts and figures used wherever needed? Is the language objective and specific?
5. *Is it considerate?* Does the message focus on the reader's interests and needs? Does the language express the reader's viewpoint and include the reader in the action?
6. *Is it correct?* Is the language level correct for the reader? Are grammar, spelling, punctuation, and capitalization correct?
7. *Is it courteous?* Does the message sound sincere? Is the language positive?

P3: Postconditions

1. *Ask another person to proofread the message if (a) it is not satisfactory at this point or (b) it has special importance.*
2. *Revise the message if it is not satisfactory at this point.* After revising the message, proceed again through P1 (preconditions) and P2 (procedure).
3. *Rewrite the message entirely if it is still not satisfactory at this point.* While rewriting, refer to the revised message now being discarded only for facts. Avoid using an unsatisfactory revision for guidance on organization or expression. When you must rewrite a message, remember that you are starting over.

When carefully followed, the Three P's System will work well. At first you will spend more time than you will after you become accustomed to it. Here is a paragraph from a long report that was proofread using the system. A corrected copy follows.

Sixteen women and six men shopped regularly at the Fan Market. Incomes ranged from $15,000 to $55,000. Income level and sex showed no correlation. 3 women and one man had incomes between $15,000 $25,000 and six women and men two had incomes between $25,000 and $35,000. 4 women and two men had incomes between $53,001 and $45,000, and three women and one man had incomes bwtween $45,001 and $$55,00 0.

The sixteen women and six men who shop regularly at the Fan Market have incomes ranging from $15,000 to $55,000. Income level and sex show no correlation. Three women and one man have incomes between $15,000 and $25,000. Six women and two men have incomes between $25,001 and $35,000. Four women and two men have incomes between $35,001 and $45,000, and three women and one man have incomes between $45,001 and $55,000.

The next step in business writing, preparing attractive copy, is as important to the professional as a well-written message.

PREPARING ATTRACTIVE COPY

Why is the appearance of a written message important?

Tom Sellars has just finished a memo on financing public radio that his supervisor expects to see in the next half hour. Proofing it hurriedly, Tom notices a few mistakes. Since he does not have time to retype it, he simply crosses out the incorrect figures and inserts the correct ones. Later on that day the memo is returned to him with this curt message attached: "When this is in satisfactory form, then I will read it."

As do most readers, Tom's supervisor is responding to the physical appearance of a message. On the basis of it, receivers usually react—at least initially—either positively or negatively. To test this observation, notice what happens the next time you read a letter or memo. If the letter or memo looks attractive, your first impression will probably be positive. But if it looks messy or otherwise unattractive, you may have the opposite reaction. You may wonder if the writer is careful or really intelligent or simply doesn't care.

How to Prepare Copy

Good-looking messages require careful copy preparation. Usually, written messages are either typed or printed whenever they are important enough to be recorded. Although most messages that today's managers write are prepared for mailing or routing by nonmanagerial employees, this process is changing. Now an increasing number of managers are using word processors to write, print, and send their own final copy.

Because computers permit them to work faster and to have access to more information, managers have begun to recognize that using computers increases management effectiveness. If you do not already know how to use a word processor, learn! You will quickly see that the quality of your work will improve. Probably this is the result of your direct involvement in the entire writing process from start to finish. If, however, you do not have access to a computer, then check the work of those who prepare your messages before you sign or approve them. For example, even if you trust your assistant to be precise, still look over every message carefully before it goes out. (See Chapter 6 for more details on using word processing equipment.)

Checkpoints for Preparing Copy

Here are four points to check before approving a message for mailing or routing:

What points should you check before mailing a written message?

1. *Do the pages look clean?* Remove any visible erasures, corrections, or smudges. Sometimes this may mean retyping the message.
2. *Does the copy look sharp?* Copy should be dark, contrasting sharply with the paper. Quality paper and a new typing ribbon should accomplish this for you.
3. *Is the copy balanced on the page?* Frame the message with blank spaces on all sides of each page. Center the message slightly high on the page—called the "picture frame" effect.
4. *Are standard layouts and formats used?* Readers expect to see standard layouts and formats. Those that are nonstandard distract attention from the message. (See Chapter 16 and Appendix B.)

Other graphic elements also affect the reader's impression of the message. These include:

1. Design of letterheads, memo forms, and envelopes.
2. Quality of reproduction or printing.
3. Paper type and color.
4. Type style and ink color.

Most firms standardize selection of these items, requiring their use throughout the company. Because a change in any of them may affect everyone, supervisors usually have to approve such changes.

SUMMARY

1. Effective business communication, whether its purpose is to inform, persuade, or build goodwill, is the product of careful planning.
2. The steps to good message planning are (a) identifying the purpose, (b) determining the content, (c) organizing the content by priority, (d) setting a time schedule, and (e) devising a system to monitor progress.
3. A critical element in designing effective business communications is writing for the reader. Accomplish this by identifying (a) your relationship with the reader, (b) the position the reader holds, (c) the reader's reading level, (d) the reader's interests, (e) the reader's knowledge of the subject, (f) the reader's background, (g) if the reader has strong feelings about certain subjects, (h) the reader's unspoken needs, and (i) if the reader needs information quickly.
4. The goal of effective business writing is to write so the reader will understand. When preparing a business message, this goal is achieved through the writer's appropriate selection of (a) words, including both denotation and connotation and improved word selection; (b) sentence structure, including structure and use of connectives; and (c) paragraph structure, including development and coherence.
5. Credibility is gained in business messages through (a) objectivity; (b) fairness, which includes showing different viewpoints and giving complete information; and (c) avoiding unrelated matters.
6. Giving proper emphasis to points in a message includes both structure and design. The use of key ideas, repetition, and proportion are examples of structural considerations. Examples of design considerations are use of headings, white space, and color.
7. Ease of reading—readability—is an important property of effective business messages. The readability level of a written message can be found by using formulas such as the Gunning Fog Index.
8. The final stage in preparing a professional, written business message involves (a) proofreading, perhaps using the "Three P's System," and (b) checking final copy preparation to ensure a clean look, balance on page, and standard layout and format.

Review Questions

1. What advantages do written business messages have compared with those sent by telephone or in person?
2. What are the steps in planning and achieving writing objectives?
3. Why should we analyze the reader before sending a written message?
4. Which four of the nine questions involved in reader analysis stand out most in your mind? Why do you think this is true?
5. Why should we prefer concrete nouns and pronouns to abstract ones in cases where there is a choice?
6. Can you think of a situation in which you heard or read adjectives and adverbs being used that overstated the situation? If so, how did you react to this misuse of language?
7. What difference is there between deductively and inductively organized paragraphs?

8. Why do you think the supporting details within a paragraph need organizing? Isn't it enough to just state the facts?
9. Does being objective add to the credibility of messages? If so, can you name at least two ways you can be objective?
10. How could you be unfair in business writing by giving incomplete information?
11. What two main ways are available to emphasize messages? Give two examples of how to do each.
12. What is readability? How can you measure it?
13. How does the Gunning Fog Index work? Briefly explain the steps involved.
14. What are the four methods of proofreading? Give one advantage for each.
15. What are the checkpoints for preparing attractive copy? Explain the importance of each one.

Exercises

1. List three verbs that show more action than the underlined word in each of these sentences:

   a. Agnes went to her noon appointment with the personnel director.
   b. Lars talked with Diane about the Stears project.
   c. Marvin Jenks came to the four o'clock meeting.
   d. Vennie looked at her work schedule.
   e. Connie smiled when she heard they had gotten the contract.

2. Examine the simple sentences following in each part of this exercise. Then rewrite the sentences to form compound, complex, or compound-complex sentences as indicated. You may add connectives when needed.

   a. The Jorgensens charged the purchase to their credit account. Marilyn then posted the charge on the record. (change to a *compound* sentence)
   b. The accounting staff needs another auditor. Sara Scranton applied for the job. (change to a *compound* sentence)
   c. A $55 balance was due. Olga paid it. She then bought a new radial tire for her car. (change to a *complex* sentence)
   d. Hilda Turner gives the orders here. She is the manager. (change to a *complex* sentence)
   e. The holiday season begins tomorrow. We will prepare for it. Afterward we will celebrate. (change to a *compound-complex* sentence)
   f. Helena Schmidt works in France. Josep Aulbert works in Austria. They exchange visits once a year. (change to a *compound-complex* sentence)

3. The following paragraph contains only simple sentences. Rewrite it so that it has at least one of each of the four sentence types: simple, compound, complex, and compound-complex. Use connectives wherever appropriate.

   Roberto and Joan spent two weeks campaigning for Alderman Pemberton's reelection. Both are busy with their jobs. They asked their neighbors to vote for the alderman. They passed out leaflets in South Philadelphia. They spoke to voters during rush hours. They posted handbills on telephone poles in the district. First, they got a permit to do this. Joan appeared on a local television program to promote the cause. Roberto promoted it among union members. Both Roberto and Joan believe the alderman is doing a good job.

4. Write *deductively* and *inductively* arranged

paragraphs using the information presented. First, write a main idea (topic sentence) from the suggestion. Next, write a deductively arranged paragraph using your topic sentence and the suggested ideas for details. Then, rearrange the paragraph inductively. You may add words to smooth the thought flow.

Suggestion for Main Idea
K-C Company's new Zippy paper towel is the best on the market.

Suggestions for Paragraph Details
The towel will absorb 20 percent more than other towels on the market. It is more tear resistant than any of the five leading brands and will not get "soggy" when wet. The towel is more durable than those of any competitor. It comes in five new designs. Each towel is 15 percent larger than any major brand.

5. Find the parallelism problems in the parts of this exercise that follow and then rewrite them in a parallel form.

   a. Not only will we debit the account, but also making the disbursement is necessary.
   b. Shelley will choose the gift, arrange the retirement party, and the guests must be invited by her.
   c. Where we go and the things we do are often unplanned.
   d. (headings in a report)
      A. Finance Charges Increased
      B. Decrease in Profits
      C. Inventories Remained Steady
      D. Costs Fell Slightly
   e. (headings in a report)
      A. Selling for High Prices
         1. Planning the Presentation
         2. Making the Delivery
         3. Buying for Lower Costs
      B. Salvaging for Resale
      C. Should Manufacture for Best Design
         1. Use Buying Plan
         2. Sell Old Stock

6. Apply the procedure for finding the Gunning Fog Index to the two paragraphs that follow. Find one reading grade level for the combined paragraphs.

   Millions of travelers enter the continental United States each year. Along with the usual souvenirs, they often bring many varieties of prohibited agricultural products. Currently, a number of these contraband products carried by travelers get through without detection.

   Many of these agricultural products may carry pests not found in this country. Because these pests may not have natural enemies in the United States, they can flourish. The Mediterranean fruitfly is a prime example. This enemy of fruit growers has appeared in the country several times during this century. Thus far, we have been able to eradicate them each time using scientific methods. But can we always do this?

7. Applying what you know about readability, rewrite the two paragraphs in Exercise 6 so they are easier to understand <u>but</u> do not lose any of their meaning.

8. Make a photocopy of the first of the two paragraphs that follow or type it on a sheet of paper. Then proofread so that when the corrections you suggest are made, the copy will read like the second paragraph.

   Enter the new United Bank serve yourself sweepstakes is easy. Firstly conduct a transattion at any Serve Yourself Banking Center in area your between August 1st and September 30th. each transaction is actually an entry in the sweepstakes. Whether you check your balance or make a deposit, payment transfer or withdrawal of cash, you are entered automatically. Winners willbe notified before October 1st by mail.

   Entering the new United Bank Serve Yourself Sweepstakes is easy. Simply conduct a transaction at any Serve Yourself Banking Center in your area between August 1 and September 30. Each transaction is actually an entry in the sweepstakes. You are entered automatically whether you check your balance or make a deposit, payment, transfer, or cash withdrawal. Winners will be notified by mail before October 1.

9. Select a news story from the front page of *The Wall Street Journal*. Do a Fog Index on two or three paragraphs. Complete the same exercise with a story from the front page of a local newspaper. Is there a difference? If so, is it what you expected? Explain your findings.

10. Select an editorial or column from *The Wall Street Journal, Barron's, Forbes, Fortune,* or *Business Week.* What persuasive techniques, such as word choice and organizing for emphasis, do you find in it?

CHAPTER 4

STYLE AND TONE IN LANGUAGE

Many things have style—furniture, clothes, jewelry, automobiles. People also have style, often a noticeable one—an athlete or entertainer comes to mind. And a business executive has a managerial style. If you look for the word in the dictionary, you'll find it broadly defined as "a distinctive form or type of something."

ABOUT STYLE

Writing too has style. For example, compare these two excerpts from business letters:

> Pursuant to your request of the fourth instance for merchandise parcels, we beg to say that your gracious order has forthwith been shipped posthaste.

Does writing style change with time?

> Your order No. 311 was shipped this morning by railway express.

To our ears, the first excerpt sounds indirect, stilted, and wordy, whereas the second appears direct, informal, and concise. Perhaps we react this way because we are not used to the style of the first excerpt, which is typical of most nineteenth-century business messages. In contrast, we are perfectly familiar with the style of the second, as it embodies the virtues of late twentieth-century style.

Just as the times in which we live affect writing style, so does where we live. For example, business messages in the United Kingdom preserve a certain formality in expression that Americans and Canadians no longer use, and messages from Japan are couched in language that is more indirect and formal than that in most other countries. In writing to readers in other countries, we should always keep these stylistic distinctions in mind and try to meet their expectations.

In addition to time and place, other factors affect your writing both in its style and tone. Among these are your education, preferences, and likes and dislikes, in other words, who you are.

ABOUT TONE

What makes tone effective?

Tone in writing refers to the way you express yourself. What you elect to say *and* how you say it determines your tone. In business messages, the most effective tone to strike is friendly, conversational, objective, and businesslike.

When used excessively, however, these positive qualities may become negative. For example, if a message is inappropriately friendly or personal, the reader may feel the writer is being overly familiar or intrusive. Nor should conversational language become chatty and trite and business language too stilted or formal. Also, in trying to sound objective, a writer may convey instead an image of indifference.

Like style, setting the right tone is a delicate matter. Anything in a message that draws attention to itself may distract the reader's attention from what really matters: the contents. To avoid potential barriers, always seek a balance between extremes. For example, in a memo on the loan sales market, you want to sound neither impersonal on the one hand nor insincere on the other.

The major elements that affect style and tone are the subject of this chapter. Each of them—language level, bias, clarity, conciseness, accuracy, sincerity, positiveness, and vividness—is important in constructing effective business messages. As you become more aware of the effects of your own tone and style, writing should improve dramatically.

GENERAL LANGUAGE LEVELS

Recently, *The New York Times* published an article about unofficial dress codes for men in the office. For example, many companies required male employees to wear suits and ties. Some guidelines were even more specific, for instance, banks requiring men to wear blue suits and black shoes. Individuals who did not conform to the dress code were sometimes viewed as not inspiring confidence or not representing the company as they should.

Just as certain clothes are considered inappropriate in offices, so is certain language considered equally inappropriate in business messages. In both instances, the result is a loss of credibility and respect. When used correctly, language accurately reflects the degree of formality inherent in the situation. Thus, we can arrange language along continuum between "formal" and "informal." Compare the uses of formal and informal language in the different communication situations that are shown in Figure 4-1.

The elements determining language level are vocabulary, phrasing, sentence and paragraph length, and punctuation. If you are using strictly formal language, you would include more complex words and phrasing. At this level, you would also avoid first- and second-person pronouns, such as *I, we,* and *you.* In their place you would use the third-person pronouns *he, she, it,* and *they.* Also you would avoid informal shortcuts such as contractions. Your paragraphs too should be thoughtfully constructed and fully developed. Sentences should average 25–40 words and paragraphs 200–300 words. Naturally, as a result, punctuation will be more complex.

Formal language in a business message can be quite useful where the occasion or the reader demands it. For example, suppose you

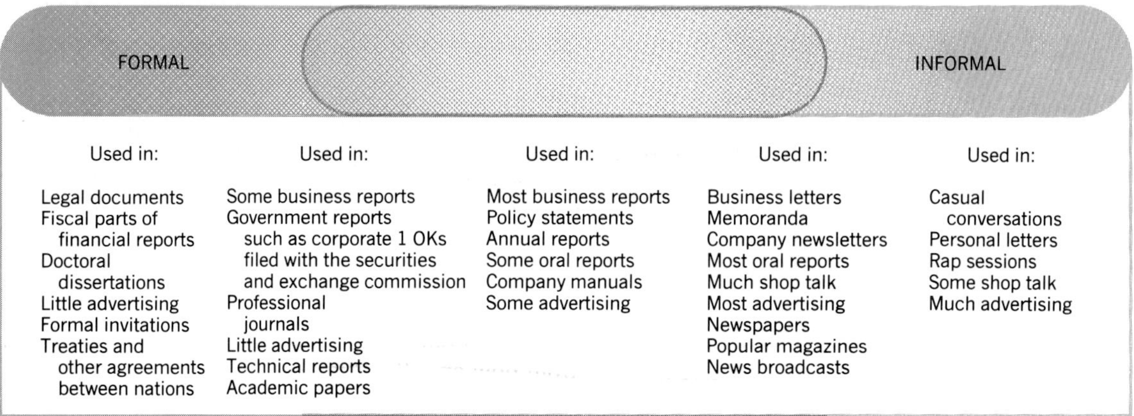

FORMAL
INFORMAL
Used in:
Legal documents
Fiscal parts of financial reports
Doctoral dissertations
Little advertising
Formal invitations
Treaties and other agreements between nations
Used in:
Some business reports
Government reports such as corporate 1 OKs filed with the securities and exchange commission
Professional journals
Little advertising
Technical reports
Academic papers
Used in:
Most business reports
Policy statements
Annual reports
Some oral reports
Company manuals
Some advertising
Used in:
Business letters
Memoranda
Company newsletters
Most oral reports
Much shop talk
Most advertising
Newspapers
Popular magazines
News broadcasts
Used in:
Casual conversations
Personal letters
Rap sessions
Some shop talk
Much advertising

FIGURE 4-1 Accepted uses of language levels. (Notice that the levels overlap considerably.)

Right now, do you use formal or informal language more often?

have to write an unfavorable auditing report. You are aware that your message may be used in some future legal proceedings. Also, you are familiar with the traditional language of accounting documents. Both of these factors cause you to decide to adopt a formal style, as the following excerpt from your report shows:

> Because of the effect of the failure to provide for deferred income taxes described in the preceding paragraph, the financial statements of ABC Company referred to above and taken as a whole are not reasonably stated in accordance with generally accepted accounting principles.

Because of its complexity and difficulty, writers of business messages tend to use formal language only in special circumstances such as in legal documents. Even here, however, the trend is to use less formal language. For example, insurance policies and loan agreements are sometimes written in informal language.

Most of the time, then, business messages are informal. This does not mean that they are ungrammatical; business writing is shaped by its purpose and audience and cannot afford to be stuffy or academic. Said differently, informal language is conversational. When we speak or write it, we use shorter and simpler words and phrasing than we do on formal occasions. Informal sentences and paragraphs are short, with sentences averaging 10 to 20 words and paragraphs averaging fewer than 175 words. Figure 4-2 shows acceptable uses of formal and informal language in business messages.

UNBIASED LANGUAGE

The message on the bulletin board concerned the company's new safety procedures. It contained the following sentence: "An increased

Formal and Informal Language

Do you know when you are speaking or writing formally? Informally? Here are some examples of formal and informal usage both of words and sentences that commonly appear in business messages. For your own writing, it would be useful for you to become aware of the formality or informality of specific words.

Formal	*Informal*
appertaining	belonging
ascertain	learn, find out
henceforth	from now on, after this
heretofore	up to now
pursuance	carrying out
statute	law
prior to	before
undersigned	signer (or use name)
vigilant	watchful
wherewithal	means, necessary means

Formal	*Informal*
The undersigned will ascertain prior to the deadline how the statute applies.	I will find out how the law applies before the deadline.
Henceforth, we need the wherewithal to be vigilant.	After this, we need the means to be watchful.

FIGURE 4-2 Formal and informal words and sentences.

awareness of safety procedures will lead to fewer accidents for the worker and lower insurance premiums for his employer." Underneath the message, someone had scrawled, "Don't women workers suffer accidents around here, or is that only a male privilege?"

Why is the use of biased language a problem in business?

Obviously, the original message is not only biased but inaccurate. Until recently, such language was common in the workplace. In ways both subtle and nonsubtle, language helped to support the stereotype that businesspeople were white, Protestant, and male.

Certainly, language was not the only factor in creating this stereotype. However, as women and minorities asserted their rights in the workplace more vigorously, many people in business began to be more sensitive to biased language in the messages they sent and received.

Although greater sensitivity exists, the problem has hardly vanished. As a writer of business messages, what can you do? Most important, you need to recognize the problem and to be watchful about its appearance in your own writing. The following discussion on using unbiased language is adapted from Judy E. Pickens, ed., *Without Bias: A Guidebook for Nondiscriminatory Communication*, 2nd ed. (New York: John Wiley, 1982).

Sexual Bias

Sexist language is probably the most common form of bias in business communication. The following five guidelines should help you to eliminate it from your messages:

Guide 1 *Include all people in general references by using asexual words and phrases instead of masculine and feminine words.*

Is sexual bias more common in business than other types?

Rather than This	*Try This*
man-made	synthetic, artificial, constructed, manufactured
man-sized	husky, sizable, large, requiring exceptional ability
man-hours	hours, total hours, staff hours, working hours
mankind	people, humanity, human beings, human race
for the lady of the house	for the homemaker, for the consumer

Note: To avoid using *he* when a generic singular pronoun is needed, use one of these techniques: (1) reword the sentence to remove unneeded gender pronouns; (2) change the case from singular to plural; or (3) replace the masculine pronouns with *one, you, he or she,* or *his or her.* Avoid using the same technique repeatedly in a passage, however, because it will result in a monotonous sameness in the message.

Rather than This	*Try This*
Each employee completes his timesheet at the end of his shift.	Each employee completes a timesheet at the end of the shift. OR All employees complete their timesheets at the end of their shifts. OR Each employee completes his or her timesheet at the end of the shift.

Guide 2 *Refer to women and men equally and make references consistent.*

Use the full name the first time you refer to a person in a message, but then use either the first or the last name in later references.

Rather than This	*Try This*
Sam Purdy and Miss Brown	Sam Purdy and Julia Brown OR Mr. Purdy and Miss Brown
Sam Purdy and Julia Brown were recently promoted. Purdy has been with the firm since 1980 and Julia since 1978.	Sam Purdy and Julia Brown were recently promoted. Purdy has been with the firm since 1980 and Brown since 1978. OR Mr. Purdy has been with the firm since 1980 and Ms. Brown (or Miss or Mrs. as appropriate, if she prefers) since 1978. OR Sam has been with the firm since 1980 and Julia since 1978.

Guide 3 *Avoid unnecessary labels and stereotypes. Use generic titles or descriptions for both men and women.*

General expressions refer to both sexes. Use them both in titles and descriptions of men and women.

Rather than This	*Try This*
lady executive/banker	executive/banker
male secretary/nurse	secretary/nurse
ladylike	well mannered
authoress	author
aviatrix/comedienne	aviator/comedian
just like a man/woman	(avoid using)

Guide 4 *Avoid using "man" or "woman" as a suffix or prefix in job titles.*

Rather than This	*Try This*
businessman/businesswoman	business executive, manager, entrepreneur
chairman/chairwoman	presiding officer, the chair, head, leader, moderator, coordinator, chairperson
foreman	supervisor, manager

Rather than This	*Try This*
salesman	salesperson, sales clerk, sales representative

Guide 5 *Use parallel language when referring to people by sex.*

Rather than This	*Try This*
the ladies and the men	the women and the men; the ladies and the gentlemen; the girls and the boys
man and wife	husband and wife

Racial and Ethnic Bias

How do racial and ethnic bias differ?

When the company magazine published an article about Susan Kim's achievements as a computer salesperson, she was naturally quite pleased, that is, until she read the following sentence, "Breaking with tradition, Susan Kim chose a career where she had to be aggressive and fiercely competitive." Sometime during the following week, Susan had lunch with the magazine's editor. Between the first course and the entree, she explained to him how in praising her, he had implicitly endorsed the stereotypic view of Asians as passive and docile.

Susan's experience was not unusual. Since the business world exists inside the larger environment, society's prejudices will be found there too. The following are some guidelines to help you avoid racial and ethnic bias in your own message.

Guide 1 *Avoid using qualifiers that reinforce racial or ethnic stereotypes.*

Do not add information that suggests that a person is an exception to a racial or ethnic norm.

Does This Sentence . . .	*. . . Contain This Hidden Stereotype?*
John Jones, a well-groomed black student, works as a part-time clerk.	Blacks are poorly groomed.
No retiring, quiet job for her, Betty Wong chose a dynamic career as . . .	Asians are shy, docile.
José Rodriguez, a steady and even-tempered worker . . .	Mexican Americans (or other people of Hispanic ancestry) are volatile, unpredictable.

Guide 2 *Avoid citing racial identification or ethnic origin except when pertinent to the message.*

If This Identification Is Inappropriate . . .	*. . . Is This Phrasing Any Different?*
Judy, an outgoing white woman	Mary, an outgoing black woman

When proofreading messages, be alert for any bias whether overt or subtly implied in the context.

CLARITY

Teresa Moscone included in her memo to her supervisor the following sentence, "Objective consideration of the phenomena compels the conclusion that a considerable element of the unpredictable must be taken into account in order to predict with any degree of accuracy the outcome." When Teresa's memo was returned, she saw that her boss had underlined this sentence and written in the margin: "Translation please."

What happens when you send unclear messages?

Business misunderstandings result more often from unclear messages, such as Teresa Moscone's, than they do from either bad feelings or lack of goodwill. Unclear messages require the receiver to become a mind reader, having to guess the intended meaning or, failing that, to ask for a clarification or "translation" from the writer. Sometimes an entire message may be unclear. In such instances, the reader cannot derive any meaning at all. When this happens, he or she may simply disregard it, feeling too frustrated to ask for clarification.

Concrete and Abstract Expressions

Should you never use an abstract expression?

As we have previously explained, readers find it easier to understand messages that contain a high percentage of concrete expressions. You will recall that concrete words refer to actual objects about whose meaning a general consensus exists. In contrast, abstract words refer to qualities whose meanings are somewhat different for everybody. Therefore, because you always want your business messages to be clear, use concrete words or expressions wherever possible. These three guidelines should help you to raise your percentage of concrete expressions:

1. Add a word or phrase to an abstract term to define it more fully. For example, change *progress* to the *corporation's progress* or to *economic progress*.

2. Make the abstract term less abstract by explaining its meaning in the sentences that follow its introduction. For example, changing "progress" to "economic progress" may still only incompletely clarify what you mean. You may also have to specify the type of economic progress. Is it short term or long? Is it small or large? or what?
3. Use the most specific concrete term you can when it is important to your message's meaning. For example, if you are referring to the costs for buying a building, state if it is an *apartment house,* an *office building,* a *duplex,* and so forth.

Specific and General Language

Have you ever heard the saying, "to be clear, be specific"?

Suppose you find a note from your boss in your mailbox that says, "Let's meet later this afternoon to discuss the Cutler contract." Would you know when to step into his or her office? Certainly, not from the message itself. You will either have to ask your boss or risk coming by at an inappropriate moment. Either way you will probably lose some time in clarifying exactly when your appointment is.

In contrast to the problems that vague language causes, specific language helps daily business to proceed efficiently and effectively. Here are some commonly used words that, because they are too general, confuse rather than clarify situations. Try to avoid them in your own messages.

above named	as in the above
as soon as possible	at an early date
at your convenience	in due course
in due time	of the above date
order has gone forward	give this matter your attention
under separate cover	without further delay

Simple Expressions

Sometimes we think that long, complex words are more impressive than simple expressions, especially when we are directing our message toward someone "important." In one such instance, a bank executive wrote a memo to the vice president in charge of credit operations in which she spoke of "facilitating the amelioration of the interest rate structure." When they next met, the vice president asked innocently if in her memo she was referring to easing interest rates? Embarrassed, the executive nodded yes and escaped to the safety of her own office, where she vowed from then on to use ordinary English in all her communication.

No list can contain all possible applications of this principle, but the following examples should give you some guidance in choosing simple rather than complex expressions.

Rather than This	*Try This*
advise	write, tell
ascertain	find out, learn
constitute	are, be, is
deem	think
desire	want, wish
disclose	show
effect (verb)	cause
endeavor	try
ensue	follow
execute	do
facilitate	make easy
forward	mail
insufficient	not enough
subsequent	later
supply	send
sustain	suffer
terminate	end, stop
transpire	happen

How often do you use the words in the left column?

One caution: Not all long or complex words are inappropriate, and not all of them have simple and short equivalents. In general, however, choose a simple word unless one that is complex is also more precise and meaningful.

Unfamiliar Words, Foreign Expressions, and Jargon

Do you know what *piscatorial* means, or *circumambient?* What about *terpsichorean? tesselate?* Even though these words may be found in any English dictionary, most people are not likely to know their meaning. But what if you do know the definition of piscatorial (of fishers or fisher-like)? Should you use it in a business message even when it is appropriate? The answer is no because you risk your reader's misunderstanding. Instead, choose a more commonly known synonym. Reserve unusual words for the special situations where they are necessary and where your reader will understand them.

Are you impressed by someone who uses unfamiliar words?

This does not mean, however, that you should not use technical terms. They are an entirely different matter. For example, if you are an accountant, in your messages to other accountants, you would naturally speak of accruals and reversing entries. And even if your message's receiver is not an accountant, you may still use these terms because of their accuracy or for legal purposes. Only, in such situations, you will have to explain their meaning if you think your receiver will not otherwise understand you.

Foreign expressions are another category of words your readers may not understand. Therefore, you should avoid them unless no accurate equivalent exists in English or legal reasons compel their use. Substitute English phrases for the following list of commonly used foreign expressions.

Have you ever been confused when someone used one of the terms in the left column?

Rather than This	*Try This*
ad nauseam	to the point of disgust
à propos	to the point or purpose
caveat emptor	let the buyer beware
coup de grâce	a finishing stroke
de facto	in fact, actual
in toto	as a whole, entirely
ipso facto	by the fact itself, by that very fact
magnum opus	a great work
modus operandi	procedure
non sequitur	it does not follow
quid pro quo	one thing in return for another
sine qua non	a necessary thing

The rule about foreign expressions is not absolute. Foreign technical terms are an exception. For example, *de facto* and *ipso facto* are both legal and financial terms. Since they are almost universally used in certain professions, they represent a kind of shorthand beside which English explanations may be clumsy.

Jargon is the language peculiar to a profession, trade, or group. Depending on its use, a word may sometimes be jargon and sometimes not. For example, if you described a fellow employee as an "activator," you would be using business jargon; but if you were referring instead to a nuclear reactor's "activator" core, you would be employing a technical term.

Are fad words similar to jargon?

Within your own trade, if you use jargon in a message, readers will understand you. But if the receiver of a message is an outsider, try another expression or else define your jargon.

Fad words, sometimes called *buzz words,* are closely related to jargon. These terms and phrases are business slang. Like ordinary slang, they are popular for a time and then either are incorporated into the language or disappear. *High-visibility concept, RAM modality, bottom line* are some current business buzz words. When you read this, you may not even know their meaning because other words have replaced them. This is one problem to keep in mind when using a buzz word in a business meeting. Even as you write it, it may no longer be popular or is so overused that it is virtually meaningless. While buzz words can create rapport, you need to be careful that your reader will understand their meaning. Sometimes a buzz word is limited to a particular field and outsiders are unfamiliar with it.

Instant words! What are they?

Instant words are also closely related to jargon. They are created by shifting an established word's function in a sentence, making a verb into a noun or a noun into a verb. The first instance, called *nominalization,* changes a verb, the action word of a sentence, into a noun by attaching "tion" or "ment," as in "Labor cost escalation will not allow a *maximization* of profits this year." The second form of instant word making creates verbs out of nouns by adding an "ize," as in "Writers who do not *prioritize* word choice will *jargonize* their reports."

By adding these suffixes, you create strange and unreliable words. Instant words not only raise eyebrows and cause chuckles, but they are also easily misunderstood—the listener or reader thinks he or she should know what the word means because it sounds familiar. Experienced businesss communicators recognize this habit and avoid it in their messages.

Finally, remember that when choosing any word, someone is going to read it. Thus, an experienced writer always asks, "Does this word improve my communication with the reader?" Your answer determines the best choice.

CONCISENESS

To be concise is to express a message completely in as few words as possible. Being concise results in increased effectiveness and probably decreased costs, whether in time or money. Wordy expressions and redundancies are the major problems to overcome if you want to communicate concisely.

Wordiness

Wordiness simply means using too many words to say too little. For example, you may write this sentence in a letter to a customer: "In compliance with your request, I am sending you a large number of shipment forms." The information in this sentence might, however, be put more concisely as "As requested, I am sending you 500 shipment forms." Notice that the first sentence takes nearly twice as many words as the second.

The following list contains examples of commonly used wordy phrases. Because wordiness occurs so frequently in business communication, the list could easily be five times longer.

Wordy	*Concise*
according to our records	we find
after the conclusion of	after
are desirous of	want to
are of the opinion that	believe, think
as a general rule	generally
at the present time	now, at present
at such time, at which time	when
attached find, attached herewith is, attached hereto	attached, attached is, here is
attention is called	notice, please note
by means of	by
consider favorably	approve
due in large measure to	because, since
during the time, during which time	while
every effort will be made	we can, we will try
for the reason that	because, since
held a meeting	met
in a careful manner	carefully
in a situation in which	when
in accordance with	by
in accordance with your request	as you requested
in addition to the above	also
in spite of the fact that	even though
in the amount of	for
in the near future	soon
in view of the fact that	because, since
inquired as to	asked
kindly advise	please call, please write
let us hear from you	call us, write us
not in a position	cannot, unable
of the opinion that	believe, think
on the occasion of	on, when
other things being equal	normally, usually
pending receipt of	until
pertaining to	about, of
please forward	mail
reason is due to	because
remember the fact that	remember
this will acknowledge receipt of	thank you for sending
until such time as	until

If you listed the wordy expressions you used today, how long would the list be?

Sometimes you can omit certain wordy phrases entirely without changing the meaning. For example, compare these sentences:

Wordy This is to inform you that your shipment was sent today.
Concise Your shipment was sent today.

Would you ever need to add not pare, words?

In your own messages, try to delete any empty, or meaningless, phrases you at first included through oversight. Once in a while, however, you may find that you need to add, not pare, words. For instance, suppose you need to write a note to a worker explaining why he or she was not promoted to head of the advertising department of your company. Here some extra words, coupled with an inductive structure, may soften the blow. (See Chapter 9 for a fuller discussion of this strategy.) But, unless you have a good reason to add words, as in this instance, keep your business messages concise.

Redundancies

Sometimes we repeat something in a message to emphasize it. This technique is especially useful when the idea is important. For example, in recommending against your company's adding a new product to the soft drink market, you may point in your memo on the subject to the decreasing size of the market. Since this is the main reason for your opposition, it is a good tactic to repeat it several times in the memo, particularly at the end.

Should all redundancy be removed from messages?

In contrast to deliberate repetition, *careless* repetition will detract from your message's effectiveness. Sometimes use of such redundancies also suggests that you do not really know the English language. For example, if you mention in a letter to your salespeople that one of their number is "a popular salesperson who is well liked," you are letting yourself open to your reader's ridicule, for the redundancy makes it appear that you do not know what *popular* means. The following is a list of some common redundancies to avoid in your messages.

adequate enough
always and ever
assemble together
awkward predicament
basic fundamentals
big in size
close proximity
combined together
complete monopoly
completely eliminated
consensus of opinion
depreciated in value
each and every
entirely complete
few in number
final completion
first and foremost
gather together
grateful thanks
important essentials
instructional training
last and final
mutual cooperation
necessary requisite
ordered sequence
pair of two
past history
positively certain
refer back
repeat again
reverse back
surrounded on all sides
true facts

ACCURACY

Because we communicate in business to achieve results, accuracy in expression is critical. Just as an omitted decimal point can cause $50.00 to be read as $5000, so can an ill-chosen expression alter the meaning of your message. Euphemisms, overstatements, figurative clichés, and colloquialisms, are four major causes of inaccuracy in business messages.

Euphemisms and Overstatements

Euphemisms are "nice" words that we substitute for unpleasant terms that seem (to us and to others) distasteful or offensive. In general, euphemisms are less accurate than the words they replace. For this reason, use them only when the original term appears unpleasant enough to detract from the message. For example, if you want improved performance, the euphemism "had another setback" may be a better strategy than telling your office manager that he or she "has failed again." Or, in discussing the recent state of an industry, you might decide to use the euphemism "decline," instead of the more accurate "recession," so as not to alarm people and set off an industrywide panic. In contrast, euphemisms such as "terminated" for "fired," "laid to rest" for "buried," and "golden years," for "old age" may not only call attention to themselves, but also appear pretentious or insincere to many readers.

In what ways do euphemisms and overstatements decrease accuracy?

Overstatements are descriptions that exceed reality. As discussed in Chapter 3, most stem from the unnecessary use of the superlative form of adjectives and adverbs. For example, instead of saying that his company's mainframe computer was *more powerful* than a competitor's (which was true), one salesperson prepared a mailing to potential customers in which he claimed his computer was the *most powerful* on the market (which was untrue). Eventually, such overstatements seriously diminished this salesperson's credibility.

Another form of overstatement occurs when we use adjectives that are simply too strong for the situation they are supposedly describing. For example, notice how often you and the people around you apply the words *fantastic, unique,* or *amazing* to people or things that are in no way fantastic or unique or amazing. While these words may be useful in advertising—where their absence would be perhaps viewed as a lack of confidence in the product—you should use them sparingly in business messages. Both you and your reader know they are meaningless and, consequently, not to be believed.

Figurative Clichés

Clichés are stereotyped or trite expressions worn out by overuse. Figurative clichés convey metaphorical rather than literal relationships. For example, if you tell a worker in your department to "bust your back" or "shake a leg," he or she will of course interpret this figuratively, and if so inclined will take your advice and work harder. However, sometimes readers may assign literal meanings to something you meant only figuratively or, because such terms are clichés, not really hear what you are saying.

Can you think of a couple of reasons not to use figurative clichés?

Another reason to avoid figurative clichés in your messages is that they are culture-bound. For example, suppose you are dealing with Mr. Aki Yashimo, a Japanese manufacturer of television sets. He sends you an invoice for a large delivery and you reply in a letter that you "can't make head or tails" of his figures. Probably, he will not understand you. And, so another exchange of letters will be needed to clear things up. In general, then, avoid using figurative clichés in any international communication. Moreover, even in domestic messages—those within North America—be careful to use them minimally. Most readers would tend to believe that a message that is cliché ridden is written by someone who thinks in clichés. The following is a list of commonly used figurative clichés.

a rude awakening
bed of roses
blood is thicker than water
bone to pick with
bury the hatchet
by leaps and bounds
don't give a hoot
exception that proves the rule
fill the bill
grin and bear it
happy as a lark
in the nick of time
it goes without saying
keep the wolf from the door
leave no stone unturned
let the cat out of the bag
make a bundle
never spoke a truer word
play the game
pride and joy
pull yourself together
putting the cart before the horse
say the word
shake a leg
shoulder to the wheel
stand your ground
stick to your guns
strike while the iron is hot
take the bull by the horns
turn over a new leaf
up to no good

Colloquialisms

Colloquialisms are informal expressions—sometimes regional or ethnic in origin—that we use instead of standard speech. Usually they crop up in conversations, but some people may include them in their written messages as well. An example of the difference between colloquial and standard speech is:

Colloquial Bob Davis couldn't feel but what Jenny Burke was wrong.
Standard Bob Davis felt Jenny Burke was wrong.

Written colloquialisms can create problems because they are so informal that many readers will see them as examples of illiteracy. For instance, if you use "no account" instead of "worthless" or "fixin' to" for "about to," readers may disregard these phrases and the rest of your message as well.

Should we avoid using all colloquialisms? If not, why not?

Other colloquialisms, however, are useful because they are as accurate as their standard English equivalents and are not too informal. For example, it is perfectly acceptable to write that "the bailout plan for the company fizzled" instead of "the bailout plan for the company failed." The following is a list of some common colloquial phrases to avoid in your messages.

Rather than This	*Try This*
all done	completed, finished
all the farther	as far as
anywheres	any place
around this time	about this time
as to (when used for *about*)	about
be most happy	be glad, be happy
better than (when used for *more than*)	more than
but what (when used for *but that*)	but that
no good	worthless
nowheres	no place
of no account	worthless

A final word about the lists in this section: we recommend against using the listed words and phrases because they can lead to miscommunication. But if you do decide to use a listed colloquialism (or a buzz word or a euphemism or even some slang) in a message, you're not necessarily breaking any essential rule. Just remember that if you ignore the guidelines, your language should meet the demands of both the receiver and the occasion. Thus, in certain situations, if you think a cliché will get your message across more effectively, use it. Some writers "hedge their bets" by placing quotations marks around these expressions to show readers they have used them consciously.

SINCERITY

Conveying sincerity is one of the most difficult tasks you will encounter in business writing. Yet it is also one of the most necessary. Having honest intentions is not enough; somehow your message has to convey this too. The major elements that confer "a ring of truth" on a communication are showing confidence, safeguarding confidentiality, refraining from excessive flattery, and avoiding displays of unnecessary humility.

Showing Confidence

How does showing confidence relate to sincerity?

Maria Daly wondered why her boss in the furniture section of a large department store almost always rejected the recommendations Maria sent her in weekly memos. It wasn't that she disliked her boss, far from it. Nor were her ideas bad, or so her colleagues told her. What, then, was wrong? Eventually, Maria showed some of her memos to a trusted and successful business acquaintance. After reading them, her friend said, "Maria, if I were your boss, I don't know that I would believe in your recommendations either. You sound so hesitant."

Sending messages that lack confidence is certain to cause readers to doubt you. In contrast, appearing confident can help you to reach your objective. The following guidelines should add to the self-confidence you transmit in your business messages.

Guide 1 *Appear certain of the result.*

Showing confidence about achieving the desired result can help you to achieve it. Notice the difference between the confidence level of these statements:

Lacks Confidence	*Sounds Confident*
Would you like to see our new fall catalog?	Call us today at 000-0000 for a copy of our new fall catalog.
When you can spare the time, please stop in to see our new spring suits.	Join us Thursday for the open house celebration of the arrival of our new spring suits by Halsey.

Expressions such as *would you like to* and *when you can spare the time* are hesitant and doubtful. So are *if you would like to* and *you should consider*. These statements destroy the success-oriented tone of good business writing.

In trying to appear certain of what you say, could you wind up sounding overly confident?

Guide 2 *Avoid overconfidence.*

Sounding overly confident can be more of a problem than a benefit. If you appear to take too much for granted, a reader might find you presumptuous. Consider these examples:

Overconfident	*Confident*
Naturally, you'll agree with my assessment of the oil market.	My assessment of the oil market shows . . .

In the example on the left we can ask, "How does the writer know the reader will agree?" The self-centered tone of an overconfident statement is irritating and may lead readers to discount the message.

Guide 3 *Avoid expressions of certainty that actually convey doubt.*

On the surface, such expressions as "I am sure," "we hope," "I trust," and "we just know" appear to be confident. But in reality, they mask the writer's uncertainty. Consider these examples:

How can expressions of certainty actually convey doubt?

Implies Doubt	*Implies Confidence*
We just know that you will want to take advantage of our special subscription offer today.	To take advantage of this special subscription offer, just sign and return the enclosed card today.

The seller in the example on the left cannot "know" that the reader will buy, and the reader is well aware of it. Moreover, implying something that someone does not have—whether it is knowledge or trust or desire—makes receivers feel the writer of the message does not really respect them enough to let them make a decision on their own. In other words, readers can see these kind of statements as a form of coercion.

Guide 4 *Avoid statements of dismay, surprise, or shock.*

Expressions such as "we were astonished to hear" and "your money problems are unique" are rarely true. Readers know it and react negatively to such a false note. Consider these examples:

How do statements of dismay, surprise, and shock relate to sincerity?

Insincere Tone	*Sincere Tone*
We were shocked and dismayed to learn that you selected Brand X instead of our Deep South Cottonseed Oil.	Thank you for considering Deep South Cottonseed Oil. Please notify us when you next solicit bids. We are eager to offer you the best price-production combination.

In comparing the two examples, ask yourself, "Which damages future dealings?" Whereas the writer of the message on the left adopts a tone of outrage, the writer on the right sends a message that is positive, constructive, and sincere.

Writers of responses to complaint letters often make this mistake. "We can hardly believe it," they exclaim, "when you say our hair dryer malfunctioned." Receivers of such messages disbelieve both the surprised tone and the suggestion in it that the company's hair dryers *never* malfunction. For one thing, the consumer owns one that did. For another, it is impossible for anyone to conceive that complaint departments are ever surprised. In any case, omit expressions of shock, dismay, and surprise from your business messages.

Guide 5 *Avoid speaking to harass or demand.*

Could those who harass or demand actually be trying to sound confident?

Some attempts at sincerity sound more strident than believable, and they also harass the reader or demand that he or she take some action. Compare these two examples:

Harassing and Demanding	*Nonharassing or demanding*
You absolutely must pay your bill by June 21 to avoid a late payment charge.	Please pay your bill by June 21 to avoid a late payment charge.

As you can see, the statement on the left provokes anger, whereas that on the right is simple and straightforward, eliciting in the reader a similar response.

Safeguarding Confidentiality

What does it mean to safeguard confidentiality?

Sally Meyers started off a note to a colleague in her company with "Your assistant told me that . . . ". In response, she received a note that was brief and to the point. It said, "Sally, stop nosing about. If you want to ask me something, ask me, not my assistant." As the preceding example shows, discretion in an office is important and so is the sense others have that you are discreet. Many company records, reports, and correspondence must remain confidential for business, personal, or legal reasons. For example, information about a firm's new fall fashions must be kept secret from the competition. Similarly, information on employment records needs safeguarding both to preserve employees' rights and to avoid lawsuits.

Even when we are discreet, a few ill-chosen words can imply the opposite. For instance, statements beginning with "I heard that . . . " may suggest a writer who listens to gossip and hearsay. In the same vein, "We saw you at . . . " can suggest someone who pries. Therefore, try to avoid these expressions and others like them.

Avoiding Excessive Flattery and Humility

Although you should always show respect for your reader, excessive displays will seem insincere. Most of the time they embarrass the reader and lead him or her to speculate on the writer's motives. For example,

> I know a person of your importance is busy, but will you take a few minutes of your valuable time to . . .

would be better as:

> We need your opinion as an authority in the field. Will you please take a few minutes to . . .

How can the use of flattery and humility be overdone in business writing?

Other examples of these overstatements are *You are surely one of the world's leading authorities in* or *You are held in such great esteem.* Both sound insincere. Only compliment someone when the situation justifies it. Your sincerity will be appreciated.

The same cautions apply to displays of excessive humility. For example,

> Will you please take a few minutes to . . .

is surely better than

> May I kindly beg a favor of you?

Similarly, expressions such as *Will you kindly be good enough to, I shall be eternally grateful if,* and *I am just a mere clerk but . . .* humble the writer unnecessarily. Instead of doing this, ask directly for what you want and justify your request.

KEEPING YOUR READER WITH YOU

So far in this chapter we have focused on the more general facets of style and tone. Now let's consider some of the finer points of keeping your readers' attention. Basically, this involves creating a positive rapport with them, showing that they can trust your messsages to be informative, businesslike, *and* readable.

To achieve such a rapport, avoid making your readers struggle for information or feel your message is not really directed to them. Thus, try to keep your reader with you by being positive and using vivid language.

Positiveness

The supervisor of the accounting department was angry. He felt that the workers under him were sloughing off. So he posted a memo by the copy machine, where everyone could see it. The message said:

What role does being positive play in business writing?

> *No more lateness.*
>
> *No loitering by the coffee machine.*
>
> *No two-hour lunches.*
>
> *No departures before 5:00* P.M.
>
> *Is this understood? For your benefit, I hope it is.*

What do you suppose the reaction was to this message? Did it achieve the supervisor's object—to have his department shape up—or did it have another effect—to cause resistance to him and his authority? More likely, it had the second effect.

The supervisor might have approached his problem differently. Instead of adopting a negative attitude toward his workers, he might have communicated with them positively, trying to be supportive, constructive, patient, other-directed, fair-minded, adult, and action oriented. For example, he might have taken each of them aside and discussed the problem, beginning with an appreciation of the individual's situation. As a result he might have discovered that one man had trouble getting to work on time because he had to take his children to nursery school. Or another may have had to leave early because her mother was ill and alone. Then, having clarified the situation for himself, the supervisor might have written a memo to his staff, being firm yet as supportive as possible. In his memo he might have said something like, "Thank you for being so cooperative and open during our talk," instead of, "I've listened to everybody and I'm tired of hearing excuses."

If you find yourself in a similar situation, write from the reader's viewpoint and limit the number of negative expressions you use.

A far simpler situation to handle positively occurs when someone is the receiver of good news. In such instances use descriptive adjectives liberally and be specific in details. For example, suppose a salesperson in your office is promoted to Midwest sales manager. Your letter of congratulations might include the following sentiments: "Congratulations, Josh, on your promotion to district sales manager. Frances Thomas often calls you her one-person sales force. That's a real compliment to your hard work and skill."

Writing from the Reader's Viewpoint

How could you possibly write from someone else's viewpoint?

The best business messages never lose their focus on the reader, observing the situation as he or she sees it. Since readers (like everyone else) respond to their own interests, this technique works well. For example, suppose you want Amanda Schroeder, a customer, to buy more paperbacks for her discount chain store than usual this month. To reach your objective, write her a letter about the benefits she will receive by buying now. Since you know she is especially interested in increased profit potential, emphasize this possibility. But also discuss other issues of *importance to her*, such as discounts on volume orders and your new company policy about returns.

Besides highlighting the reader's interests, focus on him or her by using the pronouns *you* and *your* rather than *I* or *me*. For example,

Rather than This	*Try This*
I shipped the six dozen sweaters this morning by air express.	Your order for six dozen sweaters was shipped this morning by air express.

We and *our* are also effective when referring to you and your reader because they emphasize the two of you as a unit.

Personalizing a message by using the reader's name also makes the reader feel your constant awareness of him or her, as in the following example:

> Therefore, your $300 refund should arrive next week, Mr. Lopez. Thank you for . . .

But because direct address can sound insincere if you overuse it, employ it sparingly. Once or twice in a letter or memo should be the maximum.

Avoiding Negative Terms

Perhaps few of us would be as blunt as Ben Franklin was in a letter to a former friend:

> You and I were long friends; you are now my enemy, and I am
> Yours,

Right now, how often do you choose positive over negative terms in your writing?

Although Dr. Franklin must have felt justified in his anger, on the basis of this letter, he would have had a difficult time persuading his former friend to do anything for him in the future. Similarly, angry statements in business writing generate ill feelings and may remain in the personal and public records long after the anger itself is gone. Even veiled anger can cause trouble. The best rule is to let your anger subside before writing your message.

Also avoid using the word *not* (and its contracted form, as in *won't, can't, couldn't,* and *mustn't*) in a message too often. Often it is just as easy to express an idea positively as negatively, for example, *remember* rather than *don't forget.*

In addition, avoid using inherently negative expressions. They either accuse the reader unjustly or interject an unwanted note of sorrow. Examples are *claim* (the verb), *neglected, failed, hardly, scarcely, regret, unfortunately,* and *sorry.* Here is an illustration of how these negatives work:

> You failed to enclose a check to pay for the supplies.

The verb *failed* accuses the reader of neglect and may provoke anger. Instead, just ask for a check to pay for the supplies.

Vividness

Like striking clothes, vivid or lively language makes an impression. Readers read more attentively and with greater enjoyment if a writer uses strong images as well as words that are as precise as a well-cut gem. As it happens, however, many businesspeople still associate dullness with objectivity. But this book doesn't advocate bland language.

Through Word Use

Word usage is an acquired skill. Some people handicap themselves by constantly recycling a limited number of words; their speech and writing is marked by the exhaustion of these overworked terms. Good communicators select from a broader base of language. The words you use should be precise, but they can also be chosen for qualities of vividness—the ability to create lively mental pictures.

How can skilled word usage result in vivid language?

To your own collection of specific nouns, add action verbs and mix in a few well-selected descriptive adjectives and adverbs. They are the textures and colors of your writing. But do not sprinkle them in your messages carelessly. Otherwise, they would be calling attention to themselves and not to the communication's content. Rather, use them subtly, just below the reader's consciousness. The following recommendations show the difference between bland and lively writing styles:

Bland Barry Lyndon was employed with this company for a period of three months in the summer of 198__, during which time he had a very good record of being on time. He took only one day off. His supervisors wrote in their reports that he was "intelligent," "hard working," and "always rushing around."

I can therefore, due to his good record, recommend him for a position in your company.

Lively Three months may seem a short time for a young man to work with a company, but Barry Lyndon proved himself to us in that time. In fact, time is a good touchstone to use in describing him. He was never late to work, was rarely absent, and seemed to be able to do more in a day than anyone else in the plant. His supervisors noted his enthusiasm and habit of always rushing from place to place. When he was told he didn't have to work so fast, Barry smiled and said, "There's so much to do. I guess I'm just in a hurry."

It's refreshing to recommend a young person with these qualities to you. His record (and the good feelings he left behind) makes me want to help him as he hurries to meet with success.

In trying to make your writing more lively, also recognize the limitations that the communication itself imposes. Not all business messages lend themselves to enlivenment. For example, legal documents or a memo announcing the new company policy on parking seem to resist liveliness. Or do they?

Through Use of Active Voice

Using the active voice helps the reader to "see" the relationship between the subject of the sentence and the verb. If the subject *does* the action of the verb, we say the verb is in the active voice. If the action is, however, *done* to the subject, that is, if the subject *receives* the action of the verb, we say the verb is in the passive voice, as the following two examples show:

Subject Verb

Active: Miss Valences paid the insurance premium.

Subject Verb

Passive: The insurance premium was paid by Miss Valences.

The first thing to notice about these sentences is that the second one is longer. If you use the passive voice, you will need at least two words to describe the action. One of them is a form of the verb *to be*. The other is the passive participle of the verb. Examples are "was paid," "are given," and "were chosen."

Why is active voice generally preferred in business writing?

A second characteristic of the passive voice is that it is less lively than the active. If you use passives extensively, your message will be tedious. For example,

> After the check *was deposited* and the insurance premium *was paid*, Miss Valences *was reminded* that other obligations *would have to be met*.

A third characteristic of the passive voice is it deemphasizes and sometimes even omits the doer. Any action—for instance, imagine riding a bike—is hard to visualize without someone doing it. This works for readers too. What they cannot visualize easily, they won't remember as clearly. For example:

> New employees will be assigned to their stations after they have been given their instructions

is less clear than either

> Give the new employees their instructions and assign them their stations,

or

> After I give the new employees their instructions, Kiefer will assign them their stations.

In summary, use the active voice for most of your business writing. It will make your sentences clearer, crisper, and more vivid. Sometimes, however, the passive voice is preferable. For example, you may not always wish to draw the reader's attention to the doer. If you are sending bad news, you may not want to identify who is the cause of it. Thus, the first sentence below uses the passive voice deliberately. Compare it with the second, where the voice is active and the words are fewer.

> Your request for a loan extension has been taken into consideration, but because of changing interest rates, signature loans are not extended now beyond 60 days.
>
> Because of changing interest rates, we won't extend your signature loan beyond 60 days.

Which message might upset the reader more? Both contain the same bad news, but the first cushions the effect slightly by obscuring who has refused the loan and by cloaking what has happened with extra words like fat on bone. Learning to use language as subtly as this is what studying business writing is all about.

Summary

1. What a business writer chooses to say and how it is said are referred to as style and tone.
2. The levels of language used in business range from formal to informal.
3. A major concern among modern business writers is avoiding sexual, racial, and ethnic bias.
4. Clarity is expressed in business writing by using concrete terms, specific language, and simple expressions, and by avoiding the use of unfamiliar words, foreign expressions, and jargon.
5. To be concise in business writing, limit wordiness and avoid using redundancies.
6. Accuracy of expression is very important in business writing. When trying to be accurate, use euphemisms wisely, avoid overstatements and figurative clichés, and use only desirable colloquialisms.
7. Sincerity in business writing is demonstrated by showing confidence, safeguarding confidentiality, and avoiding excessive flattery and humility.
8. Unless your reader is attentive, the complete message may not get through to him or her. So to keep your reader with you, be positive and write vividly.

Review Questions

1. Why are style and tone the two most important qualities of business messages?
2. Which of the general language levels is appropriate for business writing? Explain.
3. In what ways can business writing appear to be biased? Give an example of each.
4. What four techniques can you use to make business writing clearer? Give an example of each.

5. How do wordiness and redundancy affect conciseness in business writing? Give two examples of each.
6. How do euphemisms, overstatements, figurative clichés, and colloquialisms affect accuracy in business messages? Give two examples of each.
7. What three techniques can you use to add sincerity to your business messages? Give an example of each.
8. How can writing from the reader's viewpoint make readers more attentive?
9. How can you avoid negative expressions in business messages? Give two examples.
10. What value does vivid language have in business writing? Which is more vivid, active or passive voice? Explain.
11. Is the use of foreign words an error in business messages? Explain your response.
12. When is formal language justified in business communication? Give two examples.
13. What is changing a verb into a noun to make a new word called? Give three examples.
14. When is it correct to use the passive voice in business messages? Give two examples.
15. Are fad words useful in effective business writing? Explain your answer.

Exercises

1. Name the types of bias shown in each of the following sentences and then rewrite each as an unbiased statement.
   a. Each employee's union dues are deducted from his paycheck.
   b. Julia Garner and Edgar received raises.
   c. Jerry Herrington is a male secretary.
   d. Cynthia Tricou and Larry Miloni are our new salesmen.
   e. Gretchen is both a girl Friday and her husband's better half.
   f. Hanna LaFada, an even-tempered Italian, will negotiate the contract for management.
   g. Susan Amani, a hard-working black woman, heads the payroll department.
2. Locate the wordy expressions in each of the following sentences and then rewrite the sentences using more concise expressions.
   a. As a general rule, a grievance is filed first.
   b. The plan at the present time is to file the grievance at a later date.
   c. Attached herewith is a form to write the grievance on.
   d. Each of these clerks came into contact with Mr. Largess in the hallway.
   e. Feel free to withhold the check first of all if you so desire.
   f. We are now in a position to give consideration to your plan.
   g. Our lawyer sent a message to the effect that the information is of a confidential nature.
3. Locate the undesirable colloquialisms in each of the following sentences and then rewrite the sentences to eliminate them.
   a. Crowded conditions force us to store goods anywheres that space is found.
   b. Ric will be most happy to take your order.
   c. Lelia will get through with the inventory tomorrow.
   d. We do not know but what she will arrive late.

e. Such mistakes happen in this day and age.
f. All these old records are no good.
g. When you are all done with the interviews, please sound out the records before hiring anyone.

4. Rewrite each of the following sentences to give them a more positive tone.
   a. You neglected to enclose the invoice.
   b. We are unable to find the merchandise you claim you sent.
   c. Don't forget to meet the guests in the foyer.
   d. I hope you will file the papers on schedule.
   e. You are not the Schlesinger representative, are you not?
5. Rewrite the following sentences in active voice.
   a. Susan was told about the award by Gaye and Phil.
   b. A decision was made by the board of directors.
   c. The truck is driven only by Miranda.
   d. Business ethics should be practiced by everyone in the chamber.
6. Rewrite the following sentences in passive voice.
   a. Lemuel drove the car to the garage.
   b. Gayle threw the crumpled invoice into the wastebasket.
   c. Therefore, we deny your request.
   d. For these reasons, we chose another option.
7. Using the diagram of language levels presented in Figure 4–1 as your guide, locate five examples from formal to informal language in periodicals in the business library.
8. Compile a list of 25 colloquialisms related to business that could interfere with clear communication.
   Hint: Check the *Dictionary of American Slang* and H. L. Mencken's *The American Language.* Be prepared to present and defend the entries on your list.
9. Look through recent copies of *The Wall Street Journal* or other business newspapers or magazines—*Forbes, Fortune, Barron's* and *Business Week,* for example. Compile a list of 25 special business applications of language, such as jargon, buzz words, and clichés.
10. Many words in English, such as housewife and salesman, contain a sexual bias. List 20 of them. Then compile a second list of 20 acceptable alternatives.

PART 2

COMMUNICATION TECHNOLOGY IN APPLICATION

CHAPTER 5

THE FUTURE TODAY: BUSINESS COMMUNICATION TECHNOLOGY

Traditionally, people in offices have communicated with each other through face-to-face meetings, the telephone, interoffice mail, and the postal system. In many offices today, these are still the most common ways in which people send messages, but they are no longer the only ways.

What is a paperless office?

Computers have carried business communication into the Electronic Age. Nearly every office has been affected by electronic communications. Figure 5-1 shows an *electronic office* workstation environment. Because some people use computer screens extensively in working with messages and records, these offices are called *paperless* offices.

We are in a decade marked by the use of new technologies designed to meet traditional communications goals—all intended to increase quality and productivity. These rapid advances in the technology of business communication require both employers and employees to reassess their communication goals as well as their methods of achieving them.

FIGURE 5-1 IBM display workstation with display screen. (Courtesy of International Business Machines Corporation.)

As business communicators, we must be familiar with these technologies. This means understanding the equipment available to us—its advantages and disadvantages. In this context, consider once again the basic communication model discussed in Chapter 1. No matter how futuristic its design, the function of communication technology remains the same as that shown in the model. Electronic machines exist to assist us in delivering spoken words, written messages, and graphic images. In other words, they perform the same functions as do the long-familiar telephone or typewriter. The difference lies in performance—the new machines are simply far more efficient than are the old.

What strategies should you pursue to use the new technology effectively?

To use the new technology most effectively implies the adoption of two strategies: we need to have a working knowledge of what it can do for us, which means being familiar with its advantages and limitations, and we must anticipate potential barriers arising from its use.

For these reasons, the primary discussion of the electronic office will focus on word processing and related communication advancements. Descriptions of the basic equipment and how it functions will give you an overview of the rapidly changing area of business communication technology. The chapter will conclude by considering the effects of these technological changes on the business communication process, noting general trends and anticipating possible barriers.

Of the new machines to enter the office, the computer is the most important. Businesses use it for accounting, record storage, research, and planning. The computer is also a component in almost all the communications advances that involve preparing and distributing memos, letters, proposals, and reports through internal and external networks. As the computer screen in Figure 5-2 shows, managers can use the computer's capabilities in nearly every business activity. And this is only the beginning.

WORD PROCESSING

How can a word processor be "user friendly"?

Word processing equipment can be used to simplify repetitive aspects of the writing process. For example, a word processor permits you to add or delete information or move ideas about in a message as you are composing it. Consequently, you can produce your message faster and with far less effort than if you had used a typewriter and correction materials. Moreover, a word processor is so easy to learn to use—it is even termed "user friendly"—that many executives and managers are preparing their own messages on the computer using word processing software.

FIGURE 5-2 Managerial workstation function chart. [From Marly A. Bergerud and Jean Gonzalez, *Word/Information Processing: Concepts of Office Automation*, 3rd ed. (New York: John Wiley, 1987).]

In its simplest form, word processing can be used systematically throughout the writing of a document. The writer can use word processing to draft ideas, to revise efficiently, and to produce letter-quality copy. Thus, you can use it to organize your first ideas concerning the Mexican debt, to revise drafts following review by the Legal Department, and, then, to check the final copy of your report for typographical errors. As you will soon see, the computer can even help you distribute the report.

Will word processing make writing obsolete?

In this section, the discussion of word processing concerns the basic computer equipment and how it functions in the modern electronic office. A simple reminder, before we explore the variety of expanding technology, is appropriate. As you read about the advantages of the new communication tools, *remember* that effective writing is still the product of skilled and thoughtful writers. (For an expanded discussion of the applications and techniques of word processing, see Chapter 6.)

Word Processing Components

The most elementary word processing system requires a number of interconnected physical devices, called *hardware*. Although the manner in which this hardware is linked or used varies, the tasks the components perform do not. Word processing tasks include:

What are the basic tasks of word processing?

1. *Inputting*, or the activity of putting data (words) into the system. This job is usually done with a keyboard, although other devices are available.
2. *Processing*, or the activity of working with the data (words) in a variety of ways. The central processing unit (CPU) does this "work."
3. *Storing*, or the process of housing the data for immediate or future use. The two storage areas are (a) temporary—memory areas within the CPU itself—and (b) permanent—external devices—such as floppy and hard disks.
4. *Outputting*, or the activity of delivering the processed data to its destination—generally a screen (called a monitor) or a printer.

Basically, the hardware needed to execute these tasks are a keyboard for input, the CPU for processing, disk drives for storage, and a screen or printer for output. Depending on the user's requirements, the tasks performed by these devices vary. However, the memory in the CPU, or central processing unit, coordinates all of them.

At the center of the modern managerial workstation is the computer terminal. The minimal terminal is composed of a keyboard and a monitor. If you want your computer to perform special tasks such as

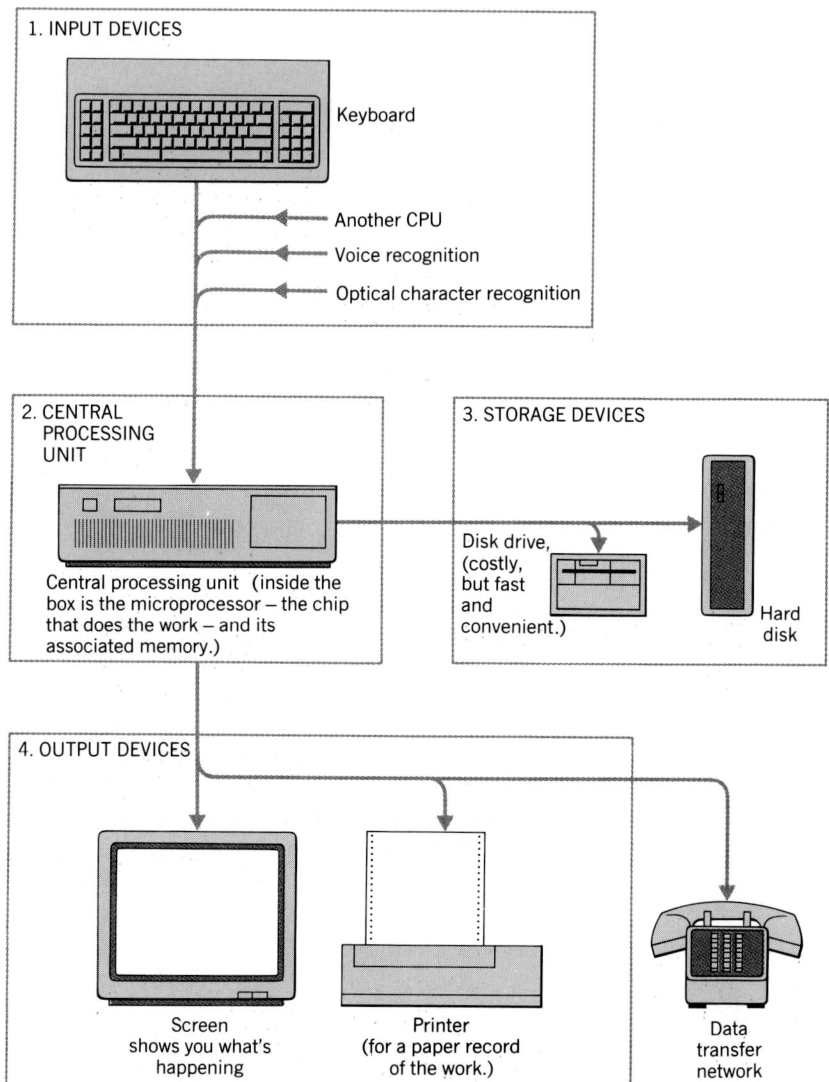

FIGURE 5-3 Basic word processing components.

printing copies of documents, you may add other devices, or *peripherals*. Figure 5-3 shows these basic word processing components.

Two basic types of office computers are the *shared* and *stand-alone*. In a shared terminal, the CPU is used by other terminals on a shared basis. But with a stand-alone terminal, the CPU is independent or built into the machine. A microcomputer is an example of a stand-alone terminal; the two types of stand-alones, display and non-display, are shown in Figure 5-4.

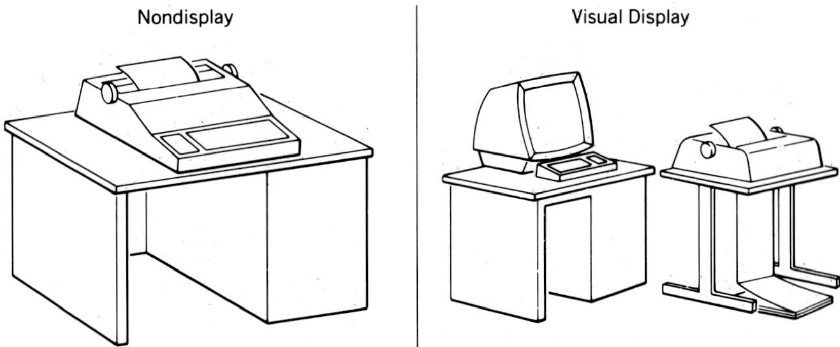

FIGURE 5-4 Diagram of display/nondisplay stand-alone systems.

Besides an initial savings in equipment cost, the advantage of a shared system is that information can be easily transferred from one terminal (or workstation) to another simply by pressing a key or two on the keyboard. As is said, computers can "talk" to each other in a shared system. With a stand-alone system, though, more computing power is in the hands of the user because the system is independent; it is the stand-alone system that has put automation on everyone's desk.

Input Options

How many ways can you put information into a word processor?

Suppose you want to use your word processor to write an analytical report on the trade deficit. First, you have to input or enter the data. You can enter it in one of four ways: (1) by keyboarding, (2) by optical character recognition, (3) by transferring the information from another computer, or (4) by using your own voice. Let us examine each of these separately.

Keyboards

If you can type, then keyboarding should present no problems, for it is similar to typing on a standard typewriter. The only difference is that the word processor's keyboard has some special command keys, such as the function keys. The two types of keyboard most commonly used are *membrane* and *full stroke.* A membrane keyboard has a flat surface without raised keys and resembles the new cash registers in many supermarkets and fast-food restaurants. Keys are touch sensitive, so you merely press the "key area" to enter a character. One problem you may have with a membrane keyboard is speed. This is because touch typing—typing without looking at the keyboard—is difficult. In contrast, the keys of a full-stroke keyboard move when you depress them, enabling you to touch type. Consequently, you can keyboard faster with a full-stroke keyboard than with a membrane.

Optical Character Recognition (Scanners)

An optical character recognition (OCR) reader is a device that scans or "reads" pages of written information and enters them directly into the computer's memory—just as if you had keyboarded them manually. The advantage of an OCR system is that it can input data 25 times as quickly as the fastest typist. But OCR equipment also has disadvantages. At present, it is expensive, it cannot read all printed documents, and it requires that you proofread carefully for errors. These disadvantages may, however, be only temporary, for the technology of these scanners is constantly and rapidly improving.

Direct Transfer from Computer to Computer

Can computers "talk" to one another? If so, how does it work?

Word processing equipment is able to transfer data both internally and externally. For example, you can move a block of information from one file area to another in a computer or send it to an entirely different file or computer. You are able to perform this second operation because computers can be connected to one another to form networks. These networks can be thought of as either *permanent*, when linked by a "hard-line" for continuous interchange, or *temporary*, when connected by a telephone device—or "modem"—for the duration of a single call.

Like a standard phone line, hardline connections, or local area networks, can be used to link computers physically. This linking enables many people in an office or building to continuously share information or share the same sources, such as personnel records.

The modem is a device that uses telephone equipment to join computers separated by long distances. It does this by translating the computer's pulsing signals—binary code—into the more leisurely cadence of the human voice—analog tones—for which telephones were originally designed. The basic modem system consists of two modem units connecting two computers, using advanced telephone technology. Basically, the source modem receives the first computer's code and translates it into a telephone signal. This signal is then sent to the second modem that, in turn, transforms it back into computer code for the second computer.

Both hardline and modem networks permit more rapid transfer of information than if it is contained in physical documents such as books. Major disadvantages are the high costs of equipment and personnel training and the problem of preserving the privacy of information transmitted in this way.

Touch Screens and Mice

The touch screen (see Figure 5–5) is a time-saving innovation available on some computers. It allows a user to input commands by simply touching the appropriate section of the display screen. A "mouse" (see Figure 6–1 in next chapter) is a hand held device that

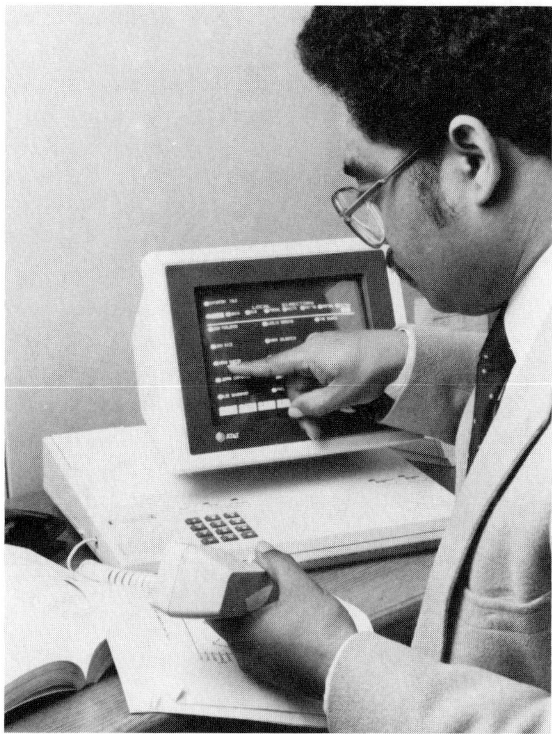

FIGURE 5-5 Touch screen on an AT&T Personal 510 terminal. (Courtesy of American Telephone & Telegraph Corporation.)

allows the user to execute various commands without the necessity of a keyboard.

Voice-Activated Computers

At present, the applications of voice recognition computers are limited. The next generation of computers may, however, eliminate manual keyboarding entirely, replacing it with voice-activated computers, or "typewriters with ears." These would allow people simply to speak messages for input into the computer. Increasingly, such changes in technology will require us to emphasize an older communication skill—dictation.

Processing Information

How does RAM differ from ROM?

The "intelligence" of word processing equipment is located in its central processing unit, or CPU. This is where information is received, stored, and processed. A refined collection of computer chips, the CPU operates two types of memory. *Read-only memory*, or ROM, is a permanent part of the unit and guides the rest of the system. A manufactured product, it cannot be altered by the user. In contrast, *random access memory*, or RAM, is the temporary storage area. In this location, nothing is really permanent, so the user can easily add, delete, or correct RAM.

However, since ROM is usually not designed to handle anything beyond the most general operations of the system, it will require instructions for more specialized tasks, such as adding a column of figures or reordering a sentence. Using a "software" program, the user enters these special application commands.

What are the basic types of business software?

Business software comes in four basic types: (1) *word processing* programs that can be used to write and revise messages; (2) *data bases* that can be used to store, manipulate, and retrieve data; (3) *spread sheet* programs; and (4) *graphics* programs for visual presentation of numerical data. Because word processing is the most important application of technology in business communication, a variety of machines exist. Some, called *dedicated word processors,* are designed exclusively for preparing written messages. Other machines with broader applications allow users to process numbers and images as well as words. *Mini-* and *microcomputers* (sometimes referred to as personal computers or PCs) are examples of this type of machine. Recently, manufacturers have developed larger integrated software packages for minis and micros, thus permitting users to engage in all four basic activities at the same time.

Storing Information

Where does the computer store information?

After you enter data into the computer, you need to be able to retrieve it when you want. This means that it has to be stored. Information may be retained in the computer's RAM or outside the CPU. Remember, however, that RAM is only a temporary storage area: if you turn the machine off, you will lose the data stored there. Thus, to save information permanently, you must transfer it to another storage place.

Two standard storage media for computer information are *soft* and *hard* disks. The soft disk (often called a floppy disk) looks like a small phonograph record inside a cardboard envelope. When you need to store information, you insert the disk into the machine's disk drive, removing it only when you no longer need to save anything for future use. In contrast, the hard disk, also called a "Winchester disk," is usually part of the machine itself, although you can also attach it as a peripheral. Whereas floppies can only store several hundred pages of data (at most), hard disks can retain thousands of pages of copy.

Output Options

In computer language, *output* is any words or data processed by the CPU. These are available whenever you need them for review or reproduction. The primary output for word processing equipment is the *monitor*, or display screen. This is where you can see your data as you enter and edit it. Most businesspeople use the cathode ray tube or CRT monitor, also called a visual display terminal or VDT. A second type of monitor, an LCD (liquid crystal display), is popular in lap or briefcase computers because of its compact size and light weight.

The second most important output of word processing is printing. When you complete a message, hard copies can be produced on a printer directed by the CPU. Two basic types of printers are the *impact* and the *nonimpact*.

Impact printers resemble typewriters: they create characters physically by striking an inked or carbon ribbon against the paper. *Letter quality* and *dot matrix* are two types of impact printers. Letter-quality printers employ typing elements, thimbles, or print wheels to produce copy. They are slower and more expensive than dot-matrix printers, but the quality of their copy is the same as that produced by a conventional typewriter. In contrast, in a dot-matrix printer, a cluster of pins forms the characters, that is, the characters themselves are composed of small, characteristic dots that create fully formed letters when clustered together. Some dot-matrix printers "double strike" characters (print them twice), giving better looking copy called *near letter quality*. Figure 5-6 compares letter-quality, near-letter-quality, and dot-matrix printing. Because of their mechanical nature, impact printers tend to be both noisy and relatively slow, ranging from 10 characters per second to 400 or more characters per second.

What advantages do laser and inkjet printers have over letter-quality and dot-matrix printers?

Since it does not rely on a device striking paper, a nonimpact printer prints more quietly. Also, the newer versions print considerably faster than do impact machines. The two types of nonimpact printers used today are *inkjet* and *laser*. Inkjets form characters by spraying a fine stream of ink onto the paper, whereas lasers employ a light beam to etch characters onto light-sensitive paper. Then a special toner and heating unit fix the image. Both types are astonishingly fast. While inkjets are not as fast as laser printers, lasers can reach speeds of 600 pages a minute. In other words, a laser printer could print this book in about a minute.

A third form of nonimpact printer is now available, ICP or intelligent copier/printers, which combines laser, computer, and photocopying technologies. Through a communication link to an ICP, a document and any accompanying graphics stored in a word pro-

The sentence you are reading was printed with a letter-quality printer.	The sentence you are reading was printed with a near letter-quality printer.	The sentence you are reading was printed with a dot-matrix printer.

FIGURE 5-6 Comparison of letter-quality, near letter-quality, and dot-matrix printing.

cessor can be transferred to it for copying. Also, ICPs permit users to do "desk top publishing," that is, prepare camera-ready copy for professional printing jobs.

NETWORKS: THE BASIS OF ELECTRONIC MESSAGE DISTRIBUTION

Suppose you have used your office word processor to create, edit, and print a letter of inquiry to a large and important vendor 2000 miles away. The next step is to forward your letter to the person. In the past you have transmitted such messages by mail, or, if you were in a hurry, by phone. But each of these delivery systems has presented problems. The postal service has been slow—the last letter you sent to this vendor took over 10 days to arrive—and once it even lost a critical shipment order request. As for the telephone, you've tried that too, only to be frustrated at having to make an average of four calls before getting through to the vendor. For these reasons, you are now ready to try the office's new *electronic mail/message system* (EMMS).

What is an EMMS? How does this system work?

This system stores and delivers messages such as yours that otherwise would be sent through the mails or transmitted orally over telephone lines. Here is how it works. Either by keying or speaking, you send your message to a specified individual (in this case, the vendor) who has a computer storage "mailbox" in the message system. If your office uses voice mail, you simply send the system's phone number, log into the system, and then transmit your letter to the vendor. The sound waves you produce in this way are converted into digital pulses that are then stored on a hard disk for retrieval. When your vendor calls the voice store-and-forward system, he or she discovers that your message is waiting. Whenever time permits, the vendor can listen to your message, which is produced as reconstituted speech. Afterward, he or she has the option of saving it for reference or forwarding it to others in the company.

Besides its time-saving aspects, EMMS can be a less intrusive way of sending messages than traditional methods, particularly the telephone. For example, you neither have to locate your receivers nor interrupt them at a bad moment. Instead, they can review stored messages at a convenient time. Also, communication between offices in different time zones such as Western Europe and North America becomes easier with EMMS. Finally, senders and receivers reduce their handling of physical documents.

The key to electronic mail—and to many of the recent innovations in business communication—is the *network*, or shared system. Although we may link computers in a variety of ways, basically networks may be described as close or distant. In close communication, data are transmitted between workstations located nearby, such as in one company in one office building. The system that links them is referred to as a *local area network,* or LAN. In distant communication, data are transmitted among computers, terminals, and word processing stations that are far apart. The system that links them relies on telephone, microwave, or microwave and satellite technology and is referred to as a *wide area network,* or WAN.

TELECOMMUNICATIONS

Traditionally, we have used telephones and telegraphs to communicate quickly over great distances. We still do. Yet the "electronic office" has created many new ways of linking communication. For example, microwave relay stations, cellular telephones, fiber optics, lasers, and space satellites allow businesses to communicate anywhere in the world.

As a business communicator, you have access to an astonishing number of communication devices and services to help you shrink distance and time. These range from facsimile duplication—in which replicas of printed pages or pictures are sent over telephone lines—to Express Mail and private couriers who guarantee 24-hour delivery of documents. Figure 5-7 presents an overview of the present telecommunication media.

Some of the most potentially productive of these advances have occurred in *teleconferencing*, or the electronic linkage *at the same time* of individuals or groups in scattered locations. Its basic components are the telephone, the computer, and the television camera. These elements can be combined to create a variety of *teleconferencing networks.*

The advantages of teleconferencing are enormous. For example, suppose you are the chief engineer of an oil company that has developed a drilling problem off the coast of Argentina. If this had happened several years ago, you and a team of specialists might have flown from Dallas to Argentina to deal with the situation. Today, however, using teleconferencing, you might "travel" instead to the conference room in your office with your team of advisors and confer there with the engineers in Argentina. Moreover, if you need to "call in" other experts, you can simply "plug them" into your meeting electronically. This more cost-effective and time-saving way to solve problems puts greater emphasis on careful planning, accurate data analysis, and productive group decisions.

How can a manager "travel" through teleconferencing?

A convenient way to discuss such networks is to divide them into voice, video, and computer conferencing, which rely on telephone, television, and computer technology, respectively. With each, space satellites may be employed.

TELECOMMUNICATIONS

Data Transmission Networks	Telephone technology used to create permanent and temporary networks for the transmission of audio, video, and computer signals using modems. The medium of transmission can be either hard lines (including fiber optics) or microwave signals. The latter rely on recent advances in electronic broadcast technology such as microwave relay stations and earth satellite communication.
Facsimile	An office machine that allows users to send pages of information and data by reproducing them. FAX, as it's often called, also relies on telephone media for delivery.
TWX and Telex	These acronyms are standard references for the telewriter and teleprinter services of Western Union such as the United Press News Wire.
PBX and PABX	Technology is turning the telephone switchboard (the PBX, or private branch exchange) into a microcomputer and the office telephone into a data processing terminal. The newer equipment, the private automated branch exchange (PABX), using digital techniques, allows such innovations as automatic dialing and computer networking.
Microform and Microfiche	One of the reasons the automated office is called the "paperless" office is because company records are no longer retained in hard copy. Both microform and microfiche processes—the first using rolls of film and the second aperture cards—allow miniaturization of records using photographic techniques. The gain is reduced storage space (a microfiche card can hold 98 pages of $8\frac{1}{2}'' \times 11''$ copy) and, using telephone networking, remote access to records from distant locations.
Teleconferencing	Application of *data transmission networks* to conduct meetings for which participants do not have to be in the same location.

FIGURE 5-7 Technology systems available to deliver business messages.

Voice Conferencing

Years ago, the telephone party line allowed a number of people to talk together at the same time. Voice conferencing, or *telenet*, is based on the same principle. In this type of network, five or six people in different locations can hold a conference call using only conventional telephone equipment.

What are the advantages of voice conferencing?

Obviously, voice conferencing saves time. Suppose you have an opportunity to invest a large sum of money in a certain company's stock. This opportunity arose only this morning and you have to make a decision before the stock market closes today. Although you are familiar with the company's performance, you would like some last-second advice from four or five people whose judgment you trust. Not all of them are in your own office. Formerly, you would have had to spend time trying to reach each of them separately. Now, however, you can arrange a conference call and listen to your advisors' exchanges. Then, on the basis of your discussions, you can decide whether to buy.

One disadvantage of basic voice networks such as this, however, is that calls must be reestablished each time a meeting is held. In your own situation, this was not a problem because you had to decide so quickly. But at other times you will need to speak to people several times. You can, however, avoid this problem by using *dedicated* lines. Installed by the local phone company, you can lease these systems for 24 hours a day. With a dedicated line, much like the famous "hot line" between the U.S. president's office and the Soviet premier's, you would no longer have to reestablish a connection each time you need to make a conference call to the same people.

All telephone conferencing networks have a time-lapse framework called *store and forward*. This feature is useful if conference members need to be absent when a call is made. With it, messages are recorded for replay in the same way as on a telephone answering machine. As a result, receivers can review them and respond when it is convenient. The advantage of the store-and-forward feature lies in the freedom it gives receivers, allowing them to decide when to communicate.

Video Conferencing

Suppose you want to see the people you are talking to in a conference call. Sometimes this provides an important clue about their reactions to your proposal to expand into the health care business or to cut back basic research for the next six months in the cosmetics company you own, or whatever the call is about. For example, telephone conferencing does not permit you to see the irritated look that passes over the face of one participant or the supportive smile of another.

How does video conferencing work? In its most advanced form, each participant enters a separate television studio, usually in *fixed* locations. In it are cameras and microphones to transmit messages and monitors to receive them.

Most companies, however, use either *one-way or two-way ad hoc or fixed networks*. (Ad hoc networks are not fixed and therefore may be moved.) At present, one-way networks are more popular, perhaps in part because they are less expensive than two-way systems. In one-way networks the relation between sender and receiver is similar to that between a TV news anchorperson and the home audience. Thus, if your company has a one-way system and the president uses it to send a message to employees in a number of different locations, they can see and hear the president but cannot respond immediately. In contrast, the relation between sender and receiver in a two-way system is comparable to that between a TV news anchorperson and a reporter at the site of a story. Both have equal access; that is, they can converse back and forth with each other. Thus, if your company has a two-way system, managers in different offices around the country can converse with each other almost as if they were in the same room. The previously mentioned conference on the troubled oil rig is an example of two-way networking.

How does video conferencing work?

A less frequently used type of video networking is *interactive broadcasting*. This system is a kind of hybrid in that it uses one-way networks and telephones or computers. With it a conference leader can broadcast a one-way message both orally and visually, and receivers can respond by way of a computer or telephone link. This interactive approach greatly reduces the risk of miscommunication inherent in a one-way system.

If you are thinking about using a visual networking system in your office, you need to consider not only the type of network, but also the speed at which signals are sent. Two types of systems control the speed. The first, *full motion*, sends them at a rate comparable to that of frames in television or movies. The second, *slow scan*, transmits signals at a rate similar to that of slides in a slide presentation. For most conference applications, the time lapse between individual pictures in slow scan is from 5 to 12 seconds. Naturally, full-motion systems cost more than do slow scans.

In general, video conferencing has more applications than do voice systems. However, it is also more expensive than voice per teleconference—two-way systems are more costly than are those that are one way, and both are far less expensive than if each participant enters a separate TV studio.

Computer Conferencing

How might a comuter conference differ from a telephone conference?

Computer conferencing—an application of the same technology used for electronic mail—links distant terminals in a multiuser network. For example, suppose you work for an investment house with branches around the world. Using computer conferencing, out of the company's main office "A" in New York you "speak," that is, send and receive messages, to branches "B" in Chicago and "C" in Hong Kong. You may also want to send graphic information to aid in your discussion. If you send it to the other branches, they should receive it almost instantly.

The speed with which graphics may be received is one advantage of computer conferencing. Another lies in its "store-and-forward" application—receivers do not have to be present when a message is sent. For this reason, the system is sometimes referred to as an "electronic bulletin board."

The system's major disadvantage is that if participants are on line at the same time, the network's overall efficiency is limited to the speed of the slowest typist. To diminish the problem, enhancements are available to transmit data that have already been entered, such as documents, graphics, and spread sheets. As these enhancements are perfected, computer conferencing will also increase.

Space Satellites

Today's businesses are using space satellites in teleconferencing hookups of all types: voice, video, and computer. Companies may own or lease satellites. (Usually, companies lease satellite "time" from telephone companies, who offer the time as a service to customers.) The great advantage of satellites is that they can transmit messages anywhere in the world in a few seconds. Thus, even though satellites are costly, some companies use them extensively.

What are satellite uplinks and downlinks?

In a satellite network, the source establishes an *uplink*, which allows it to transmit messages to the satellite. Then the messages are sent by the satellite through a *downlink* to their destination. So a minimum network consists of one uplink and one downlink. If a company wants a one-way communication to more locations, it can add downlinks. If, however, it wants a two-way communication, it adds uplinks as well.

The basic cost of a one-way satellite teleconferencing program is based on some combination of program production, uplinking video transmission, satellite time, and downlinking. Usually, the first four are computed hourly, whereas the expense of downlinking depends on the number of sites to be reached. If more uplinks are added, all related expenses will also increase. Figure 5-8 shows how all components of teleconferencing interact with each other, and Figure 5-9 shows how a teleconference is organized.

In summary, using teleconferencing, businesses can send and receive quality information with extraordinary speed. In addition, these systems can save money and effort, especially that spent on traveling. However, costs are still high. Nevertheless, for many large corporations the improved ability to analyze data compensates for the higher costs.

Some managers and employees are apprehensive at first about using teleconferencing. With familiarity, they seem, however, to lose their fears. Some workers worry that networks will replace them. But

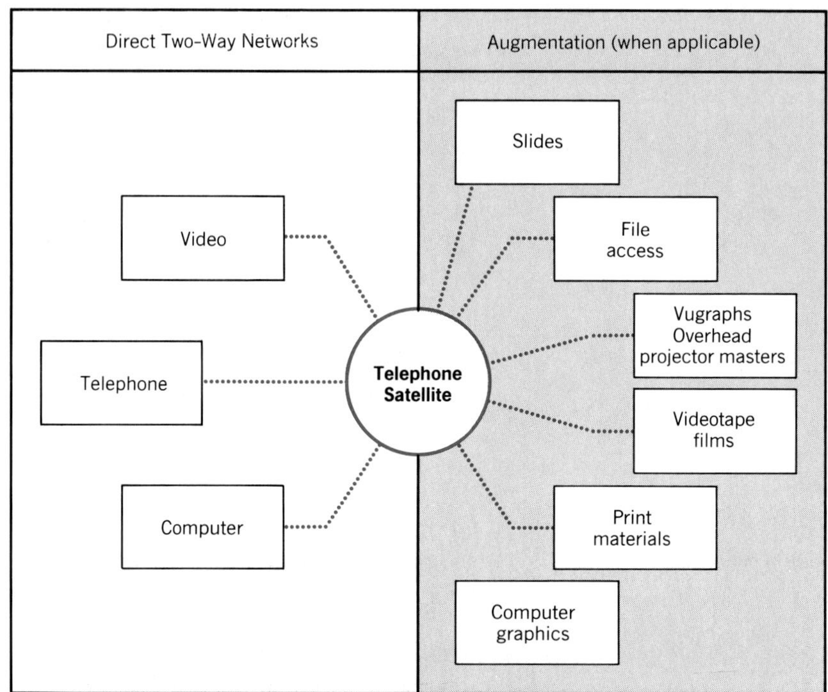

FIGURE 5-8 How basic components of telecommunications networks interact.

so far companies are finding that, while certain jobs are eliminated and others are changed, still more are created.

TRENDS AND BARRIERS RELATED TO TECHNOLOGY

How does the new communication technology affect business managers? At first, its influence seemed to be limited to reducing or eliminating the time employees spent typing and to providing people with easier access to company records. Then managers began to notice more subtle effects: more communication seemed to be occurring, the office was less formal, and the general quality of messages was improved. Now, as we become more familiar with the new technology, we see that these effects are truly widespread and deep. Basically, they influence how all business is conducted.

What changes is technology bringing to business communication?

In the process, LANs and WANs have changed management's expectations and procedures, including the basic organizational structure itself. The following is a list of the most significant trends in business communication affecting both large and small companies as computer technology is integrated into the workplace.

- Distance is no longer a major barrier. The importance of personal contact between people has been replaced with face-to-face communication. Communication across the country, or even around the world, has become as easy as communication with the office down the hall.
- The organizational structure has become more streamlined as managers have increased direct contact with subordinates. Since this also means fewer transfer stations (people who pass messages on), the organization itself is more flattened.

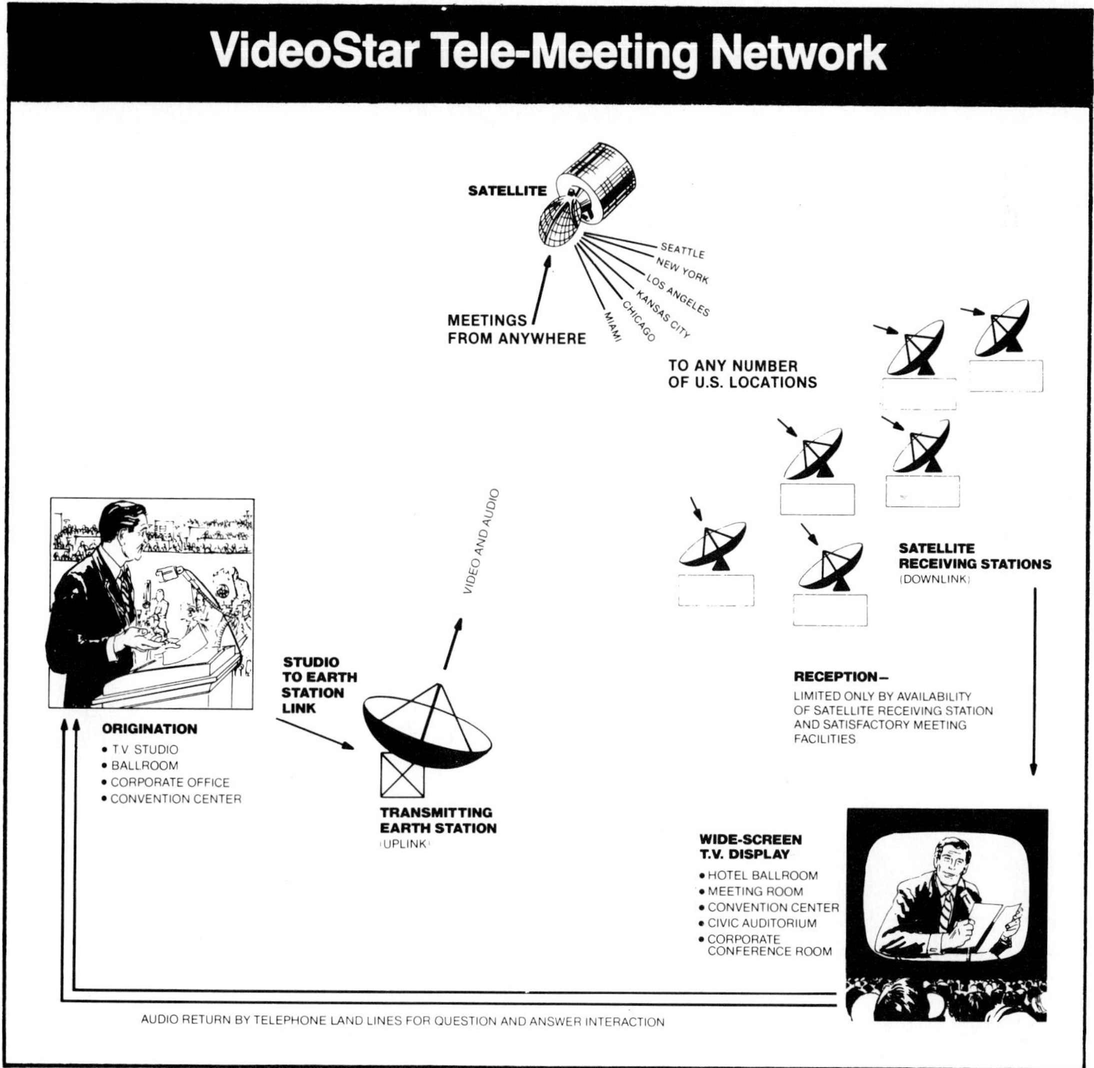

FIGURE 5-9 Organization of a full-motion teleconference. (Drawing used with permission of *Communications News.)*

- More people in an organization have access to more information. This reduces the "information float"—the rate of information flow—and tends to change the traditional role of managers as primary information sources.
- The time required to make decisions has decreased because managers have access to increased information resources. Time to consider decisions, though, has also decreased because of increased pressure to act quickly.
- The timeliness and quality of information is increasingly important as more people have access to more sources of information. The difficulty is that more information doesn't necessarily mean better information.
- The implementation of projects, particularly those depending on communication or involving scheduling time, has been enhanced.
- Teamwork in organizations has increased. More people, with a broader range of skills, can have input on projects. In fact many newer organizational charts are designed around computer links.
- Finally, as technology increases in scope, managers are required to learn more about the communication process at all levels.

Could technology actually create communication barriers?

In Chapter 2, we discussed business communication barriers. Certainly, the electronic office will create its own set of barriers—those specifically related to the interaction between people and machines. (The study of this interaction is called *ergonomics*.) Already, we can identify some of these new barriers. One is *technophobia*, or the fear of the new technology itself. As we have seen, this problem can often be resolved through familiarization and education.

But what about other, more subtle barriers: most people familiar with computers understand that human beings enter and direct the information that these machines use. Yet we all have a tendency to assume that *any* computer output is accurate. Such assumptions can easily cause us to overlook obvious sources of error.

Thus, the new communication technology is a challenge as well as a boon. Perhaps our work will be easier on the mechanical level, but speed, for example, is hardly the only goal of work. What matters more is the quality of the messages we transmit through the technology. Computer users have coined the phrase "garbage in, garbage out." In other words, this new communication technology can only be useful if messages are well planned and managers understand how the new technology affects their tasks.

As business communicators, we should always be aware of the potential that technology has to create new communication problems. When such barriers arise, approach them as you would any other communication problem. Apply the problem-solving methods of analysis and application described and illustrated in Chapters 1 and 2.

SUMMARY

1. Recent advances in business communication technology, especially in the area of computers, have created the electronic or paperless office.
2. The goals of this chapter are to (a) become familiar with the new technology and (b) anticipate its effects.
3. Word processing is a systematic approach to writing. The components of a basic word processing system are (a) input, which can include keyboards, optical character recognition readers, direct transfer, touch screens and mice, or voice-activated computers; (2) processing, which includes the central processing unit and software programs; (3) storage on either soft or hard disks; and (4) output to either monitors or printers.
4. Electronic mail/message systems distribute written and oral business messages to people who don't necessarily have to be present to receive them. EMMS systems are based on (a) local area networks or (b) wide area networks.
5. Telecommunications, which incorporates numerous communication technologies, has a wider variety of options than does EMMS. Teleconferencing, which allows people to communicate across vast distances at the same time, includes (a) voice conferencing, or telenet; (b) video conferencing; and (c) computer conferencing.
6. Space satellites, supporting a variety of telecommunication systems, ensure fast, global message transmission.
7. Since communication is such an important part of business, the new technology has had a number of effects. Some of these influences, such as technophobia, have created new communication barriers that may be solved by (1) anticipating them, and (2) applying communication problem-solving methods described in Chapters 1 and 2.

Review Questions

1. What is a paperless office? Why do you think the term evolved as it did?
2. In the paperless office, which of the new machines has evolved as the most important? Discuss your answer briefly.
3. What are the four major word processing tasks? Describe each one.
4. What difference is there between shared and stand-alone computers?
5. What difference is there between membrane and full-stroke keyboards?
6. How does an optical character recognition reader work?
7. What are ROM and RAM and how do they differ?
8. How would you distinguish between letter-quality and dot-matrix printers?
9. What is an electronic mail/message system? How does it work?
10. How does a local area network work and how does it differ from a wide area network?
11. How could teleconferencing change the work life of a manager who travels extensively?
12. What is a telenet? How does it work?
13. How does interactive broadcasting work in a business situation?
14. What use could computer conferencing be put to in a company that has several branch offices?
15. Can you name two trends in computer technology that may affect managers today or in the future?

Exercises

1. Go to the library. List and review at least six journals, magazines, and newspapers that feature articles on business communication technology. Be prepared to discuss your findings in class.
2. As part of the same library investigation described in Exercise 1, review the most recent books on business communication technology. Now answer this question: Which resource—books or periodicals—is the best source of information on this subject? Cite examples to illustrate your conclusion.
3. Keyboard arrangement differs among microcomputers and among word processors. Assume that you have been asked to study keyboard designs to determine whether any particular one is easiest to use or most efficient. Conduct the research and write an informal report of your findings.
4. A number of communication trends related to technology were noted in the chapter. Select two of them and answer these questions for each: What specific type of communication barrier do you think this trend will lead to if any? How would you recommend alleviating it?
5. Review the steps a message goes through when it is sent by an electronic mail/message system from an office on the East Coast to one on the West Coast. List each piece of equipment used and explain its function.
6. List the types of written messages you, as a student, have to produce. With your list, visit two local stores that sell different brands of microcomputers. Obtain literature, ask questions, and request a hands-on demonstration of each brand. Write a report on what you have learned. Which would you recommend a student purchase? Why?
7. As an alternate to Exercise 6, do the same research, but this time pay particular attention to the networking capabilities of the equipment. Write a report on what you have learned. Which would you recommend a company with 10 widely separated offices purchase? Why?
8. A basic argument against using interactive teleconferencing is that users are uncomfortable with it. Find two or three recent articles on this issue and answer these questions. Do you think this is a real issue? Will it hamper the development of teleconferencing or is it just a temporary problem that time will solve? Be prepared to cite and discuss your research in class.
9. In the library, read about the effect of the first typewriters on business. Prepare a short report on the similarities (and differences) between what occurred then and the effect of word processors today. Does history teach us any lessons?
10. List the major word processing software available today. Combine your list with those of others in your class. Divide the class into as many groups as there are programs on the list. Now assume that each group represents the company that owns that program.

    For your next class meeting be prepared to describe (or demonstrate) the capabilities of "your" product. After each group has made its presentation, ask the entire class to vote on which product is believed the best value for a small retail business to buy.

CHAPTER 6

NEW SKILLS FOR OLD: WORD PROCESSING AND DICTATION

In this chapter we will focus on two applications of business communication technology: word processing and dictation. Both require special training. Yet, once learned, they can save you time and increase your efficiency.

Are word processing and dictation both new technologies?

Dictation is not a new technology—in fact, it has been in use throughout this century. Nevertheless, it shares some characteristics of the new word processing technology and may even be said to "cooperate" with it: for when a dictator records a message for later transcription, the result of this act is a store-and-forward situation similar to that in teleconferencing. Moreover, once this dictated message is stored, telecommunication technology can hasten it on its way.

Even though it is not part of the new technology, dictation does have a place in it, one that should grow in importance. Recall for a moment the discussion in the last chapter on voice-activated word processors, the "typewriters with ears." When this technology becomes available, basic dictation techniques will most likely be used in inputting. Just as skilled dictators do now, users will need to organize information by using raw data in the dictation process so that the machine can prepare "perfect" copy. This also means "telling" the machine when to capitalize and what punctuation to add or how to spell unfamiliar words.

WORD PROCESSING: THE BUSINESS WRITER'S NEW TOOL

Randy Ellis has to write the personnel section of the "Initial Study Report" for the office analysis group project he has helped to complete. In this report he needs to include findings, conclusions, and recommendations for improving personnel policies in his office. If he chooses, he can write the report in longhand and give these notes to his assistant to type. He then can use this typed draft to edit and revise the report copy. The last step toward producing the final copy of his report is to return this revised copy to his assistant for retyping.

Or Randy can use a new technology to produce his report. This technology will let him write and revise his report without assistance from anyone. He can type as fast as he is able, and the words appear instantly on a screen similar to that of a television. He does not need to return a carriage or pause to hyphenate at the end of a line. He does not need to throw away a page and retype to correct an error or change what he has written. If he decides to add a sentence, he can put it in where it belongs, and the words after it will adjust automatically to make room. If he sees a misspelled word, he can go to that word and type in the correction, wiping out the wrong letters. If he decides a paragraph will work better in the middle of the report than at the beginning, he can move it. The sentences around the added paragraph will move to make room, and the paragraph will be deleted from the beginning of the report.

All this activity is controlled by Randy with the help of an insignificant looking box. But this box contains electronics that control everything else. Randy has entered the world of the automated office—the Computer Age—for this insignificant looking box contains a microprocessor, a computer. This box enables Randy to use a machine and what is called word processing to automate many functions in the writing process.

Writing Methods for "Fingertip Thinking"

Why is word processing called "fingertip thinking"?

You want to write a letter to a TV station requesting that it cover an important press conference your company is going to hold on its new plan for toxic waste disposal. Since your assistant is out, you decide to compose the letter yourself on your new word processor. Yet, although you know how to use the machine, you still hesitate before sitting down in front of it. The problem is that, somehow, you still think of typing as a clerical task: you are a manager—and typing your own work is not something you should be doing. Still, you reason, the keyboard is faster and more efficient than the pen, and you even saw your boss using a word processor the other day.

So you sit down at the keyboard and type, and what you have written appears in front of you on a screen—not on the familiar sheet of paper. (See Figure 6-1.) You discover that the speed of recording your thoughts is limited only by the speed of your fingers on the keys. Settling in, you also see that learning to use a keyboard while you think will take time. Already you know enough not to expect to be proficient at it the first time.

Later, as you become more experienced, you will feel able to write down unrelated thoughts and to compose and experiment as much as you wish. Because word processing shows the changes you make instantly and can be used to revise *immediately*, it gives you freedom to draft and edit extensively without worrying about retyping.

If you tend to polish as you work, you may draft a sentence or a paragraph using the word processor and then edit the material. You'll evaluate each word and write transitions that make the parts flow together. In this way, you might rewrite a paragraph five times before you are satisfied with it. Then you will start the next paragraph, going through the same process.

In contrast, if you write as quickly as possible without worrying about smooth phrasing or whether you should use the phrase "at the same time" instead of the word "simultaneously," you will keyboard

FIGURE 6-1 Writer using an Apple MacIntosh with a "mouse" to prepare a business report.

a lot of words and then return later to polish them and fill in the details.

No matter which way you compose your message, you will still write faster and more easily using word processing than if you had employed the traditional pen and paper or typewriter.

Writing with the Word Processor

What word processing features must you know to enter information into the system?

If there is any area where automation has clearly improved upon the old ways of doing things in the office, word processing is it. Some of the word processing features that make writing easier include cursor controls, automatic return, word wrap, and scrolling.

Cursor Controls

The cursor is a patch of light that may be in the shape of a rectangle, square, or triangle. Its purpose is to tell you where you are on the screen. As you type, a letter or space appears where the cursor was as it jumps one space to the right. Figure 6-2 shows how the cursor looks on the screen.

If you want to change what you have typed, you move the cursor through the text to the appropriate place. Every word processor has four cursor control keys (or combinations of keystrokes) that move the cursor in each of the four directions—up, down, left, or right. On

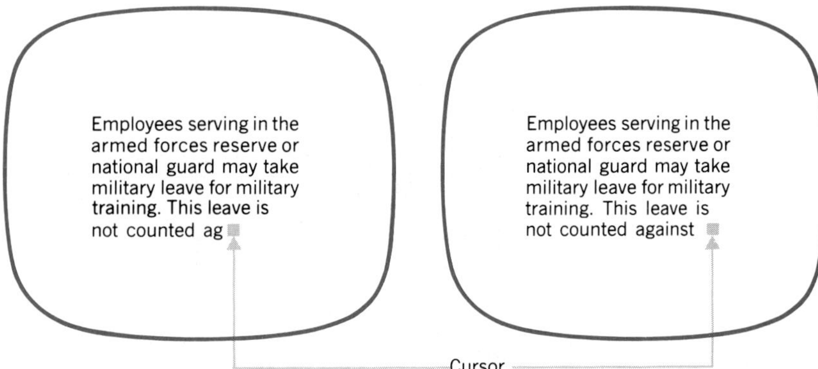

FIGURE 6-2 The cursor shows your location in the text. [From Steven P. Golen, C. Glenn Pearce, and Ross Figgins, *Report Writing for Business and Industry* (New York: John Wiley, 1985).]

some machines the cursor controls move the cursor one letter at a time, forward or backward. On others you use command keys, such as "Home" or "End" to move the cursor by word, line, paragraph, screen, or file.

Automatic Return

A favorite feature for users is the automatic return. Each time the cursor reaches the end of a line on the screen, the machine automatically moves the cursor to the next line. Thus, you do not have to pause in your typing to strike a Return key. If you end a line, however, before you reach the line ending on the screen (for example, a paragraph ending), you signal this ending to the machine by striking the Return key. The processor indicates the end of the paragraph, usually with an onscreen marker of some type.

Word Wrap

If you cannot complete a word on a line, word wrap automatically takes the letters typed on the first line and puts them on the next line so the complete word now is on the second line. Some machines will alert you when a word cannot be completed on a line and give you the option of hyphenating it. Some of them even suggest where you should place the hyphen. Figure 6-3 shows the effect of word wrap.

Scrolling

The screen displays a limited number of lines. As you type and fill it with text, a line of your report moves off the screen at the top to make room for a new line. This feature is called scrolling. To review any

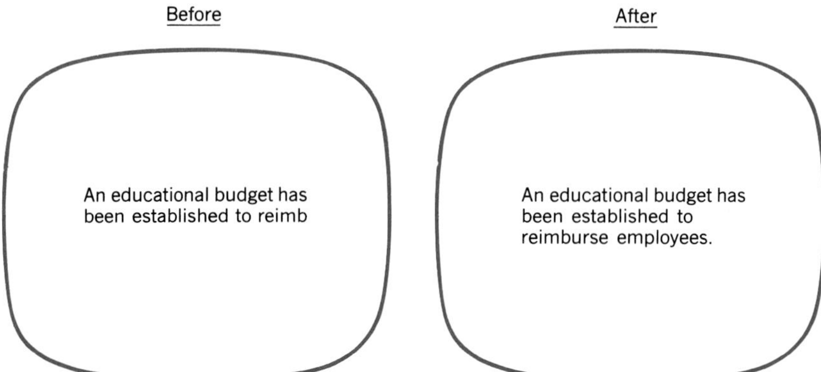

Before
An educational budget has
been established to reimb
After
An educational budget has
been established to
reimburse employees.

FIGURE 6-3 With word wrap, a word that will not fit on one line is carried forward automatically to the next line. [From Steven P. Golen, C. Glenn Pearce, and Ross Figgins, *Report Writing for Business and Industry* (New York: John Wiley, 1985).]

Could you compare scrolling to turning loose leaf pages?

portion of your report that is off the screen, you use various scrolling commands available on your machine. All word processors let you scroll at least by screenfuls. Most will let you scroll to the beginning or the end of your text in a single action. Some will allow you to scroll a specified number of lines or to a specific line number. For long business reports, it is helpful to be able to scroll at high speed or by screenfuls.

Scrolling and cursor movements let you locate any spot in your text quickly. Therefore, whenever you want to make a change in your report, all you need do is move the cursor to the point in the report where the change is to be made. Then use the machine's add or delete features to edit your text.

Editing Text

What are the basic editing features in word processing?

Taking words out, putting them in, correcting spelling, even removing or adding pages of information can occur at any point in the process. This ability to change what you want whenever you want is the key to the value and popularity of word processing. The features on the machine that make this possible include *overtyping, backspacing, deletion, insertion, block moves,* and *search and replace.*

Overtyping

In overtyping, you move the cursor to a word previously typed that you want to replace. Any character then typed at the cursor will substitute for the existing character. Overtyping is best used in making corrections on words just typed.

Backspacing

On some machines a Backspace key moves the cursor to the left, deleting characters as it does so. Backspacing is useful for making corrections while you are typing.

Deletion

Using delete functions available on your word processor, you can discard text by letter, word, line, or larger blocks. To delete a character, position the cursor on it and strike the Delete key. That character disappears and the remaining characters shift to the left to close the space. Striking the Delete key a second time removes the character now positioned at the cursor. If your machine has the Delete Word key, you can remove an entire word with one keystroke. Other delete functions that are available on some machines are Delete to End of Line, Delete Sentence, Delete to End of Sentence, Delete Paragraph, Delete to End of Paragraph, and Delete File. In addition, some machines will highlight exactly what you want deleted before the words actually disappear. This gives you an opportunity to check yourself before actually executing the function. Figure 6-4 shows the effect of the delete functions on a word processor.

Insertion

Inserting additional words into text you already have written is one of the most useful functions a word processor performs. To insert words or lines into an existing text, you need to put the machine into what is called Insert mode. In this mode, some machines allow you to insert new words into the middle of the text simply by typing them there.

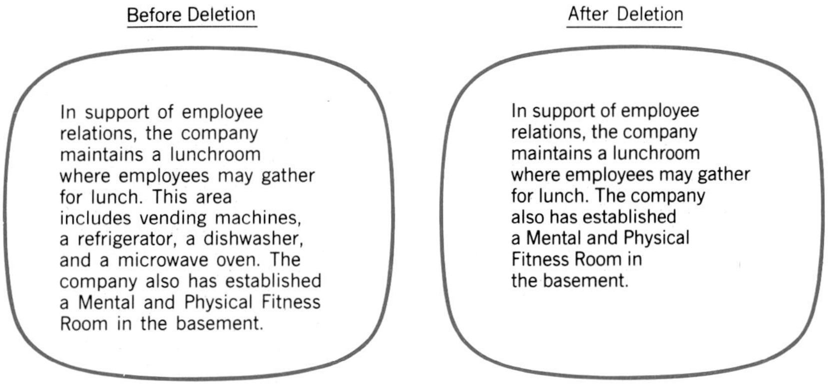

Before Deletion
In support of employee relations, the company maintains a lunchroom where employees may gather for lunch. This area includes vending machines, a refrigerator, a dishwasher, and a microwave oven. The company also has established a Mental and Physical Fitness Room in the basement.
After Deletion
In support of employee relations, the company maintains a lunchroom where employees may gather for lunch. The company also has established a Mental and Physical Fitness Room in the basement.

FIGURE 6-4 Unwanted words are removed simply by striking a key. [From Steven P. Golen, C. Glenn Pearce, and Ross Figgins, *Report Writing for Business and Industry* (New York: John Wiley, 1985).]

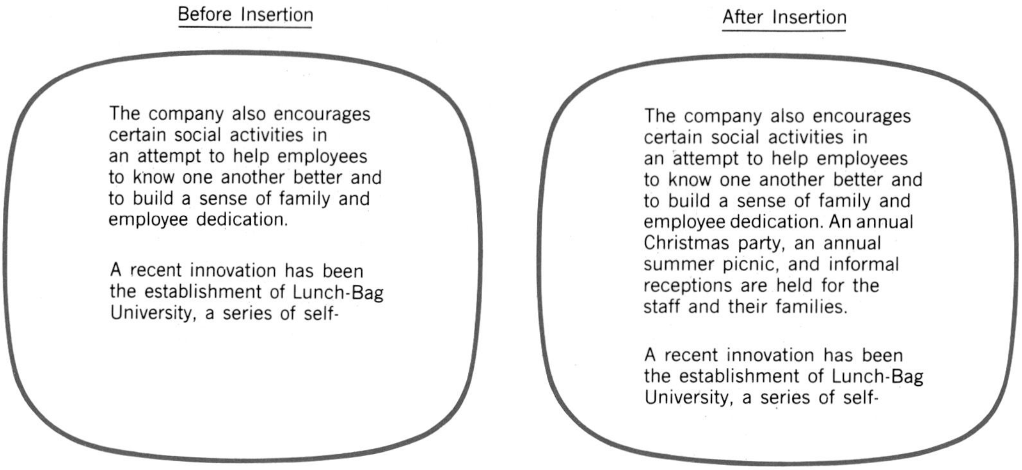

Before Insertion	After Insertion
The company also encourages certain social activities in an attempt to help employees to know one another better and to build a sense of family and employee dedication. A recent innovation has been the establishment of Lunch-Bag University, a series of self-	The company also encourages certain social activities in an attempt to help employees to know one another better and to build a sense of family and employee dedication. An annual Christmas party, an annual summer picnic, and informal receptions are held for the staff and their families. A recent innovation has been the establishment of Lunch-Bag University, a series of self-

FIGURE 6-5 Inserting new text is easy, too. [From Steven P. Golen, C. Glenn Pearce, and Ross Figgins, *Report Writing for Business and Industry* (New York: John Wiley, 1985).]

The rest of the text automatically adjusts to the right as you add each new character. Other machines create a blank space on the screen where the insertion is to occur. You type the new text and then reformat so any remaining blank space is closed up. When the machine is in Insert mode, the Overtyping option is unavailable. Figure 6-5 shows the ease of inserting text with a word processor.

Block Move

How important is it to be able to move blocks of copy on the screen?

Changing text character by character or even word by word may be too slow, especially when large blocks of text are involved. The Block Move lets you move large sections of text from one location in your report to another. To do this, mark with the cursor the beginning and end of the section of text to be moved. On some machines, the block designated will be highlighted.

The next step is to move the cursor to the location where you want to insert the block of text. The Block Move command causes the text to appear at the cursor while the section of text disappears from the original location. Some machines offer a Block Copy option that allows you to duplicate a block in the text without removing that section of text from the original location. Figure 6-6 shows an example of a Block Move of copy.

Search and Replace

Most word processors have a search routine that allows you to type a word or a phrase and then have the processor search for each reoccurrence of it in your report. If you want to replace this word with another word, the processor will search for the original and replace it with the substitute. For example, in creating a report you might abbreviate or code some words that are repeated often. Then at the end, you can have the machine search for the abbreviation and replace it each time with the complete word.

Some programs will make the substitution automatically at every occurrence. Others will highlight each occurrence and let you decide each time if you want to make the substitution at that location in your text.

When you use the features available with a word processor, the job of editing and revising your report is faster and easier. Once you are satisfied with what you have written, you are ready to prepare the report for printing.

Formatting for Print

What do the formatting features allow you to do?

As it did with writing, editing, and revising, the word processor can help you arrange the format properly before you print the finished report. The formatting features available on most word processors include *automatic pagination, headings and footings, centering, right-justified margins,* and *hyphenation.*

Some word processors allow you to footnote or create indexes, headings, and subheadings in a report format as you enter text.

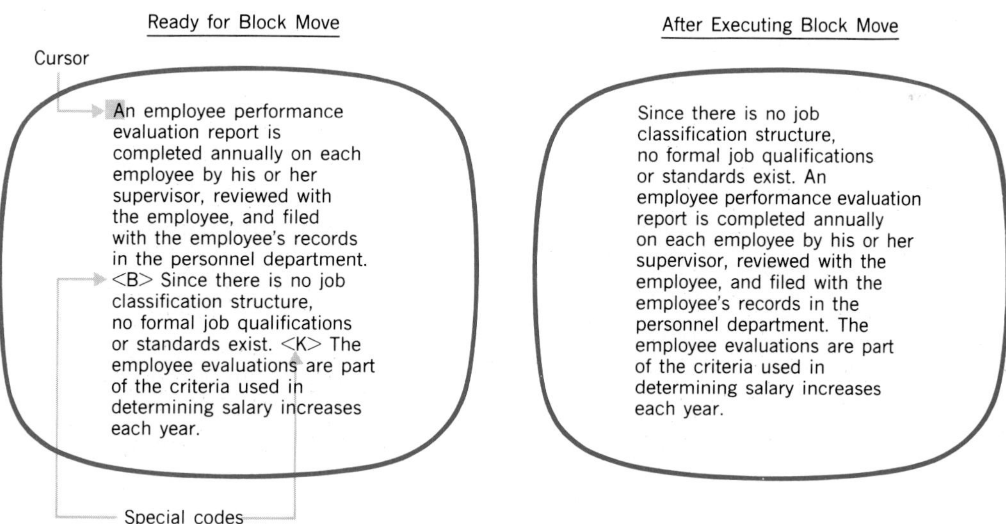

FIGURE 6-6 The first screen shows text marked as a block to be moved, with the cursor positioned to show the location to which the block is to be moved. The second screen shows the same copy after the block move has been completed. [From Steven P. Golen, C. Glenn Pearce, and Ross Figgins, *Report Writing for Business and Industry* (New York: John Wiley, 1985).]

Automatic Pagination

Many word processors will automatically number printed pages for you. Most also will let you omit the number on page one, and some will let you designate where it should appear on the page. In addition, some machines will adjust lines on a page automatically to prevent a "widow line"—a single line of a paragraph occurring at the bottom or top of a page.

Headings and Footings

When producing long reports, you may want to print some identifying name or title at the top of each page. Word processors will do this automatically for you. Simply give the machine the information you want to appear on each page. As each new page is printed, this information is inserted. In reports with footnotes appearing at the bottom of the pages, some machines will format and print them on the correct page.

Centering

With a word processor, you can type the words for a line, press a key or two, and your line is automatically centered. Just think! You no longer need to count the letters in a title, divide by 2, and backspace from centerpoint to center a line.

Right-Justified Margins

The right margin is justified when the last word of each line ends at the same position, flush with the right margin. Most machines can justify the right margin for you as your report is printed. And most insert extra spaces between words until all lines are the same length. Some, however, provide for incremental spacing that inserts small spaces between letters and words to fill out the line evenly. Figure 6-7 shows copy with the usual ragged-right margin and the same copy with the justified right margin.

Hyphenation

How can hyphenation be a formatting feature?

Word wrap eliminates the need to hyphenate a long word that does not quite fit on a line. At times you may, however, want to hyphenate a word. If editing and revision change the line ending, this hyphenated word may then appear in the middle of a line. Some word processors eliminate this problem by automatically removing hypens from a word that is moved from the end of a line in editing.

When writing-editing-printing with a word processor, you have the ability to be in complete control of your communications as you prepare reports from original thought to final printed copy. As a business manager, the machine you will most likely use as a word

Ragged Right Margin
All hiring of new employees is done within departments by the appropriate officers. Compared to those paid by other companies in the industry, salaries are competitive. Employment testing may or may not be done, depending on the departmental policy and the specific job involved.
Justified Right Margin
All hiring of new employees is done within departments by the appropriate officers. Compared to those paid by other companies in the industry, salaries are competitive. Employment testing may or may not be done, depending on the departmental policy and the specific job involved.

FIGURE 6-7 Report copy printed with a ragged-right margin has a left-justified margin. But copy with a right-justified margin has both margins justified. Were the line of writing longer in the example at the right, the blank spaces between words would not be as wide as some of them are. [From Steven P. Golen, C. Glenn Pearce, and Ross Figgins, *Report Writing for Business and Industry* (New York: John Wiley, 1985).]

processor is a microcomputer. Hundreds of word processing programs are available for these computers. The challenge is to find the right program for you.

WORD PROCESSING SOFTWARE FOR MICROCOMPUTERS

Word processing software is the package of instructions that tells the word processing equipment what to do. Software is made up of two parts: a text editor and a text formatter. Generally, the editor allows for input and corrections of text, whereas the formatter prepares text for output to a printer or a screen. The key to selecting a software package is to know your word processing requirements.

Matching Requirements to Software

What guidelines should you follow in selecting a software program?

Knowing your requirements, you can begin matching your needs with features available in the word processing packages. A list of functions you need to consider in selecting word processing software is provided in Figure 6-8.

The hundreds of software packages available for microcomputers offer a variety of options and functions. Also, they come in a variety of price ranges. "You get what you pay for" may not be the best rule to follow when purchasing software if you will never use much of "what you get." For example, you may hear that a certain word

A CHECKLIST OF FUNCTIONS
FOR WORD PROCESSING SOFTWARE

All word processing software packages are not alike. The following list includes many of the features you should consider before purchasing a package. Have the vendor demonstrate all the functions before making a decision.

Cursor Movement
- Up/down/left/right
- Tab
- Scroll up/down/left/right
- Jump to mark
- Screen top/bottom/left side
- Begin/end of text
- Work back/forward
- Sentence back/forward
- Line back/forward
- Paragraph back/forward
- Block back/forward
- Page back/forward

Insertion
- Character
- Word
- Line/block
- Dynamic
- Open end
- Swap adjacent characters

Deletion
- Character
- Word
- Line
- To word end
- To line start
- To line end
- Block
- All text

Block Operations
- Label block beginning
- Label block end
- Define multiple blocks
- Copy block
- Move block
- Delete block
- Limit to block size

Search/Replace
- Once
- Specified number
- Every occurrence
- Continue
- Whole words only
- Partial match
- Backwards
- Without regard to case

CRT Display
- Word wrap-around
- Text printed as displayed
- On-screen help messages
- Upper-/lowercase displayed
- System status line
- User tab set
- Decimal tab
- Displays page break
- Reverse video
- CRT screen size (characters by lines)

Storage Operations
- Diskette
- Hard disk
- Disk buffering
- Displays directory
- Rename files
- Copy files/documents
- Delete files/documents
- Backup files/documents

Formatting
- Margin set—
  - Top
  - Bottom
  - Left/right
  - Multiple
- Spacing—
  - Proportional
  - Double
  - Operator selectable
  - Subscripts
  - Superscripts
- Footnotes
- Automatic hyphenation
- Justified right margin
- Line centering
- Multicolumnar
- Page heading
- Page footing
- Page numbering
- Alternating page number format
- Lines per page
- Ribbon change

Printing
- Underline
- Bold face
- Font change
- Overstrike
- Special characters
- Partial document
- Stop printing

Other
- Spelling checker
- Single sheet feed
- Pause during print for sheet insertion
- Multiple originals
- Merge data/text files
- Simultaneous printing and editing
- Security protection
- Communications

FIGURE 6-8 Functions available with word processing software programs. (Used with permission of Geyer-McAllister Publications.)

processing package is *the best available*, perhaps Wordstar from MicroPro or a similar package. Although Wordstar is an excellent, powerful package that will perform a wide range of functions, you may never need to perform all of them. Therefore, perhaps you do not need the best, or perhaps you do.

Still, the question remains: How do you choose? The situation is made even more complex because the software market is so dynamic, with companies introducing new products and updating old ones almost daily.

Who has the best information about software programs?

The best source of current information about software programs is periodicals. These include general business magazines and newspapers, as well as more specialized periodicals in business communication and office automation. Naturally, computer and computer software magazines are also excellent sources. So are consumer magazines that evaluate products.

After only a brief survey, you will discover that the number of periodicals about computer software is almost as bewildering as the number of products themselves. To find your way through them, check the appropriate indices of periodical literature for descriptive and comparative articles.

A second source of information is personal contact. For example, members of local computer clubs can describe products from the perspective of personal experience. Also, retailers who sell software packages should be able to answer your questions as well as demonstrate their products. Another source of information may be coworkers who have needs similar to yours. Finally, computer hardware and software companies or their representatives can answer your questions and supply you with literature on their products. But be aware that they have a vested interest in their own products.

As a business communicator, you are naturally most interested in software programs for *word processing*. But you may also want to invest in other related software, such as

Can you name four types of software that is related to word processing?

1. *Spread sheet*: organizes numbers in rows and columns. These data can then be printed or processed mathematically by the computer.
2. *Data management*: allows data to be accessed and cross-referenced between data bases.
3. *Graphics*: converts numerical data into visual representations, such as charts and graphs.
4. *Integrated*: combines these applications for multi-purpose uses: Word processing, spread sheets, data management, and graphics.

Software packages are written to run on specific computer operating systems, and these systems are not standard. Thus, not all programs can be used on all computers. This means that although you may have found the perfect software program, it may be incompatible with your computer.

Finally, in selecting a software program, you should also look at the documentation. *Documentation* is the written instructions software manufacturers prepare for the user. Some documentation manuals are written in "computerese" that is almost impossible to translate into English. For example, if the documentation for a package that interests you tells you to "*sysgen* disks after formatting," you might reconsider buying this particular package.

What should you look for in software documentation?

What should you look for in documentation? Mostly, be aware that it has two functions: (1) it assists new users in learning how to use the software program and (2) it is a reference guide. In its first function, it assists new users at each stage of operation until they are familiar with the program and quite literally can "use" it. In its second function, it assists the now experienced users when they need specific information that is either too detailed to memorize or related to rarely performed operations. In other words, documentation should remain helpful to you even as your skills improve.

Some programs also have supplementary documentation. (This is documentation not written by the manufacturer.) In general, supplementary documentation indicates that a particular program is popular. Thus, for the popular *Wordstar* or *Pagemaker*, a number of handbooks exist. These range from handy "crib sheets" of basic commands to sophisticated instructions on how to customize the programs by changing the coding system for how the computer processes data. Besides being an index of popularity, supplementary documentation may also be a valuable resource if you encounter difficulties that the original documentation itself does not discuss. So, in choosing software, take into account whether it has supplementary documentation.

In addition to the software available to handle basic word processing activities, other programs are also available to help you evaluate and edit your writing.

Looking at Optional Software

Packages are available to check your spelling, grammar, and punctuation, and to note any trite expressions you may have used. These electronic dictionaries or spelling checkers can help you proofread your writing. After you write your report, submit it to the spelling checker. When the checker does not "recognize" a word, it flags it on the screen for you to correct yourself. Some spelling checkers even suggest possible correct spellings. Dictionary packages also can flag words that are overused in a report.

Programs also are available that flag objectionable expressions.

How could optional software improve your writing?

One such program, called "Punctuation and Style," sold by Oasis Systems, contains commonly misused phrases and even suggests substitutions. Another, called "Grammatik," available from Aspen Software, detects repetitions, certain punctuation errors, and forbidden expressions such as slang. A popular software package for analyzing your writing is "Writer's Workbench," developed by Bell Laboratories. It points out weak, passive construction in your writing and also calculates the length of sentences and words so you can determine how readable your text is. While all these programs can be useful, at this stage of their development, they are somewhat cumbersome to use and tend to be rule-bound.

What can utilities do for you?

Besides programs specifically designed to support word processing, you might also look into related programs, referred to as *utilities*. Such programs assist in other tasks such as formatting disks (preparing them for use) or purging (eliminating) old files. Among the most useful is a new group of utilities called *macros*. By allowing you to reconfigure the keyboard—change the functions of certain keys—to meet your own needs, macros speed up many of the computer's activities, including word processing itself.

Basically, they operate like "super function" keys, letting you automate repetitive word sequences or commands. For example, with macros you could program your name and address—or entire "boiler plate" or repeated paragraphs—so that two keystrokes could enter them into your text at any time.

Composing on a Word Processor

You have a word processor and have selected the right software for it. Now, using the system, you are aware of a new freedom—to move words around with almost magical ease and to do the same with sentences, paragraphs, and even ideas. Not only are these tasks easier, but also the way you perform them is different. Before the word processor, you wrote something and then edited or revised it. Now, with your word processor, these formerly step-by-step operations have become simultaneous; that is, you type in information and rearrange, change, and edit it in one continuous operation.

How has word processing changed the way we write?

In this sense, word processing has changed the way we write. Freed from continuously coping with the *mechanics* of writing, we can spend more time with the *act* itself. Perhaps another way to see this is as a division of labor between the writer and the machine: word processors do what machines do best—repetitive activities—which permits writers to do what they do best—focus on selection, arrangement, emphasis, and style. Already we can see the effects of this "alliance": we can write more and better copy.

To understand how this writing happens, it may be useful to

COMPOSING TEXT ON A WORD PROCESSOR

LEVEL I: Generating Initial Text

Goal: To input (enter) basic information about subject.

This period is devoted to generating and sorting out ideas; you might not even know how things will turn out at this stage. If not, let it develop itself. Warning: The key to this type of approach is your ability to recognize when the subject and major points emerge. Enter all available information, initial thoughts, and notes. Complete sentences, developed paragraphs, transitions, or even an outline are not necessary. Do not bother to stop to correct spelling or punctuation.

WP SKILLS:
Enter and save text/basic cursor movement.

LEVEL II: Structuring Text

Goals: To establish the general format of the ideas and identify further needs.

Check the order of development of information and identify any omissions that may require additional research. Draw conclusions and write an introduction or lead paragraph. At this point the subject and major points should be clear and focused.

WP SKILLS:
Block moves/read and write files/scrolling/search and replace/reformatting.

LEVEL III: Refining Text

Goal: To develop ideas fully.

Work with material to refine necessary background, frames of reference, definitions of terms or concepts, facts, dates, names, references, illustrations, and other material to develop ideas for the reader. Can also begin refining language and deleting spelling and grammatical errors.

WP SKILLS:
Insert/delete characters, lines, and blocks/reformatting.

LEVEL IV: Draft Editing

Goal: To use a hard copy to gain perspective.

Check structure again—it's easier to leaf through pages of copy than to scroll. Find a balance between the purpose of the work and its shape.

FIGURE 6-9 Levels of editing when composing written messages on a word processor.

Mark those places that require further development. Be ruthless about condensing copy and deleting useless words and phrases. Also edit for word choice, sentence length, redundancy, necessary transitions (block moves can leave logical lapses in thought), and overall form. If text is not satisfactory, repeat level III.

WP SKILLS:
Print copy.

LEVEL V: Copy Editing

Goal: To use available software to find and remove basic copy errors.

Use appropriate auxiliary programs to check spelling, grammar, style, and punctuation. Remember, though, the final choices are yours.

WP SKILLS:
Use auxiliary programs.

LEVEL VI: Printing

Goals: To select appropriate layout for final printed copy.

Consider visual appeals such as layout, type styles, headings, centering, underlining, spacing, paper length, page numbering, double strike (boldface), pitch (number of characters per inch), top and bottom margins, indentions, justification, and overall look in terms of probable reader response.

WP SKILLS:
Know printer and specific "embedded" commands.

FIGURE 6-9 continued

divide the word processing activity into smaller units. Figure 6-9 shows the six levels of editing that comprise the writer's task and the skills used at each.

At level I, *generating initial text*, try to get as much of the text on screen—and into the computer's memory—as quickly as possible. Although an outline might help you to sprint even more quickly, it is not a necessity. You may just as easily develop the message's final form while you write.

At level II, *structuring text*, begin to revise your message, editing, blocking, and shaping it. Write your introductory and concluding paragraphs.

At level III, *refining text*, clarify and support your ideas. Fill out your paragraphs and begin to correct spelling and grammar errors. Print a paper copy to work on. Switching from the screen to the printed page requires a change of perspective and is an extra step, but it's worth it for several reasons. First, you can usually see errors more easily on the printed page than on a monitor. Moreover, editing a screenful of illuminated words can be subtly deceptive. Because of its clean and neat appearance—after all, the machine has erased the traces of previous versions—you may incorrectly assume your message is perfect. In contrast, when you work with hard copy, you see the corrections—paragraph 2 switched with paragraph 6, the word *erased* changed to *delete,* the addition of a row of figures, and so forth. These traces act as reminders that this message has been worked over and in fact may need more attention. In other words, a final draft should be a function of quality, not tidiness.

At level IV, *draft editing,* this is precisely what you do with the printed copy before you. The printed draft allows you to read through the entire message quickly and to check its overall structure. In this way you can easily see the relationship between the various parts—something that is more difficult when looking at a monitor that usually can only show one "page." You can then add any transitions you need as a consequence of previous changes.

Truthfully, do you think your writing could improve if you followed these six steps when composing?

In printing such a draft copy, you might do it at the end of your word processing session. This way you can make changes at your leisure. When you return to the machine afterward, it will be simple to make the corrections as well as to take care of any other problems you found. Another advantage of printing a paper copy at the end of a work session is that you have time to think about your message—away from the machine. Then, if you make your corrections at the start of the next session, this operation returns you to the context of the message before you actually resume writing.

At level V, *copy editing,* all the computer does is simplify standard writing practices. Various software programs can quickly check your spelling, punctuation, style, and grammar. Be careful, however, not to depend too heavily on some of these systems.

For example, although there is an accepted spelling of words, usage or style may call for applications that a checker would call wrong. In the following example, a copy editing program would probably "correct" the first italicized item by joining the two words into one: "I have two copies of the operations manual on my desk. Take the *copy right* next to the telephone and check the *copyright.*"

At level VI, *printing,* you may be introduced to another aspect of editing—page design. Previously, even the most demanding writers rarely retyped a page to see how it looked with wider margins, different spacing, or an alternate type face. Now, because of the new technology, business communicators have developed a new appreciation of page layout and design to enhance readability. Word processors, whether connected to letter-quality or dot-matrix printers, can quickly lay out a page in innumerable ways. Within the limitations imposed by your equipment, try to choose the most pleasing, easiest to read, and most suitable look for your message.

In summary, composing business messages in the electronic office involves more than faster and better typing. It also allows you to work more efficiently, and, perhaps, more creatively.

DICTATION: A WAY TO INCREASE PRODUCTIVITY

Adrienne Kent is a sales manager for a large pharmaceutical company. Thirty-four field representatives, servicing seven western states, report to her. For this reason, Adrienne spends much time traveling between sales territories. Today she is flying from San Francisco to San Diego. During the flight, she uses her portable tape recorder to dictate a memo summarizing yesterday's meeting with her San Francisco representative. (see Figure 6-10) When she completes this memo, she will prepare her monthly report to the home office and begin roughing out her speech for next week's regional sales meeting.

After Adrienne has dictated her messages, all she will have to do is arrange to have them transcribed, that is, typed. She can do this in a number of ways. She can (1) give the tape to her assistant on her return to the office, (2) send it ahead to the office, either mailing it or transmitting it by telephone, (3) leave it with a public stenographer in San Diego to transcribe, or (4) if she has the time, transcribe it herself on her portable, lap computer.

Coupled with Adrienne's knowledge of dictation techniques, the portability of dictation equipment has converted travel time into

FIGURE 6-10 Dictation is convenient. (Photo of Dictaphone Exec-Master courtesy of Dictaphone Corporation.)

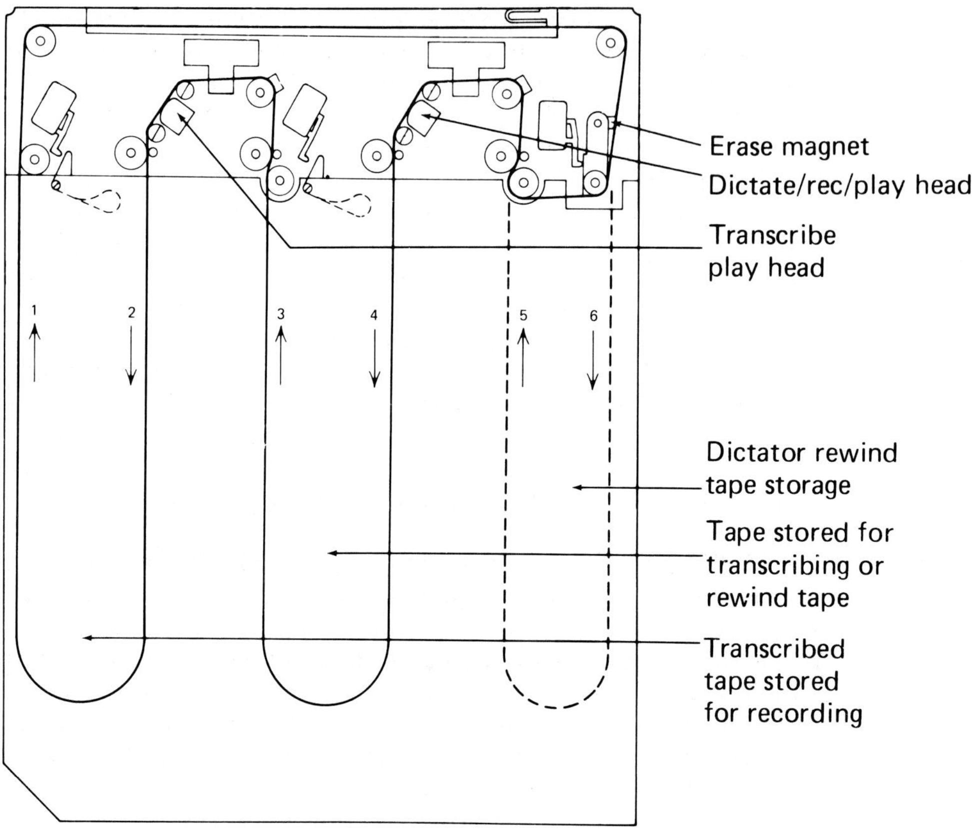

FIGURE 6-11 Drawing of the inside of a Dictaphone Thought Tank System 193, a dictating/transcribing unit. (Courtesy of Dictaphone Corporation.)

productive time for her. But, even if she did not travel so much, she could still dictate letters, memos, and reports directly to a stenographer who would take her words down in shorthand for later transcription. No matter where Adrienne and other business communicators are, however, dictating messages saves time and increases productivity.

Dictation Equipment

Would endless loop or discrete dictation media be better for you at this time?

The two types of dictation equipment available are *endless loop media* and *discrete media*. All endless loop media equipment uses magnetic tape to store the information and does not have to be replenished. The typist can begin typing (transcribing) the information before the dictator finishes dictating it. Figure 6-11 shows how an endless loop dictation system operates. Endless loop equipment is used only in centralized dictation systems.

In contrast, discrete media equipment uses a recording unit with a removable storage medium—usually a cassette tape—that is placed manually into the "playback" (transcribing) unit when the dictated information is typed. Figure 6-12 shows a transcribing unit that uses a cassette tape for recording dictation. Three types of discrete media equipment are *centralized systems, portable units*, and *desk-top units*.

The two types of centralized dictation systems are *telephone line* and *private wire*. With the telephone line system, you use a telephone handset or some other dictation device to dial the telephone number of the word processing center. The recording unit in the center switches on automatically, and the dictator then may begin dictating the message. With the private wire system, you make the connection to the recording unit in the center by flipping a switch located on a microphone or control box on the dictator's desk. The control box is wired directly to the recording unit in the center. Figure 6-13 shows a centralized dictation system that uses cassette tape as the recording medium.

Portable dictation units are especially useful for people such as Adrienne Kent who travel frequently or who spend time away from the office for other reasons.

The magnetic recording media employed in the portable units can be mailed easily to the office for transcription into page copy. A typical portable unit uses some type of cassette tape, and the units are available in a variety of models. Figure 6-14 shows a portable dictation unit.

FIGURE 6-12 Desk-top transcribing unit that uses cassette tape to store dictation. (Photo of Regent Standard courtesy of Harris Lanier Corporation.)

FIGURE 6-13 Integrated systems, such as the Dictaphone Nucleus System, allow dictation and transcription over ordinary telephone lines. (Photo courtesy of Dictaphone Corporation.)

What is the advantage of a combination dictation/transcription unit?

A desk-top dictation unit provides an alternative to the portable unit. To use this system, you dial a telephone number and are connected directly to the recording unit. You then can dictate your message, which will be recorded for transcription by a typist. The types of desk-top units vary according to the function(s) they perform. For example, some units will only record dictation, whereas others only play back recorded information. Another type is a combination dictation/transcription unit, where dictation and playback can occur on the same machine. In most companies where desk-top units are used, they perform only a single function. After information has been recorded on a single function unit, the dictation medium is removed and sent to the typist who then transcribes whatever has been dictated. Figure 6-10 shows dictation being recorded with a portable dictation unit. Then, Figure 6-15 shows a stenographer transcribing dictation from a desk-top unit.

Regardless of the dictation system and devices you use, knowing how to prepare for dictation and how to dictate effectively make your use of it more efficient. Consequently, your messages themselves will be more informative and more persuasive.

Dictation Techniques

Knowing how to communicate effectively with the person who will transcribe the information you dictate can help to prevent confusion. Many managers do not know how to dictate properly, however. When dictating information directly to a stenographer who takes shorthand notes, you can answer immediately any of his or her questions about the intent of the message or how to prepare it for distribution. But when you record dictation, this interchange is less direct. For example, any garbled dictation or missing instructions take time to clarify.

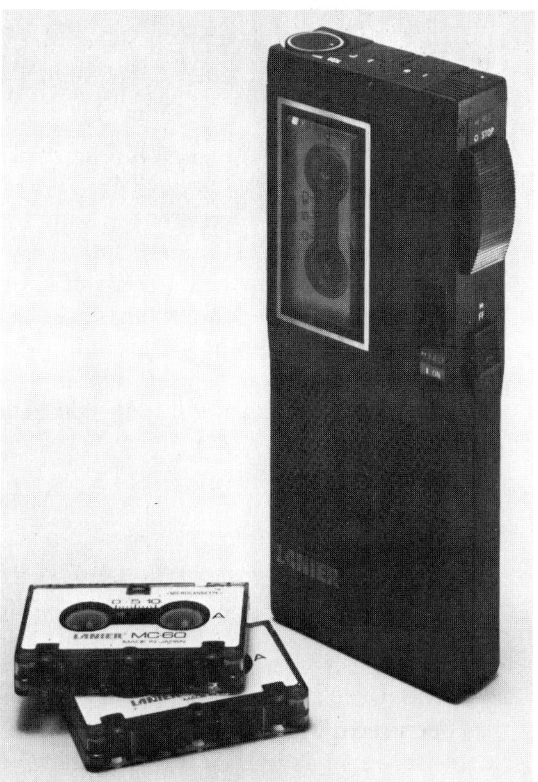

FIGURE 6-14 Harris Lanier's Pocket Caddy, a portable dictation unit that uses microcassettes. (Photo courtesy of Harris Lanier Corporation.)

FIGURE 6-15 A stenographer transcribing a dictated message.

What preparations need making before you dictate a message?

Because machine dictation is used widely as a method of input into a word processing system, today's managers should know how to operate dictation equipment. Recorded dictation can be processed faster and at lower cost than dictation directly to a secretary. Instructions for operating specific brands of equipment are provided by the vendors who sell the equipment. With proper instruction and practice you can quickly improve your ability to dictate. The first step is to organize yourself for dictating before you actually begin to dictate. The following checklist will help you in this preparation stage:

CHECKLIST OF PREPARATION STEPS FOR DICTATION

1. *Gather all necessary reference materials.*
   a. Materials to be gathered include the letter or memorandum you are answering, previous correspondence or reports needed for reference, and names and addresses.
   b. For certain kinds of communication, you may need a membership directory of an organization or trade association or a foreign language dictionary.

2. *Establish a purpose for the communication.* You should be clear about why the dictation is necessary. For example,
   a. Are you trying to get, give, or record information?
   b. Are you going to acknowledge receipt of any information?
   c. Are you going to tell someone about something that might require immediate action?
   d. Are you going to make a recommendation or a referral?
3. *Make some type of outline.* An outline helps you to organize your thoughts and decide what ideas to communicate and how best to present them. Be sure your outline is adequate before starting to dictate.
   a. Jot down an outline on a piece of paper or
   b. Underline important points to which you plan to respond in the letter or memorandum you are answering or
   c. Jot down marginal notes on the letter or memorandum to which you will refer while dictating.
4. *Consider your reader.*
   a. What background and experience does the reader have?
   b. Will he or she react to your message as you wish?
   c. Will you satisfy the reader's needs for information, or will he or she have more questions after reading your response?
5. *Have an extra recording medium available.* If you are using a desk-top unit for dictation, have an extra recording tape ready in case you need it.

Once you are completely organized, you are ready to dictate. The instructions in the following checklist will help you with the actual dictation:

CHECKLIST OF DICTATION TECHNIQUES

1. *Identify yourself*—name, position, and department, for example.
2. *Name the type of document*—letter or memo, for example.
3. *Name the type of stationery to be used*—letterhead or plain paper, for example.

4. *Give special instructions.* Include letter and punctuation style and spacing to be used if other than a standardized style already agreed upon.
5. *Give the number of copies needed.*
6. *Identify the priority for processing*—rush or routine.
7. *Name the type of copy being dictated*—rough draft or final copy.
8. *Give and spell out receiver's name and address.*
9. *Dictate the material in the order in which it should be transcribed.*
10. *Spell all proper names, unusual and technical words, and words that sound alike.*
11. *Give special instructions.*
    a. Capitals: say "all caps" if entire word(s) is (are) to be capitalized, "initial cap" if only the first letter in a word is to be capitalized.
    b. Indentions.
    c. Paragraphs.
    d. Tables: give format to be used. For example, "arrange this in three-columned headings; type in initial caps and underline each heading."
    e. Underlining.
12. *Note any unusual punctuation.*
    a. Hyphens.
    b. Commas used to set off words such as those in a series or in quotations.
    c. Other marks: semicolon, colon, exclamation point, dash, slash, or parentheses, for example.
13. *Give closing information.* Include name, title, and/or department.
14. *Describe any enclosures.*
15. *Note any distribution of copies.*
16. *Give any deferred corrections or changes.*
17. *Give instructions for retaining the recording medium used to store the dictation.*
18. *Identify the end of document.*

Finally, dictation, because it transforms oral messages into written ones, requires special precautions to avoid errors. It is always good advice to never sign or initial any document without proofreading it first. This is especially true in dictated messages. The following checklist will help you avoid these common mistakes:

CHECKLIST OF POST DICTATION REVIEW STEPS

1. *Include all relevant information.* Using your initial outline, be sure all information required is present.
2. *Determine accuracy of information.* Are all data correct? Pay particular attention to
   a. Numbers and calculations.
   b. Routing information, including all addresses.
   c. Reference to enclosures.
3. *Confirm spelling.* Naturally, all words should be spelled correctly, but pay particular attention to
   a. People's names, such as MacDonald and McDonald.
   b. Transposed letters, such as "hte" or "nad."
   c. Capitalizations, such as "Ca" instead of "CA."
   d. Misuse of homonyms, such as "capital" and "capitol" or "fare" and "fair."
4. *Ensure that grammar is correct and appropriate.*
5. *See that style and tone are appropriate to the situation.*
6. *Make final layout and typing look neat and professional.*
7. *Sign or initial the document.*

People using most word processing systems still rely on written copy or dictation as the primary methods of getting information into the system. However, new technology is providing a way to end this time-consuming step. The challenge facing business communicators is to evaluate and apply the new technology—both written and spoken—so that messages can be prepared and presented most efficiently and effectively.

SUMMARY

1. Word processing is the most important new technology in business communication. Messages can be entered directly, by keyboarding, or indirectly, by using dictation equipment.
2. Word processing automates repetitive writing tasks, such as (a) composing messages, (b) editing and revising, and (c) preparing final copy.

3. Word processing equipment includes dedicated word processors and microcomputers (Also called personal computers).
4. Word processing features include (a) special functions, such as cursor movement, automatic return, word wrap, and scrolling; (b) editing functions, such as overtyping, backspacing, deletion, insertion, block moves, and search and replace; (c) automatic formatting functions, such as page numbering, headings and footings, centering, justification, and hyphenation; and (d) auxiliary software programs, for example, dictionaries and spelling checkers, guides to readability, grammar and style, and automation of keyboarding and commands.
5. Dictation is a common form of message input that requires special equipment and training.
6. Dictation equipment can be either endless loop or discrete media. The latter form includes centralized systems and portable and desk-top units.
7. The key to successful dictation requires both careful preparation and good technique.

Review Questions

1. To what does the phrase "fingertip thinking" refer?
2. How do the cursor control keys work on a word processor?
3. When referring to word processing features, what is meant by "word wrap" and "scrolling"?
4. Which two editing features on a word processor would be most helpful for you if you were writing a business report? Explain your answer.
5. What is meant by the term "formatting for print"? List four common formatting features.
6. Is it possible that one software package could be best for all situations? Explain your answer.
7. What are the four types of word processing related software? Briefly explain what each one does.
8. What is software documentation? Why is that important in selecting word processing software?
9. What are the six steps recommended for composing on a word processor?
10. Which word processing skills are needed when structuring and refining text while composing on a word processor?
11. How do draft editing and copy editing differ when composing on the word processor?
12. How has the portability of dictation equipment made managers more productive?
13. What are the two types of dictation equipment? Distinguish between them.
14. Why is it important to prepare for dictation before actually doing it? List the five basic steps in preparing for dictation.
15. What kinds of errors does post-dictation review alleviate?

Exercises

1. Review the steps you now go through in writing a report. Given what you now know word processors can do, make a list of requirements you would have at present for a word processor in the writing process.

2. Visit stores where word processors and microcomputers are sold and study the features of available equipment. Compare the list of requirements you prepared in Exercise 1 with the features of the equipment and write a report about what you have learned. Explain which type and brand of equipment you would prefer to buy and defend your choice.
3. Using word processing equipment, enter the copy given here into the system exactly as it is printed and store it:

   Annual leave is accrued at the rate of 4 hours per full pay period worked. Permanent parttime staff earn proportionate leave. Wage employees earn no leave. Permanent, full-time employees earn 1 bonus day for each year of service after the first year with a maximum of 12 bonus days. Permanent, parttime staff earn proportionate bonus days. To receive credit for 1 year of service, an individual must have been employed for a majority of the year. Therefore, if employed before July 1, employees receive credit for the year of service. Permanent, full-time employees may carry a maximum of 40 annual leave days (320 hours) from 1 calendar year to another. The maximum carry-over leave for permanent, parttime staff is proportionate. Permanent staff are paid for all unused annual leave upon termination.

   Sick leave is accrued at the rate of 5 hours per pay period. A maximum of 6 sick leave days may be taken per year as family sick leave. There exists no limit to the amount of sick leave that may be accrued. Employees with 5 or more years of service are paid for 25 percent of their accrued sick leave upon termination.

4. With the copy you entered and stored for Exercise 3, perform the following tasks:
   a. Delete the word *full* from the first sentence.
   b. Insert a hyphen between *part* and *time* in each occurrence of the word written *parttime*.
   c. Delete *majority of the* from the line that reads "an individual must have been employed for a majority of the year."
   d. Delete *Therefore* from the beginning of the next sentence and capitalize the letter *i* in *if*, the next word.
   e. Add the following sentence after the sentence, "Permanent, part-time staff earn proportionate bonus days.": "Bonus days are credited on January 1." (Do not include the quotation marks.) Now, store this revised copy of the report section.
5. Using word processing equipment, format the copy stored in Exercise 4 to print as follows:
   a. Justify the right margin.
   b. Insert the heading, "Initial Study Report," to appear as it would on every page of a multiple-page report.
6. Print the copy formatted in Exercise 5. Then reformat for output so the right margin is ragged—*not* justified. Print the copy again, this time with a ragged-right margin.
7. Notice that the copy you entered into the word processor and stored in Exercise 3 is written in formal style. Now your task is to recall that text from storage to rewrite it in informal style. To do this, use personal pronouns throughout. One more thing: remove all passive verb forms from the text and replace them with active verb forms.
8. Assume that you work as a manager for First Line Corporation, a wholesale distributor of books sold at retail bookstores. Your company is about to install microcomputers in all managers' offices for their use in writing their own reports. The decision has been made to install the same brand and model of computer in every office. You have been asked to research the problem and write a report in which you examine possible choices and recommend the purchase of a particular

brand. Do the research and write the report on a word processor. (You may add information to this situation as long as what you add does not conflict with information already written in the exercise.)

9. Keyboard arrangements differ among microcomputers and among word processors. Assume that you have been asked to study these keyboard designs to determine whether any particular one is easiest to use or more efficient. Conduct the research and write an informal report of your findings.

10. You can research this problem at the company where you work. If you do not work, you can visit a company to collect data or collect them in a department at your college or university. Now, the problem is to determine whether a particular department should buy a dot-matrix or letter-quality printer, or both, for printing the reports produced on word processing systems in the department. You will need to research the capabilities of the printers and the needs of department members. Write a report of your findings addressed to the department head.

11. Visit a computer store that sells computers that use integrated business software packages. Then, using word processing equipment, write a report describing what the packages will do. Be sure to include advantages and disadvantages of using an integrated package.

12. Compare the time it takes to write a longhand draft to the time it takes to dictate the same information. To do this, time yourself while you write and then dictate the following letter:

    Dear Ms. Jarvis:

    Thank you for sending the current catalog of merchandise you sell at Indigo Products. I received it only two days after you shipped it.

    The catalog you sent does have several types of carved and painted Peruvian gourds that I like. However, the available colors are unsuitable for the color scheme in my newly redecorated living room, where they would be used. You have listed that you have red, yellow, and brown shades, but I need blue or purple shades to match the color scheme in the room. Do you have gourds in shades of either color? The specific design on the gourds does not matter, but the color is important.

    If either color is available, will you please send a description of it so that I can place an order. I'd appreciate receiving the information by April 1 so that I can order and receive the merchandise by May 1, the date my home will be shown on the La Mesa Tour of Homes.

    Sincerely yours,

13. Assume that you are the manager at Balton's Books, a local bookstore. You received a telephone inquiry from J. Fred Magici who lives in a small town 45 miles from your city. You agreed to order a book for him entitled *What You Should Know About Microcomputers*. Your supplier just wrote you that the book is out of print, but a similar book entitled *How to Use Microcomputers Effectively* is available at the same price. You decide to dictate a letter to Mr. Magici to explain the situation and ask if he will accept the available book as a substitute. You can have the book shipped directly to him from the publisher with overnight delivery by Express Mail if he wishes.

    Now, consult the checklist of preparation stages for dictation in the chapter. Then follow the steps to prepare to dictate the letter. Perform the tasks in each step as required for this situation.

14. Assume that you are prepared to dictate the letter to J. Fred Magici in Exercise 13. Now dictate the letter on whatever type of dictation equipment is available to you. In doing so, follow the steps in the checklist of dictation techniques given in the chapter.

15. Using whatever type of dictation equipment is available to you, dictate the following memorandum. In doing so, follow the steps in the checklist of dictation techniques given in the chapter.

    To: Sally Bernois, Inventory Supervisor

    From: (Your Name), Word Processing Center Supervisor

    Will you send me a checklist of our inventory of software packages held in stock for our Apple II and TRS-80 personal computers.

    We are considering buying several new types of software packages but first need to know what we have in stock and how many of each.

    Can you send the checklist by Friday, Sally? If we receive it by then, we can take advantage of a 20-percent discount now being offered by the vendors.

PART 3

COMMUNICATING THROUGH LETTERS AND MEMOS

CHAPTER 7

WRITING ROUTINE REQUEST LETTERS AND MEMOS

Jane Beck is a district sales representative for a national office automation manufacturer. This morning is a typically busy one for her. She needs to advise one of her salespersons about an important deal he is in the midst of negotiating. She has to tell her staff of an upcoming meeting. A disgruntled customer needs soothing. The vice president of finance wants a detailed explanation about why a complex ordering system she is proposing is necessary. Also, someplace in between, Jane needs to confirm a speaking engagement she has agreed to in Dallas next month.

Because this morning's calendar is so full, the first thing Jane must do is decide which is the most efficient mode of communication for each of these situations. For example, she can easily walk down the hallway to talk with the sales representative in his office. She can call the angry customer and try to find a solution to his problem. Since there are 10 sales representatives in the office, calling each one about the upcoming meeting would be too time consuming. Typing a rough draft of a memo about the meeting for her assistant to polish and distribute to them would take only a few minutes. Since she has already spoken once to the vice president about the new ordering system, it might be better to respond to his comments in writing. This way he will have time to assess her arguments before they next meet about the proposal. As for the speaking engagement, Jane can ask her assistant to write a letter confirming it and describing the topic of the speech.

Having decided the best way to communicate each of her messages, Jane can now deal with the actual communication. In your own business environment, you will also have to become, as Jane is, familiar with the situations that require written communication. In this chapter we will discuss how to plan and write letters and memos in which you make routine requests. Before doing that, though, we should discuss how to set the purpose for any correspondence, regardless of its type.

SETTING THE PURPOSE OF CORRESPONDENCE

What are the reasons to write business messages?

In every business message you will ever write, you will be doing one or more of three things:

1. *Informing someone*—very often in response to that person's earlier request.
2. *Persuading someone*—usually to take some action or to provide some assistance.
3. *Building goodwill with someone*—often by acknowledging that person's comments, achievements, or other actions.

How do letters differ from memos?

No matter which of these things you do when corresponding, generally you will use a *letter* to convey your message to someone outside your organization. If, however, you write to someone within it, you will prepare a *memorandum,* or *memo,* regardless of whether you are writing to the president on the floor above you or to an accounting clerk in the downtown office. Furthermore, even if you are addressing co-workers, you should prepare memos as carefully as any letter. Otherwise, some may be offended by an improper style or tone, careless punctuation, or information that is either inaccurate or incomplete.

Proper style and tone in memos probably bears a bit more discussion, given their importance. Both should be adjusted—finely tuned, even—according to two factors:

1. *The reader's rank and status within the company.* When you are writing to someone in a position above yours, your style should usually be more formal than when you are writing to someone in a position below yours. Of course, in making this adjustment you need to take into account the degree of formality in communications already established with the company—what people expect—and your relationship with the reader, the second of the two factors.
2. *The reader's relationship to you.* Generally, you are more likely to have closer personal relations to people within your company than without. Consequently, the tone or "sound" of what you say in a memo will reflect this closer relationship. This type of tone is necessary for you to sound sincere and therefore credible. Further, remember to dwell on the positive aspects of the relationship to keep the tone positive.

Letters and memos also have standard layouts. It is important that you become familiar with them so that the reader will not be distracted by hard-to-follow formats. (See Appendix B for a detailed explanation of the proper formats.)

Determining Your Objectives

Whether you are preparing a letter to a department store that sells some of your company's products or a memo to the head of advertising suggesting a new campaign, you will probably be trying to do one or more of the following:

1. Seek ideas or facts.
2. Obtain action.
3. Send ideas or facts.
4. Direct action.

5. Instruct.
6. Encourage.
7. Promote goodwill.

Do general and specific objectives serve the same purpose?

These goals are your *general* objectives. Naturally, however, you will also have ones that are *specific.* Choosing a specific objective will help you to focus your letter or memo. For example, if you realize that your specific objective in writing a memo to someone in your division is to congratulate him or her on a promotion to office manager, then you would exclude from it a distracting discussion of a project of mutual interest. The following are specific things you might want to do. (Each one correlates with its counterpart in the preceding list of general objectives.)

1. Request credit information on a new customer.
2. Order goods.
3. Provide a job reference for a former employee.
4. Sell a product.
5. Give directions on how to complete a travel voucher.
6. Appeal for donations to a charitable organization.
7. Congratulate a fellow employee on his or her job promotion.

To ensure your message's success, make sure that you have only *one* specific objective for your letter or memo. Otherwise, the strength of what you want to say will be diluted. Once you have mastered this, however, you can include secondary objectives. For example, in requesting credit information on a new customer from another firm, you might also want to promote the goodwill between the two companies. Perhaps your words of praise for their new procedure used to handle these requests would be appropriate in this context. Make sure, though, that these secondary objectives do not overwhelm the primary ones.

Anticipating the Reader's Reaction

You know what you want to achieve in your letter or memo. Should you now go to the word processor or typewriter? The answer is: Not until you have analyzed your reader's needs, attitudes, and background. (See Chapter 3 for a discussion of these matters.) By doing this preanalysis, you will be able to anticipate his or her reaction more accurately. No matter who the reader is, he or she may be

What are the *possible* reactions to a message?

Pleased
Displeased
Neutral, that is, interested, but neither pleased nor displeased
Uninterested

Of course, a reader may experience a combination of these reactions. This is why it is useful to anticipate the response you'll get before actually writing.

For example, your co-worker may feel pleased yet at the same time a little displeased by hearing from you. Relations between the two of you have been strained since you had a disagreement over a personnel matter. Knowing that he or she might react in this mixed way, you decide to use even warmer words than usual in praising this person's achievement. Both the words themselves as well as the order you select in presenting your ideas—in this case, which qualities of his or hers you choose to praise first—might overcome any displeasure that might have been felt toward you.

PLANNING ROUTINE REQUEST LETTERS AND MEMOS

Certain types of messages generally invoke a positive response, or at least one that is neutral, in readers. A *routine request* is typical of this type of message. A request is considered routine because the writer expects the reader to grant it without having to be persuaded. Sometimes this situation occurs because the reader's job may involve possessing the information you need and distributing it.

For example, if you write a memo to the company's librarian, asking whether the library contains any articles on the use of liquid hydrogen in space shuttles, you are making a routine request. Or suppose your company requests an adjustment in price for some damaged cloth you received. Here you are requesting assistance, not information. The situation, however, is essentially the same. Like the librarian, the customer service department of the fabric manufacturer has the job of answering requests such as yours. In the end, what makes a request routine is that the writer can expect the reader to comply with it because of its nature.

What steps should you follow in writing a routine request?

In writing a routine request, follow a *deductive* or *direct* plan similar to that outlined in Chapter 3:

1. *Make the request.* Be direct and state it in your first sentence or paragraph.
2. *Include the necessary details.* If you need to explain the request, do so in the paragraphs following your initial statement of it. State any condition or details the reader will need to comply with it—such as shipment number—if a quantity of goods is involved.
3. *Close with a clear statement of the action you desire.* Be explicit, but ask courteously. For example, if you want another company to pay an overdue bill, politely request that it be done by the date you specify.

A diagram of this plan is shown in Figure 7-1.

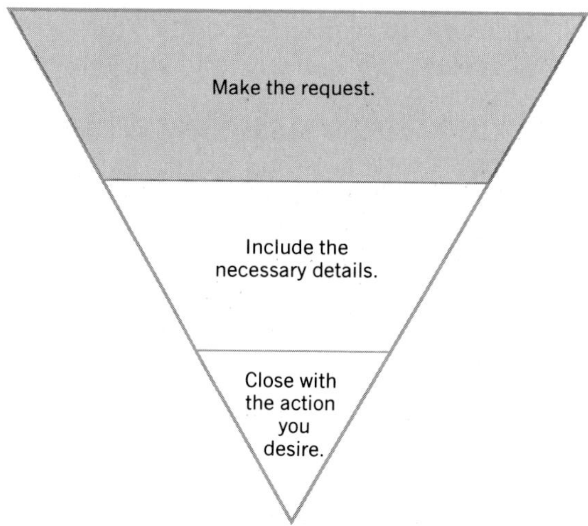

FIGURE 7-1 Diagram of deductive plan for making routine requests.

The following is a letter of request. Imagine that you are asked to critique it. Do you see any problems in organization or in anything else?

Dear Sirs:

When I attended the fall conference of the Personnel Administrators Association in Falls Church, I met one of your salesmen, Jean Jordan. Ms. Jordan was staffing your exhibitor's booth.

Ms. Jordan was very helpful in providing answers to my questions regarding your films and filmstrips. Due to the fact that our company is expanding our training section, many of the films you market might be beneficial. In fact, having viewed the film "Supervision: It's All in the Mind," it is clear that the film would be a valuable addition to our training library.

Would you send a copy of said film to us? Bill for said film, and a check in the amount of $59.95 plus the postage will be forthcoming.

Thank you in advance for your cooperation.

Sincerely yours,

Critique

One problem you should notice immediately is that this letter should be—but is not—organized deductively. It should be because it is a routine letter of request that the company distributing the film will react to positively. But the writer waits until the second paragraph to state the objective. To make processing simpler, always express your request first in a routine letter like this one.

The letter also has other problems. The writer

1. Begins with a salutation that is too formal, "Dear Sirs," which many people now think is also sexist.
2. Uses a sexually biased job title—"salesmen"—to refer to the sales representative. (line 3)
3. Uses two wordy expressions: "Due to the fact that" and "In the amount of." (lines 6 and 13, respectively)
4. Commits a grammatical error when a participial phrase—"having viewed the film"—modifies an expletive—"it." (line 10)
5. Includes several formal and outdated expressions: "said film," "Bill for the said film," and "will be forthcoming." (line 12 for the first two expressions and line 14 for the third)
6. Punctuates a courteous request with a question mark. (line 12)
7. Ends with the presumptuous "Thank you in advance." (line 15)

Now that the illness is diagnosed, what is to be done? To improve this letter, we need to look more carefully at how to write opening statements, use details, and make closing statements. Only after a complete discussion of each of these aspects will a revised draft of this letter be shown.

Writing Opening Statements

Should you open with the subject in a routine request?

Because they are emphatic, you will naturally want your opening paragraphs to provide the correct emphasis for a routine request. In fact, you might think of the opening paragraph as the place to present the letter's (or memo's) *subject*. You can only achieve such an emphasis if this paragraph is clear, concise, and courteous. Remember the following points as you write your first paragraph:

1. *State your request in the first sentence.* After reading the first sentence, your reader should know *what* you are writing about—and perhaps even *why*. Avoid lengthy lead-ins, for they delay the reader from discovering why you are writing. The following are some effective and ineffective openings:

   Ineffective I read with interest about the availability of your new spring catalog. Your advertisement provided some excellent comments.

   Effective Please send me a copy of your new spring catalog that you recently advertised. I am interested in several items mentioned in it.

Ineffective I just learned that the report on traffic congestion in Houston is available. You can understand the public's interest in the contents of this report.

Effective Please send me a copy of the report on Houston's traffic congestion. I am interested in learning what the city's administration has discovered.

2. *Subordinate references to previous communications.* How many letters or memos have you read that have begun with either "This is to answer your letter of" or "I have received your memo of"? Sometimes, as these openings indicate, we need to refer to previous communications. Such statements, however, should not appear at the beginning of your message because the reader will then focus too much attention on them. For example, compare the following two openings:

Ineffective We have received your inquiry of January 10. As a result, we are enclosing a copy of our brochure on tax-sheltered investments.

Effective A copy of our brochure, "Tax-Shelters in Today's Business," is enclosed. It contains answers to the questions you asked in your letter of January 10.

3. *Keep your opening paragraph short.* Readers are quickly bored reading a long paragraph, and a lengthy opening paragraph is particularly treacherous in this respect. Therefore, make it three sentences or fewer. In fact, you may feel that it only has to contain a single sentence. If so, don't be afraid to employ this strategy: such paragraphs are perfectly acceptable in business writing.

4. *Be courteous.* Never demand action; ask for it. Also, ask politely. Whenever possible, use "please" in the opening. A courteous approach is much more likely to gain you what you want.

Can you name five points to follow when writing openings for routine requests?

5. *Write from the reader's viewpoint.* Even though you are asking the reader to do something, you can still consider the request from his or her viewpoint. By doing so, you might realize that the reader also could gain something from the request. If this is true, you might describe this benefit. For example, your request might result in a large sale for another company. In your letter to the firm, you might mention this, thus raising the chance that your message will not only be viewed favorably but also be acted on swiftly. If, however, you cannot find that the reader will benefit, then avoid beginning your request with an "I" word because it somehow emphasizes a distance between the two of you that even a reference to shared benefit would decrease if not eliminate. For example, compare the following "writer-centered" and "reader-centered" openings:

Writer centered	I would appreciate your sending me a copy of your speech that was given at the Managers' Roundtable last Thursday.
Reader centered	Would you please continue your efforts to tell others of the benefits of performance appraisal by sending me a copy of the speech you gave at the Managers' Roundtable. I would then share the information.
Writer centered	We would like to receive a copy of your latest financial statement so that we can consider your request for credit.
Reader centered	Your request for credit can be considered just as soon as we receive a copy of your latest financial statement.

Including Details or Explanation

Suppose you write a letter in which you order 5000 compact discs from the manufacturer. A week later, you receive a reply: "To process your order, we need to know whether you want to purchase the XFM or the TSI model."

Many beginning writers forget that the reader must have certain information to act on a request. In writing your letter or memo, make sure that you ask all your general questions in the opening paragraph and then follow them with each specific question. Also, try to include the details or explanations that your reader needs to respond to your request. Insert these in the body of your letter or memo. You should also include any special circumstances or justifications for your request.

Can you name four ways to organize the details of a routine request?

How should you organize this information? Depending on the circumstances and your own inclinations, you can choose to organize it in *chronological, priority, inverse priority,* or *spatial* order.

Suppose you decide to arrange your reasons and explanations *chronologically,* that is, in the order in which they occurred. Frequently, some events have caused you to make a request. For example, you may have had several experiences with a product that moved you to make a large order if the manufacturer can ship it by a certain date. To emphasize the necessity of promptness, you might show in sequence how late delivery can set off a whole chain of events that will negatively affect future orders. Perhaps you might even arrange these events in reverse order, showing the worst possible effect and tracing its development backward in time. Use this reverse order only if it will make the consequences of lateness clearer than would a forward chronology.

Not all information can be organized chronologically. In such cases, you might organize it by priority or inverse priority.

Priority implies importance. In a *priority* sequence, you list the most important reason for your request to be granted and follow with the next most important reason and so on until you have given all the needed information. In *inverse priority* sequence, you start with the least important reason and end with the most important. While few routine requests follow this order, many persuasive messages do because what is said last lingers longest in the reader's mind. (For a further discussion of writing persuasive letters and memos, see Chapter 10.)

The last way you might organize your letters or memos of request is in a *spatial* sequence. This refers to a physical order, as in from left to right, bottom to top, or inside to outside. For example, in describing the damage done to a newly purchased company automobile, you would start with one physical point of reference and list the damage, moving logically through a particular spatial order. This attention to organization of information helps your readers remember key points more accurately.

Writing Closing Statements

Susan Roblowski is writing a memo to her boss trying to persuade him that she needs to take a vacation during the next couple of weeks, not in the spring as she had originally planned. In writing the memo, she finds herself working hardest on the final paragraph. Since it is the last thing that the boss will see, she feels that it needs to be as emphatic as possible about why this vacation is necessary both for Susan and for the effectiveness of the department.

As she reworks the paragraph, she suddenly remembers that she has forgotten to mention that her most important client will also be away at the same time, making any sales to her impossible. So Susan includes this piece of information in the memo.

The next day, she receives this reply: "You have my permission to take your vacation during the next two weeks. I didn't want to approve your request, but your last paragraph convinced me."

What are the five guidelines for writing closing statements for routine requests?

In writing your own final paragraphs, try to use the same guidelines as Susan. These include the following:

1. *Say clearly what action should be taken.* You may have said in general terms what you wish the reader to do. You still, however, need to be specific. If you have not mentioned earlier what the reader should do, your closing paragraph should contain an attempt to motivate him or her to action. You can do this in three steps:
   a. Say clearly what action or answer is needed.
   b. Make the action easy to perform if you can or as easy to perform as you can.

c. Give a date by which the action should occur if that is important.

Suppose you want the reader to contact you. If so, say exactly how you wish him or her to accomplish this. If you want to be telephoned, include your number; if you want a response by letter, include your address and perhaps a preaddressed reply envelope. Finally, say by what date your reader should perform the action you have requested. Make sure you give a reason for the date. Otherwise, the reader may think you set it arbitrarily simply to motivate him or her. For example, in asking a printer to have bound books by September 30, you might say that this date must be held or you will lose the all-important Christmas sales at the bookstores. The following are examples of effective and ineffective final paragraphs:

Ineffective	I need this information soon so you should send it as soon as possible.
Effective	As the information is needed for a report due October 5, would you please send it to me at the above address by October 2. A preaddressed, stamped envelope is enclosed for your use.
Ineffective	To supply this requested information, you need to contact me by September 5.
Effective	Please call me at (617) 555-0000 by September 5 to provide the answers I requested for this project. Your cooperation will be appreciated.

2. *State appreciation by using the future tense.* Suppose you are writing a memo asking that each employee submit his or her travel expenses to you by the end of next week. At the end of your memo, you write, "Thank you in advance." Then you decide to delete this and substitute a phrase that states your appreciation in the future tense: "We will appreciate your answering this request by . . .". You decide to delete the former because, reading it over from the receiver's viewpoint, you are struck that it might seem a form of subtle coercion rather than a courteous remark.

3. *Sound successful when describing the desired reaction.* You are writing a memo to Jake Morris, the head of the mailroom, requesting a swifter delivery of the morning mail. In closing, you write: "We hope you will be able to assist us." Somehow the tone of the remark is a little "off." At first, you don't know precisely what is wrong, and then, you realize: it suggests you are not confident he can help you. Since this is hardly the impression you want to give, you substitute a phrase such as, "When we can return the favor, please let us know," which implies confidence that he will act as requested.

4. *Refer to the reader by name.* By using the reader's name—personalizing—in the final paragraph, you demonstrate that he or she is a person to you. This "friendliness" will help to reinforce goodwill on the reader's part.
5. *Keep it short.* If you have been thorough in the body of your letter or memo, that is, if you have discussed most details, then your closing paragraph should seldom be longer than three sentences.

Forming the Complete Message

To summarize: A well-written routine request contains an opening paragraph that concisely and clearly identifies your purpose. This opening is followed by the body of the message that presents in some form of logical sequence the additional information necessary for the reader to respond. Finally, the request closes with a specific statement of the action you desire and how the reader can best perform it.

In the revised draft of the letter that began this discussion, notice how the deductive organization, conciseness of expression, and the strategy of making the request seem helpful to the reader all work together in creating a more effective request. Figure 7-2 shows the revised draft.

WRITING SPECIFIC TYPES OF ROUTINE REQUEST LETTERS AND MEMOS

Suppose a steel company you are dealing with decides to raise its per ton price. Naturally, you need to know more about the change in price than this. Since the information you desire is complex, you decide to write a letter to the manufacturer asking for more specific information about the increases and how they will affect you.

What are the five specific types of routine requests?

Generally, we write several types of routine requests. These include requests for (1) information, (2) assistance, (3) adjustments, (4) goods and services, and (5) credit. As we have stated previously, each has the same characteristic—the writer can expect the reader to react positively or at least neutrally to it. Consequently, you should arrange your letter or memo deductively. Since the five types also differ from one another in various ways, we shall discuss each in greater detail.

Asking Others for Information

Frequently, someone else may have some information you need to perform your duties. Suppose a giant West Coast observatory has information about comets that you need for a space research project. To get this information, you can be direct in your letter of request. So

SMITH AND COMPANY
439 Forest Hill Parkway
Alexandria, Virginia 00000

July 9, 19--

Sales Department
Universal Film Labs
628 Monument Avenue, N. W.
Washington, DC 00000

Ladies and Gentlemen:

Will you please send us a copy of your film, "Supervision: It's All in the Mind."

At the recent fall conference of the Personnel Administrators Association, I talked with your sales representative, Ms. Jean Jordan. She was very helpful in answering my questions about films and filmstrips.

Our company is presently expanding its training section, and based on the information Ms. Jordan supplied, we will probably be ordering additional films in the future.

Please bill us at the above address for the price of the film, $59.95, plus postage. We will appreciate your sending the order by June 1, in time for the start of our next training session.

Sincerely yours,

George Abbott
George Abbott
Personnel Specialist

FIGURE 7-2 Routine request in mailable form.

first you write a general statement that tells the reader what information you are seeking. In the paragraphs that follow, you are even more specific in describing your needs. Moreover, because the requested information is detailed, you decide to arrange the explanation in numbered statements. All the information about one of these statements cannot be contained in a single paragraph, so you add paragraphs as needed before going on to the next statement. You know such a format will make it easier for your reader to respond because it functions like a shopping list in which each item is clearly defined and can easily be checked off. Finally, you write your closing paragraph. In it, you repeat the deadline you set at the beginning for receipt of the information. Also, you mention a benefit your reader may not know about—that your company has some rare photographs of comets the observatory doesn't know exist. You will be glad to lend them for as long as six months. Then, when you write your appreciation for the reader's assistance, you are careful to use the future tense.

The letter that follows shows an ineffectively written routine request for information. Can you locate some of its problems?

What advantage can you see in the first draft–critique–revised draft format?

First Draft

Dear Mr. Cortez:

With reference to our recent telephone conversation, please find enclosed a copy of the real estate plan for the proposed subdivision in Orange County. As you can see, the planned subdivision is going to have several interesting features.

We will have a large recreational complex for the owners of homes in the subdivision. This area will include an Olympic-sized swimming pool, three (3) tennis courts, and a general-purpose playing field. We also plan to have each building lot be from one (1) to three (3) acres.

You are an outstanding builder in Orange County, and we would be exceedingly delighted and pleased if you would be one of the builders of homes in our planned community. We cannot offer you any special deals because there will be other builders in the subdivision, but we will do everything we can to assist you if and when you build in our community.

In closing I would like to say that once you have reviewed the plans for the subdivision, please advise whether you wish to pursue further discussions regarding your possibly building in this subdivision. If there are any questions, please do not hesitate to call us at (000) 000-0000.

Respectfully yours,

Critique

This letter is a routine request for the reader to tell the writer whether he wishes to discuss further the possibility of building in a planned subdivision. Yet, even though the request is routine, the writer does not arrange the information deductively. For example, the actual request is found only in the last paragraph. Further, the writer

1. Uses vague wording. We do not know the date of the telephone conversation. (line 1) Nor do we know when a response is expected. (last paragraph)
2. Uses clichés and wordy expressions such as, "with reference to," "please find enclosed," "in closing I would like to say," and "do not hesitate." (lines 1, 2, 17, and 21, respectively)
3. Uses redundancies, such as "delighted and pleased," and "if and when." (lines 12 and 16, respectively) In addition, the use of double notations for numbers in documents that are not contracts is redundant. (lines 7 and 9)
4. Praises insincerely. (lines 11–12)
5. Uses words incorrectly, such as "advise." In this letter, it seems to mean "to tell or explain." However, it really means to "give advice." (line 18) Also, "please advise" is too formal an expression and is a cliché.
6. Uses words with negative connotations such as "deals." (line 14)
7. Uses a too formal complimentary close, "Respectfully yours."

A corrected version of this letter might read as follows:

Revised Draft

Dear Mr. Cortez:

After you have reviewed the enclosed real estate plan for the proposed subdivision in Orange County, will you please call me to discuss your possible participation in the Orange Grove subdivision. As we discussed by telephone on March 23, the subdivision will have many interesting features. We plan to have building lots from one to three acres. To attract affluent homebuyers, we are planning a large recreation area that includes an Olympic-sized swimming pool, three tennis courts, and a large general playing field.

Your reputation as an outstanding builder in Orange County is widely known. Consequently, we would be delighted to have you join with the other builders who have committed to building in this planned community.

Your letting us know of your interest in building in this planned subdivision by April 15 would be greatly appreciated, Mr. Cortez. We will finish the preconstruction advertising shortly after that date.

Sincerely yours,

A similar request for information in memorandum format is shown next. Do you see any problems in it?

TO: All Department Heads
FROM: Gerald McKay, Personnel Office
SUBJECT: Ongoing Rewrite of Job Descriptions

As you know, our organization has been involved in a very unique long-term project to re-write the job descriptions of all salaried personnel. This project will culminate with the publishing of a performance appraisal guide to be used in the evaluation of said salaried personnel.

We first began this project by asking all department heads to prepare the preliminary job analysis guides and then to validate these guides through a variety of methods. Most department heads used interviews. Some of you, however, used questionnaires and observation. The result of these efforts bring us to this point in time.

We are writing now to ask each department head to send his validation results summary. In fact, you should send two copies of the summary to Gerald McKay in the Personnel Office. These summaries are needed very soon so that the remainder of this project can be completed.

Thanks in advance for your help and assistance.

Critique

Since this is a routine request for information, it should be organized deductively. The writer, however, waits until the third paragraph to make the request. He also

1. Spells inconsistently—"rewrite" is spelled without a hyphen in the subject line and with one in line 2.
2. Is redundant. For example, "very unique" and "first began" are redundancies as is "help and assistance." (lines 1, 6, and 17, respectively)
3. Uses outdated, formal expressions, such as "said salaried personnel." (line 5)
4. Uses sexually biased language, such as "his" as the pronoun referring to department heads. (line 12)
5. Uses his own name instead of the pronoun me in a superficial attempt to strike an undesirably formal tone. (line 14)
6. Uses present instead of future tense to express appreciation. (line 17)

A revised version of this memo follows:

Revised Draft

TO: All Department Heads
FROM: Gerald McKay, Personnel Office
SUBJECT: Request for Validated Job Analysis Guides Summary

Will you please send me two copies of the summary of the validated job analysis guides that you recently completed. To complete the project on rewriting job descriptions for salaried employees, we will need your summaries by June 15.

As you know, we have undertaken this project to develop performance appraisal guides for all salaried employees. The project will be completed soon, and your cooperation in developing the guides and validating them is appreciated.

You should send the summaries to me at the Personnel Office. Soon thereafter, we can all look forward to the successful completion of this long-term project.

Seeking Assistance from Others

You need to ask a co-worker, Molly O'Day, to explain a new investment strategy. Should you ask her orally or in writing? Usually, it is simpler to talk with somebody in requesting assistance, yet occasionally you may prefer to write a memo or letter.

How does seeking assistance differ from seeking information?

Generally, the assistance you request will be a part of the reader's regular responsibilities. Therefore, you should organize such letters and memos deductively. Like requests for information, they should begin with a statement of what you need. Sometimes you can make your request in the first paragraph because what you are requesting needs little explanation or justification.

For example, if you are working with a fellow employee on gathering information about the investment plan, you hardly need to justify your request for her assistance. At other times, however, you may need to provide the reader with some additional information or justification. Of course, you would discuss these issues in the paragraphs that follow the opening one. Your last paragraph should include any information about deadlines (time limits for action) and any offers on your part to return the favor. If properly stated, such offers will help build goodwill between you and the reader. The following letter is a routine request for assistance. What do you think of its style and tone?

First Draft

Dear Ms. Kelley:

Attached herewith are three (3) copies of an Offer to
2 Purchase and Agreement covering the proposed sale of approximately 20 acres of land owned by the undersigned.

Upon your review and approval of the provisions contained in subject contract, please execute all three (3) copies, returning two (2) to this office. The remaining one (1) copy is for your files. Also remit to this office your deposit check in the amount of $20,000 made payable to the undersigned. Upon our receipt of said contract and deposit, we will immediately and at once begin processing for formal approval of the sale of this land.

Also attached are copies of the Department of Highways' plans showing the subject property and the adjacent Main Street widening project improvements. I wish to state that I intend to forward to your attention maps showing possible building sites in the Main Street vicinity under separate cover.

Cordially yours,

Critique

This request—to sign the contract and return it and a deposit—is the routine closing of a business transaction. Therefore, it should be arranged deductively. Moreover, because it is not a legal document, for example, the letter's overall style should be less formal and the tone more personal. The writer also

1. Uses redundancies, such as ''immediately and at once'' and double-number notation. (lines 10, 1, 5, 6, and 7, respectively) The sentence in line 6—''The remaining copy . . . '' —repeats part of the previous sentence.
2. Uses wordy phrases, such as ''in the amount of'' and ''I wish to state that.'' (lines 8 and 14, respectively)
3. Uses outdated, wordy, formal expressions, such as ''attached herewith,'' ''by the undersigned,'' ''subject contract,'' and ''under separate cover.'' (lines 1, 3, 5, and 16, respectively) You might argue that all these expressions are clichés as well.
4. Uses a complimentary close—''cordially yours''—that is too personal in comparison with the tone of the rest of the letter.

The following is a revised draft of the letter:

Revised Draft

Dear Ms. Kelley:

Will you please review the enclosed Offer to Purchase and Agreement that covers your purchase of approximately 20 acres of land that I own. If you approve, please sign two of the three copies and return them to me.

You will also need to send a check made payable to me for $20,000 as a deposit on this property. After receiving the signed contracts and check, I will begin formal processing of the sale.

For your information, I have enclosed a copy of the Department of Highways' plans for widening Main Street near this property. I am also sending you in another package a map showing building sites in the Main Street area.

I look forward to hearing from you within the ten days specified in the contract.

Sincerely yours,

Making a Simple Claim or Requesting an Adjustment

A shipment of clay pots your company has received is defective: apparently the entire shipment is unusable. Since the manufacturer is responsible, your request for an adjustment is routine in that the company will want to know about the defective shipment to discover what went wrong and avoid a repetition.

Is making a claim any different than requesting an adjustment?

Thus, you can organize the message deductively. In addition to making the request in the first paragraph of the letter you send to the clay pots manufacturer, you will also want to supply any information the reader may need to correct matters. While being informative, also try to be objective. Even though this problem will cause delays in your own production schedule, placing blame will not solve it. For example, you could write, "Your workers have done a careless job here." A much better approach would simply be to say that the "pots in this shipment are defective." Be specific in the adjustment you are seeking—in this instance, replacement of the defective items.

The following letter is a routine request for an adjustment for goods received in a damaged condition. What suggestions for revision can you make to the writer?

First Draft

Gentlemen:

SUBJECT: Order No. 2334 Damaged in Transit

Reference is made to the above-captioned subject. This was damaged in transit because of careless packing.

When we ordered the clay pots, we specified that they were needed by April 1 due to the fact that the spring growing season would begin shortly after that. So, when your shipment arrived on March 27, we were extremely pleased with your promptness.

However, when we unpacked the shipment, we found nearly all of the pots were broken. The shipping company's truck driver said he took extra care in driving so it has to be your fault. In fact, we noticed that you didn't even put padding between the pots.

We must demand a new shipment immediately and at once. As it is, the pots will arrive late because of your carelessness. Needless to say, you can see we're steamed about this incident. We can hardly believe that it happened since we never have had this problem with your company before.

Send the shipment as fast as you can, and we won't go elsewhere in the future.

Cordially,

Critique

Although the writer may have reason to complain about the service received on this damaged order, this request for an adjustment is routine and should therefore be arranged deductively. In addition, the tone of this letter is negative—angry and demeaning. Certainly, after looking it over, the reader would be less disposed to help solve the problem. The writer

1. Uses a salutation that many people consider to be sexually biased.
2. Employs a negative tone throughout. For example, look at the use of inflammatory language such as "careless packing," "it has to be your fault," and "never have had this problem." (lines 2, 10, and 17, respectively)
3. Uses implied threats, such as "demand" and "won't go elsewhere." (lines 13 and 18, respectively)
4. Uses stilted, formal expressions, such as "reference is made" and "above-captioned subject." (line 1 for both)
5. Uses an inappropriate colloquialism—"steamed." (line 15)
6. Is wordy and redundant, as in "due to the fact that" and "immediately and at once." (lines 4 and 13)
7. Uses vague references, such as "this" in line 1, which refers to the subject line. Also, no mention is made of how many pots remained unbroken and what would be done with them.
8. Uses an inappropriate close—"cordially"—that is too informal for the formal salutation and contrasts sharply with the letter's angry tone.

The following is a suggested revision of this letter:

Revised Draft

Dear Sir or Madam:

SUBJECT: New Shipment Needed Immediately

Will you please reship our order number 2334. When the shipment of clay pots arrived today, most of the merchandise was broken.

When the order was received on our shipping dock, we immediately inspected the contents since we could hear rattling coming from the container when it was moved. We found that 86 of the 100 pots were broken and unusable. One possible explanation for the damage was the lack of padding between the pots.

Since the spring growing season is already upon us, we would appreciate your rushing the reshipment by April 10 or sooner. In the meantime, we'll keep the 14 usable pots, and you can bill us for them. If you would like the broken ones, just tell us when you send the reshipment; otherwise, we will discard them.

Sincerely yours,

Placing an Order for Goods or Services

Are orders usually placed by letter or memo? Please explain

If you work for a large company, you usually fill out a purchase order form whenever you need to place an order for goods or services. Or sometimes you have your sales representatives order for you. If, however, you work for a small company or one that seldom places orders, you might write a letter to acquire the goods or services you want.

Since the reader will be "pleased" by your order, you should organize it deductively. In the first paragraph, clearly state that you are placing an order. Include in the following paragraphs any details the reader should know to fulfill your request. Also remember to keep these details subordinate to your main objective, which is to place an order. For example, you may want to compliment the reader about the product or service provided or explain how you learned about it. Although you should build goodwill in both tone and content, if you see that too great a proportion of your letter is about this specifically, delete some of these details, so that your expression of goodwill is concise. Also, reserve it for your final paragraph.

If your order is the least bit complex, list the items. Your reader will find this format easier to follow than if you had inserted the information 'within' a paragraph. Or you might arrange the information in columns like those on standard order forms.

Your order should also include the method of shipment you want, for example, air, ship, truck, and how you intend to pay. In general, the type and amount of purchase as well as where it is produced will essentially determine the shipping method. If you are ordering 1000 television sets from Taiwan, probably they will be sent first by ship and the rest of the way by truck or train. In such instances, you should leave the shipping method to the reader's discretion. But if size, amount, and distance are not factors, you may choose to indicate a preferred method.

When buying goods or services, what are the options for payment?

Usually, you have several options for payment. You can enclose a check, be billed for the order, or have the goods shipped C.O.D. ("collect on delivery"). So that no misunderstanding arises, say exactly how you plan to pay. For example, if you are enclosing a check, don't simply send it without saying for the record that payment is enclosed. Also, regardless of what method of payment you choose, indicate the total amount of the purchase so that this information is part of the record.

The following is the first draft of an order letter. Read it to see if it has any problems.

First Draft

Dear Sirs:

We are planning to participate in the annual "Spring Festival Jubilee" in Dubuque by holding a sale on April 1. This sale will be just one part of our involvement in the community's activities for the "Spring Festival Jubilee."

In recent months, several of our regular customers have asked for books we don't carry. So we thought we would order some copies of those books.

Please send us 8 copies of *How to Win Big in the Stock Market,* 25 copies of *Writing Winning Resumes,* and 6 copies of *Looking for a Pot of Gold.* We have enclosed our check for these books and have computed the purchase price based on the copy of the catalog we have from you.

We need these copies as soon as possible. Your usual swift attention to this order will be appreciated.

Sincerely,

Critique

When readers receive orders for goods or services they normally sell, they should be pleased. Consequently, such letters should be organized deductively. This letter, however, is not. Instead, in the second paragraph, the writer vaguely hints that he or she is placing a book order. Finally, the third paragraph gets to the point. The writer also

1. Uses a too formal and sexually biased salutation: "Dear Sirs."
2. Presents incomplete information in the third paragraph. (lines 9–14)

3. Omits important information, such as authors' names in addition to book titles, the cost of the order, and the date of the catalog from which the order was placed. The writer should mention this date in case the company has since printed another catalog. (lines 9–14)
4. Use clichés, such as "as soon as possible." (line 15)

The following is a revised book order:

Revised Draft

Dear Mrs. Gianinni:

Will you please send us the following trade books:

8 copies *How to Win Big in the Stock Market* by
James K. Broker @ $8.95 a copy

25 copies *Writing Winning Resumes* by Charlotte
Zurich @ $5.75 a copy

6 copies *Looking for a Pot of Gold* by Herman
Silverton @ $6.35 a copy

Our check for $253.45 is enclosed. We based our prices on those shown in your fall 1987 catalog. If these prices have changed, please bill us for the difference.

Please ship these books by United Parcel Service as we will need them for our sale during the "Spring Festival Jubilee," which begins April 1. You may bill us for the shipping charges.

Sincerely yours,

Asking for Credit

You have lived in your own home for ten years and are in excellent financial condition. As part of your recent remodeling, you are ordering a large number of products from a local home furnishings dealer. Since you are certain that your financial condition merits a favorable response, you decide to make a direct request for credit from the vendor.

When should you use a deductive plan letter or memo to ask for credit?

Many firms that offer credit terms ask applicants to complete financial disclosure statements. Nevertheless, you might anticipate the type of information desired and shortcut matters by submitting it with your request. Be prepared, however, to complete the various forms as well.

The following is the first draft of a letter requesting credit. What are the problems you see in it?

First Draft

Dear Mr. Devereaux:

I was in your store the other day and saw a living room set that my wife and I think is out of this world, and I want you to know that I would just about break a leg to have it to make my wife and me happy for making our home look smarter than a castle.

The set contains nine pieces—a three-piece sectional sofa, two chairs, two end tables, and a two-piece coffee table—which you call the Jefferson Manor group, and I am prepared to buy it if I can get it on credit terms for the $900 purchase.

Enclosed please find a financial disclosure statement that your clerk gave us to complete and that my wife and I have completed.

Sincerely yours,

Critique

This letter is simply a routine request for credit that accompanies the financial disclosure form. Since the reader will be pleased to have a potential customer and is likely to grant the credit, the writer should organize the request deductively. Yet, he does not. Instead of asking for credit in the first paragraph, he waits until the second. In addition, the writer

1. Writes sentences that are too long. For example, the three sentences average 42 words each, whereas 15 to 20 words would be a desirable average length.
2. Organizes his thoughts so they ramble and sometimes seem incoherent.
3. Uses wordy clichés, such as "enclosed please find" (line 11) and "smarter than a castle." (line 5)
4. States the obvious. In the last sentence, he mentions that he and his wife have completed the form. We can safely assume that he would not return one that was incomplete because this would hardly serve his purpose.

The following is a revision of this request for credit:

Revised Draft

Dear Mr. Devereaux:

Will you please open a line of credit for my wife and me.

A completed copy of your standard financial disclosure statement is enclosed. Your regular one-year repayment plan at 18.5 percent simple interest is our choice of available plans.

We wish to buy your nine-piece Jefferson Manor Group living room set priced at $900. The group is just what we have been looking for, and we look forward to making the purchase.

Sincerely yours,

ROUTINE REQUESTS CHECKLIST

1. Ask these questions when you write the opening paragraph of your request.
   a. Does my subject line get my request off to a fast start? If a subject line is included, the first paragraph should be understandable without it.
   b. Do I make my request in the first sentence and place my details in later paragraphs?
   c. Is my opening swift enough? The reader should not have to read three or four sentences before knowing what my objective is.
   d. Do I emphasize the reader's viewpoint?
   e. Do I subordinate references to previous communications?
   f. Is my opening paragraph short—one to three sentences?
2. Ask these questions when you write the body of your request.
   a. Do I ask all the necessary questions?
   b. Do I include all necessary details?
   c. Are all my explanations and reasons clear?
   d. Do I include any benefit to my reader?
3. Ask these questions when you write the closing paragraph of your request.
   a. Is it short?
   b. Do I word the desired action clearly?
   c. Do I make the desired action seem easy to perform?
   d. Do I clearly say and justify when the desired action should be taken?
   e. Do I emphasize the reader's viewpoint?
   f. Do I tell the reader, if appropriate, how to reach me?
   g. Do I express my appreciation in the future tense?

The checklist above should help you write clear and concise routine requests. After you have drafted one, evaluate it by applying the checklist.

SUMMARY

1. We write letters and memos in business for a variety of situations. In correspondence and every business message, our primary purpose is to inform, persuade, or build goodwill with someone.
2. By setting general and specific objectives before attempting to write a letter or memo, you will do a better job with the finished product.

3. Before beginning to write a letter or memo, you should determine the purpose and anticipate the reader's reaction to it. (That reaction will be one of pleasure, displeasure, neutrality, or no interest.) You can then organize the letter to capitalize on the expected reaction or to counter it.
4. Many business requests are routine. Therefore, the reader will react to them either favorably or neutrally. Organize such requests deductively.
5. The deductive format used for routine requests requires a three-step approach: (1) begin with the main idea or request, (2) provide the necessary details, and (3) close with a clear action statement.
6. Opening statements in routine requests should be short and to the point. References to previous communication should be subordinated to the primary purpose. Courtesy and reader benefits should be emphasized.
7. The body in a routine request should include only the details or explanation necessary to make clear the request. Usually, you only need explain the situation briefly.
8. Closing statements in routine requests should be clear. That is, you should courteously make clear what action you wish the reader to take.
9. Five specific types of routine requests are (1) requests for information, (2) requests for assistance, (3) requests for adjustments, (4) orders for goods and services, and (5) requests for credit.
10. When requesting information, start with a general statement of what you need and supply necessary details in the second and subsequent paragraphs. Use a listing format if you have several specific requests or one that is complex.
11. When seeking assistance, make your specific request in the first paragraph. Be sure to justify any deadlines you give.
12. If requesting an adjustment, ask for it in the first paragraph. Cite the reasons for the error objectively and say what specific adjustment you want.
13. When placing an order, say what your purpose is in the opening paragraph. In following paragraphs, give all the details needed to process your order, including the method of shipment and manner of payment.
14. Asking for credit is considered a routine request when your company's financial position is sound. Thus, ask for the credit in the opening paragraph. Also, give any additional financial information that you can supply.
15. After composing your first draft of a routine request letter or memo, compare it to the routine request checklist at the end of the chapter.

Review Questions

1. What are four general objectives that writers of letters and memos might have? Give a specific example of a letter you might write to convey each of the general objectives.
2. What are the four major reactions a reader might have to a letter or memorandum? What is the value in knowing these reactions when organizing your ideas before you write either a letter or a memo?
3. What criteria would a reader or a writer use to determine whether a request is "routine"?
4. What is the justification for using a de-

ductive or direct approach in writing routine requests?

5. What are the three major steps to follow in writing a routine request?
6. What five specific types of routine requests do businesss people prepare frequently?
7. Why should you keep opening and closing paragraphs in routine requests short?
8. What are four guidelines for opening paragraphs in routine requests? Write an opening paragraph in which you ask for a copy of a speech the reader has given at a meeting you attended.
9. What are the three parts to a closing that ask for action? Write an action close that contains all three.
10. In a routine request for information, why is the statement "Your assistance in answering these questions will be appreciated" better than "Your assistance in answering these questions is appreciated"?
11. How would it help the reader if you use numbered questions or separate paragraphs for each detailed question in a routine request for information?
12. What would you inquire about when writing a routine request seeking information on a job applicant? Requesting a line of credit?
13. What major details should you cover in a letter ordering goods or services?
14. Should you place "blame" for a problem in a routine request for an adjustment? What is the value of taking a neutral or third-person approach when describing the problem for which you are seeking adjustment?
15. If you send credit information in a letter asking for credit, will you still have to complete a financial disclosure form? Explain your answer.

Exercises

1. As manager of an electronics dealership, you often receive requests from charitable organizations for donations of radios, television sets, and other electronic equipment. A local nonprofit retirement home has asked you to donate a television set to place in its recreation room. You agree to do this but need to know whether it wants a portable or console model. Write a letter to get this information. Address: James Oliver, President; Yarborough Senior Citizens Center; 8765 Franklin Street; Yarborough, Massachusetts 00000.
2. As personnel director of Oriental Express Insurance Company, you are in charge of employee orientation. Each new employee receives an orientation booklet, but your company's is now three years old and needs revising. Before you undertake this revision, you want to look at orientation booklets from other companies. Write a form letter requesting a copy of an orientation booklet or other orientation materials that a company might have. Offer to send a copy of your booklet after you have revised it.
3. As personnel director of Oriental Express Insurance Company (Exercise 2), you also believe that new employees can provide valuable assistance in revising your orientation booklet. Consequently, write a form memorandum to solicit information from employees who have been with Oriental Express for one year or less. Inquire about the adequacy of the various

sections of the present booklet and ask for specific suggestions for improvement. You will need their suggestions by October 10.

4. Small and Inverness, an accounting firm, has decided to advertise for business. You were hired as the new advertising director and are now designing an advertising program. You need a 15-minute appointment with each of the firm's 15 account supervisors to discuss their ideas about how best to advertise the firm. Write a form memorandum to be routed to each supervisor.

5. You have just moved from San Francisco, California, to Lynchburg, Virginia. Two weeks before moving, you bought a new 10-speed, 26-inch Model 96 Twixt bicycle for your son's birthday. You delayed unpacking the bicycle for assembly until you completed your move to Lynchburg. When you unpacked the bicycle yesterday, you discovered that the rear brake assembly is missing. Twixt bicycles are not sold in Virginia, and your son's birthday is two weeks away. Write a letter to San Francisco asking that a rear brake assembly be express mailed to you. Enclose a copy of your sales receipt. Address: Twixt Bikes Unlimited; 422 Arcadian Way; San Francisco, California 00000.

6. You recently graduated from Southwestern University in Dallas, Texas, and took a job as a management trainee with Optimal Oil Company. You work in the research and development division in the home office in Dallas. You decide to apply for a BankNational Credit Card through your local bank, Major National Bank. So you pick up an application and fill in all the required information. Write a letter to accompany your application, requesting that an account be opened in your name. Address: Cynthia Trecou, Supervisor; BankNational Credit Card Department; Major National Bank; 33154 San Antonio Road; Dallas, Texas 00000.

7. You are a chemist with Robertson Pharmaceuticals Company, a manufacturer of prescription drugs. You are developing a new drug that will relieve asthma symptoms. The drug works best in time-released capsules, and the granules of the active ingredient must be coated in zilfin. Zilfin is sticky when wet, and you do not know whether the production department can manufacture the drug in that state. Write a memorandum to the production manager, Lily Tao, asking her assistance in preparing sample capsules of the product in your laboratory. The objective is to determine whether your manufacturing design will work. Enclose a drawing of your design. Address: Lily Tao, Manager; Production Department; 18 Bridges Lane Building.

8. You are employed by a manufacturing company and supervise the second shift in the shipping department. At the end of your shift on the last payday, one of your employees was robbed on the way home from work. As it happened, the employee, James McLean (social security number 000-00-0000), had already endorsed his check, which was taken by the robber. You have talked with Shirley Beggs, the Payroll Department Manager, and she has asked you to follow up the conversation with a written request that a new check be prepared for McLean within the next two days. Write a memo to Beggs, recounting the circumstances and ask that the new check be prepared and sent to McLean.

9. Select one of the courses you are enrolled in presently and assume the instructor has asked you to arrange for a guest speaker. The speaker will talk on one of the major topics discussed in the course.

Write a letter to a possible speaker (real or imagined) asking that he or she come to speak to your class. Provide information about the topic to be covered, date, location, and so on.

10. As the office manager of Tate and Tate, Attorneys-at-Law, you ordered some carpeting for the offices. When the sales representative, Michael Swain, quoted you prices, he stated that the $\frac{3}{4}$-inch padding was $1.19 a square yard. You received the carpeting and it has been installed. Today, the invoice arrived from Atlas Carpet Outlet, and the dealer has charged you $1.49 a square yard for the 37 square yards of padding you purchased. Write a letter requesting a correct invoice to reflect the quoted price. Include a copy of the invoice. Address: 493 East Broad Street, Knoxville, Tennessee 00000.

11. As an assistant to the Director of Personnel, you must obtain some films on employee motivation techniques. You have located three films that seem very appropriate. Write to the film distributor and order them. You wish to be billed for the films and postage and need them by the first of next month. (Note to student: Use real titles and locate an actual distributor. To do this, research the various film catalogs in the audiovisual department of your college library.)

12. As president of your area homeowners' association, you arrange to have speakers at your meetings. Recently, a local newspaper article reported that the town's board of supervisors is considering a request for a change in zoning for the area near your subdivision. Such a change would have a detrimental effect on property values in your subdivision. Write a letter to the chairperson of the board of supervisors requesting one of the supervisors attend your September 13 meeting to speak about the zoning change. Your meetings are held at 7:30 P.M. in the auditorium of the Glenwood Recreation Center on Valencia Avenue. Address: Gerald T. Lewis, Chairperson; Batavia Board of Supervisors; City Hall; Batavia, New York 00000.

13. Brad Daughtrey, owner of Daughtrey Office Supplies, has written a letter to order some products that you distribute. Daughtrey has been a long-time customer of your firm (Century Stationery and Sundries) but has not placed an order in some time. In fact, the order he has placed has come from one of your catalogs that is now out of date. Consequently, two of the items he ordered are no longer available, but you do carry items that are similar. He ordered 12 gross of the medium-point indelible accountant's pens and 10 reams of the single-sheet thermal-duplicate copier paper. You now stock only fine-point marking pens ($3.30 more per gross) and roll-type thermal-duplicate copier paper ($1.19 more per roll, each roll equivalent to one ream). Write to ask how Daughtrey wishes to proceed on his order. Address: 391 Academy Drive, Las Vegas, Nevada 00000.

14. The offices of the three vice presidents of your firm, Jansen Computer City, are being redecorated. The vice presidents have talked with you, the administrative office manager, about what they would like, but you think they should also talk with Beth Kinney of Kinney Interiors, the interior decorator your company has contracted with. Write a memorandum to each vice president offering to set up at their convenience 30-minute appointments with the interior decorator. Ask for times during the first week in November for such appointments. The three vice presidents are Jane Brock, Per-

sonnel; Henry Morganstein, Finance; and James Pearce, Marketing.

15. The three vice presidents in Exercise 14 have responded to your memorandum. Each has indicated that the appointment with the interior decorator is a good idea. They have suggested the following times and dates for a possible meeting with the interior decorator:

    Brock: 11/3, 9:45 A.M.; 11/4, 10:30 A.M.; 11/6, 9:00 A.M.

    Morganstein: 11/3, 3:30 P.M.; 11/4, 9:35 A.M.; 11/7, 2:00 P.M.

    Pearce: 11/3, 1:30 P.M.; 11/6, 11:15 A.M.; 11/7, 1:15 P.M.

    Write to the interior decorator to request she or one of her associates arrange to meet with each vice president or to have one of her associates at one of the times indicated. The purpose of the meeting will be to obtain in-depth information on decorating schemes, colors, and so on. Address: 793 Keystone Parkway, Scranton, Pennsylvania 00000.

16. At a recent meeting of the Windy City Personnel Administrators, you learned of an exemplary employee hospitalization program that a local company has developed. You think the plan may have some merit for your consulting firm of Dewee, Helpem, and Howe. You want to obtain further information from the personnel administrator who mentioned the program during the meeting. Write a letter to arrange a meeting to discuss this hospitalization program in depth. You would appreciate knowing about such things as coverage, deductibles, employer contributions, and so on. Address: Marianne Woodson; Director of Personnel; Windy City Temporaries; 581 Michigan Avenue, Chicago, Illinois 00000.

17. The company that administers the hospitalization plan described in Exercise 16 could also provide valuable information about it. Write a letter requesting printed information on the hospitalization program. Although you want no sales representative to call at present, you would set up an interview after reviewing the literature (and after you've talked with Woodson at the Windy City Temporaries). Address: Medicalcare, Inc.; Medical Arts Building; 6992 Collier Drive; Milwaukee, Wisconsin 00000.

18. Rita Jenkins has applied for a position in your data processing department. In her resume, she indicated that she worked for three years as a programmer/analyst with SpectroVision, Inc., a position similar to the one she has applied for with your company. As the administrative assistant to the director of personnel, one of your duties is to write former employers of applicants to obtain employment histories. Write to SpectroVision to request information about Rita. Inquire about job competence, interpersonal skills, and punctuality. Address: Steven Robertson; Data Processing Department Manager; SpectroVision, Inc.; Ruthers Mill Road; Richmond, Virginia 00000.

19. As Office Manager for Reusch Electronics, you monitor the telephone activities of the various offices within departments. Your telephone system provides a record of calls made from each number, including number of calls, time of the calls, and numbers called. After some preliminary checking, you have discovered that a substantial number of employees are making personal calls, many of them long distance. Write a form memo to be distributed to all department heads, asking them to assist you in monitoring the calls made by their subordinates. Attach to the memorandum the list of calls from the various offices of

each department to substantiate your claim about telephone abuse.

20. Your company, Marshall Distributors, has been incorrectly billed by a collection agency for items never purchased. After some investigation, you find that another company, Marsh Distributing, Incorporated, is located in your city. That company deals in antique collectibles and the items that you are being charged for would be used when displaying antiques in a showroom. Your company distributes architecture supplies, such as design pads, blueprint paper, and the like. Write to the collection agency and ask that they remove your name from their collection list. Suggest that an error has been made in identifying the company liable for the items purchased. Address: Bill's Collection Agency; 739 Railroad Street, San Angelo, Texas 00000.

21. A new temporary help agency has opened a branch in your city. In a recent letter, it describes its services as covering rush orders, vacations, and peak times. It also describes a new service whereby it keeps employees on its payroll, handling all the "red tape" involved with government record keeping, and so on, but the employees are originally chosen by the company for which they work. This program would allow the company to recruit its own workers but contract with the temporary help agency to carry the workers on the payroll of that agency. Although you do not need temporary workers, the second program sounds interesting. Write to the temporary help agency requesting some literature and having a sales representative call. Address: Management Support Systems; Hammer Building; Tulsa, Oklahoma 00000.

22. Your main office has promoted a branch sales manager to sales manager. She will be moving to Charleston next month, and you have been placed in charge of arranging the welcoming dinner for her. In the past, your company has always gone to a local beef and seafood restaurant for such occasions, but your last experience was unpleasant. You have decided to try a different restaurant but don't know which one to choose. Your company policy has been to return to a particular restaurant and thus you have always been able to obtain low dinner rates. Prepare a form letter to be sent to several area restaurants, asking whether they could handle your banquet on the 20th of next month. Approximately 50 people will attend this function, but future banquets might be larger. You would like to have a cash bar for about a half hour before the banquet. A meal in the $20 to $25 range would be appropriate—this price would include tax and gratuity.

23. You own a small gourmet shop in downtown Cleveland. On occasion, you need to order a variety of items from a distributor in Dayton. You have a six-month-old catalog of the products the distributor handles, but the order blank is missing. You need 500 paper bags (size A) and 1000 paper bags (size D). The prices for these bags are 2.3¢ and 8.4¢ each, respectively. You also need some wrapping paper; one roll of the 24-inch-wide brown paper at a cost of $5.60 will be sufficient. Since the holiday season is rapidly approaching, gift boxes will be in demand. The distributor handles three sizes: one pint, one quart, and half gallon. You think the prices have remained the same: $20 per hundred for the smallest size, $22.50 for the middle size, and $24 for the largest size. You don't care how the order is shipped but would appreciate receiving it within ten days. You

want to be billed for the goods. Write an order letter. Address: Dayton General Supplies; 3579 Spring Garden Drive; Dayton, Ohio 00000.

24. Your credit terms allow your customers to take a two percent discount if they pay their money within ten days of the date of the invoice. However, some of your customers take the discount even if they pay after the ten-day limit. While a few dollars and cents discount does not seem very important, if all your customers were allowed to take it, the amount would be significant. Consequently, you need to have a form letter that requests the customer remit the remaining balance on the account because an incorrect discount was taken. Some explanation of why you are seeking such a small amount of money from a customer would be desirable. Write the form letter. You will sign the letter since you are Customer Accounts Manager.

25. From time to time your company receives requests to ship merchandise on credit to a new customer for whom you have not yet established credit. Information is needed from the potential customer before you can ship the goods that have been ordered. Generally, all you need is a recent financial statement or the following information: income in last fiscal year, present cash balance, present amount of accounts receivable, present amount of accounts payable, amount of other current liabilities. Prepare a form letter that can be sent to these potential customers upon receipt of their initial orders.

CHAPTER 8

WRITING FAVORABLE RESPONSE AND GOODWILL LETTERS AND MEMOS

In the last chapter we discussed how to make routine requests. All such requests need answers. In this chapter we will show the way to answer them, that is, how to write *favorable responses.* We will also discuss the strategies you might use in writing *goodwill messages.*

PLANNING FAVORABLE RESPONSE AND GOODWILL LETTERS AND MEMOS

Suppose you are a salesperson in a major auto dealership. A potential customer writes you a letter requesting some information about a new import, a Korean-made economy model that has only been recently introduced on the market. Naturally, you are going to respond favorably to this request and send along the desired information—in fact, you are going to do it today—for answering this letter is part of your job and answering it quickly is being on top of your job. Also, as an experienced business communicator, you understand the value of treating routine requests like this in a more than routine manner. You want not only to make a sale but also to create goodwill. Therefore, your response will be both thoughtful and thorough.

In this instance, building goodwill is a secondary goal—you still must first answer the potential customer's request. But sometimes creating goodwill may be the primary purpose of your written communication. For example, you may write a letter congratulating a fellow employee who has gotten a job with more money and more responsibility at another dealership. Still, whether you are answering a letter of request or writing to express goodwill, you should follow the steps in this deductive organization to make your message more effective:

What are the steps in writing a favorable response or goodwill message?

1. *Deliver the news.* Begin with either your request or an expression of goodwill, depending on which is the subject of the message. The rule is simple: the more direct you are, the better.
2. *Include details or explanation.* Include all the information necessary to make the message complete. Be careful, however, to include only relevant details.
3. *Close positively.* End on an optimistic, affirmative note. Sometimes you may need to close with a request for action, where you seem optimistic that the reader will want to carry out your request. At other times a general statement of goodwill is appropriate.

Figure 8-1 diagrams these steps.

Writing Opening Statements

Most effective communicators will agree that the first sentence and paragraph are the most important. Here is where you accomplish the

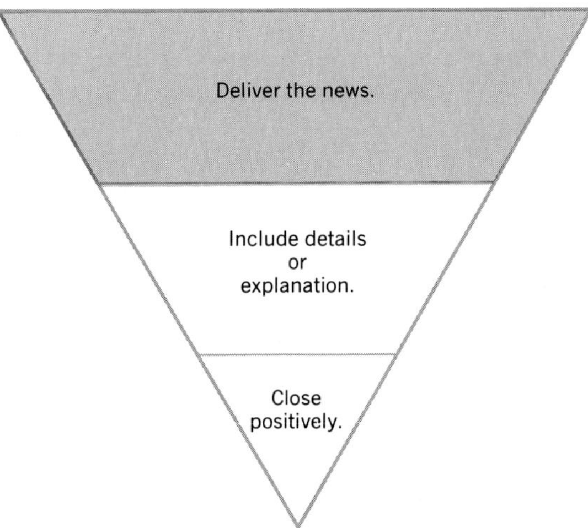

FIGURE 8-1 Diagram of deductive plan for favorable response and goodwill letters and memos.

main part of your mission—to deliver the request—or if goodwill is your primary goal—to express it.

Can you name the checkpoints to follow when writing openings for favorable response or goodwill messages?

As you write your opening statement, check that it

1. *Delivers the news in the first sentence if possible.* Previously, we suggested stating it in the first sentence or paragraph. If your first sentence can contain it, that would be preferable. Sometimes, however, this may be impossible. If so, the first sentence should function as a lead-in to the request or declaration of goodwill, which should then follow immediately.
2. *Is positive and cooperative in tone.* Good communicators want to establish a tone that makes them seem positive, cooperative, and agreeable.
3. *Is short.* Short openings are more emphatic. If your opening paragraph is more than two or three sentences in length, it may be too long. In this case, either delete details or transfer them to another paragraph; do the same for an explanation.
4. *Takes into account the reader's viewpoint.* See the request or expression of goodwill through your reader's eyes. It is an excellent check against establishing a false tone or inserting inappropriate content.
5. *Avoids or subordinates references to previous correspondence.* Try to exclude references to previous correspondence, especially clichés or stereotyped statements such as "in reference to your request." Generally, such statements are unnecessary unless previous messages need to be referenced to clarify your purpose.

Nevertheless, if you must refer to previous correspondence, subordinate it to the main point of your message.

The following are some appropriate opening statements:

> Here is the free copy of *Fifty Ways to Save on Home Heating Costs* you requested.
>
> Yes, Janice, I'll be glad to help review the legal aspects of your proposed budget for next year.
>
> A check for $50 is enclosed to reimburse you for the overcharge on the tapes you ordered.
>
> The new Zippy Model 250 electric blanket you ordered was shipped by parcel post today. You should receive it within ten days.
>
> Here is the new Amex credit card you applied for last month. We are delighted to be able to offer you this convenience.
>
> We appreciate your doing business with us at Internal Auditing Associates this year. The cooperative spirit you have shown has made us think of you as a friend as well as a valuable customer.
>
> Congratulations, Jessica, on your promotion to assistant vice president in charge of finance.
>
> Please accept our sympathy in this time of bereavement. Our thoughts and good wishes are with you and your children.

Including Details or Explanation

Suppose you are the employee in the large heating firm who answered a request for a copy of a pamphlet with the sentence suggested previously:

> Here is the free copy of *Fifty Ways to Save on Home Heating Costs* you requested.

In looking over this first sentence, you feel you want to add some details that will help the reader to solve some of the problems mentioned in the letter of request. So you write this second paragraph:

> Every one of these methods has proved effective in small and large residences in all parts of the country. Even in the extreme cold of Point Barrow, Alaska, one family saved 50 percent on their total heating costs by following the suggestions in points 34, 41, and 44 alone. Moreover, within just two years, they recovered the full cost of materials and installation. Even so, they estimate that they can save another 20 percent by following some of the other suggestions in the booklet.

As this response shows, the details or explanation in a favorable response or goodwill message should always be concise. Yet such a communication should also be complete, including in it all relevant details so the reader is left with no unanswered questions.

Where do details go in a favorable response or goodwill message?

Sometimes you can begin specifying these details in the first paragraph in the sentences that follow the statement of purpose. At other times, you may, as in the example, put them in a second paragraph. No rules exist concerning this, except to say that (1) your details or explanation should follow a recognizable organization as discussed in Chapter 7 and (2) shorter paragraphs are more emphatic than are longer ones. Simply put details where they would least interrupt the thought flow. Of course, consider too how many details you want to include. For example, one reason you decided to begin a separate detail paragraph on the home heating booklet is because you had a number of points to make. Putting all these details in the first paragraph would have tended to overwhelm your opening statement.

If your details are numerous, you might have to add a third paragraph, or a fourth even. Most favorable response and goodwill messages, however, are about simple, straightforward subjects. Therefore, they are relatively brief.

Adding Resale and Sales Promotional Ideas

Suppose you are writing a favorable letter in response to a request to purchase a blender advertised in your store's fall catalog. In the detail section of your letter, you might want to reassure the customer about the quality of the blender he or she is purchasing. Such reassurance is called *resale*. Even though you naturally have a vested interest in anything you sell—such as this blender—you have found that the technique works because customers naturally assume that a store's staff are authorities on what they sell. Resale occurs most often in favorable responses that grant simple claims or adjustments, but, as you have seen, you can also use it when you fill an order. Where you place resale depends on the situation. Generally, responders put it in the body of the message, but sometimes it may fit perfectly well into the opening and closing statements.

What is resale?

What is a sales promotion?

Sales promotion is something else you might want to add to a favorable response. For example, suppose a customer inquires about a computer you are putting on a special sale. Once you have responded to the request, you decide to promote some of the software programs you also sell that he or she may use with the computer. Or you might want to describe the kinds of service contracts available. When should you add promotional details to a favorable response? The answer is both practical and simple: Do it when the opportunity is present. Thus, in selling a computer, it is natural to promote software because the computer has to have software or it is unusable.

In contrast, because they do not come naturally out of the message's subject, some sales promotions may seem either awkward or irritating and can even cause ill will. For example, to promote the purchase of riding boots when filling an order for dinnerware is not taking advantage of an opportunity.

As with resales, vendors are the message writers who most often insert sales promotion into favorable response or goodwill messages. However, effective communicators are careful not to use expressions of goodwill only to make a sale, lest they kill the sale and the goodwill, too.

Where does promotional material go in your communication? That too depends on the specific situation. Yet almost without exception you will find yourself putting it in either the final sentences of the body or the first sentences of the closing statement.

Writing Closing Statements

What are the two types of closings for a favorable response or goodwill message?

What should you put in your closing statement? Depending on the circumstance, in a favorable response you can make a *general* request or ask for *action.* For a goodwill message, however, you should always make a general closing. (Even if you do suggest an action in a goodwill message, do it only to be courteous or as an offer of help.) The following are two general closings. Notice how they round out a message with a statement of goodwill and how tone is as important as content:

> Thank you very much for your order. We look forward to serving you again.

> Everyone in the office looks forward to your return to work. Meanwhile, take care of yourself, Joyce.

How could you make good use of deadlining?

In contrast to a general request closing, an action request means that you ask the reader to respond with a specific action. If appropriate, also ask for the action to be performed within a certain time. Called *deadlining,* this technique is the best way to get a reader to respond when you need it, if time makes a difference to you. Deadlining is most effective when you tell your reader why you are setting a time limit. The following are some action request closings. Notice how the third and the fourth use deadlining.

> If you need my help with reviewing the vouchers, Millie, stop by my office upstairs. I'll look forward to seeing you then.

> Just call at extension 7433 to set a time we can get together to discuss the attorney general's ruling. After hearing from you, I'll ask Donald to prepare an abstract of the *Mackling* decision you need to know more about.

> Both your tow trucks can be operational by the time the tourist season starts May 15. All you need do is call us at (000) 000-0000 by May 1 to give us permission to install the pollution control devices you asked about in your letter.

I plan to go deep sea fishing with members of my fishing club on June 20. So, will you please send the request for a replacement by June 15.

What are the guidelines to follow when writing favorable response or goodwill messages?

The following specific guidelines should help you write effective closings for your favorable response and goodwill messages:

1. *Be positive and strike a "closing" tone.* Remember that both closings as well as openings are in an emphatic position. Thus a positive closing is especially important because it is the last thing the reader reads. Also, you should sound as though you are finishing the message: The reader should feel as if you have fully completed what you wanted to say and not that you simply stopped abruptly, jamming on the brakes for no apparent reason.
2. *Sound successful.* You wish to appear as if you anticipate mutual success—what is good for you is good for the reader as well. To achieve this tone, feel confident and use expressions that show it.
3. *Write from the reader's viewpoint.* As in most business communications, you need to see things from the reader's viewpoint to be truly effective. Try to refer to the reader by name and if possible tailor what you can to his or her interests.
4. *Be specific in action request closings.* This guide can be expressed quite simply: If you need a specific response, ask for it specifically.

Putting Together the Complete Message

You have already seen how details were added to the first example of an opening statement. Figure 8-2 shows the complete letter: opening statement, details, and closing statement.

WRITING SPECIFIC TYPES OF FAVORABLE RESPONSE LETTERS AND MEMOS

What are the five categories of favorable responses?

The number of favorable response subjects can be organized into five main categories: (1) sending information, (2) offering assistance, (3) granting a simple claim or adjustment, (4) filling orders for goods or services, and (5) granting credit.

Sending Information to Others

Suppose you are part of an engineering team in a space technology company. You are designing a rocket and need some information from another company about a new fuel it has tested successfully. Since your two companies are working together on the project, you anticipate that your request for these data will be granted. So you are

April 11, 19--

Mr. Morley J. Tutley
829 Valdosta Avenue
Ypsilanti, MI 00000

Dear Mr. Tutley

Here is the free copy of "Fifty Ways to Save on Home Heating Costs" you requested.

Every one of these methods has proved effective in small and large residences in every part of the country. Even in the extreme cold of Point Barrow, Alaska, one family saved 50% on their total heating costs by following the suggestions given in Points 34, 41, and 44 alone. Moreover, they recovered the full cost of materials and installation within just two years. Even so, they estimate they can save another 20% by following other suggestions in the booklet.

After reading the booklet, you may have further questions. If so, just write us or call our toll-free hotline, 800-000-0000. We'll be glad to answer your questions. Or if you prefer, call or visit your nearest home heating dealer, where you can get both information and materials. A list of dealers certified by the institute is enclosed.

Sincerely yours

Kim J. Luan

Kim J. Luan
Heating Consultant

Enclosures

FIGURE 8-2 Favorable response in mailable form.

extremely surprised when it is not. Your superiors try to achieve what you could not do—get these data—but their efforts meet with no success either, at least for the moment. Meanwhile, you have to go ahead with your design, seeking other sources of information—which may not be so state of the art—until the obstacles are removed. But even if they are, your work has been delayed at best and at worst adversely affected because you do not have access to the necessary information.

Whether you are building a rocket or are deciding to take over another company, you need the right information upon which to base any decision you may have to make. This means that you must have complete access to the data you want. If in any way your freedom to obtain it is restricted, so too will your decision be restricted and perhaps even seriously flawed. To state matters more extremely—but no less accurately—without such free access to information, nobody would be able to conduct any business.

Why will the need for information in the future be even more critical than it is today?

Moreover, in the future the need for information should become even more critical to success in business. This trend would occur because many of the new technologies require that people dealing with them be familiar with the process of using them as well as the enormous amount of information they can produce.

No matter what your job is, a large portion of it will consist of providing information. Because of the fast pace of business life, it will also frequently have to be quickly dispatched. In business, more often than not, information that arrives late is virtually useless. So when your boss or a customer asks for some data by a certain time or date, be sure to meet the request if you can. If you do, they will probably return the favor when you ask them for information about the new retirement plan, or about the oil situation in the Persian Gulf, or whatever.

Of course, everybody, including yourself, has his or her own motives for responding to a request or an inquiry for information. For example, perhaps you want the account executive whose office is next to yours to tell you what he or she knows about developing TV commercials. Or perhaps you answer a request about property in the neighborhood promptly and very thoroughly too because you perceive a potential customer.

In any office where you work, it might be useful to ask yourself: Who is sending out information around here? If the answer is "not me," then you have a problem. Quite simply, you are being ineffective, for every good businessperson is aware of the truth of this simple maxim: Only by helping others meet their goals will they help you meet yours.

Now let's turn to some specific examples of responses to requests. In each case, a first draft is followed by a critique and then by a revised draft. Here is a response to a request for information. Do you see any ways in which the communicator does not make the most of his or her opportunity?

First Draft

Dear Miss Sampson:

This letter is in reference to your inquiry of October 7. We are glad we might interest you in our products.

Please find enclosed a brochure with the information you requested. The wallboard is made from both white oak and yellow pine. The only size offered is 4′ × 8′. Colors include the natural finish, tan, antique green, and white. Shipment is made at our expense by truck or rail. Yes, the 100-year life of the glue is guaranteed.

Please be advised, too, that prices are included on the enclosed brochure. With kindest regards,

Yours truly,

Critique

Judging by this letter, the writer will probably lose the opportunity to make a sale of wallboards. For one thing, the tone is wrong—at first, self-centered, later, indifferent. Perhaps this is in large measure the effect of the writer's style, which is formal to the point of being stilted and riddled with clichés as well. Most important, the good news arrives late, occurring in the second paragraph instead of the first.

The following is a list of the letter's problems and some suggestions about how to improve them:

1. The writer should transfer his or her news from the second paragraph to the opening sentence.
2. The first sentence is obvious and may easily be omitted.
3. The second sentence (line 2) shows self-centeredness. If left in, it should be recast into a sentence that is reader centered.
4. The details in the second paragraph (lines 3–8) are jumbled and disorganized. The word flow also is too jumpy and needs smoothing. Perhaps a list that answers the reader's inquiry point by point would help solve these problems.
5. The writer uses such formal and clichéd expressions as, "please find enclosed," "please be advised," and "with kindest regards." (lines 3, 9, and 10, respectively) "With kindest regards" is both formal and clichéd, and old fashioned as well. (line 10)
6. The writer fails to include sales promotional material in the final paragraph.

The following is a revised draft of this response:

Revised Draft

Dear Miss Sampson:

Here is the information you requested about the "New Era" wallboard you saw advertised in the April 15 issue of *Construction News:*

1. The wallboard comes in both a sturdy white oak and a finely grained yellow pine.
2. The size is a standard 4′ × 8′ panel.
3. Colors include white oak and yellow pine if you prefer the natural wood tones as many of our customers do. Other colors available are brushed rose, antique green, and oyster shell.
4. We pay all cost of shipment by truck or rail, whichever you prefer.
5. Yes, the 100-year life of the glue is fully guaranteed in writing.

Complete information on the wallboard is given in the enclosed brochure—prices, all specifications, and samples of color and wood grains. If you need finishing nails, saws, or any other tools or materials to install your "New Era" wallboard, please take a look at the brochure, which contains complete information on those items as well.

We appreciate your inquiry and look forward to the opportunity to serve you. Shipment is guaranteed within two days after receiving your order, or we will pay for the merchandise ourselves.

Yours truly,

Offering Assistance

Of course, offering information is a form of assistance. For example, suppose you are your firm's real estate expert and your boss, Bob LeClerc, asks you to give him some information about applying mortgage pools to commercial properties. He needs these data because the firm is considering a major expansion into commercial mortgages.

Where do requests for assistance come from?

Requests for assistance can come, as in the example, from within your office or from the outside. Where it comes from should not affect your decision about whether to offer your help. In deciding this, the only factors to consider are (1) the legitimacy of the request and (2) your ability to help.

Although the requests you receive in any business day will vary, they will have one thing in common: each requestor believes you will be able to fulfill his or her request. Most often, it will involve something in your area of expertise. In the following memo, J. Stuart Laws answers a request for assistance from Amanda Fishbein. Do you see any problems with his response?

First Draft

To: Amanda R. Fishbein, Personnel Assistant
From: J. Stuart Laws, Corporate Legal Counselor
Subject: Meeting

Per your recent request, I am glad to be able to inform
2 you that I will help. Meet me in my office this Friday at 10:30.

You probably don't know it, but you have to do some things
4 now that you never had to do before. I'll clue you in when
you get here.

6 Meanwhile, get the following information together and bring
it with you: the procedure you used this year to advertise
8 jobs to minorities and how did you make sure place of residence
was disregarded. See you Friday.

Critique

Perhaps Mr. Laws's perception of his position within the company accounts for his tone, which is curt, presumptuous, demanding, condescending, and negative. Still, superior rank is no excuse for adopting such a tone (nor, for that matter, is there ever any reason to). That he may be unaware of his errors or have made them carelessly is a similarly poor explanation and one that, if publicized, will hardly stem the ill feelings this message is sure to provoke. In addition, the style is inconsistent, ranging between too formal and too informal. Finally, Mr. Laws provides too few details for Ms. Fishbein to prepare properly for their meeting.

The following are specific errors and some suggestions for correcting them:

1. The subject line is too general and vague.
2. The opening phrase, "per your recent request," is both stilted and obvious. Nothing is lost by omitting it. In the same sentence, "I am glad to be able to inform you" is wordy. (line 1) It can also be omitted.
3. "Meet me in your office. . ." may sound demanding and does not recognize that the reader may have another commitment. (line 2)
4. "You probably don't know it" is condescending. In the same sentence, the wording "some things," is vague. (line 3 for both)
5. "Clue you in" is an undesirable colloquialism that can also sound demeaning. (line 4)
6. "Get the following information together and bring it with you" is wordy as well as demanding. (line 6)
7. The final paragraph shows nonparallel structure.

8. The closing statement, "see you Friday," is not only flippant, but it also ends the memo abruptly.

The following is a revised draft of the memo:

Revised Draft

To: Amanda R. Fishbein, Personnel Assistant
From: J. Stuart Laws, Corporate Legal Counselor
Subject: Meeting for EEO Report Preparation

Can we meet in my office (Suite 245) this Friday at 10:30 A.M. to complete Section 6 of your annual equal employment opportunity report?

You will need to provide two items of information that were not required last year:

1. The procedure followed in advertising available jobs to minorities.
2. The procedure followed to assure that an applicant's place of residency was disregarded in hiring practices.

Please bring this information to the meeting along with information you normally include in this section of the report.

I look forward to meeting with you on Friday, Amanda.

Granting a Simple Claim or Adjustment

Suppose you are in charge of the appliance department in a department store famous for its customer service. A woman who purchased one of your most expensive toasters says it was faulty and wants reimbursement.

Should you grant the customer's request? The answer is yes, if you believe that the toaster was faulty due to a manufacturing defect and not because it was mishandled by the customer. It is also yes if you don't know how it was damaged but because of the store's policy, you believe maintaining goodwill is more important than the price of the toaster.

What makes a claim *routine?*

Having decided to grant the woman's claim, you now have to consider whether you will do it wholly or partially. If you decide to meet it *fully,* the claim is simple or *routine.* In this situation, you decide that it is routine, so you organize your letter of response deductively, beginning it by granting the customer's request. (In organizing such a letter—or memo—follow the guidelines established at the beginning of this chapter.) Also, having decided to reimburse her, do it graciously in a spirit of goodwill. Too many adjusters grant claims grudgingly and end up losing money *and* the customer's goodwill. The following is a response to a simple claim. What problems do you see in it?

First Draft

Dear Mrs. Marable:

We are in the process of granting your claim at the earliest convenience.

Please know that we have had no desire to inconvenience you. In fact, it was a surprise to hear that such a well-made drop lever would break in normal usage. Yours is the first such claim we've received on this model.

May we take this opportunity to thank you for your business. If you should have any questions, feel free to write or call.

Sincerely yours,

Critique

The major problem of this letter is its tone. Notice that the second paragraph implies that it is the reader who is at fault. This strategy is poor at best, for eventually it will result in losing the customer. Some specific problems are:

1. The opening sentence states the purpose indirectly.
2. "In the process of," "may we take this opportunity," and "feel free to" are wordy expressions. (lines 1, 7, and 8, respectively)
3. "At your earliest convenience" (line 1) is both too general and a cliché, and "may we take this opportunity" and "feel free to" are clichés.
4. The tone of the entire second paragraph is negative and should be rewritten to express a more positive and reassuring response.
5. The final paragraph should, but does not, contain an attempt to resell the product.

The following is a revised draft of the letter:

Revised Draft

Dear Mrs. Marable:

A new Model #64 Sunrise electric toaster was shipped to you this morning by parcel post. You should receive it within five days.

Your new toaster has a drop lever that is reinforced with a magnesium alloy plate that will withstand 20 pounds of pressure. Only 1 pound of pressure is needed to lower two slices of bread into the toasting chamber.

We are delighted to hear that you enjoy using the Sunrise model. Tests performed by Consumer Laboratories showed that this model does indeed brown toast more evenly than any competing model on the market today. We appreciate your business and look forward to your next visit to Finest Goods.

Sincerely yours,

Filling Orders for Goods and Services

Some business writers confuse *acknowledging* orders with *filling* them. These activities are not the same, even though both are favorable responses calling for deductive organization. To acknowledge an order is to let a customer know you received it, and you might begin with "Thanks for your order; we're glad to have you as a customer," or something similar. You might then go on to tell the customer when to expect the goods and perhaps add some resale and sales promotion before closing. Some firms send acknowledgments to "first timers"—new customers—and "long goners"—customers who place orders after a long absence—because, as easy as these letters are to write, they are powerful goodwill builders.

What part do packing lists and invoices play in filling orders?

Filling orders is done another way, and you will sometimes see exceptions to this general practice: companies do not write letters when filling orders for goods or services. Instead, they send forms called *packing lists* to verify orders when shipping goods and forms called *invoices* to request payment for goods or services.

Two exceptions are noteworthy, however. Letters are sent by firms that do not use forms, generally small businesses or those that seldom fill such orders. And letters are sent occasionally, though never routinely, to build goodwill. These letters may accompany the shipment and packing list or the invoice, or they may be mailed separately.

The following is a separately mailed letter. It fills the order placed in the letter included in the section, "Placing an Order for Goods or Services," in Chapter 7. Do you see any problems with it?

First Draft

Dear Mr. Smith:

Thank you for your letter. You have been one of our best customers for a long time, and we appreciate your orders.

Our records indicate that you wanted shipment by United Parcel Service, and your wish was carried out yesterday. Your check enclosed with the order is for the correct amount.

Thank you. Good luck.

Sincerely yours,

Critique

This letter establishes a good, reader-centered tone. Its style too is generally informal. The major problem is it does not open with the subject—which is to fill a specific order. Instead, it starts with an effective reader-centered paragraph of acknowledgments designed to build goodwill. Although the content of this opening is excellent, it emphasizes a secondary purpose at the expense of the primary one.

The following are some specific problems:

1. "Thank you for your letter" and "our records indicate" are clichés and should be omitted. (lines 1 and 3, respectively)
2. The specific amount of the check should be mentioned. (line 5)
3. Either move the opening paragraph to the last paragraph or omit it and take advantage of the opportunity for sales promotion and sell your products in assertive language that will also build goodwill.
4. "Thank you" and "good luck" are each abrupt and, combined, make for a curt closing.

The following is a revised draft of the letter. The twist is the writer knows no invoice will be sent because the customer has already paid. Thus, the ordered items are restated here for accuracy and easy reference, even though the customer may have received a packing list with the merchandise.

Revised Draft

Dear Mr. Smith:

The following Private Press books were shipped to you by United Parcel Service yesterday as you requested. You should receive them by Thursday, perhaps before you get this letter.

8 copies of *How to Win Big in the Stock Market,* #36 @ $8.95 each	$ 71.60
25 copies of *Writing Winning Resumes,* #21 @ $5.75 each	143.75
6 copies of *Looking for a Pot of Gold,* #42 @ $6.35 each	38.10
Total	$253.45

Your check for $253.45 sent with the order is correct, and we are glad to pay shipping charges because you paid in advance.

A flyer announcing a new motivational book just published —*Thinking Big, Winning Big*—is enclosed. The initial response has been so great that already we have ordered a second printing. If we receive your order for 25 copies or more by December 1, you are entitled to a 30 percent discount. So place your order today, Mr. Smith, and take advantage of this rare offer. Of course, your complete satisfaction is guaranteed, or we will gladly refund the full purchase price.

Sincerely yours,

✳ Granting Credit Terms

Credit is what makes the industrialized countries of the free world "go round," and its uses seem to grow daily. Because credit stimulates sales and customer loyalty, many businesses are willing to grant credit to worthy customers. Moreover, the attractive interest rates of the last 15 years have acted as an added incentive to the use of credit. Not only are many companies willing to let you charge your portable computer or compact disc player, for example, but they will also allow generous repayment terms to add to their profits from the interest. Today increasing numbers of people use credit cards to buy anything from pocket calculators to private jets for business. (Even students who do not work can get major credit cards quite easily, and the Japanese, famous for paying cash, have begun to say, "Charge it.")

Do businesses usually issue credit cards to other businesses?

A company will issue its own cards or it will honor major credit cards such as American Express, Visa, MasterCard, and Discover. These cards are really just a convenience, for many firms that do not offer cards of their own will still grant credit terms. For businesses, however, credit lines—open accounts, usually with 2/10, net 30 terms, after which time interest accrues if the debt is unpaid—remain the most widely used form of credit.

Whether you are responding to a request from a consumer, a fellow employee (credit unions), or a representative of another business, you first have to decide if you will grant it. Suppose you decide that you will; the next question is, Can you grant it as requested? If you can meet the full terms of the request, it is routine and you should organize your response deductively. Since the subject is that you are granting credit terms, always begin your message with this good news.

The following is a response to a request for credit. Do you see any problems in it?

First Draft

Dear Mr. Lovejoy:

I am happy to extend credit terms to cover the purchase of the furniture group I tentatively sold you earlier. Your credit record appears to be good.

I trust our relationship will be mutually beneficial.

The terms are that a monthly payment is due on the first day of each month. Interest is 15.5 percent. For your convenience, a coupon book is enclosed.

The Jefferson Manor Group you chose will be delivered within two days after you call to set a delivery date. This set will blend with almost any decor, perhaps the reason it has become our most popular living room group. Thank you for choosing Abacus Furniture Company for this purchase. I look forward to a continuing business relationship.

Yours sincerely,

Critique

Although the writer organizes the letter deductively, two problems detract from its effectiveness: the tentative and therefore negative tone of the first two paragraphs and the lack of details in the second. Yet the third paragraph is not ony adequately written but it also includes a mention of resale to reassure the customer about his purchase. However, the writer does not seize the opportunity to promote any other products. The following are some specific problems:

1. Self-references, such as the use of "I" three times in the first two paragraphs, should be omitted. (lines 1, 2, and 4)
2. Expressions that show doubt instead of self-confidence, such as "tentatively," "appears to be," and "trust" should be omitted. (lines 2, 3, 4, respectively)
3. "For your convenience" is a cliché and should be omitted. (line 6)
4. The credit limit, interest rate, use of the coupon book, and method of payment require fuller explanation. (lines 4–7)

The following is a revised letter:

Revised Draft

Dear Mr. Lovejoy:

Your application for a credit account is approved for your use in making purchases at Abacus Furniture. We are glad to open the joint account for you and will mail the monthly statements to your home address as you requested.

Your statement will arrive during the second week of each month, and the minimum payment is due in our office by the last day of the month. All you need do is fill in and return the appropriate coupon from the enclosed booklet, along with your check or money order. You may maintain a balance up to $2000, on which simple interest accrues at 15.5 percent yearly.

Free delivery of the Jefferson Manor Group you chose can be made within two days after you call to set a delivery date. This furniture set will blend with almost any decor, just one reason it has become our most popular living room group.

Thank you for choosing Abacus for this purchase, Mr. Lovejoy. When you again need furniture or accessories, be sure to visit our store. We are always glad to serve your needs and look forward to a continuing business relationship.

Yours sincerely,

Favorable responses are perhaps the easiest messages to write. Basically, this is because it's always nice to deliver good news. Still, remember to be thorough. Include all the necessary details so the reader will neither have to call nor write for more information. Also, if you are handling problems with products or services, mention resale items. Remember, too, to include appropriate sales promotional material whenever you can in a manner that is forthright but that also has nothing awkward or overly aggressive about it.

WRITING SPECIFIC TYPES OF GOODWILL LETTERS AND MEMOS

What type of letters and memos don't we bother to write?

One of the oddest business phenomena is that the letters and memos people should write are the very ones they don't. Too frequently, we write only if we want something: a job with that military contractor, a sale of that commercial property, a payment for that shipment of designer clothing. In doing so, many business writers fail to distinguish between their short- and long-term goals. This means that once they have achieved, for example, the sale of a commercial property, they fail to follow through and pursue other sales with the client or his or her associates. Perhaps this omission can be traced to a quality many businesspeople have only insufficiently cultivated—that of attending to the finer points of interpersonal relationships.

Goodwill messages represent the business equivalent of followthrough. People have numerous reasons for "forgetting" to go beyond the immediate situation. For example, some have difficulty extending thanks or congratulations; others are negligent; still others have been spoiled by the telephone and other devices that allow them to avoid writing letters and memos. Nevertheless, the goodwill message—the thank you note or acknowledgment, the congratulatory message and letter of condolence—is an indispensable element of effective business.

What are the advantages of writing such messages? Often, they are pleasant surprises to people. For example, suppose you send a note of congratulations to a business acquaintance on the birth of her daughter. Since she is someone you only occasionally do business with, she is both pleased and surprised to hear from you. Naturally, she is also aware that you may in part want to promote a favorable impression on her and through her on her company. Still, your note makes no specific demands on her, and she remains gratified by your interest.

In general, you should take time to say "thank you," "congratulations," and "we're thinking of you." People enjoy doing business with those who do.

Expressing Thanks and Acknowledging Others

At the right occasion and the right moment, a simple expression on your part of thanks or an acknowledgment can build much goodwill. For example, you may write a note congratulating a salesperson in your division for having spectacular December sales. Or you can thank the head of office services for being quick in getting you the special lamp you needed to counteract the effects of the harsh office lighting. Or you may simply write to acknowledge receiving an order to purchase 1000 head of cattle or to tell a customer that you are pleased to have done business with his or her company this year. If, in these messages, your *primary* purpose is to build goodwill, then you will ask for nothing in return from your reader. (Do not construe this statement to mean that goodwill is never a secondary purpose. It often is. In fact, goodwill is—or should be—a secondary purpose in every letter or memo you write in which it is not primary.)

When is goodwill primary in a letter or memo? When is it secondary?

To be effective, such messages require a sincere tone. Without it, you create either suspicion about your motives or actual ill will. Be especially aware of tone as you read the following letter of acknowledgment. Do you see any problems with it?

First Draft

Dear Ms. O'Reilly:

Beyond any shadow or shade of doubt, you have been one of our very, very best customers during the past seven years. Just imagine what pleasure it has been for us to have done business with the same wonderful, ladylike person you are! I only wish every customer met your standards of promptness and correctness.

Although I have never seen your fine retail store, I hear that the best description is "sheer elegance." As soon as I can take time from my busy schedule, I'll drive over to take a look. Meanwhile, I wish you the very best in all that you do.

Cordially,

Critique

This draft is an exaggerated version that shows nearly all the mistakes such a letter or memo can contain. Although you probably will never see a message that is so wrong, remember that one incorrect word or phrase can invalidate a goodwill message. In this particular letter, at least the organization is deductive and the writing style appropriately informal.

The following are some specific problems:

1. "very, very," "just imagine . . . same wonderful, ladylike. . . ," "sheer elegance," and "very best" are overstatements that strike an insincere tone and should be omitted (lines 2, 3, 4, 8, and 10, respectively)

2. The repeated use of "I" (lines 5, 7, 8, and 10) as well as such words or phrases as "for us to have," "I'll," and "from my busy schedule" are writer centered and create a selfish tone that should be eliminated. (lines 3, 9, and 9, respectively)
3. "Shadow or shade" (line 1) is redundant and either one word or the other should be used.
4. "Ladylike" is sexist and should be omitted. (line 4)
5. Negative comparisons with other customers should be deleted. (line 5)
6. "I hear that" implies the writer responds to gossip or has been prying and should be omitted. (line 7)

The following is a revised draft of this letter:

Revised Draft

Dear Ms. O'Reilly:

Filling your orders for the past seven years has been a pleasure, and we are grateful for your business.

Your regular orders, placed accurately, have allowed us to supply you with the right merchandise in time to meet your needs. Further, you have paid on schedule every time, making it possible to keep the records of your account up to date at all times.

You have our best wishes for continued success with your fine retail store. We look forward to another seven years—and more—of a rewarding business relationship with you.

Cordially yours,

Congratulating Others on Special Occasions

What special occasions call for congratulations?

Effective managers and communicators know what's happening around them in ways that encompass more than strictly business events. They know that the people they work with have both private and public lives; that is, in their private lives, they have birthdays, get married, have children, and so forth. And in their business lives they successfully complete major projects and reports, move to better jobs in other companies, or get promoted within their own. Effective communicators know how to send the right messages to commemorate such happy events so that goodwill increases.

The following is a congratulatory message. Do you see any problems with it?

First Draft

To: Sol Manning, Sales Manager
From: Doris Lawrence, Personnel Manager
Subject: Many Happy Returns

I just wanted to take a few minutes to put in writing what you already know, I'm sure, and that is congratulations on your promotion. Now that we are peers, I want to welcome you to the fraternity of managers here at the company. You will do a great job, I know.

Critique

Technically, this message does begin with the news in its first sentence. But this news is "weakened" by its position in that sentence, for it occurs after two wordy introductory clauses. Morever, the entire message seems to lack substance because the style is almost impersonally formal. In addition, the writer's condescending manner can put you off. The following are some specific problems:

1. The subject line is too general or vague.
2. "To put in writing" is unnecessary because the letter itself is proof of this fact; it can be omitted. (line 1)
3. The message is so brief as to seem that it was written just to get it out of the way. Also, in choosing to use one paragraph, the writer cannot set thoughts off from each other for emphasis.
4. "What you already know" and "I'm sure" are presumptuous phrases and can be deleted. (lines 1 and 2, respectively)
5. "Now that we are peers" is condescending, even though this may not be the writer's intention. (line 3)
6. "Fraternity" is a sexist word and should be deleted. (line 4)

The following is a revised version of this memo:

Revised Draft

To: Sol Manning, Sales Manager
From: Doris Lawrence, Personnel Manager
Subject: Congratulations on Your Promotion

Congratulations, Sol, on your promotion to sales manager. The announcement of your selection arrived on my desk just this morning.

Your cooperative spirit has made working with you during the past five years a pleasure. And your record as the top real estate salesperson for the past three years assures everyone that outstanding performance is rewarded in this firm.

Should you need any information on working procedures between sales and personnel, please let me know. If you want to meet for a discussion of the procedures, call my office at Extension 0000. I'll be glad to meet you for lunch or in your office or mine. Meanwhile, I look forward to helping you recruit and train salespersons who will strive to excel in their jobs.

Sending Condolence in a Time of Grief

What situation might call for extending condolence?

In business situations it may be appropriate to send a message of sympathy to someone you work with, a client, or a customer. The occasion may be the death of a close friend or relative or a serious illness or injury. Even a pet's death might warrant a message.

Any such message should attempt to reassure and comfort. Therefore, organize it deductively and adopt a positive tone. This translates as: avoid dwelling on the event that caused the grief and concentrate instead on the possibility of a happier future.

The following is a condolence letter to a client on the death of her husband. What problems do you see with it?

First Draft

Dear Mrs. Mendes:

In reference to the recent death of your husband, whose obituary we read in yesterday's newspaper, we were sorry to hear the news. You must have been hurt very much by this sorrowful event, and you have our deepest regrets.

Our hearts go out to you as you carry on with your life. Kindly be advised that you should feel free to call on us for assistance at any time.

Sincerely yours,

Critique

Although obviously well intended, this letter contains mostly negative references and anticipates little relief or recovery. As such, it represents the most common errors writers of condolence messages commit. Moreover, the writing style is inconsistent, wavering between too much formality and too little. The following are some specific problems:

1. "Sorry" and "deepest regrets" create a negative tone; they are also negative reminders and should be omitted. (lines 2 and 4, respectively)
2. "In reference to" and "kindly be advised" are phrases that are

simultaneously obvious, wordy, overly formal, and clichés. As such, they should be omitted. (lines 1 and 6, respectively)

3. "Hearts go out to you" and "feel free to" are also clichés and should be deleted. "Feel free to" is also wordy. (lines 5 and 6, respectively)

The following is a revised draft of the letter:

Revised Draft

Dear Mrs. Mendes:

You have our sympathy in your bereavement following the death of your husband.

Our association with the two of you during the past few years has been more than a fulfilling business relationship. It has been a friendship as well.

Should you need any assistance, just call us at the office (000-0000) or at home (000-0000). We will gladly help in any way possible. Meanwhile, we look forward to hearing that you are feeling well again.

Very sincerely yours,

In summary: we write goodwill letters and memos to express happiness or sorrow. Nevertheless, whatever your purpose, you should emphasize positive ideas instead of negative ones. With the exception of condolences, these messages are usually a pleasure to write because you are the bearer of good news. If you are sensitive to the opportunities around you, you will discover that you will write them often.

The following checklist should help you to form and evaluate your favorable responses and goodwill messages. By consulting it regularly, you can ensure that they will have the desired effect.

CHECKLIST FOR FAVORABLE RESPONSE AND GOODWILL LETTERS AND MEMOS

1. Ask these questions when you write the opening paragraph of your letter or memo.
   a. If possible, is the news delivered in the first sentence?
   b. Are "slow" openings avoided? (Slow openings are those where the news is preceded by unnecessary information, such as "This is in reply to your request of July 3.")

   c. If convenient, is the reader's name mentioned in the sentence with the good news? (If you use the name here, then do not use it again unless it is a long message. To overdo this type of personalization is to sound insincere.)
   d. Is the news delivered in positive, cheerful, sincere, reader-centered language?

2. Ask these questions when you write the body of your letter or memo.
   a. If a favorable response, are all answers given to questions originally asked? Also, are answers provided to questions not asked but raised as a result of information provided?
   b. If a goodwill message, is the language positive and forward looking? Is the message reassuring?
   c. Are all necessary details included? Are explanations and reasons stated clearly and concisely?
   d. If a favorable response, has resale been included if appropriate, either here or in the closing? Is the same thing true for sales promotional material?
   e. If a goodwill message, have all demands on the reader been avoided, both directly and through implication?
   f. Is the "you" (reader-centered) approach used throughout?
3. Ask these questions when you write the closing paragraph of your letter or memo.
   a. Is it short? (Unless you included some body material, such as resale or sales promotional material in this paragraph, the closing should be short.)
   b. If a favorable response and action is to be taken by the reader,
      (1) Is the desired action stated and easy to perform?
      (2) Is the time period when the desired action should be taken stated clearly and courteously? If appropriate, is the reason for the time given?
   c. If a favorable response, has resale been included if appropriate and if not included in the body? Is the same thing true for sales promotional material?
   d. If a goodwill message, is it forward looking and positively stated?
   e. Is the reader-centered approach used?

SUMMARY

1. Favorable responses are answers to routine requests. Use a deductive (direct) plan to write both them and goodwill messages. Both deliver good news.
2. The recommended three-step deductive plan for writing favorable responses and goodwill messages is (a) deliver the news, (b) include details or explanation, and (c) close positively.
3. The opening statement, which is in the most emphatic position, is especially important in these types of correspondence because it contains the subject.
4. The details or explanation might be called the body of a favorable response or goodwill message. This is where you should explain the subject fully.
5. Resale material reassures the reader about goods or services after the purchase; include it in favorable responses when problems have arisen. Sales promotional material is designed to promote a product or service related to that under discussion. Use it in favorable responses whenever the opportunity arises.
6. Both general and action request closings are appropriate for favorable responses, depending on the situation. But always close a goodwill message with a general closing.
7. Although the subjects of favorable responses are as diverse as are jobs and job duties, you can organize them into five general categories:
   a. *Sending information to others.* Write these messages whenever you can supply the information as requested.
   b. *Offering assistance to others.* Write these messages whenever you can give the help requested.
   c. *Granting a simple claim or adjustment.* Write these messages whenever you can grant a claim or make an adjustment as requested.
   d. *Filling orders for goods or services.* Write these messages whenever you can fill an order as it was placed. The letter or memo may accompany the order or may be mailed separately.
   e. *Granting credit terms.* Write these messages in response to an application or other type of request for credit terms in situations where you can meet the request fully.
8. The primary purpose of a goodwill message is to build goodwill; you make no demands on the reader in it.
9. As with favorable responses, the subjects of goodwill letters and memorandums vary widely. The following are probably the most common types written in business today:
   a. *Expressing thanks and acknowledging others.* Write these messages to say thanks for a job well done or to acknowledge receipt of an order.
   b. *Congratulating others on special occasions.* Write these congratulatory messages on special occasions such as promotions or marriages.
   c. *Sending condolences in times of grief.* Send these messages of sympathy when a friend or relative has died.

Review Questions

1. What are favorable responses and when should you write them?
2. What are goodwill messages and when should you write them?

3. How can you make a favorable response more than just a routine answer?
4. Why should you use a deductive plan when writing favorable responses and goodwill messages?
5. How many steps does the organizational plan suggested for use in writing favorable responses and goodwill messages have? Name and define each of them.
6. Why is the opening statement in a favorable response or goodwill message especially important? How can you be sure yours is effective?
7. What is resale material? Write an example of appropriate resale for a type of favorable response.
8. What is sales promotional material? How and where should you use it in favorable responses?
9. What is the difference between general and action request closings? Write an effective closing for a memorandum in which you congratulate a co-worker for receiving a promotion.
10. Do you make any distinctions between sending information and offering assistance to others? If so, what are they?
11. What is it about a claim that makes it simple or routine? Can you name a situation in which a claim may not be either simple or routine?
12. Do all companies handle orders for goods or services the same way? Explain your answer.
13. Why do you think goodwill messages often fail to work? Why are they very effective if handled properly?
14. Why should you congratulate clients, customers, or co-workers on special occasions in their private lives? Isn't this prying or snooping? Explain your answer.
15. Why do we write deductively organized condolences? Isn't the form too straightforward, too direct? Explain your answer.

Exercises

Favorable Responses

1. You are the credit manager for Top Dollar Department Stores. Today, you received a credit information request from the credit manager at Minton Department Stores. Harriet McKenzie has applied to open a credit account with Minton and gave your store as a reference. Write a letter to the credit manager at Minton telling him that Ms. McKenzie is a good credit risk. She has a $2000 credit line with your store and has owed as much as $1500 on the account at one time. She has always paid her monthly installment payment within 10 days of receiving a statement. Address: George J. Macklin, Credit Manager; Minton Department Stores; 682 Waverly Lane; St. Paul, Minnesota 00000.
2. You work as a district sales supervisor for McGuire and Associates, a manufacturer of track lighting fixtures. Recently, the company hired a new marketing manager, Gabrielle LeVoy, who is your immediate superior. This week, you received a memorandum from Mrs. LeVoy telling you that she wants to meet with you for about an hour next week to discuss a new marketing program designed to boost sales. You should send a memorandum suggesting a convenient time for the meeting, she said. Any weekday morning between 8 and 11 A.M. is convenient for her. She mentioned that she

would like your reaction to the program and would like you to share any ideas you have as well. Because sales in your district have been down 5 percent this year, you are eager both to take care of the problem and to make a good impression on Mrs. LeVoy. Write a memorandum to schedule the appointment as she requested.

3. You are traffic control manager for Birdland Industries, an importer of fine avian porcelain. Your company is located in the heart of the downtown business district, where it owns a parking lot adjacent to your main office building. Parking spaces in the area are scarce and expensive, so Birdland gives free parking privileges to all employees as a fringe benefit. Yesterday, you received a letter from Amy Lowe, the personnel director of Lacey Department Store, located just two blocks away. Ms. Lowe wants to know whether Lacey can rent a block of 50 parking spaces for its employees. If so, her assistant director, James Jacobs, will be glad to coordinate with you so you don't have to deal with 50 individual employees. Write a letter to Ms. Lowe telling her that the spaces are available and that you will rent them as a block for an annual fee. Explain all necessary details, including the price, and enclose a contract for Ms. Lowe's signature. Address: Ms. Amy L. Lowe, Personnel Director; Lacey Department Store; 334 S. Michigan Avenue; Chicago, Illinois 00000.

4. You work as public relations director for PBM Industries, a manufacturer of computer software packages specializing in word processing programs. This week, you received a letter from a college student asking for information about your best selling word processing program, WriteSmart. He said that his business communication instructor had recommended the program highly one day this semester while comparing writing on the computer to other methods of writing. Send two color brochures to meet the request, along with a cover letter. Because you have begun to get many such requests, prepare the letter as a form with variables to handle individual requests so you won't have to continue writing the same letter again and again. Address: Mr. Abdul Khalim; 43 Johnson Hall; Shell Coast University; 988 Lincoln Avenue; Venice, Florida 00000.

5. As the director of advertising for PBM Industries, the firm mentioned in Exercise 4, you received a memo yesterday from the executive vice president, Manuel Richards. He said bluntly that he doesn't like either of the color brochures you use in advertising the WriteSmart word processing program. They don't get the message across as effectively as they could, he said, and they are printed on cheap-looking "slick" paper. You don't know what he means by "don't get the message across," and the paper you use is very high quality. In fact, you suspect the executive vice president of trying to intervene in a specialized area he knows little about. Yet he holds a position in the company well above yours, so you know you must handle the problem diplomatically. Send a memorandum acknowledging that you received the information and ask for a 30-minute appointment to discuss the brochures, including their use as part of your overall advertising program for WriteSmart.

6. Three months ago, you were hired as a manager trainee in the sales department of Markels, Incorporated, a wholesale distributor of children's toys located in Wilmington, Delaware. Today, Mabel O'Neill, manager of foreign accounts and your supervisor, handed you a letter from Lin Ching, president of a toy store in Taipei, Taiwan. While the letter is writ-

ten in broken English, you can understand most of it. Mr. Ching wants information about your line of Ugly Muggins dolls, which he heard about (or saw?) while on a business trip to Singapore. You are preparing to send the information as Mrs. O'Neill requested, but one part of the letter bothers you. You can't decipher a reference to "wanting watch simple mechanism." After consulting with several members of your department, you decide that he may be asking to see samples of the merchandise, which you can send only on request and only to companies in foreign countries if they prepay. Write Mr. Ching a letter sending color brochures and a price list. Offer to send samples of any particular Ugly Muggins he wants to see if he will prepay. You can refund his money if he decides to order or return the samples. Address: Mr. Lin Ching, President; Ming Yuan Toys; 87 Tzeschu; Taipei, Taiwan.

7. You live in a small town in a farming region in North Dakota and own and operate your own business, Central Feed and Seed Store. Most of your sales are made to farmers who buy large quantities of feed for livestock or seeds for planting in the spring. This week, you received a letter from a customer who lives in a remote corner of the county about 30 miles away. The customer, who does not have a telephone, asked that you please deliver 10 tons of your Formula X hog feed to his residence by the end of the month, which is three weeks from now. His supply is running low, but he expects to have enough to last until that time. He said he would come to your store to take delivery were not both his trucks needing repair. Write a letter acknowledging the order and telling him when to expect your drivers to deliver the feed. Include a bit of resale on Formula X feed, which is a brand you formulated yourself. Also, include some sales promotion. Perhaps he would like to take advantage of an early sale on corn seed now that it's March and planting time will be here soon. Address: Mr. Lars Jorgensen; Route 1, Box 803; Manning, North Dakota 00000.

8. You are a broker for Watkins, Watkins, and Jenks, a regional brokerage house in Atlanta specializing in municipal bonds. This week, you received a call from the city manager of a small town in South Alabama asking that you call him to discuss the possibility of your handling the sale of a bond issue. You have called—four times, in fact—and each time you begin the discussion, he gets interrupted and asks you to call later. By this time, you think you probably will never get him the information he needs by telephone because of the interruptions. Next month, you are driving to New Orleans for a conference and can easily stop by his office on the way. So, you call for an appointment, but his secretary says that he isn't in and that he schedules his own appointments. She says she will ask him to return your call, but he hasn't returned any in the past. So you decide that he's either avoiding you or is a very busy man. Choosing to believe the latter but not wanting to be aggressive, you decide to write him. Send him all the information he needs about your company, bond rates, and the procedures you use for the sale and issue of municipal bonds. Tell him about your trip to New Orleans and indicate that you can stop by his office if he wishes. Address: Mr. Johnny Walkerton, City Manager; City of Broughtown; P.O. Box 000; Broughtown, Alabama 00000.

9. You are the bicycle dealer mentioned in Exercise 5 in Chapter 7. Write a letter to accompany the rear brake assembly that you are sending by Express Mail today. Also include a bracket wrench (stock

number 39) and 12½-inch Willy bolts (stock number 45-1) that are needed for the assembly. Be sure to include some resale in it, too. Address: Timothy L. Waxen; 3622 Lexington Avenue; Lynchburg, Virginia 00000.

10. You are the production manager, Lily Tao, mentioned in Exercise 7 in Chapter 7. Write a memo to the chemist, Abraham Minkovitz, who wants your assistance in preparing sample capsules of the asthma symptom–relieving drug. Agree to meet in his laboratory and suggest that the meeting be held either Monday or Tuesday of next week.

11. You are the claims manager for Finest Products Company, a retail discount store. Two weeks ago, a customer bought a microwave oven that is guaranteed against defective parts for one year. The customer, who lives on a ranch about 60 miles away, returned the oven today with a letter saying that the oven will not heat. He requested that you either repair it or send a replacement. You check the oven and see that the electric circuitry does not work and cannot be repaired. Write a letter to the customer saying that you are shipping a new oven by parcel post tomorrow. Include both resale and sales promotional material in your letter. Address: Walter Abbott; Route 1, Box 805; Depot City, Wyoming 00000.

12. You are employed as the director of finance for the roads and highways department in your state and report directly to the state secretary for roads and highways herself. In this job, you supervise managers of finance in several regional offices. Your general policy is to correspond with them by memo when time permits. Yesterday, you received a memo from one of the regional managers, Jack Logan, asking for your interpretation of a section in the state code used to govern reimbursements to employees who travel on state business. When one subordinate petitioned for reimbursement for expenses incurred on a trip to Houston recently, he included a dinner at $72.50, along with a valid receipt. When the manager told him that the limit for a single meal is $50.00, he said that according to a memo sent from your office last month, the limit has been increased to $75.00. Jack Logan doesn't remember any such memo and doesn't believe it exists or that the code has been changed. Yet, he wants to know if it has been changed and if you sent such a memorandum. Write the manager to tell him that he is right. The limit is still $50.00. Some discussions about increasing the limit to $75.00 have taken place, and you understand that rumors of these discussions have been widely circulated by the grapevine. Perhaps, the subordinate got the news that way.

13. You own and manage a small real estate firm in LaJolla, California. Last month, you (tentatively) sold a $500,000 oceanfront property and are representing both buyer and seller. At this point, you are doing all the things necessary to close the sale within the 90-day time limit. The buyer, a wealthy business consultant from Maryland, called earlier today to say that he was shocked when he just happened to look at the option to buy he signed last month. The binder he paid should have been $10,000, not $20,000 as stated in the agreement. He didn't know about it until now because his assistant handled the transaction and even wrote the check to bind the agreement. You told him you would check into the matter right away. You then called the seller immediately, and she told you that the buyer is correct about the oral agreement; when she received the contract with the $20,000 binder, she thought you and

the buyer had decided to offer a larger amount to induce her to grant him the option.

You explain to her that, no, a mistake was made that nobody caught until now. She then refuses to return the $10,000 now but does agree to return it if the buyer is unable to complete the purchase before the option expires. Otherwise, the full amount can be applied to the purchase at the closing. You thank her and call the buyer immediately. He says, "Great," but he wants it in writing from the seller, and please send it by Express Mail. Then you call the seller again, and she agrees to sign such a letter if you will write it. Wiping the perspiration from your brow, you agree to write the letter this morning and bring it to her house this afternoon at 3:15 for her signature. Address: Mr. J. Lawrence Crimpton, President; Crimpton and Associates; 405 Bayfront; Annapolis, Maryland 00000.

14. You manage the shipping and receiving department of Gander Brothers, Incorporated, a manufacturer of electronic components that are used in brand-name computers. Three weeks ago, you shipped an order for 20,000 MX disk drives to one of your best customers. Then yesterday, the sales manager brought you a letter from the customer explaining that all the 4X2 spindles that are part of the disk drives were not shipped and that you've gotten him into trouble with one of the firm's best clients. He asks you not only to ship the spindles by air express today, but also to write the customer to explain your responsibility for the problem. Meanwhile, the sales manager will write as well. Quickly now, write a letter to accompany the spindles that must be taken to the airport for a flight that departs three hours from now. In your letter, deliver the spindles, explain how the problem occurred (How did it occur?), accept responsibility, and explain what you have done to ensure that the problem will not recur. Address: Mrs. Marjorie M. Manning, Manager; Production Department; WinWith Computer Company; 11 Warehouse Road; East Orange, New Jersey 00000.

15. You are a sales representative for Better Firs Company, a wholesaler of ornamental trees and shrubs. Your firm purchases from growers in Florida and Texas and sells to retailers in a five-state region. Today, you received a memo from a fellow sales representative, Lola Lilburn, telling you that you have invaded her territory. When she visited a client in Bluefield, West Virginia last week—Wentworth Ornamentals, Incorporated—the owner told her that you had taken their quarterly order two weeks ago. You are surprised because you thought Wentworth is located in Bluefield, Virginia, and is therefore in your sales territory. But when you check the map, you see that indeed it is located in West Virginia. Write a memorandum to your fellow sales representative saying she is correct and that you have filed a requisition to have the commission from the sale paid to her. Along with your explanation, perhaps you should send a copy of the requisition and promise to be more careful in the future.

16. You work as a credit manager for WorldCard Company, a giant credit card firm that has 4.6 million cardholders who can use the card for purchases at 850,000 locations worldwide. Your job is to supervise employees who process applications for cards. For efficiency, you notify both successful and unsuccessful applicants with form letters that have variables for entering individualized information. While you think the letter used to notify the unsuccessful applicants is

very good, you think the one used to successful applicants is very poor. It is so poor, in fact, that you decide to discard it entirely (and forget it, too, if possible) and write a new one. Write the new form letter in which you deliver the card, explain its use, welcome the new customer, and include any appropriate enclosures.

17. You own the local cable television company, BG Cablevision, that you manage yourself. You employ 20 technicians who hook up new subscribers to the service and make repairs when necessary. The work these technicians do is invaluable, of course, and job openings are hard to fill. In addition, they do most of the goodwill building for the firm because they have most of the contact with your subscribers. In other words, you want to keep these technicians happy. As it happens, one of the technicians asked you yesterday whether you might offer them a discount and credit terms, something you have never done before. After thinking it over and checking the financial records, you decide that you can do it. You call in the technician who approached you and explain that you will announce an offer in a memorandum next week. Now, how much discount can you offer and what credit terms? For example, if they subscribe to the basic service and one movie channel, what can your offer be? Can it be better if they subscribe to the basic service and two movie channels, and so forth? Also, will you extend the service to the ten other employees who work in the office? And what offer will you make the four technicians (and three office workers, if appropriate) who now subscribe to the basic service? Make your decisions and respond to their request in a memo with the best offer you can afford to make.

18. You work as accountant and credit manager for Better Goods Company, a firm located in a suburban shopping mall that sells high-fashion women's clothing. Although Better Goods is a small company, you do offer store-brand credit cards for making purchases on credit terms. Because this service is really a convenience offered to regular customers who live within 50 miles of your city, you recently turned down an application from a woman because she lives 600 miles away in another state. Then this morning, you received a letter from her telling you that she will be moving to your city within three months. She then says graciously that she would like a card when she gets there. Write her a letter telling her that you will reactivate her application and will issue her a card when she moves to town. All she need do is come by the store and pick up the card at that time. Or you will mail it to her at her new address after she moves in. Address: Mrs. Clara Cassiday; 2121 Wembley Court; Davenport, Iowa 00000.

Goodwill Messages

19. You are the president of Richland Fabricating Company, a builder of metal tanks for storing liquids underground. You have just received a large order from Mason Fuel Company. This company has placed orders regularly for five years now and always has paid you on time. Write a goodwill letter to the president of Mason thanking her for doing business with your company. Address: Elaine Gruver, President; Mason Fuel Company; P.O. Box 946; Columbia, South Carolina 00000.

20. You are the marketing director for Sherburne and Company, apple growers and packers in upstate New York. You specialize in growing Adam's Apples, a delicious seedless variety of red apple Mr. Sherburne, the owner and president, developed himself and made famous. As it

happens, you are in the enviable position of having more demand for your product than you can supply. Because Mr. Sherburne does not want to risk the reputation of the "best apples in all New York State," your marketing strategy has been to supply steady customers only. Any customer who does not take shipment of the order you reserve for her or him each year is replaced by another from your waiting list. Last week, you received a letter from the owner of Adam's Steak House, a famous San Francisco restaurant you dropped from the list three years ago. He wants to feature the applies on the restaurant's menu next year, thinking that "Adam's and Adam's" is a natural winner. He mentions that one of his best friends in "all the Bay area" is Peggy Padow, a life-long friend of Sherm Sherburne. You show the letter to Mr. Sherburne, and he says, "Peggy Padow is indeed one of my best friends, and I hate to say no. We *must* maintain our policy, though." He then asks if you have enough excess apples to fill the order on a one-time basis, but the answer is no. "Well, you'll know how to handle the owner of the steak house, but I also want you to write Peggy for me. Acknowledge her recommendation and thank her for thinking of us." Write the letter for Mr. Sherburne's signature. Address: Ms. Peggy Padow; 48 Market Square Place; San Francisco, California 00000.

21. You own and operate a convenience store in one of the best locations in Milwaukee. Up to three years ago, you were grossing $2 million annually with net profits of $200,000 to $300,000. Then, sales dipped by 30 percent in one year and have continued to decline to the point that you grossed less than $1 million this year and lost $150,000. As one of your assistant managers put it, "the bottom fell out." Everyone has been working hard to reverse the trend, however. You have renovated the store, put in more parking spaces, and upgraded your product line throughout, for example. And you haven't lost a single employee, although all of them took a 20 percent pay cut this year to help out. It's the year end now, and you're sitting in your office thinking how lucky you are to have such loyal, hard-working employees. You've told them many times how much you appreciate what they've done, but you want to do something more. The answer flashes through your mind. You can make it official, so to speak, by writing them a sincere memorandum of appreciation. You can put it in writing. So now, go ahead and write this memo to all employees, who number 20 clerks, three assistant managers, and one associate manager.

22. You are sales manager for Spicy Chicken Restaurants, a fast-growing retail franchiser. Last month, your company awarded its one-hundredth franchise. Write a letter to the new owner of the franchise congratulating him on receiving the franchise. Address: Ralph C. Snodgrass; Spicy Chicken Restaurant; 1369 Ocean Drive; Bridge City, Louisiana 00000.

23. You learned last week that an old friend, Mary Sue Tanner, was promoted. Mary Sue, a botanist, is a civil servant who works for the federal government's agricultural department near Allentown, Pennsylvania. The promotion means she will move to Beltsville, Maryland, near Washington, where you live. You're very happy for Mary Sue, knowing that this particular promotion took years to qualify for and more years for a vacancy to occur. You're happy too that you may get to see her more often. Write a letter congratulating Mary Sue on her promo-

tion to GS-15 (a high civil service job grade). Anticipate getting together more often and offer to "show her around" the capital area.

24. You own and manage a retail flower shop in Washington State. One of your suppliers, an orchid grower, is also a good friend. You have just learned that his wife died last week in a tragic automobile accident. Write a letter of condolence expressing your sympathy. Address: Harry J. Soccer, President, Washington Orchid Growers, Incorporated; Vashon, Washington 00000.

25. You are a trial lawyer working for a St. Louis law firm, Megerton, Battle, and Jacobsen. Recently, a senior partner in a rival firm, Kotlotski and Williams, has been wooing you to take a partnership in that firm. In fact, the suitor is Karen Williams herself, who is famed in this part of the country as a brilliant trial lawyer. Yesterday, you learned that the Williams's son, Ellery, was killed in the crash of a small plane near Lagos, Nigeria. Tragically, all six passengers, the pilot, and the co-pilot were killed. Write a letter of condolence to Karen Williams and her husband. Ellery was their only child. Address: Karen and Jason Williams; 66 Mayfield Park Way; St. Louis, Missouri 00000.

CHAPTER 9

WRITING UNFAVORABLE NEWS LETTERS AND MEMOS

In business as elsewhere, no one likes the bearer of bad news. As one chief executive candidly told a vice president who had brought the news that the company had lost a multimillion-dollar bid to build a new airplane for the Navy, "If you want to get ahead, learn to bring the right news, which is good. Leave the bad news for someone else."

The problem with bad news is twofold. First, nobody likes to receive it. Second, on receiving it, people tend to blame the messengers, either associating them with the message itself or holding them in some way responsible. Sometimes receivers also react angrily and may vent this on the messenger; at other times they may express disappointment and feel discouraged. As a result of these feelings, they may strike out against those who have, for example, refused to extend them credit or rejected their request for information or assistance. This type of response can take many forms—from a complaint letter to a blocked promotion.

But, despite the warning of the chief executive cited in this example, if businesses are to run at all, some people must tell or write bad news and others must hear and read it. Further, and most important, such messages must be honest.

In many instances, putting bad news in the form of letters and memos creates distance between senders and receivers. For example, if you write to a worker rejecting his or her disability claim, you are spared witnessing her immediate response. Yet physical distance does not grant you immunity from being sensitive and diplomatic. In other words, you need to exercise tact. This means that you are not simply a reporter, telling someone what a decision is, but your responsibility also includes ensuring that he or she understands the reasons for it.

In writing such messages, you need to adopt an inductive or indirect approach by putting your explanation before the negative information (the refusal). Thus, you must justify your news before actually saying what it is. Here, though, you will need to watch for the difference between indirectness that softens the "harshness" of the news and indirectness that attempts to disguise the bad news with fancy wording and long sentences. This second approach may result in both agitating readers and destroying not only your own credibility but also your company's as well.

PLANNING UNFAVORABLE NEWS LETTERS AND MEMOS

In organizing unfavorable messages, the most important thing to remember is your reader's natural reluctance to hear bad news. All the following steps to help you plan such messages reflect this concern with your reader's reaction:

What five steps make up the unfavorable news plan?

1. *Open with a buffer statement.* Buffer statements, as their name implies, cushion the reader's initial reaction. They do so by establishing a common ground between the two people: the writer and the reader. By opening with a statement that touches on some positive aspect of the subject, writers smooth the transition to the next step.
2. *Give reasons for refusing.* Help the reader to anticipate the bad news by giving the reasons for it. State your most convincing reasons first—from the reader's viewpoint. (Your most convincing reason is the one your reader would consider the strongest.) If you have only one reason, state it at this point. But if you have two or more reasons, save at least one of them to include with the material in step 4.
3. *Refuse.* You can state your refusal directly, or you can imply it. In implying it, however, never be vague.
4. *Give additional reasons for refusing.* If you want to do the best possible job with your refusal, then give additional reasons for your decision if there are any. You may find it appropriate to offer some alternative instead of or in addition to more reasons for refusing. In such situations, refer the reader to someone who may be able to assist, or offer your own substitute method, procedure, product, or service. (This gesture may include a compromise suggestion.)
5. *Close with a positive statement and tone.* If you have offered your reader an alternative in step 4, you may need to close your message with a request for action. In fact, you should do this if you need a response about the alternative you suggested. For example, you may request that the reader accept your compromise plan. If, however, you need no response from the reader, close with a positive statement that is consistent with the other ideas in the message. Also, you may include here resale of goods or services or promotional material.

This five-step plan is an example of a type of *inductive* or indirect organization and is diagrammed in Figure 9-1. In contrast to a deductive message, where you begin with the news and then explain or give details, here you start with the details or reasons for your decision and only afterward do you actually say or imply clearly what this decision is. (For a discussion of inductive organization, see Chapter 3.)

How, though, do you determine if news is unfavorable? Obviously, if you reject a company's serious takeover bid, its management is going to perceive this news as being extremely unfavorable. If, however, you tell a jewelry dealer that a shipment of wristwatches will be several days late, he or she may not view this news as being especially bad. In fact, existing inventory may be adequate to fill all

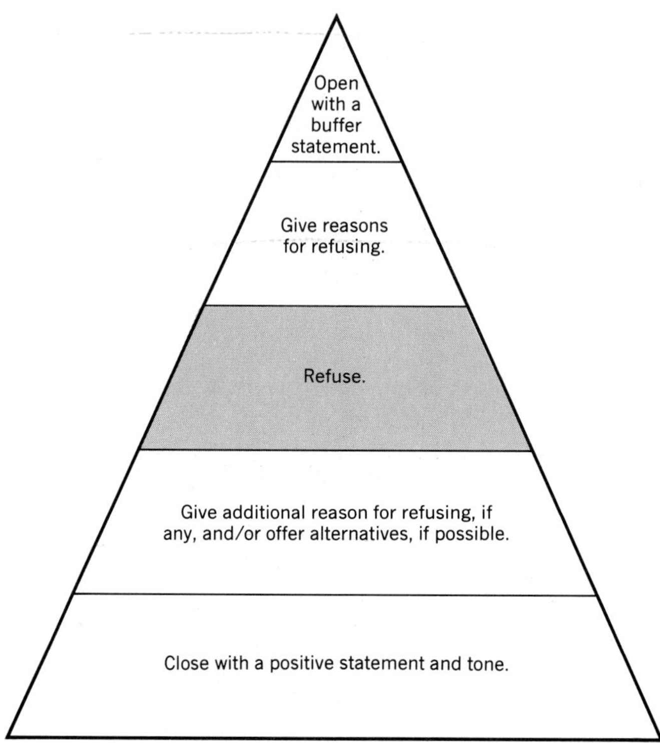

FIGURE 9-1 Diagram of inductive plan for unfavorable news letters and memos.

needs until the late shipment arrives. Still, you should use the inductive pattern when writing the jeweler so that the negative news (however slight) does not affect your working relationship.

In both these cases, you will need to project yourself in the role of reader in determining whether you are going to write an unfavorable message. Sometimes, you may not really know how "bad" the news will be, as is probably the case with the jeweler. But when it is unexpected news—a substantive change in what you assume the reader expects to hear—treat it as unfavorable news.

Writing Opening Statements

Why is an opening statement especially important?

Here, as in all forms of correspondence, the opening statement sets the tone of the entire message. However, opening statements in unfavorable responses can create more ill will than just about anything else you write. So you need to be especially careful in composing them. The following suggestions should help:

1. *Be careful with a subject line.* A subject line in this type of opening should not present the negative news first. This means you can only use a "general" type of subject line, such as "Response to

Request for an Installment Loan.'' Of course, you need to include a subject line in all memos because it is regarded to be a necessary part. But you have the option not to use one in a letter.

2. *Be positive.* Naturally, effective business writers always try to write positive opening statements. With negative responses, they try even harder.
3. *Write to the point or subject.* Otherwise, your reader will suspect you of trying to create a smokescreen.
4. *Sound supportive.* Whatever the contents of your buffer statement, it should sound friendly. The reader should immediately receive two messages: that you have thoroughly considered the situation and that you care about it and his or her interests as well.

The following are examples of effective opening sentences:

> Your customer opinion survey sounds promising! Reading about your carefully planned study led me to discuss it with our marketing manager.
>
> Thank you very much for expressing such a strong interest in our Labor Day VCR promotion at Electronics Unlimited.
>
> We are glad that you were able to walk away from your automobile accident last month.
>
> You made the right choice when you decided to purchase our top-of-the-line BestRite refrigerator.
>
> We appreciate your interest in helping our company operate smoothly. As employees, all of us benefit by such concern.
>
> We are glad that you are recovering quickly from the injuries you sustained on the job two weeks ago.

Reducing the Negative Effects of Refusals

Suppose you have to tell an employee that he or she is fired. You are fully aware of how serious the situation is, but you are certain the decision is the right one. After some consideration, you decide it would be kindest to discuss the matter in person before writing a memo ''for the record.'' After the discussion, the person thanks you, saying he or she felt your directness to be a form of kindness. In fact you were kind in other ways, in that you were clear, straightforward, considerate, sincere, and honest.

How can directness be ''kind'' in a refusal?

Directness that is ''kind'' in the ways just described is the best strategy for delivering bad news. Thus, even though you follow an indirect plan in organizing such messages, your language throughout should be direct. This way, the reader will not have to both deal with his or her reactions and sift through the reasons for your decision at the same time, trying to understand them.

Avoid Overly Direct, Negative Approaches

You are furious with Sandy Quincy, a co-worker, for a mistake he has made that might cost you a new account. So you write him a memo about it, in which you accuse him of "carelessness unbecoming a professional." Since then, he has not spoken to you and looks the other way when you approach.

In unfavorable messages, try to avoid accusations such as this one. Like your co-worker, readers will surely be angry with you as a result. Statements that arouse anger and even provoke resentment in readers include

Can you name several words that can arouse anger in a refusal?

1. "You *neglected* to enclose a receipt with your request."
2. "We *cannot understand* why you have *failed* to use the proper procedure."
3. "You *claim* you included a check with your letter."
4. "Therefore, we *certainly* will not accept these terms."

In each of these statements, the italicized expressions provoke the reader. They are more likely to worsen the problem than to solve it.

Imply the Refusal Itself or Use Passive Voice

Surely everyone in business wants to maintain that happy state of having his or her interests agree with those of others. But when major interests differ, the situation is always negative, and often everyone is adversely affected. For example, if you refuse a customer a refund on a color TV, on the surface he or she appears to be the only person who loses. Yet, you lose too because your business suffers a loss of goodwill as a result of your refusal. Your choice, forced though it may be, is to risk trading the goodwill for the refund.

One way to reduce the negative effects is to imply the refusal itself whenever possible. For example, suppose the head of a department, Shena Moore, asks you to release confidential information about an employee who wishes to transfer to her department. Because of current law against such disclosures, you have to refuse the request. You could put the refusal this way: "Because the information you want must be kept confidential as required by federal law, the request must be denied." Or you might imply the refusal, "The information you requested must be kept confidential as required by federal law." Mulling over the two possibilities, you decide that the implied refusal is as clear as the direct one and also softer, so you go with it. Perhaps either way would be effective, but you're sure about the second version.

Another example of the superiority of the implied refusal over one that is direct is shown in the following example.

Suppose that a top importer of teas from the East, Sativ Bhatia, asks you for an appointment on January 16 to discuss a contract between your two companies. You are eager to talk with him, but your daughter's wedding is on that date. First, you think of writing a direct refusal such as, "I will be in Wilmington attending my daughter's wedding on January 16. Therefore, I will be unable to meet with you on that day." In looking this over, though, you see that an implied refusal might be more effective, so you write instead, "I will be attending my daughter's wedding in Wilmington on January 16 but can meet with you on January 17 or 18." Not only is your implied refusal less harsh than the direct one you had contemplated, but it also suggests an alternative. This way, you lead the reader quickly through step 3, the refusal, to step 4, where the content of your message improves considerably.

How can you imply a refusal?

Notice again the clarity of both these implied refusals. In contrast, an unclear implied refusal may anger your reader and also cause both of you to have to exchange another set of messages to clear matters up. Sometimes writers "straddle the fence" between direct and indirect refusals with annoying results. For example, "The information you requested must be kept confidential as required by federal law. To release it would be illegal. Therefore, the request must be denied." Here, by repeating the bad news—called a *double whammy*—the writer adds to the negative effect. In addition, by belaboring the subject, he or she postpones advancing the reader to the part of the message offering more reasons and/or possible alternatives.

In this discussion, we do not mean to suggest that implied refusals are always better than stated ones. Sometimes stated refusals are, in addition to being the only way to communicate the news, also completely effective. For example, "The request must be denied" probably is perfectly acceptable to most people. Yet these more direct responses sometimes also go too far. When they do, they can indicate to readers, for example, that although you are capable of meeting their request for financial help to build a neighborhood playground, you are strongly opposed to granting it. In this context, statements such as "We certainly will not do what you ask" are insulting.

But isn't it a bad idea to use passive voice in letters and memos?

Another point to remember about stated refusals is that, as suggested earlier, they can be quite harsh. A way to soften such a refusal when you need to use it is to employ passive voice, as in "The request *must be denied.*" Because it is less direct than the active voice, passive voice softens the statement in much the same way as an implied refusal does, just not as much.

One final note for those who want to work at the "art of fine refusals": Avoid using pronouns that refer directly to the reader or yourself in a stated refusal. For example, "The request must be denied" is better than "*Your* request must be denied" or "*I* must deny *your* request." This latter type of reference tends to personalize the refusal, a negative act, and can put the reader on the defensive or leave you looking like a villain of some sort.

Offer the Reader an Alternative

Even if you are unable to fulfill a request, you might still help your reader. For example, suppose you own a wholesale shoe business. You sell shoes to retailers who then sell them directly to consumers. One day you receive a letter from a man who says he has seen some shoes in the window of your store and wants to buy them even though it said on the door, "Wholesale Only." He wonders if you might make an exception. In reply, you write a letter saying that you only sell to retailers. After declining his request, however, you do include the name, address, and telephone number of a local retailer who sells your shoes. In this instance, you are making a *referral*, sending the reader to someone else who might help him.

How can offering an alternative improve an unfavorable news message?

Similarly, you might also offer *substitutions*, *compromises*, or *alternative methods or procedures* when appropriate. Providing readers with options—offering recourses—increases goodwill. Also, it may increase your profits, as when a once refused customer uses you for another project or recommends you to someone else because you are "a person who takes time to help."

Writing Closing Statements

Recently, the head of personnel for a high-technology company revealed that she received nearly 200,000 job applications in a single year. Her department, she continued, handled refusals with extreme care. Asked why, she said, "Casually handled, they can translate into untold losses to us in customers and sales. We really watch ourselves here. Our goal is to have the people we can't find jobs for know the reasons for our decision and still feel good about us." In this context, closing statements are especially important because they are the final impression you make on the reader.

Why are closing statements especially important?

The following suggestions may help in creating them:

1. *Be positive.* Like all openings, all closings should be positive in every message you write. In negative messages, a positive closing is absolutely essential to counteract the refusal itself.
2. *Emphasize goodwill.* Include a goodwill gesture by focusing on a positive aspect of the subject.
3. *Use the reader's viewpoint.* Write from the reader's viewpoint using words like "you" and "your." Imagine yourself to be the reader of your message as a way of avoiding offense.

4. *Make your words flow smoothly.* A smooth word flow keeps attention and implies confidence in yourself. If you achieve this type of flow, your reader will not only pay careful attention, but also will be less likely to question your decision.

The following are some examples of effective closing statements:

Good luck with your project. I believe you will really enjoy working with Mary Davis.

All models listed in the enclosed brochure have the same features as the XTC-1000 VCR. After you have reviewed our literature, please call John Willis on our sales staff at 000-0000 with your questions. When the cold weather arrives, you should be sitting in your warm home, watching your favorite movie on your new VCR.

Next month marks your tenth year with our company. Because you have maintained a safe driving record during the entire time, we are able to reduce your insurance premium by 20 percent. Congratulations on your good driving.

During our Thanksgiving Jubilee, the SpeedEasy washer and dryer that interested you will go on sale. So we look forward to seeing you again the week of November 20. Meanwhile, enjoy the many conveniences featured in your new SpeedEasy refrigerator.

Please continue reviewing those company policies you feel need to be strengthened. With the concern of employees such as yourself, our company will meet the demands of a competitive industry.

WRITING SPECIFIC TYPES OF UNFAVORABLE NEWS LETTERS AND MEMOS

The following typical business situations may require you to send unfavorable news: requests for information or assistance, order problems, claims or adjustments, requests for extension of credit, and requests for changes in policies or procedures.

Refusing Requests for Information or Assistance

What will be the subject of half or more of your unfavorable news messages?

Do you know that half—or even more—of the unfavorable messages you will write in business will consist of refusals to give information or assistance? (If you are already a manager, notice how often you write such refusals.) The reason is simple: the needs of customers, clients, and business associates often differ from your own. Luckily, many of the problems are small enough to enable you to work the problem out to everyone's satisfaction. Whether the refusal will cause much or little grief, the tone of your writing should remain the same, reflecting a professional, yet willing and cooperative, spirit.

Consider the following draft of a memo to an internal auditor, refusing his request for information about a line of cosmetics. Look for any problems with it you can find.

What about the organization of this first draft makes it deductive?

First Draft

To: Jackson Pallock, Internal Auditor
From: Mabelline Yurich, Sales Supervisor for Cosmetics
Subject: Response to Request for New-Life Cosmetics Sales Records

In reference to your request for last quarter's sales records for our line of New-Life Cosmetics, I am unable to give them to you by March 12 as you requested.

According to Section 6 of our policy manual (copy attached), "only the vice president of sales may release classified sales records internally or externally." Cosmetics sales records are classified. The vice president of sales, Jack Grayson, is vacationing and cannot be reached until he returns to work March 17. Jack's assistant, Ms. Mary Smith, told me that the records that you are desirous of can be sent immediately in toto if Jack approves their release when he returns next Thursday. She asked me to tell you that unfortunately we must hold your request in abeyance until he returns.

I am sorry this happened, Jackson. If you need information on man-hours spent on sales, I can fill the bill now. Otherwise, we will meet your request in due time if it is approved. You'll still have time to complete your audit by March 30, though.

Critique

This memo is incorrectly organized deductively. Consequently, the refusal becomes a rebuff. The direct quote from the policy manual is so objective as to be cold. After it, the apology in the closing paragraph sounds false. Finally, the closing sentence is presumptuous and seems particularly insensitive given the reader's very legitimate needs.

The following are some specific problems:

1. "In reference to your request" is wordy and a cliché. (line 1)
2. Jack Grayson is not referred to as "Mr.," whereas Mary Smith is referred to as "Ms." The contrasting usage may be interpreted as being sexually biased. "Man-hours" is definitely sexually biased. (lines 7, 9, and 15, respectively)
3. "Are desirous of" is formal as well as wordy. (line 10)
4. Saying the records can be sent "immediately" is vague; some people don't interpret the word to mean "now." (line 10)
5. "In toto" is a foreign expression that is unnecessary because an American term can easily be substituted. (line 10)

6. The connective "unfortunately" contributes to the negative tone. (line 12)
7. "Hold your request in abeyance" is too formal as well as wordy. (line 12)
8. "Sorry" contributes to the negative tone and also seems insincere. The writer apologizes for something she cannot control. (line 14)
9. "Fill the bill" is a figurative cliché. (line 15)
10. "In due time" is vague. (line 16)

Figure 9-2 shows a revised draft of the memo.

Most often, when would you have to refuse assistance?

Refusing assistance is much like refusing information. Usually, assistance is refused for one or more of the following reasons: it would take too much time, it would cost too much money, or the person addressed does not know how to help or is unable to do so for some other reason.

The following letter of refusal represents a rejection for assistance; in this case, the writer cannot speak at an insurance club meeting. Do you see any problems with it?

First Draft

Dear Mrs. Winokur:

I received your request directed to my secretary that I come speak to your insurance club on March 10, which was received with warmest regards.

I was in an insurance club such as yours when I was in college, so I want you to know that I think well of them. Insurance is the name of the game in business today, and I am thoroughly excited about seeing graduates such as you prepare for service in the field. People who get into this field will surely find that it is right for them and will find it much more rewarding than they had imagined beforehand.

I do hope that you will be able to find someone to speak at your meeting. I will be in Omaha, Nebraska, the entire week of March 10 and therefore cannot be with you at the same time. You'll find somebody, I know, because many insurance agents are interested in college insurance club members just as I am. Our district manager in Richmond, Mary Cox, may consent to do it, so why don't you call her?

By the way, we have the right insurance policy for you should you ever decide that you want outstanding coverage designed to meet your specific needs. Good luck with your projects.

Cordially yours,

To: Jackson Pallock, Internal Auditor

From: Mabelline Yurich, Sales Supervisor for Cosmetics

Date: March 5, 19--

Subject: Response to Request for Cosmetics Sales Records

Mary Smith and I have reviewed your request to see last quarter's New-Life Cosmetics sales records by March 12. She is an assistant to Jack Grayson, Vice-President of Sales.

Mary and I checked Section 6 of our policy manual and confirmed that Jack must give permission for any internal or external release of classified records. All cosmetics sales records are classified. At this time, Jack is vacationing and cannot be reached until he returns to work March 17. Mary said these records are complete, though, and can be sent to you the day Jack returns if he approves their release.

Should you need any unclassified records to help finish your audit on time, I can send them now. Records such as those of staff hours spent on selling cosmetics are unclassified. Just call me at Extension 0000 if this material will help.

FIGURE 9-2 Memo refusing information (in mailable form).

Critique

What on earth could make a letter "pseudo-hip"?

Although the writer's style is informal enough, but not too informal, his or her tone ranges from pompous to patronizing to "pseudo-hip." The following are some specific problems:

1. The letter is not inductively organized. The refusal, which is implied and stated, precedes the reason for it. This order should be reversed. (lines 11–13)
2. The opening statement, "I received your request," states the obvious. In the same sentence, "which was received with warmest regards" is misplaced; "with warmest regards" is also an outdated expression. (lines 1 and 2, respectively)
3. Overuse of the word "I" focuses attention on the writer instead of the reader. (lines 1, 4, 5, 6, 11, 12, 14, and 15)
4. "I want you to know" is preachy and should be deleted. (line 5)
5. "Thoroughly excited" is an overstatement and should be toned down or omitted. (line 6)
6. "Will surely find," "will find it much more rewarding than they had imagined," and "you'll find somebody, I know" are presumptuous and should be omitted. (lines 8, 9, and 14, respectively)
7. "I do hope" is insincere, and the reader may interpret it as expressing doubt rather than encouragement. (line 11)
8. Following a poorly handled refusal, the attempt at sales promotion in the last paragraph will probably anger the reader. (lines 18–20)
9. "Good luck with your projects"—the closing sentence—changes the thought flow abruptly; some readers may find it flippant as well. (line 20)

The following is a revised draft:

Revised Draft

Dear Mrs. Winokur:

Beta Eta Xi is an outstanding insurance organization, and I appreciate your invitation to speak at your career-day program this year. The schedule of activities you sent looks both appropriate and timely.

On March 10, the day your program is being held, I will be in Omaha, Nebraska, attending a seminar on changes in insurance laws. These changes affect our policy writing procedures here at the Williamsburg Agency, so we need to know about them to serve our clients' insurance needs properly.

Mary Cox, our district manager in Richmond, is an excellent speaker. I talked with her last Friday about your needs, and she said she will be glad to speak to your group. Ms. Cox lives in Richmond, so it will cost nothing for her to speak at your seminar. If you agree with this choice, just call Ms. Cox at 000-0000 by February 15 to give her time to prepare thoroughly. Whenever you need further support with your programs, write us or call at 000-0000. We will gladly do whatever we can to assist.

Cordially yours,

Handling Problems with Orders for Goods or Services

What are some of the problems you face when handling orders?

If you receive an order you cannot fill, the prospective buyer deserves to know why. Problems with orders include cancellations, substitutions, and back orders or delays. When you can, offering a substitute may be your best option. This substitute should be closely equivalent in quality and price to the original order.

If your best substitute is not equivalent, then consider delaying delivery until you can provide the original goods or services. Such a delay should be reasonable—two weeks, perhaps three or four, depending on the buyer's needs. Also, if you offer a substitute or a delay, permit the buyer to accept or reject the offer.

Finally, you may cancel the order completely. Although this may be necessary, it is the least effective option. If, however, you must cancel, refer your customer to an alternative source if possible, giving the full name, address, and telephone number of the other supplier.

The following is a letter refusing part of an order of merchandise:

First Draft

Dear Mr. Royalton:

We wish to say that we appreciate your order Number 8181, which we are now attempting to fill.

We can't send the Jamaican ginger, however, because it is out of stock at the moment; but we do have everything else on the order. We're going ahead and shipping the remainder of the order this afternoon. Because Jamaican ginger is the best available and many customers will buy only that type, we feel it the better part of wisdom not to substitute another type.

We will have another supply of Jamaican ginger within 30 days, and we will ship it at that time unless we hear otherwise. We will gladly substitute Indian or American ginger or will send a 30-day supply to last until the Jamaican ginger arrives. If either option is preferred, call us toll free at 1-800-000-0000. We will be most happy to follow your instructions to the letter.

Yours truly,

Critique

The writer fails to include the good news—that the company is shipping everything *except* the Jamaican ginger. Nor is the letter written, as it should be, from the reader's viewpoint. In several places, the writer might easily have substituted "You" for "we" (see lines 9–10, for example). Another problem is that the refusal precedes the reasons for it; in other words, the organization is deductive instead of inductive. Some specific problems are

1. The writer fails to say how the order is being shipped or how quickly the substitute can be sent.
2. "We wish to say that" and "going ahead and" are wordy and may be omitted. (lines 1 and 5, respectively)
3. "Which we are now attempting to fill" expresses unnecessary doubt instead of confidence and should be modified. (line 1)
4. "At the moment" is wordy, a cliché, and should be omitted. (line 4)
5. "Better part of wisdom" and "to the letter" are figurative clichés and should be deleted. (lines 7 and 13)
6. "Be most happy" is an undesirable colloquialism. (line 13)

The following is a revised draft:

Revised Draft

Dear Mr. Royalton:

Your purchase order Number 8181 is now being filled and the goods will be shipped this afternoon by Paulus Freight Lines. Thank you for placing your order with us.

Because of a rainy harvest season, our fall supply of Jamaican ground ginger has been delayed 30 days. Since our stock of this ginger is now depleted, this part of your order will be delayed until the new shipment arrives. Since many of our clients' customers will buy only Jamaican ginger, we are reluctant to ship another type.

Your ginger will be shipped by April 30. If you prefer, however, you can have Indian or American ginger shipped now. You may order a 30-day supply of either or you may substitute the order entirely. If one of these options is better for you than waiting until April 30, please call us toll free at 1-800-000-0000. We will ship the order prepaid by air express within 24 hours after receiving your instructions.

Yours truly,

Refusing Claims or Adjustments on Goods or Services

Does the strategy change if you are rejecting only part of a claim?

If you have to reject a claim entirely, follow the inductive method of organization. But what if you are only rejecting part of it? Then, still follow the same strategy. You may feel that you will never have to write such a letter or memo. However, most people in business do send them occasionally. For example, real estate dealers and supervisors in utility companies sometimes have to refuse to return nonrefundable deposits or fees.

The following is a letter refusing to grant an insurance policy claim. Do you see any problems in it?

First Draft

Dear Mr. Chan:

We were informed by you this morning that you are requesting an additional $500 as reimbursement compensation for repairs to your sports car, which is insured with this business concern.

All Ways Insurance is always willing to ascertain information from clients to help the company make just and fair decisions on claims. Your case is no exception. Upon inspection of your Fiat sports car last month after the accident but prior to the repairs, our appraiser estimated that the damage could be repaired for the amount of $1500. She recommended three shops that would fix your car for that amount but told you that you could have it repaired wherever you like as long as the cost did not exceed our estimate, and I received notification from Jiffy Automobile Repairs who stated that they had given you a $1500 estimate. Therefore, pursuant to the regulations of our policies in handling claims, you became the party responsible for paying the override when you had the car repaired at Old Faithful Repair Studios. All Ways Insurance Company denies your request.

Your business heretofore has been appreciated. Call on us whenever we can be of assistance again.

Sincerely yours,

Critique

The letter's formal style creates a message that is stiff and detached. Moreover, it is unresponsive, blunt, and self-centered. The writer blames the reader for the problem and thinks that the reader should handle it, not the insurance company.

The following are some specific problems:

1. "Informed," "business concern," "ascertain," and "prior to" are too formal and should be omitted. (lines 1, 3, 4, and 7, respectively) So are "received notification," "pursuant to," "party," and "heretofore." They should be omitted as well. (lines 11, 13, 14, and 17, respectively)

2. The opening statement is obvious. (lines 1–3)
3. "Reimbursement compensation" and "just and fair" are redundant. (lines 2 and 5, respectively)
4. The first and second sentences in the second paragraph imply that the company always does the right thing. (lines 4–6)
5. "Your case is no exception" is insulting. (line 5)
6. The third and fourth sentences in the second paragraph are too long; the fourth also rambles. (lines 6–12)
7. "For the amount of" is wordy. (line 8)
8. Avoid the use of "policies" in a letter; policies are internal, not external, guidelines. For that reason, the same term may be used in memos. (line 13)
9. The refusal is too close to the end of the letter to permit the reestablishment of a good tone. (lines 13–16)
10. "Override" is jargon. (line 14)
11. The refusal in the last two sentences in the second paragraph is too direct: "you became the party responsible" and "denies your request." (lines 14–16) Also, these clauses repeat the refusal; both statements are not needed.
12. The closing sentence probably will evoke anger; in large part, this is because of poor writing earlier in the letter. (line 17)

Revised Draft

Dear Mr. Chan:

We were glad to learn that your Fiat has been repaired and that you are again able to drive it to work.

When our appraiser, Judy Nix, inspected the damage to your car on August 1, she estimated that it could be repaired for $1500. She then gave you a check for that amount and recommended three shops that would fix the car. When the managers of the three shops sent us copies of their estimates, we saw that Jiffy Auto Service offered to repair your Fiat for $1488. Had you been unable to get your car fixed for $1500, we would have reappraised the damage to see whether payment of an override was justified.

You will still continue receiving the $50 yearly "safe driver" deduction given those like you who have not caused an accident. Then, next year, you will be eligible for a $100 deduction if this safe driving record continues.

The enclosed pamphlet, just published by the American Driving Association, gives tips for long-distance traveling by car. Because you do travel regularly in your work, I thought you would enjoy reading it.

Sincerely yours,

Refusing Claims or Adjustments Against the Company

What types of claims are internal and therefore are made in memos rather than letters?

In addition to claims on goods or services, people may make claims directly against a company from within it or outside it. Thus, in answering them, you will either write letters or memos. Claims from outside the company vary widely as to type, depending on the nature of the business. While the same is true inside the company, two common topics are requests by employees for reimbursement of travel expenses and for compensation for on-the-job injuries and personal losses.

If a refusal involves legal issues—such as a client under contract requesting money he or she claims an entitlement to—a lawyer should represent your company's interests. But when claims violate company procedures or policies, a financial officer is usually the one to refuse to grant all or part of it.

What revision suggestions can you make for this refusal to grant a claim for travel expenses?

First Draft

To: Mark Johnson, Salesperson
From: Maria Cillias, Controller
Subject: Reimbursement for Travel Expenses

As per your request, we are processing your request for reimbursement of travel expenses for your December 2 to 5 trip to Denver.

Your attention is called to two items for which you are seeking reimbursement: tolls and taxicab fares. You listed tolls totaling $10.50 and taxicab fares totaling $27.50 on the request form but neglected to enclose receipts for these expenses. Company rules require that receipts be attached to the form for all expenses for which you seek reimbursement except meals and tips.

To facilitate reimbursement of your travel expenses, will you kindly advise us whether you can furnish these receipts. When you comply with this constraint, we will reimburse you without further delay.

Critique

This memo's style is stilted and its tone too negative. Some specific problems are

1. "As per your request" and "your attention is called to" are wordy clichés, and should be deleted (lines 1 and 3, respectively)
2. "Neglected" accuses the reader of causing the problem. (line 5)
3. "Kindly advise" and "comply with this constraint" are too formal; the latter is also wordy and should be omitted. (lines 9 and 10, respectively)
4. "Facilitate" is too abstract and should be omitted. (line 9)

5. "Without further delay" is both vague and a cliché and should be deleted. (line 11)

The following is a revised version of this memo, written in a less formal style and a more positive tone:

Revised Draft

To: Mark Johnson, Salesperson
From: Maria Cillias, Controller
Subject: Response to Request for Travel Expense Reimbursement

Your request for reimbursement of travel expenses for your December 2–5 trip to Denver is now being reviewed for processing.

In looking over the form you submitted for reimbursement, we noted that you listed tolls and taxicab fares, but no receipts were attached. Company procedures require that receipts be submitted for all refunded expenses except meals and tips. Will you please send us the receipts for $10.50 in tolls and $27.50 in taxicab fares. Then, we can send you a check for $56.35, the full amount of your request.

We will issue your reimbursement check within two days after receiving the receipts.

Refusing to Extend Credit Terms

Have you ever refused credit terms to anyone? If so, how did you go about doing it?

Suppose you are a furniture dealer and you have just reviewed a request by a young married couple for an installment loan. The loan will finance some furniture they want to buy for their first home. In investigating their financial situation, you see they are already extended. So, reluctantly, you decide to refuse the sizable loan they requested. According to current disclosure laws, you need to give the applicants a complete explanation of why you are refusing credit. How should you organize the letter and write it?

The following letter is addressed to the young couple refusing their request. An alternative—a smaller loan—is offered that can help them, yes, but it can help you as well. Look at this first draft to see if it has any problems:

First Draft

Dear Mr. and Mrs. Mertz:

I do trust that you are enjoying your new Chesapeake living room suite that you bought from us last month. Let us know if it doesn't meet your expectations.

When I learned that you plan to furnish your apartment as soon as you can save the money, I suggested that you apply for credit with us so that you could furnish the entire apartment now. Your decision to do so seemed wise then.

8 Your credit application has been reviewed according to our modus
operandi. Your credit rating and credit references are favorable,
10 although combined together you have bought little on credit in the
past. However, your present debt-to-income ratio is too high to allow us
12 to give you $5000 installment credit as you requested.

You are eligible for $2000 credit, though, according to the above-
14 mentioned plan. Is that suitable? If it is, come in after the conclusion of
any workday and buy whatever you wish as long as it doesn't exceed
16 $2000. At your convenience choose that new bedroom suite, or what-
ever, pursuant to this agreement.

Sincerely yours,

Critique

On the surface, this letter seems inductively organized, but a closer scrutiny reveals that it is really deductively structured. Moreover, the general tone is negative. After reading it, the couple will probably never want to do any business with this furniture dealer again.

The following are some of the letter's problems:

1. The verb "trust" immediately implies doubt about whether the Mertzes are enjoying their new living room furniture. So does "let us know if it doesn't meet your expectations." (lines 1 and 2, respectively)
2. "Your decision to do so seemed wise then" implies prematurely that the credit will be refused. Such a clear hint destroys the inductive organization. Although more explicitly repeated later, this first refusal precedes the reasons for it. (line 6)
3. "Modus operandi" is a Latin term and should be omitted and an American phrase substituted. (line 8)
4. The clause "although combined together you have bought little on credit in the past" is a negative reminder with "combined together" being a redundancy. Since the couple's credit rating and references are favorable, the writer should avoid any mention of such negative considerations. (line 10)
5. "Debt-to-income ratio" is financial jargon that customers may not understand. (line 11)
6. "Above-mentioned" and "pursuant to this agreement" are too formal. (lines 13 and 17, respectively)
7. "After the conclusion of" is wordy and should be shortened. (line 14)
8. "Is that suitable" is a negative suggestion; "as long as it doesn't exceed $2000" and "pursuant to this agreement" are negative reminders in this context, reprimanding the readers without cause. (lines 14, 15, and 17, respectively)

9. "At your convenience" is vague and a cliché. (line 16)
10. The last paragraph leaves the impression that the writer doesn't really need the couple's business, in which case the couple should have been refused credit completely. If, on the other hand, the writer does want their business, the paragraph should include special terms and a strong appeal to buy.

The following is a revised draft of this letter:

Revised Draft

Dear Mr. and Mrs. Mertz:

Your application for a $5000 installment loan to buy furniture from us has been reviewed by Joan Lanham, our credit supervisor. Thank you for making the application.

Ms. Lanham first checked each of your credit ratings and found them favorable. Next, she checked your credit references and found them favorable also. Then, she compared your monthly expenses with your monthly incomes. This comparison showed that your monthly expenses of $1200 leaves you $175 when deducted from your $1375 monthly income after deductions. A $5000 loan at 18 percent annual interest for 48 months would cost you $187 monthly, $12 more than you have left after paying the bills. Based on these figures, you would be unable to assume payment of a $5000 loan.

You are eligible, however, for a $2000 loan at 18 percent annual interest for 48 months. On this loan, your monthly payment would be only $75. We encourage you to accept this loan so that you can purchase many of the furnishings you want now. If you accept this agreement, we will gladly review your application after 24 months to see if you are eligible for an additional loan then.

The Chesapeake bedroom suite you looked at last month is on sale now at 20 percent off—a $400 savings. This classic suite will match perfectly the living room suite you bought from us last month. Please stop by the store this week after work to take advantage of this offer, which expires Saturday. We are open Monday through Saturday until 9 P.M.

Sincerely yours,

Refusing Requests for Changes in Policies or Procedures

How do policies and procedures differ?

Policies are guidelines set by the company for conducting business. For example, one company may require a two-year wait before an employee is eligible for a paid vacation, whereas another may offer it the first year. Procedures are the methods the company uses to put its policies into effect. For example, one company may ask that its employees fill out a vacation request form two weeks before the anticipated time away. Others may merely require that you tell your boss when you want to take time off. Changes in policies always require the consent of the company's officers, perhaps even the board of directors if it is a corporation. Sometimes, changing procedures may also require the consent of company officers. Since changes in procedure and policy are internal issues, all refusals are generally written in memo form.

The following memo refuses a request for a new vacation schedule. Meeting the request would have required a change not only in departmental procedure, but also in company policy as well. Do you see any problems in it?

First Draft

To: Donna Crenshaw, Account Executive
From: Ernest Smithson, Account Supervisor
Subject: Response to Rquest for a Change in the Vacation Schedule

Your trip to Paris sounds exciting. Many people are taking such trips. You want to switch your vacation to June 16 to 30 from May 1 to 15 so you can take the trip. But five people already chose that date. Only five people may vacation at one time.

I checked with everyone in the department. Nobody is willing to change.

I already checked with Mr. Jones to see if we can let you go anyway. He said no.

You may switch to another two-week period. Your parents may change their plans. However, keep your choice between May 16 and August 30. Also, do not choose August 1 to 15.

I must know about any change by March 1, the deadline for setting vacation dates.

Critique

Although the writer has made two attempts to accommodate the reader's vacation plans, his negative tone gives the impression that he really does not care about fulfilling her request. His curtness and inability to express his ideas completely contribute to this impression. Some specific problems are

1. Too many short sentences and paragraphs make the memo sound curt and sometimes insulting.
2. "Many people are taking such trips" and "your parents may change their plans" are both rude and inconsiderate. (lines 1 and 9, respectively)

3. The language about the available vacation dates is confusing. (lines 10–11)

The following is a revised draft of the memo written to clarify the vacation dates and improve the curt tone and incomplete expression of ideas:

Revised Draft

To: Donna Crenshaw, Account Executive
From: Ernest Smithson, Account Supervisor
Subject: Response to Request for a Change in the Vacation Schedule

Your choice to vacation in Paris this summer with your parents does sound exciting. They were thoughtful to invite you to join them.

As we discussed when you chose your vacation dates, only five people in the department may vacation during any two-week period. When I received your request to change your vacation from May 1–15 to June 16–30, I checked to see how many people are scheduled for vacations then. The roster showed that five people had already requested June 16–30.

Next, I asked each of these five people if he or she would make a change. Having planned their vacations already, all of them declined. Then, I asked Mr. Jones if we could make an exception and let you go anyway. He declined, saying it was important that we meet the two-thirds' staffing requirement all summer to serve our customers adequately.

You may reschedule your vacation for another two-week period if that will help. Any other period between May 16 and August 30 is acceptable except August 1–15, when five people are scheduled already. If you wish to make such a change, please tell me before March 1, the deadline for setting this year's dates.

The following checklist should help you to evaluate your first drafts of letters or memos containing unfavorable news. After you have finished the draft, check it against each point on the list. Then, revise accordingly.

CHECKLIST FOR UNFAVORABLE NEWS

1. Ask these questions when you write the opening paragraph of your letter or memo.
   a. Is the buffer statement relevant to the purpose and subject of the letter or memo?
   b. Is the buffer statement positive in tone and content?
   c. Have you avoided implying that a "positive" response follows?

   d. Have you avoided implying or stating a "negative" response?
2. Ask these questions when you write the body of your letter or memo.
   a. Has at least one good reason for refusing been given *before* the unfavorable news?
   b. Have all necessary details and background information been included?
   c. Are answers to direct questions given? Also, are answers to questions not asked but needed included?
   d. Is the tone reader centered, especially in the section where you present the reasons that support the unfavorable news?
   e. Is the negative decision clearly implied or stated?
   f. Is an appropriate alternative offered if possible?
   g. If appropriate, are resale and sales promotion included?
3. Ask these questions when you write the closing paragraph of your letter or memo.
   a. Have all negative references to the problem or decision been avoided?
   b. If any action is to be taken by the reader,
      (1) Is the desired action clearly stated?
      (2) Is the action easy to perform?
      (3) Is the time period for taking the action clearly and courteously stated?
   c. Are insincere statements (such as "When we can be of further assistance, . . ." when you have flatly turned down a request) avoided? Is the letter or memo courteous?
   d. Is goodwill prominent in the tone and content? For example, is any statement of gratitude expressed in the first person, future tense ("I would be grateful . . .")?

SUMMARY

1. Avoid being too indirect and obscure when writing unfavorable news letters and memos. Yet, avoid being too direct and negative. Telling the truth without being blunt or vague works best.
2. Use the following five-step organizational plan for delivering unfavorable news: (a) open with a buffer statement, (b) give reasons for refusing, (c) refuse, (d) give additional reasons for refusing and/or offer an alternative if possible, and (e) close with a positive statement and tone.
3. To reduce the negative effects of refusing requests, avoid being too direct, imply the

refusal whenever possible, and offer the reader an alternative if you can. Implied refusals should be clear, and any alternative offered should be realistic.

4. Types of unfavorable letters and memos include the following: (a) *refusing requests for information or assistance* are written when your needs and interests differ from those of your readers; (b) *handling problems with orders for goods or services* may be written when cancellations, substitutions, and back orders and delays are involved; (c) *refusing claims or adjustments on goods or services* may be written when you deny an adjustment on goods sold or services rendered; (d) *refusing claims or adjustments against the company* may range from personal requests to individual suits against the company for injuries or personal losses; (e) *refusing to extend credit terms* may be written by people who work for lending institutions or branches or for businesses that finance the sale of their own goods or services; and (f) *refusing requests for changes in policies and procedures* usually are written by company lawyers or financial officers.

Review Questions

1. What is the twofold problem with unfavorable news? Explain your answer.
2. What is meant by the statement, "In many instances, putting bad news in the form of letters and memos creates distance between senders and receivers"? Explain your answer.
3. What are the five steps in the unfavorable plan for writing letters and memos? List and briefly discuss each.
4. What does it mean to say that the suggested plan for delivering unfavorable news is "inductive"? What difference does it make whether you use this or some other plan?
5. Briefly, in your own words, explain how you determine whether news is unfavorable?
6. Why must you be especially careful about the content of subject lines in unfavorable messages?
7. What do you think might be the result of being caught "creating a smokescreen" in an opening statement for an unfavorable message.
8. What is your reaction to this statement: "Directness that is 'kind' in the ways just described is the best strategy for delivering bad news." (See page 253)
9. How can you be overly direct when writing refusals? Give an example.
10. Which is better in your opinion, an implied or a stated refusal? Does either or both have drawbacks? Explain your answer.
11. Can you yourself benefit from offering an alternative? If you say yes, give one or more examples. If you say no, defend your answer.
12. Why is it important to write closing statements for unfavorable messages from the reader's viewpoint?
13. What typical business situation might lead to your writing "half or more" of all the unfavorable letters and memos you write? Why do you think this is so?
14. What types of problems may cause you to write an unfavorable letter about orders for goods or services?
15. How do policies and procedures differ? Describe a situation in which you may have to write an unfavorable memo about one or the other, or both.

Exercises

1. Your company just received a request from the Neighborhood Beautification Committee of Wentswood. The committee is asking that all businesses in Wentswood erect fences around their buildings and repave their parking lots. You believe that the committee is doing a good job. However, you must decline this request. You did repave your parking lot last year, but erecting a fence is too expensive for you to do at this time. Write a letter refusing the request. Address: Neighborhood Beautification Committee of Wentswood; 1001 Dennison Parkway; Wentswood, Kentucky 00000.
2. You work for WRSF-AM radio station as an advertising account executive. John Williams, the president of Parkersburg Civic Club, wrote the station manager asking that someone speak to the club. The topic is radio advertising, and the presentation is to be made at the next monthly meeting. The station manager asked you to do it, but you will be in Charleston on business at the time of the meeting. No one else at the station can do it either. The club is one of the most prominent organizations in the city, and the station would have gained valuable public relations if you could have made the presentation. Write a letter explaining the situation. Address: John Williams; 1267 Lapsburg Highway; Parkersburg, West Virginia 00000.
3. You work as a marketing representative for Duxbury Computer Company. Recently, you sold a new computer system to Total Automobile Parts Company. As a part of the sales agreement, you agreed to train one of the firm's employees to use the equipment. Then today you received a letter from Total's president asking you to train three of that firm's employees. Besides not having agreed to do this, you have no available training spaces. Write a letter refusing the request. Address: Lydia Perkinson, President; Total Automobile Parts Company; 88 Lyons Parkway; Savannah, Georgia 00000.
4. You manage the mail-order department for a large retail merchandising firm. Each year, you publish an expensive catalog of your merchandise. Five years ago, you had to begin charging $2.00 for copies of the catalog to recover some of the expense of producing it. This year, the cost went to $7.00, and you wrote all your catalog customers telling them about the increase. Yesterday, you received a request for a new catalog from a customer accompanied by a $2.00 check. You must refuse the request and ask for an additional $5.00. If you prefer, return the $2.00 check and ask for a $7.00 check. Address: Mabel Kowalski; 188 Philadelphia Street; Pittsburgh, Pennsylvania 00000.
5. You buy merchandise and equipment for Tas-T Bakery in Lima, Ohio. This year, you asked for bids for 50 delivery trucks. The successful bidder was a firm in New York City, and you placed the order last month for delivery in four months. Now a new competitor has taken so much of your business that sales are off 25 percent. So you believe it wise to buy only 25 delivery trucks at this time. Perhaps you will be able to order the other 25 next year. Send a letter to New York to tell them the news. Address: Tom Brownlee Auto Mart; 413 East 121 Street; New York, New York 00000.
6. You own and manage the Bestways Tax Service, a firm that prepares both individual and business tax returns. Most of

your business comes from individuals, and your busiest season is January through April. In January, you receive a letter from a local home for senior citizens (men and women ages 65 and older). The supervisor of the home requests that you give free tax counseling in February and March to 50 residents of the home. The commitment will require about 200 work hours for your seven tax counselors. Write a refusal letter in which you include at least one alternative. Address: Brenda Bushway, Supervisor; Bozeman Home for Senior Citizens; 888 Stafford Street; Bozeman, Montana 00000.

7. As sales manager for Lucky People Fashions, you offer a close-out sale of your slow-selling merchandise each year. Your inventory space at the factory is too small to allow you to store this merchandise. This year, you offered a 50 percent discount on men's jackets and pants with the agreement that no merchandise could be returned. Today, you received a letter requesting permission to return six dozen Number 5768 Trimline jackets that a customer was unable to sell. Write a refusal letter. Address: Johnny L. Davenport, Manager; Paris Best Fashions; 2424 Lawrence Avenue; Topeka, Kansas 00000.

8. You are sales manager for Computerville, a local dealer specializing in microcomputer sales. Last month, one of your representatives sold an Orange III microcomputer to a restaurant in the city. Two weeks ago, one of your technicians went to the restaurant to repair the microcomputer, which had broken down. Your sales agreement with the customer reads that a customer will not tamper with the machine when it breaks down but will call the company to send a technician to repair it. The technician saw that the casing on the machine had been pried open and that the seal was broken. She told the restaurant owner that this violated the sales agreement and left a bill for $200 for repairs. Today you received a letter from the customer saying that the guarantee is still effective and that he will not pay the bill. Write a letter refusing to cancel the debt and include a copy of the sales agreement. Address: Hugh M. Willoughby, Owner; Round-O-Loin Steak Restaurant; 411 North Gates Avenue; Rochester, New York 00000.

9. You manage a local retail credit company. Two weeks ago, a young couple came into your office. They plan to add a room onto their home for a child they are expecting in six months. You saw that they really wanted the new room, so you asked them to complete a credit application. When you checked their credit references, you learned that they have made payments on some accounts as much as 120 days late. Write a letter refusing to lend them the $5000 they want. Address: Judy and Glen Pearson; 45244 Huntington Beach Boulevard; Long Beach, California 00000.

10. You own your own vehicle leasing company. Four years ago, a friend who lives in another state bought a new van from you on a lease/option agreement. While he did make the payments, he sometimes paid as much as 90 days late. The debt has now been paid, but it cost you in both interest and stress. Now, he has written you with plans to buy a camper. Write him a letter that will refuse the request but maintain your friendship. Address: Jerome Topping; 906 West Avenue; Lewiston, Maine 00000.

11. You own and manage a plumbing supplies company. Recently, you granted credit to a new customer, Wellsville Fixtures Company. Your decision was based

on information supplied by Wellsville. Although your credit check did not uncover a problem, you learned by chance that this company's manager gave you false information about having bought merchandise on credit terms before. As yet, Wellsville has not purchased anything on credit terms from a supplier. Write a letter retracting the offer to sell goods on credit terms. Ask that the firm buy from you for cash. Address: Walter Roush, Manager; Wellsville Fixtures Company; 105 North Lane; Wellsville, New York 00000.

12. You work for a large paper manufacturer as personnel director. One morning, Percy Hamberg, an employee, came into your office and asked for information about another employee who wants to buy a sailboat from him. He wants to know if the other employee can afford to pay for the sailboat and asks about the man's income. You tell Percy that the information is confidential and refuse to disclose it. This week, you received a memorandum from the same employee making the same request. Write Percy Hamberg telling him once again that the information is confidential.

13. You are production manager in an office furniture factory. Yesterday, you received a memorandum from the marketing manager, J. Terence Moore, asking that you manufacture 475 Scepter desk chairs for next month's promotional sale. Your stock of the special aluminum alloy needed to make the chairs is depleted; a new supply will arrive in three months. Write a memorandum explaining the situation. Offer to make the chairs from steel alloy stock that you do have in inventory.

14. As vice president for a large investment company, you just received a request from the supervisor of the word processing center, Baxter Lanager. He tells you that the center's work load is two weeks behind schedule. One answer is to allow employees to work on weekends, which they will do if paid double-time wages. Your company has always had a policy of never paying double-time wages. Also, you think it will set an example that employees in other departments might expect to follow if you grant this permission. You are willing to hire additional temporary employees if the supervisor can document the problem. Write a refusal memorandum.

15. As president of an automobile parts manufacturer, you received a memorandum today from Laura P. Zeigler, an assembly-line employee. Last month, she tore her work uniform on a piece of equipment on the assembly line. She asked her supervisor to pay for a replacement. The supervisor refused, saying that the equipment is safe and that the tear must have been caused by carelessness. Write a memorandum to the employee telling her that the authority to make such a decision has been delegated to her supervisor. However, you will ask one of the vice presidents to discuss the incident with her supervisor.

16. Your fraternity has just received a request from a local volunteer rescue squad station to participate in a fund-raising event for the American Cancer Society. The members of the rescue squad plan to sell Brunswick stew to the public on Saturday, October 20. To prepare the stew, at least 15 people are needed to stir it, beginning Friday night, October 19, at 11 P.M. and continuing until 7 A.M. the following morning. Your fraternity has a history of contributing time and energy to various fund-raising projects. On this weekend, however, you have a banquet and awards ceremony on Friday night

and a formal dance on Saturday night. Write a letter refusing the request. Address: Will Johnson, Chief; Lee Hill Rescue Squad; 2120 Lee Hill Drive; Eugene, Oregon 00000.

17. As general manager of Commonwealth Microfilm Systems, a firm that sells and services microfilm equipment, you must renew the annual service contract of one of your largest and most important customers. This customer has recently been complaining about excessive equipment breakdowns, which he attributes to the poor performance of your service department. After investigating his complaints, you discovered that the second shift has been operating the equipment, and the additional usage has increased breakdowns. To service the equipment properly under these conditions, you must allocate 10 additional service hours per week to the account, and you must increase your spare parts inventory by 20 percent. To cover these costs, you must raise the price of your service contract from $10,000 a year to $14,000 a year. Write a letter to the company: explain the high rate of equipment failure, and tell them of the new service contract price. Address: Paul Jones, Manager; Beltway Research Group; 1010 Lee Highway; Arlington, Virginia 00000.

18. You are a professional recruiter in the Employment Services Department of Northeastern Electric and Power Company. Your vice president of personnel brings you the resume and transcripts of his friend's daughter. She graduated with a 2.1 grade-point average (on a 4.0-point scale); her resume does not show any involvement in extracurricular activities. Although you feel some pressure to accommodate a friend of your vice president, you have no positions for which this person qualifies. Write a letter for the signature of your vice president, saying you currently have no job openings. Address: Jane Wright; 15 Lakewood Drive; Manhattan, Kansas 00000.

19. You are the general marketing manager for Interpace Corporation, a manufacturing concern located in Princeton, New Jersey. John Scott, an employee with five years of service, recently transferred into your department. He had been attending school at night for the past two years, working toward a B.S. degree in marketing. The corporate benefit package has always reimbursed employees for courses that relate directly to the job or apply to a specific job-related degree. But you recently received a memo from the company personnel director outlining changes in the educational reimbursement program. Effective immediately, the company will only pay for courses that directly relate to the job. You also recently received a standard approval form from John, listing the courses he selected for the upcoming semester: marketing management and organic chemistry. Write a memorandum to John, telling him of the new policy. Tell him that the company will not pay for the chemistry course but will pay for the management course.

20. You are the contracts manager for the Florida Department of Highways. Each month, you open highway construction projects for competitive bidding by contractors and award projects to the lowest bidder. Before advertising projects, you calculate a confidential cost estimate for each one, and if the low bid exceeds this estimate, you refuse to award the job. On Project 409-85, the lowest bid exceeded the cost estimate. Write a letter to the lowest bidder refusing the bid but asking him to submit another bid when the job is advertised again next month. Address:

Bob Jones, President; Jones Construction Company; 1070 Willis Circle; Pensacola, Florida 00000.

21. You are a claims representative for an insurance company. At the beginning of the month, you received a questionable claim. A man who does roofing work slipped while on the job and broke his leg. Upon investigating the incident, you discovered that the claimant has a history of drinking on the job. According to three witnesses, the day he fell was one of those days. Since your company does not cover injuries resulting from intoxication, you will not cover the claim. Medical expenses, lost time on the job, and lost wages are the responsibility of the injured worker. Write a letter denying the claim. Address: Phil Smith; 13 Mill Street; Huntsville, Alabama 00000.

22. As a sales representative for the computer software firm, DiscSales, you just received your annual merit increase. However, you are dissatisfied with the amount. This past year, you assumed additional job responsibilities: you serviced several accounts left unattended by a sales representative who took another job, and you increased the profitability of those accounts. In addition, you regularly attend management development courses in an effort to become a better employee. Write a memo to your supervisor, Jennifer Williams, explaining why you are not completely pleased with your review.

23. As supervisor of New Life Insurance's secretarial force, you have been approached by several typists who want the company to purchase word processing equipment. They claim, and rightfully so, that the present system of typing, proofreading, and retyping entire documents is inefficient. However, the budget for your department was cut as the result of lagging company profits during the first quarter. Although second quarter profits increased, third quarter profits are questionable. Write a memo to your staff explaining that the cut budget does not allow buying new equipment at this time.

24. You own a mail-order book club. Recently, one of your customers has returned several books, claiming that pages come unglued and fall out of the books. With each return, you send the customer a new book. After examining the most recently returned book, you notice that the binding of the book has been abused—as if the reader folds the book in half when reading it. Few books could withstand such treatment. In front of you is another such book from the same customer. Write this individual a letter, refusing to exchange this and any other book that displays marks of improper handling. Address: Todd Winston; 9187 Boca Street; Columbia, Missouri 00000.

25. As one of the largest employers in your area, your company receives dozens of inquiries from students each day. These graduating students are evaluating your firm as a prospective employer. Frequently, students ask about your compensation and benefits package, the components of which are extremely confidential. While being careful not to discourage the interests of these qualified students, explain your situation. Write a form letter refusing such requests but providing an alternative if possible.

CHAPTER 10

WRITING PERSUASIVE LETTERS AND MEMOS

Persuasion is the art of moving people by their own agreement to a belief, position, or course of action. In business, persuasion is either *overt* or *covert*—open or concealed. The salesperson who tells you that a blouse is pure linen and a great buy is openly trying to persuade you to do something—in this case, buy the blouse. Similarly, the boss who calls you in and announces that you are performing below expectations and he or she thinks you have more talent than this is openly trying to persuade you to change your attitude first and then your behavior. So is the co-worker who wants to persuade you to join the union and gives six reasons why you should.

Frequently, however, business persuasion is more subtle. Thus, a salesperson who gives you free instructions on the use of a VCR may be doing so to persuade you to buy one, but never once does he mention this as the purpose. Or your boss may lavishly praise your ability to write reports quickly, expecting to persuade you to volunteer to draft on short notice a report on economy car fuel standards. And the same co-worker who wants you to become a union member may act coldly because you have resisted his or her attempts until now. Although everyone knows that covert persuasion is really a form of manipulation, it often works, as do more overt tactics.

Generally, when persuasion is effective, it is because all participants see the benefit of the changed belief, position, or course of action. For example, Alan Dorsey, an assembly-line worker, raised his performance from substandard to above standard after his boss, Jack Olliff, spoke to him about the raise such a change would bring, which he eventually received. As for the boss, he got better quality work, which resulted in numerous benefits to the department, not the least of which was greater profitability.

What is the evidence that effective persuaders know the person they are trying to change?

Effective persuaders know the person they are trying to change. That is, they see things from his or her viewpoint, and this ability gives their strategy its power. For example, the manager who got his employee to raise his work level appealed to the man's competitiveness and sense of pride, saying that with some work he could be the best performer on the line.

Persuasiveness in business writing works similarly. First, you need to see your request through the reader's eyes. If you were Betty Janes, the assistant vice president of marketing in a large cosmetics firm, how would you react to a request for a more aggressive advertising campaign for a new shampoo? What would be your concerns about such a campaign? your objections? What about it might appeal to you?

In addition, persuasive messages must be specific. Thus Betty Janes wants to know if by aggressive you mean the firm should change the model for its ads? Or do you want more TV instead of magazine coverage?

As you can see, to write effective persuasive messages requires strategy—perhaps as much or more as does writing unfavorable messages. If you don't have a carefully conceived plan of attack, you risk confusing rather than clarifying; you may even turn off the person you are trying to convince. The following discussion explains how to use the various persuasive strategies to achieve your goals.

PLANNING PERSUASIVE LETTERS AND MEMOS

What do the letters A-I-D-A stand for?

The A-I-D-A approach—Attention, Interest, Desire, and Action—serves as an excellent guide to writing persuasive letters and memos. Inductively—indirectly—organized, it allows the writer to justify an action before requesting the reader take it. The subject—the request for action—comes at the end of the letter or memo in this type of inductive design.

Here is how A-I-D-A works:

1. *Open with an attention-getting statement.* The opening statement should arouse the reader's curiosity by relating to an area of interest relevant to him or her. Or it could relate to the person's needs in some way or perhaps be complimentary. Be positive and brief and be sure this opener talks about some aspect of the topic.
2. *Interest the reader in the topic.* Next, use appeals or arguments that will engage the reader's interest in the topic. Focus on a central appeal—the one that will interest your reader the most. Put it first among the appeals, thus emphasizing its importance in the message. Then follow with supporting appeals that act as other selling points.
3. *Build up the reader's desire to act.* After you have captured the reader's interest, keep it by presenting more reasons (supporting appeals) why the actions would benefit him or her. Also, use words and images that enable readers to see themselves enjoying these benefits. If appropriate, anticipate and downplay any obstacles that would prevent the reader from acting, such as a product's high price or low quality.
4. *Close with an action request.* Ask the reader *directly* but courteously to take the desired action. A confident and positive tone shows your certainty that the action is desirable and that it will be taken. Suggest a specific time he or she should act. Then, if needed, make it easy to do by including such inducements as business reply cards, a toll-free telephone number, a coupon, or whatever is appropriate for the situation.

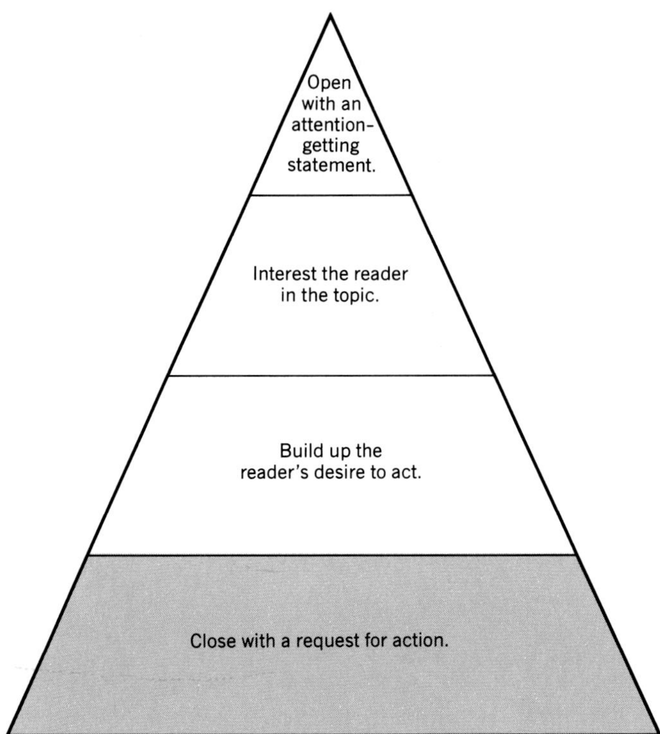

FIGURE 10-1 Diagram of inductive plan for writing persuasive letters and memos.

Is the A-I-D-A plan inductively or deductively organized? How can you tell?

The steps in this indirect—inductive—plan are diagrammed in Figure 10-1. A-I-D-A is no magical plan for success. But if you carefully develop each step and remain aware of the reader's viewpoint, you will most probably write an effective message. Certainly, the ultimate test is whether the reader does what you want. Even better would be action accompanied by these words, "You read my mind!"

The next several sections are meant to help you learn to create that "you read my mind" response. Writing openings is covered first, the appeals (central and supporting), and then closings.

Writing Opening Statements

From writing other messages, you already know that the first statements are critical in gaining rapport and focusing the reader's attention on the subject of your letter or memo. In fact, the opening and closing generally are read very carefully by the reader. Thus, in persuasive messages, the first words of the first statement are the most emphatic, and the closing words in the final statement are next.

What guidelines should you follow in writing opening statements for persuasive messages?

Your first words should signal your genuine interest in the reader. Here are some suggestions for composing opening and closing statements:

1. *Be positive.* Because of its position, the opening statement sets the tone for the entire message. Therefore, use it to stress the positive effect the message's subject will have on the reader. How he or she reacts to your opening statement determines the person's view of the remaining text.
2. *Sound cooperative.* Make your reader feel as if you can easily accommodate diverse interests and needs.
3. *Keep it short.* The reader should be able to identify quickly the subject of the message and the benefits he or she will receive by acting in the desired manner.
4. *Use the reader's viewpoint.* Center your message on the reader's needs and interests, not on your own.

The following are examples of attention-getting opening statements from persuasive messages:

> Have you ever finished reading a new book on management and then suddenly got the message?—The entire volume sums up to be a single blinding flash of the obvious!
>
> You're curious about high technology. You're generally aware and keenly conscious of the need to keep abreast of what's happening across the frontiers of "high tech"—all fields, not just one.
>
> With just a little help from you, we can land a $100,000 sale here in the Topeka office. Here's the situation:
>
> I'll bet it's happened to you at a business meeting . . . or during an employment interview, for certain.
>
> Thanks for your expert leadership. Last month was one of record sales in four of our five divisions.
>
> Have you checked the price stickers in new car showrooms lately? If you haven't, you're in for a surprise—a shocking one!

Each of these examples is effective because the writer has used a positive tone and has focused on the reader's viewpoint. Notice that several are purposefully vague to arouse the reader's curiosity and engage his or her attention. Another device for capturing interest is a humorous opening statement: James Thurber said, "The conclusion you jump to may be your own." But will you take the time now to investigate carefully the career of life insurance sales and service?

The trick in creating an effective opening statement is not to appear to try too hard. The following is an opening that simply yearns for the reader's attention:

> That's right! For the next 30 days only, you can order famous Johnson Company DORA-LIFE DOORMATS at ½ OFF OUR REGULAR PRICE!!!

Can an opening statement be overstated?

Here, too many attempts to catch the reader's interest—large print, underlining, and exclamation points—fight against each other rather than cooperate. The result is the opposite of what the writer desires.

Finally, the style and tone you choose to adopt for opening statements also depends to a large extent on the type of request and the audience. Selling a product or service by mail generally calls for a "jazzier" tone, especially if it's mass produced and therefore less personal, than does a special request for a favor, for instance. Too, the style may be more informal—chattier—when selling a product or service.

Choosing and Writing Persuasive Appeals

Suppose you want to persuade a discount house to take back 1000 lamps you ordered for your office because employees don't seem to be using them. What appeals could you use to persuade the store to make an adjustment? You might appeal to the store's desire to maintain good customer relations. After all, you have bought in bulk in the past and you will continue to use them in the future. Or, you could simply say that for one reason or another, you deserve the adjustment. Here, unlike the appeal to maintaining good customer relations, you are concerned with only your own interests, not those of the store.

Why judge an appeal by looking at it from the reader's viewpoint?

Which of these appeals should you make? In persuasive letters or memos, always look at an appeal from the reader's viewpoint. To be effective, it should seem attractive to his or her interests. Any logical or tasteful reason that will motivate the reader to act on your behalf is appropriate. Any that simply benefits you is not. Naturally, if an appeal benefits both of you, add it to your list. For these reasons, in writing to the store, appeal to their sense of fair play and do not contend you deserve the adjustment.

Also, remember that of all the appeals you can make to readers, self-interest is probably the strongest motivator. So, if possible, focus most on the rewards they will reap in performing the action. Figure 10-2 lists the characteristics of effective persuasive appeals. Depending on the situation, the subject, and your strategy, you can use any item on this list as either a central or a supporting appeal.

Selecting Central and Supporting Appeals

Suppose you own a small investment counseling firm that both advises clients about investments and invests for them. Now you are expanding your services to include tax return preparation and want to write a letter telling your clients of this change. Naturally, you

POSSIBLE APPEALS FOR PERSUASIVE LETTERS AND MEMOS

1. Gaining sense of satisfaction
2. Giving comfort or convenience
3. Saving time, money, effort, or merchandise
4. Creating and maintaining goodwill
5. Increasing health benefits
6. Adding prestige, exclusiveness, or distinction
7. Gaining attractiveness (beauty and style of product, physical appearance)
8. Adding taste or wholesomeness
9. Gaining safety or security
10. Getting durability

FIGURE 10-2 Qualities to consider when writing persuasive appeals.

want to also solicit their tax business. Your list of appeals might include

1. Guaranteed correctness of the returns.
2. Reliability of your service in the past.
3. Knowledge of your clients' financial backgrounds.
4. Efficiency of conducting more financial business in one place.
5. Lower prices than the competition.
6. Quicker service than the competition.
7. Expertise in preparing returns.

Is a central appeal the most persuasive one you can think of?

Of these, which is the most central, that is, the one that is the most persuasive? Your answer might be that some clients would react to one appeal, whereas others may react to another, and so forth. On the other hand, you can't write a separate letter to each client, so you are going to have to choose one of the seven as the appeal that you believe will work best for most clients.

Among the appeals listed, the first and the seventh are necessary to attract any customers at all. However, since all your competitors can make the same offers, neither can constitute your central appeal. In contrast, the second appeal represents an advantage some of your competitors are unable to offer. However, some probably can; for example, a bank. The fifth and sixth appeals are certainly attractive, but clients may consider them important only in combination with other appeals. In contrast, the third and the fourth appeals are each strong incentives that you may offer exclusively. The third seems especially powerful because you already counsel these clients about their investments and invest their money for them. Therefore, you might choose "knowledge of your clients' financial backgrounds" as your central appeal.

Use the same deductive procedure as you just employed to find the best central appeal for every persuasive message you write. In making your choice, think about your clients' or customers' needs and how you can best serve these needs. Of course, you can only know for certain if you have chosen effectively after the receiver responds to your appeal. Nevertheless, this procedure does work, as witnessed by the thousands of business writers around the world who use it daily to great benefit. Problems occur only when you have too little information on which to base your appeal.

Once you have chosen your central appeal, all the others may become supporting appeals, if appropriate. Again, use the deductive approach in judging if appeals are supportive.

For example, in the list you have already examined, the first and seventh appeals are necessary if you want any business and so should be supporting appeals. So should the second and the fourth, because they provide you with an advantage over some, if not all, competitors. As for the fifth and sixth appeals, if your prices are low and your services quick, then include them. But if they are not, don't.

You should be aware that just as you can have too few supporting appeals and be unconvincing, you can have too many. Too many of these appeals lead to an exhausting length and an oversold reader. While this may rarely happen in other situations, it can easily be the case with selling products or services. A good guideline—not a rule—is to limit the supporting appeals to five to seven, at most.

Writing Appeals

The following persuasive appeal is based on the analysis performed in the last section. Notice how the first paragraph develops the central appeal and the second and third paragraphs provide the supporting appeals—all directed to the reader.

Our clients have been asking us to prepare their state and federal tax returns ever since we opened for business in 1980. Many of them tell us that we know more about their financial needs than anyone else and therefore they want us to prepare their tax returns. This makes sense because we do counsel you and our other clients about your financial investments and make investments for you. Your investment portfolio is reviewed weekly in this office, and we can use this up-to-date knowledge of your financial background to determine exactly what tax deductions are available to you.

To make certain that you get the best possible service, Janice Moriarity has joined our staff to work full time in offering this new tax service. Janice has fifteen years' experience in preparing tax returns. She is also a Certified Public Accountant and has a university degree in tax accounting. The correctness of your returns will be guaranteed.

You will get the same reliable service that you have received from us in the past. We will review your tax records each time your investment portfolio is reviewed and will keep all these records in the same file. In addition, you can enjoy the convenience of doing more of your financial business in one place—no more running around the city at tax time to find someone to prepare your returns.

How is an appeal emphasized to make it the central one?

Notice that the central appeal not only appears first but that more is written about it than any of the other appeals. Both its position and the number of words devoted to it emphasize that it is the central appeal. Also notice that the supporting appeals continue its work—persuading the reader to take the action you will request in the closing. If all the appeals do their job, then readers should be ready to do what you suggest by the time you actually request it.

Writing Closing Statements

In closing your message, your reader has a final glimpse of you, your request or offer, and your company. At this point, you either strengthen your grip on the reader or lose it entirely. Use the following recommendations to ensure the effectiveness of your closing statements:

What are the guidelines to follow in writing closing statements for persuasive messages?

1. *Be positive.* Like the opening statement, the one you close with is in an emphatic position. Because the reader sees the closing last, end on a positive note.
2. *Strike a closing tone.* Your closing statement should sound properly final, as though you finished rather than quit. Too often, closings sound chopped off, leaving questions in the reader's mind or leaving him or her to notice that you didn't finish what you were saying.
3. *Sound successful.* To inspire confidence, use expressions that suggest you possess it. (For review, see Chapter 4, particularly.)
4. *Use the reader's viewpoint.* In the end of your message, as in the rest of it, continue to center on the readers' interests and needs.
5. *Request specific actions if appropriate.* If you want readers to take a specific action, make a specific request. For example, ask them to sign and return an enclosed form or call a special number. More often than not, you will also want them to act by a certain date.

Persuasive messages always require a request-for-action closing statement. The following are examples of effective closings:

> Choose from several convenient order plans outlined in the enclosures. Fill in and mail the enclosed order form today!
>
> Will you please call me at Extension 0000 by Monday to give us time to complete all the arrangements for Friday's meeting.

> Call me personally at 000-000-0000 collect, or mail the enclosed postage-paid reply card now, so we can arrange a personal meeting. At that time, we'll be happy to prove how well our system works. You may then have questions, and we'll be glad to give you answers.
>
> Please call or write us with your approval by October 14 to allow time to get the completed program to the printers on schedule. The telephone number is 000-000-0000, and the address is the same as that given in the heading of this letter.
>
> So, please look over what we have to offer. When you're ready to order, please fill in one of the order forms in the back of the catalog and mail it to us with your purchase order. Thank you.

How can you use the imperative mood to write a closing statement for a persuasive message?

Used positively, the imperative mood that people employ to command others, for example, "shut the door," becomes a courteous but vivid request for action. All the examples use the imperative in this way. Thus, "choose from," "fill in and mail," "call me," "call or write," and "look over" are, in the context, not harsh commands but confident requests. When they do sound harsh upon rereading them, soften them a bit by saying "all you need do is fill in and mail" or "just look over." Adding "please" in front of the phrase is sometimes right, too. Remember, though, that too much "softening" can erode the confidence you are showing. "I wonder if you will" is just too soft.

Another tip in writing these closings is to use deadlines, an idea first mentioned in Chapter 7. In persuasion, setting a time or date by which to take an action can motivate the convinced reader to go ahead and do it rather than procrastinate. Through deadlining, you can move this action up on a person's calendar of things to do. Too, when appropriate, offer some incentive to act by a certain date—10 percent off—or justify the deadline you set—in time for start-up of the new program. Reward and reasoning can work wonders.

Putting Together the Complete Message

Now that you have written your appeals and have composed opening and closing statements, you are ready to put them together into a complete persuasive message. Figure 10-3 shows one possible version. Note that the complete message follows the A-I-D-A approach. In all your messages of this sort, follow this general outline.

WRITING SPECIFIC TYPES OF PERSUASIVE LETTERS AND MEMOS

What are the types of persuasive messages managers often write?

Managers commonly write six types of persuasive letters and memos. These are (1) appeals to buy goods or services, (2) appeals by memo that sell services or ideas, (3) special requests for information or

PROFESSIONAL ACCOUNTING, INCORPORATED
9 West Avenue
Overton, MA 00000

November 4, 19--

Mr. Enos Brown
1213 Franklin Drive
Overton, MA 00000

Dear Mr. Brown

Serving your financial needs since 1982 has been a pleasure. Now, there is a way to serve these needs more fully.

Our clients have been asking us to prepare their state and federal tax returns ever since we opened for business in 1980. Many of them tell us that we know more about their financial needs than anyone else and therefore they want us to prepare their tax returns. This makes sense because we do counsel you and our other clients about financial investments and also make investments for you. Your investment portfolio is reviewed weekly in this office, and we can use this up-to-date information to determine exactly what tax deductions are available to you.

To make certain that you get the best possible service, Janice Moriarity has joined our staff to work full-time in offering this new tax service. Janice has fifteen years of experience in preparing tax returns. She is also a Certified Public Accountant and has a university degree in tax accounting. The correctness of your returns can therefore be guaranteed.

You will get the same reliable service that you have received from us in the past. We will review your tax records each time your investment portfolio is reviewed and, in addition, will keep all these records in the same file. You can enjoy the convenience of doing more of your financial business in one place--no more running about town at tax time to find someone to prepare your returns.

Ms. Moriarity is ready now to begin reviewing your investment portfolio, but she needs your permission to go ahead. So that she will have plenty of time to get acquainted with the information in your file and begin studying your needs thoroughly, will you please give us your consent to go ahead by January 1. All you need do is sign the enclosed form and mail it in the attached postage-paid, return-reply envelope.

Sincerely yours

Susan Adams

Susan Adams, President

tt

Enclosure

FIGURE 10-3 Persuasive letter in mailable form.

sistance, (4) requests to grant complex claims, (5) appeals for donations or contributions, and (6) appeals to pay debts. (See Chapter 12 for a discussion of persuasive employment messages.)

Solicited and Unsolicited Appeals to Buy Goods or Services

How does a solicited appeal differ from an unsolicited one?

Letters—and, infrequently, memos—that sell goods or services may be either *solicited* or *unsolicited*. In a solicited sales letter, you respond to inquiries about goods or services, which sets up an invitation to sell. Since readers are already interested, you do not have to worry about getting their attention, except to note what you are responding to in the opening. (Avoid the obvious statement as an opening, though: "this letter is in response to . . .".) You do, however, need to respond positively to each question they ask. This includes any inquiries about real or alleged shortcomings of your product. In such circumstances, if you need to deal with negative information, subordinate it in the discussion. For example, if a customer asks you if your refrigerator has 9 cubic feet of freezer space, but it does not, you might respond: "The KOOL-1 has 8 cubic feet of freezer space, which easily accommodates a family of six" instead of "Our KOOL-1 refrigerator does not have 9 cubic feet of freezer space." As you can see, the first example turns the negative information around by confronting the reader's real concern—whether the refrigerator is big enough for his or her family.

What is direct mail advertising?

In contrast, the unsolicited sales letter avoids any mention of unfavorable information. This written equivalent of the cold sales call is used in situations where you make the *first* contact. The reader has made no prior inquiry. Called *direct-mail advertising*, the unsolicited sales letter is widely used in business. You may at different stages of your career write such requests to millions of people, to small groups such as members of a ski or hiking club, or to individuals. For example, in deciding whether you can afford to advertise your new medical supply business by direct mail, consider the nature and the size of your audience, the type and cost of your products, and the cost of preparing and mailing the letter and any enclosures. Only after weighing each of these factors can you decide whether such a mailing would be profitable.

Defining Your Audience

Suppose you write a letter in which you try to sell the concert violin your small company is producing. You are tailoring your letter to the reader's needs; in addition, you can send the same version of the letter to violinists who belong to the musicians' union because you know that they have basically similar criteria in deciding the kind of instrument they want.

In contrast, when writing to mass audiences, you may need to vary both your central and supporting appeals to suit the special interests of subgroups. Most frequently, it will be your central appeal that you will have to change. For example, suppose you want to sell solar-powered water heaters to homeowners. Members of high-income subgroups may be most interested in the tax deduction they can receive if they buy the heater. If so, then the best central appeal for them is this deduction. In contrast, members of low-income subgroups may be most interested in the money they will save on utility bills by buying it. If so, then the central appeal for them is these savings.

In deciding which appeals works for whom, business communicators evaluate demographic and psychographic factors. In this example, income—a demographic factor—turned out to be instrumental in deciding how to appeal to the various subgroups. (See Chapter 1 for a discussion of the demographic and psychographic factors used in business communication.) Figure 10-4 lists the ten most important.

When you screen an audience, what factors should you consider?

Demographics and psychographics are also useful if you are trying to decide whether to mail a letter to a certain group. Often you can do this by *screening the audience.* Screening assures that a mailing reaches the people who are potential customers. For example, suppose you wish to sell portable radios by mail. First, you might screen an audience to ensure that those to whom you write are adults who are legally obligated to pay for the radios they buy. Next, if owning radios might appeal to people in a certain age group, you might further screen the audience by age. You might even rank them as *best, or "hottest," prospects; next best;* and so on. Then, if you believe that people who travel often might have a special interest in portable

FACTORS THAT DEFINE YOUR AUDIENCE

1. Age
2. Sex
3. Vocation
4. Income
5. Marital status
6. Dwelling status
7. Geography
8. Education
9. Ethnic background
10. Personal interests

FIGURE 10-4 Factors to consider when screening an audience.

radios, you might screen the audience further for a list of frequent travelers. In this way you may continue screening until you have designated the people who are the best candidates to buy your radios. The result of this process is decreased selling costs: you don't waste money on those who are not potential customers.

Besides screening an audience yourself, you can buy a mailing list that has been screened for the demographic and psychographic factors that interest you. Some companies exist to sell such lists, and companies offering credit cards sell them too.

Helping the Reader Visualize

Can you think of ways to help readers "see" something in their minds?

Expert sellers know that people are always more willing to spend their money on something they can "see" in their minds. Thus, in writing a letter selling sporting goods, you should make your readers visualize themselves using that tennis racquet or those sneakers—not paying for them. Moreover, readers should sense your interest in their needs and your belief that the product you are selling will satisfy them.

To help readers visualize using your product or service, carefully describe it in vivid language and even include a well-designed brochure with your letter if appropriate. Put yourself in their place: How will what they see help them lose 25 pounds, make $100,000, become a money manager, or whatever? You'll wind up using such terms as *just imagine, see yourself,* and *look at.*

Overcoming Special Objections

Sometimes audiences need special help in overcoming several kinds of strong resistance. Most special objections involve *low quality* or *high price.* For, if the quality of a particular tennis racquet is high, the price you charge for it may also be high. Similarly, if the price of a racquet is low, its quality may be equally low.

What factors do most special objections involve?

The best method of handling special objections to low quality is to offer guarantees on the product or service, or swift correction or repair in the event problems occur. Generally, the better your guarantees, the more you will be able to overcome resistance. High price can be handled with low or no down payments, discounts, deferred buying plans, and emphasis on the tax deductibility of some purchases.

Regardless of how you overcome special objections over the high price of a product or service, avoid mentioning the cost in either the opening or closing statement. Even if you offer a terrific bargain, most readers would prefer neither to start nor to finish a persuasive letter thinking about money.

Let's see how this advice about handling special objections to cost works specifically. Remember the letter on page 289 about selling a new tax preparation service? Assume that the price of this service may be a special objection because some competitors are lower-priced. To overcome this problem, you might insert the following paragraph, offering deferred payments, above the closing paragraph:

> If you prefer, we will gladly add the cost of preparing your returns to your monthly deferred payment for maintaining your investment portfolio. We estimate that most of our clients' monthly payments will increase by only about $5.00, depending on the amount of time required to prepare the return.

What role does convenience play in inducing others to take an action?

Another way to inspire readers to act is to make it convenient for them. For example, if you are soliciting inquiries about your home health care service, enclose with your letter a business reply card or a toll-free telephone number. If you are seeking an order for a new pocket calculator, include an order form and a self-addressed envelope with your letter.

The following letter attempts to sell a group of college students on the idea of coming in to look at the newest model of a specific car. Do you see any problems with it?

First Draft

Dear (Student's Name):

Tired of heretofore missing the bus to classes? Tired of walking to the college day after day?

The time has come to terminate that experience by buying an Arrow! Cadet Motors has the newest model of Arrow. The car is a sleek, slant-backed model, ready to take you around Springfield or up to Chicago. Arrow's 4-cylinder, 125-cubic-inch engine powers the most advanced ideas in sporty and economical cars. This configuration makes Arrow look good.

Smirk at your friends. Acquiesce to their compliments. Avoid long gas lines. You can choose between a three-speed automatic transmission that gets 50 miles to a gallon of gasoline and a five-speed manual transmission that gets 60 miles to a gallon.

Features of the car include two fold-down, bucket-shaped, contoured front seats; a rear seat; a trunk; and pretty upholstery.

For students at Northside College who have approved credit, we have a special offer—no money down and low monthly payments. Those first 25 Northside students who come in to see the car will receive a free sweater. Stop by or call in to place your order. You'll get off on riding in your new Arrow!

Sincerely yours,

Critique

The writer fails to follow the persuasive correspondence plan. For example, the request in line 3 to buy the car is direct; it is not an introduction to the idea. (Anyway, cars are too expensive to sell outright in a letter, so the writer should focus on the idea of the students coming in to see and test drive the Arrow.) Also, the writer seems not to have designated a central appeal. The best writing in the letter is the attempts to make readers visualize owning the car, although even these might be more effective by the use of greater specificity. (lines 5, 9–12) The following are some other problems:

1. The ideas in the first paragraph are negative reminders as stated. "Smirk" and "acquiesce to" also have negative connotations. (line 9)
2. "Heretofore" is too formal. (line 1)
3. "Terminate" is too abstract. (line 3)
4. "Configuration" is too complex a word in this context. (line 7)
5. The fourth sentence of paragraph 3 contains a factual error; it is the car, not the transmission, that gets the gas mileage. (lines 10–12)
6. Paragraph 4 offers a list of the car's features without actually selling them. (lines 13–14)
7. Instead of only making an action request for readers to visit the showroom and perhaps test drive the car, the writer adds a second attempt to sell the car outright. Further, a specific date for the visit should be added. (line 18)
8. "Get off on" is a figurative cliché. (line 18)

The following is a revised draft of the letter:

Revised Draft

Dear (Student's Name):

Put away those rain-soaked shoes and discover that there's more to being mobile than a moped.

Cadet Motors has a stylish new car for you and a plan to help you buy it now.

Arrow is a new minicompact you can afford to drive. The five-speed manual transmission model gets an outstanding 60 miles to a gallon of gasoline—a feat unmatched by any other car on the road today. At the present price of gas, you can cruise around Springfield or up to Chicago for just 2 cents a mile! If you would rather not shift gears, you can choose the three-speed automatic transmission model, which gets 50 miles to a gallon. That performance, too, is unmatched in its class.

Along with economy, you get performance and looks. Arrow has a powerful 125-cubic-inch engine that will accelerate to 50 miles an hour in just 7.6 seconds. You'll be charmed by the interior as well. The car has two bucket seats, contoured for hours of comfortable driving. And the 4-cubic-foot rear seat is ideal for carrying luggage and large stereo speakers—and groceries! A roomy trunk and attractive triple-weave upholstery lend Arrow its practical appeal.

How does the car look from the sidewalk? The new Arrow is a sporty, slant-backed model that closely resembles an expensive European sports car. Compare its sleek styling shown in the enclosed brochure to the ordinary, box-shaped cars that so many people drive today.

You can own an Arrow much more easily than you might think. As a Northside College student with approved credit, you can drive away in your new Arrow with no down payment. Monthly payments are as low as $87.50, and you may take up to five years to pay.

Starting Monday, the first 25 Northside College students who come in to see the new Arrow will receive a free pocket calculator. Stop by our showroom at 9 Chamberlayne Avenue anytime between 9 A.M. and 9 P.M., Monday through Saturday, to see this great new car. Be sure to test drive it while you're here.

A college education will tell you that this is no deal from which to walk away.

Sincerely yours,

Memos That Sell a Service or Idea

Can you think of a service or an idea you may want to sell by memo?

Suppose you want to sell Jason Kupzik, a new employee in your firm, a service—membership in the company's credit union. Or, conversely, you may want to sell the new arrival an idea—to allow you to join an already crowded study group he is organizing on corporate financial trends. One way to approach him is to write a persuasive memo. If you decide to do this, then follow the A-I-D-A approach just as you do when writing any other persuasive letter or memo.

The following is a memo selling Jason on the company's credit union:

First Draft

To: Jason Kupzik, Financial Analyst
From: C. O'Dell Aprisner, Credit Union Supervisor
Subject: Financial Services at Company's Credit Union

Congratulations on assuming the duties of your new job as a financial analyst with the company.

As a new employee, you are entitled to become a member of the employee credit union, which exists solely to serve employees. The credit union's low interest rates enable employees to purchase items ordinarily unaffordable. And you can join by investing as little as $50 monthly. Not only is membership in the credit union affordable, but the office is conveniently located in the building.

Please stop by our office and talk with us about joining the program. We look forward to meeting you.

Critique

Although this memo's tone, style, and word flow are good, a couple of other problems exist. First, it lacks critical information. Second, the writer should pay closer attention to developing a central appeal and several supporting appeals.

The following are some specific problems:

1. Specifically, the reader needs to know, What are the "low interest rates"? Where is the office's convenient location? (lines 5 and 8, respectively)
2. The writer should show fully how the reader would benefit from membership, including an explanation of how the specific items "ordinarily unaffordable" would be purchased by joining the credit union, such as cars, furniture, and home improvements. These themes—appeals—not only are not sold, but they also are never mentioned. (lines 5–6)

The following is a revised draft of this memo:

Revised Draft

To: Jason Kupzik, Financial Analyst
From: C. O'Dell Aprisner, Credit Union Supervisor
Subject: Financial Services of Company's Credit Union

Congratulations on assuming the duties of your new job as a financial analyst with the company.

As a part of our orientation program for new employees, let me introduce you to the company credit union. The credit union exists solely to serve you and other employees. Once you become a member, you can borrow at the lowest interest rates available anywhere today—10 percent annually. Members can borrow as much as $5000 at a time and can take as many as five years to pay. Just imagine driving that new car you've been wanting or getting that new furniture for your home or apartment. Perhaps you've already tried to save enough cash to make such a major purchase but just needed the right plan to make your savings program work. The credit union offers a plan that works every time.

By investing as little as $50 monthly, you can become a credit union member. Your money is safe when invested in the program because every penny you invest is guaranteed by a federally insured protection plan. You won't need to rush around town on your lunch hour to make financial transactions; the credit union office is right here in the building.

In addition, a full 10 percent annual interest rate, compounded daily, is paid on all your deposits.

A brochure containing details about how the credit union investment program works for you is enclosed. This month, we are making a special offer to employees who wish to apply for membership. By depositing as little as $50, you will receive *9 percent* interest on all deposits made during the next 12 months.

Please stop by the credit union office in Room 114 before April 30 to talk with us about the program. We look forward to meeting you then.

Special Requests for Information or Assistance

What makes a request "special"?

We have already discussed routine requests (see Chapter 7). As you remember from that discussion, whenever the action you request is part of the reader's normal job duties, then it is routine. In contrast, whenever you request an action that is not part of it, then yours is a "special" request. In such situations, you should follow the persuasive correspondence plan in writing any message of this type.

Remember that such requests work best if you appeal to the reader's self-interests. The following is a request for information. (The questionnaire that accompanies it is shown in Figure 13.3 in Chapter 13.) Do you see any problems with this letter?

First Draft

Dear Ms. Magnuson:

We are conducting a survey among men and women across the country pertaining to life insurance needs. The objective of the research is not only to find out what your needs are but providing for them as well.

Your name was selected in a computer-derived random sample from a list of our customers who now have automobile insurance with Trumpeters. We value your business and now seek utilization of your opinions about other insurance that customers like you might need.

Your initial outlay will be to take a few minutes to complete the enclosed questionnaire. You have our assurances that your answers will be held in strictest confidence and will be used only for bona fide research purposes. No salesman will call on you as a result of your sharing your opinions with us.

Please complete and return the questionnaire as soon as possible. A postage-paid envelope is enclosed for your convenience.

Sincerely yours,

Critique

Because this letter is ineffective, the reader is likely to ignore it. The opening statement tries to interest her in the topic without first arousing her attention. Nor does the letter develop any appeals;

instead, it simply asks the reader to fill out the questionnaire. The writer is fairly effective, however, when he or she attempts to overcome any resistance by assuring that the information will be kept confidential and promising that no salesperson will call (lines 9 and 11, respectively). Yet the failure to reveal how the researchers will use their information undermines these assurances. Also, the style is too formal, and many problems of tone exist.

The following are some specific problems:

1. Basically, the letter should be reorganized using A-I-D-A, beginning with an attention-getting opening statement, a clear statement of purpose—which includes how the survey takers will use the information, appeals to action, attempts to reduce the reader's resistance to granting the request, and a closing request for action.
2. "Pertaining to," "utilization of," and "you have our assurances" are overly formal and wordy and should be omitted. (lines 2, 6, and 9, respectively)
3. The second sentence in paragraph 1 fails to follow parallel construction. (line 2)
4. The objective stated in the second sentence of the first paragraph implies a hidden motive. The reader may wonder why the writer wants to provide for her needs if no sale is contemplated. (line 2) Later, the writer again implies this with "that customers like you might need" and "your initial outlay." (lines 7 and 8, respectively) As a result, the assurances in the third paragraph seem suspect.
5. "Computer-derived" and "initial outlay" are jargon undesirable in this usage. (lines 4 and 8, respectively)
6. "Strictest confidence" is redundant and should be omitted. (line 10)
7. "Bona fide" is an unnecessary Latin expression. (line 10)
8. "Salesman" is sexually biased. (line 11)
9. "As soon as possible" and "for your convenience" are both classic clichés. (lines 13 and 14)

The following is a revised draft of this letter:

Revised Draft

Dear Ms. Magnuson:

Would you exchange one favor for another if it were very easy to do?

We will deduct $5.00 from your July automobile insurance premium payment if you will take about five minutes to give us your opinions. And it will not cost you a penny.

For several years now, many of our customers have been asking us to offer them a life insurance plan. They want more complete insurance coverage from the company that insures their automobiles. At first, we were reluctant to do this, believing that we should continue to specialize in automobile insurance. But now we wonder if perhaps we can better serve our customers by offering broader coverage. Therefore, we are considering offering a life insurance plan.

You can help by telling us whether we should offer this extended coverage and, if so, what type coverage you think should be offered. The enclosed questionnaire makes it easy for you to share your opinions. No salesperson will call on you as a result of your answering this questionnaire. Also, your answers will be kept confidential and will be used only for research purposes.

All you need do is complete the questionnaire and mail it in the enclosed postage-paid envelope by June 15. Then, $5.00 will be deducted from your premium before a statement is sent to you in July.

Sincerely yours,

In writing a special request memo, use the same strategy as for a special request letter. The following memo asks for an appointment to discuss a flexible work schedule in a word processing center. Do you see any problem with it?

First Draft

To: Janet Schich, Director, Employee Services
From: Carroll Jauber, Director, Word Processing Center
Subject: Advantages of Flexible Work Schedule

I need your help with a big problem that I have in the word processing center.

About 80 percent of the center's employees are homemakers who find it difficult to work the 9 A.M. to 5 P.M. work schedule we keep. As a result, we have often had to lower our job requirements just to get enough employees to fill the jobs we have had available.

Now our competitors in the area, CopyRight Company and CompuText Industries, have adopted a flexible work schedule in their word processing centers. Their employees can report for work as early as 6 A.M. or can stay as late as 7 P.M. Also, they can work as little as 30 hours a week if they choose. Consequently, our competitors are stealing our employees who are homemakers.

Were we to adopt a work schedule like theirs so that we could compete with them effectively, we would need to hire five more employees. We could do this without increasing the total number of hours worked a week. So, without increasing our labor costs, we could offer our employees greater freedom in choosing the hours they will work. Therefore, those homemakers who now work for the center will be encouraged to stay on with us, and other qualified homemakers will be encouraged to apply for a job with us.

Adopting these changes will cut our turnover rate. Your department will then enjoy a lower cost of hiring and training new employees.

I look forward to hearing your feelings about this proposal.

Critique

The writer probably is effective in developing the reader's interest in the topic and in creating a desire to take action (steps 2 and 3 of A-I-D-A). In addition, the writing style is appropriately informed and the word flow is smooth. Some specific problems, especially in tone and organization of ideas, are

1. The opening statement is self-centered and focuses on a negative thought—the problem. (lines 1–2)
2. The idea that competitors steal employees who are homemakers needs to be supported by facts. (lines 7–12)
3. If the writer mentioned the reader's benefits before requesting the desired action, the plan presented in the fourth paragraph would be strengthened. (lines 13–20)
4. The closing statement fails to suggest any specific action. (line 23)

The following is a revised draft of the memo:

Revised Draft

To: Janet Schich, Director, Employee Services
From: Carroll Jauber, Director, Word Processing Center
Subject: Proposed Flexible Work Schedule

I have a plan that will reduce your hiring and training costs and will reduce the employee turnover rate in the word processing center at the same time.

About 80 percent of the center's employees are homemakers who find it difficult to work the 9 A.M. to 5 P.M. work schedule we now keep. As a result, we often have had to lower our job requirements just to get enough employees to fill the jobs we have had available.

Now our competitors in the area, CopyRight Company and CompuText Industries, have adopted a flexible work schedule in their word processing centers. Their employees can report for work as early as 6 A.M. or can stay as late as 7 P.M. Also, they can work as little as 30 hours a week if they choose. Consequently, our competitors are stealing our employees who are now homemakers—8 within the last month alone.

We could adopt a flexible work schedule to allow us to compete with them without increasing our labor costs. Just by hiring five more people, we could allow our employees to work fewer hours if they choose. Yet the total hours worked in the center would still remain the same. Homemakers who already work here would be encouraged to stay on with us. Also, other qualified homemakers would probably be encouraged to apply for jobs.

Hiring these new employees and changing to a flexible work schedule will result in your department's enjoying a lower total cost of hiring and training new employees. At the same time, the center's turnover rate will be reduced.

May I have an appointment with you, Janet, to discuss these proposed changes? I will be in Santa Barbara on business all day Wednesday but will gladly meet with you on any other day next week. Please call me at Extension 000 to confirm a time.

Requests to Grant Complex Claims

How do simple and complex claims differ?

Claims on goods or services can be simple or complex. A simple claim is one that both the writer and reader can justify (see Chapter 7). For example, according to your company health plan, an insurance company will pay 50 percent of each visit you make to a doctor's office. In filing your claim after such a visit, you accompany it with a simple and routine letter of request since you know the reader will automatically grant it. In a more complex claim, however, the reader might question or resist taking action for one reason or another, but the writer feels justified in making it anyway. For example, suppose a tax service that makes certain guarantees about the quality of its work prepares your return. Later, you discover that your return was prepared incompletely. Therefore, you feel justified in seeking an adjustment, even though you know that getting what you want may be difficult. In writing your claim letter, use the persuasive plan as a guide.

The following is a first draft of such a letter. Do you see any problems with it?

First Draft

Dear Mr. Grantham:

Your "know all the latest changes in the tax codes" advertisement was the first and foremost reason for my selecting Reliable Tax Consultants to prepare my federal tax return this year.

On February 3, I had my return prepared by one of your tax consultants, Jack Custou. Mr. Custou reassured me that you guarantee correct computations of all entries on returns, but nevertheless he would accompany me to the tax office if my returns were audited.

Wouldn't you know what would happen? On November 20, my return was audited, and Mr. Custou went with me to the tax office as promised as mouthpiece for your company. While all entries on the return were computed correctly, the auditor told me that I could have deducted an additional $400 for an office that I maintained in my home and $300 depreciation on a personal computer that I purchased last year. I quite distinctly remember asking Mr. Custou about both these deductions when he prepared my returns, and he said that federal regulations did not allow for such deductions.

Because Mr. Custou did not "know all the latest changes in the tax codes," I feel that the fee in the amount of $75 that I paid your company to prepare the return should be reimbursed posthaste. Enclosed please find a copy of your advertisement guaranteeing your services. I'll expect payment soon.

Sincerely yours,

Critique

The major problem with this letter concerns its tone, which is demanding throughout. In addition, the closing paragraph is disorganized, and the action request is nonspecific. Some other problems are

1. Quoting the advertisement in the opening statement gets attention negatively by indicating that a complaint is coming. Closing the letter by repeating the quote compounds matters. A reference to the idea might be less irritating. (lines 1 and 17, respectively)
2. "First and foremost" and "but nevertheless" are redundant. (lines 2 and 6)
3. The first sentence in the third paragraph is unnecessary and should be omitted. Besides, it's flippant and presumptuous. (line 8)
4. The connotative meaning of "mouthpiece" is demeaning. (line 10)
5. The third sentence in the third paragraph contains 42 words, and the first sentence in the last paragraph contains 37. Both are too long for easy reading. (lines 10 and 17, respectively)
6. "Quite distinctly" is didactic—preachy. (line 14)
7. The connective "and" is incorrect; "but" should be substituted. (line 15)
8. "in the amount of" is wordy. So is "enclosed please find," which is a cliché. (lines 18 and 19, respectively)
9. "Posthaste" is demanding, outdated, and indefinite. "I'll expect payment soon" is also demanding and indefinite. (lines 19 and 20, respectively)
10. The second sentence in the last paragraph is misplaced. (line 19)

The following is a revised draft of this letter:

Revised Draft

Dear Mr. Grantham:

Your advertisement that your tax consultants keep up with the latest changes in the tax codes led me to select your company to prepare my federal tax return this year.

Jack Custou, one of your consultants, prepared my return on February 3. At that time, he reassured me that you guarantee that the return is computed correctly. He also said that he would accompany me to the tax office if the return were questioned.

On November 20, the return was audited, and I was called to the tax office to explain several deductions. Mr. Custou went with me as promised and explained how the deductions were computed. While the auditor agreed that they were computed correctly, she also said that the tax code would have allowed me to deduct an additional $700. I could have deducted $400 for an office that I maintained in my home and $300 depreciation on a personal computer. When I asked Mr. Custou about these deductions when he was preparing the return, he said they were not allowed.

Because the consultant did not know about these changes in the tax code, the $75 fee I paid for preparing the return should be reimbursed. Therefore, will you please send this payment by December 31, the close of the tax year.

Sincerely yours,

Appeals for Donations or Contributions

Have you ever tried to persuade someone to donate or contribute something? If so, were you successful?

Always write appeals for donations or contributions as persuasive requests. Such appeals range from requests for money to those for clothing, food, or some other goods or services.

The following letter asks for donations for the State Science Museum's programs. Do you see any problems with it?

First Draft

Dear Ms. Jenkins:

Building renovation costs totaled nearly $1 million; operation costs were $2 million. That was last year, though. The costs for this year promise to be even higher.

At the State Science Museum, we need money: to pay operating costs and to lure special exhibits to the area. Since we are a major tourist attraction, we must keep up our appearance, maintain a qualified staff, and conduct exciting programs. To do each, we need your help.

With a tax-deductible contribution from you, we will continue to serve the state and the nation as a center for the display of man's technological and scientific feats.

We look forward to receiving your generous contribution.

Sincerely yours,

Critique

Although this letter is an appeal for money, it focuses too much on money and on "we" (meaning the museum). The writer pays no attention to the reader's viewpoint except for mentioning that contributions are tax deductible. Additionally, the closing offers little inducement to act. Some specific problems are

1. The opening paragraph fails to attract the reader's attention because it is unconcerned with her interests, focusing instead on money and self.
2. "We" appears far too frequently. (lines 4, 5, 6, 8, 9, and 12)
3. Paragraph 2 presents good ideas but fails to translate maintenance and special exhibits into reader benefits.
4. "Man's" is sexually biased. (line 11)
5. The closing statement sounds presumptuous and contains no action request. Nor does it attempt to make acting easy or beneficial for the reader. (line 12)

The following is a revised draft of this letter:

Revised Draft

Dear Ms. Jenkins:

As manager of a company devoted to the development of high technology, you have shown how much you value science. We think too that you prize great contributions to science and technology and appreciate the women and men who performed great feats to make our world more comfortable.

The State Science Museum stands as a monument to scientific advancement. People from all states tour the museum. And students from kindergarten to college visit the special exhibits, listening to highly trained guides explain scientific concepts.

Since the museum serves science by making people aware of its importance, we thought a company with your goals would like to help us meet ours. Your contribution would ensure that students of all ages will have a place where detailed displays and exhibits enhance classroom discussions.

Because of the way the State Science Museum is organized, a corporation like yours may contribute to a specific area—the Air and Space Division, for instance. Or you may contribute to a general fund, which allows the museum to develop special areas and programs. In either case, you may make your donation in a single payment or in four equal payments spread over the next year.

Along with an explanation of what can be done with a $100, $200, $500, or $1000 donation, the enclosed brochure outlines our special programs. Will you please read the brochure, and then visit the museum too if you have time. Once you witness our commitment to science, we think you will want to help. To do that, all you need do is mail your contribution in the enclosed envelope by December 15, the closing date for this campaign.

Sincerely yours,

Appeals to Pay Debts

What are the stages in the collection process?

In the collection of debts, use a three-stage process involving *reminder, inquiry, and persuasion.*

Reminder Stage

Throughout this stage assume that your customer intends to pay on time. Therefore, you are merely writing to prompt payment. First, send only a statement of the amount due. If your customer pays within the stipulated time, then you have no problem. But, when the due date passes without payment, you may send another copy of the statement as a reminder. Either stamp this "Second Notice" or include a brief routine letter—using the direct approach discussed in Chapter 7—reminding the customer or client that payment is due. If you have no time to send a second reminder, or if you think it wise to move more quickly for any reason, then proceed to the inquiry stage.

Inquiry Stage

Once you decide that something may be preventing the customer from paying on time, write an inquiry letter. Perhaps your statement has not been received, or some other simple reason is behind the nonpayment. Still, assume the customer intends to pay you. So write to ask for your money or an explanation by a certain date, but avoid any hint of exasperation. Use a direct—deductive—plan when writing.

Although Chapter 7 discusses routine letters of this type, we have included an inquiry letter here so you might more conveniently study the collection process. Do you see any problems with the letter?

First Draft

Dear (Buyer's Name):

Since you have received bills regarding your account of $350, we wonder why you haven't paid.

In order for us to pay our bills, we need our customers to pay on time. Your account is now 60 days overdue.

So please send us a check today for $350, and we can let our bookkeeper balance your account.

Sincerely yours,

Critique

Although the style is appropriately informal, this letter's tone is not quite right. For example, it fails to consider oversight as a possible reason for the buyer's nonpayment. Also, the company's self-interest is too obvious and dominates the entire letter. The following are some specific problems:

1. The opening statement, "We wonder why you haven't paid," is overly aggressive, immediately placing the reader on the defensive. (line 2)
2. "In order to pay our bills" introduces a self-centered appeal and is condescending; customers realize that retailers pay bills with sales-generated revenue. (line 3)
3. "So we can let our bookkeeper balance your account" also emphasizes self-interest, even though overdue accounts do inconvenience bookkeepers. (lines 5–6)

The following is a revised draft of this letter:

Revised Draft

Dear (Buyer's Name):

Your payment of $350 for the VCR you purchased from us on Independence Day is still overdue, although the date for payment was August 4.

If the problem is just an oversight as it appears to be, or if your check is in the mail, please disregard this notice.

Write or call, though, if you have a reason for not having paid your balance. One of our credit supervisors will gladly discuss the matter with you.

Sincerely yours,

If the owner fails to respond properly to your inquiry, advance to the persuasive stage.

Persuasive Stage

You have sent your reminders and your inquiries and nothing has happened. Now you need to prod, which means writing persuasive appeals following the A-I-D-A approach.

What are some effective type of appeals to use in collection messages?

Use all or some or one of the following appeals. Each one can make a good central or supporting appeal as the situation calls for it.

1. *Appeal to integrity.* Such an appeal addresses the customer's sense of fair play or honesty—the idea that if people owe debts, they should pay them.
2. *Appeal to economic self-interest.* Such an appeal invokes the vision of the consequences of nonpayment. Some of these might be possible loss of credit with your firm, loss of a good credit rating, and the cost of paying for the account's collection by legal means.
3. *Appeal to pride.* Such an appeal may be both positive and powerful—the idea that paying the debt is a way to keep self-esteem.

How do mild and urgent appeals and an ultimatum differ from one another?

If you need to follow through completely, this stage includes three steps. In the first, you write a *mild appeal,* pointing to the benefits of payment and asking for it by a certain date. In the second, you issue an *urgent appeal* to pay by a certain date. Use the reader's viewpoint in writing it to paint vivid pictures of the consequences of nonpayment. In the third, issue an *ultimatum.* Say that this represents a final attempt to collect the debt before you take appropriate action. This action may consist of turning the account over to your lawyers or a collection agency. At its most extreme, it may include suing the customer if this becomes the only way to collect the money. Since relying on legal means to collect a debt destroys goodwill, do not introduce this tactic until you are ready to use it. Usually, in the first two steps of this persuasive stage, credit managers write the letters. But, for the final step, a company officer—perhaps the treasurer or a vice president—usually is the writer. The idea is to apply the authority—and added pressure—of high office.

The following is a mild appeal to collect an overdue debt. Do you see any problems with it?

First Draft

Dear (Customer's Name):

The success of credit depends on paying customers. Some people, however, fail to pay their debts, and all consumers suffer the consequences.

When we sold you a VCR several months ago, we thought that you would pay your bill promptly. Yet since you haven't responded to our inquiries about the status of your account, which is now 75 days past due, perhaps we made a mistake extending credit to you for such an expensive purchase.

Your failure to pay causes serious problems. Not only will you lose the privilege to buy goods from us on credit, but we will have no choice but to report your delinquent account to the Credit Bureau Association. If you fail to pay at that time, we will pursue legal action against you to recover our money.

So send a check for $350 immediately, or we will take serious action.

Sincerely yours,

Critique

While the style is acceptable, the letter's tone—which makes the reader seem devious and irresponsible—is deplorable. Moreover, the threat of legal action is probably premature, and the early threat of serious action offsets the effectiveness of the request that the reader act. The writer does, however, follow the A-I-D-A plan. The following are some specific problems:

1. The opening paragraph first distinguishes between good and bad customers and immediately puts the reader in the latter category. It also commits the outrage of trying to make the reader think the future of credit itself rests on this one account.
2. "Fail" and "failure" are too negative; they bluntly associate the reader with the negative act and will make it more difficult to collect in doing so. (lines 2, 12, and 9, respectively)
3. "We thought" and "mistake" are condescending. (lines 4 and 7)
4. Paragraph 3 is entirely too aggressive. "We will have no choice but to report" falsely refuses to allow the writer any alternative. Also, the threat of legal action is premature. By mentioning it too soon, the writer risks unnecessarily the chance to restore goodwill once the matter is resolved. (lines 11 and 13, respectively)
5. The final paragraph consists of another threat. Simply requesting the balance by a certain date in an expectant and positive tone is sufficient.

The following is a revised draft of this letter:

Revised Draft

Dear (Customer's Name):

As you know, credit brings business to life. It allows customers such as yourself to purchase particular products without having to deplete savings.

We were glad you were able to use credit to purchase a VCR during our Independence Day Sale. After all, you have been an excellent customer since opening your account two years ago. Now, though, payment of your account is 75 days overdue. Although we have not received a response to our inquiry, we believe that you intend to pay the debt.

This oversight is causing serious problems, however. The matter can result in the loss of your privilege to buy goods from us on credit terms. Also, as a member of the Credit Bureau Association, we are required to report to the bureau all accounts that are 90 days overdue. Such an action could affect your good credit standing.

To avoid serious consequences that result from late payment, please send us a check for $350 by October 1. That will place your account in good standing once again and will allow you to continue buying merchandise from us on credit.

Sincerely yours,

In summary, no matter what your topic is, in writing persuasive messages, use the A-I-D-A approach. Then, if your style, tone, and content are appropriate, you should achieve the desired result. The following checklist should help you to evaluate any of your persuasive messages during the writing process:

CHECKLIST FOR PERSUASIVE LETTERS AND MEMORANDUMS

1. Ask these questions when you write the opening paragraph of your letter or memo.
   a. Does the first statement intrigue the reader enough to continue reading?
   b. Does reader interest dominate the content and tone?
   c. Is the action request itself avoided?
   d. Considering demographics and psychographics, is the tone pitched correctly for the audience?
   e. Is the language clear, and is there a logical transition to the body?
2. Ask these questions when you write the body of your letter or memo.
   a. Is the action you will request now clear in the reader's mind?
   b. Is the central appeal presented first and talked about most among the appeals?
   c. Is the central appeal fully complemented by the supporting appeals?
   d. Is the tone confident but not overly so?
   e. Are any special objections anticipated and a plan presented to overcome them?
   f. Are any enclosures introduced toward the end of this section?
3. Ask these questions when you write the closing paragraph of your letter or memo.
   a. Is it short—two or three sentences?
   b. Is the action request
      (1) Clear and easy to perform?
      (2) Made in a courteous, straightforward, self-confident manner?
      (3) Stated specifically, including the time or date the action should be taken by?
      (4) Gracious and put in terms of reader viewpoint?
   c. Does it include a final "punch line," on available benefits—a reference to the appeals—if appropriate?

SUMMARY

1. Persuasion is the art of moving people by their own agreement to a belief, position, or course of action. Persuasion in business is both overt and covert.

2. The most widely used strategy in writing persuasive business letters and memos is the A-I-D-A plan: attention, interest, desire, and action. This plan is a type of inductive (indirect) approach.
3. An opening statement—"attention" step in the plan—in a persuasive letter or memo should be positive and short, sound cooperative, and use the reader's viewpoint of the situation.
4. The body—"interest" and "desire" steps—is where you build the case for the action you want the reader to take. This is done with a central appeal, the most persuasive argument, and supporting appeals, minor arguments that support the central appeal.
5. The closing statement—the "action" step—is where you specifically request the action you want the reader to take.
6. Six common types of persuasive letters and memos are the following:
   a. *Appeals to buy goods or services* may be solicited or unsolicited. When selling by mail, you will need to define your audience to target their interests as a whole and the interests of any subgroups, if they exist. Further, you will need to get them to visualize themselves using the product or service and help them overcome any special objections they may have to taking the action you want.
   b. *Memos that sell a service or idea* are fairly common in internal persuasive writing. Use the same procedure you use in selling goods or services in letters.
   c. *Special requests for information or assistance* ask for an action that is not a regular job duty for the reader.
   d. *Requests to grant complex claims* differ from simple claims in that a reader will likely question a complex claim unless it is fully justified.
   e. *Appeals for donations or contributions* range from requests for money to requests for clothing, food, or some other goods or services, including your time, as in volunteer work.

   f. *Appeals to pay debts* comprise three stages: reminder, inquiry, and persuasive. The first two stages call for using the direct (deductive) plan of routine requests; the third calls for using the persuasive plan.

Review Questions

1. How is persuasion effective in business letters and memos? Include a definition of persuasion in your response.
2. How does the A-I-D-A approach work? Discuss each step in the process.
3. Is the A-I-D-A strategy deductively or inductively arranged? How does it differ from the unfavorable news plan?
4. Why is an opening statement important in a persuasive letter or memo? List four guidelines you should be careful to follow when writing opening statements.
5. What is a central appeal? Explain how to choose a central appeal from among a list of appeals.
6. What are supporting appeals and what relationship do they have to the central appeal?
7. When writing closing statements, why is it that "you either strengthen your grip or lose it entirely" at this point?
8. What difference is there between a solicited and an unsolicited appeal to buy goods or services?
9. How does a writer go about defining an audience? On what basis is an audience defined?
10. Why do you think it is important that your reader visualize him- or herself using a product or service? Have you any

idea what difference that can make?

11. What is meant by "special objections"? How can they be anticipated and overcome?
12. Can you really sell an idea in a memo? If yes, give two on-the-job situations in which you might do this. If no, why not?
13. How do special and routine requests for information and assistance differ? Which plan should you use to write each?
14. How do simple and complex claims differ? Which plan should you use to write each?
15. What are the three stages in the debt collection process? Define each stage.

Exercises

1. Business at your furniture store has fallen off 40 percent. The cause of the problem is a nationwide recession. Unemployment is especially high in your area. Experts agree that economic conditions should improve in about four months. You have information to show that it will improve in your area along with nationwide recovery. Write your major furniture supplier to ask for a four-month delay in making payments on your account. You will gladly pay interest charges on the balance during that time. Address: J. P. Ownby, Credit Manager; White Hall Furniture Company; 749 Pine Lane; High Point, North Carolina 00000.
2. The apartment you rent needs repairs. The plumbing fixtures leak, the paint is peeling from the walls, and several windows are broken. The owner of the building in which you live is a local bank that is noted for spending little money to maintain its rental units. Write the bank's real estate manager to request repairs. Persuade her that the bank will benefit by making the repairs and then maintaining the apartment thereafter. Address: Elvira M. Jessup, Supervisor; Real Estate Division; Valley National Bank; Grand Rapids, Michigan 00000.
3. You work for Tomaz Research Associates as a research analyst. One of your clients, Willis Audio Shop, asked you to study the effects of declining recorded music (records, tapes, compact discs) sales in its market area. You prepared a questionnaire that will be mailed to the shop's customers to get their opinions. Now write a form cover letter to accompany the questionnaire. Persuade the customers to take 10 minutes to complete the questionnaire and return it to you within two weeks.
4. While on a visit to Toronto, you found a chair in a store there that you liked so much that you bought it. The chair is an unusual design that you have never seen before. When it arrived by railway express one month later, you unpacked it eagerly. Although the shipping carton was not damaged and the packing was done correctly, both arms have fallen off the chair. The product carried no guarantee, but you feel that the company should replace it or pay for repairs. Write a persuasive letter to the store manager. Address: Alex LeMeire, Manager; Toronto Furnishings Limited; 1121 Bloor Street; Toronto, Ontario 000 000.
5. While visiting Albuquerque on business, you had a suit cleaned by a dry cleaners near your hotel. Because you didn't wear the suit as planned at that time, you inspected it only after arriving home. When you did look at it, you found a 4-inch burned spot on the left leg of the trousers. Then you found a similar burned spot on the lapel of the coat. You cannot wear the suit again, and it cannot be repaired. Write a letter to the cleaners

asking for a check to pay for another suit. The suit cost $350 and is three weeks old. Ship the damaged suit to the dry cleaners for inspection. Address: Lamont Cleaners; 81 West Lomas Boulevard; Albuquerque, New Mexico 00000.

6. You serve as director of the Yarborough Senior Citizens Center, a home for people aged 65 or older. The residents of the center told you that they would enjoy having a color television set in their recreation room. The center is a nonprofit operation, and no funds are available to buy the television set. Write a letter requesting that a local business donate a television set to the center. Address: Sandra Albermarle, President; Yarborough Electronics; 159 Center Street; Yarborough, Massachusetts 00000.

7. You serve as a volunteer worker for Helping Hand, a local charitable organization. Your job is to administer the record-keeping system. Currently, records are kept manually, which is an inaccurate and time-consuming method. You wonder if a large company in your city might donate a used microcomputer for your use. Another solution is for the company to allow you to keep your records on its system; if this can be done, you would manage all the data and maintain the records yourself. Write the letter. Address: Pierre Meyer, President; Little Town Distributing Company; 9870 Pearl Road; Cleveland, Ohio 00000.

8. You own and manage a women's formal wear store, which just opened for business. As a part of your advertising campaign, you decide to write a letter to women whose engagements are announced each week in the local newspaper. You should describe your product line and service. Also, you might wish to offer a special discount or some other incentive to get them to visit the store. Write the form letter.

9. As sales supervisor for a large lighting fixtures company, you just received an order for 200 Model 98 antique brass porch lamps. The buyer is one of your best customers. While you will be glad to fill this order, these lamps have been selling slowly for other customers. Besides that, you recently imported a different line of antique brass porch lamps from Copenhagen, Denmark. These lamps are selling better than any such lamp you have ever stocked, but they cost $10 more per unit than the model the customer ordered. Because the customer has a small store, you know that an additional order is unwarranted. Therefore, you decide to write a letter to persuade the customer to buy the new model instead. Address: M. Mary Renquist, President; Pine Bluff Lighting Company; Pine Bluff, Arizona 00000.

10. You have just opened a house cleaning service with a staff of 25 employees. This service will appeal best to people who earn between $25,000 and $40,000 yearly. As a part of your advertising campaign, you bought a mailing list of names and addresses of individuals and couples who might buy the service. Now you are preparing to write a form letter to persuade them to become customers. Write the letter and include an introductory offer as a special incentive.

11. As sales representative for a music store, you specialize in selling keyboard musical instruments. Also, you are responsible for seeing that your customers pay their accounts. Six months ago, you sold a piano to a young couple whose son is taking music lessons. They paid one-half of the $3500 price and agreed to pay the remaining $1750 in three months. You sent them a statement three months ago

and followed with an inquiry letter six weeks ago. You have heard nothing from them. An additional problem is that they live 300 miles away and have never answered their telephone when you have called. Write a first-step persuasive appeal letter to the couple. Persuade them to pay the debt. Address: Mario and Annie Lipitzer; 4321 East Van Buren Street; Colorado Springs, Colorado 00000.

12. Assume that you are the sales representative mentioned in Exercise 11. You received no response from the Lipitzers. You checked to see if they still live at the address they gave you, and they do. However, they still do not answer the telephone when you call. Write an ultimatum telling them to pay you or you will turn over the account to your company's lawyers for collection.

13. You manage the personnel division for a large investment counseling service in your city. The company has three branch offices in addition to the main office in which you work. When you were closing the office yesterday, you noticed a stack of confidential contracts laying atop a work table. When you picked them up to put them away, you also noticed three employee information files on the table as well. The next day, you ask the supervisor who did it. She doesn't know. Then you call the supervisors at the three branch offices and learn that they have had the same problem you're having. You decide to write a form memorandum to all personnel employees. Remind them of the need to secure all confidential files before leaving work each day. Also, remind them of the procedure to follow in securing confidential files.

14. You work as a marketing representative for a data processing vendor in Birmingham, Alabama. You are about to try to make a large sale to a local company that you have visited several times already. You believe that if a systems engineer from the Chicago office would come to Birmingham and accompany you on the next visit to the firm, you could make the sale. This is an unusual practice, but this is a special situation. Write a memorandum to the sales manager in the Chicago office making the request. Address: Alexander Hallman, Sales Manager, Chicago Office.

15. You work as a senior internal auditor at Drexler Industries in Madison, Wisconsin. As a part of your job, you often write reports to upper-level managers. Most of these reports contain statistical data. To help you prepare more effective tables and figures for these reports, you want to attend a computer graphics seminar that will be held in Houston, Texas. The seminar is entitled "Applying Computer Graphics to Accounting Problems." Write a memorandum to your supervisor, Amy D. Lowe, asking her to give you the time off from work to attend the seminar and to grant permission for reimbursement of your expenses.

16. With a business degree and 15 years' work experience at a *Fortune* 500 company, you decide to enter the consulting business. Your area of expertise—preparing and delivering oral presentations—is a field in which most professionals need guidance. And your presentation will help: you provide detailed handouts, demonstrate the use of audiovisual equipment, and conduct one-on-one workshops. Your fee, $1000 for a one-day session, falls at the high end of the pay scale, but you know that your experience entitles you to that amount. Write a form letter announcing and selling your service.

17. You work in public relations for the Lexington Ballet. Although the Ballet cur-

rently lacks the funds to lure prestigious acts to town, you know that engaging first-rate performers would enhance the appeal of your organization. Write a form letter soliciting contributions for your project. Companies that contribute over $500 will be given eight complimentary tickets—good for any Saturday evening performance during the next year. The tickets are located in a choice section of the theater. In addition, the names of contributing companies will be listed in the program. Such contributions are tax deductible.

18. Your organization, the American Red Cross, has been overwhelmed with requests for assistance as a result of severe flooding in your state—in fact, so many requests have come in that you need assistance. Many people are without shelter, food, or clothing. And with cleanup expected to take up to six months, it will be a long time before some people are able to return to their homes. Write a form letter to the major companies in your area asking for their tax-deductible contributions. The Red Cross needs help immediately.

19. You direct community relations for P.M., Incorporated, and you have received the request for donations discussed in Exercise 18. Although your company needed little persuasion to help remedy the problem, you feel that more should be done. Write a memorandum, a copy of which will be sent to each employee of the company, asking for personal contributions: cans of food, articles of clothing, and so forth. Some employees themselves may have been victims of the flood; others may have relatives who were.

20. On a recent trip to Washington, D.C., your parents bought you an art print from Printer's Gallery. Since the store offered to frame the print at a 50 percent discount, your parents decided to have it done there. The gallery promised to mail it to your home address the following week. The package arrived, and when you examined the contents, you noticed fingerprints in one corner. Write a letter to the store, asking that it reframe your print (cost valued at $80) and pay the mailing and insurance costs involved (about $20). Address: Printer's Gallery, 0010 Wisconsin Avenue, N.W., Washington, D.C. 00000.

21. Several months ago, your company, Graphic Design, decided to create a luncheon area for its employees. In your capacity as employee liaison, you bought two coffeemakers, a microwave oven, and various utensils, with the provision that employees would be responsible for keeping the serving area clean and washing their own dishes. You have recently discovered, however, that several employees are neglecting to take care of this area: coffee spills have stained the counter, and silverware and coffee cups lay in the sink for several days before anyone washes them. Write a memo to your employees, explaining the problem and encouraging them to keep the kitchen area clean. After all, they did agree to do just that.

22. When you built a deck on the back of your house, you purchased lumber from Jones Lumber Company. The salesperson, John Muir, assured you that at the building site his employees would unload the lumber from the truck by hand rather than by dumping it, which damages the lumber. When the delivery truck arrived the following week, the driver intended to dump the wood. However, you persuaded him to unload it by hand, and he agreed, provided that you could help. As a result, you feel you should be reimbursed the $45 delivery

charge since you helped unload the lumber. Write a letter to the store, asking to be reimbursed the cost of delivery. Address: Jones Lumber Company, 10 Rose Avenue, Richmond, Virginia 00000.

23. For the past three weeks, you have noticed people in your department taking more than the allowed hour for lunch. In fact, some employees are taking as much as one and one-half hours. This practice hinders production and damages the morale of those who follow regulations regarding lunch. Write a memorandum to employees in your department (Finance), explaining the problem and asking them to monitor their own lunch breaks.

24. Your company has just published a new magazine, *The Dynamics of Management*. Aimed at midlevel, moderately experienced managers, the magazine offers various theories of management from well-known managers. In addition, the publication analyzes such issues as how to get the most employee participation in the company, the success of women managers in business, and what makes a successful manager. Write a form letter, which you will send to managers at various companies, soliciting subscriptions. The magazine is published monthly at a tax-deductible yearly rate of $36.

25. Your job at Levitz Advertising involves writing marketing reports, which you prepare on a typewriter. You know from experience that using a word processor would increase your productivity. Write a memo to your supervisor, Lenny Speight, stating your case. Persuade him to allow you to review word processing equipment and submit a proposal for his consideration.

PART 4

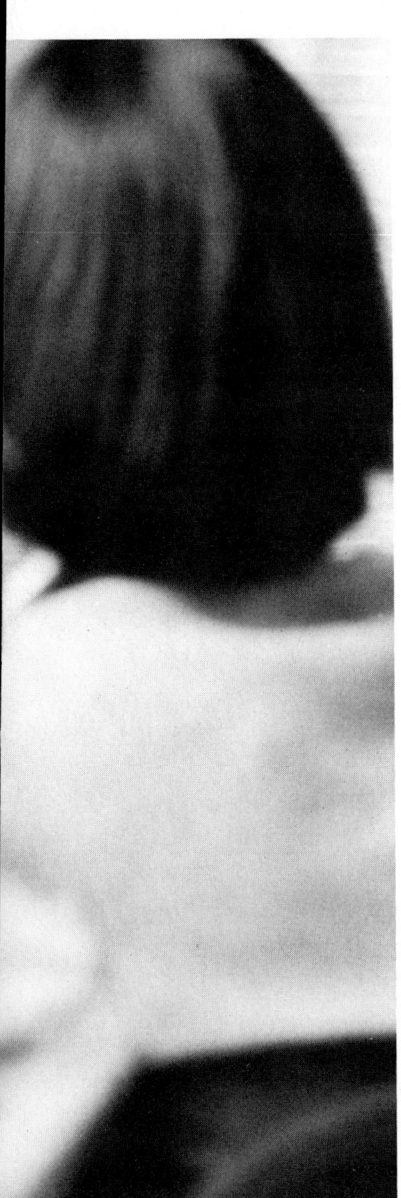

COMMUNICATION ABOUT EMPLOYMENT

CHAPTER 11

FINDING EMPLOYEES: THE EMPLOYER'S ROLE

> Publisher seeks assistant production manager for its rapidly expanding trade paperback division. Tremendous growth experience for "go-getter" who can work in exciting "pressure cooker" atmosphere. 6 mos to 1 yr related exp pref'd. Send resume with salary requirements to Box 2777, THE TIMES 19811.

When Joseph Hamlein came across this ad in the classified section of the paper, he was uncertain whether to add it to his list of job possibilities. On the one hand, he really wanted to work in production. But he had just graduated from business school and had no job experience. However, he had done some production work on a voluntary basis for his school's *Business Review*, so perhaps he could list this on a resume.

But what did the ad mean by a go-getter? Did the firm want somebody energetic and outgoing? Or someone like himself who was quiet yet enjoyed getting things started rather than going into situations where practices were long established.

Joseph wished he could see inside the head of the person who had placed the ad and discover what he or she was really looking for in filling this job. But, of course, that was impossible. So, hesitating only for a moment, Joseph added the publishing company to his job prospect list. He just might be able to convince the firm that he was the person it was looking for.

In this chapter we will do what Joseph was unable to do: analyze how employers go about finding the right employees. Thus, this chapter is written from the employers' point of view. Knowing the way employers approach the employment process should help you make your own job search successful.

HOW THE PROCESS WORKS FOR EMPLOYERS

If interviewed on the subject, most people in senior management positions would concede that in the end a company's success depends on the people it hires. Naturally, the managers whose responsibility it is to recruit, screen, and hire applicants appreciate this fact more than anyone. In addition, in this capacity, these managers will use almost every communication skill this text discusses. The better their mastery of these skills, the more effective these managers will be in finding and hiring qualified applicants.

What five steps are involved in finding new employees?

The employment process is truly just that: a process that begins with advertising a job opening and ends with welcoming the newly hired employee. Figure 11-1 shows the five steps that comprise this employment process. By following each step, employers can do a thorough job as well as keep up with their progress in that process. Also note that most applicants never complete the entire process.

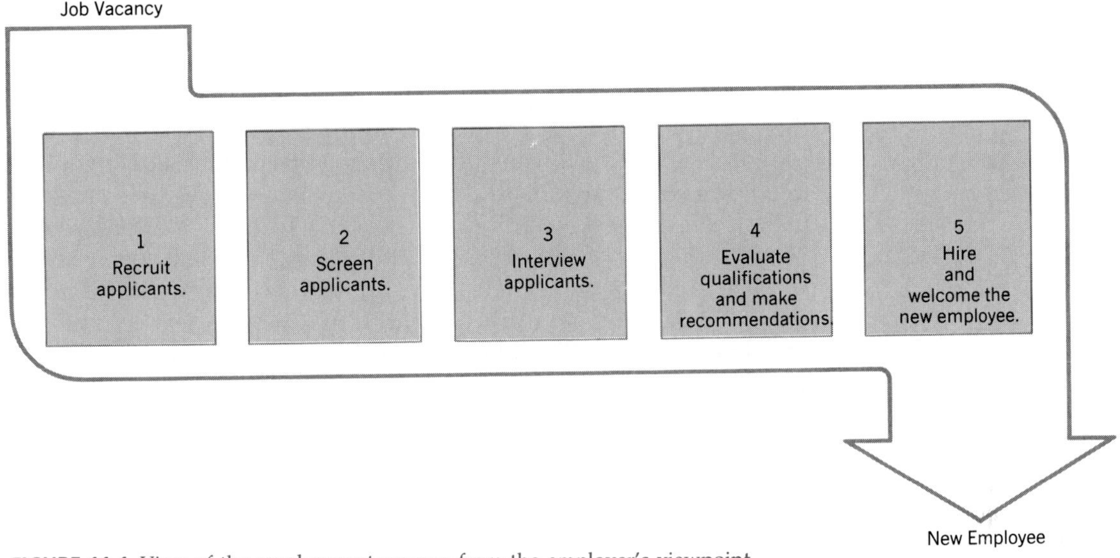
Job Vacancy
1
Recruit applicants.
2
Screen applicants.
3
Interview applicants.
4
Evaluate qualifications and make recommendations.
5
Hire and welcome the new employee.
New Employee

FIGURE 11-1 View of the employment process from the employer's viewpoint

Either they stop pursuing the job themselves or the employer screens them out.

Employers hire applicants to fill new positions and to replace people who vacate positions for one reason or another. If you need to hire employees, you should know how to plan, analyze, and make decisions. In addition, you should have both excellent speaking and writing skills, for you will have to act as liaison between the company and the applicant. Thus, you will advertise job openings, screen applications, conduct interviews, evaluate qualifications, make recommendations, and, finally, hire and welcome new employees. If you have done your job properly, the people you welcome to the company will be the best qualified applicants at the best possible prices for you.

LEGAL CONSIDERATIONS FOR EMPLOYERS

Suppose you are about to recruit some new employees. Even before you start this process, you need to be aware of the provisions of the federal Uniform Guidelines on Employees Selection Procedures. By following these provisions, employers protect themselves legally against charges of discriminatory hiring practices and also protect the applicants themselves against such discrimination.

Which two major laws affect employment practices?

The two major laws affecting hiring that you should be familiar with are the Age Discrimination in Employment Act (ADEA) and the Civil Rights Act of 1964. Along with their supplementary legislation, they protect applicants and employees of any company that has more than 15 people working for it (20 for ADEA). Basically, these laws forbid any employer to use information that may discriminate unfairly among job applicants. The most common types of such information are age, sex, race, religion, color, and national origin.

In addition, if your company has a contract or does certain types of business with the federal government, you must comply with other federal laws and executive orders. These are the Vocational Rehabilitation Act, the Vietnam Era Veterans' Readjustment Act of 1974, and Executive Order 11375.

How does the four-fifths rule work?

The main concern of these laws is not how information is gathered but how employers use it. If employers use applicant information improperly, then they are guilty of illegal discrimination. Moreover, in proving that such discrimination exists, lawyers need only show that practices, though seemingly fair, are actually discriminatory in their effect. The "rule-of-thumb" measure for discriminatory effect is called the *four-fifths rule.* This rule states that a hiring procedure is discriminatory if the selection rate for the "protected [minority] group is less than 80 percent of the rate for the non-protected [majority] group." If this condition exists, then the employment process is said to have an *adverse impact.* The company must then show either that its selection process is valid or that the applicant does not possess a *BFOQ—a bona fide occupational qualification.* (A BFOQ is a cited qualification that an applicant must possess to be eligible for hiring for a particular job.) The validity of an employment process can be established with construct, content, or criterion validity procedures.

To ensure that you are complying with the various laws, write or call the U.S. Department of Labor for copies of federal employment laws and guidelines. In addition, you might consult a lawyer to review any documents you write that have any reference to these laws.

RECRUITING APPLICANTS

Jim Davis's assistant has been promoted to regional marketing manager, so you must hire a new marketing management associate for him as quickly as possible. Before you set the recruitment process in motion, your first step is to update the information you have about the job itself. You need to know what duties the new marketing management associate will have to perform and the personal qualifications he or she should have. After talking to Jim and seeing the

Career Opportunities

General Telephone Company of California

September 26, 19--

Position Title: Marketing Management Associate

Location: General Headquarters
General Telephone Company of California
100 Wilshire Boulevard
Santa Monica, California 00000

Start Date: December, 19--

Duration of Program: One Year

Salary: $30,000 per year

Job Responsibilities:

The marketing management associate will have an initial six-month assignment which will consist of establishing an overall marketing plan for the telephone answering services market. Subsequent assignments within the marketing department for the following six months will be geared to the associate's interest in developing either as a specialist or generalist. Following successful completion of the program, the Associate will be eligible for permanent placement within the GTC organization.

Program Purpose:

This program is geared toward the development of high potential employees interested in long-term managerial careers within the marketing department of GTC.

Qualifications Sought:

Recent graduates with a bachelor's degree in marketing or an MBA with a marketing emphasis are eligible for this program. Candidates must possess strong written and oral communications and presentation skills, plus analytical planning and organizational abilities. Candidates must have the ability to work independently in project completion with limited supervision. Prior experience (paid or unpaid) in financial/marketing activities such as pricing analysis, capital management, and cost flow layouts would be desirable.

Application Procedure:

Applicants may forward a complete resume by November 1, 19--, to:

Management Staffing Office
General Telephone Company of California
P.O. Box 889, RC 3221 A
Santa Monica, CA 00000

AN EQUAL OPPORTUNITY EMPLOYER

FIGURE 11-2 A typical job announcement. [From Steven P. Golen, C. Glenn Pearce, and Ross Figgins, *Report Writing for Business and Industry* (New York: John Wiley, 1985).]

kinds of work other marketing management associates perform, you add such items as appropriate college education and a familiarity with telephone answering services to the updated information.

Once you have reanalyzed the job, use this current information to update or prepare a *job description* and a *job specification.* A job description contains information about the job, describing its duties and responsibilities. For example, familiarity with telephone answering services would be part of the job description. In contrast, a job specification details the personal requirements the job demands, such as a college degree in marketing.

Using your job description and specification, you should now be able to prepare a job announcement and perhaps a display or classified advertisement. Supported by appropriate company literature, these documents form the core publications for recruiting applicants for a position.

Preparing Job Announcements and Advertisements

What types of information does a job announcement contain?

Essentially, a job description and a job specification each describe half a job. When combined, however, into a *job announcement,* they provide applicants with a more complete description of the job. Figure 11-2 shows a sample job announcement for the marketing management associate's position mentioned earlier.

Perhaps you can find a marketing management associate for Jim Davis within your company. Some companies, in fact, require in-house job posting before outside recruiting can begin. Therefore, you might post the job announcement on the bulletin board of each floor and also include it in the firm's monthly newsletter. Outside the company, send it to the various employment agencies you have dealt with, to college recruitment offices, and to individual applicants whose names you have on file from previous interviews.

In addition to the job announcement, you may prepare classified and display ads to insert in professional and trade journals as well as in the local newspapers. *Classified ads,* which appear only in the section of the newspaper or magazine with the same name, usually contain between four to six lines and describe the duties of the job and also tell applicants where to apply. Figure 11-3 shows a simple classified advertisement.

STORE MANAGER — energetic, enthusiastic individual to manage shop in Grove/Libbie area. No nights, some Sats. Mail resume to 0000 Patterson Ave., Richmond, Va. 00000

FIGURE 11-3 Classified job announcement.

COMPENSATION &
CLASSIFICATION ANALYST

A challenging opportunity for self motivated individual with proven analytical skills is open with the Office of Employee Relations Management. Duties include

- auditing and classifying jobs
- performing occupational series studies
- conducting manpower utilization studies
- management consulting

Candidates should possess a demonstrated background in personnel compensation and classification as well as the ability to communicate in a clear and concise manner, both orally and in writing.

We offer a challenging work environment and attractive benefits package. Salary $00,000 - $00,000. Apply to

VIRGINIA STATE HEALTH DEPARTMENT
Room 110 James Madison Bldg.
109 Governor St., Richmond, Va. 23219

by 5:00 p.m. September 20, 0000. Include position #2515 on form.

Equal Opportunity Employer.

FIGURE 11-4 Display job advertisement.

In contrast, *display ads* are longer, often contain the company's logo or other artwork, and may appear in other sections of a magazine or newspaper besides the classified. Figure 11-4 shows a sample display advertisement.

In writing job recruitment documents, try to describe the position, such as the marketing management associate's opening, clearly, interestingly, and as completely as space allows. Use short sentences, descriptive adjectives and adverbs, active verbs, and precise nouns. (For the job announcement, you will have to divide the information into well-organized, easy-to-follow categories set off from each other by descriptive headings.) A measure of your success will be the quality, not the quantity, of applicants your ads attract.

Using Company Publications to Recruit

Most large companies produce a variety of publications that provide useful information about themselves. Often these publications contain information the other recruitment documents omit. For example, serious applicants can find out much about the financial operations of a company from its annual reports, whereas general information pamphlets, brochures, and flyers are informative about internal organization, site locations, and so forth. In addition, company newsletters and magazines provide information about employees and employee-management relations, another area of interest to prospective employees.

Thus, with skillful use of primary and supporting recruitment documents, you can give applicants a balanced view of your company's organization, management, and employees. In this way, candidates can make a realistic decision about whether they truly want to become part of the company, and that in turn will make your own job of screening easier.

SCREENING APPLICANTS

Are blue-collar and white-collar jobs gotten in the same way?

Most companies you will work for have standard application procedures. Applicants for blue-collar positions—nonmanagerial jobs, for the most part—usually complete an application form. (More specifically, blue-collar workers are paid mostly for the physical work they do.) The form is a fill-in-the-blank report in which prospective employees merely supply the requested information. Naturally, different jobs may require different questions, but always be sure that all your forms comply with Equal Employment Opportunity Commission guidelines.

In contrast, applicants for white-collar jobs—which include managerial, professional, and nonmanagerial office positions, for the most part—may or may not complete an application form (white-collar workers are paid mostly for their knowledge and mental skills; many of them do physical work, but it is seldom strenuous). They will, however, have to prepare resumes. Usually, an application letter as well as recommendation letters accompany a resume. (See Chapter 12 for a complete discussion of the application package for white-collar employment.)

After filling out an application form or a resume, both blue- and white-collar applicants may have to undergo tests that measure their qualifications. Some typical tests are aptitude, skill, interest, inventory, and medical examinations. For example, an individual applying for the position of typist may have to take a typing skills test but not one that measures his or her interests. Employers will also usually verify information that the applicants furnish. In general, the various selection methods depend on the vacant position.

As a rule, the more your firm plans to pay a new employee, the more information you will require in deciding to hire someone. Similarly, the more complex the job or the more responsibility the successful candidate must assume (for example, regional sales manager), the more time you will take screening applicants.

Classifying Applicants by Qualifications

Why would you classify an applicant as unqualified?

Suppose you have received a substantial number of applications for the marketing management associate's position in your company's marketing department. How do you begin reviewing them? First, classify each applicant as unqualified, undecided, or qualified. Applicants who lack the *basic* qualifications you have listed on the job specification are clearly unqualified and can quickly be eliminated from the pool of applicants. For example, those without the necessary bachelor's degree or MBA mentioned for the marketing management associate's job would fall into this category.

In contrast, applicants with the basic qualifications for the job but without some desirable credentials, such as recent work experience, fall into an undecided category. Also, put candidates who fail to show clearly whether they are qualified in this category. Finally, place all people who meet your requirements in the qualified category.

After this initial classification, return to the undecided category, sort through the applications, and once again divide them into qualified or unqualified. Now, you are left with these two categories.

Notifying Applicants About Status

Now you are ready to notify the candidates of their status. Although you can use the telephone, letters work better. By writing, you can more carefully evaluate your message before sending it.

First, write your *refusal letters* to the unqualified candidates. Use the guidelines established in Chapter 9 for conveying unfavorable news to organize the letters. If time permits, write an original letter to each applicant, explaining the reasons for your decision. But if you cannot write such a letter, then use a word processor and a letter-quality printer in composing form letters. This way, the letters will at least have the appearance of being original.

Next, for all qualified applicants, telephone them or send out *interview invitation letters* to set up interview dates and times. (Modern hiring practice does call for interviews to be granted to all qualified applicants, in most cases.) The invitation should include all the information that applicants will need to get to the interview, including time and place, exact address of the interview, and the name and location (floor and office number) of the interviewer. (Follow the guidelines for favorable news given in Chapter 8 to organize these letters.)

A word of caution: After reading your letter, all candidates should know that actual hiring occurs at a later stage of the process.

INTERVIEWING APPLICANTS

Why should you set goals before you begin interviewing applicants?

You've issued the interview invitations and received acceptances, so now you can begin preparing for the initial interviews. The key to successful interviews is organization. To be well organized, you will first have to set your goals. In doing this, keep in mind the type of interview you are planning and how you want to conduct it.

Goals of Interviews

Many managers ignore this stage and are left with mixed results at the end of the interview. To make certain that you get the information you want, therefore, jot down your goals immediately. Even though the specific questions you ask may vary, knowing what your goals are should keep you on track throughout any interview.

The ultimate purpose for setting interview goals is to help you narrow the field of applicants. In this initial interview, concentrate on how closely the candidate's qualifications *fit* the requirements you have detailed in the job description and job specification. (Later in this section, we will discuss what the right questions are to ask during such an interview.)

The following checklist shows the four goals of initial interviews:

CHECKLIST OF INITIAL INTERVIEW GOALS

1. Get answers to questions that arose when you read the application package.
2. Get details about each applicant's background—work experience and education, for example—that will supplement and explain information in the application package.
3. Learn about each applicant's personality, while remembering the restrictions the BFOQ may place on consideration of it.
4. Explore any additional relevant information that comes up in the interview or appears in the application package.

Types of Interviews

What are the two basic types of interviews?

Usually, a *standard* interview is held in the personnel offices of the company with a company representative meeting with one applicant. In this type of interview, your objective is to acquire the information described in the initial interview checklist. Sometimes, however, you may for one reason or another hold a *nonstandard* interview. For example, you may ask the advertising director of the company to join you in interviewing a particularly well-qualified applicant, or you could meet with the candidate somewhere else. Currently, the most common types of nonstandard interviews are campus, hotel/motel, and panel. A new type that may grow increasingly common is the computer interview.

Campus Interviews

Suppose you are looking for entry-level accountants, and several universities have soon-to-be graduates who are especially well qualified. Rather than pay the expenses for individual candidates to visit your company, which may be hundreds of miles away from these schools, you might find it more economical to travel to the universities to interview the students. After screening these applicants, you probably would ask several to visit your company at your expense for further interviewing.

Hotel/Motel Interviews

When applicants work in high-demand, low-supply specialty areas, such as some "high-tech" positions, companies must travel to where the best qualified applicants live to compete with other companies for these prospective employees. Since many of these specialists tend to be concentrated in certain regions of the country, you might decide to interview them from a hotel or motel suite nearby.

Panel Interviews

In a panel interview, usually three or more experts in different fields within the company question the candidate. The purpose of these interviews is to measure an applicant's qualifications in depth. Sometimes too the panel format functions to achieve consensus about candidates. Obviously, though, the high cost in time and money makes it relatively rare. Panel interviews are generally reserved for upper-middle or top managerial jobs, those requiring great expertise and/or those requiring the ability to function under stress. For example, if you were hiring someone to head a bank's branch office in Hong Kong or an ice cream company's production plant, or someone to supervise traffic control at the nation's busiest airport, you might conduct a panel interview.

Computer Interviews

Today, a few employers are already interviewing by computer. Essentially, they are using computers linked through telephone lines to conduct a teleconference. As you and the applicant ask and answer questions, written messages are transmitted from one computer screen to the other. During such sessions, the contents of a document, such as a recommendation letter or resume, may also be transmitted. Perhaps in the future, computer interviewing may become popular as a way to screen applicants initially, especially when they live far away from your company. At this point, however, the quality of the information you receive from a computer terminal is quite restricted, especially when compared with a face-to-face interview.

Conducting the Interview Session

Can you explain the difference between structured and unstructured interviews?

You have written your goals down on a yellow pad and have decided to interview the candidate in your own office. Now you have to consider whether to use a structured or unstructured interview. Your choice should depend on the degree of control you wish to maintain. If you want full control, plan a *structured*, or directive, interview and, therefore, write out all your questions beforehand. The advantages of this approach are twofold: your interview should run efficiently, in that you won't waste time on tangents, and you can easily compare applicants' qualifications afterward.

In contrast, if you decide on an *unstructured*, or nondirective, interview, you will have less control during its execution. Here you want to open discussion—and so you do not prepare all (or most) of your questions in advance. (You should, however, plan for the information you need to gather.) Although unstructured interviews require more of your time and effort to conduct, they do have this advantage over structured ones: because the applicants can talk more freely under less stressful conditions, you can learn more about their communication abilities and depth of job-related knowledge.

Two types of questions can be used in interviews: closed questions and open questions. Closed questions require specific answers, and are especially useful in a structured interview. Open questions, however, require thoughtful, in-depth answers and are especially useful in an unstructured interview. The checklist on the following page contains questions you might ask during both types of interviews. Notice how different the types of questions are for each. At the same time, note that you will need to ask some of both types of questions in a typical job interview, regardless of the basic format used.

The Overall Procedure

Like written or oral reports, interviews have a *beginning*, a *middle*, and an *end*.

CHECKLIST OF TYPICAL INTERVIEW QUESTIONS

Closed Format

1. How did you find out about this job opening?
2. Are you willing to relocate if hired?
3. Why did you leave your last job?
4. What is the best professional journal in your field?
5. How did you spend your spare time when in school?

Open Format

1. How did your education prepare you for this job?
2. How do you get motivated to do a good job?
3. What is your idea of a successful career?
4. What three or four words would you use to describe yourself? And why would you choose these words?
5. What is the most important question you think I could ask you about your ability to handle this job? And why do you think it is the most important question?

Why is it important to recognize that an interview has a beginning, a middle, and an end?

The beginning of an interview is especially critical because it is here that first impressions are established, which set the tone for the remainder of the session. Because the applicant's tension is likely to be greatest at this point, you should try to create a calm, relaxed mood. Do this by choosing a comfortable setting, such as a sofa, if your office has one, or a comfortable chair for the applicant. In the same vein, start out with "small talk"—general conversation about noncritical topics. You'll find it easier to move smoothly into the important questions of the interview if you begin with casual comments picked up from the applicant's resume. Talking about the success of the basketball team at the applicant's college can easily lead into a discussion of the person's educational qualifications.

The *middle of the interview* should focus on questions and answers. Naturally, you want to ask the right questions, but you also have to ask them in the right way at the right time. Even in a structured interview, these factors are important, and a certain flexibility on your part is necessary. For example, suppose you receive an answer to your third question about relevant experience that really answers your fourth question too. If this occurs, you should be ready to skip to your fifth question about future ambitions, and so forth. Although experience helps more than anything, the following guidelines will assist you in asking and answering questions in the middle part of the interview.

GUIDELINES FOR QUESTION AND ANSWER SESSIONS

1. Ask leading questions to encourage discussion when appropriate.
2. Time or pace the questions to allow just enough response time before moving on. Return the conversation to the subject if the applicant strays.
3. Use only the time you reserved for the interview. Get as much information as you can.
4. Rephrase a question or move on if the applicant is unable to answer. Long, awkward pauses are embarrassing.
5. Avoid wasting time by asking questions to which you already know the answers.
6. Ask follow-up questions to explore an issue further. For example, if you learn an applicant had a personality conflict with his or her last supervisor, you might ask, "What did your supervisor do that bothered you most?"
7. Avoid tricky questions or ones that might entrap the applicant. An atmosphere of trust yields the best responses.
8. Record responses for later review without allowing this procedure to interfere with the interview.
9. Remain neutral when asking or answering questions or when listening to answers. Be pleasant and encouraging, but avoid agreeing or disagreeing with opinions.
10. Speak distinctly; do not mumble while taking notes.
11. Ask the applicant to explain any unclear response.
12. Follow a flexible procedure. No two interviews can ever duplicate each other, but you can get the important answers in many ways.

After you have acquired all the information you need, *end* the interview. A good way to begin to close is to ask an applicant if he or she has any questions that the interview hasn't answered. If there are none, then tell the candidate what to expect next. For example, you might call if the need exists for another interview. Or you will have to interview other applicants before making a decision. Whatever your next step is, tell the applicant the date by which you will make your hiring decision.

Figure 11-5 shows a general procedure for conducting a 30-minute interview. As you study this plan, notice that the organization is structured loosely enough to permit flexibility on the interviewer's part.

THE INTERVIEWER'S PLAN

Objectives of the Interviewer:
1. Evaluate the Candidate
2. Stimulate the Candidate's Interest in the Firm
3. Maintain the Goodwill of the Candidate

Structure of an Interview (30 min.)

Time	Interviewer's Activity	Interviewer's Purpose
4–5 min.	1. Reading résumé	1. Notice grades, academic achievement, extracurricular activities
	2. General comments Résumé Weather "Why did you decide to study at ____ ?"	2. Establish rapport Put candidate at ease Ask questions candidate can answer easily so he or she gains confidence
16 min.	3. Information gathering	3. Decide whether to ask the candidate back for a second interview
	a. Open questions—requiring explanatory answers "How do you spend your leisure time?" "Tell me about your college experience." "What courses did you like?"	a. Determine candidate's motivations and habits
	b. Closed questions—requiring short factual answers How does a candidate act in certain situations? Focus on past behavior	b. Determine if candidate's apparent attributes are reflected in reality
	c. Listening techniques Echo (repeat phrases) Eye contact Silence	c. Show acceptance
	d. Behavior observations Interested? Enthusiastic? Poised? Assertive?	d. Pierce through candidate's nervousness to substance of what the candidate is like
5 min.	4. Answer questions	4. Sell the organization
1 min.	5. Summary and close	5. Tell the candidate when and how he or she will hear from the organization
4 min.	6. Write up evaluation	6. Write while impression is fresh

FIGURE 11-5 The interviewer's plan. (Joan W. Rossi, "Make Your Students Interview Ready," *The ABCA Bulletin*, September 1980, p. 3.) Reprinted with Permission.

Handling Stress During an Interview

Should you always try to reduce stress in an interview?

If people really want a job, they are bound to feel some stress during the initial interview. Will you like them, they wonder? Will they slip and say something stupid? The questions of this type are many in a typical applicant's mind. Sometimes stress can sharpen the senses. More often, though, you will need to reduce the applicant's anxiety. The most effective interviewers use small talk at the start of the interview for this purpose. They are also friendly and supportive throughout the session. If appropriate, they may even offer candidates a soft drink or coffee as a tension-easing gesture.

But what if you want to see how a candidate deals with stress because the job for which he or she is applying is fast paced and requires an employee to function under tense conditions? For example, jobs in sales, claims adjustments, and many management positions often call for stress interviews. In these instances, simply allow normal tensions to go unchecked and then build on that tension by asking probing questions as needed. If such an approach doesn't work well enough, you can appear cold and unfriendly as well.

Taking Notes During an Interview

Could using an applicant evaluation form lead to less note taking during an interview?

In general, unless you have an excellent memory, you will need to take some notes during the interview. The trick is to do your note taking inconspicuously; otherwise, you will distract the applicants and cause them to be uneasy when they should be relaxed. Common note-taking pitfalls are (1) stopping too often to take notes, (2) talking as you write, or (3) emphasizing the special importance of an answer by reaching for your pen. To avoid these hazards, many interviewers use an *applicant evaluation form.* Figure 11-6 is a sample of this form.

As you can see, using an application evaluation form (Figure 11-6) eliminates the chore of taking extensive notes during the interview. Instead, as soon as the interview is over and while your impressions are still fresh, you can complete the form.

An applicant evaluation form is easy to fill out, saves time, prevents distractions during the interview, and provides objective evidence about the applicant. However, it doesn't always permit you to present the best information. For example, you can't record the applicant's in-depth responses on a form. Thus, when these kinds of reactions are important, you may also have to take notes during, or immediately after, the interview.

Holding Follow-up Interviews

Suppose that you have interviewed all the candidates but that you cannot choose among three of them for the position of assistant treasurer of your company. Your next step is to do follow-up inter-

APPLICANT EVALUATION FORM

Applicant's Name ______________________ Position __________

Overall Appraisal	Poor		Average		Good
1. Initial impression	1	2	3	4	5
2. Personal demeanor	1	2	3	4	5
3. Preparation for interview	1	2	3	4	5
4. Ability to express self	1	2	3	4	5
5. Level of maturity	1	2	3	4	5
				Total	_____

Career Qualifications					
1. Academic preparation	1	2	3	4	5
2. Professional experience	1	2	3	4	5
3. Knowledge of job	1	2	3	4	5
4. Leadership ability	1	2	3	4	5
5. Career potential	1	2	3	4	5
				Total	_____

Personality Impressions

These judgments are not absolutes, merely impressions. You do not have to complete every one, or, if you wish, you may expand your responses on the back.

Dominance:	Aggressive/passive
Self-regard:	Positive/negative
Self-confidence:	Strong/weak
General behavior:	Friendly/shy or hostile
Interactions:	Spontaneous/guarded or reticent
Feelings about change:	Accepts or enjoys/negative or fearful
Endurance:	Sticks to tasks/gives up
Overall evaluation:	Consider abilities to perform job tasks, form relationships with peers and future career success. Use back of sheet if required.

Would this person be an asset to the company?
What should this applicant's hiring priority rating be on a 1 to 10 scale?

Interviewer ______________________ Date __________

FIGURE 11-6 An applicant evaluation form for interviewer.

views with the three candidates. In many companies, second or even third interviews are held regularly for top managerial positions.

What role does a follow-up interview play?

Instead of simply repeating the first interview, try to enlarge the scope of your inquiries. For example, you may probe for more detailed information about each of the three's qualifications. You might also enlarge the size of the interview by inviting the manager who will supervise the successful applicant. Also, you may want to arrange meetings with the people with whom the applicant will work if hired. And if you haven't done so already, you might want to get up a tour of the appropriate plant facilities.

EVALUATING QUALIFICATIONS AND MAKING RECOMMENDATIONS

After holding all the interviews you need, you must evaluate the information gained so you can recommend hiring one of the applicants. In deciding, rely only on written, oral, and observed data. Generally, some of the data are more easily analyzed than others. Thus, you will probably find that you may quickly evaluate written data, such as that on resumes, application forms, and letters of recommendation. Similarly, oral evidence, such as answers to your interview questions, is easy to appraise if the questions have evoked meaningful responses. Of course, the answers in unstructured interviews are more difficult to compare with one another than are those that result from structured sessions.

What information can you get from a recommendation letter that you may not get otherwise?

Of all the evidence you have to consider, *recommendation letters* contain the only information that you did not in some way originate. Either you or an assistant may request them directly, or applicants may send them to you unrequested. Employers today usually do want to see such letters. Generally, most recommendations are favorable, perhaps because the information they contain may be used in legal disputes.

Still, the content should appear credible. If it does not, then refuse to assign it much value. In contrast, a well-written, apparently sincere recommendation may be a rich source of useful information about an applicant. Compare the data in the accompanying box to see

---

CONTRASTING RECOMMENDATIONS FROM THE SAME EMPLOYER

Janice enjoys working in an active environment. She accepts responsibility and likes to get involved with solving production problems as they occur. Because she works well with others, Janice can direct other employees' work effortlessly and continue her own work at the same time.

George is a quiet man who is happiest and most productive when working alone. He is patient, responsible, and requires little supervision. When working on long-term projects and those requiring detailed thinking, George is at his best.

---

how two favorable recommendations can sharply differ in the portrait they paint.

Based on your evaluation of the evidence you have, you must make a recommendation to hire or not to hire each applicant you have interviewed. Once you have decided, then your recommendation report usually goes to the person who will supervise the successful applicant, and this supervisory person will make the final decision. In some instances, your report may merely consist of a copy of a completed applicant evaluation form. In others, you may write a detailed report. How much you do will probably depend on the number of applicants involved, the time pressure encountered, and the importance of the job itself. Remember that, legally, an employer must provide objective criteria, such as whether and how much prior experience is required, to job applicants. Then the employer must base hiring decisions on these criteria. So include all available evidence to support any opinions involved in offering a recommendation.

HIRING AND WELCOMING THE NEW EMPLOYEE

After an eventful interviewing process, you have recommended hiring a particular applicant for a managerial position. The department manager has concurred with your choice. Now you need to notify each applicant you interviewed. Usually, you call or send a telegram to the person you wish to hire. Then you send a confirmation letter.

Since the job offer is favorable news, follow the plan for organizing such messages suggested in Chapter 8. Be sure to include all the details the applicant will need to decide whether to accept your offer.

Of what value is a counterproposal?

Suppose the applicant decides he or she wants the position but doesn't like the terms you are offering. If this happens, you will have to determine whether you can negotiate or want to offer the job to another person. Usually, when your terms are unacceptable, the applicant will respond with a counteroffer. If you decide to accept it, write a second favorable news letter stating your agreement to the terms. If, however, you want to counter with a compromise offer, then write a persuasive letter following the A-I-D-A approach suggested in Chapter 10. Or, if you are unwilling to accept the counterproposal or to offer a compromise, write a refusal using the inductive plan for such messages outlined in Chapter 9. In the refusal, you can ask the candidate to reconsider your original offer or you can rescind it. If you choose to rescind the offer, then offer the job to the next best qualified applicant and continue the process until you fill the position.

After your job offer has been accepted, you will have to write refusal letters to all the unsuccessful candidates. Once you have

What can you do to make a new employee feel welcome in the company?

written them—using the suggested format for unfavorable messages in Chapter 9—your job is *almost* done. One last step remains, however, that many employers often overlook: welcoming the new employee to the company. You can accomplish this task with a welcoming letter that follows the favorable news design discussed in Chapter 8. If your company has a job orientation program, explain in the details section of your letter how and when orientation will take place. If you have no such program, however, then include information about orientation in this letter. Orientation will include such information as where and to whom to report and what to expect during the first few days on the new job.

SUMMARY

1. This chapter describes how employers advertise jobs and then fill them.
2. Employment is a process in which employers recruit, screen, interview, evaluate, hire, and welcome new employees.
3. Employers follow equal employment laws to select the best qualified applicant and to avoid legal problems.
4. When recruiting applicants, you may use a detailed job announcement drawn from the job description and job specification for the position. In addition you may use classified and display job advertisements.
5. Company publications containing general information about the company and its employees are useful in recruitment as supporting material. These publications include newsletters, magazines, and brochures.
6. Screening applications occurs after you have advertised the job and people have applied for it. In screening, the first step is to classify the candidates as unqualified, undecided, or qualified. Then reclassify those in the undecided category as either qualified or unqualified and notify all applicants about their status.
7. The next step is to hold initial interviews with qualified applicants. The first stage in this step is to write down the interview goals so you can know what to achieve in the process.
8. You probably will hold a standard interview in most cases. This type of interview takes place in the company's office between you, the interviewer, and one applicant.
9. Many types of nonstandard interviews are held for one reason or another. Such interviews include campus and hotel/motel, panel, and the new computer interviews.
10. The interviews themselves are either structured or unstructured. In a structured interview, you will plan carefully and ask specific questions designed to get precise answers. In an unstructured interview, the questions should be designed to provoke thought and elicit discussion.
11. Like oral and written reports, interviews have a beginning, a middle, and an end. At the beginning you should set a positive tone to ease the applicant's tension. Then, in the middle section, questions

and answers should follow. At the end, you should close the session by telling the applicant when to expect your decision.

12. Unless you conduct an interview specifically to measure stress, you should try to control and/or reduce this factor.
13. Instead of taking notes during the interview, you might complete an application evaluation form immediately afterward. Even if you use such a form, you may still have to write.
14. If you are unable to make a recommendation to hire after the initial interview, hold one or more follow-up interviews.
15. After all interviews are completed, you must then evaluate the applicants' qualifications, compare them to one another's, and make recommendations to hire and not to hire. In most cases, you will consider written, oral, and observed evidence. The final decision, however, should be made by the person to whom the new employee will report.
16. The last step in the process of filling a vacancy is to hire the best qualified applicant available under conditions you consider acceptable. After you have filled the vacancy, notify the unsuccessful applicants you interviewed that you have hired someone else. Then write a letter welcoming the new employee to the company, including in it information about orientation.

Review Questions

1. In what way can an applicant find help with a job search by studying the employer's role in the employment process?
2. Why do most job applicants never complete the entire employment process shown in Figure 11-1?
3. Which laws primarily affect equal employment opportunity? What type of protection do they give job applicants?
4. What are job descriptions and job specifications? What role do they play in recruiting job applicants?
5. What differences exist in the makeup and use of job announcements and classified and display job advertisements?
6. How are company publications used in recruitment? Generally speaking, which ones provide what types of information?
7. How are applicants classified by qualification once applications for a job begin to arrive?
8. Why set interview goals? Name four goals for an initial interview.
9. What is the difference between a standard and a nonstandard interview? Which one is held more often, and why do you think this is the case?
10. Have you ever heard of a computer interview? What can an employer gain by holding these interviews?
11. How do structured and unstructured interviews differ? Under what circumstances should you hold one or the other? Can you name two closed and two open questions you would ask that do not appear in the checklist on page 331?
12. Can you name one or two questions you might ask an applicant during an interview that would be fair in one situation but unfair in another? Explain your answer.
13. When would you want to control stress in an interview, and when might you prefer to promote stress? What would you do differently in the two situations?

14. Do you think an applicant evaluation form is really useful for recording results of interviews for managerial positions? Explain your answer.

15. Why do you think the person who will supervise a job applicant if hired is usually the person to make the actual hiring decision?

Exercises

1. Find three current job descriptions and job specifications for a position in your career field that you would like to have. You might get them from local companies or employment offices, a college career placement office, or a library. Then analyze these documents to see whether you are now fully qualified to fill the position. If not, will you be qualified upon completing your present plans? Prepare a short report to explain the situation and your plans to fulfill any deficiencies.
2. Prepare a job announcement for a position in your career field that you would like to have. To do this, you will need at least one job description and one job specification to provide the basic information. (If your instructor agrees, you might use those obtained to complete Exercise 1.)
3. The Age Discrimination in Employment Act and the Civil Rights Act of 1964 are the two major federal laws affecting fairness in employment. Get abstracts or complete copies of the acts to analyze. Then prepare a short report summarizing their effect on discrimination in employment in your career field.
4. Find a record of any laws in your state that supplement the federal age discrimination and civil rights acts mentioned in Exercise 3. Then summarize the content of these acts in a short report. Include an explanation of why you think this legislation is or is not needed in your state.
5. Call or visit a firm that employs people in your career field and ask for copies of the company publications. Then prepare a short report evaluating each publication. Include the types of information it contains, the major purpose it serves, and how it can be used in the company's recruitment efforts.
6. Set up a simulated standard employment interview in your class. If convenient, you might ask an employer or personnel officer to conduct the session with students. Otherwise, students can play all the necessary roles. Record the interviews either on audiotape or videotape (videotape if possible). Evaluate the success of these interviews in a short report. Include all changes each participant should make for future interviews.
7. Clip a job display advertisement from the newspaper or a magazine. Choose a field you work in now or are interested in getting into later. Assume that you have applied for the job and classified yourself as unqualified, undecided, or qualified. If you classified yourself in the undecided category, reevaluate the situation and reclassify yourself as unqualified or qualified. Now, write yourself an interview invitation letter if you are qualified for the job; if unqualified, write yourself a refusal letter.
8. Assume that you work for R. E. Penter Group, a local manufacturer of robots for industrial use that are sold throughout the country. You have just finished screening six applicants for a job as district sales supervisor for a tristate area. You want to interview three of the six applicants (the other three do not have the five years of sales experience re-

quired). Write an interview invitation letter for use as a form to invite the three for an initial interview. Then write a refusal letter also for use as a form to notify the unsuccessful applicants.

9. Based on your present qualifications for a job you would like to have, write yourself a recommendation letter. Be as objective as possible. In class, your instructor may decide to have you share the information in your letter with other class members. If so, your classmates will cross-examine you about your qualifications.

10. Assume that you work for EmCee Microphonics Company as the personnel director. EmCee is a middle-sized manufacturer of microphones and speaker systems for teleconferencing facilities. Now, assume that your employment process is the same as that discussed in this chapter and that you just hired Mohan Ali as a junior accountant in the payroll department. Write a letter welcoming Mr. Ali to the company, including information about a job orientation program in which he will participate during the first week.

CHAPTER 12

FINDING A JOB: THE APPLICANT'S ROLE

Lenny and Julia are two recent college graduates who are looking for their first jobs. Lenny, a marketing major, has written to several companies inquiring if they have any vacancies. Yet, even though he has done this, he has not really considered the type of position he wants, nor has he prepared a resume. Julia, on the other hand, a finance major, knows that she wants to work for a major investment firm. To obtain a job in her chosen field, she has composed a resume that highlights her education and work experience. Each week she looks at the finance section of the classifieds and talks to acquaintances who may be helpful, including her instructors in finance. Moreover, she has recognized that the job search is a step-by-step process, much of which complements the prospective employer's routine you have just learned about in Chapter 11. At the end of several weeks, Julia has interviews set up with three prospective employers, whereas Lenny has none.

What are the five steps to follow in finding a suitable job?

In this chapter, you will learn, as Julia did, the step-by-step job search process that can help you reach your goal—finding the right job. As Figure 12-1 shows, this process consists of five steps. To be successful, you will need to become familiar with each of them.

LOCATING JOB VACANCIES

The first step in your job search process involves identifying job vacancies. Where do you look for them? Usually, you turn first to the classified section of the local newspapers. However, only a small

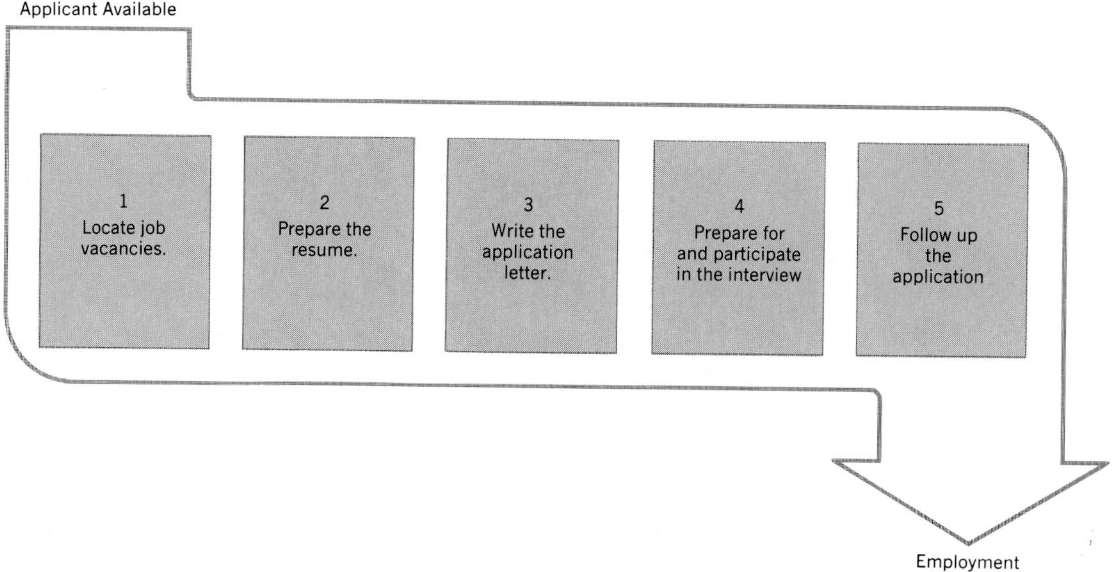

FIGURE 12-1 View of the employment (job search) process from the applicant's viewpoint.

percentage of available jobs appears in the classifieds. Other sources are professional and trade journals, college and university placement offices, employment agencies, personal contacts, and contacts with the companies themselves. Let us look at each of these separately.

Newspapers

Newspapers are the most popular source of job leads. Local newspapers carry announcements for positions in a specific geographic area, whereas large city newspapers often announce jobs in distant places. National papers, such as *The Wall Street Journal,* advertise positions in the entire country and abroad.

How do blind and signed ads differ?

As discussed in Chapter 11, newspaper ads are of two types: classified and display. When only a box number is given, the ads are termed *blind ads.* (See Figure 11-3.) When the name of the company that has the vacancy is mentioned, they are called *signed ads.* (See Figure 11-4.)

A signed ad offers an advantage: because you know the company's identity, you can tailor your application letter and resume accordingly. A blind ad, however, does not permit this. In addition, the company does not have to acknowledge your letter, so you may never know why you were not contacted if you do not receive a response. (Some companies actually run blind ads to determine the state of the job market.)

Whether you answer a blind ad is up to you. Several more promising sources are available.

Professional and Trade Journals

Some professional journals have job placement columns and even classified sections. Most also print announcements of professional activities such as meetings, workshops, seminars, and conferences. Attending any of these activities can lead to potential job contacts by providing you with the opportunity to meet company officials or recruiters. This is especially true when the activities include job placement booths.

How can you find the professional journals in your field?

How can you find the professional journals in your field if you are not already familiar with them? You can find them in *Ayers,* the *Working Press,* or the *Business Periodicals Index.* Or you can locate them in an encyclopedia of associations, such as the *Career Guide of Professional Associations* or the *Directory of National Trade and Professional Associations.*

Although trade journals and in-house publications do not include advertisements for employees, they do contain timely information. For example, stories on retirements, new plant and office locations, and plant expansions and relocations all mean that jobs may be available.

College and University Placement Offices

A third source of job information is your college or university placement office, whose services range from job referrals to career counseling. Visit the placement office on your campus to find out what it can do for you.

Employment Agencies

How do government and private employee agencies differ?

Employment agencies—both public and private—are a fourth source of job information. Public employment agencies exist at all levels: federal, state, and local. The U.S. Office of Personnel Management is in charge of federal employment of applicants for every type of federal job, including managerial positions. In addition, each state is in charge of placement services for all its citizens. (Federal law requires the states to do this.) Traditionally, the states have directed these services mostly toward blue-collar employment. However, state agencies do provide information about managerial positions often enough to justify making inquiries to them. Local or city agencies perform similar functions, although their services are more geographically limited.

Unlike government agencies, private employment agencies are in business to find jobs for their clients, so they charge for their services. For some jobs, employers pay all or part of the agency's fees; for others, they pay nothing and the applicant pays the fee. Because different agencies perform different services—for example, some find people jobs in health care services whereas others do the same in accounting and finance—be sure to find the one that best meets your special needs. Then, when you contract with the agency, read your agreement carefully or consult a lawyer before signing it.

Personal Contacts

Personal contacts are another excellent source for finding the right job. Begin by contacting people you feel will be able to help you find job leads. For instance, if you are interested in finding a job in advertising and your neighbor is an executive in a local advertising company, talk with your neighbor. Explain what you want and ask for his or her assistance. If he or she cannot help, ask about any acquaintances who might be able to do so. Then, when you call or write these contacts, start by explaining who referred you to them. If you do this, you are developing a *network* of job sources that you can use throughout your career.

How could you develop a network of job sources?

When using networking, keep accurate records; that is, find out exactly which jobs are available and obtain the correct spelling of the names of the individuals you are to contact and their job titles.

Building an effective network takes endurance and the right timing. You may end up making a large number of calls, but the payoff comes when the person on the other end of the line replies: "Yes, we are looking for someone. Please send us a resume, and we will set up an interview."

Organizational Contacts

Another way to find out where the jobs are is to call or stop by companies in your area or in areas where you may want to relocate. If the company is not hiring at the time, ask for the name and title of the person in charge of hiring. Later, you might want to send him or her a letter as a follow-up to your visit. (Follow-up letters are discussed later in this chapter.)

Or you might send unsolicited or "prospecting" application letters to the companies rather than call on them directly or telephone. Again, you do not know if a job is available, so it is best to ask to have your letter held for reference if no openings exist at present. (Unsolicited letters are also discussed in more detail later in the chapter.)

Suppose that by using all these sources you have turned up a couple of jobs you feel qualified for and are interested in. You can ask your college or university to send a copy of your placement file to these prospective employees. However, since the file usually presents your qualifications in a form that may be unsuitable for the position you are seeking, you will want to prepare a resume and application letter to send in advance of it.

PREPARING THE RESUME

What makes up a two-part application package?

The second step in your job search process is to prepare a resume. This is a historical account of your education, work experience, skills, and other job-related personal information. Your resume and the application letter you will compose later form the *two-part application package.* In preparing this package, your goal is to present your qualifications for the position you are seeking so that an interview will follow. Your chances of being invited to such an interview virtually depend on the effectiveness of the application package.

Analyze Your Qualifications

Suppose you are ready to begin writing your resume and application letter, but you don't know where to start. The answer is to start with yourself. "Take stock" of *who you are, what you know,* and *what you have done.* Figure 12-2 shows a sample resume worksheet. In conducting your own self-examination, you may use the headings on this worksheet as a guide to the kinds of information you need to supply for a resume. Although you may decide not to include all the data in your responses to each section, you can create a "rough draft" resume that shows who you are and what you can do. Then, after you have completed your own worksheet, you can go on to prepare a resume.

RESUME WORKSHEET

Heading

Name

Local address and telephone number (with area code)

Permanent address and telephone number (assuming it is different from your school address)

Job Objectives/Career Objectives

Short-range objective (for example, programmer/analyst)

Long-range objective (be as specific as possible)

Educational Background—beginning with the most recent and working backward to your high school

Name of school

Dates attended, including months

Degree(s) earned or expected (be specific—Bachelor of Science in Business, not just Bachelor of Science)

Anticipated graduation date

Major and minor fields of study

Relevant courses

Overall grade-point average and/or grade-point average in major

Scholarships, awards, and other academic honors (including number of semesters on dean's list, graduation honors)

Co-curricular and extracurricular activities, including elected and appointed offices and dates of membership

Internships, cooperative education experiences, special class projects

Professional memberships

Percentage of college expenses you paid for

FIGURE 12-2 A resume worksheet.

Work Experience—including full-time and part-time paid experiences as well as volunteer work

Employer (including address and telephone number)
Position
Dates employed (including months)
Duties performed and responsibilities assumed
Skills used or learned on the job
Awards or special recognitions

Military Service

Branch of service
Dates in service
Rank when you left service
Duties performed and responsibilities assumed
Skills used or learned
Type of discharge
Awards or special recognitions

Special Skills

Keyboarding skill (words per minute)
Knowledge of business machines and computers
Ability to program in various languages
Proficiency in reading, writing, and speaking a foreign language
Certificates, licenses, diplomas

Personal Information

Willingness to travel
Willingness to relocate (including geographical preference)
Activities in civic groups (including offices held)
Honors and awards other than scholastic
Hobbies and interests

References

Names, addresses, and telephone numbers of at least three people who can attest to your ability and knowledge.

FIGURE 12-2 continued

Become Familiar with Types of Resumes

Application letters interpret the information in resumes so you should prepare your resume first. Using sentence fragments—clauses and phrases—a resume describes, discusses, and explains your qualifications for a job. Some people refer to resumes as personal data sheets; however, resumes are much more than that. For example, an excerpt from a personal data sheet relating to an applicant's work experience might read:

> Smith and Barney Architects, 92 South Broad Street, Richmond, Virginia. Architect's Assistant. May 1984 to present.

As you can see, only the name of the employer and a job title are given. In contrast, a resume not only identifies but also describes the same data:

> *Architect's Assistant.* Smith and Barney Architects, 92 South Broad Street, Richmond, Virginia. May 1984 to present.
>
> Assist in organizing designs, obtain information on zoning ordinances, and prepare work schedules for blueprint printing.

Clearly, a resume provides much more information about your qualifications than does a personal data sheet.

In deciding what information to put into your resume, that is, what to transfer from your worksheet, remember that your goal is to obtain an interview. In other words, avoid including information that may stand in your way. For example, if you have a low grade point average or have left a job because of a disagreement with your employer, you might exclude this information from your resume. You can handle such delicate topics better in an interview, where you can explain your position more completely.

Do general and personalized resumes perform the same function?

In composing a resume, you may follow the form of either a *general resume* or a *personalized resume.* Submit a general resume when you are applying to more than one company or for a variety of related jobs, such as in sales. As its name implies, in a general resume, present your qualifications so that you appear to be a good candidate for a number of positions or companies. Figure 12-3 shows a general resume.

On the other hand, use a personalized resume when you are applying for a specific job or to a specific company. In a personalized resume, you tailor the information so that you appear to be the best qualified person for this one job or for this one company. Usually, personalized resumes are more effective because they permit employers to see more easily how you might best meet their needs. Figure 12-4 shows a personalized resume.

WILLIAM E. WEBB

Candidate for Bachelor of Science in Business
Administration and Management
Virginia Commonwealth University
May, 1987

Position Sought: Entry-level Manager in Human Resource Development

Personnel-Oriented Education

Will receive Bachelor of Science in Business Administration and Management with major in Personnel from Virginia Commonwealth University, Richmond, in May, 1986. Attended September 1982 to present.

Personnel and Related Coursework:	Personnel Administration; Salary Administration; Job Analysis and Evaluation; Seminar in Personnel; Stress in Management; Industrial Psychology; Adult Psychology.
Honors:	Dean's List--six semesters; will graduate Summa Cum Laude. GPA in Major-3.8; overall-3.5 (4.0 basis).
Co-curricular Activities:	Student Member of American Society of Personnel Administrators, VCU Chapter; 1984 to present (Vice President, 1985-86).

People-Related Work Experience

Pizza Station
439 South Broad Street
Richmond, Virginia 23288

Counter Clerk and Cashier
(Part-time--April 1982 to present)

Assist customers in placing orders, maintain customer goodwill during rush periods; handle cash receipts and disbursements.

Personal Information

256 Grove Avenue
Richmond, Virginia 23222
804-555-2134

Willing to travel/relocate
Special interests in guitar playing and racquetball

Contributed over 50 percent toward college expenses through part-time employment while attending school full time.

References

Upon request, references will be supplied by the Virginia Commonwealth University Placement Office, 901 West Franklin Street, Richmond, VA 23284.

FIGURE 12-3 A general resume.

MARGARITE PEREZ'S QUALIFICATIONS FOR

MARKETING REPRESENTATIVE WITH FOODWHIZ, INC.

Immediate Objective: Marketing Representative

Long-term Objective: Director of Regional Marketing

EDUCATION

Bachelor of Science in Marketing, Northwest University, Bangor, Maine, to be awarded June, 1987.

Program included courses in market analyses, marketing research, and marketing strategies.

Co-curricular Activity: Student member of American Marketing Association, September 1983 to present.

EXPERIENCE

Sales Representative--Exercise Department. Down-N-Under Sporting Goods, Oxford Mall, Bangor, Maine. September 1982 to September 1987 (part-time during school year; full time during vacations).

Assisted customers in selection of exercise clothing and equipment; prepared weekly sales representatives' work schedule; assisted manager in selecting line of women's exercise apparel. Received "Outstanding Sales Representative of the Month" award three times.

Temporary Office Worker. We-Help-Ur Company, 981 West Main Street, Bangor, Maine. November 1981 to August 1982 (part-time).

Performed general office work on an assigned basis for various clients.

PERSONAL INFORMATION

Address until June 1, 1987
Rhoads Hall, Room 426
Northwest University
Bangor, Maine 02911
207-555-4933

Address after June 1, 1987
497 Salem Boulevard
Bangor, Maine 02912
207-555-7944

Willing to travel and relocate in Northeast.

Member of church choir; teach Sunday School to elementary-age children.

Hold certificates in CPR and YWCA Lifesaving.

FIGURE 12-4 A personalized resume.

Margarite Perez
Resume
Page 2

REFERENCES

Ms. Marie Brown
Manager--Exercise Department
Down-N-Under Sporting Goods
Oxford Mall
Bangor, ME 02913
207-555-6944

Dr. Mildred Longo
Chairman, Marketing Department
School of Business
Northwest University
Bangor, ME 02911
207-555-5549

Mr. George Jackson, Manager
We-Help-Ur Company
981 West Main Street
Bangor, ME 02913
207-555-8412

FIGURE 12-4 continued

Draft the Resume

What are the six types of information a resume contains?

Whichever resume you choose to prepare—and you can, of course, do both types—it can contain as many as six types of information, arranged in various ways: (1) heading, (2) job or career objective, (3) education, (4) work experience, (5) personal information, and (6) references. Naturally information in these sections will vary from person to person and, if you are composing a personalized resume, from job to job. Still, in preparing them, you may follow some general guidelines.

The Heading

You can choose your heading from a variety of formats. Generally, the heading "Resume" should be avoided since the reader will immediately recognize the document as being a resume. So, come right to the point with a heading similar to one of the following:

WILLIAM E. WEBB

Candidate for Bachelor of Science in Business
Administration and Management
Virginia Commonwealth University
May, 1987

or

MARGARITE PEREZ'S QUALIFICATIONS FOR
MARKETING REPRESENTATIVE WITH FOODWHIZ, INC.

or

MARILYN J. BOSTON

2323 Piney Road
Idaho Falls, Idaho 87344
801-555-3794

Or, in a variation of the last example, many people choose to put their name alone at the top of the resume and their address and telephone number under "personal information."

In designing your heading, you can center it, using upper- and lowercase letters as in the examples. Or you may choose to type your heading at the left margin. Both locations are equally acceptable and are shown in the sample resumes in this chapter.

Job or Career Objective

How do long- and short-term job objectives differ?

At some point in the selection process, you will probably be asked: What are your short- and long-term goals? Even if your long-term goal is only tentative, it will reflect something an employee may judge rather significant: the degree of your understanding of career paths. Thus, whether you choose to include a career objective on your resume, you should nevertheless think about it before your interview.

If you do include a career objective in your resume, place it immediately after the heading. Here you have two options: you may include an immediate job objective or both a short- and long-term objective. For example, if you are applying to Jones Products, Inc., for a programmer/analyst position, you might write the following job objective in your personalized resume:

Job Objectives Position as programmer/analyst with Jones Products, Inc.

Or, if you were sending a general resume to various medical supply companies, you might include the following job objective:

Immediate-Term Objective Sales representative—medical supplies.

Or, if your career path is clearer, you might indicate both short- and long-term objectives:

Short-Term Objective Position as programmer/analyst with Jones Products, Inc.

Long-Term Objective Progression to systems analyst

Whichever approach you choose, avoid vague and meaningless statements such as "Position in Sales with Prosperous Company" (who would want to work for a company that isn't prosperous?) "Career Objective: Manager Trainee" (who would want a career as a manager trainee?). Be alert also to such empty phrases as "A Challenging Position," "Position Dealing with People," and "A Progressive Company." These and similar phrases only reveal a lack of knowlege about your field of interest.

The next two sections of your resume deal with education and work experience. Which you place first depends on your answer to two questions: (1) Is education or work experience a bigger asset for the job you are seeking? (2) Regardless of the job, which is the bigger asset? Since most recent college graduates view their education as their more important asset, we shall discuss this section first.

Education

In describing your education, present your most recent experience first and continue in reverse chronological order. Include the following information for each school you have attended:

Name of college/university Avoid abbreviations as they are easily misunderstood.

Address Include at least city and state.

Degree Because names of degrees, such as bachelor of science, are self-explanatory, you do not have to follow them with the word "degree" (such as Bachelor of Science degree). If applicable, include your major and minor.

Dates attended, including months Do not account for summer months when you were not enrolled; for example, "September 1985 to May 1987" is better than "September 1985 to May 1986, September 1986 to May 1987."

Graduation date Indicate "degree in progress" if you are uncertain of your exact graduation date.

Grade-point average Indicate your grade-point average for your overall studies, or your major area of study, or both. For clarity, include the base for the grade (such as 3.2 on a 4.0 scale). As explained earlier, do not include your grade-point average if it is low; instead, discuss it during the interview if the subject comes up.

Should you put anything else in the education section? The answer depends on your own situation. For example, if you have participated in co- or extracurricular activities, you can include them in this section. In doing so, also indicate dates and elected or appointed positions. And if you want to go into greater detail or want to emphasize these activities, you might put them under a separate subheading: "Co- and Extra/Curricular Activities."

In addition, you may want to include various honors, awards, and scholarships under "education." Being on the dean's list, graduating with honors, and holding membership in honor societies are especially applicable. If your honors and awards are numerous or otherwise impressive, you might choose to emphasize them by listing them in a separate section immediately following education.

Since you will probably send college transcripts, you do not need to include long lists of your courses. Two situations exist, however, where you might consider a limited list:

When should you emphasize education on a resume?

1. If you have no work experience, you probably need to stress your education. Therefore, a listing of relevant courses may be useful. For example, suppose you are seeking work as a computer programmer. You might then list the programming courses you completed as well as state that you majored in information systems. (In your application letter, which accompanies the resume, you may discuss some of the material covered in these courses.)
2. If you have completed courses outside your major that enhance your education, you might include them in a brief list. For example, suppose you are looking for a job in marketing and you have majored in this subject in college. But, since you have also taken courses in psychology, you might then emphasize them by listing each one. Later, in your application letter, you could explain how they would help you perform in the marketing position.

Another category you may include under education is internships, work-study programs, cooperative education experiences, and educational projects. For educational projects, you might briefly describe a specific long-term project completed for an independent study course. However, do not include single-class projects such as ones you might participate in during a business policy course. If warranted, you could set aside a specific section for the projects you do include. And, if your work-study or cooperative education experiences were paid positions, you could place them either under "work experience" or "education."

Also, list under education any special licenses, certificates, or skills you possess such as fluency in Spanish. Depending on their relevance, you might also list such assets under "personal information."

Finally, although you probably will not include your high school education in this section—college assumes high school—you may describe it because of one of the following reasons:

1. Outstanding academic honors, such as valedictorian, *Who's Who*, National Merit Scholarship winner, or the like.
2. Outstanding athletic or co- or extracurricular honors or activities, such as class president, outstanding athlete, or club officer.
3. Reputation of school, for example, if it is a school for gifted and talented students.

Work Experience

Why do different people handle work experience differently on a resume?

For many college or graduate school students, work until now will either have been "part-time on a continuing basis"—working part time while attending school full-time—or "full-time on a limited basis"—working full-time during vacations. Perhaps one or both of these situations describe your own experience. Whether you need to include every job in this section of your resume is subject to some debate. On the one hand, some people prefer to account for all their work experience. On the other hand, others prefer to include only the most relevant or only the excellent work experiences. If you remember that the purpose of a resume is to secure an interview, then omitting the "less than excellent" experiences seems prudent. However, if you have already graduated and begun a career, you will need to include all the jobs you have had since you graduated.

Once you have decided which work experiences to include, you need to determine the order of presentation. This order may vary. Usually, people use reverse chronological order. Yet by putting your most valuable work experience first, you may show your abilities to the best advantage.

In listing your jobs, include the following information in the order shown:

Job title or position held

Company name and address

Dates of employment, including months

Immediate supervisor

Description of duties/responsibilities (stated briefly)

This format is illustrated as follows:

> *Sales Representative—Exercise Department.* Down-N-Under Sporting Goods, Oxford Mall, Bangor, Maine. Supervisor: Zola Painter. September 1984 to present.

> Assist customers in selection of exercise clothing and equipment; prepare weekly sales representative work schedule; assist manager in selecting line of women's exercise apparel. Received "Outstanding Sales Representative of the Month" award three times.

For some jobs, such as waiter or stock clerk, you can omit a description of the duties involved because everyone knows what they are. (Also, you may want to use the limited space available for more important information.) But for other jobs, you'll need to explain the duties briefly, using short phrases and clauses that begin with action verbs. For example, in describing your summer job in a shipping company, you might state one of your duties as "processing invoices using automated equipment." Some verbs that might be useful in such descriptions are shown in the checklist on the next page.

When detailing your activities, include references to your accomplishments—"Selected sales representative of the month three times"—and responsibilities—"Supervised 10 employees when manager was sick." In these descriptions, avoid using long sentences and personal pronouns such as I, me, my. Do, however, employ the correct verb tense—past for former positions and present for current.

In this section, you might also put any military experience you have had. If so, include your rank, branch, discharge date, duties, and special recognitions such as promotions. You may also choose to include an internship here rather than in the education section. Volunteer work may fit here nicely too, especially when it is related to the job you are seeking. In describing it, you may want to add the note "volunteer work" so the reader will not mistakenly think you were paid.

Personal Information

Is this the section of your resume where you disclose that you like children and have lots of energy? The answer is probably no. Unless a personal characteristic, such as citizenship or national origin, is a bona fide occupation qualification (see Chapter 11), omit it.

What good might it do to include personal information on a resume?

But, if you did not include your address and telephone number in the heading, put it here, along with your zip and area codes. And if you are going to graduate soon and then be returning home, indicate both your current and permanent addresses and the date you can be reached at home.

Your participation in out-of-school activities, such as civic or church groups, may also go in this section. In inserting this information, avoid names of groups that indicate race, religion or national origin. For example, instead of mentioning that you are a member of the Valleyview Baptist Church Choir, simply state that you sing with a church choir.

DESCRIPTIVE VERBS FOR USE IN RESUMES

Use the following action verbs to describe your participation in work experience and co- and extracurricular activities. The verbs are arranged in five easy-to-use categories.

Planning	*Directing*	*Advising*
Create	Administer	Advise
Design	Approve	Apprise
Develop	Authorize	Communicate
Establish	Control	Confer
Estimate	Coordinate	Consult
Formulate	Delegate	Contribute
Initiate	Direct	Cooperate
Organize	Implement	Counsel
Plan	Instruct	Endorse
Program	Manage	Inform
Research	Motivate	Interpret
Summarize	Recruit	Recommend
Write	Supervise	

Executing	*Servicing*
Arrange	Adjust
Check	Assist
Classify	Expedite
Evaluate	Inform
Examine	Insure
Improve	Issue
Interview	Provide
Investigate	Report
Perform	
Prepare	
Process	
Study	
Use	

Suppose you like to study foreign languages, collect first editions, and are a member of a local group that devotes itself to helping the elderly care for themselves in their homes. Should you list these interests and activities? You might, especially if they seem relevant to the work you want. For example, suppose that you would like to work in an area of international business. Then, your liking for foreign languages and your expertise in them are a valuable asset.

If you are also willing to travel or relocate, then say so in this section. The percentage of your college expenses that you earned yourself, the date of your availability to begin work, and any special skills, certifications, or licenses that you have may go here too. For example, if you are certified in lifesaving, registered to officiate a sport such as tennis, or can read American Sign Language, you may list these skills. Of course, when these special skills are relevant to the job, you should include them without hesitation. As for other, less relevant skills, you may add them to show the range of your abilities and interests.

Should you include references to your health, marital status, height or weight, or religion in this section? Generally not—for two reasons: first, such information may violate Equal Employment Opportunity Commission regulations, in which case the employer should not have asked you for it; and, second, such information probably has nothing to do with your occupational qualifications, which is why the employer shouldn't ask for it. However, when height or weight or other such information is a bona fide occupational qualification, as with height and weight when applying for a modeling job, such information is acceptable.

References

The reference section always ends a resume. In it, write the names, addresses, and telephone numbers of at least three people to whom employers might speak. If you do not include this information, state that it is available upon request or is included in your school placement files. If you are responding to an opening that you know exists, providing the actual references will speed up the evaluation process. But, if you are only "prospecting," this information is not critical.

What do references attest to concerning your job credentials?

Whom should you select as references? Mostly, it is preferable to choose individuals able to attest to your ability and knowledge. Therefore, current and former employers, immediate supervisors, and college professors are your best choices. If the relationship between you and a person you use as a reference is unclear, include a short notation—such as "former employer"—immediately after the information about that person.

Naturally, you should obtain the permission of the people you plan to list as references before including them. You might also consider giving them a copy of your completed resume. This reminder of who you are might be helpful if these people are called for a reference. Similarly, you might alert them to which companies you are applying and keep them informed of the status of various applications.

Prepare the Final Copy

What six things should you pay attention to when preparing final copy for a resume?

In preparing the final copy of your resume, you should keep in mind several things. First, no one form for a resume is best—the one that presents your qualifications clearly, concisely, and attractively will be "best" for you. Thus, the sample resumes included in this chapter show several possible formats.

Second, use headings to introduce the sections dealing with education, work experience, personal information, and references. Here you may employ simple topic headings, such as "Education" and "Work Experience." However, talking headings or more descriptive captions are preferable. For example, "Specialized Training in Accounting" is more informative than is "Education." In either case, make your headings grammatically consistent.

Third, remember that the physical appearance of the resume is important because it reveals something about your organization and presentation skills. Therefore, create a professional format by using uniform indentations and capitalization, and by underscoring when organizing your information. For short items, employ rows and columns; for longer items, arrange them in lines extending across the pages. As large blocks of information are unattractive and difficult to read, leave blank spaces between various segments of material. Although dates are essential, play down their presence by placing them just after the address of your employer so that more important data attract the reader's attention.

Fourth, type your resume on white or "off-white" $8\frac{1}{2}'' \times 11''$ bond paper. If you are preparing a general resume, reproduce it on a good-quality copier or have it printed. For most resumes, black ink is preferred. Do not use unusual paper, colored stock, or off-sized paper. Some readers do not like deviations from traditional resume formats.

Fifth, most employers agree that resumes from soon-to-be-graduated students should be one to two pages in length, preferably one page. Try to keep your resume to one page, but if it is longer than two pages, review what you have written and delete less important material.

Finally, when you have finished, proofread your resume. Then, proofread it again, reading backward one word at a time. Next, have a friend proofread it too. The value of proofreading cannot be overemphasized: one error may lead a prospective employer to think you would be similarly careless on the job.

Consider Special Resumes

Suppose you arrange the information on your resume in a reverse time sequence—from the most recent to the least recent events. If you organize it in this way, you are composing a *chronological resume.* Although this is the traditional approach to resumes, one serious disadvantage is that your most recent work experience may not be the most relevant for the particular job you are seeking. This is especially so for college seniors with limited work experience. But, if you have extensive work experience that shows steady progress in your career development, a chronological resume best presents that growth. Figure 12-4, shown previously, is a chronological resume.

What are three "special" approaches to preparing resumes?

A second approach to resume organization is *functional.* A functional resume groups skills or major job duties and responsibilities under topical headings, such as "supervisory skill" and "decision-making activities." After these topical listings, you can then add a history of your work experience. This approach is particularly useful to people who have varied experience or who are switching careers and "taking" certain skills with them. In contrast, the functional resume will not be as much help to people with limited work experience. Figure 12-5 shows the functional resume approach.

A third approach is the *targeted* resume shown in Figure 12-6. Here the job objective at the top clearly identifies the position sought. This objective is followed by specific statements about the applicant's skills as they relate to this job. Frequently, applicants place these statements under the heading "Capabilities," but any other descriptive heading would also be appropriate. After this section, the targeted resume concludes with the work experience and education sections. In the end, its effectiveness depends on how clearly you identify and state your qualifications in the "capabilities" section as they relate to the position you seek.

To evaluate your resume, whatever its approach, use the following checklist. By comparing each of the areas in your resume to it, you can be more confident that you have presented yourself properly to your prospective employer.

RESUME CHECKLIST

General Content

Omit information about qualifications that might be considered negative.

Omit information that is not relevant to requirements sought.

State job objective clearly and concisely to tell reader what type of employment is sought.

Be sure that section immediately following job objective contains information about most important qualification for position sought.

MICHAEL GRANSTAFF

1204 Foxcroft Road
Stillwater, Oklahoma 34895
405-555-6745

JOB OBJECTIVE:	Programs Director
PUBLIC RELATIONS:	Maintain personal contact with 140 customers in four-state region by scheduling office visits, dinner engagements, golf outings, and sporting events. Organized banquet for top-level management and primary customers. Designed and distributed framable poster against drunk driving for local civic group.
ADMINISTRATION:	Conduct daily price surveys, compile and evaluate information to determine market prices. Administer purchase, sale, and exchange contracts for supply and distribution of 1.5 million barrels of refined petroleum per month. Researched hardware and software for microcomputers and made recommendations on what to purchase.
TRAINING:	Trained new employees on scheduling tactics. Wrote training manual for schedulers. Trained employees on use of microcomputers.
DATA PROCESSING:	Entered daily supply and distribution schedules in on-line terminal for accounting, credit, and planning reports. Gained full knowledge of microcomputer hardware and software.
WORK HISTORY:	
January 1986 to Present	Marketing Representative, Freed Fuels, Inc. Stillwater, Oklahoma
May 1983 to January 1986	Scheduler, Adams Refining Company Oklahoma City, Oklahoma
EDUCATION:	Bachelor of Science in Business Management Oklahoma State University, Stillwater Degree awarded May, 1983. GPA--3.2 (4.0 basis)
UNIVERSITY ACTIVITIES:	Interfraternity Council--Treasurer, Chief Justice Sigma Alpha Epsilon--President, Alumni Chairman
PERSONAL:	Willing to relocate in Southwest Member of Backridge Jaycees
REFERENCES:	References supplied upon request.

FIGURE 12-5 A functional resume.

MARILYN J. BOSTON

2322 Piney Road
Idaho Falls, Idaho 87344
801-555-3794

JOB TARGET: OFFICE AUTOMATION MANAGER WITH KELLY ADVERTISING

CAPABILITIES:

*Familiar with automated office technologies
*Analyze office procedures for increased productivity
*Delegate routine work effectively
*Design and sketch office layouts
*Write complete and clear reports and correspondence
*Program in Basic and COBOL
*Operate IBM-PC
*Instruct others on use of application software

ACCOMPLISHMENTS

*Elected Vice President of Phi Beta Lambda, business fraternity
*Selected as Student Representative to School of Business Undergraduate Curriculum Committee
*Received award as Outstanding Office Automation Management Student
*Maintained A+ average during college education and appointed to Dean's List for eight semesters

EDUCATION

Idaho State University, Pocatello, Idaho 87411
Will receive Bachelor of Science in Office Automation Management in June, 1986. Attended June 1984 to present.

Ricks College, Rexburg, Idaho 86455
Received Associate in Science in Information Systems in June, 1984. Graduated Magna Cum Laude.

WORK EXPERIENCE

Data Entry Clerk September 1985-present	Bank of Idaho 444 Monument Avenue Idaho Falls, ID 87342
Word Processing Operator June 1984-August 1985	Parson's Legal Service 558 Hillshire Lane Idaho Falls, ID 87343

REFERENCES--Supplied Upon Request

FIGURE 12-6 A targeted resume.

Education

Give name and address of each college/university attended along with dates of attendance.

Indicate degrees earned or anticipated.

Indicate overall grade-point average or grade-point average in major.

Avoid list of courses completed.

Indicate honors, awards, scholarships, and so forth.

Include co- or extracurricular activities and offices held.

Describe internships, cooperative education programs, and special projects.

Work Experience

Give names and addresses of employers along with names of immediate supervisors and dates employed.

Indicate positions held.

Describe job duties/responsibilities with verbs in active voice parallel form.

Personal/Other (includes information in heading)

Omit information that is not relevant or that could be used for discriminatory purposes.

Include information on willingness to travel/relocate and percentage earned toward college expenses if relevant.

Provide mailing address and telephone number with area code.

Describe hobbies and interests only briefly, if at all.

Mention special skills possessed and certificates/licenses held if relevant.

References

Include at least three references with titles, addresses, and telephone numbers or make them available upon request.

Format

Make sure that resume is no more than two pages long, preferably one page long.

Make sure that resume is printed or typed in black ink on $8\frac{1}{2}'' \times 11''$ white or "off white" paper.

Make sure that resume is consistent in heading styles, indentions, and underlining.

Make sure that resume has been proofread at least two times by author and once by someone else.

WRITING THE APPLICATION LETTER

In your application letter—the second part of the two-part application package—you tell the reader why you are writing and what position you are seeking. This letter gives you the opportunity to highlight your abilities, experiences, and education, especially in relation to the employer's needs and to the job you want. In effect, the application letter is a sales letter in which you "sell" yourself and your qualifications to obtain an interview.

The question is: What do you say in this letter? Broad disagreement exists about its content. Some people suggest that an application letter is nothing more than a brief cover letter that identifies the position sought, refers to the enclosed resume, and requests an interview.

Conversely, others contend you should use the letter for an in-depth explanation of your education and experience that your resume only outlines. Still others insist that prospective employers rarely read these letters, and you should not even bother to send one. As the prospective employers must at least know what job you are seeking, this last position appears logically insupportable.

What role does the application letter play in a job application?

You have the choice of whether to view the application letter as a cover letter accompanying your resume or as an opportunity to present your qualifications for the job. Whatever you decide, be aware that employers will often pick up your application package, skim the letter, and browse through the resume to see if you meet their minimum job requirements. If your letter is poorly written, they may not even look at the resume. Or, conversely, if they read the resume first and see you meet the minimum requirements, they may then read the application letter more attentively—since it is there! From these two scenarios you can see that an application letter has excellent *potential* to help you achieve your goal of getting an interview.

Use Solicited and Unsolicited Letters

How do solicited and unsolicited application letters differ?

Two types of application letters exist: *solicited* and *unsolicited.* You write a solicited letter when you know that a job is available—through personal contacts, newspaper ads, or the like. This type of letter is easy to write because you know the employer's identity, needs, and the job's duties.

In contrast, you write an unsolicited letter—also called a "prospecting" letter—when you do not even know if an opening exists. Basically, such a letter identifies you and the type of work you seek, asks the prospective employer to consider your application if an opening exists, and requests an interview. If no opening exists at the time of writing, the letter closes with a request that the reader file the application for future consideration.

An unsolicited letter has two major disadvantages:

1. Because companies often do not have openings when you write, you waste time and money.
2. Because your letter is unsolicited, they are not obliged to answer. (Many do respond with a form letter and may also keep your application on file.)

Still, even with these drawbacks, unsolicited letters may bring results.

Draft the Letter

Whether you write a solicited or unsolicited letter, follow the persuasive format explained in Chapter 10. Thus, you should begin with an attention-getting first paragraph. Then, try to create some interest in your qualifications and arouse a desire to talk with you. Close with a request for an interview.

Opening the Letter

Why would you sometimes open an application letter one way, sometimes another?

The opening paragraph marks the major difference between the two types of application letters. This is because in an unsolicited letter you have a greater need to catch and hold the reader's attention. In contrast, the reader of a solicited letter is already attentive because the letter is written in response to his or her request.

The solicited letter should indicate the position sought, how the opening became known to you, and what your qualifications are. The following is a typical opening of a solicited application letter:

> Please consider my application for the position as programmer-analyst that you advertised in *The Wall Street Journal* on November 20. My bachelor's degree in information systems and two years' experience with Accutron Corporation fully prepare me to perform the job as you have outlined it.

In writing the opening paragraph of an unsolicited letter, you may use one of three approaches. The first is to start with a description of the requirements associated with a specific job and then show how you meet them. For example,

> The manager of an automated office must understand automated office technologies, systems analysis techniques, and supervisory methods to achieve organization goals. After you have reviewed my qualifications detailed below, you will see that I have the necessary preparation to perform as a manager in your automated office.

You can also begin by presenting your major qualifications for the position you are seeking. The prospective employer then can readily perceive that you are qualified to do the job. The following is an example of this approach:

> When you need a person skilled in programming languages, adept in using various application software, and familiar with personal computers, please consider my qualifications.

Or you can use a "catch" phrase or sentence that identifies your major qualifications. If you use this approach, be careful that you stay within the bounds of good taste and that what you say is relevant to the position you seek. In any case, it may be more appropriate to employ such an opening for positions where creativity is important—such as marketing and sales. The following is a sample of this approach:

> *Français, Espãnol, Deutsch*: three languages in which I'm fluent would be valuable for an international marketing representative in your oversees division.

Whatever approach you use in your opening paragraph, it must achieve three goals: (1) identify clearly that you are applying for a job, (2) identify clearly the job or type of job you want, and (3) lead naturally and logically into the rest of the letter.

Presenting and Relating Major Qualifications

Why should you interpret facts from the resume in the application letter?

Although the first paragraph of an application letter may be the most difficult to write, presenting major qualifications and relating them to the job you want form the heart of the letter. Frequently, this discussion of qualifications is also the weakest part of the application letter. Mostly, this weakness occurs when a writer merely *repeats* facts from the resume instead of *interpreting* them in relation to the employer's needs and the job's requirements. This problem is compounded when beginners try to mention everything in the resume—names, skills, dates, and so forth.

In presenting such material, keep in mind the purpose of both the resume and application letter. Your resume is a historical account of your experiences, education, and other qualifications for employment. In contrast, your application letter interprets these qualifications in relation to a particular job. Your goal in the letter is to identify the major qualifications and present them to the reader. Notice how the writer of the following application letter accomplishes this goal:

> From my study of office automation concepts, I've become acquainted with the various automated office technologies that can improve office productivity. In addition, techniques for analyzing office procedures and selecting appropriate methods were discussed and practiced in class activities. Standards of performance for office personnel were identified and methods for measuring that performance were studied. As a result,

> working as your office automation manager, I would be able to assist in streamlining the office operations to improve your information flow to other functional areas of the organization.

Also, in trying to meet the employer's requirements, avoid empty phrases such as "I feel I can perform the job" or "I believe my qualifications are adequate for the position." Instead, be specific. Describe what you can do for the company. And, if you are familiar with its operations, indicate this also.

Near the end of this part of the letter, refer readers to your enclosed resume. Of course, they know it's there. But referring to it now serves a purpose—it permits you to summarize the other qualifications that make you the "complete" candidate. The following are two examples of effective references to an enclosed resume:

> When you review my enclosed resume, you will see that I have excelled academically even though I have worked throughout my college years.

> An examination of my enclosed resume will provide insight into my many "people-oriented" activities that would enhance my performance as a financial counselor with your firm.

Asking for the Interview

You have reached the final paragraph of your application letter. Now you must ask for the interview. Since the reader will hardly be surprised at your request, don't be indirect—"Would you like to discuss my qualifications further?" Instead, ask openly, "May I have an interview so that we can discuss what I can do for your company as one of its marketing representatives?"

Who should call or write to set up the job interview?

Some people recommend that the writer show initiative by suggesting that he or she accept responsibility for setting up the interview, as in the following example:

> I will call you on October 20 to set up a convenient interview time.

Others find such an approach too forceful or aggressive because it may put the employer in the unenviable position of having to tell you over the telephone that such an interview is not desired. So, if you decide to close in this way, consider both the positive and negative attitudes that result from such straightforwardness and be prepared for occasional rebuffs.

Another way to end is to let employers take the initiative and contact you. If you plan to close in this way, indicate when you can be called and include your telephone number—with the area code if it differs from the employer's. Although your resume has your telephone number on it, inserting the number in this last paragraph saves employers time in locating the information. If you are writing an unsolicited letter, also add the date you are available for employment.

Suppose you want to express gratitude because you have asked employers to call you or to consider you for the position. Then use the future tense rather than the present tense, which is presumptuous. Thus, "I will appreciate your considering my qualifications" is better than "Thank you in advance for considering me."

Apply General Guidelines

You are now ready to edit the first copy of your application letter. Perhaps your most difficult editing task is to achieve the right balance between pompousness and humility or between seeming too casual and appearing too desperate. You can achieve this balance by concentrating on presenting and interpreting your qualifications. Then the tone of your letter will be properly businesslike. Also, although you should employ personal pronouns such as "I" and "my," try to limit their use, especially at the beginning of sentences and paragraphs. In this way, you avoid striking a self-centered tone. For the same reason, focus your remarks on the reader by employing "you" and "your" when relating your qualifications to the reader's needs.

Another thing to be watchful about: Delete any criticisms of current or past employers if these have somehow strayed into your letter. Avoid, too, any discussion of the reasons you are leaving a present job—if you are—or suggesting a salary—unless the ad you may be answering requests that you do. Generally, it is best to deal with the last two items during the initial interview—if they come up.

How long should the application letter be?

Ideally, your letter should be no more than a page long. If, however, you need two pages, include the appropriate heading for the second page. (See Appendix B for examples of such headings.) Remember, too, to address your letter to a specific individual, not to a department such as the personnel department or to a position such as personnel director. If you don't know the person's name, call the company to find out. If the firm is large, find an organizational listing in the reference section of your library.

Finally, if you are sending an unsolicited letter, consider the day on which it will arrive. Monday and Friday are the busiest workdays, so plan to have it arrive on Tuesday, Wednesday, or Thursday, if possible. Also be aware of shortened workweeks due to holidays. During these times, employers may be too preoccupied with the more hectic pace of the office to attend to your letter.

Prepare the Mailable Letter

In preparing your final copy, follow traditional guidelines for letter style. Few potential employers overlook errors of this type. Thus,

1. Use an acceptable letter style, such as one illustrated in Appendix B. Include your return address at the top of the letter.
2. Type each application letter individually—even if you are enclosing a printed photocopied resume.
3. Type the letter on $8\frac{1}{2}''$ × 11″ white or "off-white" bond paper. Do not use your current employer's letterhead paper.
4. Both type and *sign* your name at the end of the letter. Be sure to sign legibly.
5. Include an "enclosure" notation, but do not use typist reference initials even if someone else typed your letter; this particular letter is from an individual rather than a business.
6. Use a "business size" (no. 10) envelope for mailing.
7. Prepare the resume and application letter on the same color and quality of paper, using the same color ink.

Use the following checklist to evaluate your application letter:

APPLICATION LETTER CHECKLIST

General Content

First Paragraph

Indicate specific position sought.
Indicate source of information regarding job vacancy.
Preview major qualifications.

Following Paragraphs

Avoid chronological recap of education and work experience.
Link statements about qualifications directly to employer's needs or job requirements.
Support statements about qualifications with examples or facts.
Make reference to enclosure prior to closing paragraph.
Do not discuss salary, reasons for leaving previous employment, and negative remarks about employers.
Minimize use of "I"; stress reader benefits.

Closing Paragraph:

Request an interview.
Give telephone number and time to be contacted.
Give date of availability for interview and employment.
State appreciation using future tense.

Format

Address letter to specific individual.
Type letter individually in black ink on $8\frac{1}{2}'' \times 11''$ white or "off-white", bond paper.
Arrange letter attractively using an acceptable letter style.
Format return address at top of the letter.
Include enclosure notation.
Sign letter in black ink.
Prepare appropriate mailing envelope.
Ensure that letter is one page in length.

Three sample application letters are shown in Figures 12-7, 12-8, and 12-9. The application letter in Figure 12-7 is written to accompany a resume illustrated earlier in this chapter (Figure 12-3). Likewise, the application letter in Figure 12-8 would accompany the resume shown in Figure 12-4, and Figure 12-9 illustrates an application letter that would be mailed with the resume shown in Figure 12-6.

Keep a Mailing Log

What is a mailing log used for in the job application process?

To keep track of your job-hunting activities, use a mailing log. When different job applications are at different stages of development, such a record will alert you to where things actually are. For example, if you send an application to a chemical company but do not receive a response in two weeks, you will—because of the mailing log—know to inquire about it. The position may have been filled, your application may have been mislaid or never received, or the employer may have been too busy to respond.

Whatever the problem, you will need to find out what is happening to keep your job hunt going. Figure 12-10 illustrates a sample log.

Although you do not have to send follow-up letters or make follow-up calls, they can make a difference—sometimes. For example, they can start the next move, reinforce earlier messages, and solve problems. If you want to write such a letter, follow the favorable correspondence plan outlined in Chapter 8. (A sample follow-up letter appears later in this chapter.)

PREPARING FOR AND PARTICIPATING IN THE INTERVIEW

If your application package is effective, employers may call you for an interview, and you have achieved your initial goal. Your next step is to convince them that you are the best candidate for the job when you go for the interview.

256 Grove Avenue
Richmond, Virginia 23222
April 23, 19--

Ms. Jane M. Brock
Vice President - Personnel
SpectroVision, Inc.
Ruthers Mill Road
Richmond, Virginia 23226

Dear Ms. Brock:

Are you in need of an entry-level manager in personnel who is well grounded in personnel and psychology and who has participated in many activities of the American Society for Personnel Administrators? If so, please consider my qualifications.

In May I will receive my bachelor's degree in Business Administration and Management from Virginia Commonwealth University. My concentration in my degree work was in personnel. In addition, I have completed several courses in psychology, including industrial psychology and adult psychology. The concepts I have mastered in my personnel courses and the background in understanding motivations of adult workers would enhance my performance in your personnel division. I have also been an active member of the VCU chapter of the American Society of Personnel Administrators. My participation in the activities of that organization has brought me in contact with many personnel administrators who have provided additional insight into the area of human resource development.

After reviewing my enclosed resume, you will see that I also have worked in a "people-oriented" position, thus helping me to develop my interpersonal skills so necessary in personnel administration.

Please call me at 555-2134 to discuss the possibility of my working in your personnel division. If no openings are available at this time, I would appreciate your placing my application on file for later reference.

Sincerely yours,

William E. Webb

William E. Webb

Enclosure

FIGURE 12-7 Application letter.

Rhoads Hall, Room 426
Northwest University
Bangor, Maine 02911
April 5, 19--

Mr. Michael Kennedy
Chief Personnel Officer
Foodwhiz, Inc.
2444 North Wabash Avenue
Bangor, Maine 02913

Dear Mr. Kennedy:

Please consider my qualifications for marketing representative that you advertised in the April 4 issue of The Bangor Press. My degree in marketing and my extensive experience as a sales representative provide a sound background for this position.

My degree work in marketing emphasized the latest techniques in market analysis and research and stressed developing viable marketing strategies to capitalize on the marketing mix. With this sound background in the theory of marketing, I would be able to assume fully my duties after just a short period of orientation.

As a sales representative with Down-N-Under, I became familiar with sales techniques, understanding fully the need to address the customer's needs rather than simply relay product information. This understanding of addressing customers' needs led to my being named "Outstanding Sales Rep" three times.

As you will see from my enclosed resume, I have been a member of the American Marketing Association and am willing to travel or relocate.

May I have an interview so that we can discuss what I can do for your company as one of its marketing representatives? I can be reached between 2 p.m. and 4 p.m. any weekday at 555-4933. I look forward to talking with you.

Sincerely yours,

Margarite Perez

Margarite Perez

Enclosure

FIGURE 12-8 Application letter.

2322 Piney Road
Idaho Falls, Idaho 87344
May 8, 19--

Mr. George Kelly
General Manager
Kelly Advertising, Inc.
105 North Higgins Avenue
Idaho Falls, Idaho 87343

Dear Mr. Kelly:

The manager of your automated office must understand automated office technologies, systems analysis techniques, and supervisory methods to achieve organizational goals. After you have reviewed my qualifications detailed below, you will see I have been prepared to perform as the automated office manager you advertised for in last Sunday's Idaho Falls Tribune.

In a month, I will receive my Bachelor of Science in Office Automation Management from Idaho State University. From my study of office automation concepts, I've become acquainted with the various automated office technologies that can improve office productivity. In addition, techniques for analyzing office procedures and selecting appropriate methods were discussed and practiced in class activities. Standards of performance for office personnel were identified and methods for measuring that performance were studied. As a result, working as your office automation manager, I would be able to assist in streamlining the office operations to improve your information flow to other functional areas of the organization.

When you review my enclosed resume, you will find that I have excelled academically even though I have worked throughout my college years. That work has been in information processing and data processing, so I'm familiar with the types of problems that automated office employees might experience

Please call me at 555-3794 to arrange a time when we can further discuss your opening for an automated office manager. I can be reached after 1 p.m. during the week.

Sincerely yours,

Marilyn J. Boston

Marilyn J. Boston

Enclosure

FIGURE 12-9 Application letter.

Employer	Initial Contact	Follow-up	Response	Special Notes
Lockheed	Application package 9/1	Send letter 9/15	Job filled 9/20	Will be hiring again in January. Contact: W. Ely.
Northrop	Application package 9/2	Send letter 9/16	Yes	Interview to be scheduled. If not, letter 9/20.
Aero-Jet	Inquiry 9/5	Send letter 9/20		If no response by 10/10, drop lead.
Grumman	Inquiry 9/6	Application package 9/12	Favorable 9/10	Received job description. May be hiring November.
Boeing	Application package 9/6	Call 9/15	Interview on 9/18	Spoke with Grace Levering. Research company further.
Aero-Nutronics	Résumé only 9/9		No 9/16	Not hiring now. Could have opening in March.
Marquart	Application package 9/10	No Follow-up		

FIGURE 12-10 Mailing log.

What is the key to success in the interview?

Preparation is the key to success in the interview. So be prepared:

- Prepared with knowledge about the company.
- Prepared with answers to questions you will certainly be asked.
- Prepared with information about yourself that was unsolicited but that you feel is important.
- Prepared with questions for the interviewer.

In short, *preparation* means "doing your homework."

Gather the Necessary Information

Most of the information you will need for the interview you already know because this information is about yourself. You can be certain that the interviewer will ask many questions. Most of these questions will center on your career goals, qualifications, education, and work experience.

Besides the questions you will have to answer, you should have several to ask yourself. After all, you too are doing some evaluating, deciding whether you really would like to work for the company, and so forth. In general, don't ask questions about salary, vacation benefits, and retirement plans. Focusing on them may imply that you seem more concerned with "what you are receiving" than with the job itself. The following checklist shows some possible questions you might ask.

QUESTIONS YOU MAY CONSIDER ASKING IN AN INTERVIEW

1. Would I receive any special training before beginning work?
2. In what ways does your company support the professional development of its employees?
3. What career path would be available for me, assuming I do well in this position?
4. What have you liked most/least about working for this company?
5. In what ways does your company support and encourage the further education of your managerial/technical personnel?
6. Does your company provide training seminars and workshops? How are people selected to attend these activities?
7. How is performance appraised for employees in positions such as this one?
8. What type of support personnel and services are available to assist me in the performance of this job?
9. Why is this position available? Is it a new position or was someone promoted or dismissed for it?
10. Can you explain the management style or philosophy of the company—MBO (Management by Objectives), quality circles, and so on?

Complete Last-Minute Details

What materials would you take with you to an interview?

Once you feel confident about the interview, you should gather some materials to take with you. For example, carry one or two copies of your resume, especially if you know you will be talking with persons other than the interviewer, such as department heads and supervisors. If you have a portfolio of work samples, such as advertising copy you have written for a class project, take that too. When you have a number of materials to carry, you may put them in a briefcase. But generally, a pen and some note paper is sufficient. (Do not, however, take notes during the interview; the paper is for jotting down names and other important points afterward.)

Naturally, you will have to dress correctly for the interview. Many books and articles have been written on this subject. Just remember that you don't have to wear an expensive outfit, only one that is appropriate for the situation. Also take care of details such as carefully polished shoes and manicured nails. (See Chapter 19 for more information about the effect of dress on first impressions. Other nonverbal communication information in the same chapter should also be helpful.)

If the interview is to be held locally, you may want to check it out a day or two in advance to see exactly where the company is located and to estimate how long it takes to get there. Nothing is as unnerving as being late to an interview, so check out your route carefully.

Participate in the Interview

How much early should you arrive for an interview? Why?

On the day of the interview, arrive 5 to 10 minutes early. Take this time to "catch your breath" and calm yourself. On meeting your interviewer, greet him or her with a firm handshake. Pay close attention to all interviewers' names and titles so you can use them either during the conversation or in later communications.

During the interview your most important task is to act professionally. Thus, try to answer all questions both thoroughly and accurately. Be natural too. When you have the opportunity, expand your responses to incorporate ideas you have wanted to include in the conversation. If you do not know or have forgotten the answer to a question, don't panic. Simply explain that you do not know if the first company that employed you used such an accounting procedure or that you no longer remember whether the day care center you worked at after school was solely financed by federal funds. Then, if either seems important, offer to find the answer and furnish it later. If it is nonessential, the interviewer will decline your offer.

As explained in Chapter 11, your interview may turn out to be structured, unstructured, or some combination of the two. Consequently, you will be asked open or closed questions, or both. (See Chapter 11 also for the types of questions to expect.) Whatever the structure of the interview and the types of questions, focus your answers—and your own questions—on the job and your qualifications for it.

Remember that federal laws govern the types of information interviewers may solicit from you. Mostly, this means they should not touch upon your religion, national origin, marital status, or any other information not directly related to your ability to do the job.

Whatever happens, try to maintain your composure. The best way to accomplish this is to realize your own value: you can handle the job and you are perfectly capable of explaining why. If, however, you start feeling nervous or anxious, take a deep, silent breath.

Sometimes you will do this when faced with an unusually difficult question. Then, also ask for a moment to think it over. Throughout, simply concentrate on succeeding.

When the interviewer offers you a chance to make some final points, use the opportunity to summarize your qualifications and ask the questions that still need answers. If time seems to be running out, explain that you want to make certain points that could affect the hiring decision. Such a statement will usually get you the few minutes you should need.

Who should close an interview?

The interviewer has the responsibility to close the conversation. At this point, you need to follow his or her lead. Close cordially, but don't linger. If you want to make a last-minute point, do it briefly. The interviewer probably has a busy schedule and will appreciate your thoughtfulness. Exit on cue and with a handshake. The interview is officially over, but your business is incomplete until you thank the receptionist or other assistant for any special arrangements or assistance that has been provided.

The following are a few additional comments about the interview:

1. Remember to maintain normal eye contact throughout.
2. Remember that many interviewers find gum chewing and smoking unprofessional.
3. If you are at lunch or dinner, you probably should decline an alcoholic drink.
4. Be alert to your "body language," since slouching is viewed as a sign of indifference.
5. Keep the interview on your good points—never say anything bad about your current or former employers. If the interviewer asks about some negative situation, do not try to cover it up or sidestep it. Rather, explain the circumstances in an honest, objective manner rather than make excuses or blame others.
6. Let the interviewer bring up the topic of salary. Avoid giving a definite figure; however, a knowledge of the job, company, and similar salaries will assist you if you are forced to give a specific salary requirement.
7. Listen carefully and actively. Keep your mind on the interview.

FOLLOWING UP THE APPLICATION

As soon as you can after the interview, "debrief" yourself. That is, reflect on how the interview went; list some things that you did well, and those that need improvement, including the questions for which you did not prepare adequately.

Rhoads Hall, Room 426
Northwest University
Bangor, Maine 02911
May 3, 19--

Mr. Michael Kennedy
Chief Personnel Officer
Foodwhiz, Inc.
2444 North Wabash Avenue
Bangor, Maine 02913

Dear Mr. Kennedy:

Thank you for the opportunity to interview with you last week for the position as Marketing Representative with Foodwhiz, Inc.

I thoroughly enjoyed our tour of the manufacturing plant and office facilities and appreciated your explanation of the duties and responsibilities of the position as Marketing Representative. The position does seem to be the right challenge for me, and the benefits and incentive programs at Foodwhiz are excellent.

You mentioned during our conversation that you wanted to review my college transcript. I have asked the Registrar at Northwest to send a copy to you immediately. If you haven't received it within a day or two of this letter, please call me and I'll follow up on my request.

Mr. Kennedy, the visit with you left me feeling positive about the possibility of working for Foodwhiz. I would appreciate an opportunity to join your staff and look forward to hearing from you.

Sincerely yours,

Margarite Perez

Margarite Perez

FIGURE 12-11 A follow-up letter.

Why should you send a thank-you letter after an interview?

Within a day or two, send a thank-you letter—even if you don't think you will be offered the job or would accept it if it were offered. The letter serves a variety of purposes, including

1. Reminding the prospective employer that you are still interested and available.
2. Giving you the opportunity to reemphasize your qualifications or mention a pertinent fact that was overlooked in the interview.
3. Providing you with a slight advantage over those applicants who do not write such a letter.
4. Demonstrating your good business manner.

Thus, the "thank you" letter reinforces your application. Even if you would not accept an offer at this time, you may be applying at a later time for a position with the company.

Use the following three-part format for the letter:

Paragraph 1	State your appreciation for the interview and, if appropriate, request that similar appreciation be extended to others who participated in the interview.
Paragraph 2	Review your qualifications or provide additional information.
Paragraph 3	Say that you look forward to hearing from the prospective employer.

Verifying the spelling of the names and titles of various people reinforces nonverbally the fact that you can handle stressful situations.

A sample follow-up letter appears in Figure 12–11. Be sure to record on your mailing log the date on which the letter was sent.

With this letter, you have completed the job-finding process. Now you have only to wait for a response.

SUMMARY

1. The job search process is a step-by-step procedure that can help a job applicant achieve a successful objective—employment.
2. The first step in the job search process is to locate job vacancies that may be appropriate for you.
3. Sources of job leads include newspaper advertisements, professional and trade journals, college and university placement offices, public and private employment agencies, personal contacts, and contacts with organizations.
4. Before you prepare a resume, you must gather information regarding your education, work experience, co- and extracurricular activities, achievements, skills, and other personal characteristics.
5. The resume and application letter form the two-part application package. The re-

sume is written first and presents a historical overview of your skills, education, and experience. The application letter is written next and interprets the information on the resume for a specific employer's needs and job requirements.

6. General resumes are designed to be used when applying to a number of firms or for a variety of different but related jobs. Personalized resumes are written with one job or one company in mind.
7. In order, the six major parts found on most resumes are (a) heading, (b) job/career objective, (c) education, (d) work experience, (e) personal information, and (f) references.
8. Information presented in a resume under "education" includes names and addresses of schools attended, dates attended, graduation date, grade-point average (if it is high), honors, scholarships, awards, and co- and extracurricular activities.
9. "Work experience" information on a resume includes names and addresses of employers; dates of employment; immediate supervisor; positions held; and description of major duties, responsibilities, and achievements.
10. Personal information included on a resume is left to the discretion of the applicant. Information about civic activities, special skills and licenses, and hobbies and interests are generally included.
11. Chronological, functional, and targeted resumes are special types that you may consider writing.
12. At least three people who can attest to the applicant's abilities should be available as references. If listing the references on the resume, include their addresses and telephone numbers.
13. Application letters are either solicited or unsolicited. Whichever the case, each has three major sections: an attention-getting opening paragraph, a middle section in which you present and relate qualifications, and a closing paragraph in which you request an interview.
14. Accuracy in content and preparation of the resume and application letter is vital.
15. When called for an interview, be prepared to answer a variety of questions, to volunteer relevant information that has not been requested, and to ask questions regarding the employer.
16. Each interview should be followed with a "thank-you" letter, which also restates your major qualifications.

Review Questions

1. What is meant when the job search is described as a process? What are the five steps in the process?
2. Describe five sources of job leads and rank them according to their possible value to you. Be prepared to justify your ranking.
3. What criteria should you use to evaluate the information to include on your resume?
4. When should you use a general rather than a personalized resume?
5. Why is a job objective included on your resume?
6. What type of work experience should you include on a resume? When should you include volunteer work?
7. Who should you choose as references and why?
8. Why is accuracy in spelling, punctuation, grammar, and format so important when preparing the resume and application letter?

9. What is meant by the following sentence: "In an application letter, interpret the facts presented on your resume—do not simply repeat them."
10. What are the similarities and differences between unsolicited and solicited application letters?
11. What four approaches can you use in the opening paragraph of an application letter?
12. What three items should you include in the closing paragraph of an application letter?
13. What type of information should you prepare before attending an employment interview?
14. Why should you prepare questions to ask during a job interview?
15. What specific purposes does a follow-up "thank-you" letter serve? What type of information should you include in it?

Exercises

1. Invite a professional who is experienced in interviewing job applicants to a class meeting. You might ask a personnel officer, someone from your college placement center, or someone from a local business. Using role playing, ask this person to interview members of your class. Class members who are not interviewed should prepare critiques for an evaluation session to follow each interview. If possible, videotape these interviews for later analysis.
2. Complete a "resume worksheet" for yourself. Use the resume worksheet in this chapter as a guide.
3. Visit your college/university placement office. Find out what services it offers, what sources of job vacancies it has, and what procedures are followed to prepare a job placement folder. Then prepare a report to present to your classmates on the placement office.
4. Locate and talk with two private employment agencies. Find out what types of employers they normally service, what they charge, and what resume services they provide. Prepare a report for your classmates.
5. Clip a promising job advertisement from the newspaper and prepare a resume of your credentials to suit the requirements of the job.
6. Write a letter of application to accompany the resume you prepared in Exercise 5.
7. Write an unsolicited application letter to accompany the resume you prepared in Exercise 5. Rework the resume so that you could send it with the unsolicited application letter.
8. Using the job opening you identified in Exercise 5, learn what you can about the company. Note how you would use the information you uncover when you write your application letter and as you prepare for the interview.
9. Interview three human resource representatives to determine what they look for in resumes and application letters. Prepare a questionnaire to inquire about such topics as what information is wanted under work experience and the effect of spelling and grammar errors.
10. Prepare 10 questions that you might ask in an interview. Using the information you uncovered in Exercise 8, prepare answers to questions listed in Chapter 11 that might be asked of job applicants.

EMPLOYMENT CASE PROBLEMS

The following cases are designed for your use in studying and learning about employment as a process. Various activities are suggested following each case.

A DO-IT-YOURSELF CAREER PLAN

In their Behavior Management class, a group of students heard their professor make several suggestions concerning career employment. She had told them that their chosen employment should be selected differently from the employment that they fit into their class schedules to pay some of their college-related expenses. Her advice was directed at having each student make a career employment plan before he or she began job hunting. Their first postgraduate employment then would be the first step of their total planned work experience rather than a job taken just because it was available.

She explained that many people get started in work they do not like. Some begin with an employer they find unsatisfactory and for various reasons are unable to make a change to something they like better. It is probable, she explained, that each student would work 40 or more hours a week for as long as 45 or 50 years. How unfortunate it would be to spend all that time doing something the students did not like and from which they derived little satisfaction. All it took to avoid such a problem was to make a career plan and follow it carefully.

In a discussion later that day, several students decided that they liked the career plan idea well enough to try it. Their first step was to visit the professor during one of her office hours for more information. They were told that a good way to create their plans would involve the following steps:

- Inventory their skills, knowledge, experience and interest.
- Research the available employers—government, industry, education, social services, and so forth—that interest them.
- Research the types of work each category of employer provides.
- Analyze all the data and make some preliminary choices of which type of employer they would like to work for.
- Narrow the choices to three or four that could be researched thoroughly.
- Research the chosen employer/type of work choices.
- Narrow again to the one or two most preferred employer/type of work choice.
- Contact people employed in similar work for their advice.
- Make a final selection, if possible; or if no preference is found, return to making more choices and repeat the research steps.
- When the final selection has been made, contact one or more employers to obtain that employment.

The professor explained that the plan would require some time and effort, but if carefully and thoroughly done, the plan could have a lifetime payback.

The students who had gotten this advice proceeded to follow it, making the university library their first stop. Each one made a personal skills, knowledge, experience, and interest inventory. Then, they selected references starting with the *Dictionary of Occupational Titles (DOT)*, reading the descriptions of the job duties to see if they were of interest. Other government and industry publications were also read. Data gathering took several hours and resulted in each student's compiling a large volume of notes. Analysis and choices would be based on these notes.

Student Activities

1. Since statistics indicate that people change career paths several times during their lives, of what value is such a detailed career plan?
2. Other than library sources such as the *DOT*, what sources of information about employers and types of jobs could a person research when preparing a career plan?
3. Prepare your own preliminary career plan by completing the first seven steps listed in this case.

THE SUMMER "VICE PRESIDENT"

Joe Edwards was being interviewed for an executive trainee program at Abrams Manufacturing Corporation. He had obtained the interview by responding to a signed advertisement in *The Wall Street Journal* and following up his initial mailing of an application letter and resume with a telephone call. The interview had proceeded to the point where Ms. Graves, an employment interviewer, was questioning Joe about his summer jobs while completing his bachelor's degree at a southern university.

In response to a question concerning his work at Colossal Corporation's Florida facilities, Joe had asked for a few minutes to recall the pertinent details. Ms. Graves then told him to think about it for a few minutes while she ordered some coffee. Joe's thoughts turned to the company and the work he had done there.

During the summer of his junior year, he had applied for several internships in various parts of the country. Two companies made offers. The one he had accepted was in Florida near several resort attractions that he wanted to visit. The job described sounded routine and relatively unexciting, but Joe had decided he could tolerate it in order to enjoy a Florida "vacation" with all expenses paid.

At Colossal Corporation, Joe was employed in an engineering division that was doing part of the design work on a major defense contract that Colossal was fulfilling. The design work involved the navigation equipment for a military aircraft. Colossal had subcontracted part of the design and development work to other companies and was, in turn, a subcontractor to the company producing the complete aircraft.

Joe's work involved obtaining all the blueprints and other data submitted by Colossal's subcontractors, sequencing them in their proper place as part of his employer's engineering specifications package, renumbering them in a Colossal Corporation format, and mailing the completed package to Massive Aircraft Company, the aircraft manufacturer. In fact, the job was a clerical task, and Joe's title of Engineering Specifications Clerk reflected the nature of the work. However, Joe was well paid, soon mastered the essentials of the job, and did it effectively.

Now, Ms. Graves had provided their coffee, and her inquiring glance at Joe invited him to share these details with her. Instead, Joe proceeded to invent and describe a job to go with the title of "Engineering Specifications Coordinator," which he had put in his resume. As he spoke, the job got bigger and bigger. His imagined responsibilities expanded as did the importance of the work until Joe essentially was single handedly keeping Colossal Corporation running. When he finally stopped creating this imaginary position, Joe noticed that Ms. Graves was smiling. She entered a very brief notation on his resume (which Joe could not read) and proceeded to other items in his resume.

As the interview closed, Joe left the company with a strong hunch that he had invented himself out of the running for the job he had applied for. If he had been able to read Ms. Graves' comment, he would have been certain of it. She had written "Very inventive/not suitable for this position—possible PR candidate?"

About a week later, Joe received a polite but definite "don't call us" letter from Colossal Corporation.

Student Activities

1. Why do you think Joe embellished the description of his summer employment at Colossal Corporation? Do you believe that Joe felt that other candidates embellish their credentials so he should also? Prepare to defend your answer in an informal debate or brief extemporaneous oral presentation.
2. Should Joe have told Ms. Graves before leaving that he had embellished the job requirements he had performed at Colossal? Should Joe have written to Ms. Graves following the interview to explain his embellishment? Prepare to defend your answers in an informal debate or brief extemporaneous oral presentation. If you think he should have written Ms. Graves, then write the letter for Joe's signature.
3. How best could Joe have avoided embellishing the work he had performed at Colossal Corporation? Did his embellishment result from his not being prepared for the interview or his lack of knowledge of what goes on in an interview? Research the issues concerned and prepare a brief extemporaneous oral presentation, complete with an outline for the instructor's examination.
4. Do you believe job embellishment, either in an interview or on a resume, is acceptable under certain circumstances? If you answered "yes," under what circumstances? If you answered "no," plan a rebuttal to those who answered "yes."

Note: In preparation for all the activities, be sure to include information on the legal and ethical questions involved.

THE CHAMELEON CANDIDATE

Jerry Mathern arrived early at Environmental Conservators for a job interview. Jerry's application letter and resume, sent to the company's Vice President of Industrial Relations, had resulted in an invitation to visit Environmental's headquarters in a nearby West Coast city at company expense. The letter stated that Jerry would be interviewed for as many as three different positions because the company was expanding and had several openings. Aware of the need to make a good first impression, Jerry had researched the company and knew how and when it had been organized, what products and services it provided, and where it had located its facilities.

While waiting for the promised interview, he reexamined some informative material given him by the motel clerk when he had checked in the evening before. It had impressed him to know that Environmental was interested enough in him as a candidate to begin preselling the firm to him even before he actually visited the company. The material presented the company in a highly favorable light. His previous research in Standard & Poor's *Corporation Records* and Moody's *Industrial Manual* and the *Business Periodicals Index* was confirmed by data in the company publications. Jerry became convinced that he could find suitable career employment at Environmental Conservators—so convinced that it impaired his judgment.

During the day on two occasions, in the morning and after lunch, Jerry met with executives who had positions to fill in their departments. Although he knew that one of them was his best opportunity, he was not satisfied to concentrate on it. Instead, he let his eagerness to work for the company hurt his chances rather than help them. He tried urgently to fit himself into all three positions even though one of them was not well suited to his education and experience and another was completely unsuited.

Jerry's degree in Business Administration had prepared him, in general, for several kinds of work if he had an interest in them and a willingness to learn how to do the work. His concentration in marketing and his considerable ability to present his ideas to others convincingly were most applicable to one position for which he had interviewed. Environmental had recently developed an effective and relatively inexpensive technique for monitoring the ground water around industrial facilities to determine if any factory wastes were escaping into the water. All companies handling potentially contaminating substances were required by Environmental Protection Agency regulations to guard against contaminating their environments. Thus, such a monitoring service was required. Companies could do it for themselves or contract for it. As Jerry was told, Environmental's engineers and cost analysts believed they could do it cheaper on contract than potential customers could do it for themselves. It was an ideal job for Jerry, and he realized it as soon as the details were explained to him. He made a strong case for getting the job by carefully matching his preparation and abilities to the requirements.

However, he also attempted to match his credentials to an administrative position in the company's engineering laboratory even though he had no real interest in the work. At another interview he also made a strong, if insincere, attempt to present himself as the ideal candidate for a position for which he was temperamentally and academically unsuited. This position involved contract performance monitoring and preparation of customer billing. In fact, Jerry was so obviously unsuited for this position that the manager trying to fill it later reprimanded the employment manager for sending Jerry as a candidate.

The results of the three interviews from the managers having the various jobs to fill were sent to the employment manager. Unluckily, the manager read the most negative summary first, then the one from the engineering laboratory. By the time he got to the favorable summary, written by the executive needing a customer contact person, he was seeing Jerry as a "chameleon candidate," uncertain of what he really wanted to do and willing to try to convince others of something he really did not believe himself. As a result, the employment manager wondered if Jerry would be willing to concentrate on the customer contact position if he were hired to do it. He decided to call in other candidates for that manager to interview before making a final selection.

Jerry Mathern went home feeling mixed emotions. He knew that he would accept immediately the customer contact position if it were offered to him. However, if he were offered either of the other two positions, he would have to trade off his desire to work for Environmental against his lack of enthusiasm for the work itself. "Why didn't I only go for the one position I really wanted and tell them I wouldn't want either of the others," he wondered. It was a question he would ask himself many times as he waited for a letter from Environmental Conservators.

Student Activities

1. Why do you believe Jerry fell into the "trap" of interviewing for positions for which he was not qualified? Was his being interviewed for such positions his fault or the fault of the executives at Environmental? What could he have done to avoid interviewing for those other positions? Option A: Research these questions and prepare a short letter report addressed to your instructor in which you define the issues involved, draw conclusions, and make recommendations. Option B: Research these issues and prepare to debate the issues in class as an individual or, if so instructed, as a member of a team.
2. If Jerry had to interview for the other two positions, should he have done something during those interviews to disqualify himself from being considered for those positions? Should he have acted, in other words, in a manner that would have been detrimental to his being considered for those positions that he had no interest in? Plan a short, extemporaneous presentation in which you explain your position to other class members. Prepare an outline for your instructor's evaluation.
3. What, if anything, should Jerry do following the interviews to reverse the beliefs of the employment manager? For example, should he write the employment manager rather than wait to receive a letter? How might Jerry avoid similar situations in future interviews? Prepare a response for class discussion in which you bring notes to class to guide you as you argue your position. And if you think Jerry should write the employment manager before receiving a letter, write the letter for Jerry's signature. How can Jerry avoid similar situations in future interviews?

A VISIT TO SLIPPERY RECRUITERS, INC.

Throughout her college years, Jill Carpenter had thought about job hunting for a career position. Despite repeated reminders that time for making a well-planned search was running out, she had never gotten around to doing it. During both her junior and senior years, she had seen her classmates involved in job hunting, but Jill never did so.

Now she was just a few weeks from receiving her bachelor's degree. Suddenly, she realized that she had no employment plans or prospects.

What to do? Let your fingers do the walking! Jill flipped through the telephone book Yellow Pages and stabbed her finger at the listings for "employment agencies." It struck Slippery Recruiters, Inc., which claimed to be a "nationwide comprehensive recruiting service" with an office near Jill's university. She telephoned them and was told that they had handled "many" graduates in her degree field and presently had "several" job listings waiting to be filled. In answer to her question, Jill was told that the "placement fee" was paid by the prospective employer but that Jill might be charged a nominal fee for other services. Feeling that this might be her best bet and perhaps her only chance for employment without wasting time, Jill asked for an appointment.

She felt some concern when she arrived at the Slippery Recruiters, Inc., premises. It didn't look like what she had expected a branch of a national company would be: two small third floor offices in a rundown building on a street of poorly maintained buildings. James Brewster, the branch manager, explained to Jill that the present location was temporary until a new suite in the Mid-town Centre was ready for occupancy. Business was so good the firm just could not wait for the suite to be completed and had taken this substandard location to get some of its many clients placed in career positions. Of course, all the furniture and equipment would be replaced when it occupied the new offices.

Jill was then introduced to Marianne Onofree who would handle her placement details. Marianne quickly determined that Jill had made no previous preparation for job hunting and told her that she would need a resume, a letter of application, and a description of the type of position she would like to have. She also would have to decide what size and type of company she preferred and in what part of the country she wanted to work. Marianne was friendly but firm—until Jill could provide these items, Slippery could not place her in any of the several positions it had available. Marianne then asked Jill to make another appointment for the following week to which she would bring the required items.

Jill was then faced with a problem, since these were exactly the steps she had not taken during her junior and senior years. Could Marianne help her? Yes—happy to, but there would be some nominal fees. So they proceeded to draft the resume and the letter, with Jill supplying the information and Marianne recording and working the information into a finished form. She then sent Jill to James Brewster to discuss her desired position, company, and location while she sent Jill's resume and letter to the secretarial staff. Since she had not seen any other staff members, Jill assumed they were in another office.

James Brewster interviewed Jill for about 25 minutes, filling out a series of forms as they talked. He avoided answering Jill's repeated questions concerning what positions Slippery had on file, stating that he first needed the basic information from Jill to match her to a position. Sending a company an unsuitable applicant could result in Slippery's losing that company as a client. Jill was then asked to return in two hours to examine her finished resume and a computer analysis of her interview data.

When she returned, Jill was met by Marianne Onofree, who told her that James Brewster had been called to a client company. He had taken a copy of Jill's resume with him for discussion. She gave Jill 50 photocopies of the resume and letter with a list of companies to which she could mail them. In addition, she gave her five pages of a computer printout that summarized the information she had given James Brewter. Of course, an itemized bill for "placement services" totaling $378.10 was also included.

Jill was shocked by the amount of these "nominal" fees: $100 for preparation of resume, $.50 per copy for duplication, $75 for placement research interview, $125 for a computer research scan, and charges for several other items. A growing feeling of having been very naive and very foolish engulfed Jill as she began to realize that she could have done for herself everything that Slippery Recruiters, Inc., had done. And she could have done it at a fraction of the cost. She realized now why her classmates had done their own placement services with some help from the college placement office personnel.

Student Activities

1. Should Jill have gone to an employment agency when she first became concerned about her employment prospects? What should Jill have done before contacting an employment agency to prepare herself for the initial meeting with the employment agency's representative?
2. What information should Jill have obtained from the employment agency before agreeing to discuss job openings? Would Jill have been correct in demanding that a contract be signed that outlined the responsibilities of all parties involved?
3. What steps should Jill now take to locate and obtain suitable employment?

PART 5

COMMUNICATING THROUGH WRITTEN REPORTS

CHAPTER 13

PLANNING THE REPORT PROCESS AND COLLECTING DATA

Steve Petri's boss is famous within the company for his brusque manner that seems to cut through to the core of problems. Working for him is both tense and challenging, for he always demands the most from the people reporting to him. Yesterday he called Steve into his office and asked him to prepare a report on the rapidly accelerating rate of consolidation within the airline industry and how it was affecting the medium-sized airline carrier Steve's boss was thinking of acquiring. "Something about them is bothering me, Steve. I've got a hunch they're in trouble somehow. I want you to find out if I'm right. A lot's riding on this. One week, okay?"

Today, Steve sits in his office, a huge stack of papers about recent developments in the airline industry in front of him. If he has a weakness, he admits to himself, it's doing reports. Somehow he's never really mastered the process to his satisfaction. Looking down at the papers in front of him, he realizes that in the next week he is going to take a self-imposed crash course in this subject. On a yellow pad, he writes his first question: "What does my boss really want to know?" The learning process has begun.

This chapter is designed to help you avoid the kinds of problems Steve Petri is experiencing. In it, you will learn how to prepare reports—orderly written or spoken communications of meaningful data to one or more people. Good reporting requires more than writing ability. Other communication skills—reading, listening, speaking, and observing—are just as necessary for writing effective reports. A report may be verbal or written. In fact, your manager may sometimes ask for both for the same project.

What are two objectives of reports?

In preparing a report, you have two objectives: (1) to provide managers with information, such as the status of a particular airline, and (2) to aid them in decision making, such as whether to buy the airline. The first part of this chapter examines the report process itself. In it we discuss writing for the report audience and defining the problem or subject.

The collection phase of any research project involves gathering data from *primary* or *secondary* sources, or both. In business, primary data consist of original source material, such as that derived from interviews or questionnaires. In contrast, secondary data consist of materials filtered through an intermediate source, such as books, periodicals, and microforms. To prepare many reports, you will have to collect both kinds of data. The second part of this chapter discusses methods of gathering primary and secondary data. In it we discuss techniques to aid you in each.

WRITING FOR THE REPORT AUDIENCE

In composing a report, you must first consider who will receive your message. This may seem obvious, but many writers—because of their own involvement in the project—forget the reader. Consequently, they assume that he or she has the same basic understanding of the crude oil and petroleum industry or of the booming market for compact discs as they do. Therefore, they omit important information from their reports. For these reasons, you need to analyze your audience each time you write a report. The following checklist contains some questions you may ask yourself in such an analysis.

AUDIENCE ANALYSIS CHECKLIST

1. What does my audience want to know?
2. For what purpose is the audience using my report?
3. Will more than one person read it?
4. If there are two or more readers, who are they?
5. Will the audience understand the vocabulary or language I plan to use?
6. What is my audience's educational level?
7. What is my audience's background and experiences?
8. How much knowledge of the topic does my audience have already?
9. Does the audience have a positive attitude toward my subject?

Why is audience analysis important in report writing?

Having information about your audience will help you determine the report's content and organization. For example, if the audience is unfamiliar with your topic, you may have to include more background material. Or you may have to define certain technical terms so they will understand you. Or you may have to add various visual aids to help them interpret the data. From first to last in the report process, then, you need to be sensitive to your audience's needs.

DEFINING THE PROBLEM

Is it really necessary to define a report problem? Why or why not?

Each report you write has at its center a problem that needs solving. The key to your success is to understand fully what this problem is. Naturally, you should state the problem at the beginning of the report. However, defining it may not be so easy. You can begin by (1) conducting preliminary research, (2) limiting the problem, (3) determining its scope, (4) identifying the factors involved, and (5) depending on the nature of the problem, formulating the hypothesis.

Conducting Preliminary Research

When you are asked to write a report, naturally you are either familiar or unfamiliar with the subject. If you are familiar with it, you can clearly define the problem. For example, suppose you are an accountant who is asked to write a report on a company's financial situation. Since you have done many similar reports, you are easily able to define the problem, locate the right information, and write a report in a way that satisfies your client's needs.

In contrast, if you are unfamiliar with the subject area, you may not have such a clear idea of the nature of the problem. For example, if your area is corporate law and you are asked by a senior partner in your firm to report on some recent public interest rulings, you may have more difficulty defining what problem you are addressing. In such situations, you may need to do some preliminary research into the background of the problem.

What is the relationship between a report authorizer and a report writer?

First, make sure you understand specifically what the *authorizer*—or person granting permission or requesting the study—wants from you. Does he or she simply want some information? Or are you supposed to make a recommendation? Sometimes the authorizer may also be unfamiliar with the subject and, therefore, unable to assist you. If this happens, then read background material or talk to people who really know the subject. As you read, talk, and collect this preliminary background information, think constantly about its relationship to your problem. In this way you should begin to define it with more precision. If your reader's knowledge of the subject area is limited, you may also have to include some of the background data in the final report.

Limiting the Problem

You have begun to get familiar with the problem or purpose of your report. Yet it still seems so broad—you could write a 500-page book on the subject—then obviously you will have to *limit* it to the precise problem area you want to study.

What? Why? When? Who? Where? How do these questions relate to limiting a report problem?

One way to do this is to ask yourself these five questions:

1. *What* do I want to do?
2. *Why* am I doing it?
3. *When* do I have to have it completed?
4. *Who* (or what) am I going to study?
5. *Where* is the geographical area I need to study?

Let's see how answering these five questions helps to set limits on a problem.

Suppose Beta Sporting Goods, a Chicago-based company, is thinking about expanding to another location. The company's owner, a man who likes to consider all the options, asks you to look into the situation and write a report to be delivered within a month. In returning to your office, you immediately write down the five questions and your answers to each:

1. *What:* A study of three possible expansion sites.
2. *Why:* To determine whether the expansion is feasible.
3. *When:* Within the next two years.
4. *Who:* Beta Sporting Goods.
5. *Where:* Chicago, Illinois.

In answering these questions, you have limited the problem to three expansion sites within the next two years in the Chicago area. Now you can write a precise statement defining your problem, such as

> The purpose of this report is to analyze three possible expansion sites within the Chicago, Illinois, area for Beta Sporting Goods and to determine whether expansion is feasible within the next two years.

You have written your problem statement in declarative form. If you want, you may put it in *interrogative* or *infinitive phrase* form. For example,

> What is the feasibility of Beta Sporting Goods expanding in one of three locations within the Chicago, Illinois, area within the next two years?
>
> Problem: To analyze three possible expansion sites within the Chicago, Illinois, area for Beta Sporting Goods and to determine whether expansion is feasible within the next two years.

Determining the Scope

In analyzing your problem, keep in mind its *scope.* Scope refers to the report's boundaries. In other words, you need to determine which areas to study and which to not. In doing this, you can then identify how thoroughly you need to research the subject to solve the problem. Moreover, if you have defined its scope, your reader will also know what to expect from your report. The following is an example of a scope statement on Beta Sporting Goods:

Does the scope set unnecessary boundaries for the report problem? Why or why not?

> This report will analyze three expansion sites for Beta Sporting Goods. Each site will be evaluated and compared based on certain criteria. No attempt will be made to study future economic conditions that may influence the sporting goods market for the next 10 years.

Let's take another example. Suppose the record company you presently work for is considering buying a new copying machine for under $4000. Your supervisor has asked you to investigate this situation. After some preliminary research and some thought about the problem, you have written a problem statement. Next, you have limited your study to three copying machines. Your scope statement might then resemble this:

> The study will focus on evaluating three copying machines priced below $4000. A comparison of these machines will be based on analysis of their costs, operating features, and special input-output qualities. This study will not include a comparison of their physical features such as their weight, dimensions, and color, because all three copying machines have fairly similar physical features.

Note that both these scope statements are tentative; that is, you may add or delete items as you continue to research. Yet, at the same time, a scope statement itself helps you identify the limits of this research.

Identifying the Factors

How do factors relate to the report problem? What purpose do they serve?

You've written a succinct scope statement; now you have to identify the *factors* involved in the problem. Factors are extensions of the original problem that you will examine separately according to how each contributes to solving your problem. Sometimes they are called elements, descriptors, criteria, or categories. Whichever term you prefer, try to identify all of them. Your analysis will form the basis of any conclusions you draw and any recommendations you make.

Factors also provide a framework for the collection phase of the report process. As you will see, they can serve as a tentative outline too. Therefore, you may have to add or delete some of them as you enter the collection phase. (See the second part of this chapter for a more detailed discussion of collecting data.)

To see what factors are and how they relate to a problem, let's return to the Beta Sporting Goods example. What factors in the preliminary research could you list that might help solve your problem? Some of them might be

1. Cost
2. Site selection
3. Competition
4. Demand
5. Employee availability
6. Traffic flow

Of course, you can think of other factors or subfactors (for example, under employee availability, you might insert managerial and sales personnel). But that is not the point. What is, is that the problem now seems more structured, more orderly. With these items you can begin your research. Notice too that they extend the problem's scope.

CHECKLIST FOR DETERMINING FACTORS

1. Develop a sense of curiosity—explore.
2. Ask the authorizer or others familiar with the problem for possible factors. Seek multiple viewpoints.
3. Try to identify possible factors based on your own understanding of the problem.
4. Indicate possible factors from your preliminary reading and review of the literature.
5. Once you have identified a factor or two, ask yourself what-if questions: What are the causes and effects? Do comparisons and contrasts exist?
6. Keep an open mind about including other factors that may arise during your research.

The above checklist should help you discover the factors for any type of report problem.

Formulating the Hypothesis (If Applicable)

Sometimes a report problem requires you to analyze alternative solutions. In such situations, instead of identifying factors, you should form hypothesis statements. Behind such statements lies the assumption that you are going to test some alternative solutions during your research to decide which, if any, is best. Whether your hypothesis turns out to be accepted or rejected, the reasons for acceptance or rejection constitute your findings.

You may write either *directed* or *null* hypothesis statements. A *directed* hypothesis focuses your research and analysis and predicts the result—the alternative solution—you expect to occur. For example,

> Using individualized instruction for in-service managerial training will result in higher achievement than will using the traditional large-group instruction.

Why do researchers prefer null to directed hypotheses?

In contrast, a *null* hypothesis states that no differences exist between or among solutions. In research—especially formal primary research—the null hypothesis statement is used more frequently than is the directed. For one thing, it gives a more objective test statement. For another, it tends to reduce the researcher's bias about the results. Two ways of writing a null statement for the managerial training project are

1. No significant difference in achievement will result when using individualized instruction for in-service managerial training than when using the traditional large-group instruction.
2. The type of instructional method used in in-service managerial training will have no effect on achievement.

Once you have defined your problem, your next step is to collect data. Since this step can be both complex and time consuming, you should approach it systematically.

COLLECTING SECONDARY DATA

Exactly what is a bibliography? Where does the information for it come from?

In doing research you need to be aware of all the sources that will help solve the problem. Thus, you should prepare a bibliography for your research area of written–secondary–sources of information.

Preparing a Bibliography

In this context, a bibliography is simply an open-ended list of all available sources that may contain data you believe relate to your subject. The purpose is to list all the sources you will review later. These might include company publications, general reference books, trade and technical books, periodicals, and government documents. (See Appendix C, Business Research Reference Sources, for a detailed compilation of sources that may be useful to your research.)

Scanning Company Publications

Company publications are developed, produced, and written for a specific organization, namely, the company itself. These sources may include newsletters, bulletins, brochures, pamphlets, handbooks, manuals, company records, and reports.

Reviewing General Reference Books

General reference books range from almanacs to biographies. Two major guides to specific reference books in your area of interest are the *Guide to Reference Books,* 9th ed. (American Library Association, 1976; 1980 and 1982 supplements available), by Eugene Paul Sheehy and *Where to Find Business Information* (John Wiley & Sons, 1982) by David M. Brownstone and Gorton Carruth.

Finding Books

Other sources that you can add to your bibliography are books related to your topic that are located in the library. Use the library's classification system to find what you want. Books may be classified (cataloged) either in the Dewey Decimal or the Library of Congress system.

In beginning your search through the catalog, you may be unaware of any specific books or authors in your research area. However, because you do know the subject area, you can consult the subject catalog. If you cannot find any books under your subject heading or those closely related, consult the *Subject Headings Used in the Dictionary Catalog of the Library of Congress.* This guide usually is located near the card catalog files. Use it to find related subject headings.

Your local library will probably not have many books in your subject area. To find out about others, you can consult three different sources: *Cumulative Book Index, Publishers' Weekly,* and *Subject Guide to Books in Print.* The *Cumulative Book Index* includes books published since 1928 by author, title, and subject area. *Publishers' Weekly* lists books, pamphlets, and paperbacks that are published each week. *Subject Guide to Books in Print* identifies books presently available in the United States.

How can an interlibrary loan service help you with your research?

If you do not find the books you need at your library, you may be able to get them from another library near you. If not, your librarian may be able to borrow them from some other library through what is called an *interlibrary loan service.*

Finding Periodicals

Is a book a periodical? If not, explain the difference.

Periodicals, sometimes called serials, are those magazines, journals, and newspapers published at regular intervals, such as weekly or monthly. You will find periodicals contain the most current data about your research topic. You can find appropriate articles in them by checking various indexes. Two of the most helpful ones for business research are the *Business Periodicals Index* and the *Business Index.* The *Business Index* is a microform index. For newspaper sources, consult *The Wall Street Journal Index, The New York Times Index,* or the *National Newspaper Index.* This last source indexes five national newspapers and is a microform index.

If you do not find enough material through the indexes that relates to your research topic, consult either the *Ayer Directory of Publications* or *Ulrich's International Periodicals Directory.* These directories contain the names of periodicals that relate to your subject area. Also, once you have found some related articles, browse through the references at the end of them. Usually, authors will list here the sources they have consulted in preparing their articles. Some of these may be useful.

To find out what libraries hold the periodicals you want, consult the *Union List of Serials in Libraries of the United States and Canada.* This resource provides you with a comprehensive list of periodicals and the libraries that hold them. This list is updated by the *New Serial Titles.*

After identifying which library has the periodicals you need, you can ask your librarian if copies of the periodicals can be borrowed through the interlibrary loan service. You should note that some libraries will not lend the entire periodical, but they will make photocopies of articles contained in them.

Finding Government Documents

Various federal, state, and local governmental agencies publish a vast amount of data of interest to researchers. For example, the state commerce department and the research divisions of state universities are two places where you can find data related to many areas of interest to a business researcher. In addition, you can find publications from your state, as well as other states, by consulting the *Monthly Checklist of State Publications.* When you are searching for U.S. Government publications, the first place to look is in the *Monthly Catalog of United States Government Publications.* In this guide, current publications for all federal agencies are listed. Monthly and annual indexes also are prepared. Another source to help you find the various periodicals available from the federal government is the *Index to United States Government Periodicals.*

Technological Developments

What role has technology played in research?

New technological advancements are providing researchers with the opportunity to find data quickly and accurately. Two that libraries now use are microforms and computerized literature search services.

Microforms

With the amount of data increasing each day, microforms have been developed to reduce their size and make them easier to file through a photographic process. The two common microforms are microfilm and microfiche. Many libraries carry only microforms of periodicals.

Microfilm comes in 16mm (millimeter) or 35mm reels that contain data viewed in sequence on a reel-to-reel reader. In contrast, microfiche comes in 4 inch × 6 inch cards that contain data printed in a grid format. The viewing process allows you to gain access to the data randomly rather than in sequence as with microfilm. You can make copies of data located on either form if the microform reader you use has a photocopy attachment.

Computerized Literature Search Services

Until recently, we located most secondary materials manually by using reference guides to lead us to magazines, books, pamphlets, and so forth, which we then read or leafed through. Now computers are easing this time-consuming process. For example, you may use computers to access various files or data bases for your subject area. This results in a computer-produced bibliography that often contains abstracts (brief descriptions of the contents) of the citations in the data base. A review of these abstracts will save you time because they permit you to decide whether or not to locate and read the entire article.

How do you go about conducting a computer search for information?

Before conducting a computer search, you should establish a search strategy. Thus, you will need to determine key word descriptors (words that relate to your research area) for your topic because the computer will search through all citations in the data base that contain them. In addition, you have to decide the data bases you want to search and set publication date limitations. Obviously, if your topic is too broad and has no cut-off dates, you will spend more time and money than is really necessary. If you need assistance, your librarian will work with you to determine the best strategy. (For a list of popular data bases, see sources in Appendix C.)

Suppose your search effort has turned up a number of excellent sources. Next, you will need to know how to record the data that will help solve your problem.

TAKING EFFECTIVE NOTES

You may know some people who view recording or note taking as a routine or passive process requiring only a pen and a stack of index cards. But to gain the most from this phase of the report process, treat it as an active and thought-producing operation that can contribute to your knowledge. In other words, question and critique what you read. If you do, you will start to understand how the data relate to your problem.

Once you begin the actual collection process, use the checklist on page 406 as you read, think about, observe, and review your data. Answering these questions should enable you to screen secondary data more effectively so that you may find the information you need to solve your problem.

Once you have the right data, you should follow a systematic and orderly plan to take notes. Such a plan includes the following steps:

What are the seven steps in note taking?

Step 1 *Review the factors.*

Earlier, when you analyzed your research problem, you began to identify factors relating to it. Now you should review them and let them serve as the starting point for locating related data.

CRITICAL EVALUATION OF DATA CHECKLIST

1. Are the data *directly* related to the problem or are they just interesting to know?
2. Will the data have a definite effect on solving the research problem?
3. Will the report audience need the data to make a decision about the results of the research study?
4. Are the data related to the current factors being studied and do they support or refute these factors?
5. Could these data be subfactors of the factors being studied or could they be new factors?
6. Do these data lead in any directions other than that of the problem itself?
7. Are these data current or are they too old to use?
8. Are the data from valid and reliable sources? For example, what reputation does the publisher or author have?
9. Are the data accurate? If opinions are presented, are they supported fully?
10. Do the data include all aspects of a particular issue?

Step 2 *Prepare a tentative list of factors.*
This list will show you how your factors relate to one another as well as provide a foundation for your written outline. As you find additional factors or subfactors, write them in the appropriate area on your list. Your original concepts about your research project may change as you begin the research phase. Revise or recheck key ideas throughout your research phase.

Step 3 *Scan the source for major or related factors.*
If the source is a book, you might review the table of contents or index for factors. If it is a periodical, you might concentrate on the major headings and their topic sentences. By providing a general overview, this process will help you to determine the data worth pursuing.

What two purposes does a bibliography control card serve?

Step 4 *Prepare a bibliography control card.*
Once you determine that a particular source contains data you want to record, prepare a 3″ × 5″ index card. Make such a card for every source you use. Because they will be keyed to your note cards, these will serve as controls. As such they will have two purposes. First, you

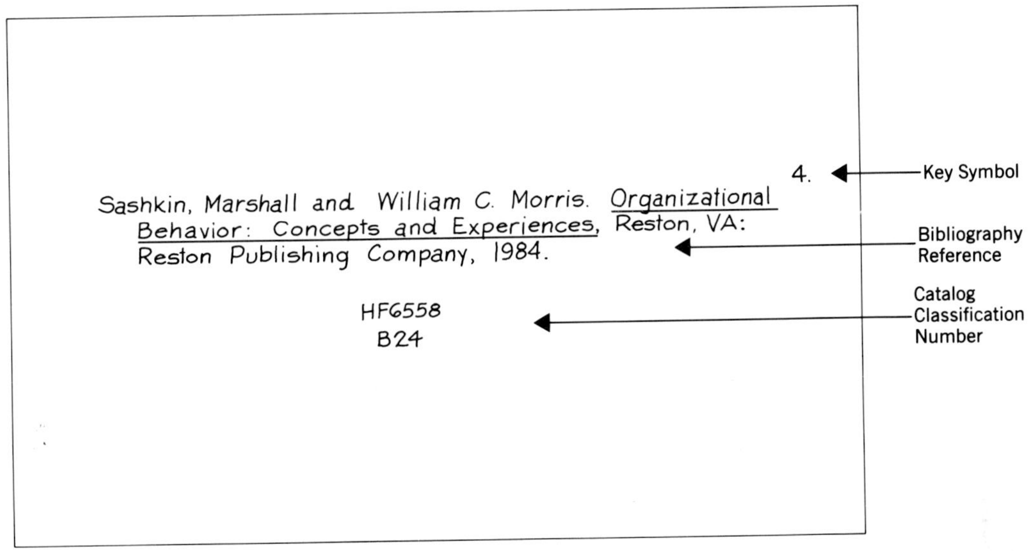

4.
Key Symbol
Sashkin, Marshall and William C. Morris. Organizational Behavior: Concepts and Experiences, Reston, VA: Reston Publishing Company, 1984.
Bibliography Reference
HF6558
B24
Catalog Classification Number

FIGURE 13-1 A 3″ × 5″ bibliography control card.

only have to write the bibliographical reference once on a control card with a corresponding key symbol. This key symbol helps with organizing the information. Second, when you have completed your search, all you need to do to type your bibliography is to alphabetize these cards.

You can base the key symbol system on numbers or letters, or a combination of the two. Whichever system you use, assign each source its own symbol (e.g., 1,2, . . .). On each card, write the entire bibliographical reference. For example, periodical sources should include the author(s), article title, name of magazine or journal, volume and number of issue, date of publication, and page numbers. (See Appendix D for the proper format for writing bibliographical entries.) Also, you should write the catalog classification (call) number of your control card in case you need to locate the source again in the library. A bibliography control card for a business text is shown in Figure 13-1.

Why prepare just one note per card when taking notes?

Step 5 *Prepare one note card for each factor.* For your actual note taking, use a 3″ × 5″, 4″ × 6″, or a 5″ × 7″ index card. In preparing it, write the key symbol for the source in either of the upper corners. Then, write the factor (or key word) near the top of the note card. Leave space and next write the page number and the corresponding note, as shown in Figure 13-2. To make organizing data easier, prepare a separate note card for each new factor or subfactor. Even when the same factor is discussed in two different sources, prepare separate note cards for each source. You will find

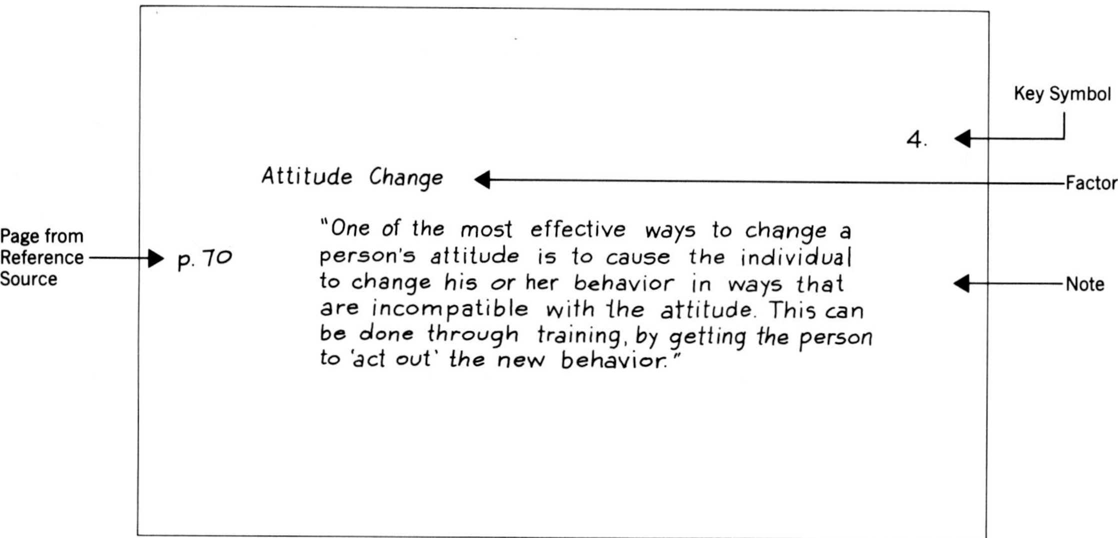

FIGURE 13-2 A 4″ × 6″ note card.

that one comment per card should provide maximum flexibility in terms of organizing data.

Step 6 *Determine the type of note.*

The note that appears on the card in Figure 13-2 is a *direct quotation.* Three other types of notes are *paraphrasing, outlining,* and *summarizing.*

In notetaking, what four types of notes are there?

In a direct quotation note, copy the quote word for word without changing the punctuation or spelling. If you choose to omit some words, use ellipses to show that they are missing. Three spaced periods (. . .) at the point of omission represent ellipses. In a paraphrasing note, write the idea in your own words. Even though you are quoting indirectly, you still need to footnote the source in your report. (See Appendix D for a discussion of footnote documentation.) In an outline note, record the key word(s) from a paragraph, page, article, or chapter in an organized format. In a summary note—which is similar to but usually longer than a paraphrased note—condense the main ideas from all or part of an article or book chapter. For both outlines and summary notes, also acknowledge your source.

Whichever type of note you use on a card, consider writing some of your own ideas or comments on it whenever appropriate. In doing this, you may more clearly see the relationship of the note to your overall problem.

Step 7 *Arrange note cards in a logical order.*

The last step of note taking is also the first step of your organizational phase. As you record a note for a factor or a subfactor, include it with your other corresponding notes. From this arrangement, combined with a tentative list of factors and subfactors, you should be able to prepare your writing outline. (See Chapter 14 for a discussion of the organizational phase of report writing.)

At what point should you stop searching for information?

When you find the same data repeatedly in different sources, close your data search. At this point, you probably have collected two or three times the amount of information necessary to solve your problem.

Nevertheless, useful secondary data—from books, journals, or government documents—may not be current or specific enough, or may not be available to help you solve a problem. Or the data may only help you solve part of your problem. For example, in deciding whether to take over another company, you will have to rely mainly on primary sources such as interviews.

COLLECTING PRIMARY DATA

When collecting primary data from original sources conducting personal interviews or preparing and administering questionnaires can be time consuming as well as expensive. Similarly, time and money availability may also affect which research method you will use.

Primary Research Methods

You can collect primary data by experiment, observation, survey, or some combination of these.

How do experimentation, observation, and surveying differ from one another?

Experimental research seeks to determine whether change in one factor causes change in another. For example, suppose the manager of a bus company wanted to know whether lowering the fare between two cities would increase the number of riders. To find out, he or she decreases the fare for a week to measure its effect (factor A) on the number of customers (factor B).

A major consideration in conducting this experiment is to develop a research design that ensures that any change in the number of riders is due only to the fare reduction. That is, if you were conducting this experiment, you would have to consider such outside influences as similar fare reductions by competing bus lines or unusual changes in the weather, and so forth. Many research designs exist, and you should become familiar with the techniques and the limitations of these designs before conducting experimental research.

Observational research involves watching respondents' actions or the results of their actions. The data can be gathered firsthand by observation, where, for example, you count how many male customers buy a specific brand of toothpaste at a local supermarket, or it can be done mechanically, as for example, in videotaping the same activity. Obviously, such research can only record external actions, not internal ones, such as why a particular type of customer prefers one brand of toothpaste to another. If you collect observational data, you must be as consistent, accurate, and objective as possible.

Survey research is a way of collecting data by asking questions or posing statements that respondents answer on questionnaires or during interviews. The purpose of such research is to determine such things as opinions, attitudes, beliefs, or perceptions about various work situations, issues. policies, procedures, or products. In business, this method is frequently used because it is the only way researchers can collect the type of information needed.

Combining research methods is something you might consider in collecting your data. For example, you might conduct an experimental study to test the effectiveness of large-group instruction versus individualized instruction in your company's training program. In addition, you might survey the participants' attitudes about each of these methods of instruction, either by having them complete a questionnaire or by conducting personal interviews.

Validity and Reliability

What does it mean to have valid and reliable data?

In any research study your objective is the same: to collect *valid* and *reliable* data. *Valid data* measure the factor or factors you intend them to measure. If your results are invalid, your interpretation of them will also be invalid. Some things that may adversely affect validity are giving unclear directions or using ambiguous questions or statements on questionnaires and surveys.

In contrast, *reliable data* measure people, actions, and situations consistently and accurately. One way to prove reliability is to be able to reproduce the results of your study at a later time. You can increase validity and reliability by exercising care in sampling design and by properly developing your questionnaire or surveys.

Sampling Procedures for Survey Research

Can sampling a population save time and money? Explain.

When designing a survey for a particular purpose, you will need to define the survey's population or all the members of a group you wish to survey. For example, a population for a study on student interest for an entrepreneurs' club could be every business major in a college. Or for a study of voting patterns on the budget deficit, the population could be all the registered Democrats or Republicans in a state. If you were to question each member of the population, you would know what the responses are for everyone in it. Attempting to question the entire group, however, could be costly and time consuming. Instead, you can use a *sample* of respondents from it.

In sampling you need to select a representative subgroup of a population. To be representative, the sample must have characteristics that are similar to those of the entire population. If your sample is truly representative, you will then be able to generalize your findings to the larger group.

Once you identify the population for a study, you will have to determine how to choose the sample.

Selecting Sampling Methods

What are the three types of random sampling? How do they differ from one another?

Three common types of sampling methods are *simple, systematic,* and *stratified random sampling*. For each, you need a list, directory, or roster that identifies all the members of the population. For example, one such list might contain the names of all the real estate brokers in California.

Simple random sampling involves selecting a sample where every member of the population has an equal chance of being chosen. For example, you could place all the names of California's real estate brokers in a container and then pull out the number of names that would be representative of the entire group. Or you can use a table of random numbers. (For tables of random numbers and instructions on how to use them, consult a statistics text or reference book.)

Systematic random sampling is similar to the simple random sample technique except in one respect: with systematic sampling, you pick your sample based on some predetermined interval. In other words, you would choose every *n*th member of the population from the list for the sample. Thus, you might select every sixth name on your real estate brokers' list, or every tenth, or whatever.

Stratified random sampling consists of dividing the population into subgroups based on similar characteristics. After this, you make a simple random selection within each subgroup to form the sample. In the case of the real estate brokers, you could stratify them according to sex, geographical location, educational level, or a combination of these subgroups.

In selecting the proper sample, you should be aware of the relative proportion of the subgroup to the total population. For example, suppose that the list of brokers' names consists of 70 percent males and 30 percent females. Suppose too that you want a sample size of 1000 brokers. Then you would select at random 700 names from the male subgroup list and 300 names from the female. As you can see, the use of stratification offers you the opportunity of having more representation in the sample based on certain population characteristics.

Questionnaire Development for Survey Research

You've identified your population and selected your representative sample. Now you are ready to determine the answers you need to solve your research problem. In other words, you will have to plan, design, and select a series of questions or statements. Your sample's responses will provide the data you need to solve the problem, and a questionnaire will contain your list of questions or statements. As you have done with every other part of the report process, you must compose the items on it with the problem in mind. Also, the items must be geared to the population—its interests, needs, and knowledge. Therefore, audience analysis is critical at this stage.

You may be seeking facts or opinions. For example, you may want to know how a new hair spray is selling (fact) or if a new management procedure seems preferable to the old (opinion). You might derive your items from factors such as a review of related secondary data, a talk with people familiar with the problem, or your own experience. But however you design the questionnaire, your questions or statements must give you the appropriate, or valid and reliable, data.

How does a panel of experts validate a questionnaire?

One common way of proving the validity of a questionnaire is to use a panel of experts. These panel members may be professionals or practitioners who are familiar with the target population or the problem, or both. For instance, if you conduct a study on a company's personnel practices, you might include instructors of personnel management and personnel directors on the panel. These experts will review the content, clarity of the directions, vocabulary difficulty, item arrangement, ambiguities, and length of the questionnaire before using it. The reliability of the questionnaire can be determined statistically. Although the statistical analysis is beyond the scope of this book, you should become familiar with various statistical methods that are appropriate. Very often, these methods require you to conduct a pretest or pilot study. To do this, you would administer the questionnaire to a group of people who are similar to the members of the population to see if the questionnaire gives reliable results. If it does not, you can revise it before administering it to the sample group.

In addition to the points already discussed, follow these guidelines as you develop the questionnaire:

1. Word the items in a parallel manner so that respondents will interpret them the same way.
2. Be careful to choose the right words. Common problems in wording are the use of abstract words, jargon, ambiguous or general expressions, and negative terms. When you must include abstract words or technical jargon, define them in the question or statement. If you must use general expressions such as *frequently,* then include specific reference points like *once a week* to clarify them. Here is an example of a well-worded question:

How frequently are you required to make oral presentations of your written reports?

Very frequently (almost daily)	1. ____
Frequently (once a week)	2. ____
Occasionally (once or twice a month)	3. ____
Seldom (once or twice every 3 to 6 months)	4. ____
Rarely (once a year)	5. ____
Never	6. ____

Note: Notice that the response column is placed at the right of the responses. This fits more naturally with the way in which people fill out questionnaires than does placement at the left.

Why should you phrase questionnaire items positively?

Phrase questionnaire items positively and let the respondent agree or disagree with the items as they think appropriate. (Positive phrasing provides consistency and seems to interfere less with the respondent's freedom to respond truthfully than does negative phrasing.) Here is an example:

> Resistance to change is an important concern [instead of saying "*not* an important concern"] when deciding whether to install a new computer system:
>
> 1. yes ____ 2. no ____

3. Design items that require a response to only one aspect of an issue in each item. In other words, do not include compound questions or statements in a questionnaire item. For example, avoid a question such as the following:

   > Do you favor leasing or purchasing a computer system?
   >
   > 1. yes ____ 2. no ____

   This structure will confuse the respondent because you are asking two questions. Instead, pose separate questions.

4. Word items so that they do not suggest or influence a particular response. For instance, a question such as "Do you believe Gamma Corporation would provide the best aftersale computer service?" suggests a particular response. Instead, ask "Which company do you believe would provide the best aftersale computer service?" Then, you might include the possible responses.

5. Include *only* items that you need answered to solve the research problem. As a courtesy, do not waste the respondents' time by asking "nice-to-know" items—related items not necessary to solve the problem. If respondents detect that you are doing this, they may question the seriousness of the study and cease to answer the remaining questionnaire items.

6. Phrase each item in a way that avoids damaging the respondents' pride or bringing up their biases. In other words, ask sensitive questions indirectly. Thus, be careful when asking questions about age, income level, education, church affiliation, political party membership, or any other personal characteristic. Age and income level are especially sensitive items. One way to get more accurate responses to this type of question is to give a range interval from which to choose. For example, give intervals such as "20 to 30," "31 to 40," and so on for age and "$10,000 to $14,999," "$15,000 to $19,999," and so on for income. These intervals should be mutually exclusive; that is, no overlap should exist between them.
7. Design items that request current and easily remembered data. When respondents must rely too much on their memories, they may either guess or not respond at all. Either way, their answers would be invalid and unreliable.
8. Arrange the sequence of items so the questions start in an easy and nonthreatening way. (When respondents see that the first few questions are complex or threatening, they may decide not to complete it.) Also, group the sequence of items in a logical and coherent order. If possible, group together all items about a particular topic or subject. This grouping will help the respondent think more logically about the issues involved and will show that you care enough to have planned the questionnaire thoughtfully.
9. Design the overall format of the items in a way that will help you to tabulate, organize, and evaluate the data easily. The easier a questionnaire is to complete, the easier it will be to deal with the data once you have them. Devise a coding system, especially if a computer analyzes the data. To show how coding works, assume that you are surveying commercial bankers to determine the type of bank in which respondents are employed. You ask the question:

    In what type of bank are you employed?

    National 1. _____

    State 2. _____

How do open- and closed-ended questions differ?

In this example, each response is coded with a number: 1 or 2. These codes make both manual and computer tabulation and analysis much easier. (See the next chapter for a further discussion of coding techniques.) Questionnaire items can be written in two types of formats: *unstructured* or *open-ended responses* and *structured* or *close-ended responses*.

Unstructured or Open-Ended Response Items

Unstructured or open-ended response questionnaire items permit respondents to answer in their own words. This type of item is useful for gathering general data or, more important, for identifying issues or problems you may not have considered.

The following is an example:

Please indicate the one major problem area in your office.

____

In answering, respondents might indicate problem areas, such as low productivity or morale or outdated equipment. However, open-ended questions will have to be evaluated individually, no small task when hundreds of questionnaires are involved.

The following questions that might be asked about a bank officer's perceptions in evaluating and declining a loan are additional examples of unstructured or open-ended response items:

1. If your first impression is that a loan request is weak, how will you proceed to investigate the loan request? ____
2. When you decline a loan, how much consideration if any do you give to its effect on a family or community? ____
3. What alternatives and/or suggestions to the loan applicant do you give when you decline his or her loan? ____

Structured or Closed-Ended Response Items

What are the three types of closed-ended responses?

Structured or closed-ended response questionnaire items provide respondents with a set or list of possible responses from which to choose. Three common types of structured or closed-ended response items are *dichotomous items, multiple-choice items,* and *rating scales.*

Dichotomous items allow only two alternatives, such as "yes-no" or "male-female." The following is an example:

Do you own a personal computer?

1. yes _____ 2. no _____

Sometimes these items include a third response, which is neutral. This third item is used when the respondent may not have an opinion ("no opinion") or may not know the answer ("don't know").

Multiple-choice items provide three or more alternatives that identify all the responses possible for each item. You should include an "other" category in cases where you do not know all the alternatives. The item that follows is an example:

Please check your present position in your public accounting firm.

Partner 1. _____

Manager 2. _____

Senior staff 3. ____

Junior staff 4. ____

Other (please specify ______) 5. ____

A *rating scale* is a type of multiple-choice item where the alternatives are based on some continuous scale. The following is a rating scale based on a frequency of writing business reports:

How frequently do you write business reports?

Very frequently (almost daily) 1. ____

Frequently (once a week) 2. ____

Occasionally (once or twice a month) 3. ____

Seldom (once or twice every 3 to 6 months) 4. ____

Rarely (once a year) 5. ____

Never 6. ____

When you need to know respondents' attitudes toward a particular issue, you can use either a *Likert scale* or the *semantic differential scale.* A Likert scale permits respondents to identify their degree of agreement or disagreement with a statement by selecting a response from a list of alternatives. The following is an example:

Computer information systems is one of the most important courses in the business curriculum.

1. Strongly agree ____ 2. Agree ____ 3. Neither agree nor disagree ____ (neutral response) 4. Disagree ____ 5. Strongly disagree ____

In contrast, the semantic differential scale allows respondents to show their attitude about an issue by choosing a response from a seven-point scale. The scale has bipolar adjectives at each end, for example, large-small. Because of this, it can indicate precise degrees of feeling about a statement. Here is an example:

Please indicate your attitude toward Theta Corporation's management development program by selecting one alternative for each of the following scales:

good : ____ : ____ : ____ : ____ : ____ : ____ : ____ bad
useful : ____ : ____ : ____ : ____ : ____ : ____ : ____ useless
successful : ____ : ____ : ____ : ____ : ____ : ____ : ____ unsuccessful
adequate : ____ : ____ : ____ : ____ : ____ : ____ : ____ inadequate
important : ____ : ____ : ____ : ____ : ____ : ____ : ____ unimportant

A complete questionnaire about insurance needs that uses a Likert scale is shown in Part I of Figure 13-3. The questionnaire is designed to be mailed to respondents, and a cover letter requesting

INSURANCE PLAN QUESTIONNAIRE

Directions: Please check the appropriate answer for each statement in both Part I and Part II of this questionnaire about family insurance needs.

Part I

	Desirable	Important	No Opinion	Not Important	Undesirable
1. Anyone between the ages of 18 and 55 can enroll in the plan.	a. ______	b. ______	c. ______	d. ______	e. ______
2. My spouse can enroll in the plan for an additional 50 percent premium.	a. ______	b. ______	c. ______	d. ______	e. ______
3. My child or children can enroll in the plan for an additional 25 percent premium for each child.	a. ______	b. ______	c. ______	d. ______	e. ______
4. Cash benefits up to $200,000 will be paid if I die from any illness or accident before reaching age 55.	a. ______	b. ______	c. ______	d. ______	e. ______
5. Cash benefits up to $200,000 will be paid if I die from any accident after age 55.	a. ______	b. ______	c. ______	d. ______	e. ______
6. Cash benefits up to $100,000 will be paid if I die from any illness after age 55.	a. ______	b. ______	c. ______	d. ______	e. ______
7. Questions will be asked about my health before I can enroll.	a. ______	b. ______	c. ______	d. ______	e. ______
8. I may cancel the policy within 60 days after I enroll.	a. ______	b. ______	c. ______	d. ______	e. ______

Part II

1. I am: a. Married ____ b. Single ____ c. Divorced or separated ____
   d. Widowed ____
2. I am: a. Under age 18 ____ b. Age 18 to 35 ____ c. Age 36 to 55 ____
   d. Over age 55 ____
3. I have: a. No children ____ b. One child ____ c. Two children ____
   d. More than two children ____

FIGURE 13-3 A sample questionnaire.

that respondents fill out and return the questionnaire is shown in Chapter 10.

The following is a checklist to follow when conducting survey research.

CHECKLIST FOR DEVELOPING A QUESTIONNAIRE

1. Have I properly structured the items in my questionnaire?
2. Have I worded the items in a parallel manner?
3. Did I use words that are not abstract, jargon, general expressions, or ambiguous?
4. Does each item ask only for a response to one aspect of an issue?
5. Is each item free from suggesting or influencing a particular response?
6. Are all items necessary?
7. Have I worded sensitive questions indirectly?
8. Am I requesting current and easily remembered data?
9. Does my sequence of items start in an easy and nonthreatening way?
10. Can the items be coded easily?
11. What type of questionnaire items am I planning to use?
    - Unstructured or open ended?
    - Structured or closed ended?
        - Dichotomous?
        - Multiple choice?
        - Rating scale?
12. Is my questionnaire valid and reliable?
13. Has a panel of experts reviewed my questionnaire for possible problems?
14. Have I pretested my questionnaire on a small representative group?
15. Have I properly identified the population for my study?
16. Have I selected the proper sampling method?

Common Survey Techniques

After you have developed a questionnaire, you can choose three ways of gathering the data. These three methods are *mail questionnaires, personal interviews, and telephone interviews.*

Mail Questionnaires

This technique requires you to prepare, print, and distribute questionnaires by mail to a group of people. You can survey a large number of people and in a wide geographic area by using this technique.

Are mail questionnaires more or less costly to administer than interviews?

The cost of administering a mail questionnaire is relatively inexpensive compared with doing personal or telephone interviews. In addition, this technique is convenient for the respondents because they do not have to be in their offices or at home to be contacted. They can complete the questionnaire at their leisure. Still, you face several limitations when using this technique. First, the response rate is usually low. Second, respondents do not have the opportunity to seek clarification about questions or statements. Third, the person who completes the questionnaire may not be the one to whom you mailed it. Finally, you may take more time in mailing questionnaires and waiting for responses and still not get the information you need than if you had conducted personal interviews.

Personal Interviews

Under what circumstances should you interview in person?

The main purpose of personal interviews is to acquire detailed data in a face-to-face situation. This technique encourages respondents to answer in depth. Also, if they cannot understand a question or statement, they can ask the interviewer for clarification. Conversely, if the interviewer fails to understand a response, he or she can also ask for an explanation. It is, however, time consuming to establish contact and then to interview members of the sample group. Also, training interviewers and paying for their travel expenses (if any) may prove costly. Finally, you must be very careful to ask each item in the same way and in the same order to eliminate any bias. (When using this technique and that of telephone interviewing, see Chapter 20 for a discussion of interviewing and Chapter 19 for the skills involved in listening.)

Telephone Interviews

Is telephone interviewing just a cheap way to get information?

Obviously, you can contact respondents more quickly and at a lower cost by telephone than by personal interviews. Moreover, although you cannot see the person you are interviewing, you can still ask for and give explanations. If you use this technique, structure the interview so that administering it will not consume too much time, as people resent talking at length over the phone to someone they do not know. Another limitation is that some individuals do not have telephones and others have unlisted numbers. Thus, using the phone book to locate your sample will increase the possibility that your survey will be flawed.

SUMMARY

1. A report is an orderly written or spoken communication of meaningful data to one or more people.
2. Reports can provide managers with information or aid them in decision making.

3. The audience needs to be analyzed when planning the research.
4. Defining the problem involves conducting preliminary research, limiting the problem, determining the scope, identifying the factors, and, depending on the nature of the problem, formulating hypotheses.
5. In conducting preliminary research, consult with the report's authorizer, read background material, if needed, and for the same reason, talk to experts.
6. Ask *what, why, when, who,* and *where* when limiting the problem.
7. Factors are key words that will help you solve the problem.
8. A hypothesis predicts the problem solution you expect to occur.
9. You can collect data from either secondary or primary sources.
10. Secondary data comes from intermediate sources such as books and periodicals.
11. Primary data come from original sources such as interviews and questionnaires.
12. The first step in collecting secondary data is to prepare a bibliography.
13. Microforms and computerized literature search services are available to aid your search of secondary data.
14. Effective note taking is an important skill for researchers.
15. Three primary research methods are experiment, observe, and survey.
16. Experimental research seeks to determine whether a change of one factor causes a change in another.
17. Observational research involves examining the respondents' actions or results of their actions.
18. Survey research provides a means of collecting data from respondents by asking questions or posing statements to be answered on questionnaires or during interviews.
19. Data are valid when they measure the factor or factors they intend to measure.
20. Reliable data are those that are measured consistently and accurately.
21. A percentage of a population can be selected by using sampling methods.
22. Questionnaires may contain either unstructured or structured response items.
23. Unstructured response items leave the respondent free to express any response in his or her own words.
24. Structured response items provide the respondent with specific responses from which to choose.
25. Three survey techniques are mail questionnaires, personal interviews, and telephone interviews.

Review Questions

1. What is a report? What purposes does it serve? Give some specific examples of reports with different purposes.
2. What effect does audience analysis have on effective reporting?
3. What are some of the outcomes of analyzing an audience effectively?
4. Why is it important to define clearly the report problem?
5. What five questions can you answer to help you in limiting a report problem? Give an example.
6. Why is it important to determine the scope of a problem?

7. What is the purpose of identifying factors? formulating hypotheses?
8. Explain the role that technology has played in secondary research.
9. Why is it important to develop a computer search strategy?
10. Compare and contrast the use of computer searches with manual searches.
11. Why should you systematically approach note taking?
12. Why are validity and reliability important when conducting primary research? Can you have one without the other? Why?
13. How does a population differ from a sample?
14. What are some of the major concerns in questionnaire design? Give an example of each.
15. What are the situations that would require you to use either mail questionnaires, personal interviews, or telephone interviews?

Exercises

1. Using the following broad topics, write a problem statement for each topic that limits it precisely:
   a. Inflation accounting
   b. Consumer price index
   c. Capital budgeting
   d. Word processing
   e. Commercial lending
2. Using the problem statements you wrote in Exercise 1, make a list of some factors that apply to each problem. If you cannot identify any from your own knowledge, you might then do some preliminary research.
3. Write a scope statement for each problem statement you wrote in Exercise 1.
4. Select one of the problem situations in Exercise 1 and determine who the audience might be. Make a list of major concerns you need to be aware of when analyzing this audience.
5. Locate the card catalog in your local library. Compile a bibliography of books on one of the following areas:
   a. Office of the future
   b. Worker productivity
   c. Price-level accounting
   d. Computer graphics
   e. Executive development programs
6. From the list of areas in Exercise 5, select one and prepare a bibliography of 10 recent articles indexed in the *Business Periodicals Index* or *Business Index*.
7. From the same list in Exercise 5, select one and prepare a bibliography of 10 recent articles indexed in *The Wall Street Journal, The New York Times Index,* or the *National Newspaper Index*.
8. Choose a specific date, such as your birthdate. Then, locate a newspaper on microfilm for that date. Locate the major business, world, fashion, entertainment, and sporting events printed in the newspaper on that date. What changes have taken place since that date?
9. From the following improper questionnaire items, give the reason why each is improper and then correct the item:
   a. Having a competitive attitude is not important for a beginning salesperson.
      1. yes ____ 2. no ____
   b. Are quantitative and verbal skills necessary for a computer programmer?

c. Do you read *Management World* often?
d. What is your salary?
e. When did you buy your first bicycle?

10. Prepare three to five statements or questions for a questionnaire for the following types of structured or closed-ended response items:
    a. Dichotomous
    b. Multiple choice
    c. Rating scale
    d. Likert scale
    e. Semantic differential scale

CHAPTER 14

SORTING AND SUMMARIZING, INTERPRETING, AND OUTLINING DATA

When Mary Singer was promoted up from the ranks a year ago, she had no idea she would be so quickly involved in critical management decisions. Yet, only three months ago, the president of the company asked her to prepare a report on whether it would be advisable to spin off the medium- and heavy-duty truck division and concentrate instead on the sale of more profitable aerospace products.

Since then Mary has been gathering secondary and primary data: interviewing experts, poring over the company's books, investigating the advantages of spin-off versus selling the truck manufacturing division outright, exploring what the change would mean to stockholders and workers, and so forth. Now she feels ready to begin to interpret, organize, and outline her data. Mary knows that this is the second stage of the report writing process.

In this chapter we will discuss three aspects of report preparation: (1) sorting and summarizing, (2) interpreting, and (3) outlining the data gathered in the collection phase of the report process. Sorting and summarizing consists of classifying, editing, coding, tabulating, and computing summary statistics. In contrast, interpreting concerns evaluating both statistical and nonstatistical information. When both these processes are completed, it is possible to outline, or determine, the report's proper organizational plan, headings, and outline symbols.

SORTING AND SUMMARIZING DATA

In the last chapter, you learned to collect your research data with the framework of a defined problem. Thus, when you identified the factors or wrote a hypothesis statement to define the problem, you developed a sense about the type of data you needed to collect. Similarly, you began to know the type of analysis you would apply to those data. Actually, as you began to identify the factors that led to defining the problem, you also began the sorting and summarizing phase of report writing. These same factors provided you with the framework to begin collecting the appropriate data.

How does note taking in research relate to sorting and summarizing data?

During this sorting and summarizing phase, you were organizing the data for a thorough evaluation and interpretation. In fact, when you began to take notes from this magazine article or that book, or any other secondary sources you may have used, you sorted and probably summarized these notes in some logical arrangement. Combined with the tentative list of factors and subfactors, this arrangement helped you to organize your collection phase. Now, having clearly stated your research problem, and taken effective notes, you are ready to analyze further the secondary data you've collected.

Because secondary data are usually qualitative, you can analyze the data as you collect it. In contrast, primary or original data are usually quantitative, and consequently, they should be sorted and summarized after the collection phase. For example, if some of your primary data consist of responses to a questionnaire, you will have to wait until the necessary number of respondents have answered before you can interpret the information from them. For primary data, you will need to *classify, edit,* and *code* to prepare the data for analysis. After this sorting is complete, you will want to summarize the data by *tabulating* them and *computing summary statistics.*

What three steps constitute *sorting* data? What two steps constitute *summarizing* data?

Classifying Data

To classify material, you have to identify mutually exclusive intervals or groups of data by dividing them into related and manageable amounts. In other words, you should group data systematically. Let us see how to do this with both structured, or close-ended, and unstructured, or open-ended, questionnaire responses.

Structured responses lend themselves naturally to a classification system. This is because the responses group the data. For example, items with two alternatives may be classified as "yes-no" or "male-female." Multiple-choice items may be classified into three or more alternatives, such as "rarely," "often," and "very often." And rating scale items can be classified into a list of alternatives.

Are structured and unstructured responses equally easy to classify?

In contrast, with unstructured items, you cannot know in any way what responses you will get. That respondents can freely use their own words to answer an item automatically makes possible a wide variety of answers. Therefore, in contrast to structured responses—where you have designed a classification system into the items themselves—unstructured responses may only be classified after you receive them.

For example, consider the following unstructured questionnaire item and response:

Item Please indicate the one major problem in your office.
Response It seems as though every time I begin typing a report, the typewriter breaks down.

Only after reading this response would you be able to classify it. Thus, you might devise the category "equipment problems" for this response and any similar ones. Whatever the response, take care to classify it into a meaningful group.

Editing Data

You've classified your data; your next step is to edit them. Editing requires that you check carefully to see if any problems exist in the data. Most typically, data are missing—no response to an item—or are inaccurate—the respondent has checked response "B" throughout most of the questionnaire. If data are missing, decide what you want to do with the response. Possibilities include classifying it as a "nonanswer" response, eliminating it from your analysis, or contacting the respondent to obtain a clear response. In contrast, if a respondent has responded repetitively to a series of items, these data may be inaccurate. If you think so, you may decide to eliminate them from your analysis.

Coding Data

Does coding really make the sorting phase of research easier to do? Explain.

In coding, you assign a number to each response classification. This classification is necessary if you plan to analyze the data using your computer. If so, you might combine classifying and coding with the preparation of closed-ended response items. Consequently, when you decide on the alternatives for response items, assign a number to each alternative at the same time.

The following is a classified and coded questionnaire item:

Please check your age category.

21–30 1. ____

31–40 2. ____

41–50 3. ____

51–60 4. ____

Over 60 5. ____

Tabulating Data

Tabulating data means counting the number of responses in each response classification for each statement or question in your questionnaire. You can do such tabulations manually or with your computer. If your sample is large, a computer tabulation will save you much time and effort.

However you tabulate, the data are arranged in a *frequency distribution* that shows the number of responses tabulated for each

Age	Number of Respondents
21–30	11
31–40	32
41–50	44
51–60	10
Over 60	3
Total	100

FIGURE 14-1 A tabulation for one questionnaire item.

Item: How frequently do you write business reports?

	Age					
Alternatives	21–30	31–40	41–50	51–60	Over 60	Total
Very frequently (almost daily)	2	15	10	3	—	30
Frequently (once a week)	3	12	23	3	2	43
Occasionally (once or twice a month)	5	3	8	4	1	21
Seldom (once or twice every 3 to 6 months)	1	—	3	—	—	4
Rarely (once a year)	—	2	—	—	—	2
Never	—	—	—	—	—	0
Total	11	32	44	10	3	100

FIGURE 14-2 Cross-tabulation for two questionnaire items.

alternative to a response item. You can tabulate such responses one item at a time or two or more at a time.

How can cross-tabulation improve the quality of the data?

The tabulation for one multiple-choice item based on respondents' age is shown in Figure 14-1. If you tabulate two or more items at a time, this is called *cross-tabulation.* A cross-tabulation that combines age with a rating scale item is shown in Figure 14-2. Note that cross-tabulation indicates the relationship between or among two or more items.

If you have few data or their relationship to each other is simple, you might evaluate them immediately after your tabulation. But, if they are complex or you have many data, you can insert a step before this and compute summary statistics.

Computing Summary Statistics

What are the three types of summary statistics?

Your purpose in computing summary statistics is the same as in tabulating: to reduce the data to more manageable and meaningful forms. Basically, there are three types of summary statistics: *percentages, measures of central tendency,* and *measures of dispersion.*

Percentages

Percentages are ratios that show a relationship between one or more data-response classes to a base of 100. For example, suppose for a report on the effectiveness of insurance agents, you interview 250 of them. The results show among other things that 185 work for major insurance companies. Consequently, you would translate this relationship to a percentage, or 74 percent (185 ÷ 250), which is a ratio of 3 out of 4 working for major companies. Usually, researchers compute percentages such as this immediately after tabulating their re-

Item: What type of insurance company do you work for?

Company	Number of Respondents	% of Total
Major insurance	185	74%
Independent insurance	65	26
Total	250	100%

FIGURE 14-3 Results of a tabulation and their corresponding percentages.

sults and display these figures along with the number of responses. The results of the tabulation of insurance agents and their corresponding percentages is shown in Figure 14-3.

Measures of Central Tendency

Measures of central tendency represent the center value of a distribution of data. You can use these "averages" in determining what your findings are and their degree of importance in relation to one another and the problem as a whole. Because data tend to cluster about a point, these measures include the *mean, median,* and *mode.*

What type of average is a mean?

The Mean The mean is the *arithmetic average* of a group of responses. You can compute it by taking the sum of all these responses and dividing it by the number of them. For example, suppose a study reveals that six companies purchased the following number of microcomputers: company A bought 24; company B, 14; company C, 18; company D, 25; company E, 18; and company F, 21. To compute the mean, sum all the microcomputers (120) and then divide this sum by the number of companies (6). The mean is 20. Very often, the mean will give you a useful "benchmark" from which to view all the data in a set and the relationship to other sets of data.

If a distribution has some unusually high or low figures, the mean may not be a very useful statistic because it will be distorted. For example, suppose you had surveyed a seventh company that reported purchasing 118 microcomputers. The sum of all the microcomputers in the distribution would be 238 for the seven companies, and the mean would now be 34. As you can see, because this one company is so far out of line with the others, the mean is skewed and, consequently, yields an ineffective measure of central tendency. In such situations, you would probably need to use the second measure: the median.

The Median The median is the midpoint in a distribution of responses. Unaffected by extremes in it, the median is also easy to obtain. To find it, arrange your responses either from the highest to the lowest figure or vice versa. Then select the *midpoint* of the dis-

When is it best to use the median as the average?

tribution. For example, if you arranged each of the seven companies' number of microcomputers from the lowest to the highest, you would get the following distribution: company B, 14; company C, 18; company E, 18; company F, 21; company A, 24; company D, 25; and company G, 118. The median of this distribution would be 21. Undistorted by the unusually high number of microcomputers in company G, it is meaningful. Like the mean, the median can give you a useful "benchmark" for comparing data in a set and its relation to other sets of data.

In obtaining the median for an even number of responses, you only need to find the two middle responses, add them together, and divide your answer by 2. For example, for the original six companies, you could compute the median as follows: divide the lower middle response (18) plus the higher middle response (21) by 2. Your median would then be 19.5.

Is a mode ever a useful average? If so, when?

The Mode The mode is the *most frequently occurring* response in the distribution of responses. For example, if you wanted to find the mode for the original six companies, you might recall the initial distribution as follows: company A, 24; company B, 14; company C, 18; company D, 25; company E, 18; and company F, 21. The most frequently occurring response, and thus its mode, is 18.

One word of caution: Although the mode will give you a rough estimate of central tendency, normally the mode is the least preferred measure of it. This is because, more often than not, the mean or median will be more useful in interpreting the meaning and application of a set of data.

Measures of Dispersion

Whereas measures of central tendency deal with the center value of a distribution of data, measures of dispersion deal with its variation or spreading out. The three most common types of measures of dispersion are *range, semi-interquartile range,* and *standard deviation.*

In what way does the range measure the dispersion of data?

Range The range is the difference between the value of the highest and the lowest response in a distribution. For example, stock market quotations include the high and low prices of stocks sold on a particular day. The range for each stock is a measure of dispersion. To find the range in any distribution, subtract the value of the lowest from the value of the highest item. For the original six insurance companies (A–F), the range would be the difference between company D's number of microcomputers and company B's (25 − 14). Thus, the range would be 11. If, however, you included the seventh company (company G, 118), the range would now be 104 (118 − 14). Here, again, you can see the effect of unusual or extreme values in a distribution; to correct for them, use the semi-interquartile range.

In what way does the semi-interquartile range correct for extremes in a distribution?

Semi-interquartile Range To find this range, take one-half the difference between the highest and lowest values of the middle 50 percent of all the values. To make our computation easier, let's use eight insurance companies instead of seven, with the eighth company (H) having bought 3 microcomputers. Then the values in the distribution, arranged from lowest to highest, would be as follows: company H, 3; company B, 14; company C, 18; company E, 18; company F, 21; company A, 24; company D, 25; and company G, 118. The middle 50 percent of the values consists of companies C, E, F, and A. Consequently, the semi-interquartile range for this distribution would be 3 (24 − 18 ÷ 2).

Why is the standard deviation the most useful measure of dispersion?

Standard Deviation Standard deviation is the most useful measure of dispersion because it shows the spread or distance from the mean. The wider the spread, the more dispersed the data, and therefore the less useful in terms of locating relationships among data items. Of course, to find little or no relation is a meaningful thing to know in most situations. To compute it, use the following six steps:

1. Compute the mean.
2. Subtract the mean from each value in your distribution.
3. Square each difference you obtained in step 2.
4. Sum or add all the squared differences.
5. Divide the total arrived at in step 4 by the number of values in the distribution.
6. Take the square root of the total arrived at in step 5. This number is the standard deviation.

To see how these six steps work, consider the example of the six companies with microcomputers. The distribution of the number of microcomputers purchased by each company is company A, 24; company B, 14; company C, 18; company D, 25; company E, 18; and company F, 21. The *first step* in calculating the standard deviation of a distribution is to compute the mean. In this example, the mean is 20. The *second step* requires you to subtract the mean from each value in your distribution; this step is as follows:

Company	*No. of Microcomputers*	—	*Mean*	=	*Difference*
A	24	—	20	=	4
B	14	—	20	=	−6
C	18	—	20	=	−2
D	25	—	20	=	5
E	18	—	20	=	−2
F	21	—	20	=	1

To complete the *third step,* square each difference obtained in step 2. This means that you multiply the difference by itself in each case. These squared differences are:

Company	*Squared Difference*
A	$4 \times 4 = 16$
B	$-6 \times -6 = 36$
C	$-2 \times -2 = 4$
D	$5 \times 5 = 25$
E	$-2 \times -2 = 4$
F	$1 \times 1 = 1$

The *fourth step* is to sum or add all the squared differences. This total is 86 (16 + 36 + 4 + 25 + 4 + 1). The *fifth step* involves dividing the total from step 4 by the number of values in the distribution (86 ÷ 6 = 14.33). In the *sixth step,* you take the square root of the result of step 5 to find the standard deviation. The square root of 14.33 is 3.79 (rounded to hundredths), which is the standard deviation. Actually, you could determine the square root without mathematical computations by consulting square root tables found in the appendix of most basic statistics books. You can also use a pocket calculator with a square root key.

To make the characteristics of a distribution clear for your report audience, compute and report as many types of summary statistics as necessary. For easy computing, employ microcomputers or other types of computers. But remember that simply reporting summary statistics is only useful when you also tabulate the data. The following checklist should help you sort and summarize them:

CHECKLIST FOR SORTING AND SUMMARIZING DATA

1. Have I placed the data from structured responses into mutually exclusive intervals and/or data from unstructured responses into meaningful groups?
2. Have I checked the data for accuracy and dealt with problems such as missing data?
3. Have I assigned a number to each response classification?
4. Have I counted the number of responses in each classification for each questionnaire item?
5. Have I reduced the data into more manageable and meaningful levels by computing summary statistics?

INTERPRETING DATA

Although you have completed interpreting the data in your report at this stage of the process, you have been interpreting material from the moment you began to define your problem. That is, throughout you have needed to think critically to gain insights to help you resolve your problem. *In everything you've done, the common denominator has been the definition of the problem.* In this section also, it remains the "glue" that holds the whole process together. Here you will learn how to evaluate and interpret the primary and secondary data now that you have sorted and summarized them. The two major ways to accomplish this are *statistical* and *nonstatistical* analysis.

What role do inferences play in data interpretation?

Statistical interpretation of data involves making inferences from them about the problem you are studying, especially in the material from your primary research. Basically, this means testing the accuracy and significance of the data and identifying relationships among them to draw valid and reliable conclusions about the problem. Any inferences or generalizations you make about a specific population should depend on the accuracy, significance, and possible relationship among your sample data. (If you need more sophisticated statistical procedures than those discussed in this chapter, consult any basic statistics text.)

Many research studies will not require that you calculate any statistics. Often, you will need instead only a few characteristics of your sample. For example, you might want to know what percentage and/or what proportion of the insurance agents you surveyed work for major insurance companies in the Midwest. Or you might want to discover the average number of microcomputers certain companies own. Either way, you could simply evaluate and interpret the statistics by describing why you used them to analyze your data. Perhaps, too, you might explain some of the implications of these data. Another possibility in evaluating and interpreting such statistics might lie in comparing them with published regional or national norms. Or you might compare them with those from related studies.

Or you could report a combination of the mean and standard deviation to show a good representation of the overall distribution. You might also use these statistics to make comparisons with similar distributions. For example, you could compare the representativeness of two sample means. Suppose that the means for microcomputers purchased by companies in two separate samples were 20 and 21, respectively, and that you found their standard deviations to be 3.79 and 10.15, respectively. The smaller standard deviation (3.79) indicates that this sample is less dispersed than is the sample with the larger deviation (10.15). The more homogeneous a distribution, the smaller the standard deviation and the more representative the sample of the population. Thus, by reporting statistics, you may derive more meaning from the data than if you simply reported the data alone.

Naturally, in evaluating and interpreting data that include statistics, you need to understand both your subject and statistical procedures. But you also should know how to reason logically, or use nonstatistical methods of interpretation.

How can you interpret nonstatistical data?

Nonstatistical interpretation of data, as we have indicated, is used primarily with secondary research. When you first defined your problem and identified its factors, you began interpreting by indicating the relationship between them. Next, throughout the collection phase, you continued this process. (See, for example, the section on collecting secondary research data in Chapter 13.)

Moreover, in taking notes about your data, perhaps you also wrote down your own ideas, suggestions, comments, and reactions. When you did this, you probably became aware too of the relations that were forming and the directions the data were leading you in. Now you can advance this interpretative process one more step by arriving at conclusions and making recommendations. When you apply logical reasoning to the results of your data analysis, you should be able to achieve these goals.

Using Logical Reasoning

What are the three parts of a syllogism?

In deductive reasoning, we move from general premises to a specific conclusion. If the premises are true, then the conclusion you draw from them will also be true. Conversely, if they are false, then your conclusion will be similarly false. A simple syllogism should show how deductive reasoning works. Its three parts are a major premise, a minor premise, and a conclusion, as the following shows:

Major premise	Word processing systems will increase efficiency in dealing with office paperwork.
Minor premise	The Porter Company has purchased a word processing system for its main office.
Conclusion	The Porter Company will increase its efficiency in dealing with that office's paperwork.

Whenever you apply deductive reasoning such as this, your reader is likely to accept it as the truth. Thus, each deductive statement of yours should be both accurate and supported by reasons.

Inductive reasoning involves moving from a specific premise to a general conclusion. In other words, it is the opposite of *deductive* reasoning. Working inductively, you identify specific research data that seem to form patterns that lead to a general conclusion. In the report process, this reasoning begins when you define your problem and identify its factors or, if applicable, when you form a hypothesis. Supported by factual data, these factors or hypotheses will then lead to a conclusion on your part.

For example, suppose you are reviewing various pension plans your company might adopt. By evaluating each, you should then be able to conclude which, if any, is best. Or suppose your company has already selected a plan subject to employee approval. Your job is to evaluate their reactions to it. After doing this, you would either generalize that they are for or against the plan.

Understanding Common Fallacies of Reasoning

In evaluating and interpreting your data, then, you should follow processes of logical reasoning based on verifiable and supportable evidence. As a researcher, you should also become aware of some common fallacies of reasoning that can adversely affect evaluation and interpretation. The five most common are *argumentum ad hominem, begging the question, false analogy, false dilemma,* and *post hoc, ergo propter hoc.*

Argumentum ad Hominem

Have you ever been the victim of "argument to the person"?

As translated from the Latin, the term means "argument to the person." In this kind of reasoning, you incorrectly associate peoples' reasoning with their personality instead of their argument. The following is an example of this fallacy:

> Because he is so loud and boisterous, Mr. Johnson can't know very much about accounting procedures.

Begging the Question

Have you ever begged the question or used a false analogy in a report?

Begging the question means offering proof that only restates the question. The following is an example:

> Anderson's hardware has fewer employees because not as many people work there now as previously.

False Analogy

False analogy means you assume two statements or ideas to be similar when they are not. The following is an example:

> Learning how to program a computer is like learning how to ride a bicycle. Once you learn, you never forget.

False Dilemma

More commonly known as the "either-or" fallacy, this implies that only two sides exist to an issue when in fact others can. The following is an illustration:

> The solution to this morale problem is either to give the people in the department more money or shorten their work hours.

Post Hoc, Ergo Propter Hoc

Have you ever read a report where the writer used the false dilemma or *post hoc, ergo propter hoc* fallacy?

This Latin term means "after this, therefore because of this." Because something precedes something else, does not mean that the former causes the latter. An example is:

> Because we have hired a graduate from Indiana University to work in the main office, our sales have increased.

Drawing Conclusions

In what way does it throw off the analysis when you present new data in the conclusions?

If your purpose in research is purely informational, you probably won't have to make any conclusions. If, however, you must evaluate any data, you will then have to not only conclude but probably also recommend as well. Remember to base both conclusions and recommendations on your evaluation and interpretation of the data. Never present new data in drawing your conclusions. If you do, you will throw off your overall analysis. Drawing conclusions implies tying your data together logically in a way that forms answers to your research problem. Thus the data should support each of your conclusions, with none of these conclusions merely restating information. The problem of misrepresenting findings as conclusions is most frequent in research studies that include hypotheses. For example, look at this hypothesis from Chapter 13:

> Using individualized instruction for in-service managerial training will result in higher achievement than will using the traditional large-group instruction.

If, indeed, you discovered a significant difference between the two methods indicating the superiority of the individualized training, then reporting it is not a conclusion but a finding. You can, however, draw a conclusion from this finding, such as:

> The findings of this study support the hypothesis that individualized instruction produces more favorable results than does large-group instruction in the in-service managerial training program.

In addition, if you are aware of other studies—that is, secondary data—that came to similar conclusions, you might cite them as support. Your own conclusions would then sound more credible.

Making Recommendations

How does making recommendations relate to solving a problem in a report?

In an analytical report, the conclusions you draw from your findings form the basis of any recommendations you make. Recommendations indicate some type of action the report audience can take using the results of the study. For example, you might recommend that:

> The individualized instruction method should be used in the in-service managerial training program rather than the large-group instruction method. In addition to producing more favorable achievement, the individualized instruction method allows in-service managers to work at their own pace. Also, these managers could work at a time more convenient to both the manager and his or her supervisor.

Note how the first sentence in this example contains the recommendation itself. The writer also implies some other advantages of using individualized instruction. Although you have more flexibility here than in any part of the research process, one constraint exists: All recommendations should logically flow from your conclusion.

OUTLINING DATA

You've completed evaluating and interpreting your data. You've even made a number of recommendations. Next, you need to organize the data so you may write your report. Such organizing is called outlining.

In making an outline, you place the material you want to include in your report into a logical and systematic pattern. This pattern should show clearly the relationship between your factors and the problem's solutions. Moreover, by reviewing the outline, you can determine if your argument or discussion is logical, that is, without gaps in its reasoning. In addition, an outline can help you see if any of the factors overlap and if each is sufficiently covered.

What purpose does an outline serve?

An outline that is effective should enable you to organize your report and serve as a guide throughout the writing phase. Referring to it, you can easily label various section and paragraph headings in the report and also prepare the table of contents and summary. Remember, your outline is an extension of the factors you identified in Chapter 13.

Deciding on an Organizational Plan

What are the four common organizational plans?

You are ready to write your outline, but how do you go about it? Remember that an outline reflects your decisions about the way to present the information in the report to its audience. In turn, this decision depends on the report's purpose and type, the nature of the data, and the audience's requirements. Whatever decision you make, your organizational outline should not change your findings, conclusions, or recommendations. It should, however, affect how you physically present your data in the report itself. The four common organizational plans you may use are *inductive, deductive, chronological,* and *geographical and functional.*

Inductive Organizational Plan

Why is the inductive organizational plan sometimes called the persuasive plan?

In the inductive organizational plan, you indirectly arrange the parts of the report, moving from the specific facts to a more general idea or concept. Another way to describe the inductive organizational pattern is to present information that your audience knows and move on to what it does not know. Thus, you start with an introduction, follow it with your findings—that is, your analysis of the data—and end with a summary, conclusions, and recommendations. If you need to convince your audience of the merits of your conclusions, for example, why it is unwise to invest in commercial real estate in a rundown section of the city, an inductive organization is the best arrangement because you will first present facts to persuade your audience to consider your recommendation. In fact, this plan is sometimes called the persuasive plan. The following is an example:

Introduction
Effects of Purchasing a Computer
Results of Leasing a Computer
Effects of Using Services of a Computer Firm
Summary of Three Computerization Alternatives
Conclusion, Supported by Findings, About Purchasing a Computer
Recommendation for Purchasing a Computer

Deductive Organizational Plan

In a deductive organizational plan, you directly arrange the parts of the report, moving from the general to the specific, or presenting the main idea first, followed by supporting, specific data. Thus, you start with recommendations and conclusions, follow them with your findings—the analysis of your data that supports these recommendations and conclusions—and end with a general summary. In other words, the deductive plan is a reverse of the inductive approach. It is used most often when an audience needs to know quickly what the major solutions are for a problem. If necessary, readers can then review and follow the logic behind your findings to confirm these conclusions and recommendations. For example, if your boss has to decide by the end of the day about bidding for some computer equipment, then a deductive organizational plan might be best to follow if you are making a report on this subject. The following is an example of such a plan:

Why do some reports begin with recommendations?

Recommendation for Purchasing a Computer
Conclusion, Supported by Findings, About Purchasing a Computer
Effects of Purchasing a Computer
Results of Leasing a Computer
Effects of Using Services of a Computer Firm
Summary of Three Computerization Alternatives

Chronological Organizational Plan

Can you combine the chronological plan with the inductive and deductive plans? Explain.

In the chronological organizational plan, you present your findings as they have occurred chronologically. Business writers often use this approach in composing informational reports, in which they present unanalyzed data in chronological order. You may also use it in combination with either inductive or deductive plans. For example, you might administer an attitudinal survey of a new health insurance plan when you first offer it to your employees. Then, after each quarter of the next year, you could readminister the survey. When you prepare your report, you might then present your data inductively, moving from the findings based on each quarter to conclusions about any changes in attitude from quarter to quarter. The following is an example of a chronological plan:

Introduction
First Quarter Production Results (January 1 to March 30)
Second Quarter Production Results (April 1 to June 30)
Third Quarter Production Results (July 1 to September 30)
Fourth Quarter Production Results (October 1 to December 31)
Summary of Annual Production Results

Geographical and Functional Organizational Plan

In a geographical plan, you present the results of your study according to relationships in physical space. Business writers can use this approach for some informational reports. For example, you might write a report for the northeastern sales manager of your toy manufacturing company on sales in each territory in his or her region. The following is an example of a geographical plan:

Introduction
Massachusetts Sales Activities
Vermont Sales Activities
New Hampshire Sales Activities
Maine Sales Activities
Summary of Northeastern Sales Activities

Is a functional plan really a geographical one? Explain.

An offshoot of this approach is the functional plan. In it, you present your information according to company divisions, departments, or other sections. For example, you might compose an outline of the activities of your company's auditing, tax, and general accounting services as a preliminary to your report on this subject to the vice president of finance. Both the geographic and functional plans may also be combined with either inductive or deductive plans.

Selecting a Type of Outline Heading

What are the three common types of outline headings?

The most important thing to remember in writing outline headings is to make them structurally parallel; that is, you should use some consistent pattern in wording topics and subtopics. Three common headings (or captions) are *topic, phrase,* and *sentence.* In selecting one of these, use it throughout the entire outline. Also, make sure the type you choose meets your audience's needs; that is, if they need more detail, use phrase or sentence headings.

Topic Heading

A topic heading consists of one, two, or three key words to indicate the specific factors your report will discuss. Such a heading is a brief, general description of a topic or subtopic. The following are topical headings for a report on managerial functions:

Introduction
Planning Function
Organizing Function
Controlling Function
Directing Function
Management Functions Summary

Phrase Heading

What are the four forms of phrase headings?

The phrase heading is an extension of the topic heading, in that it more fully describes topics (and subtopics) in a parallel form. You could write such headings in any of the following forms: *infinitive, noun, participial,* or *decapitated sentence* phrases. The following shows examples of each:

Infinitive Phrase

To Develop Long-Term Plans

To Determine Cash Requirements

To Establish Capital Budgets

Noun Phrase

Development of Long-Term Plans

Determination of Cash Requirements

Establishment of Capital Budgets

Participial Phrase

Developing Long-Term Plans

Determining Cash Requirements

Establishing Capital Budgets

Decapitated Sentence Phrase

Long-Term Plans Developed

Cash Requirements Determined

Capital Budgets Established

If you decide on the phrase outline heading, you can use any one of them, for example, participial phrases, throughout, or you can use any combination, for example, infinitive and noun phrases. Just remember, if you do, to employ parallel construction. Thus, if you have a participial form for one first-level topic, then keep it for all of them. In the same way, if you use another form for subfactors of first-level topics, then these too should be structurally parallel to one another. (They need not be parallel to subfactors at the same level in another section, however.) The following outline shows how you might try a variety of headings while maintaining parallel structure:

Do subfactors in two different sections of a report have to be structurally parallel to one another? Explain.

Presentation of Operating Budgets (noun phrase)

Developing a Sales Budget
Determining a Production Budget — (participial phrases)

Illustration of Cash Budget (noun phrase)

Cash Inflow or Generation Estimated
Cash Outflow Measured — (decapitated sentences)

Sentence Heading

Which type of heading is most descriptive—topic, phrase, or sentence?

The sentence heading states each factor in a simple, complete sentence that is usually, at the most, seven words in length. These headings provide a complete thought concisely. As such, they are more descriptive than the other types of headings, and they preview the section for the reader. An example of a sentence heading outline is:

Copies Differ in Input-Output Qualities
    Beta II Holds Slight Edge in Input Qualities
    Alpha I Allows for Diversity in Output
Copier Costs Vary Substantially
    Alpha I Has Highest Initial Costs
    Gamma III Offers Lowest Maintenance Price
    Beta II Provides Lowest Price per Copy

Using a Pattern of Outline Symbols

You have chosen the type of headings you will use and have already written them out. Still, your outline needs to look a little more systematic. One way to accomplish this is to use a pattern of outline symbols that correspond to each main topic and subtopic. In other words, identify each division by a symbol signifying its rank in the entire outline. The two most common types of outline symbols are *roman numeral–letter–number* and *decimal*.

Of what use are outline symbols?

You can choose either, depending on your preference. The decimal pattern does, however, appear more frequently in technical and scientific reports than in those dealing with business. The following are examples of the two patterns of outline symbols:

Roman Numeral–Letter–Number

I. First main division, topic, or heading
    A. First subdivision of first main division
    B. Second subdivision of first main division
        1. First subdivision of B
        2. Second subdivision of B
            a. First subdivision of 2
            b. Second subdivision of 2
II. Second main division, topic, or heading
    A. First subdivision of second main division
        1. First subdivision of A
        2. Second subdivision of A
            a. First subdivision of 2
            b. Second subdivision of 2
    B. Second subdivision of second main division
III. Third main division, topic, or heading

Used more in business

Decimal

1. First main division, topic, or heading
   1.1 First subdivision of first main division
   1.2 Second subdivision of first main division
      1.21 First subdivision of 1.2
      1.22 Second subdivision of 1.2
         1.221 First subdivision of 1.22
         1.222 Second subdivision of 1.22
2. Second main division, topic, or heading
   2.1 First subdivision of second main division
      2.11 First subdivision of 2.1
      2.12 Second subdivision of 2.1
         2.121 First subdivision of 2.12
         2.122 Second subdivision of 2.12
   2.2 Second subdivision of second main division
3. Third main division, topic, or heading

How easy would it be to convert a roman numeral–letter–number outline pattern to a decimal pattern?

Notice that both these patterns divide the information in a similar way. Therefore, only the symbols used are different. The following outline illustrates the use of the roman numeral–letter–number pattern. You can follow this outline in writing your report. If you prefer, you could use the decimal pattern in this outline instead of the roman numeral–letter–number pattern, but people rarely do so in business reports.

I. Introducing the Problem
II. Determining the Accounting Function in Banking
   A. Record Bank Assets and Liabilities
   B. Report Accounting Information
      1. Reporting to Bank Management
      2. Reporting to Customers and Potential Investors
      3. Reporting to Regulatory Agencies
   C. Maintain Internal Control
III. Evaluating Effects of Computers on Recording Function
   A. Storing Accounting Information
   B. Inputting Accounting Information
   C. Outputting Accounting Information
IV. Examining Effect of Computers on Reporting Function
   A. Provide Speed and Accuracy to Report Generation
   B. Allow Flexibility in Special Report Preparation
V. Analyzing Effects of Computers on Internal Control Function
   A. Verification of Input and Output Information
   B. Maintenance of Bank Information Security
VI. Summarizing and Concluding Remarks

Why not have a single division or subdivision in an outline?

In reviewing the outline symbols, notice that no single division or subdivision exists at any level. This is because you must have at least two or more divisions (or none). Suppose, in looking over your outline, you see that you have only one division at a level. You now have two choices: you could incorporate this single division item into a larger division. Or you could add a second division item at the same level. The following example illustrates the problem and the two possible solutions to it:

Original
II. Financing the Business
  A. Commercial Bank Loan

Possible Alternatives
II. Financing with a Commercial Bank Loan
or
II. Financing the Business
  A. Commercial Bank Loan
  B. Private Investors

Now that you have learned how to outline research data, the following checklist may be useful as a guide to ensure that you are following all the steps:

CHECKLIST FOR OUTLINING RESEARCH DATA

1. Determine a type of organizational plan.
   Inductive—specific to general
   Deductive—general to specific
   Chronological—time
   Geographical—space
   Functional—company divisions, departments, or other sections
2. Select a type of outline heading.
   Topic—one, two, or three key words
   Phrase—infinitive, noun, participial, or decapitated sentence
   Sentence—simple, complete sentence
3. Use parallel construction for each division.
4. Use a pattern of outline symbols to illustrate a topic and subtopic ranking in the outline.
5. Select either a roman numeral–letter–number or a decimal pattern.
6. Be sure that you have no single divisions or subdivisions at a level.
7. Use the outline for labeling various section and paragraph headings in your report.
8. Use the outline in preparing your table of contents.

SUMMARY

1. After collecting your data, you need to organize, interpret, and outline the material.
2. Organizing consists of classifying, editing, coding, tabulating, and computing summary statistics.
3. Interpreting concerns evaluating statistical and nonstatistical information.
4. Sorting deals with classifying, editing, and coding that data.
5. Summarizing involves tabulating and computing summary statistics.
6. Some common types of summary statistics are percentages, measures of central tendency, and measures of dispersion.
7. After sorting and summarizing your data, you can begin a more detailed evaluation and interpretation of them.
8. When evaluating and interpreting your data, use either statistical or nonstatistical methods.
9. You should also apply basic principles of logical reasoning.
10. You need to be familiar with common fallacies of reasoning that could affect your logic. The five most common are argumentum ad hominem, begging the question, false analogy, false dilemma, and post hoc, ergo propter hoc.
11. After evaluating and interpreting your data, you need to organize them into an outline.
12. Four organizational plans for writing reports are inductive, deductive, chronological, and geographical and functional.
13. After deciding on an organizational plan, you should select a type of outline heading and a pattern of outline symbols.

Review Questions

1. Discuss the importance of classifying, editing, and coding primary research data.
2. What are the benefits of tabulating primary research data?
3. What is the value of computing percentages?
4. Define mean, median, and mode. What do these measures of central tendency offer you as a researcher?
5. Why would you use a range when summarizing your data?
6. Why is the standard deviation important to determine? What does it illustrate?
7. Assume you received the following two grades along with their standard deviation: test 1: mean 82, standard deviation 4; test 2: mean 82, standard deviation 6. On which test did you have a higher standing? Why?
8. Deductive and inductive are two types of logical reasoning. What is the difference between the two? Is one more effective than the other?
9. What five fallacies are common to research reports? Why should you be aware of them? How does each affect your logic?
10. What is the relationship among findings, conclusions, and recommendations?
11. What are the advantages of preparing a writing outline?
12. What uses do the four common organizational plans have? Why should you choose one over the other three?

13. Why should you maintain parallel construction when selecting an outline heading?
14. Why should you use a pattern of symbols in your outline?
15. What is the rationale of having no single divisions or subdivisions at any level of an outline? Support your answer with an example.

Exercises

1. Based on responses to unstructured or open-ended questionnaire items, explain how to classify each of the following statements:

   a. "My boss doesn't listen to me."
   b. "I was just thrown into the new position created by the supervisor."
   c. "I can't seem to learn this new technique for preparing vouchers."
   d. "The inventory process always takes too long."
   e. "Our labor leaders don't seem to represent us well enough."

2. The manufacturing division manufactured the following motors during the past week:

Day:	M	T	W	Th	F
Motors:	75	72	80	78	76

   Calculate the mean, median, mode, range, and standard deviation.

3. The number of unit sales of microcomputers for the past five weeks were:

Week:	1	2	3	4	5
Micros sold:	20	15	14	16	14

   Calculate the mean, median, mode, range, and standard deviation.

4. A sales representative has averaged the following number of miles per gallon of gasoline during each of the last six weeks:

Week:	1	2	3	4	5	6
Miles per gallon:	25	20	32	27	25	30

   Calculate the mean, median, mode, range, and standard deviation.

5. Employees in the training department of Maxwell Industries, Inc., turned in the following accounting test scores:

92	86	91	79
81	88	85	92
89	74	90	96
94	90	72	84
79	96	84	82

   Calculate the mean, range, and standard deviation.

6. A food distribution company employs 10 sales representatives whose annual salaries are as follows:

$16,425	$21,895
24,720	19,322
22,483	28,163
34,965	25,630
62,840	23,842

   Calculate the mean, median, mode, range, semi-interquartile range, and standard deviation. Do you need to be aware of anything when reporting these statistics?

22,483	28,163
34,965	25,630
62,840	23,842

Calculate the mean, median, mode range, semiinterquartile range, and standard deviation. Do you need to be aware of anything when reporting these statistics?

7. From the following statements, discuss the type of reasoning fallacy each statement violates and why:
   a. "Our personnel problems have decreased since we started to promote only employees with 10 or more years of service."
   b. "This project will never materialize because it will be headed up by Bill Cook, who is shy and reserved."
   c. "The only problem we have is employee apathy."
   d. "We either should hire more operations employees or just close down the manufacturing plant."
   e. "This whole hiring process reminds me of a lottery. You're hired if you're lucky enough to get your name picked."
8. The two partial outlines that follow violate an outlining rule. Find the error and then correct it.
   a. I. Current Common Carrier Costs
      II. Truck Leasing Costs vs. Common Carrier Costs
         A. Equipment
   b. I. The Market for Generic Products
         A. What Types of Products Are Available?
      II. Consumer Reaction to Quality of Generic Products
         A. How Do Generic Foods Compare to Brand-Name Foods?
9. The three partial outlines that follow violate some basic rules for wording outline headings. Tell why each outline is improperly worded and then correct it.
   a. Accounting Methods Used in the Petroleum Industry
      New Accounting Method Proposed by the SEC
      Analyzing the Effects of the Change in Accounting Methods
   b. Monetary Considerations of Fringe Benefits
      Types of Fringe Benefits Offered
      Fringe Benefits and Productivity: Is There a Relationship?
   c. The Question of Actual Cost
      Analyzing Overall Performance and Riding Comfort
      Considering Operating Expenses
10. Find an article in a magazine or journal that is three pages or longer. After reading it, prepare a detailed outline of the contents of the article. Use both parallel headings and a pattern of outline symbols. Also, determine what kind of organizational plan the author or authors used.

CHAPTER 15

PREPARING VISUAL AIDS

In the last year the soft drink industry has been changing rapidly, as a spate of companies have switched from public to private ownership. Kevin King's boss has asked him to prepare a report on how the changes in the market will affect their company. Kevin has completed the search process, sorted, summarized, evaluated, interpreted, and outlined his data and is now ready to write his report. But before he does, he prepares a bar graph with the overall title, *Changes in the Soft Drink Market.* This graph shows the major companies' shares in the market before and after recent acquisitions. Naturally, Kevin has included this information in his outline; however, because he felt it was complex, he is confident that the visual aids will enhance his presentation by making the data more readily understandable to his boss.

What role does a visual aid play in a report?

In this chapter you will learn to prepare, as Kevin did, effective visual aids that simplify, supplement, and support your data when it is complex or when you need to emphasize certain critical concepts so that your audience can remember them. More specifically, you will learn how to prepare tables; bar, line, pie or circle graphs, and other miscellaneous visual aids. Finally, you will see how computer graphics may help your visual presentation.

ILLUSTRATING THE EFFECT OF A VISUAL AID

Perhaps nothing so *graphically* illustrates how a visual aid can help an audience to understand better material in a report than showing the material with and without such an aid. For example, suppose you have included the following explanation in a report on trade relations between the United States and Japan (hypothetical figures used):

> In January 1986, U.S. exports to Japan amounted to $1,285 million. One year later, U.S. exports to Japan totaled only $938 million, a 27 percent decrease in exports. However, during the same time period, Japan's exports to the United States increased from $2,540 million to $3,148 million, for a 19 percent increase in exports. The net result was that the U.S. trade deficit increased from $1,255 million in January 1986 to $2,210 million in January 1987.

Did you read this discussion slowly or quickly? Did you understand it on the first reading, or did you have to reread it? Most likely, you were confused unless you read the material slowly and carefully. Note how the addition of the visual aid shown in Figure 15-1 clarifies a slightly revised version of the discussion:

The overall change in exports between the United States and Japan in January 1986 and January 1987 is shown in Figure 1. In January 1986, U.S. exports to Japan amounted to $1,285 million. One year later, the amount of exports to Japan was only $938 million. This change represented a 27 percent decrease in exports. However, during the same period, Japan's exports to the United States increased from $2,540 million to $3,148 million. This change constituted a 19 percent increase in exports. The net result was that the U.S. trade deficit increased from $1,255 million in January 1986 to $2,210 million in January 1987.

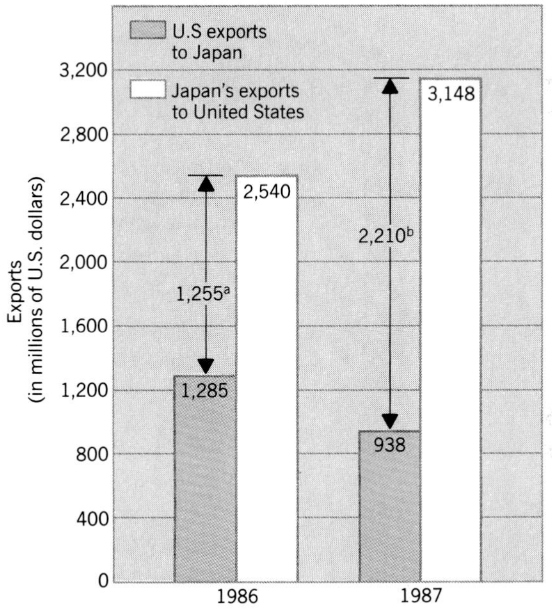

FIGURE 15-1 A narrative explanation with a visual aid.

Visual aids are especially important in clarifying statistical data such as in the example, that is, if these aids are presented effectively.

PRESENTING VISUAL AIDS EFFECTIVELY

Whether you employ a bar graph or tables in your report, to be effective visual aids must meet certain requirements. They are *identification, documentation, introduction, interpretation,* and *placement.*[1]

Identifying Visual Aids

As part of your report on the sports magazine business today, you have included a number of visual aids. How should you identify them? First, you should label them; then, you should assign each a number; and finally, you should title them. (The one exception to labeling visual aids, discussed later in this chapter, is informal or spot tables.) A common and basic form of labeling is to call each visual either a *table* or a *figure.*

How do tables and figures differ from each other?

Use "table" as the label for any visuals you want to present in tabular form consisting of columns and rows of data. Assign the label of "figure" to all your other visuals. (Sometimes—although this is infrequent—you may be asked to label somewhat differently; for example, in this text the publishers want all the visual aids, even those that are clearly tables, to be called figures.)

Next, after labeling your figure or table, number it. Do this in sequence, for example, "Table 1," "Table 2," and so forth and "Figure 1," "Figure 2," and so forth. Finally, after numbering it, include a title to describe your visual. As much as possible, this title should reflect the order of presentation and describe the table or figure accurately. Remember, many readers will skim your report, stopping to read key sections or to look at the graphics. A good example of a title is that used for Figure 1 shown within Figure 15-1 on page 449:

Comparative Exports Between the United States and Japan in January 1986 and January 1987.

Once you have completed identifying a visual, place this information either directly above or below it.

Documenting Visual Aids

Can you name three ways to document sources of data used in visual aids?

In documenting a visual, acknowledge its source. Sources are (1) *primary,* (2) *secondary constructed from narrative,* and (3) *secondary presented verbatim.* When you construct a visual aid from your own data, this is a primary source and you can document it either by (1) placing

[1] The organization of the discussion is adapted from Philip C. Kolin, *Successful Writing at Work* (Lexington, Mass.: D. C. Heath, 1982, pp. 298–300).

the words "Source: Primary" directly below it or (2) omitting all notation. Such an omission implies your own data are the source.

In contrast, when you prepare visuals from secondary sources constructed from narrative, cite the specific reference. For example, the source in Figure 15-1 reads as follows:

Source: Department of Commerce, 1987.

Finally, when you use a visual exactly as it appears in a secondary source, acknowledge the entire reference, as in the following:

Source: Jeffrey E. Long, "WP Survey: Who's Using What," *Management World,* Vol. 2, no. 4 (April 1982), p. 15, Table 3.

A word of caution: If you intend to publish your report, acknowledging a verbatim source is insufficient. You will also need permission from the copyright owner to reproduce it—or he or she has the right to sue.

What is the risk of overusing footnotes in a visual aid?

Sometimes too you may need to use footnotes within a visual to explain something about it. In such situations, use a superscript of a letter or an asterisk, for example, ^{a}, ^{b}, or *, rather than a number. Note, however, that the risk of overusing such footnotes is that the visual becomes cluttered and difficult to read, thus defeating your purpose of creating the visual to clarify or reinforce key data. Figure 15-1 has two footnotes.

Introducing Visual Aids

What are three methods used to introduce visual aids?

Never put a visual aid in a report without introducing it properly. Thus, you should refer to the table or figure before you actually present it. This reference should briefly explain its content and identify its label and number. For example, here is the lead-in sentence used to introduce Figure 1 that appears within Figure 15-1 on page 449.

> The overall change in exports between the United States and Japan in January 1986 and January 1987 is shown in Figure 1.

Notice how this lead-in emphasizes the visual's content rather than its label and number. You can also achieve the same emphasis by inserting the label and number in parenthesis at the end of the sentence:

> . . . in January 1986 and January 1987 (see Figure 1).

Or, if you want to shift your emphasis to the label and number, begin the sentence with them:

> As shown in Figure 1, an overall change in exports existed between the United States and Japan in January 1986 and January 1987.

Although many report writers prefer the first method, all three are used. Whichever you choose, employ the same way of referring to a visual in your appendix as in your text.

Interpreting Visual Aids

Why bother to interpret a visual aid? Won't the data be self-explanatory?

By interpreting, you add meaning to research data that the reader cannot get by looking at the visual itself. For example, such an interpretation would be to explain how the data contained in the visual relate to the overall discussion of your topic.

In this context, look once again at the explanation on page 449 of the change in exports between the United States and Japan. The figure itself does not include the percentages of the change. In the explanation, however, the writer underscores the change's significance by giving them. Consequently, this interpretation permits the reader to understand better just how dramatic the change is.

Placing Visual Aids

The rule here is to place a visual aid as close as possible to its introduction and interpretation in the text. In general, make your visual at least one-fourth the size of an $8\frac{1}{2}'' \times 11''$ page. Anything smaller may be difficult to read.

Where should you place a visual that is less than half a page?

If a visual is less than half a page, place it immediately after your introduction and interpretation. In typing, leave about three line spaces above and below to separate it clearly from the text.

If, however, a visual is half a page or more, put it on the first full page after your introduction. When adding a full-page visual, you can place it on the page either vertically or horizontally. But use vertical

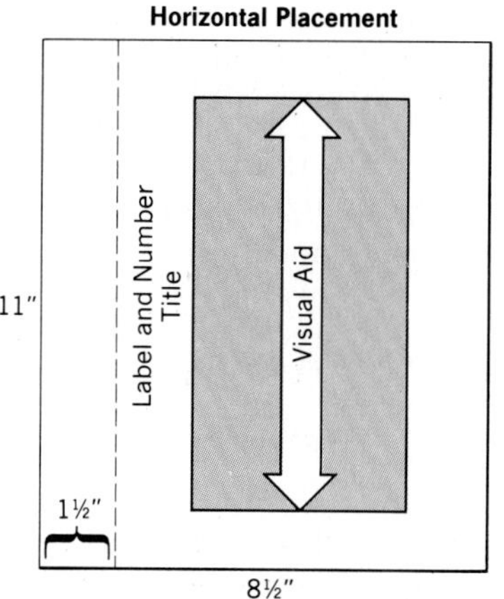

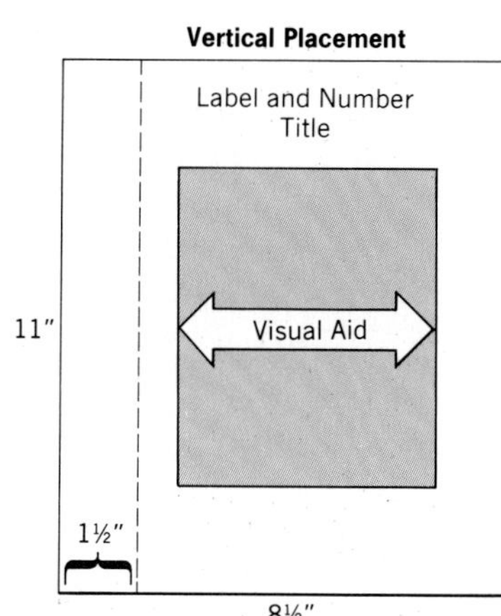

FIGURE 15-2 Horizontal and vertical placement of visual aids.

placement if the table or figure fits within the normal margins of the text of your report.

The label, number, and title for a horizontal visual should appear centered and at the left margin of the page. In contrast, those for a vertical should be centered at the top of the pages. Figure 15-2 shows both placements.

What are the three types of visual aids?

Once you know how to present visual materials effectively, you can select and construct the ones you need for your report. Several types are able to meaningfully summarize quantitative and qualitative data. They are *tables, graphs,* and *miscellaneous* visual aids.

CONSTRUCTING TABLES

Generally, report writers use tables to present quantitative data systematically in columns and rows. Somewhat less frequently, they may also be employed to show qualitative information, such as lists of words or phrases.

How do informal tables differ from formal ones?

Tables may be either *informal* or *formal.* Informal tables—sometimes called spot, or minor, tables or listings—emphasize several items by indenting them after a simple lead-in sentence. In this way, the informal table becomes a part of the regular text; that is, the table is not set aside from the text. Because of its placement, such a table does not contain a label, number, or title.

To see how an informal table works, look at the following sentence:

> Beta Corporation's 1987 quarterly operating expenses were $32,000 for the first quarter, $28,000 for the second quarter, $35,000 for the third quarter, and $37,000 for the fourth quarter.

The following informal table shows the same data:

> Beta Corporation's 1987 quarterly operating expenses were:

First quarter	$32,000
Second quarter	28,000
Third quarter	35,000
Fourth quarter	37,000

Notice that the dollar sign symbol appears only before the first figure. If you total the column, also place this sign in front of the totaled figure. Then, align the two symbols vertically. Follow the same procedure when using other unit symbols such as percent (%) or pounds (lbs).

What are the two types of formal tables?

In contrast, formal tables summarize *more* data, both quantitative and qualitative. Because of the amount of data they contain, separate them from the text. The two types of formal tables are *general* and *special purpose.*

A general table contains complex or general reference data, such as a computer printout or a list of questions used in an interview. Normally, place such tables that supplement your report text in the appendix so your readers are not distracted by unnecessary detail.

A special-purpose table contains specific data that are relevant to your text. You should place this type of table as close to the discussion of the material contained within it as possible. Use headings to indicate the row items and column categories. Place the row items—sometimes called stubs—at the left side of the table before the data columns. Figure 15-3 shows a common table format with its major parts identified.

What are the three types of table formats?

The table in Figure 15-3 uses a *ruled format*. That is, to construct one like it, you draw horizontal lines to separate the major divisions. You can, however, set up your table using two other formats: *open* and *boxed*. The following is an abbreviated example of an open format:

Position	*Number*	*Cumulative Number*
Partner	39	39
Manager	57	96
Senior staff	80	176
Junior staff	74	250
Total	250	

As you can see, the open format makes this table easy to read. However, if you have more columns than two or if your columns are spaced close together, you might use the boxed format. Here is how the information in the open table looks boxed:

Position	*Number*	*Cumulative Number*
Partner	39	39
Manager	57	96
Senior staff	80	176
Junior staff	74	250
Total	250	—

What kind of format should you use in constructing tables for qualitative data, such as instructions, guidelines, or rankings? You might list the items, letting your reader know if they are ranked or organized in some sort of priority. In doing so, follow the same rules as in a quantitative table. Figure 15-4 is an example of a table presenting qualitative data in a listing format.

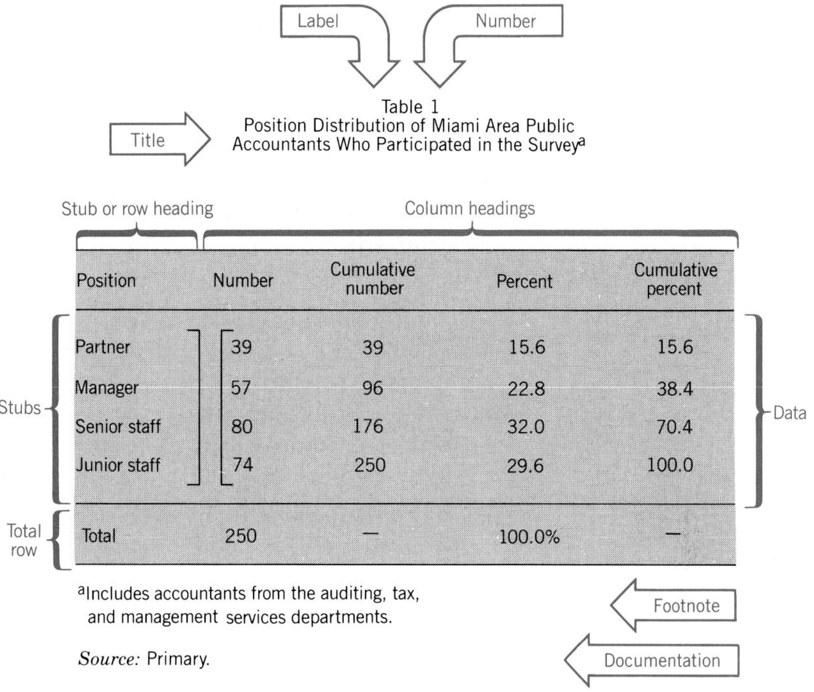

FIGURE 15-3 A common table format with major parts identified.

Table 1
The Ten Most Serious Communication Barriers in the Superior-Subordinate Relationship

Rank	*Communication Barrier*
1	Tendency not to listen
2	Lack of feedback
3	Lack of trust
4	Defensiveness
5	Personality differences
6	Information overload
7	Know-it-all attitude
8	Either-or thinking
9	Status differences
10	Resistance to change

FIGURE 15-4 A ruled table in a listing format.

One final point: No matter what form of table you use, you can save space by identifying large numbers with a phrase, such as "in millions of dollars" or "in thousands of pounds." In the same way, rather than having a column read $10,000,000," you could put "10" in the column itself and the phrase "in millions of dollars" in the column heading.

The following checklist should help you in constructing tables for your reports.

CHECKLIST FOR CONSTRUCTING TABLES

1. Are the data I want to place in a table quantitative or qualitative?
2. Do I want to use an informal or formal table?
3. Do I want merely to highlight several items? Then I should use an informal table.
4. Do I want to summarize a large amount of data? Then I should use a formal table.
5. What type of formal table do I want to use?
6. Do I want to show complex or general reference data? Then I should use a general-purpose table and place it in the appendix.
7. Do I want to reinforce a particular discussion? Then I should use a special-purpose table and place it close to the discussion.
8. Do I want to use a ruled, open, or boxed format?

CONSTRUCTING GRAPHS

What types of data do graphs show? What are the three types of graphs?

Graphs or charts are visual presentations of quantitative data. With them you can show relationships between two or more items. In constructing graphs, you help your readers to *see* the data more clearly. Three general types of graphs are *bar, line,* and *pie* or *circle.*

Bar Graphs

What are the four common types of bar graphs?

Bar graphs use rectangular bars or boxes with similar widths to illustrate the relationship among data. In selecting the appropriate type of bar graph to use in your report, consider both the nature of the data and the overall effect you wish to convey. The four most common types are *simple, grouped, segmented,* and *positive-negative.*

Simple Bar Graph

When would you use a simple bar graph?

The simple bar graph compares two or more values. Drawn either vertically or horizontally, it shows these values by the height or length of the bars. The bar graph has both a vertical and a horizontal axis, with the beginning point for each at zero.

Each bar must have the same width and each scale, equal intervals. Any variation in either will distort the data, causing the reader to misinterpret them. Figure 15-5 shows simple vertical and horizontal bar graphs, with their major parts identified.

Why would you color, shade, or hatch bars in a bar graph?

Note that the exact quantities appear at the ends of all the bars. You could also place them inside the bars, if you desire. When these numbers are unnecessary, leave them out. For additional emphasis, you might color, shade, or hatch, that is, finely line, the various bars.

Sometimes, the quantities the bars represent are at the high end of the scale you are using. If so, break it between zero and the first interval you need. Note that distortion could occur when you use a very high number for this interval. Figure 15-6 shows two types of bar graphs with Z and straight-line interval breaks.

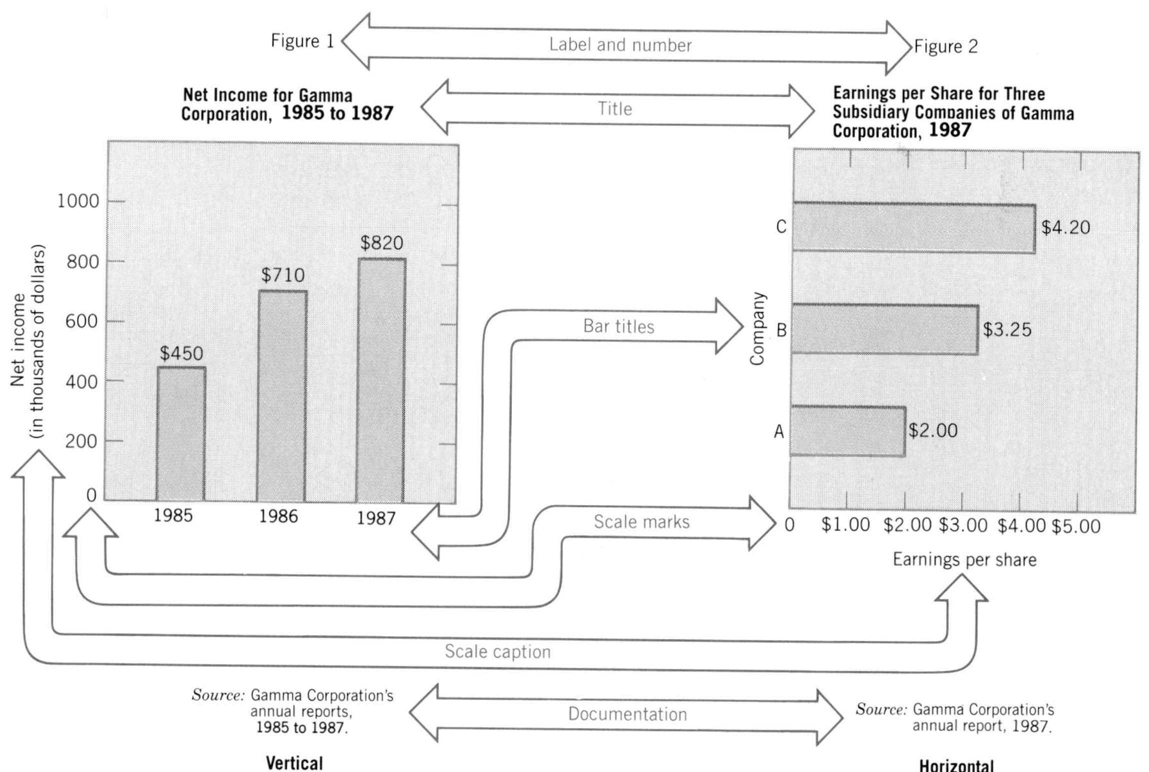

FIGURE 15-5 Vertical and horizontal simple bar graphs with major parts identified.

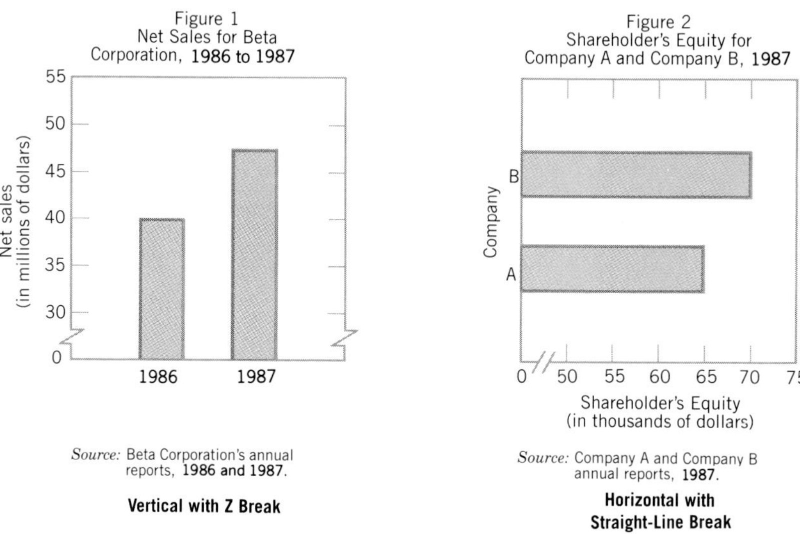

FIGURE 15-6 Vertical simple bar graph with Z break and horizontal simple bar graph with straight-line break.

Grouped Bar Graph

How do grouped and simple bar graphs differ?

A grouped bar graph compares two or more quantities over a period of time or at a specific point in time. To avoid confusion, limit each comparison group to three or fewer items.

What function does a legend serve in a bar graph?

Use colors, shading, or hatchings to identify the different elements you are comparing. Include too a legend or key on the graph to explain these designations. Figure 15-7 shows a grouped bar graph with a legend.

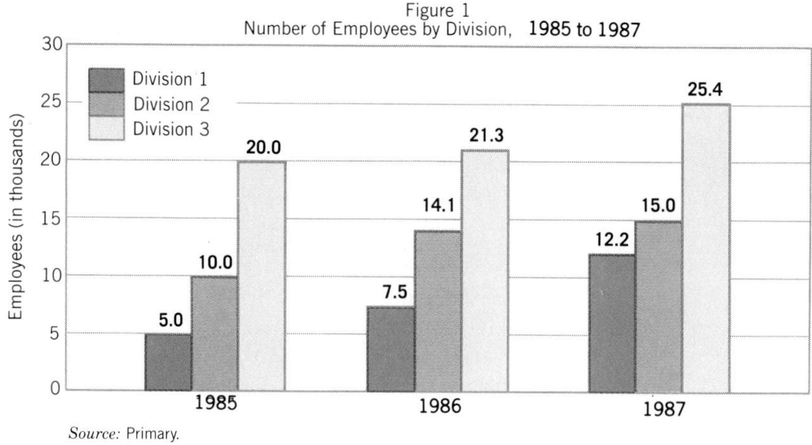

FIGURE 15-7 A grouped bar graph.

In this figure notice the different shadings to designate the three divisions. When shading, always start at the left with the darkest shade and then progress to lighter.

Segmented Bar Graph

Do the parts of a segmented bar graph always make up a whole?

A segmented bar graph shows the different parts of an item that comprise the whole. Use it when you need to compare either various parts of one item or several items. Generally, express the total amounts that are represented in the graph as absolute, such as dollars or units, but not percentages.

In a segmented graph, you can divide each bar into parts or segments corresponding to the amounts they represent. You should then color, shade, or hatch these segments and explain what they represent in a legend. Figure 15-8 is a segmented bar graph comparing three items. Notice that the bars are both shaded and hatched.

Positive-Negative Bar Graph

Positive-negative bar graphs show data that have both positive and negative values. Besides indicating this, you can use such graphs to show a series of increases or decreases in percentages. The zero point on the vertical or horizontal axis serves as the scale's midpoint. When using vertical bars, mark equal scale intervals above and below the midpoint. In contrast, when using horizontal bars, place such intervals to the right and left of the midpoint.

Thus, show increases in amounts above the midpoint on a vertical scale and to its left on one that is horizontal. Conversely, show decreases in amounts below the midpoint on a vertical scale and to its

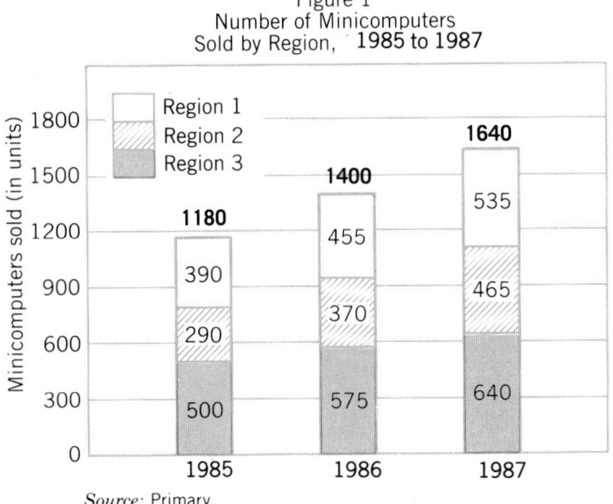

FIGURE 15-8 A segmented bar graph.

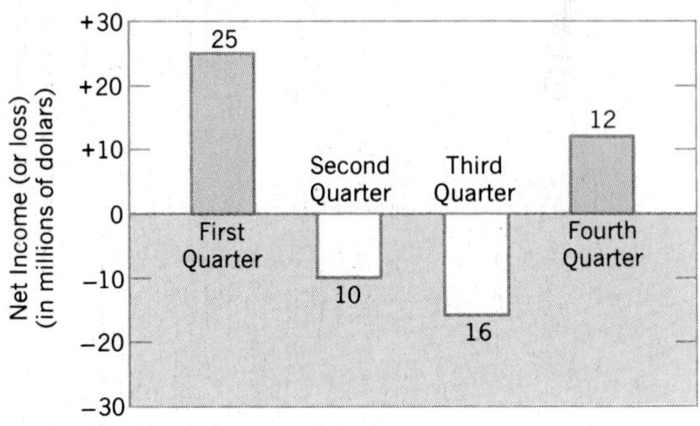

Source: Rho Corporation's annual report, 1987.

FIGURE 15-9 A positive-negative bar graph.

right on one that is horizontal. Figure 15-9 is a positive-negative bar graph with vertical bars.

Line Graphs

Can you name four common types of line graphs?

You can use line graphs to show trends—changes in data over a period of time. These graphs illustrate a continuous movement of data for a particular time period. Four commonly used types of line graphs are *single, multiple, cumulative,* and *positive-negative.*

Single Line Graph

In a line graph, which axis is Y and which one is X?

A single line graph shows one series of value. This graph has both a vertical and a horizontal axis. The vertical, or Y-axis, begins with zero and shows the amount or other value you are measuring. The horizontal, or X-axis, shows the time period or the method of classification you have chosen in plotting frequency distributions. As with a bar graph, mark the two scales in equal intervals to show relationships clearly and to present the data without distortion.

To make a line graph, place a dot for each amount you've indicated on the graph. After you have placed or plotted these dots, connect them to show the continuous movement. If the amounts are clustered at the high end of the scale, use either a Z or a straight-line break (see Figure 15-6). Figure 15-10 shows a single line graph.

Multiple Line Graph

What difference is there between single and multiple line graphs?

A multiple line graph compares two or more values over a time period or for a particular point in time. To keep the graph simple and easy to follow, try not to plot more than four series.

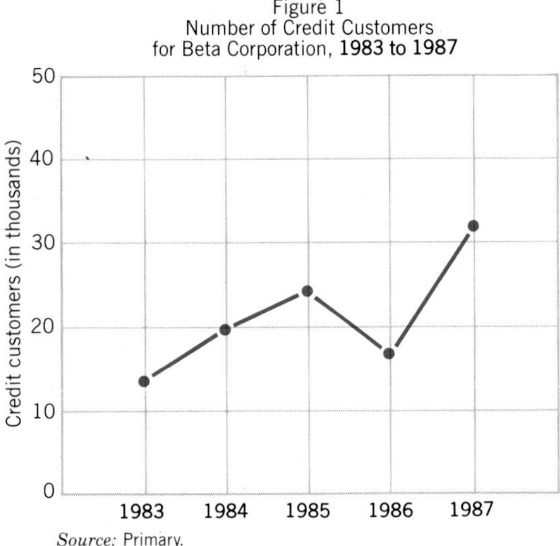

FIGURE 15-10 A single-line graph.

Because this graph has at least two lines, use some type of indicator to distinguish each line, particularly if lines cross each other. Some common indicators are single-colored lines, different-colored solid lines, dots, dashes, and combinations of dots and dashes. In a legend place a key to identify each line. Figure 15-11 is a multiple line graph.

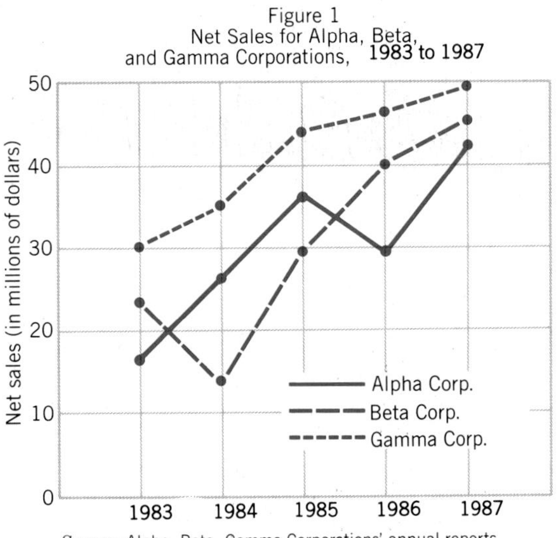

FIGURE 15-11 A multiple line graph.

Can you think of an example where a cumulative line graph would be useful?

Cumulative Line Graph

The cumulative line graph shows how the parts of a particular series of an item comprise a whole amount. In this type of graph, you can only plot one series, and the parts are stated in absolute terms, such as dollars or units.

To distinguish the parts, use color, shade, or hatching. Then, in a legend or with proper labeling, designate each part. Figure 15-12 shows a cumulative line graph. Notice that a vertical right line emphasizes the cumulative effect.

Positive-Negative Line Graph

Could you show activity in stock prices with a positive–negative line graph? Explain.

When a trend has both positive and negative values, a positive-negative line graph can illustrate changes. In this graph, the zero point on the vertical axis serves as the midpoint of the scale; therefore, mark equal scale intervals above and below this point. Then draw a horizontal line across the graph at the midpoint to distinguish the positive from the negative values. In plotting them on the graph, you clearly emphasize the positive-negative effect. Figure 15-13 shows a positive-negative line graph.

Pie or Circle Graphs

How many values do you deal with in a pie graph? How many parts? Explain.

A pie or circle graph compares the parts of one value at a particular point in time. Each part represents a portion of the total item. Include at least two parts, but to avoid cluttering and confusion, no more than eight. Label each part, and, if you want, color, shade, or hatch for emphasis. When preparing the graph, compute percentages of the

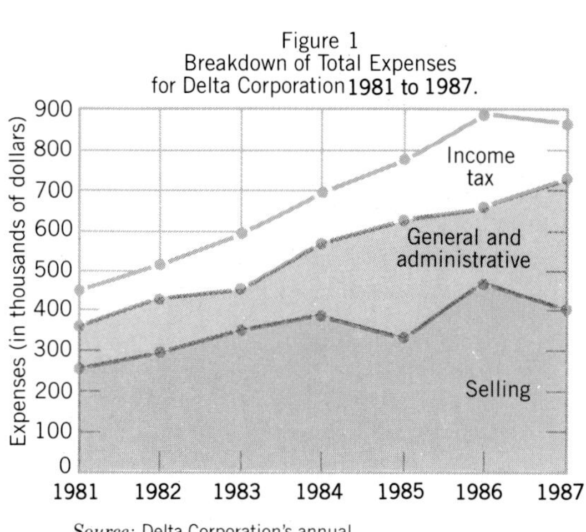

FIGURE 15-12 A cumulative line graph.

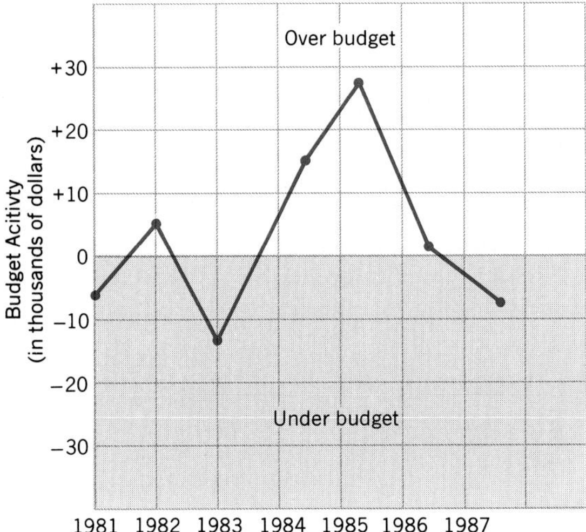

FIGURE 15-13 A positive-negative line graph.

total for each part, and then multiply each percentage by 360 degrees (the circumference of a circle).

Next, use a compass or some other round object to draw a circle with at least a 2″ or 3″ diameter. Using a protractor, mark the degrees for each part, starting with the largest at the 12 o'clock position. Then, moving clockwise, mark the other degrees in descending order of size. The only exception to this procedure is the miscellaneous, or other, category that you will include in some pie charts. Whatever its

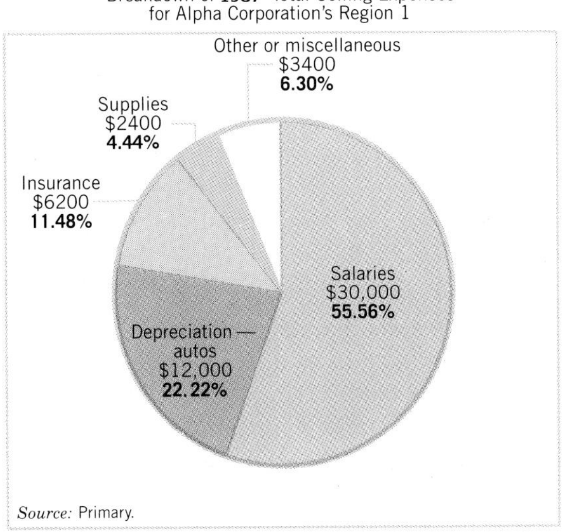

FIGURE 15-14 A pie or circle graph.

CHECKLIST FOR CONSTRUCTING A PIE OR CIRCLE GRAPH

1. Add the amounts of each part and then total them.
2. Convert each part into a percentage of the total.
3. Compute the number of degrees for each part by multiplying each percentage by 360 degrees.
4. Draw the circle with a compass or some round object.
5. Use a protractor to mark the degrees for each part, starting with the largest at the 12 o'clock position.
6. Mark the other, or miscellaneous, category at the end even though it may contain more degrees than another part.
7. Use color, shading, or hatching for emphasis.
8. Label each part, or use a legend if the parts are too small for labeling.

size, always place this segment last because it is less descriptive and therefore usually less important than other parts.

Figure 15-14 shows a completed pie or circle graph. Notice that if a segment is too small, you can draw an arrow from the label to the part, thus drawing attention to it. When constructing a pie or circle graph, use the above checklist as a guide.

CONSTRUCTING MISCELLANEOUS VISUAL AIDS

In preparing your report, you may use other visuals besides tables and graphs. Those used most commonly by business writers are *flow charts, time charts, maps, pictograms, photographs, drawings,* and *diagrams.*

Flow Charts

Why are downward directional flow arrows unnecessary in a flow chart?

A flow chart illustrates a process or procedure, such as the steps included in operating a computer or preparing a corporate tax return. In preparing one, use the conventional symbols on a flow charting template computer programmers use or use your own system of symbols. Figure 15-15 shows a flow chart using conventional symbols. Notice that you do not need to use directional flow arrows when the flow is downward, which is usually the case. Readers are accustomed to this normal downward flow. Note too that the diamond

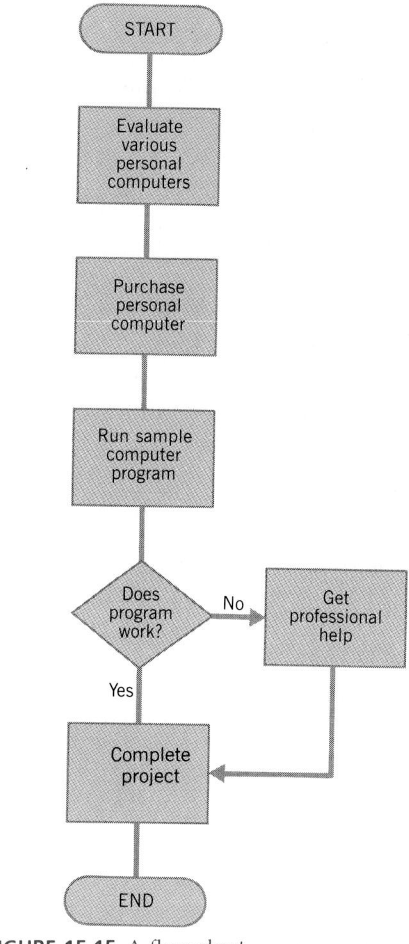

FIGURE 15-15 A flow chart.

shape is a decision symbol, permitting the process or procedure to branch to an alternative.

Time Charts

How can time charts help you plan a project?

Time charts show a schedule of activities to be completed during a period of time. Because they serve as a planning device for a project, report writers frequently use them in proposals and progress reports. In creating such charts, use either bars or lines to designate the times. Figure 15-16 is a time chart.

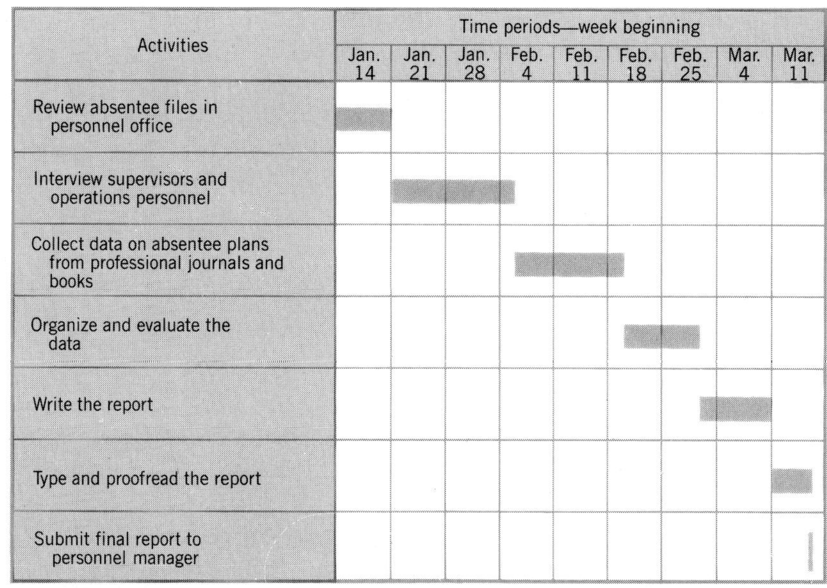

FIGURE 15-16 A time chart.

Maps

Can you think of a way to use a map in a business report?

Maps are a geographical representation of either qualitative or quantitative data. For example, a real estate developer may include in a report to potential investors a map of the area he or she wants to develop. Or a corporation may add in a report to stockholders a map showing the number and location of its franchises.

For emphasis and clarity, you can color, shade, or hatch parts of a map. Also, if these as well as other symbols represent data related to a specific geographical area, use a legend. Figure 15-17 is an example of a map.

Pictograms

Could you devise a pictogram using airplanes as the pictorial symbols? If so, explain how.

Pictograms employ pictorial symbols to represent data. Report writers use them most frequently when presenting quantitative data to a nontechnical audience such as the general public.

A common pictorial symbol is a column of stacked coins to show sales or expenditures. Or you could use cars to represent the number of cars your company has sold in the last five years, or airplanes to represent the number of air miles flown by American carriers in the past year. To avoid misrepresentation, make each symbol the same

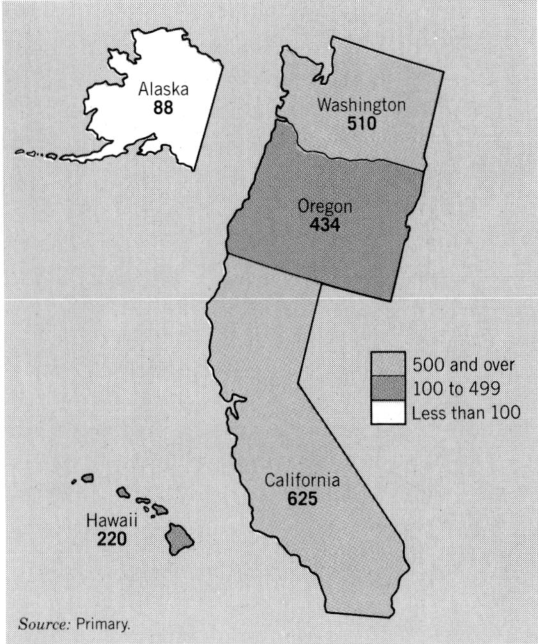

FIGURE 15-17 A map.

size and proportion. If necessary, include a legend to indicate what each represents in terms of a particular quantity. Figure 15-18 shows a pictogram.

FIGURE 15-18 A pictogram.

Photographs, Drawings, and Diagrams

Can you compare the uses of photographs, drawings, and diagrams in a single business report? If so, explain your idea.

Because photographs reveal surface detail, you can use them to show how an object or scene actually looks. For example, in a report on a problem in your company's production line, you might include a clear photograph of the problem area, that is, one without too many distractions.

Although drawings and diagrams do not include as much detail as photographs, use them in essentially the same way. For example, a drawing may present the physical characteristics of an item or an area. So you might use a drawing of a skyscraper your construction company is bidding on or one showing a piece of equipment your designers are developing to use in a rocket. In contrast, a diagram can present a brief sketch of an item or indicate how a particular process works. Thus, in addition to your drawing of the piece of rocket equipment, you may present a cutaway diagram of its inner parts. Or you might show a schematic diagram of its overall structure or one revealing how it operates. To emphasize certain parts of a drawing or a diagram, use colors, shades, or hatches. If necessary, also add arrows and labels.

USING COMPUTER GRAPHICS

What types of graphics could you produce on a computer?

With the development of computer graphics, the report writer can produce every visual aid presented in this chapter, with the exception of a photograph, more effectively and in less time. (In fact, a computer can produce a recognizable photographic approximation of the original, but not a precise reproduction of it.)

Computer graphics can transform raw data into both black and white and color visuals. Using plain English instructions, you can create these graphics on your own display terminal in the office. If you want, you may even perform "what-if" functions on it by manipulating the data to see what might be the outcome of an as-yet-to-be-made decision.

Recently, the cost of computer graphics has been declining. Moreover, you can now choose among many graphics software programs to use with your office computer. To compose visuals on a computer, you will also need at least two other pieces of related equipment: a graphics display terminal for preparation and a plotter for printing. Figures 15-19 and 15-20 show some examples of computer-produced visuals. With additional equipment you can make color or black and white transparencies of them for overhead projectors as well as 35-mm slides.

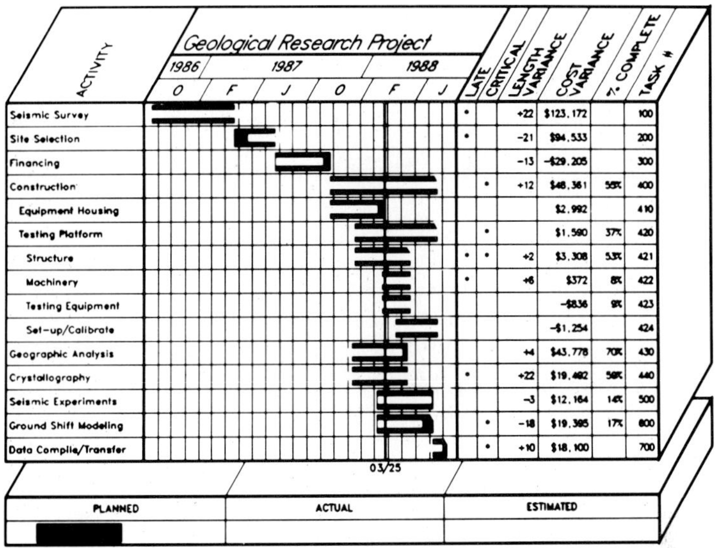

FIGURE 15-19 Example of a computer-derived graphic. (Business graphic produced by CA-TELLAPLAN. Reprinted with permission of Computer Associates International, Inc., Garden City, New York.)

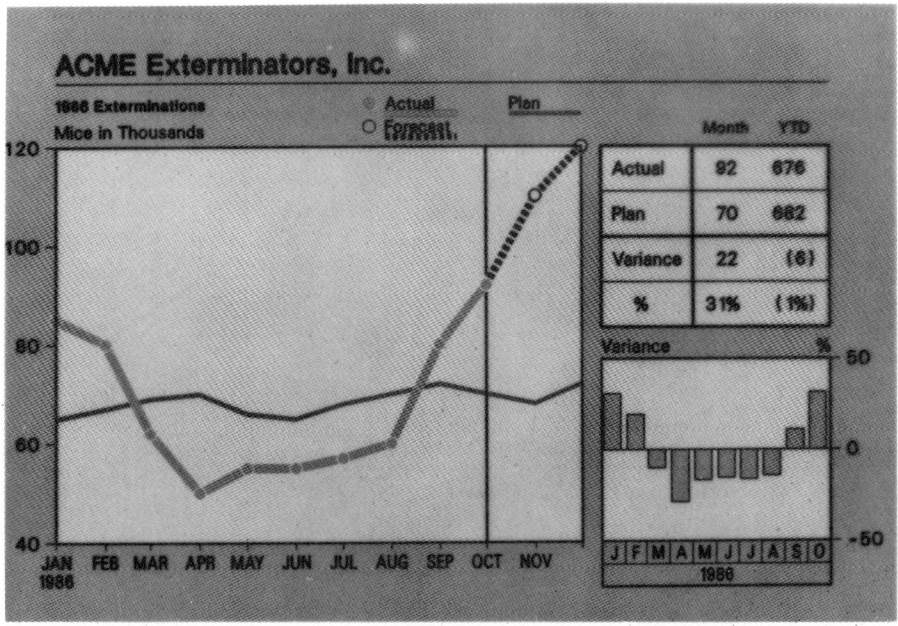

FIGURE 15-20 Example of a computer-derived graphic. (Business graphic produced by CA-TELLAGRAF. Reprinted with permission of Computer Associates International, Inc., Garden City, New York.)

If you don't have access to a computer, can you still use computer graphics in your reports? How?

What if your company does not have a computer or has not purchased computer graphics hardware and software? You can still produce such visuals by hiring an independent computer service bureau to do your work. Or you might purchase a microcomputer with graphics capabilities. At present, over 75 software programs are available for various microcomputer systems.

SUMMARY

1. Visual aids help you to simplify, supplement, and support complex data. In addition, they may emphasize critical concepts so your audience will remember them.
2. When presenting any visual aid, you should identify, document, introduce, interpret, and place it appropriately on the page.
3. You can classify visual aids into tables, graphs, and miscellaneous visuals.
4. Tables can be either formal or informal.
5. An informal table emphasizes several items by identifying them after a simple lead-in sentence and does not need to be separated from the text.
6. A formal table summarizes larger amounts of data and should be separated from the narrative.
7. You can classify formal tables as general or special purpose.
8. The three basic types of graphs are bar, line, and pie or circle.
9. When preparing a bar graph, you might choose one of the following specific types: simple, grouped, segmented, or positive-negative.
10. Four common types of line graphs are single, multiple, cumulative, and positive-negative.
11. Miscellaneous visual aids consist of the following: flow charts, organizational charts, time charts, maps, pictograms, photographs, drawings, and diagrams.
12. Computer graphics permit report writers to produce virtually every visual discussed in this chapter more effectively and in less time. With computers, you can produce black and white or color prints, transparencies, and slides.

Review Questions

1. What is the major purpose of visual aids? Why are they used in reports?
2. Describe the five common requirements for presenting all types of visual aids. Why should you complete each requirement when presenting a visual aid?
3. What are three ways to document visual aids? How does documentation differ from footnotes used in visuals?
4. Why shouldn't a visual aid just appear in a report without an introduction? What are three ways of introducing a visual aid? Which way is best?
5. When interpreting the data contained in the visual aid, all you need do is repeat the data in the narrative. Do you agree or disagree with this statement? Explain your answer.

6. Why is it necessary for a visual to be placed close to the discussion in the text? Should you ever place them in the appendix? Why?
7. What are two types of tabular presentations? When should you use each type?
8. Can you describe a situation in which you would use a table in a listing format?
9. What is the difference between a table and a graph? Is one more effective than the other? Why?
10. What is the difference between a grouped bar graph and a multiple line graph? Describe a situation in which you would use each.
11. What is the difference between a segmented bar graph and a cumulative line graph? Describe a situation in which you would use each.
12. Why would you use a positive-negative bar graph and a positive-negative line graph? Give an example for each type.
13. What is the purpose of a pie or circle graph? Describe a situation in which you would use this graph.
14. In what situation could you use each of the following miscellaneous visual aids: flow charts? organizational charts? time charts? maps? pictograms? photographs? drawings? diagrams?
15. What effect have computers had on the preparation of visual aids?

Exercises

1. Using the following data, construct a table and label it properly: 25 retailing supervisors were classified as upper management, 47 as middle management, and 38 as lower management.
2. What specific type of bar graph would you use for each of the following situations? Explain your answers.
   a. Comparing the quarterly sales of three regions for the past year.
   b. Comparing the dollar value of merchandise returned for the past three years.
   c. Showing the net income and net loss for the past five years.
   d. Comparing the breakdown of the total number of employees by division.
3. During the past five years, the following dividends were paid by Wilson Manufacturing Company: $6.20, $5.80, $4.25, $5.70, and $5.95. Prepare a simple bar graph to show these data.
4. What specific type of line graph would you use for each of the following situations? Explain your answers.
   a. Measuring the net income for the past five years.
   b. Comparing sales, expenses, and net income for the past five years.
   c. Showing the fluctuation in meeting quarterly sales quotas for the past year.
   d. Comparing the breakdown of total sales by region for the past six years.
5. Spector Computer Company had the following microcomputer sales record by region:

	Region 1	*Region 2*	*Region 3*
		(in millions of dollars)	
1985	75	84	38
1986	92	88	48
1987	118	96	65

Prepare a grouped bar graph to illustrate these data.

6. During the past six years, the following amounts were spent by each division in Belton Industries for research and development: Division 1: $29,000, $40,000, $42,000, $53,000, $62,000, and $75,000; Division 2: $34,000, $44,000, $50,000, $57,000, $64,000, and $70,000. Prepare a multiple line graph to show these data.
7. Bromowitz Carpets had the following net income (or loss) for the past five years: 1983, $55,000; 1984, $32,500; 1985, ($12,000); 1986, ($4,000); and 1987, $20,000. Prepare a positive-negative line graph using these data.
8. A department store had total monthly sales of $116,000. A breakdown of the sales by department was

Notions	$ 5,000
Ladies' wear	30,000
Men's wear	28,000
Children's wear	14,000
Sporting goods	20,000
Hardware	9,000
Shoes	10,000
Total	$116,000

Prepare a pie graph to show these data.
9. Prepare a flow chart showing the steps necessary to reconcile your checkbook balance.
10. Assume you just purchased a microcomputer. Draw and label its major parts. Then, if possible, use a graphics software program to construct your drawing on a computer.

CHAPTER 16

PRESENTING THE RESULTS AND THE FORMAL REPORT

For the past four months, Mike Green has been researching data for a report his boss has asked him to make on reorganizing the company's European clothing operations in an effort to reverse mounting losses. Mike has now completed all stages of the research process—from identifying the problem to collecting, sorting and summarizing, interpreting, and outlining the data. He has also used the office computer to produce a large number of graphics to illustrate the problem and his recommendations for solving it. (He has decided to recommend changes that more strongly combine research, styling, and production throughout Europe.) Now, however, he has to write the report itself. Given the amount of data, he knows that this may well be the most challenging part of the research process. Moreover, so much is riding on the report, for example, the future direction of the company and the fate of thousands of European workers.

Slowly Mike takes out his final outline and huge stack of note cards. Perhaps he has left something critical out, overestimated the savings in money that greater efficiency in production and marketing may bring. At least while writing he will have one more opportunity to evaluate the data and to draw further conclusions or revise others.

Like Mike Green you have gone through all stages of the research process, except for one: how to write the actual report. In this chapter you will learn to apply specific writing principles to reports. Together with the writing techniques discussed in Chapters 3 and 4, they should help you to write effective reports. In addition, this chapter presents format procedures as well as the major parts of the report itself.

APPLYING PROPER WRITING PROCEDURES AND TECHNIQUES

As with anything else you want to master, effective report writing requires practice. The following checklist suggests how you might proceed.

WRITING SUGGESTIONS CHECKLIST

1. Select a time of day for writing that will have the fewest distractions.
2. Write those sections with which you feel most comfortable first. Doing this will build your confidence in completing the remaining sections.

3. Write the first draft as rapidly as you can. Worrying about selecting the "right" word or spelling a difficult word at this point will distract you. Get your thoughts down and expect to rewrite the material later.
4. Set goals for writing different parts of the report. This approach is necessary because you will not be able to write a complete report at one sitting. Establish the time that you will complete the report and set intermediate goals.
5. Document the sources of data you present. The three ways to document data directly within a report are
   a. With footnotes at the bottom of the page (or with endnotes at the end of the report).
   b. With a full citation within the text at the point you refer to the source.
   c. With a reference to a list of sources using a key number and page number(s) within the text at the point where the reference is made.

What is an annotation used for?

You also can document data with a bibliography of sources related to the report topic. The bibliography may be just a list of sources, or you might annotate the entries. An *annotation* is a brief summary of the contents of a source.

Documentation is discussed in Appendix D. Also consult a style manual for ways to type and place documentation on the pages of the final draft of your report. Here is a list of several popular style manuals:

Campbell, William Giles, and Steven Vaughan Ballou. *Form and Style: Theses, Reports, Term Papers*, 7th ed. Boston: Houghton Mifflin, 1986.

Modern Language Association, *MLA Style Sheet*. New York: Modern Language Association, 1980.

Turabian, Kate L. *A Manual for Writers of Term Papers, Theses, and Dissertations*, 7th ed. Chicago: University of Chicago Press, 1985.

6. Edit and revise your first draft until you are satisfied with your effort. Then proofread the report using the proofreading techniques discussed in Chapter 3. You can use word processors to proofread and edit your report copy. Chapter 6 contains more information about this subject.

As mentioned, all the writing principles presented in Chapters 3 and 4 apply to report writing. Before you begin to write, you might want to review them. The principles that are especially applicable are *writing style, tense,* and *transitions.*

Selecting an Informal or Formal Writing Style

Your writing style in business reports should never be highly formal—not even when writing what is called a formal report. As discussed in Chapter 3, writing style can range from being very formal to being very informal. All business writing—except contracts, perhaps—falls somewhere between the two extremes. And the trend today is to write less formally than in the past, though report writing probably should never be informal enough to be called colloquial.

Right now, do you normally write reports in formal or informal writing style?

What is called informal report writing today is personal. Therefore, if you choose to write an informal report, use personal pronouns—I, me, my, you, your, we, our, and us—throughout. If you choose to write a formal report, then write in the third person, excluding all personal pronouns. Instead, you might either avoid using pronouns or use only impersonal ones, such as "they" when referring to desks, chairs, or whatever. (See Chapter 3 for other characteristics of formal and informal writing style, such as sentence and paragraph length.)

How do you choose between the two styles? The answer depends on your audience's requirements and the situation's formality or informality. If you are writing a longer, more formal report for someone outside your organization—such as an account officer in a bank—or for certain executives within the company—such as the vice president of consumer services—use the formal style. However, for memorandum and letter reports, adopt the informal style. (See the next chapter for a further discussion of memorandum and letter reports.)

The following examples show how the two writing styles differ:

Informal As you can see from the results of our consumer survey, your nonfood departments are an essential part of your supermarket.

Formal As the results of the consumer survey show, nonfood departments are an essential part of this supermarket.

Choosing the Proper Verb Tense

The proper tense to use in reports declares the time an event or series of events happened. Thus, in discussing the time period in which you are writing the report itself, use the present tense. Employ it, too, in reporting events that are happening now or are timeless. For events that have already happened, use the past tense. For events that will happen, use the future tense. The following are some examples of proper use of tense:

Our findings indicate . . . (present tense)

One possibility is to increase . . . (timeless, present tense)

The data I collected for this report . . . (past tense)

We will need to analyze further . . . (future tense)

Using Transition Statements

What are the two types of transition statements?

Transitions make thoughts flow smoothly, and remember, a transition directs your audience. Two types of transition statements are *transition sentences* and *lead-in sentences or paragraphs.* If you need to connect ideas between subsections, use a transition sentence at the end of the first to connect it with the next. For example, a brief summary of the first subsection and a short reference to the next can form a transition sentence, such as the following:

> (last sentence of a section on input and output qualities) Input and output qualities are very important in determining which copier to buy, but the prices paid for these qualities also command attention. (A section on prices follows.)

In contrast, as the name implies, lead-in sentences or paragraphs appear at the beginning of a subsection. Use them to introduce all the subsections of a major section. The following is an example of how to begin a major section with a lead-in sentence:

> The cost involved in owning and operating a copier can be subdivided into four categories. These categories are initial cost, maintenance, supply, and depreciation cost. (Discussions on the four categories follow.)

APPLYING PROPER FORMAT TECHNIQUES

If you can tell a book by its cover, you can also tell the effectiveness of a report by its appearance? Perhaps not. Yet your audience will definitely be affected by the way your report looks. Therefore, besides making sure your report copy is attractive, use proper headings, margins, spacing, indentions, and page numbering.

Headings

Headings show readers how the parts of your report fit together. If you arranged the headings in your final outline as suggested in Chapter 14, you might use them in your report as well. The various levels of headings are called *degrees.* Several heading formats exist. Figure 16-1 shows one of the more commonly used.

COMMONLY USED HEADING FORMATS

FIRST-DEGREE HEADING

Use first-degree headings to identify the main sections of your report. Type these headings in all capital letters centered over the copy as shown. Note that the title of the report is not a heading although you should type it in the same way as you do a first-degree heading. Note also that you need at least two first-degree headings. Triple space before and after a first-degree heading.

Second-Degree Heading

Use second-degree headings as subtopics of the main topics. Type these headings centered over the copy and underlined with the first letter of each main word capitalized as shown. (Do not capitalize the first letter of an article or a preposition except when it appears as the first word in a heading. Follow this rule for third- and fourth-degree headings as well.) Note that you need at least two second-degree headings for each subtopic, or none at all. Note also that you should triple space before and after a second-degree heading.

Third-Degree Heading

Use third-degree headings to identify subtopics of second-degree headings. Type this heading flush against the left

FIGURE 16-1 Description and placement of report headings.

margin with the first letter of each main word capitalized as shown. As with the other two headings, you need at least two third-degree headings for each subtopic, or none. Also, triple space before and after a third-degree heading.

Fourth-Degree Heading. Use fourth-degree headings to identify subtopics under third-degree headings. Type the fourth-degree heading with the first letter of each main word capitalized. Indent the heading five spaces and underline it; place it on the first line of the paragraph as shown. This heading ends with a period, after which the paragraph copy follows on the same line. As with the other three headings, you need at least two fourth-degree headings for each subtopic, or none. Also, triple space before a fourth-degree heading.

FIGURE 16-1 (continued)

Margins

What changes in margins are needed when you bind a report at the top instead of at the left?

The first page of the report body should have a 2″ margin at the top. For the remaining pages, this margin should be reduced to 1″. As for side and bottom margins in your report body, they should also have a 1″ margin. If you decide to bind the report at the left or at the top, add ½″ to the interior margin to allow for binding. For left-bound reports, the center point of the line of writing should be ½″ to the right of the center of the page. Preliminary pages—such as the table of contents and synopsis—and supplementary pages—such as the bibliography and the appendix—have the same margin as the first page of the report body. Figure 16-2 summarizes these margin requirements.

Spacing, Indentions, and Page Numbering

Within the report body, you may use either single- or double-line spacing. If you decide on single-line spacing, indent the first line of

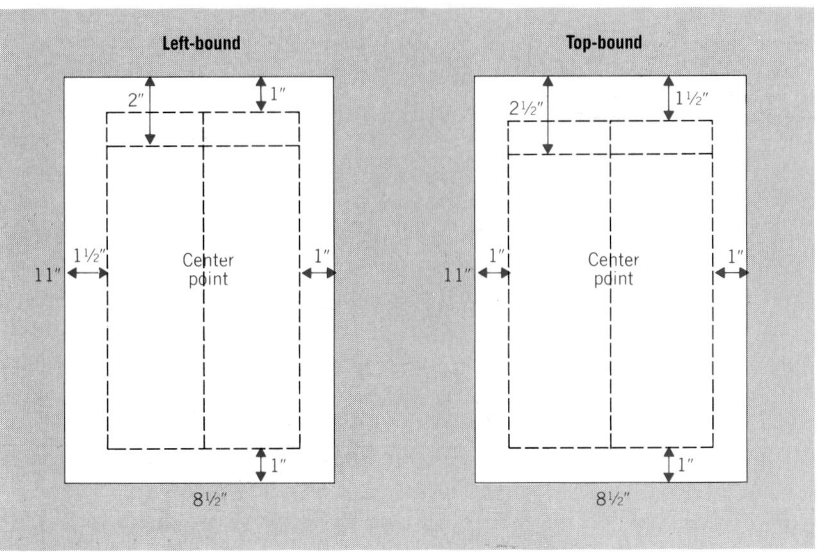

FIGURE 16-2 Margins for left-bound and top-bound reports.

each paragraph five spaces or do not indent at all. Business reports are most frequently prepared with a single-spaced format to save production costs. If your business report must be reviewed by someone else, for example, an attorney from the legal department, your report should be prepared as a double-spaced draft. If you use double spacing, indent the first line of each paragraph five spaces. Generally, double-spaced reports are prepared by those who must frequently review work in progress and make corrections. Also, they are prepared by people who work together or separately on the same report. Whether you use single or double spacing within paragraphs, double space between them.

How are preliminary, body, and supplementary report parts numbered?

Number the pages of preliminary parts with lowercase roman numerals. Although in doing so, you should reserve a number for the title page, do not type it on the page itself. But do type the correct numbers on all your other preliminary pages. Center each one horizontally ½" from the bottom of the page on which it appears. Then number the rest of your report with arabic numerals, including the supplementary pages. The first page of the report body should be "1," with the number centered and typed ½" from the bottom of the page. For the remaining pages, however, type each number in the upper right-hand corner if the report will be left-bound. Place the number so that it is even with the right margin and ½" down from the top of the page. If, however, the report will be top-bound, type page numbers at the horizontal center and ½" from the bottom of the page on which they appear.

IDENTIFYING PARTS OF FORMAL REPORTS

In what two ways do we usually organize reports?

You may organize your report inductively or deductively. If you organize it inductively, arrange the major parts in this order: introduction, data analysis (findings), summary, conclusion(s), and recommendation(s). If, however, you organize it deductively, employ this order: recommendation(s), conclusion(s), data analysis, and summary. After you have organized the body of your report inductively or deductively, add any preliminary or supplementary parts to it. Naturally, these additions lengthen your report; they also make it more formal.

Sometimes the parts you include in a report will vary, depending on its nature and your audience's needs. Still, certain ones should be included in all reports. The following outline shows all the parts you *might* put in a long, formal, and inductively organized, analytical report. An informational report, on the other hand, might include all these parts except the conclusion(s) and recommendation(s). The asterisks indicate the parts that would normally appear in most analytical reports.

Can a report part be included in one report but be left out of another? Explain.

I. Preliminary parts
- *A. Letter or memorandum of transmittal
- *B. Title page
- C. Letter or memorandum of authorization
- D. Letter or memorandum of acceptance
- *E. Table of contents
- *F. Table of illustrations
- *G. Synopsis

II. Body (or text) parts
- *A. Introduction
  - 1. Statement of authorization
  - 2. Background of the problem
  - *3. Statement of the problem
  - 4. Statement of hypothesis
  - *5. Scope of the problem
  - 6. Limitations
  - *7. Sources and methods of data collection
  - 8. Definition of terms
  - *9. Report preview
- *B. Data analysis (findings)
- *C. Report ending
  - 1. Summary
  - 2. Conclusion(s)
  - 3. Recommendation(s)

III. Supplementary parts
- *A. Bibliography
- B. Glossary
- C. Appendix
- D. Index

Preliminary Parts

Can you name the preliminary parts of a report?

Include preliminary parts to prepare your audience for understanding the information in the report body. These preliminary parts are *transmittal letter* or *memo, title page, authorization letter* or *memo, acceptance letter* or *memo, table of contents, table of illustrations,* and *synopsis.*

Letter or Memorandum of Transmittal

What purpose does the transmittal letter or memo serve?

When you are ready to deliver your report to the reader, compose a letter or memo of transmittal to accompany it. If you are sending your report to someone outside the company, write a letter; if you are sending it to someone within, write a memo.

The contents of this letter or memo depend on your audience, the research topic, and the general situation in which you conducted the investigation. To organize your message, use the direct correspondence plan discussed in Chapter 8. Some topics you might discuss in it are cost or time limitations that might have affected the results; the report's contents, especially the problem, conclusions, and recommendations. Close with an appreciation for the assignment and an offer to discuss the report's contents further.

Most of the time, you will leave the transmittal letter or memo out of your report. If, however, you do include it, attach it to your report with a paper clip. See Figure 16-3 for a transmittal memo.

Title Page

Your title page should contain the following sections: (1) the report's title typed in capital letters; (2) the name, title, and address of the individual(s) for whom you are preparing it; (3) your own name, title, and address as well as that of any co-writer(s); and (4) the date. Center each line horizontally on the page and leave equal vertical spacing between each section. Also compose a descriptive title, such as "The Effects of Price-Level Changes on Asset Valuation for Thomas Chemical Company," rather than one, such as "Price-Level Changes," that in no way indicates the report's contents. See Figure 16-3 for an example of a title page.

Letter or Memorandum of Authorization

Sometimes the person who asks for a report sends a letter or memorandum of authorization to the report writer. This document formally authorizes the writer to complete the research project. If you have received such a letter or memo, include a copy in the preliminary part of the report.

Letter or Memorandum of Acceptance

The letter or memorandum of acceptance is the report writer's reply to the letter or memorandum of authorization. The act of signing it commits him or her to prepare the report within the requirements of the authorization. If you have signed such a document, include a copy in your report.

Table of Contents

What goes in a table of contents?

In general, you should have a table of contents in any formal report with five or more pages in its body. The table of contents should contain the headings of all the major divisions of the report—and perhaps some of its major subdivisions too—and the number of the page on which each part begins. Often, a row of periods, or leaders, extends from the end of each heading to the page number. Because the table of contents assists the reader in locating a particular section, its headings should duplicate exactly those in the report. Figure 16-3 shows an example of a table of contents.

Table of Illustrations

The table of illustrations identifies the label, number, and title of the visuals included in the report and specifies the page on which they are located. If you prefer, you could divide this table into two sections: tables and figures. Also, remember to make sure the title of a visual replicates its title in the report. If you have fewer than four entries, you might consider incorporating them into your table of contents rather than preparing a separate table. See Figure 16-3 for an example of a table of illustrations.

Synopsis

Is a synopsis known by any other name?

The synopsis is a condensed version of the report body. Sometimes called an abstract, epitome, précis, or executive summary, it summarizes the report for the reader so that he or she knows what to expect. Write your synopsis after you complete the report—because at this point you too have a better idea what it is about—and limit it, if possible, to one page. (To keep the synopsis to one page, single space it even though you might double space the report's body.) Include at least the main ideas from all major sections of the body. Arrange these either deductively or inductively. Figure 16-3 shows an example of a synopsis.

Body Parts

Usually, you will divide the body, or text, of your report into three main sections: *introduction*, *data analysis* or *findings*, and *report ending*.

Introduction

What role does the introduction play in a report?

Your goal in the introductory section is to introduce the reader to the report problem and to establish both the credibility and the applicability of your research.

Statement of Authorization The statement of authorization briefly identifies the authorizer. Sometimes it also states his or her requirements. For example, the authorizer may want the report completed in a week. If you have a letter or memo of authorization, you do not need to include this statement. See Figure 16-3 for an example of an authorization statement.

Background of the Problem The purpose of this section is to provide the reader with a framework for the research problem. It is here that you might discuss the larger problem(s) that surrounds the research problem. For example, an unstable political situation may have affected the financial stability of the Third World corporation you are investigating.

Also, you might discuss the history of the condition leading to the current problem, for example, in the case of the Third World corporation, constant government interference. See Figure 16-3 for an example of this section.

Statement of the Problem The statement of the problem identifies the problem you will be solving. Such statements have to be both clear and specific. (For a detailed discussion of them, see Chapter 13.) Figure 16-3 shows an example.

Statement of Hypothesis The hypothesis is a technical statement that predicts the answer to the research problem, which the report then tests. You can write a hypothesis in either a directed or null form. (See Chapter 13 for a detailed discussion of hypotheses, accompanied by examples.)

Scope of the Problem This statement sets the boundaries for the study of the problem by answering the question, "How far reaching is this study?" Sometimes you can clarify these boundaries in your discussion of the problem statement. If so, then do not state the scope separately. (See Chapter 13 for a discussion and an example of a scope statement.)

What do you tell the reader in a section on limitations?

Limitations Limitations are outside constraints placed upon report writers during the research phase over which they have no control. Some common limitations are too small a budget, too little time for conducting the study, and the inability to acquire proper tools or materials, such as questionnaires, computers for tabulation, and so forth. Only mention limitations when they may affect or have affected the quality of your study. For example, if, in a study of the effectiveness of a certain military transport, some of the material is classified and, therefore, unavailable, this may affect your results. Consequently, you should mention this restriction. If, however, you are able to obtain the data elsewhere, then do not cite the government's policy as a limitation. However, when limitations are so great that they actually prevent you from conducting a useful study, you may decide not to go ahead.

Sources and Methods of Data Collection The discussion of sources and methods of data collection tells your reader how you gathered them. If you worked with primary data, you should describe the sample selection and the way it was collected. For example, you might explain how you established questionnaire validity and reliability and how you administered it. In addition, describe any statistical techniques you used to analyze the data. See Figure 16-3 for an example.

How do you go about defining a term?

Definition of Terms Define any term that the reader is likely to find unfamiliar. Usually, you will need to define more terms for a nontechnical audience than for one that is professional. If these terms are too numerous, you might want to place them in a glossary at the end of the report. Or if you have a couple, you may define the term when you first use it in the text. Be sure to use parallel construction if you list or enumerate terms. Also, include for each a name, class, and differentiation. Class is a common grouping for the term. Differentiation is what makes one term different from another within a class. The following analyzes how to define a term:

Term	Class	Differentiation
Inventory record	is a file	that shows the quantity and description of an item in stock.

Report Preview The report preview is a transition statement that links the introductory section with the data analysis section. In it you should mention all the major topics you will discuss in the rest of the report.

Data Analysis

The data analysis section is where you discuss your findings. Explain each finding in relation to the way you solved the research problem. If you performed statistical analysis, use a visual aid, such as a table listing your means, to present the data resulting from it. (For more information on preparing and illustrating the data analysis section, see Chapters 14 and 15.)

Report Ending

What are the three parts of a report ending section?

The report ending is the last major section of the body. Usually, you should divide this section into three parts: *summary, conclusions,* and *recommendations.* The nature of your report will determine which, if not all, of the parts to include. For example, if your purpose is purely informational—the size of the foreign car market—you probably should have only a summary. But if the report is analytical—why Japan has such a big share of this market—you will need to draw conclusions and make recommendations as well.

Summary The summary ties together the main points of the data analysis only. This section gives your reader an overview of the research findings. Do not mention the introductory parts here. A summary differs from the synopsis because the latter not only includes the data analysis but also the introductory, conclusion, and recommendation parts.

How do conclusions differ from findings?

Conclusions Conclusions are answers to the problem statement. Depending on the problem, you might draw only one conclusion or you might draw ten. Base each conclusion on your findings. For this reason, never introduce new findings here—or in any other part of the report ending.

If you have reached several conclusions, you might list them after an appropriate lead-in sentence, such as "Based on the findings of this study, the following conclusions are drawn." (For a discussion of how to draw and word conclusions, see Chapter 14.) Figure 16-3 shows a statement of conclusions.

How do recommendations differ from conclusions?

Recommendations Recommendations are actions the report writer suggests should be taken as a result of the answer(s) to the research problem. Draw these recommendations directly from your conclusions. If you make several recommendations, you might list them after an appropriate lead-in sentence, such as "Based on the conclusions of this study, the following recommendations are made."

In some reports, you might decide to combine your conclusions and recommendations under a single heading. Whether you do should depend on their number and complexity. If they are numerous and complicated, then present them separately to keep things clear. If you combine them, state your conclusions first. (See Chapter 14 for a discussion of how to make and word recommendations.) Figure 16-3 shows some sample recommendations.

Supplementary Parts

Supplementary parts provide additional related material. These parts are the *bibliography, glossary, appendix,* and *index.*

Bibliography

The bibliography (or references) provides the reader with data sources you consulted during your research. See Appendix D for a discussion of the appropriate format to use in preparing and using documentation.

Glossary

The glossary is an alphabetical list of technical or otherwise specialized terms you wish to define for the reader. In general, if you have ten or more terms to define, include them in a glossary rather than in the introduction.

Appendix

When would you include an appendix in a report?

The appendix (or appendices) contains such material as general tables or graphs, sample questionnaires, covering and follow-up letters or memos, computer program printouts, and so forth. When should you include an item in the appendix rather than in the text? If it noticeably interrupts the thought flow, then put it in the appendix. Also, if the material is not absolutely critical to the development of your main points, reserve it for the appendix. Appendices should, however, contain relevant information.

Title each appendix. For example, you might title one "Questionnaire" and another "Follow-up Letter." Then list them in the table of contents. In the case of more than one appendix, all should be further set apart from one another by a capital letter, beginning in the first appendix with the letter A, and so on. Thus, your first appendix might be "Appendix A: Questionnaire" whereas your second might be "Appendix B: Follow-up Letter."

Index

The index provides an alphabetical cross-reference by name, subject, or both to the content of your report. Include an index only when your report is extremely long and detailed. In such situations, it serves as a detailed extension of the table of contents, arranged in alphabetical, instead of page, order.

ILLUSTRATING A FORMAL ANALYTICAL REPORT

Figure 16-3 shows a formal, inductively written, analytical report. The report includes many of the parts discussed in this chapter. Some parts not shown here are discussed elsewhere in the book and have been referred to throughout the chapter. Remember to include all *appropriate* parts in each report you write.

To: Shirley B. Landry, Director
Corporate Affirmative Action

From: John Galloway, Administrator
Employee Information Systems

Date: February 19, 1987

Subject: Compliance with Equal Employment Opportunity Guidelines

The report you requested concerning the female hiring practices at Thompson Industries based on Equal Employment Opportunity guidelines is attached.

The historical employment data from the three Thompson Industries divisions were analyzed in this study. A five-year base was selected for analysis: 1982 through 1986.

The data analysis shows the Chicago and Dallas divisions were above the compliance requirements for the five-year period; however, the Atlanta Division was below the requirements.

Thank you for the opportunity to conduct this study for you. If you would like to discuss any aspects of this report, Ms. Landry, please call me.

FIGURE 16-3 Formal report.

AN ANALYSIS OF FEMALE HIRING PRACTICES AT THOMPSON INDUSTRIES, INCORPORATED, BASED ON EQUAL EMPLOYMENT OPPORTUNITY COMPLIANCE GUIDELINES

Prepared for

Shirley B. Landry, Director
Corporate Affirmative Action
Thompson Industries, Incorporated
New York, New York

Prepared by

John Galloway, Administrator
Employee Information Systems
Thompson Industries, Incorporated
February 19, 1987

FIGURE 16-3 (continued)

TABLE OF CONTENTS

TABLE OF ILLUSTRATIONS

FIGURE 16-3 (continued)

SYNOPSIS

On February 12, Shirley B. Landry, Director of Corporate Affirmative Action, authorized a study to determine if Equal Employment Opportunity hiring guidelines for females were being met at Thompson Industries, Incorporated. In addition, the study was to serve as a five-year planning tool in establishing hiring goals for females at each of the three Thompson Industries divisional employment offices.

A Computer program was developed and used to query the hiring data of each of the three divisions. Employment data for 49,453 past and present employees were searched to determine date of employment, division, and sex. Census Bureau data on the sex mix of the population surrounding each division and sex mix for applicants were used to determine what the EEO guidelines should be.

In highlight, the study resulted in the following findings:

Both Dallas and Chicago are 7 percent above the compliance figure for the five-year period.

Atlanta is 4 percent below the compliance figure for the five-year period.

Based on these findings, the Employee Information Systems Department recommends (1) developing an intensive recruiting program to bring qualified females into the Atlanta division and (2) developing a training program to train females for drafting and designing jobs in Atlanta. At the same time, Atlanta should hire 1 female for every 2 males until 32 additional females are hired. This hiring practice will bring Atlanta into compliance.

iii

FIGURE 16-3 (continued)

ANALYSIS OF FEMALE HIRING PRACTICES AT THOMPSON INDUSTRIES, INCORPORATED, BASED ON EQUAL EMPLOYMENT OPPORTUNITY COMPLIANCE GUIDELINES

PROBLEM OVERVIEW

Statement of Authorization

On February 12, Shirley B. Landry, director of Corporate Affirmative Action, orally authorized a study to determine if Equal Employment Opportunity (EEO) hiring guidelines for females were being met at Thompson Industries, Incorporated.

Background of the Problem

The EEO guidelines published by the federal government in late 1984 state that corporations advertising themselves as equal opportunity employers must maintain a specified relationship between the number of males and females hired. The relationship is expressed as a percentage and is determined by the sex mix of the surrounding population when weighted by the sex mix of the employment applicants.

Statement of the Problem

The problem of this study was to determine whether affirmative action goals established by the Corporate Affirmative Action Committee were in compliance with EEO guidelines. The results of the study will be used to determine five-year hiring goals for each of the three Thompson Industries divisional employment offices.

Sources and Methods of Data Collection

The Employee Information Systems Department (EISD) is an employee service function for the three Thompson Industries divisions. All the data about the employment life cycle of Thompson Industries employees are maintained by the EISD on a computerized data base located at the Chicago Division office. Data on newly hired employees are sent to the EISD from each divisional employment office. The data undergo both manual and automated auditing before being added to the data base. A breakdown of the current work force for each division is shown in Table 1.

FIGURE 16-3 (continued)

2

TABLE 1
Divisional Work Force Size for Each Division

Division	Work Force Size	Percentage of Total Work Force
Chicago	12,360	75.83
Dallas	3,850	23.61
Atlanta	90	0.56
Totals	16,300	100.00

A computer program was developed to query the data base. The program was designed to select only the employees hired from 1982 through 1986. The employees included in this control period were defined further by sex, division, and year of employment. The program was processed against the data base on February 5, 1986. Of the 49,453 past and present employee records queried, only 3 contained unidentifiable codes. These records were deleted from the study. The sex mix data that were used for the study were published by the U.S. Census Bureau in 1984.

DIVISIONAL HIRING MIX

Each division of Thompson Industries was analyzed for the control period to determine the ratio between females and males hired.

Chicago Division Hiring Mix

The Chicago Division employs the most people, almost 76 percent of the total work force. The historical data show that the Chicago office hired 30 percent females and 70 percent males during the control period.

Dallas Division Hiring Mix

The Dallas Division is currently the second largest, employing about 24 percent of the total work force. The historical employment data show that 35 percent of the people hired from 1982 through 1986 were females and 65 percent were males.

Atlanta Division Hiring Mix

The Atlanta Division was established as a specialized division for drafting and designing. The division currently employs only 90 people and the ratio

FIGURE 16-3 (continued)

of people hired during the control period was 18 percent females and 82 percent males. A summary comparison by sex for each division is presented in Figure 1.

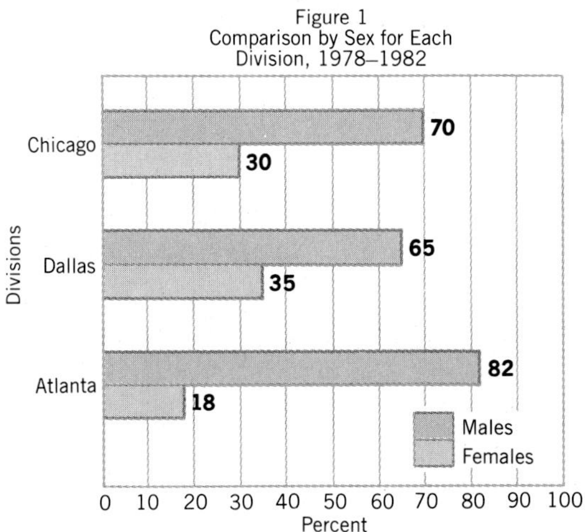

HIRING PRACTICES COMPARED WITH EEO GUIDELINES

The hiring practices for each division were compared with the EEO guidelines to determine whether the divisions were in compliance.

<u>Chicago and Dallas Hiring Practices in Compliance</u>

The hiring mix for the Chicago and Dallas divisions is in compliance with the EEO guidelines. When compared with the weighted sex mix of the surrounding population, both Chicago and Dallas are 7 percent above the compliance requirement.

FIGURE 16-3 (continued)

4

Atlanta Hiring Practices Not in Compliance

The Atlanta Division fell short of complying with the EEO guidelines by 4 percent. The explanation for the variance is that the Atlanta Division employs only high-level drafting and designing employees. The pre-employment testing statistics at Atlanta show that only 1 in 20 applicants was qualified for the jobs for which he or she applied. As a result, the choice about whom to hire was limited. A comparison of hiring practices with EEO guidelines for each division is shown in Figure 2.

Figure 2
Comparison of Actual Hiring Practices with
EEO Guidelines for Each Division

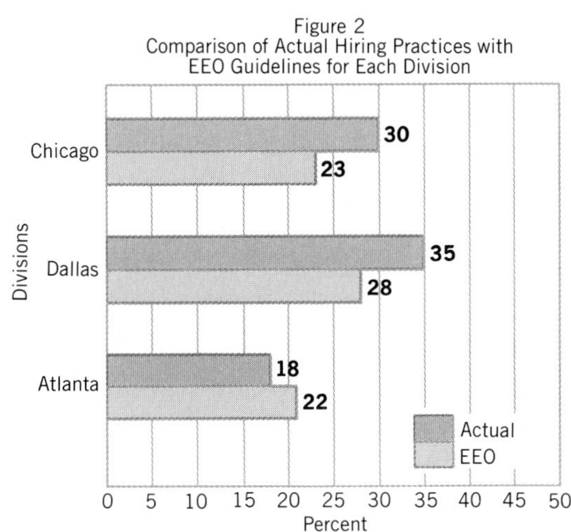

FIGURE 16-3 (continued)

5

CONCLUSIONS AND RECOMMENDATIONS

Based on the findings of this study, the following conclusions are drawn. The Chicago and Dallas divisions comply with EEO guidelines for the five-year period studied. However, the Atlanta division does not comply.

Based on the conclusions of this study, the recommendation is made that an extensive recruiting program be pursued to bring qualified female applicants into the Atlanta Division. In addition, a training program should be developed to train females for the drafting and designing positions. The EEO goals for Atlanta should be set to hire 1 female for every 2 males hired until 32 females are hired.

FIGURE 16-3 (concluded)

You can use the following checklist when preparing a formal report:

FORMAL REPORT CHECKLIST

1. *Preliminary parts*
   a. Letter or memorandum of transmittal
      (1) Write a letter when you send the report outside the company.
      (2) Write a memorandum when you send the report within the company.
      (3) Use the direct correspondence plan.
      (4) Use correspondence style and tone; avoid trite openings.
      (5) Include topics, such as cost or time limitations, major findings, conclusions, and recommendations.
      (6) Close with an appreciation for the assignment and an offer to discuss the report contents further.

b. Title page
   (1) Use a descriptive title.
   (2) Type the report title in capital letters.
   (3) Include the name, title, and address of the individual for whom you are preparing the report.
   (4) Include the name, title, and address of the report writer.
   (5) Include the date.
   (6) Center each line horizontally on the page.
   (7) Leave about equal vertical spacing between each section.
c. Letter or memorandum of authorization
   (1) Check to see what you have been authorized to complete.
   (2) If you have one, include a copy of this authorization in the report.
d. Letter or memorandum of acceptance
   (1) Check to see what you have agreed to complete.
   (2) Include a copy of this correspondence in the report.
e. Table of contents
   (1) Use a table of contents if the body of your report has five or more pages.
   (2) Include the headings of all the major divisions and perhaps major subdivisions of the report and the page number where each part begins.
   (3) Use a row of periods (leaders) that extends from the end of the heading to the page numbers.
   (4) Use the same headings in the table of contents as those that appear in the report.
   (5) Type table of contents in all capital letters and center it 2″ from the top of the page.
   (6) Center the page number ½″ from the bottom of the page.
   (7) Use a lowercase roman numeral.
f. Table of illustrations
   (1) Include the label, number, and title of each visual aid you use in the report and the page number where it is located.
   (2) Use the same titles in the table of illustrations as you used in the report.
   (3) Combine the table of illustrations with the table of contents if you have fewer than four illustrations.
   (4) Type table of illustrations in capital letters and center it 2″ from the top of the page.
   (5) If you combine it with the contents page, triple space

after the last contents entry and type table of illustrations in capital letters and center it.

(6) Center the page number $\frac{1}{2}''$ from the bottom of the page with a lowercase roman numeral.

g. Synopsis

(1) Include at least the main ideas from all the major sections in the body.

(2) Write the synopsis only after you complete the report.

(3) Limit the synopsis to one page if possible.

(4) Single space the synopsis even though you double space the report's body.

(5) Arrange the synopsis either inductively or deductively.

(6) Type synopsis in capital letters and center it 2″ from the top of the page.

(7) Center the page number $\frac{1}{2}''$ from the bottom of the page with a lowercase roman numeral.

2. *Body parts*

a. Introduction

(1) Statement of authorization

(a) Include a brief statement when you receive an oral authorization.

(b) Do not include this statement if you have a letter or memorandum of authorization.

(2) Background of the problem

(a) Include a framework within which the research problem is set.

(b) Discuss the history of the condition leading to the problem.

(3) Statement of the problem

(a) Identify the problem to be researched using clear and specific language.

(b) Answer the who, what, when, where, why of the problem.

(c) Write the statement as a question, as an infinitive, or as a declarative.

(4) Statement of hypothesis

(a) Draw the hypothesis from the problem statement.

(b) Test the hypothesis to determine the answer to the problem.

(c) Write the hypothesis in either a directed or null form.

(5) Scope of the problem

(a) Include the boundaries for the study of the problem.

- (b) Include items that might be related to the problem but will not be discussed in the report.
- (6) Limitations
  - (a) Include outside constraints placed on you over which you have no control.
  - (b) Include, among such constraints, money, time, and unavailability of information.
- (7) Sources and methods of data collection
  - (a) Discuss how you collected the data.
  - (b) Include the secondary sources you consulted, how you selected your sample, how you prepared your questionnaire, and what statistical techniques you used.
- (8) Definition of terms
  - (a) Define all terms your audience is likely to find unfamiliar.
  - (b) Define the terms using the name, class, and differentiation analysis.
  - (c) Place terms in a glossary if they are too numerous to include in this part.
- (9) Report preview
  - (a) Prepare a transition statement from the introductory section to the data analysis section.
  - (b) Include in this statement all the major topics you will discuss in the remainder of the report.

b. Data analysis
- (1) Discuss all your findings in this section.
- (2) Explain each finding in relation to the way you solved the research problem.
- (3) Use visual aids that will help the audience understand the data better.

c. Report ending
- (1) Summary
  - (a) Tie together the main points of the data analysis.
  - (b) Give an overview of the research findings.
- (2) Conclusions
  - (a) Give answers to the problem statement.
  - (b) Base each conclusion you draw on the findings.
  - (c) Do not introduce new data in this part (or any part of the report ending).
  - (d) List your conclusions with an appropriate lead-in sentence if you have several conclusions.
- (3) Recommendations
  - (a) Suggest action to be taken as a result of having answered the research problem.

(b) Draw recommendations directly from the conclusions.

(c) List your recommendations with an appropriate lead-in sentence if you have several recommendations.

(d) Combine conclusions and recommendations under one heading when there are a few of each and they are not complex.

3. *Supplementary parts*
   a. Bibliography
      (1) Provide the reader with the data sources consulted during the research.
      (2) Use an appropriate format (see Appendix D for an example).
   b. Glossary
      (1) Include an alphabetical list of technical or otherwise specialized terms you defined for the reader.
      (2) Use a glossary when you have ten or more terms to define.
   c. Appendix
      (1) Include items in this section that would interrupt the thought flow of the reading matter in the report's body.
      (2) Include such items as general tables or graphs, sample questionnaires, covering and follow-up letters or memorandums, and computer printouts.
      (3) Give a title to every appendix and label each with a capital letter beginning with A for the first appendix.
   d. Index
      (1) Include an index only when the research report is extremely long and detailed.
      (2) Arrange in alphabetical order by name and subject (or both name and subject) along with the numbers of pages where these items are located.

SUMMARY

1. Writing the report is the final step in the research process.
2. The writing phase involves applying specific writing principles, some of which were discussed in Chapters 3 and 4.
3. Use a writing style that meets the audience's requirements. This style may be either formal or informal.
4. Use a verb tense that reflects the time at which the event or series of events happened.
5. Use transitions to provide coherence to the thought flow. Transitions are especially important to use when you are presenting data.
6. Use proper headings, margins, spacing, indention, and page numbering to affect your audience positively.
7. Generally, you should divide a formal report into three main sections: preliminary, body (or text), and supplementary.
8. Although every report will not contain all the possible parts that might go in each section, you should use those parts that will aid the audience's understanding of the problem you are discussing in the report.
9. The formal report checklist at the end of the chapter details everything you should include in your report.

Review Questions

1. Discuss the effects of the report writing suggestions presented in this chapter on your work. As a student, employee, or whatever, what changes do you plan to make in the way you prepare reports as a result of this information? Explain your answer.
2. What is the difference between the informal and formal writing styles? Give an example of each. Which style is best for report writing?
3. What are two types of transitions? What are the benefits of using transitions?
4. What purpose do headings serve in a report?
5. What are the three major parts of the formal report? What purpose does each serve?
6. Which items should you include in letters or memos of transmittal, authorization, and acceptance? Explain your answer.
7. What is the purpose of a table of contents? a table of illustrations?
8. What is the difference between the synopsis (or executive summary) that appears in the preliminary parts of a report and the summary that appears in the body?
9. What is the purpose of the statement of authorization? When wouldn't you use it in a report?
10. What is the value of giving the background of the problem to the report audience?
11. What are report limitations? What effect can they have on a study?
12. Why do you define terms in a report? How should terms be defined? What is the rationale behind this format?
13. What is the purpose of the report preview?
14. What are the differences between conclusions and recommendations?
15. What is an appendix? Where should you place an appendix in a formal report?

Exercises

1. Top Brand Grocery Stores, Inc., has grocery stores in the suburbs of Portland, Oregon. During the past year, the company has expanded the health and beauty aids departments in each of its stores. The merchandise in these departments is priced slightly higher than is similar merchandise in drug and discount stores. The managers are developing a marketing and pricing plan for these experimental departments. To plan well, they need to know how many and what types of customers purchase health and beauty aids in them.

   The following data were gathered from a questionnaire given to customers who purchased these items. These questionnaires were administered at two stores between 9 A.M. and 5 P.M.

   Total customers purchasing health and beauty aids: 967

   Ages: 21 and younger, 22 percent; 22 to 30, 48 percent; 31 to 40, 18 percent; over 40, 12 percent

   Sex: females, 94 percent; males, 6 percent

   Marital status: married, 76 percent; single or divorced or widowed, 24 percent

   Employment: full-time, 72 percent; part-time, 21 percent; unemployed, 7 percent

   Frequency of purchasing items: always, 60 percent; often (every other time), 12 percent; sometimes (every third time), 20 percent; rarely (when needed), 8 percent. Two main reasons why items were purchased: time and convenience

   Write a long, formal informational report to the company's managers describing your findings.

2. You have just been promoted to the position of director of training and development at Denworth Industries. The company is located in Buffalo, New York, and manufactures specialized steel castings for the automobile industry. As one of your first assignments, the president of the company has asked you to prepare a training program for first-line supervisors in the areas of leadership, motivation, and communication skills.

   To gather the information you will need, you may have to do research in the library and perhaps interview several training directors as well.

   Write a long, formal analytical report to the president, Manuel J. Day, that includes the rationale of the new program and outlines the topics to be presented.

3. Deca Motel is a popular, high-quality, economy motel. However, during the past six months, it has experienced a decline in room occupancy. This decline follows a national trend. During this period, the price of room rates has risen slightly. Many company managers think that other reasons may possibly explain this general decline, however. To find out, you may need to do research in the library and perhaps talk to some economy motel managers. Write an analytical report for the motel's managers discussing the possible reasons for the decline. Recommend a course of action.

4. Assume that you are the supervisor of the word processing department at Owens Systems, Inc. The department operates 24 hours a day, with your employees working rotating shifts. The vice president of operations has been reading about the possible mental and physical effects that the video display terminals might have on the employees and their families. Some of the mental effects she has mentioned are insomnia, stress, irritability, depression, and lack of concentration. Some of the physical effects

are eyestrain, headaches, upset stomachs, and loss of appetites.

You will have to do some library research on the physical and mental effects of video display terminals.

Write a formal analytical report to the vice president of operations, Diane C. Velov. Analyze the possible effects of video display terminals on employees and their families and recommend possible courses of action Owens can follow to deal with this potential problem.

5. Generic products have been available in the Orchard Park area grocery stores for about a year. A variety of generic goods can be purchased that are packaged with plain labels and contain no brand names. These goods are offered by retail grocery stores at prices below those of brand-name products. As the regional director of a grocery store chain, you wanted to determine if consumers are responding to generic products as an acceptable alternative to brand-name products in your Orchard Park store. Questionnaires were distributed to customers during a two-day period from 9 A.M. to 9 P.M. each day. The data gathered with the questionnaires are as follows:

   Total number of questionnaires completed: 85

   Customer purchasing habits: bought generics, 67 percent; not bought generics but familiar with them, 27 percent; not familiar with generics, 6 percent

   Background of customers who bought generics:
   Sex—females, 77 percent; males, 23 percent
   Age—under 20, 3 percent; 20 to 30, 52 percent; 31 to 40, 28 percent; 41 to 50, 12 percent; over 50, 5 percent

   Average savings to customers who bought generics: 25 percent

   Customers who believe that quality of generic products compares well with that of brand-name products: 82 percent

   Analyze these data and prepare a formal analytical report. Make a recommendation about whether to continue stocking generic products. Send the report to the vice president of marketing, M. Aubrey Lo.

6. Compile a list of 20 common generic products that are available at four or five grocery stores in your area. Record the price of each product and then record the price of a comparable name brand. Analyze the data and prepare an informational report for your instructor. Include at least two visual aids.

7. A cosmetics buyer for a local department store wanted to determine the type of customer who purchases cosmetics. The factors involved are occupations, income levels, ages, and brands of cosmetics purchased. The buyer conducted a survey by administering questionnaires to 50 customers. The following data were gathered:

   Age: under 20, 6 percent; 20 to 29, 37 percent; 30 to 39, 32 percent; 40 to 49, 10 percent; 50 and older, 15 percent

   Family income levels: under $10,000, 34 percent; $10,000 to $20,000, 46 percent; over $20,000, 20 percent

   Occupations: professional, 29 percent; administrative, 43 percent; students, 6 percent; homemakers, 18 percent; unemployed and retired, 4 percent

   Daily use of cosmetics: 80 percent

   Average purchase range: less than $5.00, 10 percent; $5.00 to $10.00, 52 percent; $10.01 to $20.00, 32 percent; over $20.00, 6 percent

   Brand "status": extremely important, 29

percent; important, 48 percent; not important, 18 percent; no opinion, 5 percent

Assume you are the buyer who gathered these data. Prepare an analytical report for the department store manager, Sally Diaz.

8. A new company restaurant opened recently at Baxter Industries. As manager of food services, you want to determine the level of satisfaction with the new restaurant among employees who eat there. The factors that concern you are physical attributes (comfort, cleanliness, overall appearance), food (quality, portions), price, food service workers (courteous, neat, helpful), and overall satisfaction.

   You have now conducted interviews with 75 patrons (employees) to determine their reactions to the new restaurant. The following data are drawn from the interviews:

   Physical Attributes

   Outstanding, 65 percent
   Very satisfied, 22 percent
   Satisfied, 10 percent
   Not completely satisfied, 3 percent
   Not satisfied, 0 percent

   Price

   Outstanding, 25 percent
   Very satisfied, 30 percent
   Satisfied, 22 percent
   Not completely satisfied, 15 percent
   Not satisfied, 8 percent

   Food

   Outstanding, 40 percent
   Very satisfied, 50 percent
   Satisfied, 8 percent
   Not completely satisfied, 0 percent
   Not satisfied, 2 percent

   Food Service Workers

   Outstanding, 80 percent
   Very satisfied, 20 percent
   Satisfied, 0 percent
   Not completely satisfied, 0 percent
   Not satisfied, 0 percent

   Overall Satisfaction

   Outstanding, 40 percent
   Very satisfied, 28 percent
   Satisfied, 32 percent
   Not completely satisfied, 0 percent
   Not satisfied, 0 percent

   Write a formal analytical report of these findings to the vice president of finance at Baxter Industries, Allene Shaugnessy.

9. The use of celebrities in television commercials is not a recent phenomenon. Some celebrities have acted as company spokespersons for many years. However, the frequency in which advertisers choose to use them in television commercials is increasing at a rapid rate. Advertisers and their agencies constantly face the decision of incorporating celebrity spokespersons into their campaigns.

   Assume that you work in the advertising department at Bueno Industries, a company that owns 2,500 fast-food taco restaurants in the southwestern United States. The company is considering using a celebrity spokesperson to endorse its restaurants. The advertising director asked you to conduct research into the whole issue of celebrity spokespersons. Some considerations you need to research are (a) Why have celebrities been increasingly used in this capacity in the last decade? (b) What types of problems can arise with celebrity endorsements? (c) How can the effectiveness of the celebrity endorsement be measured? and (d) Are there any alternatives available to this type of advertising campaign?

Write up your findings as a long, formal informational report. Use all the major parts of a formal report, including a memorandum of transmittal to the advertising director, Sally Banara. Incorporate at least one visual aid.

10. Quality circle programs have been expanding rapidly in service-type industries across the United States and Canada. A quality circle is a small group of employees meeting together frequently to develop plans for improving all areas of their work environment.

    After reading in a business magazine about how such programs have been successful in various service industries, you wondered if it could work in your company. Assume you are an administrative manager of a large, independent, metropolitan insurance agency and you want to look into the possibility of incorporating a quality circle program at Sun Insurance Associates.

    You are responsible for 65 employees, ranging in jobs from secretaries to insurance processors. But, before you make a decision, you need to find out more about the program. How effective is it in other service industries? Have any other insurance companies tried it? What would you need to implement such a program? Would it increase productivity and employee morale?

    Prepare a long, formal, analytical report for your personnel director, Sam Billings. Present your findings and make a recommendation regarding whether Sun Insurance Associates should implement a quality circle program.

11. Many types of businesses and industries that sell a product or service look for new ways to increase their market. A tool that has experienced tremendous growth is telemarketing, and managers need to be aware of how it can be integrated into an existing marketing strategy.

    Assume you are a marketing representative with Wholesome Foods, Inc., a company that distributes health foods to various retailers. Your marketing manager, Jim Reed, would like you to look into the possibility of using telemarketing. He needs to know about its applications, how it relates to other marketing activities, and the criteria for adopting a telemarketing operation.

    Prepare a long, formal informational report on your findings for Mr. Reed. Be sure to include the rationale for telemarketing and any advantages and disadvantages of incorporating the telemarketing operation.

12. The popularity of VCRs and remote-control television has been growing at a tremendous rate. Consumers now take advantage of their time-shifting and channel-switching capabilities. Because of them, television viewing is more convenient and has fewer interruptions. But advertisers are concerned that consumers with VCRs and remote-control televisions are viewing fewer commercials. Advertisers have identified this process as "zapping," that is, the practice of fast forwarding over commercials or channel switching by remote control.

    Sandy Taylor, an owner of several furniture stores in your city, is considering using local television advertising. She has contacted you, an advertising representative for a local television station, and would like some information about the zapping problem before she makes a decision. Knowing that this potential client might not be the only one to inquire about zapping, you decide to investigate this problem thoroughly.

    Prepare a long, formal, analytical report that evaluates zapping. In it identify those viewers who zap, and what options are available to advertising personnel to reduce its effects. Send a copy of your report to Sandy Taylor.

13. Stress seems to be a common word used in today's business environment. Stress and its effects in the workplace are becoming a major health problem in the Western World. The problems stemming from it are costing businesses a great deal of money in resulting absenteeism and low productivity.

    Assume you are a general manager of a relatively new "high-tech" equipment manufacturing company. You feel the overall attitude of your employees is good, but you realize that the pressures of the job might affect some of them, including both supervisors and assemblers.

    Prepare a long, formal, informational report to submit to the president of the company, Innovations, Inc., outlining the causes of stress and how it can be reduced in a manufacturing concern. Consider its effects on both supervisors and assemblers.

14. Computers have changed many facets of daily life, including work and leisure-time activities. However, many consumers might be unfamiliar with computers because of a lack of resources, fear of the new technology, or just indifference. But this attitude does not prevail in businesses today. The use of computers by white-collar workers has increased tremendously. This trend is not evident at the middle- and top-level managerial positions, though. Most of these managers seem to be computer illiterate.

    Prepare a long, formal, analytical report on the effect of computer literacy on middle- and top-level managers. Be sure to include reasons why some managerial personnel might not be using computers. Suggest possible solutions to change this attitude.

15. Recently, the savings and loan industry has been experiencing significant disruption. Fluctuating interest rates and federal deregulation of financial institutions have created a very unstable operating environment. These problems have caused several savings and loan failures.

    Assume you are considering working in the savings and loan industry. Before you make your decision, you want to investigate the rash of savings and loan failures. You were wondering how they have affected the entire industry and what measures can be used to reduce them.

    Write up your findings as a long, formal, informational report that outlines possible solutions to your concerns.

16. Assume you are a personnel supervisor and you have been asked by the personnel director, Mrs. Jane Bellows, to determine the satisfaction of 40 employees in the Research and Development Department at Norwood Industries, a manufacturer of optical lenses for telescopes. To determine satisfaction levels, you have conducted a survey by administering a questionnaire. Of the 40 employees, 28 responded to your questionnaire. The following data have been collected:

    Sex: male, 61 percent; female, 39 percent

    Position types: professional, 68 percent; technical, 18 percent; clerical, 14 percent

    Education: college degree, 57 percent; associate degree, 32 percent; high school degree, 11 percent

    Age: 20–30 years, 43 percent; 31–40, 27 percent; 41–50, 23 percent; over 50, 7 percent

    Years in position: 0–3, 10 percent; 4–6, 23 percent; 7–10, 27 percent; over 10, 40 percent

Annual salary range: less than $20,000, 32 percent; $20,000–30,000, 50 percent; $31,000–40,000, 11 percent; over $40,000, 7 percent

Personal satisfaction: very satisfied, 36 percent; satisfied, 46 percent; neither satisfied nor dissatisfied, 3 percent; dissatisfied, 11 percent; very dissatisfied, 4 percent

Salary satisfaction: very satisfied, 32 percent; satisfied, 40 percent; neither satisfied nor dissatisfied, 10 percent; dissatisfied, 12 percent; very dissatisfied, 6 percent

Challenging job: strongly agree, 63 percent; agree, 23 percent; neither agree nor disagree, 2 percent; disagree, 10 percent; strongly disagree, 2 percent

Write a formal analytical report of these findings for the personnel director. Be sure to include at least two visual aids and an overview of what promotes job satisfaction based on a review of literature.

17. Assume you are a restaurant manager at Dailey's, a medium-priced family restaurant. The owner has asked you to look into the possibility of playing music during restaurant hours and determining what the customers' preferences are for music at each meal, that is, breakfast, lunch, and dinner.

    You have conducted a study by administering a questionnaire to 150 customers. Fifty respondents have completed the questionnaire at each meal. The following data were drawn from the questionnaires:

    Sex: males, 98; females, 52

    Age: 20–30 years old, 20 percent; 31–40, 32 percent; 41–50, 36 percent; over 50, 12 percent

Breakfast

Regularity: ate regularly at Dailey's, 80 percent; did not eat regularly, 20 percent

Of those who ate regularly: once or twice a month, 40 percent; three or more times, 60 percent

Music preference: easy listening, 51 percent; country music, 29 percent; modern music, 20 percent (No differences in music preference based on sex or age.)

Lunch

Regularity: ate regularly at Dailey's, 86 percent; did not eat regularly, 14 percent

Of those who ate regularly: once or twice a month, 26 percent; three or more times, 74 percent

Music preference: easy listening, 52 percent; country music, 30 percent; modern music, 18 percent

Sex preference: females—easy listening, 72 percent; males—easy listening, 60 percent

Age preference: 20–30 years old: modern music, 90 percent

Dinner

Regularity: ate regularly at Dailey's, 90 percent; did not eat regularly, 10 percent

Of those who ate regularly: once or twice a month, 25 percent; three or more times, 75 percent

Music preference: easy listening, 65 percent; country music, 21 percent; modern music, 14 percent

No difference in music preference based on sex.

Age preference: 20–30 years old; modern music, 86 percent

Prepare an analytical report for the owner, John Dailey. Base your recommendations on your analysis of these findings. Include at least two graphs in the report.

18. Richard Petersen, sales manager for a local cable television company, has decided to determine customers' programming preferences. Therefore, he has asked you to conduct a telephone interview with 75 current subscribers. The results of your telephone interviews are as follows:

    Cable programs watched (a respondent could indicate more than one): recent movies, 88 percent; syndicated shows, 71 percent; other movies, 63 percent; current music, 42 percent; sports, 40 percent; news, 35 percent; religious shows, 15 percent; children's shows, 10 percent; others, 8 percent

    Importance ranking of types of programming watched: 1. recent movies; 2. news; 3. syndicated shows; 4. current music; 5. other movies; 6. sports; 7. religious shows; 8. children's shows; 9. others

    Amount of cable television watched daily (mean amount of time about 3 hours): less than 1 hour, 7 percent; 1–2 hours, 25 percent; over 2–3 hours, 12 percent; over 3–4 hours, 38 percent; over 4–5 hours, 11 percent; over 5 hours, 7 percent

    Cable television versus regular television: watched more cable, 44 percent; watched about the same, 32 percent; watched less cable, 24 percent

    Weekend versus weekdays: watched more cable on weekends, 49 percent; watched more cable on weekdays, 22 percent; watched about the same on weekends and weekdays, 29 percent

    Sex: males, 30 percent; females, 70 percent

    Sex preferences: males watched three times more sports programming than did females; females watched two times more syndicated shows than did males

    Age: under 11, 3 percent; 11–18, 25 percent; 19–29, 18 percent; 30–39, 15 percent; 40–49, 28 percent; 50 and over, 11 percent

    Age preferences: respondents 19 and over watched 50 percent more news than did those under 19; respondents under 30 watched about 45 percent more current music programming than did those 30 and over

    Workers versus nonworkers: workers, 75 percent; nonworkers, 25 percent

    Workers versus nonworkers preferences: 60 percent of workers watched news regularly; 33 percent of nonworkers watched current music regularly; nonworkers watched an average of 3.5 hours per day compared to 2.6 hours for workers.

    Write a formal analytical report to Richard Petersen that describes your findings. Include at least two graphs in your report.

19. Electronic mail, an important feature in office automation, is changing the way businesses communicate. Your assignment is to research the various types of electronic mail systems available on the market. You should present both library research and interviews with representatives from at least three companies that distribute electronic mail systems. Prepare an interview guide to use during these interviews and place a copy of the guide in the final report's appendix.

    If needed, you might contact various users of electronic mail systems and determine their satisfaction with the particular system they use. Any responses they give may be inserted directly or indirectly into the report.

    Assume you are an independent office automation consultant. Prepare a long, analytical report of your findings addressed to a client, Jim Mills, Office Manager, Tailwind Manufacturing.

20. You have just been hired as a personnel specialist at First State Bank, a large bank located in your area that has 927 employees. The personnel director, Ms. Cindy Romero, has asked you to evaluate the types of complaints that result in grievances at First State Bank. Consequently, you have interviewed a manager in four departments of the bank: (a) office manager, (b) accounting manager, (c) trust manager, and (d) data processing manager. The rankings in the table below are the results of your interviews.

Complaint	*Office*	*Accounting*	*Trust*	*Data Processing*
Promotion	4	1	3	1
Layoff	8	8	6	6
Transfer	2	2	4	3
Sexual harassment	6	7	7	8
Working conditions	5	5	8	7
Shift assignment	7	4	5	5
Merit increases	3	3	2	2
Personality conflict	1	6	1	4

Note: Data are based on the last fiscal year.

You may also need to do some library research regarding grievances and how other companies deal with them. Apply your library findings to the interview findings and prepare an analytical formal report. Send your report, along with a memorandum of transmittal, to Ms. Romero.

CHAPTER 17

PRESENTING INFORMAL REPORTS AND PROPOSALS

Lisa Torres is assistant operations manager of a medium-sized hotel in San Francisco that is as famous for its understated luxury as for its attentive service. Recently, however, guests have begun to complain about rude behavior by some of the staff, particularly in the hotel's main restaurant. Lisa's boss has asked Lisa to look into the matter and report back to her at the end of the week.

After only a couple of days, Lisa thinks she has pinpointed the cause—dissension in the kitchen, which has spread to the dining room staff. She is ready to write the report, but should it be formal or informal? Lisa hesitates for a moment, reviewing her options, and then makes her decision: since she has been asked to keep it short and as the subject is small—although potentially serious—she will write an informal report.

In the last chapter, you learned how to write a formal report because that approach seems to be the most effective way to discover what goes into a report and how to put one together. Such reports, however, are less common than are informal reports. In this chapter, then, we turn our attention to informal reports and proposals, describing their characteristics and basic format. After this discussion, like Lisa Torres, you should be able to decide whether a situation calls for a formal or an informal report.

CHARACTERISTICS OF INFORMAL REPORTS

Can you name five characteristics of an informal report?

Essentially, informal reports have the same function as their formal counterparts: to transmit data to readers for either informational or decision-making purposes. (Lisa Torres's report will do both.) Moreover, they are prepared in the same way; that is, for both, you use the same process to define your problem, the same techniques for collecting data, and the same methods to create your visuals. Still, an informal report is distinguished by the following five characteristics:

1. *A length that does not exceed five pages.* Only when you have supplementary parts, such as appendices, should you extend the report beyond five pages.
2. *An informal writing style.* The writing style is usually quite informal—personal and conversational. It is characterized by first- and second-person pronouns. (For this style, follow the principles detailed in Chapters 3 and 4.) Remember also to limit the use of self-references, such as I, me, and my.
3. *Less detailed data than in a formal report.* Depending on the nature of the problem, your informal report may be informational or analytical. If it is informational, the data in it do not have to be as

detailed as do those in a formal report. Similarly, if it is analytical, your interpretation of the data can be less detailed.

4. *A deductive organizational plan.* Because managers are busy people, they often prefer to know the solution to a problem before reading the details. For this reason, many business writers use the deductive plan in informal reports. However, such a decision always rests on your analysis of the problem. If, as a result, you decide not to use the deductive plan, you can try any of the others discussed in Chapter 14.
5. *Few preliminary, introductory, and supplementary report parts.* Suppose the person who authorized a report is very familiar with the situation surrounding the problem. For example, he or she may be an expert in a specific marketing technique that you are asked to investigate. In such a situation, you might omit many of the introductory parts of your report. However, if this is the case, no clear rule exists about what to delete. To decide, review for yourself your reader's requirements in terms of audience analysis. Because informal reports are shorter and less detailed than are formal reports, you may also remove some preliminary and supplementary parts. Here again, decide on the basis of your audience's needs or requirements and the demands set by the nature of the report itself.[1]

How would you compare informal report parts to formal report parts (see Chapter 16)?

Some of the parts you might include in an informal report are

I. Preliminary parts
   A. Letter or memorandum of transmittal. Document sent by you presenting the report to the reader. Include it when you use the manuscript format for your report. (The next section of this chapter will detail the requirements for manuscript layout.)
   B. Title page. Contains the report's title; the name, title, and address of the individual for whom you prepared the report; your own name; and the date. Use this page only with the manuscript layout.

II. Body parts
   A. Introduction
      1. Statement of authorization. Reminds your reader that you have received verbal authorization to complete the project.
      2. Background of the problem. Gives the reader the framework within which to view the problem.
      3. Statement of the problem. Identifies the problem you are going to solve.

[1] See *Report Writing for Business* by Raymond V. Lesikar and Mary P. Lyons. (Homewood, Ill.: Richard D. Irwin, Inc., 1986), pp. 130–133, for another discussion of the characteristics of informal reports.

4. Sources and methods of data collection. Tells the reader how you collected the data.

B. Data analysis (findings)

C. Report ending

1. Summary. Gives the reader an overview of your findings.
2. Conclusions. Provides answers for your problem statement.
3. Recommendation(s). Suggests actions to take to solve the problem.

III. Supplementary parts

A. Bibliography (or references). Lists the sources you consulted in compiling the report.

B. Appendix (or appendices). Contains general material that is not critical to developing the report's main points or body.

FORMAT OF INFORMAL REPORTS

What four formats are used to prepare informal reports?

The four formats used to prepare formal reports are (1) memorandum, (2) letter, (3) manuscript, and (4) form. The first three may contain headings, footnotes, tables and figures, and perhaps, as needs dictate, some supplementary items. In contrast, form reports require that the writer fill in information in prearranged blocks or spaces.

Memorandum Reports

When is memo report format called for?

The memo is the most common format for informal reports, with millions of memo reports being written daily. The reason for its popularity is that within companies, people usually employ informal reports to communicate data, and the memo is an appropriate format for internal written messages. For specific information on format design and requirements, consult the following parts of this book: Chapter 16 for headings and an in-depth description of the parts of a report; Appendix D for documentation; Chapter 15 for tables and figures; and Appendix B for the memo's parts, margins, indentions, and spacing.

About spacing: Most writers use single-line spacing in the body or text of their memos. If you employ double spacing instead, be sure to indent the first line of each paragraph five spaces. Figure 17-1 shows an analytical memo report that is deductively organized.

Letter Reports

Suppose you need to prepare a report for an accountancy firm about your methods of profit sharing. For reports such as this, where your readers are outside the company, use a letter format. At the begin-

your friendly bank . . .

THE FIRST NATIONAL CITY BANK

MEMORANDUM

To: Vince Simpson, Senior Vice-President

From: Paula Miller, Supervisor

Date: July 15, 1987

Subject: Effect of the SEI Computerized Accounting System on Trust Administration

Recommendations

Our bank should remain on the SEI system, although we need to: (1) Give additional training to trust administrators now that we have switched from the old manual system. They need to understand better the reports and other system information generated by this computerized accounting system; (2) Review the input forms to determine if revisions are possible to reduce the amount of clerical work by our trust administrators.

These recommendations resulted from interviews you authorized on July 11, 1987. I interviewed seven trust administrators who have experience with both the SEI system and the old manual system. For the purpose of making this study, the administrators' various responsibilities were separated into four major categories: (1) new accounts establishment, (2) account administration, (3) asset administration, and (4) report preparation.

New Accounts Establishment

All seven administrators interviewed said that establishing a new account is more complex and time consuming under the SEI system. However, the administrators think the data available through the system are more beneficial and complete.

Account Administration

Receipts of income, principal, and disbursements are perceived to be more accurate and dependable under the SEI system by those interviewed, except one administrator who thinks no change in receipts has resulted.

Opinions about disbursements are divided almost equally. Three think that the increased clerical work required is too time consuming. The other four did not mention this clerical work as a negative factor for handling disbursements.

. .

FIGURE 17-1 Memo report

2

All the administrators believe that when transactions are coded correctly, income tax information can be obtained more readily and will be more accurate under the SEI system.

Asset Administration

Although the investment data are equally clear under both systems, administrators noted that the integrity of the investment data under the SEI system is far superior to that of a manual system. Three administrators mentioned a problem with pricing tape.

All the administrators cited the benefits to the customers and the accuracy of the investments as highly beneficial when the cash management function is computer controlled.

Report Preparation

Each administrator found the computerized reports to be both useful and timely. However, some of the reports are difficult to interpret and understand.

All the administrators reported that customer statements are more attractive, and are being prepared on a timely basis.

If you agree with my findings, Vince, I'll be glad to discuss with you the steps that will be necessary to implement a training program for our trust administrators and to redesign the input forms. I can meet with you any time this Friday.

FIGURE 17-1 (continued)

ning, include a subject line that clearly states the report's contents. The content of a letter report should be the same as that of a memo report, with one exception: your letter should contain the customary opening and closing statements that go in letters.

What is letter report format called for?

For specific information on the letter report's format and design, consult the following sources in the book: Chapter 16 for headings and an in-depth description of the report's parts; Appendix D for a documentation; Chapter 15 for tables and figures; and Appendix B for letter parts, margins, indentions, and spacing.

About spacing: Most writers use single spacing in the body or text of their letter reports. If you choose to double space, then indent each paragraph five spaces. Figure 17-2 shows an analytical letter report that is inductively organized.

August 24, 1987

John R. Tabor, General Manager
Benson Manufacturing Company
645 State Street
Florida City, FL 33034

Dear Mr. Tabor

Subject: Interest in Company Supported Financial Cooperative

On July 8, 1987, you authorized Marketing Research Unlimited to sample several of your employees' responses to determine whether they might support a financial cooperative.

Problem and Method

Several factors were considered to determine whether Benson Manufacturing Company employees could benefit from the savings and loan services that a company cooperative could offer. These factors were satisfaction of service received from present financial institutions, employee interest in borrowing money, and personal investment habits.

To find out the amount of interest in establishing a financial cooperative, I interviewed a sample of 25 employees. Of the 25, 11 presently are working as managers while 14 are not managers.

General Banking Service Favorable

Area banking services appear to be satisfactory. The employees described the services they received as prompt, courteous, dependable, and efficient. Convenience is a major factor in choosing where to get banking services.

Interest Keen in Borrowing Money

Even with the high interest rates charged by financial institutions, employee interest in borrowing money remains high. Fifty-six percent of the employees reported that changing interest rates on consumer loans have had little or no effect on their decisions to borrow money.

Even though fluctuating interest rates have affected fewer than half of the employees, the number of outstanding loans is high. Also, 10 of the 25 employees interviewed seek financial assistance every four years.

FIGURE 17-2 Letter report

John R. Tabor
Page 2
August 24, 1987

Investment Habits Irregular

With the cost of living increasing almost daily along with the fluctuations in the prime lending rate, it is not surprising that your employees' investment habits are unstable as well.

Only 44 percent of the employees have savings accounts. The high interest rates paid on money market certificates have contributed to the lack of interest in having savings accounts. The remaining 56 percent of the employees would be willing to invest in a savings account which would offer them a return of at least 7 percent.

If a 7 percent return were offered to the employees on their savings, almost one half of them would be willing to invest between $50 and $100 monthly. The employees' monthly savings investment is shown in Table 1.

Table 1

Dollar Distribution of Monthly Savings Investment

Monthly Investment	Number of Employees	Percent
Over $200	1	4
100 - 200	2	8
50 - 100	12	48
Under 50	10	40
Total	25	100

Recommended Action

This sample of 25 employees shows a definite interest in establishing a company supported financial cooperative. However, before a decision is made, I recommend that you conduct a company-wide survey to determine more precisely how many employees would support a cooperative and what financial services would be of most use to your employees.

Should you need any explanation of any part of this report, Mr. Tabor, please call me at 754-1234. Also, if you want to pursue the company-wide survey, I would be happy to conduct it for you.

Sincerely yours

Linda White

Linda White
Research Associate

Enclosure

FIGURE 17–2 Printed form report.

Manuscript Reports

When is it okay to use manuscript report format?

Sometimes your audience may prefer that you use a manuscript format for your report. Or you may prefer it. The manuscript format is like that of the long, formal report discussed in Chapter 16, with some modifications. As mentioned earlier, these modifications involve deleting a number of preliminary, introductory, and supplementary parts to achieve the shortness of length. More specifically, the letter or memorandum of transmittal and the title page are the only preliminary parts to include. As for the introductory and supplementary parts, insert only those you need. Finally, use either the inductive or deductive plan. Chapter 16 and Appendix D provide information on the format and design for manuscript reports.

Printed Form Reports

When might you prepare a printed form report?

In certain routine situations, such as yearly job appraisals of the people in your department, you might be asked to use a printed form report. Mostly, these informal preprinted reports are useful when you need similar information periodically. Some examples are periodic reports, job-related reports, and performance appraisals. A sample form periodic report is shown in Figure 17-3.

The checklist on page 521 should help you to write your informal report by describing its characteristics, what parts of the formal report to use, and the proper format.

CHECKLIST OF INFORMAL REPORT CHARACTERISTICS AND FORMAT

Characteristics

1. The report is no longer than five pages in length.
2. You plan to use an informal writing style—personal and conversational.
3. Your report is not detailed.
4. You plan to organize your report deductively. (However, you can use an inductive plan.)
5. Your report contains only those preliminary, introductory, and supplementary report parts that are necessary to convey your message.

Format

6. The memorandum format is used for writing to someone inside your organization.
7. The letter format is used for writing to someone outside your organization.

REQUISITION

GLENVIEW COMPUTER GRAPHICS CORPORATION

SUB-PURCHASE ORDER NUMBER ____________

DATE ____________

TO: ____________

QUOTER: ____________

PHONE: ____________

PROCUREMENT DEPARTMENT USE ONLY:

BID NUMBER ____________

ESTIMATE ______ CONTRACT ______

STATE PRINTER ______ STATE STORES ______

SUB. P.O. ______ STATE SURPLUS ______

DATE ______ TYPE ______

BUYER ______ NO. OF COPIES ______

MAIL ______ PHONE ______ WALK THRU ______

AGENCY BILLING CODE ______

STATE CONTRACT NO. ______ SPS ______ DATE NEEDED ______

QTY	UNIT OR MEASURE	DESCRIPTION (Color, Size, Catalog No., Make, Model, Length, Width, Height, Etc.)	BUDGET EQUIP. OR ITEM NO.	UNIT PRICE	EXTENSION
				SUBTOTAL	
				TAX	
				TOTAL	

DELIVER TO: BLDG. ______ ROOM ______ PHONE ______ SCHEDULE NO. ______

I hereby certify upon my own personal knowledge that the above estimated expenditures are necessary to perform the function stated hereon and authorize this expenditure.

APPROVED BY ____________ REQUESTED BY ____________

DEPARTMENT ____________ DEPARTMENT ____________

FUND NO. ____________

PAGE ______ OF ______ PAGES

FUNCTION ____________

LINE ITEM ____________

Form A11 Rev. 5/80

FIGURE 17–3 A Sample Periodic Report.

8. If either you or your audience prefers a manuscript form, then use it. If you do use it, send along a transmittal memo or letter.
9. The printed form format is for reports that contain similar information that is periodically requested.

TYPES OF INFORMAL REPORTS

Today many different types of informal reports exist. Some may be one-page printed forms for special-purpose reporting. Performance appraisals are an example. Usually, these are quite simple. Some informal reports may, however, be more complex and detailed. Feasibility reports are an example. The following is an annotated list of some kinds of informal reports you may have to write in your business career.

When is a report considered to be periodic?

1. *Periodic report.* A periodic report informs managers of the activities that have occurred during a specific time period. This period may be daily, weekly, monthly, or even yearly. If you have to prepare the annual report to the stockholders, then you are writing a periodic report.

How would you compare a feasibility to a justification report?

2. *Feasibility report.* A feasibility report is an analytical report that presents solutions or evaluates alternatives to resolve a problem. Its purpose is to determine whether you can put your solutions or alternatives successfully into effect. For example, you might write a feasibility report in which you investigate whether it would be better for your company to buy letter-quality or dot-matrix printers for the new office computers.

Think about it: Could a progress report also be a periodic report?

3. *Justification Report.* A justification report recommends what action should be taken to solve the problem. In it you recommend an action and then justify or explain your decision. For example, you might write a justification report to explain why it is so important for your division to have four new salespeople in the Midwest territory.

What does a process report entail?

4. *Progress Report.* A progress report informs the reader about the status of a particular project. You might write such a report during the various stages of the project, including in it what work is completed and needs to be completed. For example, if you write a monthly report about the installation of video monitors to keep managers informed, you have prepared a progress report.
5. *Process or Procedure Description Report.* A process or procedure description report gives the reader directions on how to complete

some process or procedure. Such reports usually involve step-by-step instructions and some kind of visual aid. For example, if you composed a report to people in your department explaining how to use the refined microcomputer software program in manuscript preparations, it would be a process or procedure description report.

TYPES OF PROPOSALS

What are two keys to writing a successful proposal?

Suppose you want to write a proposal to your boss suggesting a way your advertising could avoid zapping—the methods consumers devise to escape TV commercials. If your boss agrees with your idea—essentially to group compatible commercials—then he or she will send it out to the company's clients and the various networks. You think your idea is great, but you have never written a proposal before. How should you go about it? First, remember that a well-written proposal is a persuasive blend of information, organization, and reason. Moreover, the key to writing a persuasive proposal is *planning*. Two basic types are the *sales proposal* and the *research proposal*.

Sales Proposals

Naturally, you will send your sales proposals outside the company to potential clients or customers. Most of the time yours will not be the only proposal, as competitors will also want to make the sale. To be successful at acquiring this perfume company or that shoe manufacturer as your client, you will probably not only have to present excellent reasons for them to follow your suggestions, but you will also have to try to break down their resistance. This means putting yourself in their place and thinking about why they might be frightened by your idea or even hostile to it.

Since you are dealing with people outside the company, use the letter format for sales proposals. To woo them, write in an informal style. Generally, you should organize your report inductively.

Do all sales proposals look the same?

Sales proposals rarely duplicate one another in either organization or style. In fact, they often take quite different and creative directions. For example, you might decide to try some advertising technique and use professionally designed visuals aids to persuade the perfume company to go along with some of your selling ideas.

Sometimes you too might include contractual offers. Such offers would obligate your company to deliver goods or services, such as TVs or radios, by a specific time for a specific price. Whenever you include such an offer, review it carefully to make sure you can really deliver when you say you can. Even if your proposal is a bit long or a bit short, organize it according to the following inductive pattern:

1. An introduction, which describes the exact nature of the proposal.
2. A body, which describes in detail the specifications and cost breakdown.
3. A conclusion, which describes your company's ability and desire to meet the specified stipulations.

Research Proposals

Sometimes you might have to propose a design for a research project and to justify it to your superior as well. If you complete such a proposal, you will

1. Outline the precise steps to develop the project.
2. Check the research or project design for possible errors in logic and/or feasibility.
3. Have a guide to follow during the actual working stages of the research study.

Whatever your research project, the basic content does not vary. Thus, try to include each of the following 12 items in every proposal you write. (Of course, you will delete some depending on the demands of your audience and of the project itself.) Figure 17-4 shows a completed research proposal that is organized inductively.

What would you try to include in every research proposal you write, regardless of the topic?

1. *Title page.* The title page contains the proposal's title, the names of the granting body or individual and of the preparer, and the date.
2. *Abstract or summary.* The abstract or summary tells the reader exactly what you plan to do, how you will do it, and what it will cost. Limit this part to between 100 and 300 words, depending on the length of the proposal.
3. *Background.* The background statements introduce the proposed research topic. It also includes a discussion of the context of the problem. For example, you might review the literature, relating other research efforts to your proposal.

RESEARCH PROPOSAL TO RESOLVE EXPANSION PROBLEM AT

BETA SPORTING GOODS, CHICAGO, ILLINOIS

Statement of the Problem

This study analyzes three possible expansion sites within the Chicago, Illinois, area for Beta Sporting Goods and determines whether expansion is feasible within the next two years.

Scope of the Problem

This report will analyze three expansion sites for Beta Sporting Goods. Each site will be evaluated and compared based on cost, site selection, competition, traffic flow, demand, projected sales, and employee availability. No attempt will be made to study the costs of constructing a new building. This aspect will be studied in depth once a site is selected.

Sources and Methods of Data Collection

The data for this study will be collected from various market analyses of the Metropolitan Chicago area. Interviews with commercial real estate brokers as well as with various school athletic personnel will be completed. Public records also will be reviewed to gather tax information on each site and to determine if any restrictions apply to the site under consideration.

Tentative General Outline

I. Cost

   A. Land

   B. Licenses

   C. Taxes

   D. Insurance

II. Site Selection

FIGURE 17-4 Research proposal.

2

III. Competition

A. Individual stores

B. Department stores

IV. Traffic flow

V. Demand

A. Consumers

B. School Athletic Programs

VI. Projected sales

VII. Employee availability

A. Managerial

B. Sales

VIII. Conclusions and recommendations

Time Requirements

January 7	Review overall research proposal with owner.
January 8 - January 14	Discuss potential sites with commercial real estate brokers.
January 15 - February 1	Conduct a market analysis for various sites selected.
February 2 - February 3	Consult various municipal records for tax information and restrictions.
February 4 - February 8	Interview school athletic personnel located around each site.
February 9 - February 11	Organize and evaluate the data.
February 12	Review preliminary findings in meeting with owner.
February 13 - February 20	Prepare the report.
February 21	Submit final report to owner.

FIGURE 17-4 (continued)

3

Personnel

Mr. Tom Talbert will be the principal investigator in this study. He has had 12 years of experience in the market analysis area.

Budget

The following is a breakdown of the costs for completing this study:

Investigator's stipend (research, travel, report preparation)	$2500
Secretarial costs (typing, duplication)	250
Total	$2750

FIGURE 17-4 (concluded)

4. *Statement of the problem.* The problem statement clearly specifies what you intend to investigate. In it you should explain why the problem exists and the benefits that will come from the proposed research.
5. *Scope of the problem.* The scope section define the study's boundaries.
6. *Limitations.* The limitations section describes the restrictions over which you have no control, such as that some of the information is classified and, therefore, unavailable.
7. *Sources and methods of data collection.* The sources and methods of data collection section explains how you will gather and analyze your data. If you plan to use a questionnaire, include a copy of it in the appendix.
8. *Tentative general outline.* The tentative outline section details in outline form the factors you may have identified.
9. *Time requirements.* The time requirements section gives details of the exact amount of time you will need to complete the proposed project. For example, you might use a time chart to show how long each of your activities will take.

10. *Personnel.* The personnel section lists the names and credentials of the people who will conduct the research. For each, you might also include a personal data sheet in the appendix.
11. *Budget or cost requirements.* The budget or cost section provides a breakdown of all the estimated costs for the project. It should include such items as supplies, typing, duplicating, computer time, and travel.
12. *Appendix.* The appendix should contain all supporting reference documents the reader might wish to see.

Use the following checklist for preparing sales and research proposals:

CHECKLIST FOR PREPARING SALES AND RESEARCH PROPOSALS

Sales Proposal

1. Use persuasive language because the proposal will probably be competing with others.
2. Present reasons for taking a course of action.
3. Anticipate any possible reasons for rejection and provide suggestions for overcoming them.
4. Use the letter format and an informal writing style.
5. Review offers of goods and services as well as the time period to provide these and the price.
6. Use an inductive pattern.

Research Proposal

1. Use this proposal to justify a research study.
2. Outline the precise steps you will use in the project.
3. Check your research design for possible errors in logic or its feasibility to complete.
4. Use manuscript format and informal writing style.
5. Consider the following items when writing the proposal:
   a. Title page
   b. Abstract
   c. Background
   d. Problem

e. Scope
f. Limitations
g. Sources and methods of data collection
h. Tentative general outline
i. Time requirements
j. Personnel requirements
k. Budget
l. Appendix

SUMMARY

1. Informal reports do not exceed five pages, are written in an informal style, use less detailed data than do formal reports, are deductively organized, and contain few preliminary, introductory, and supplementary report parts.
2. The format of informal reports can be memorandum, letter, manuscript, or form.
3. Selecting the proper format depends on the nature of the report and the audience's needs.
4. Some common types of informal reports are periodic, feasibility, justification, progress, and process or procedure description reports.
5. Two types of proposals are sales and research.
6. A sales proposal offers goods or services to clients or customers within a particular time period and for a specified price.
7. A research proposal is a plan for designing or justifying a research project.

Review Questions

1. Which five characteristics distinguish informal from formal reports?
2. Why use a quite informal—personal and conversational—writing style for informal reports?
3. Why limit the use of self-references (I, me, my) even though the style may be informal?
4. What is the value of the deductive organizational plan in informal reports?
5. Is there any specific rule that aids a report writer in selecting the number of preliminary, introductory, and supplementary report parts? Why?
6. What role do the audience's needs play in writing informal reports?
7. Why are memorandum reports used as a common informal report format?
8. Why is the letter format used to send reports outside the organization?
9. What purpose does a subject line in a letter report serve?
10. What is a form report? What are some situations in which a report writer might use a form report?
11. What is a proposal? Why do report writers prepare proposals?

12. Why does a proposal require persuasive language?
13. What concerns does a report writer need to remember about the content of sales proposals?
14. What is the primary purpose for writing a research proposal?
15. How does the research proposal differ from the sales proposal?

Exercises

1. You have just been promoted to personnel director at Sunshine Stores, a company that specializes in low-cost household goods. The company president, Mr. Fred Cate, asked you to review the selection interview process. A selection interview is a formal, in-depth conversation with an applicant to evaluate the applicant's acceptability. His concern stems from the fact that he would like to have a consistent approach to evaluating candidates throughout this process, no matter who conducts the interview.

   Prepare a memorandum report for the president that outlines the different types of selection interviews, the correct procedures to follow, and the key qualities interviewers should seek in candidates. Include at least one visual aid.

2. The Japanese management style has resulted in the highest productivity rate in the world. What is it that makes their management style so different from western management styles? Prepare an informal report in a manuscript format that describes the key features of the Japanese management style and that compares and contrasts it with western styles. Documentation of the library information is necessary.

3. The system of flexible working hours gives employees some freedom in choosing the hours they work each day. Usually, management establishes core hours, a midday period when all employees must be present, with flexible times at both ends of the working day.

   Assume you are a management consultant, and you have been asked by a client, Galloway Industries, to look into such a plan. Prepare an informal report in letter format to the vice president of operations, Ken Bowman, that outlines the features of flexible working hours. If possible, interview an official whose company uses this plan. Incorporate these results in your final report where appropriate.

4. Assume you are a newly elected treasurer of a nonprofit organization. Its board of directors has instructed you to look into the possibility of purchasing a microcomputer for the office staff. You have decided to evaluate three different models and make a recommendation to the board. Some of the features you might need to assess are word processing capabilities, operator convenience, software, training, service, printers, and price. Visit at least three vendors and interview each regarding these features.

   Write up a memorandum report of your findings addressed to the board of directors. Include at least two visual aids to support your findings. Write the report using a deductive organizational plan.

5. The open office plan, when it was first proposed, was one solution for dealing with the dramatic changes occurring in

the office. This plan has resulted in increased productivity. It has also made the offices more accessible to all the employees. However, the plan has not worked well in some offices.

Your company is expanding and needs to remodel its office. Your supervisor has asked you to study the open office plan. Currently, your office is designed in the traditional plan. Your assignment is to evaluate the reasons why the open office plan is acceptable and why it is unacceptable in today's offices. Present your recommendation to your supervisor, Melinda Guenther.

Prepare a memorandum report using an inductive organizational plan. Include a recommendation about specific concerns that your supervisor should consider before selecting an open or traditional office plan. If possible, try to interview some employees who work for companies that have an open office plan. Include their reactions in your report where appropriate.

6. Assume you have been working for several years, and you have decided to go into business for yourself. You have saved a considerable amount of money and are interested in investing in a franchise. Prepare a short, informal report in manuscript form that evaluates the advantages and disadvantages of franchising. Include a checklist for what to look for in a franchise. You will need this report when you begin to look at the possible franchises available for consideration.

7. Assume you are a personnel supervisor and your boss, Mary E. Bartow, has asked you to develop a new employee orientation program. You know how important such a program may be because it can make a very lasting impression on employees. Considerable planning will be needed to prepare an effective program. Your assignment is to write an informal report in memorandum format addressed to Mrs. Bartow, the personnel director. You will need to conduct library research on orientation programs and develop a plan from other companies in your area, including their reactions, on orientation programs in the report.

8. Advertising by law firms has increased substantially in the last few years. As an account executive with a local advertising agency, you have been asked by your sales manager to study the issue of advertising in the legal profession for a potential client, Berne and Temple, attorneys at law. The firm is considering an advertising campaign, but it wishes to see how the public views this issue. Prepare a letter report addressed to Nick Berne, a partner, outlining how consumers perceive law firms that advertise their services.

9. Because of the highly competitive nature of many businesses and the diverse makeup of employees, conflict is often the outcome between and within companies. Conflict can be positive, but it can also be destructive, if not handled properly. You are a personnel officer with a local insurance agency. The owner of the agency has asked you to evaluate conflict in organizations. Prepare a memorandum report for the owner, James Michie Orloff, that describes the consequences of conflict and the skills involved in managing it.

10. As more and more businesses expand their operations, the need for trained personnel to cover these operations has caused the number of relocations of personnel to rise. Generally, companies' attitudes are very favorable toward the

relocation issue, but employees who relocate often have varied attitudes toward the practice. As a management consultant, you have been asked by one of your clients to study the effects of relocation on employees and their families. Write up your findings in a letter report addressed to Cindy Allen, operations manager at Certified Oil, Inc. Be sure to include what the company can do to deal with this situation.

11. Assume you are a research associate with Marketing Specialists, Inc. One of your clients, a local drugstore chain, has asked you to conduct a price comparison study. Choose five drugstores and select one as your target store. Evaluate the following product lines at each of the five stores: hair care, dental care, deodorants, shaving needs, aspirin, antacids, and beauty care. Analyze the data and prepare a letter report addressed to Millicent Cary Dare, the manager of the target drugstore.

12. Embezzlement is one of the fastest-growing office crimes in the United States. Each year, millions of business dollars are literally stolen as a result of embezzling. This problem is found in all types and sizes of businesses. As your assignment, look into this important problem. Write up your findings as an informal report in manuscript format. Library research and documentation of these data are necessary.

13. With the impact of technology in the office, a new area of concern has evolved that affects computer operators of video display terminals (VDTs). Some evidence exists regarding the physiological effects of the video display terminal on the operator. As an information processing supervisor, you have been asked by the operations manager, Jill Telper, to evaluate the potential problem of VDTs. Your supervisor has read somewhere that VDTs can cause eye strain, muscle and bone pain, and even radiation exposure. How true are these conditions? Are there others? What can a company do to alleviate these problems? These are some of the questions you want to answer in your memorandum report to Ms. Telper.

14. Perhaps the most effective and efficient informal communication network in an organization today is the grapevine. The grapevine can be both beneficial and destructive. As a management consultant, you have been asked by your client to evaluate the grapevine in organizations. This assignment requires library research on the ways a company can implement methods of handling the grapevine effectively. Prepare a letter report of your findings and send it to Sam Ziletti, general manager of Best Furniture Products, Inc.

15. Assume you are a marketing analyst with Marketing Methods, Inc. A supermarket client has asked you to find out the reasons why customers shop at a competitor, Dempsey's Supermarket. Seventy-five customers were questioned as they entered one of Dempsey's stores, and the results are as follows:

    Service: 92 percent, service was better than at other markets.

    Cleanliness: 94 percent, cleanliness was better than in other markets.

    Specialty departments: 72 percent, specialty departments same as in other markets; 28 percent, better

    Prices: 83 percent, prices better than in other markets; 17 percent, same

    Specials: 65 percent, specials better than in other markets; 25 percent, same; 10 percent, other markets better

Variety: 61 percent, variety better than in other markets; 24 percent, same; 15 percent, other markets better

Prepare a memorandum report of your findings using a deductive organizational plan. Include at least one visual aid.

16. Many offices are built and renovated each year. Two of the major considerations in these projects are the effects of color and lighting on workers in the office environment. What things does a person making the decision on the color and lighting for an office need to know? Prepare an informal report in manuscript form that describes your findings. You will have to conduct library research. If possible, talk to several office workers regarding their perceptions of color and lighting.

17. Assume you are a manager for a medium-priced restaurant, Dine Out, serving American food. You are conducting a customer survey regarding atmosphere, food and drinks, service, and satisfaction. One hundred customers have responded. The results of the survey are as follows:

Atmosphere

Decor: very comfortable, 89 percent; too mellow, 5 percent; too gaudy, 6 percent

Lighting: just right, 84 percent; too bright, 14 percent; too dark, 2 percent

Background music: just right, 67 percent; too low, 10 percent; too loud, 9 percent; didn't notice music, 8 percent; no comment, 6 percent

Food and Drinks

Temperature of dinner: just right, 82 percent; too cold, 12 percent; too hot, 1 percent; no comment, 5 percent

Overall dinner: excellent, 46 percent; good, 32 percent; fair, 14 percent; poor, 4 percent; no comment, 4 percent

Drinks: just right, 64 percent; watered down, 12 percent; didn't have drinks, 16 percent; no comment, 8 percent

Service

Timing of waitress/waiter: served at a good pace, 68 percent; too slow, 28 percent; rushed dinner, 3 percent; no comment, 1 percent

Overall performance of waitress/waiter: excellent, 48 percent; good, 37 percent; fair, 4 percent; poor, 7 percent; no comment, 4 percent

Satisfaction

Customer: will be back again, 74 percent; will not be back again, 10 percent; undecided, 16 percent

Write up your analysis of these findings as a memorandum report. Address the memorandum to Mrs. Sarah Anne Bell, owner of All-American Restaurant. Include at least one graph and use a deductive organizational plan.

18. Assume you are a sales representative for Desert Solar Water Heaters, Inc., and are preparing a sales proposal for a potential client, Ace Homebuilders, Inc. Ace is planning to develop several large tracts of homes in the Houston, Texas, area. Your purpose is to get Ace to offer solar heating as an alternative system to potential homebuyers, and you want to be Ace's supplier.

For this assignment, you will need to do some library research regarding the benefits of solar water heating. Also, if possible, talk to a distributor of solar products and include this information in the proposal where appropriate. Send the proposal to Tony Berelli, President, Ace Homebuilders, Inc., 2650 Spaceway Dr., Houston, Texas 00000.

19. Prepare a sales proposal in which you present a plan to increase sales at Champion Cement Block Company. In this proposal, state that you will investigate the competition, along with the prices they charge for their products. Mention that your company should consider expanding its operations to other local cities. Suggest several distributors at these locations. Suggest too that it promote products to related companies, such as construction companies, homebuilders, and so on. Write the proposal in letter format and send it to Joe Bill Turpen, president of Champion.

20. Prepare a sales proposal for a charitable organization on the development of an effective volunteer program. Include in the proposal such features as recruiting, screening, training, motivating, and rewarding volunteers. Make up a nominal fee for the program. The thrust of the proposal should be your explanation of how you will aid the organization in these areas. Use a letter format.

REPORT CASE PROBLEMS

The following extended—long—case studies are included to provide you with an opportunity to work on business cases that require various types of research and writing skills to solve a single problem. Essentially, these cases will test the skills you learned while studying written reports in Part 5. But in a few instances, you are asked to apply the writing skills learned in Parts 3 and 4—correspondence and employment. Also, should your instructor ask you to present a report orally as suggested in some options in several cases, consult the chapters in the next section, Part 6, Oral Communication and Special Applications.

AN IDEA WHOSE TIME HAS COME

Several members of a fraternity at a large university were having a discussion concerning a persistent problem. "We are broke again," Chuck said. "So we always are broke, or almost broke, or going broke," George answered. "Why don't we try to come up with a regular money earner instead of the one-shot things we usually do?" The idea seemed to interest several of the others, but it was Pete who posed the obvious question: "Okay, George, how do we do it? What can we do in our spare time to earn money regularly?" George had to admit he didn't have the answer, but he thought if everyone contributed ideas, they would be able to find something that would work. "All right," Pete said, "let's do that."

At the end of an hour during which everyone suggested ideas for earning money for the fraternity, Pete had composed a list:

- Telephone answering service
- Escort service
- Tutoring
- Car wash
- Odd job bureau
- Room cleaning service
- Gardening service
- On-campus taxi
- Pet grooming

At that point, the people there began discussing the ideas and discarding them one by one for one reason or another. Some were discarded because they seemed not to offer a regular income. Others did not interest those who would have to do the work. Still other ideas seemed to demand too much time. The list was rapidly reduced until only on-campus taxis and pet grooming remained. The taxi idea got a lot of interest because the campus was large, and student activities required movement from place to place. While walking was the usual practice, some people used motor bikes or bicycles. Driving was inconvenient, even for those with automobiles, because parking spaces were scarce, expensive, and inconveniently located.

For these reasons, everyone agreed that a taxi service probably would generate steady income, especially in the winter months. The idea began to look less practical, though, when Roger pointed out the liability that carrying passengers created. A phone call to Chuck's insurance agent confirmed that a standard auto insurance policy would not cover liabilities incurred in taxi service.

"Well then, what about pet grooming?" George asked without too much enthusiasm. "A lot of people in town have pets. They probably don't have time to give them all the care they need." Several people agreed that the need was there, but they weren't too enthusiastic about actually doing the grooming. "Say, wait a minute, guys!" George shouted. "We've got an idea! We don't have to do the grooming. All we have to do is pick up the pets, take them to a professional service for grooming, and then return them home afterward. Look at it this way: people don't really like spending their weekends doing a job like this. And anyway, that's the time when pet places are the busiest." "That's right." agreed Pete. "With our different schedules, we could do it during the weekdays. We'd charge a fee for our services, and we could probably get insured for carrying pets in my van."

This idea was the best they had had, so they agreed to research it further to determine if it really had money-earning potential. Everyone agreed that each of them would investigate one of the following issues:

1. How many people would be potential customers?
2. What pet care facilities existed and where were they located?
3. Besides the van and a telephone to take orders, what other equipment would they need?
4. What liability would they incur in offering this service, and what insurance coverage would they have to have to cover it?
5. How much money would they need to start the operation and maintain it for a trial period of three to six months?
6. How should they organize the operation?

After assigning these issues, everyone agreed to meet again in one week to examine the answers to these questions and decide whether to proceed.

Student Activities

1. Your instructor will divide the class into teams, each member of which will research one of the six questions. Each team member should write an analytical memorandum report of the findings for use in deciding whether to proceed with the project.
2. *Option A:* Prepare to make an oral report of your findings based on the report you wrote for Exercise 1.
   Option B: Prepare to participate in a group discussion in class in which you present the findings for the question you were assigned to answer in Exercise 1.
   Option C: Prepare to participate in a roundtable-style (small-group) discussion in which you are seated at the front of the class. Plan to present the findings for the question you were assigned to answer in Exercise 1.

THE UNQUALIFIED APPLICANT: A NEED TO KNOW THE LAW

A substantial increase in the number of commercial/industrial customers made it necessary for Comdial Corporation, located in Waltham, Massachusetts, to expand its credit administration group.

Lesley Knight, Comdial's director of industrial relations, placed a display job advertisement in the *Boston Globe* (see Figure 11-3 in Chapter 11 in the text for a sample job display ad). He believed that suitable candidates for the position were likely to be employed by a Boston-based firm. His instinct proved accurate because 20 people from that area responded to the ad.

After carefully reading the letters, resumes, and other data provided by the potential candidates for the advertised position, Mr. Knight selected seven of them for interviews. He then wrote a form letter inviting the seven for a visit.

The interviews proceeded smoothly until the fourth candidate, a male member of an ethnic minority, arrived accompanied by a member of the same ethnic group and introduced her as his wife. Mr. Knight then asked the wife to wait in the outer office while he interviewed her husband. To his surprise, the husband refused, adding that, "My wife is also my attorney."

Feeling that the attorney should not be present, Knight again asked that she wait outside. When he was rebuffed once more, he suggested that they postpone the interview. The applicant replied that if the interview were held then, no legal action would be taken because of this perceived offense. Feeling really threatened now, Knight said he felt the company's interest required a staff attorney's presence also. He then called the legal department and requested assistance. In a few minutes Jennifer O'Reilly, an experienced attorney, arrived to join the small group on the company's behalf.

As the interview proceeded, it became obvious that the candidate had falsified his resume. For example, his attorney balked at Mr. Knight's statement that he intended to call the candidate's college to verify the degree listed on the resume. Questions concerning his employment experience got similar responses. The applicant had worked there "a long time" or "quite a while," but he could not confirm the dates of employment, which were not included in the resume. Although he could remember few details, he had "done well" on all his jobs.

By now, Mr. Knight and Ms. O'Reilly believed they were being set up for a discrimination suit. Knight concluded the interview then, and the couple left. O'Reilly told Knight to write down all details he remembered of the interview for possible use in case their suspicions proved true. She asked him to clear with her any letters written to the candidate before mailing them.

Student Activities

1. Research the legal and ethical issues involved in the case and then
   a. Write a refusal letter to the candidate that Jennifer O'Reilly will approve for mailing.
   b. Prepare an analytical memorandum report for your staff members in industrial relations explaining the federal laws that might be cited if a lawsuit were to result. Include an analysis of how each might affect a company like Comdial.
2. *Option A:* Orally report to your class on the legal and ethical issues involved in the case. (Your instructor may assign this as an individual or a group project.)
   Option B: After asking your staff members to read the report mentioned in 1(b), call a staff meeting to discuss the issues. The purpose of the meeting will be to amend your interviewing guidelines to protect Comdial's interests should a similar event occur in the future. Of course, Ms. O'Neill or another company attorney must approve the guidelines. The

seven members of your staff who conduct interviews will meet with you in Conference Room A, a small room containing an oval table, comfortable chairs, and audiovisual equipment.

THE CASE OF THE UNWANTED PROMOTION

Bill LeHigh was a business college graduate working as a senior proposal cost estimator for a major missiles and electronics manufacturer. The company employed about 25,000 people at three major locations. The location where Bill worked had four plants and employed about 11,000 people performing a wide range of job duties. Bill's job required good interpersonal communication skills because he dealt frequently with different types of people in other departments within the firm. He had to obtain cost estimates from them for use by his division, which produced specialized weapons systems for the military. After obtaining these estimates, Bill used the information in preparing proposals for approval by company executives before they were sent out as bids for contracts from military branches that wanted a particular system built. If a bid was too high, the firm had little chance of getting the contract because of the stiff competition. If it was too low on the other hand, and the contract was awarded, the company would lose money.

As you can see, this job was very stressful. Some of Bill's colleagues called his work "the pressure cooker." But he seemed to enjoy it and did well.

THE COMPANY FORCES BILL TO MAKE A DECISION

In fact, Bill's superiors were so pleased with his job performance, they offered him a supervisory position when it became available. The work would be entirely different from the job he had been doing. He would be overseeing a group that monitored current contracts. The people who would be working for him collected actual costs for personnel, hardware, overhead, and other expenses. They then charged these expenses to the proper contracts to make certain that the work done did not exceed estimates. Also, this information provided a basis for billing the customer.

Bill had mixed feelings about whether to accept the new position, which he disclosed to a friend at lunch one day. On the one hand, he liked the idea of getting a promotion along with a substantial pay increase. He was also pleased that his hard work had been recognized. Too, he admitted that the offer "really turned his wife on." She would be very disappointed if he declined. And if he did turn it down, he might be labeled as someone who lacked ambition.

On the other hand, the job itself didn't appeal to Bill nearly as much as what he was doing. As he put it, "I would be shut off from all the people I deal with throughout the company, and that is what I really like about my work." In addition, he would be supervising 10 people, a responsibility that concerned him because he had never supervised anyone before.

After talking with a friend, who just

listened and helped him to clarify the issues, he deliberated as long as he could. But when the deadline came for him to accept or reject the promotion, he accepted it. Reluctantly, he gave up the proposal cost-estimating work he enjoyed because he and his wife agreed, "a better life awaited" as a result of the rewards of the new job.

After requesting and receiving permission to complete two critical proposals before assuming the new job duties, Bill moved to his new office, which was located in another building. During the first few weeks on the new job, however, he returned often to visit his former associates and to check on progress being made on unfinished work he had left behind.

BILL TRIES TO ADJUST TO THE NEW POSITION

Bill immediately began trying to learn the new job. On the first day, he met with each member of his group individually, though briefly. He then met them as a group on the second day. At this meeting, he encouraged people to suggest any problem areas that he should look into and any changes they felt should be made in the department's procedures. The subordinates spoke reluctantly and then only in generalities. Afterward, Bill concluded that very little value had come from the meeting.

Later in the week, he met for lunch with his new immediate superior, Jill Jacobsen. Between the main course and dessert, he asked for guidelines from her on how to run the new department. In return, he received only general answers from her as well. Essentially, he was free to run it as he felt it should be run, and she promised whatever support he required. This response left him unnerved; he felt he needed more guidance. The lack of structure and the responsibility that came with being so "free" bothered him. He felt he was left with a new job that he had to learn, but without any clues as to how to proceed from either his superior or his subordinates.

So Bill began to sort things out alone, feeling a bit that way too. He spent the next few weeks studying written procedures, getting to know his subordinates, examining the work flow, and learning the routine. During this time, he made no decisions that he was not forced to make. He needed time to readjust. This went on for a month, at which time he decided that he didn't want the job! The realization came late on a Friday afternoon.

BILL LEAVES THE COMPANY

Throughout the weekend, Bill pondered his situation; the more he thought about it, the more he wished he had his old job again. The job had been filled, though, so there was no turning back. After talking at length with his wife, they decided he should try to get a more suitable job with another company. So, on Monday morning he didn't go to work. Instead, he began visiting the employment offices of other companies where he felt he might be hired as a proposal cost estimator.

Three employers Bill visited were interested in hiring him. In fact, one made him an offer immediately after calling Mr. Smith, who had supervised him when he was a cost estimator. He then telephoned his wife, and they agreed that he should accept the offer before leaving for home.

Accepting the offer meant he would be making less money again, though, and he would have to drive 50 miles each way to work until they could relocate their residence.

Bill had been with the company from which he was now resigning for eight years.

Student Activities

1. Write a letter of resignation addressed to Bill's superior, Ms. Jill Jacobsen.
2. a. Research the topic, "Personality Traits of Effective Managers Who Like Their Work." Then prepare a long, formal analytical report addressed to your instructor (or the person your instructor designates).
   b. Prepare an oral report based on the written report you wrote for 2(a).
3. a. Assume that you work for Ace Consultants in your city and have been asked by Militant Merchandisers to prepare a report on "Factors to Consider When Deciding Whether to Accept a Promotion." (Militant is a huge department store chain headquartered in your city.) Prepare the final version of your study as an informational letter report documented with at least three secondary references.
   b. Prepare an oral report based on the written report you wrote for 3(a).

TROUBLE AT SYNCON: CAN COMMUNICATION PROBLEMS BE THE CAUSE?

Syncon Industries is a large electronics manufacturing company located in Cleveland, Ohio. The family-owned firm has been in business since 1920. The president, Al Norbert, has held this position since 1952, when his father, Tom, retired.

Syncon has a relatively simple organizational structure. In addition to Mr. Norbert, Bill Vestom, vice president of manufacturing; Paul Barker, vice president of marketing; Sally Davenport, vice president of finance and controller; and Maria LeClerc, vice president of personnel, make up the executive committee. All together, the employees number 785, including the executive officers. The manufacturing division, the largest, has 682 employees; marketing, 25; finance and accounting, 52; and personnel, 21.

The company has been making a decent profit each year since its beginning. However, the past year management has noticed what appears to be a morale problem in the manufacturing division. They thought that perhaps the wages paid to the employees were not competitive, but after an extensive study of the wages paid industrywide, Syncon's averaged 15 percent higher. They also studied the working conditions not only in the manufacturing areas but also in all the other divisions as well. But this study showed no problems big enough to affect employee morale. The executive committee was perplexed. They really had no idea what might be causing this problem, but they were extremely concerned because of its potential effect on operations. Maria LeClerc suggested they bring in a consultant to isolate the problem if possible and recommend some solution to it.

Betty Reynolds, a management consultant specializing in human behavior and communications, was contracted to study Syncon's problem. Mrs. Reynolds met with each executive committee member as well as each supervisor in the manufacturing division. After meeting with the 25 members of the manufacturing management team, she met with 20 nonmanagement employees. The results of these meetings indicated that there appears to be some type of communication problem existing between managers and their subordinates: what the managers thought were problems, the nonmanagers thought were not. Conversely, the nonmanagers identified problems that the managers did not think were problems at all. So, Mrs. Reynolds decided to survey the entire manufacturing division. She thought that by getting everyone's ideas about what the existing problems are—management and nonmanagement—she would be able to identify some of the key problems and, it is hoped, provide some solutions.

She began the process by developing a questionnaire and administering it to 25 managers and 557 nonmanagers. After two weeks, she received 23 managerial and 465 nonmanagerial replies. (She did not need to follow up with the nonrespondents because she had a large enough sample.) The questionnaire contained 20 communication problem areas between managers and nonmanagers that she identified from the earlier interviews as well as from her professional knowledge. Each respondent was asked to rate the seriousness of each problem on a scale of 1 to 5, 1 signifying not serious and 5 signifying very serious. The results of the responses reported as arithmetic means are as follows:

	Mean	
Communication Problem	*Mgrs. (n = 23)*	*Nonmgrs. (n = 465)*
1. Know-it-all attitude	3.1	4.0
2. Lack of credibility	3.8	3.4
3. Inadequate feedback	2.5	3.6
4. Resistance to change	4.2	3.2
5. Lack of knowledge	3.8	2.4
6. Listening	3.1	4.2
7. Prejudice or bias	3.0	3.9
8. Information overload	2.4	2.8
9. Lack of trust	2.5	3.2
10. Perceptual differences	3.8	2.4
11. Jumps to conclusions	4.1	3.4
12. Lacks understanding of technical language	4.1	3.0
13. Defensive	3.4	2.8
14. Lacks organization	3.6	2.3
15. Poor timing	2.8	3.5
16. Personality conflicts	3.1	3.9
17. Emotional reactions	4.0	2.8
18. Hostile attitude	2.9	3.9
19. Lack of interest	2.3	2.1
20. Poor spatial arrangements	2.0	2.2

Assume you are Mrs. Reynolds's research assistant and she asked you to analyze the data from the questionnaire. In addition, she needs a literature review regarding possible communication problems between managers and their subordinates. When you are analyzing the data, try to identify any patterns or trends that may be similar or dissimilar between the two groups. Consider possible solutions that you can recommend to reduce or eliminate some of the more serious problems. Prepare a long, analytical report addressed to the members of Syncon's executive committee. Include all the necessary preliminary and supplementary parts. Also, prepare an oral presentation, along with visual aids, that you will make to the executive committee.

PART 6

ORAL COMMUNICATION AND SPECIAL APPLICATIONS

CHAPTER 18

ORAL PRESENTATIONS AND ORAL REPORTS

In response to a request by his boss, Richard Chen has prepared a report on the feasibility of moving the division from its midtown office in New York City to the suburbs. After some study, Chen has concluded that such a move would save the company $4 to $5 million a year on rent. His report recommends that management search for property in Westchester County, New York, so that "We can put our money into products and people instead of real estate."

Now, three days after the study has been submitted, Chen's boss has asked him to present his conclusions and recommendations to the board of directors at the monthly meeting next Tuesday morning. Since Richard Chen has never presented an oral report—much less appeared before senior management—he is understandably nervous. Sitting at home later that evening, Richard Chen wonders how he should prepare for Tuesday.

The four basic steps in preparing written and oral reports are the same: (1) selecting a topic, (2) collecting information, (3) evaluating and organizing the information, and (4) presenting it. In this chapter, we will focus on how to prepare and deliver an oral report. After reading the material, you should feel confident when you are asked to present information orally.

SELECTING A PRESENTATIONAL STYLE

Richard Chen is not the only one who has to appear before his company's board of directors. At the end of the week, you also have to present an oral report. Again the subject is real estate, although the topic is quite different from that assigned to Chen—your topic is whether your hotel chain should acquire a rundown 200-room hotel located in a "tough" area near the commercial district in a large city. The question you have to answer is: How do I present my report?

What are the four types of presentational styles?

First, you need to consider the size of your audience, who its members are, the occasion, the type of information you are presenting, and the medium to be used. Keeping those in mind, you can then choose between these four presentational styles: *impromptu, extemporaneous, manuscript,* and *memorized.*

Impromptu speaking occurs when you are asked to say "a few words" without warning. Thus, because you have no time to prepare, your remarks are spontaneous and informal. Also, in such reports, you do not have to work to capture the audience's attention. Since it is they who have initiated the topic, what you have to say will automatically be interesting to them. Also, the informal structure encourages you to adjust your speech as you go along on the basis of feedback. However, although such reports can be lively, they pose some risks. Since you haven't carefully considered your words, they can get you into trouble. To avoid this, don't make dramatic statements, announce policy changes, or initiate long-term commitments in an impromptu presentation.

Extemporaneous speaking occurs when you have time to plan and prepare the presentation of your report. Like impromptu, it is a type of informal speaking, but you do prepare for it. Although you should devise such speeches carefully, do not, however, write them out or memorize them. Also, use only a few notes when speaking. In this way, you can appear natural—the great advantage of this spontaneous speaking—and make changes in response to your audience's reactions.

Manuscript speaking occurs when you decide to prepare completely for a presentation, writing down the exact words you will say. This means that you should study the situation beforehand. Then, as you compose the speech, polish your phrases, writing and rewriting them until you are satisfied. Next, practice aloud until you are similarly satisfied. In this way, you take advantage of the main asset of using a manuscript: it provides the chance to perfect both language and delivery.

But this style of presentation also has some disadvantages. For one thing, you cannot easily change a word or phrase or introduce a new notion while speaking. For another, it is quite difficult to appear spontaneous. In fact, you may sound "canned." Some extremely gifted speakers are, however, able to seem as if they are making up their words on the spot. They can do this because, in addition to having full command of the language and the issues, they know their audience well.

Why are memorized presentations the most difficult to present?

Memorized speaking occurs when you talk without a manuscript because you have memorized the information in it. The advantage of such presentations is that you can give your complete attention to the audience while speaking. However, you need to be careful not to offset this advantage by "going up on a line," that is, forgetting for a moment where you are in the speech because you don't know what you have just said. This can happen during a memorized speech. In fact, the likelihood that you will do this increases with the amount of material you have memorized.

Why does it happen? Apparently, the more precisely we memorize information, the less attention we pay to it as we speak.

Another disadvantage to such presentations is that they may sound too formal. Also, your chance to respond to feedback is limited and for that matter making any adjustment is difficult because every word, sentence, and illustration is fixed before you begin speaking.

Fortunately, technology has come to the aid of speakers who wish to present a carefully planned speech in a more natural style. Teleprompters are devices much like television sets that project typed pages so the speaker can see them; in short they allow the speaker to read a speech without appearing to do so. This, of course, solves major difficulties associated with manuscript and memorized speeches. If, for example, a corporate vice president wishes to make a speech to a gathering of 300 stockholders in a large meeting room, he or she could use a teleprompter situated in full view for easy reading, but that would be almost unnoticeable to the audience. The speaker would then be able to focus on effective delivery rather than on content. At this time, though, teleprompters are not adaptable to small or informal group speaking situations, nor are they widely available.

Generally, which is the most useful presentational style?

Generally, though, the best way to present oral material is to make an extemporaneous speech. This style takes advantage of the more casual atmosphere created by an informal presentation. Yet, when speaking extemporaneously, the speaker has prepared well for the presentation.

Evaluate the situation and determine the best approach. Only after you have reviewed each and have decided on your style can the actual preparation begin.

PREPARING THE PRESENTATION

Proper preparation requires three things: choosing the topic, determining the purpose, and defining the problem.

Identifying Topic, Purpose, and Problem Statement

How do topic, purpose, and problem statement differ from one another?

The *topic* is a general statement that outlines the subject. It may even become the title of the presentation if you need one. The *purpose* is your goal or objective. For example, your goal may be to deliver information about nuclear plants or persuade your audience to invest in a resort you are planning to build. Knowing your purpose should help you determine the contents of the presentation. It should also help you to evaluate afterward if you were successful. For example, if a high percentage of the audience decides to invest in the resort, your presentation must have been effective. (See Figure 18-1 for a possible setting for this type of presentation.) The *problem statement* is a brief but precise description of what your presentation is about. Usually, it defines the topic in one clear sentence.

Suppose you are making a short presentation on the company's credit union at a luncheon for new employees. In it you plan to cite a list of short-term loan services offered. First, you start with a topic. One that you come up with is, "How Your Credit Union Works for You." However, although topic statements may be general, this is too

FIGURE 18-1 Oral presentation in a formal setting.

general because you want to talk only about short-term loan services. A better topic statement, then, might be, "How a New Employee Can Apply for a Short-Term Loan."

The next step is to determine your purpose. What goal do you want to achieve? The topic implies you will talk about which short-term loans are available and then explain how to apply for them. So far, the purpose is informative. But do you also want to encourage your audience to apply for such a loan? Assume here that you do not; therefore, your purpose is only to inform, not to persuade.

Now you are ready for the next step, which is to state the problem clearly, briefly, and precisely. Based on the topic and the purpose you have identified, here is a possible problem statement: "The problem is to identify and describe the short-term loan services offered to new employees by the company credit union and to explain how to apply for such a loan." Notice how specific this statement is. It restricts the topic and thereby defines the boundaries of the presentation. As such, use it in the next stage of your preparation: collecting information and adapting it to your audience.

Collecting Information and Adapting It to Your Audience

Collect the information for your oral presentation in the same way as for written reports. (See Chapter 13 for information on planning research and collecting data.) When gathering data, try to have an excess. Knowing more about the subject than you need to will help you do a better job with both the presentation and the question and answer period, should one follow it.

Chapter 1 contains a detailed discussion on adapting material to your audience. Remember, adaptation includes carefully considering the information on their demographics, psychographics, and previous knowledge of the subject. Only after such an analysis can you shape your material to the level and character of the audience.

What are "brights"? Where can you find them?

While conducting research, also gather *relevant* quotations, anecdotes, or stories to capture the audience's attention. Your local library holds a wealth of such material. For example, *Bartlett's Familiar Quotations* contains thousands of quotes on hundreds of subjects. Consult, too, specific speakers' and toastmasters' handbooks. You can use such attention-getting material, called "brights," throughout your speech—in the beginning, the middle, and the end.

When you begin to organize the collected material, select a *general format* to ensure a good information flow.

Selecting a General Format

Experienced business speakers are aware that their audiences are going to have a harder time listening to a report than reading one. To help them follow your oral presentation, organize it according to any of the following patterns:

1. *Time or date.* The time or date pattern is chronological, where events take place in a time sequence. You present items as they happened, as is done in a story, history, or diary.
2. *Space.* The space pattern is a physical arrangement of some type. An example is to describe an office layout by beginning with a key location, such as with the receptionist's desk at the entrance. Then you would continue to the next important location, then the next, and so forth.
3. *Cause and effect.* The cause and effect pattern works on the assumption that events contribute to other events in various ways. Giving proof that shows a valid link between events is crucial to the effectiveness of these patterns. An example is using medical data to link cigarette smoking and lung cancer. You might reverse this pattern in some cases by proceeding from effect to cause.
4. *Problem solving.* This pattern follows this sequence: identify a problem, analyze data about it, and then derive a solution from the data. An example in industry is (a) to discover that an assembly-line method is slowing production in the plant (identifying a problem), (b) to study methods that might resolve the problem (analyzing data), and (c) to choose the best method to resolve the problem (deriving a solution).

5. *Inductive or deductive.* The inductive pattern begins with details and leads to the main idea. The deductive pattern begins with the main idea and continues to details. See Chapter 3 for a discussion of how to arrange information in these patterns.
6. *Basic components.* This pattern employs a parallel division of major parts of a topic. For example, you might divide a talk on food stores into four general areas: meat, produce, canned goods, and packaged goods.
7. *Comparison and contrast.* This pattern allows you to show two sides of an issue by evaluating the "pros" and "cons" or exploring similarities and dissimilarities.

After you select the appropriate format, you are ready to begin the basic development of the presentation itself—the introduction, body, and conclusion.

Putting Together the Basic Development

What are the three elements of an oral presentation?

Simply put, an oral presentation has three elements: a beginning, a middle, and an end. They are more commonly called an *introduction*, a *body*, and a *conclusion*. Together, these elements form a whole, which makes this type of message a "presentation." For listeners, the greatest value of this organization is that it segments the presentation for ease of understanding and evaluation.

The Introduction

In a speech, the first minute or two is the most critical time. It is now that listeners form their impressions of you and your message, quickly evaluating your competence, merit, and whether you are somebody who is interesting or uninteresting. If the presentation begins well, it will probably continue well with little effort like a well-oiled motor. But if it starts badly, no matter how good the remainder is, you may have lost your audience.

The introduction also serves a number of other functions. To turn a "collection of people" into a "group of attentive listeners," it should

1. *Introduce the subject clearly.*
2. *Bring the audience to a common level of knowledge about the topic so they can understand what follows.* For example, historical background, definitions of special terms, and a brief review of the events that led to your presentation can achieve this goal.
3. *Set the mood for the presentation.* Moods range from the pleasure evoked by an awards presentation for excellent service to the somberness that accompanies an announcement of worker layoffs.

4. *Arouse audience interest in the topic.* Make what follows seem worth the audience's attention. Ideally, interest in a topic grows out of a speaker's credibility.
5. *Establish a personal or professional rapport between yourself and the audience.* For example, use personal pronouns.
6. *Preview the organization of your speech.* Remember, listeners cannot read the information. If confused, an audience will quickly lose interest until the organization is firmly established.
7. *Prepare the audience for visuals.* If you are going to use visual aids, explain what they will be and their purpose in the presentation.
8. *Create a smooth transition to the body of the presentation.* Usually the opening of a presentation is the most difficult part of the speech to write. For this reason, many experienced speakers compose the introduction last, after the rest of the speech is firmly laid out. The following checklist of introductory techniques should help you get started:

CHECKLIST OF INTRODUCTORY TECHNIQUES

1. *Quotation* A phrase or passage especially well worded or relevant enough to the topic to be quoted directly. Quotations from authorities on the topic work well.
2. *Humor* A story or anecdote to please the audience. It should relate to the topic.
3. *Novelty* A surprising statement to grab attention quickly. The statement may come from the topic itself or from a relevant outside source.
4. *Mystery* An unanswered question to build intrigue.
5. *Journalism* A "real-life" incident, for example, describing an event, including names, dates, and other factual information.
6. *Statistics* Significant numerical data on the topic.
7. *Visual aid* A graphic aid to introduce the subject.
8. *Occasion* A reference related directly to either the audience or the occasion.
9. *Commonality* A direct appeal to a problem or situation shared by all members of an audience.

About humor: Nothing can capture an audience's attention more quickly or turn it off in an equal amount of time than humor. Therefore, try not to force it or be too obvious. Instead, let it grow naturally out of the topic and employ it to underscore some basic points in your presentation. Also, don't overuse it. For example, when an audience senses that a speaker is building from joke to joke, they may perceive the presentation to be a source of entertainment rather than of information. Waiting for the next punch line, they stop listening for facts.

Now that you have opened your talk, how should you move smoothly from the introduction to the body (and later from the body to the conclusion)? Use transition statements to link the various parts. What you say in them must be relevant to both the parts you are trying to link. Here your tone of voice can also cue your listeners that change is occurring. A good transition directs the audience forward, emphasizes important points, and ensures the development of the problem as each section in turn treats another aspect of it.

The Body

What is the relationship between a general format and the body of a presentation?

The main part, or body, of your presentation contains the major amount of information. Basically, the data should support your problem statement. When developing the body, pay special attention to the material's complexity. For example, do give listeners enough data to understand your major points—about the future of the International Monetary Fund, for example. Consider the amount of time available, however. That is, don't spend 20 minutes of your allotted 35 minutes on your introduction, explaining what a negotiable bond is when your audience already knows.

The body of a good oral presentation develops logically from idea to idea, following one of the general formats presented earlier in the chapter. And it prepares the listeners for the conclusion to follow. In fact, if the speaker does a good job, the listeners may well draw the conclusion before hearing it. Even if not, they won't be surprised to hear the conclusion because the facts of the body will have supported it well.

The Conclusion

If audiences form their first impressions during the introduction to an oral presentation, they form last impressions during the conclusion. Closing statements linger in listeners' minds and, if effective, shape their thinking about the topic afterward. Thus, a well-prepared conclusion should

1. Prepare the audience for the end of the presentation. Do this with the words you use and through your tone of voice.

2. Review the major points of the presentation and draw conclusions from these points.
3. (If persuading) urge members of the audience to take action or alter their opinions.
4. Leave room for feedback from the audience. A question and answer session can provide this opportunity.
5. Tie together any remaining points.
6. Disengage yourself from the audience by ending gracefully.

Below is a checklist of concluding techniques,

CHECKLIST OF CONCLUDING TECHNIQUES

1. *Summary* A review of major points of the speech.
2. *Quotation* A phrase or passage quoted from a relevant source, especially if said by someone who is well known in the field. Use the quotation to draw together the ideas presented in the body.
3. *Illustration* A real or fictitious event that shows a vivid example of the problem statement.
4. *Appeal* Either a suggestion to take action or an appeal to change a belief.
5. *Charge* A challenge to change future events through direct involvement.
6. *Statistics* A summary of relevant data on a topic.
7. *Motivation* An inducement based on an audience's psychological needs.

Once you know what to say in the introduction, body, and conclusion of your oral presentation, its basic development is complete. Your next step, then, is to prepare an outline.

Drafting the Outline

Experienced speakers use outlines to remind themselves what points to make and in what order. As you remember, most of your oral presentation will be extemporaneous. For such speeches, prepare the outline on paper or cards. When using paper, try the white standard size ($8\frac{1}{2}'' \times 11''$). When using cards, try either $4'' \times 6''$ or $5'' \times 8''$, but avoid the smaller $3'' \times 5''$ variety, which can slip from nervous hands during a presentation. Whether you use paper or cards, be sure to keep to the outline form throughout; if you start mixing forms, you will be unable to easily read and follow what you have written.

Which type of outline generally works best for presentations in most situations?

You can choose from three types of outlines: *topic, phrase,* or *sentence.* Of these, topic is the shortest, and you can put it together quicker than either of the others. However, its brevity forces you to rely more heavily on your memory.

A phrase outline contains more information about the subject than one that is topical. Here you should use verbs and direct objects, deleting all but essential words. Finally, a sentence outline is composed of complete and grammatically correct sentences. Although it also contains more information than a topic outline, transition statements may sound awkward because they are not as developed as the ideas. (See Chapter 14 for more information on outlining.)

For this reason—and because of the extreme brevity of the topical form—phrase outlines work best in most situations.

Putting Together the Outline

Usually, you will need to prepare a complete outline. Type it in capital letters. Number the pages or cards. If you wish, highlight important points in vertical columns, leaving wide margins for any special notes you might want to add about delivering the speech. For example, next to one point about the value of negative taxation, you might add "Argument weak here. Yell!"

What are the strong points of an alternative outline format?

A second, or *alternative,* format joins a full narrative style with an outline. Composed of a written introduction and conclusion, which bracket an outline, it contains enough material to keep you from feeling at a loss for information yet permits a great deal of control at the same time. Because of its flexibility, you can rearrange points, shift emphasis, or even lengthen or shorten the speech. If necessary, you can also easily supplement the body with support and reference material. Using this format, however, means you must know your subject well enough to adapt the material as you are speaking.

Figure 18-2 is an example of this alternative format. Note that the introduction and conclusion appear verbatim as you will deliver them, but the body is outlined in phrases. As stated, you can use this format to change the length of your presentation with ease. Suppose, for example, you are making a 20-minute informative speech to small-business owners considering the purchases of word processing systems, following the outline in Figure 18-2. Suddenly, the president of the group signals that you have five minutes left, just as you begin Part IIB in the body. You can then either spend less time on each remaining point or touch briefly on the major ones. In this way, you can finish on time without becoming flustered or damaging the integrity of the presentation.

WORD PROCESSING: A NEW OFFICE SYSTEM

Purpose

The purpose is to explain the development of word processing as a technology and a procedure.

Problem Statement

Word processing is a technologically based system that will influence how people manage offices and handle information.

Introduction

A hundred years ago, typewriters revolutionized the world of business. Today, word processors are having much the same effect. But, for many people, they are still strange and somewhat frightening. We need not be frightened, though, because word processing is simply a natural development of modern office procedures in combination with improved technology.

Body

I. Defining Word Processing
   A. Definitions—central elements involved
   B. Effect on personnel
   C. Cost-effectiveness and efficiency
II. Historical Perspective
   A. Development and effect of typewriter
   B. Social office structure
   C. Emergence of word processing
III. Changing Office Organization
   A. Traditional organizational chart (slide 1)
   B. Word processing center organizational chart (slide 2)
   C. Comparison

Conclusion

So you see, word processing is not new. Neither is it a gadget nor a fad. Word processing is part of an evolutionary process in handling information. This system combines existing procedures with emerging technology to bring a new order to information management and processing.

Sources

Bergerud, Marly, and Jean Gonzalez. *Word/Information Processing Concepts*, 2nd ed. New York: John Wiley, 1984.

Kleinschrod, Walter, Leonard B. Kruk, and Hilda Turner. *Word Processing: Operations, Applications and Administration*, 3rd ed. Indianapolis: Bobbs-Merrill, 1986.

FIGURE 18-2 Sample outline in alternative format.

MAKING THE PRESENTATION

You have done all the preliminary work—researched, organized, and outlined your presentation. You know what you are going to say about a new drug to combat the common cold and the way you are going to say it. But now comes the presentation itself. How should you make it?

Before the Presentation

What are the ways to practice a presentation?

First, try a practice runthrough to see how it sounds. If possible, use a tape recorder to get an idea about your pace, timing, voice quality, and thought flow. Next, say your speech before a mirror to figure out when and how to use gestures and facial expressions. If you are an inexperienced speaker, practice the presentation before friends or family to obtain their reactions too.

In such rehearsals you should receive feedback about where to vary your regular speaking tone. For example, when speaking to a large group, you need to pitch your voice to reach the person in the last row. Practice also gives you a chance to solve little problems that may occur—for instance, you may have to slow down your delivery rate. This may be necessary because you are losing your practice audience by speaking too fast or you are completing the speech in less than the allotted time. For this reason, you should know how long it takes you to read a manuscript page or card aloud. Similarly, you should know how many words a minute you speak.

You may also want to visit the location where you'll be speaking. Look everything over, practice speaking there to hear how you sound, get a feel for the place, and, if possible, test any equipment you plan to use.

During the Presentation

The great moment has finally come. You have to stand up, move to the podium, and say those all-important first words. The audience is waiting and you are more than a little nervous. Calm yourself. Take several deep breaths and concentrate on your most important task: *getting your message across to these people.* Focus on them and let all else fade into the background. You are ready to start.

Getting Started

Your audience is curious about you. They want to know right away who you are. Show them. Feel poised and expect to speak confidently. For example, as you begin your introductory remarks with a small joke that is appropriate to the subject, remember to follow your note cards or manuscript. Never begin your presentation with an apology.

Using Delivery Techniques

The human voice is a remarkable instrument. With it you can produce hundreds of inflections and a wide range of volumes and tones. Use them to deliver a smooth but emphatic message. Add interest and stress important points with your voice. The audience—without their own manuscript to refer to—needs all the guidance they can get from you.

What relationship should there be between words and gestures in a presentation?

Your posture, gestures, and facial expressions must be right for the occasion. Large- and small-body movements—the way you put on your glasses, how you lean your body against the podium or stand erect—provide visual clues about your command of the situation and the subject. Such movements should underscore your words and image. For example, if your words are confident but your movements tentative, then you may be undercutting what you want to say. Similarly, your posture, gestures, and facial expression should complement your message. For example, a slouching posture and crossed arms can defeat an otherwise confident appeal for "all of us to pull together," as can exaggerated tugging at your glasses or an overstated grimace.

In addition, watch the audience and listen to them for feedback as you speak. Observing their facial expressions, attentiveness level, body movements, and degree of eye contact should provide clues about what interests them. On the basis of these, modify or adjust your remarks.

For example, suppose all the people in the front row start fidgeting or looking at their watches. Obviously, they are losing interest in your message. What should you do? The one thing *not* to do is to continue the way you have been going. Instead, change direction and regain your audience's attention.

Handling The Jitters

Call it platform jitters, apprehension, weak knees, butterflies, sweaty palms, or just stage fright. Almost everyone who speaks before groups has one form or another of this fear. Recent studies report that fear of speaking before a group is the greatest common fear that most executives have. Thus, if you feel at least some stage fright, you are hardly alone. Still the question remains: What should you do?

Some people advise ignoring it; your fear will, they predict, diminish or even disappear. But many people suffer too much to ever get the experience needed—if indeed such an approach works for everybody. You can work at building confidence by (1) establishing rapport and (2) working through your fears about your own ability.

No experience helps more than engaging in formal or informal public speaking situations. So take every opportunity to practice your skills and add to your confidence.

Confidence results from knowing that you are prepared and are ready to face whatever may arise. Therefore, don't stint on your preparation. After you have done everything necessary to make the presentation successful, defuse your stage fright by comforting yourself with the thought that you are prepared.

How can you overcome the jitters during a presentation?

Another way to boost your confidence is to realize that most audiences want a speaker to do well. In contrast, hostile audiences are both rare and predictable. For example, suppose you are preparing a speech proposing that retirement benefits be reduced. You are going to present it before a group of retired people. Naturally, you should realize that such an audience will be hostile. In general, however, expect your listeners to support you—they will.

You can also reduce your fears by focusing on the audience. This involves thinking about what they need to know about the subject and then concentrating on explaining it clearly. Watch for signals that interest is lagging or that points are unclear; correct such problems as they arise. If you are able to direct your attention from yourself to the audience, then you can thwart the major cause of self-doubt—self-consciousness.

Even with these strategies, you are still likely to have some stage fright because you want to perform well. Experienced speakers know that a small amount keeps them alert, so don't fear a little nervousness. Try, however, to not let it get out of hand. When you start feeling increasingly nervous, take a deep breath or two, and move your head around slowly to release the tension in your neck. If you make a mistake—such as losing your place in your speech—try not to let it rattle you; instead concentrate on what you are doing. In this way, you will recover quickly and naturally. If someone else makes a mistake, such as spilling coffee on your notes or pulling the plug on the microphone, acknowledge the problem, readjust, and then go on. Handled well, such incidents actually can increase an audience's attentiveness and their openness to you and your ideas.

Using Audiovisual Aids

A sure way to capture your listeners' attention during an oral presentation is to use one or more well-prepared audiovisuals. They can make your words seem more vivid, describe your ideas more clearly, and increase the amount you can say in a given time by condensing material you might otherwise have to explain.

Suppose you are making an oral report to a group of auto dealers about the increasing market for imported and luxury sports cars. You have prepared your outline and now are wondering whether to create a line graph to illustrate the change in this market during the last ten years. On what basis should you make such a decision?

Are audiovisual aids always appropriate in a presentation?

First, consider whether the audiovisual will be *appropriate:* that is, will it add to content or interest, or will it merely be a digression? Remember, no audiovisual can substitute for you; rather, it enriches your presentation by complementing what you are saying or doing. If you decide to use such aids because they meet these criteria, place them where they will add emphasis to the other parts of the presentation. (Since the line graph enriches your speech, include it.) Also learn to use such audiovisuals when needed and otherwise keep them in the background.

Once you have selected your visuals, make sure they are visible and/or audible. Can everybody in the audience see and/or hear them? Test a visual aid for visibility and an audio aid for audibility before making the presentation. Also, remember to stand to one side of visuals when describing them.

What are the types of audiovisual aids you could use in a presentation?

In business presentations, speakers commonly use samples and models, handouts, chalkboards and flip charts (large pads of blank paper mounted on easels), desk charts, illustrations, projected material, and audiotape recordings.

Samples and Models Samples and models are the easiest visual aids to use. As you describe something to an audience, you can show it as well. If the samples or models are small and inexpensive, pass them out for the audience to look at and hold while you speak. (Note, though, that this practice can distract an audience—a disadvantage.) If they are large, delicate, or expensive, do not pass them out. Also do not pass a sample or model to members of the audience if you have only one. Keep these visual aids out of sight until you need them.

Handouts Outlines, illustrations, and reference or supplementary notes are three common types of handouts. Outlines, which show the audience the organization and content of the presentation, reduce the need to take notes. Pass out your outline before the presentation begins. Illustrations clarify confusing or difficult material. Pass them out at the time during the presentation when you are ready to present the material they illustrate. Reference or supplementary notes add information about the speech topic beyond that given in the presentation. Pass them out at the conclusion of your presentation. While handouts have many advantages, two disadvantages are that they take time to distribute and that they can distract your audience's attention.

Chalkboards and Flip Charts Chalkboards and flip charts are versatile and easy to use. Use them to show how a process or procedure works. For example, you can work a mathematical equation or develop an accounting process on a chalkboard or flip chart. Remember, though, that the time you spend writing is lost time for your audience. They must wait while you write, and you have your back to them. Also, an audience may continue looking at a chalkboard after you have gone on to another point. With a flip chart, you can guard against this problem by turning over a blank page when you are ready to proceed. Keep information clear and simple. Do not crowd words or attempt to put too much information on one board or sheet.

Desk Charts Desk charts are small visual aids, approximately 8″ × 10″ in size. You can use them in the same way as flip charts, but only with small groups. In a typical situation, a manager can meet with his or her staff and show these charts while seated at a desk. For your own use, you can prepare desk charts in advance or develop them as you illustrate points. You can easily pass a desk chart around to members of your audience.

Illustrations Illustrations include tables, charts, graphs, drawings, diagrams, photographs, pictograms, and the like. Use them in oral presentations as you would in a written report, at the point where you need a visual to support or clarify your words. The subject matter and layout of illustrations depend on the topic itself and how you present the information. The best illustrations, though, are large enough to read easily and are laid out simply. Employ color to add interest and visual emphasis to the message. With a pointer, identify the place on an illustration you are covering. Be sure too that you stand aside so you do not block the view. Chapter 15 contains details on how to select and prepare the best type of illustration for your subject.

Projected Material If you prepare them properly, you can show any type of written or drawn materials on one or another type of projection equipment. Thus, you might use opaque, overhead, slide, filmstrip, motion picture, or videotape projectors. For best results, project the material on a large screen in a darkened room.

When you use projection equipment (Figure 18-3), prepare yourself for basic problems. Because things go wrong, learn to use any equipment you may require and to correct common malfunctions.

Audiotape Recordings You can use audiotapes to get across ideas and to set or change a mood. For example, the voice and words of an authority on your subject can add credibility to your presentation. Operate the equipment yourself, except where you need to interact with the material while it is playing. If you try to do this, you may find you want to make a dramatic point at the same moment you have to lower the volume or change a tape.

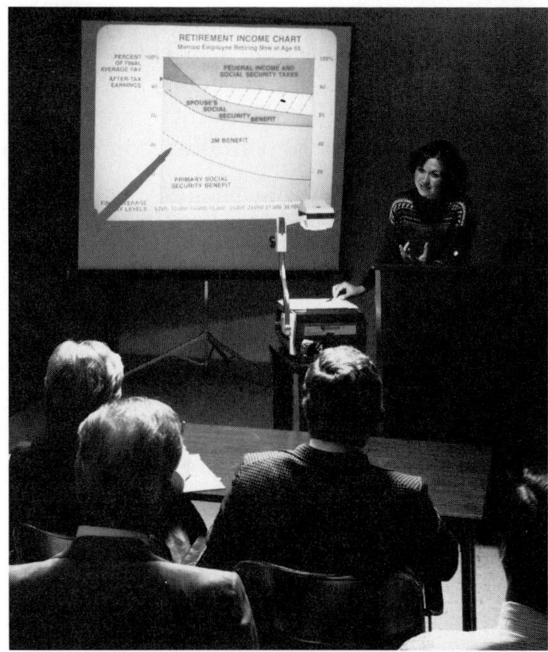

FIGURE 18-3 Use of overhead projector in informative oral presentation on employee retirement. (Photo courtesy of 3M Audio Visual Division.)

Although an oral presentation is not a multimedia event, audiovisual aids can make presentations clearer and more interesting. Choose carefully from among available aids those that fit the situation. Use the chart shown in Figure 18-4 as a guide when selecting them. When you cannot find appropriate ones, prepare your own.

After the Presentation

After your presentation, the audience has applauded enthusiastically, and you have collected your notes and put them in the large manila folder. But your job is not done—for you have allowed time for a question and answer period. You worry that you might say something that will spoil the positive impression you have made.

What can the speaker learn from a question and answer session?

Actually, question and answer sessions often follow a presentation. Such sessions give the audience a chance to clarify points for themselves and to seek further information. On your part, the session could provide a chance to obtain feedback on both the subject and the manner of your presentation. Allow sufficient time for questions and try to answer them concisely and meaningfully.

Listen to the questions to find out (1) what responses are required and (2) how well you presented your ideas. For example, the

VISUAL AIDS SELECTION CHART

Equipment	*Audience Size*	*Advantages*	*Disadvantages*
Samples and models	Limited only by sample/model size	Allow three-dimensional or multistage view	Usually expensive
Flip charts	Up to 30; depends on chart size	Inexpensive; easy to use; no projection required	Limited audience size; difficult to carry
Desk charts	Up to 5	Small enough to place on desk; easy to handle	Limited audience size
Chalkboards	Up to 30	Convenient to use; no planning required	Unprofessional appearance; cannot use colors or detailed diagrams successfully
Overhead projectors	Up to 45	Excellent for material requiring extensive discussion; inexpensive; allow speaker to face group	Projector and screen required; viewing screen may be difficult; reduced lighting may be needed
35 mm slides, films, or videotapes	Limited only by room and screen size	Give speaker professional, well-prepared image	Expensive and time consuming to produce; darkened room needed; equipment bulky and may be difficult to procure

FIGURE 18-4 Visual aids selection chart. [Adapted from a chart prepared by Lee Pitre and Larry Smeltzer in "Graphic Reinforcement for an Oral Presentation," *American Business Communication Association Bulletin,* December 1982, p. 6 (used with permission of the authors)].

question, "Wherever did you get that information on Medicaid?" could be both a direct challenge to your credibility and show disagreement with at least some of the points you made. On the other hand, "Where could I get more information about Medicaid?" may be a compliment and show an aroused interest in the subject.

ORAL PRESENTATION RATING SHEET

Section 1: Audience Rapport with Speaker (check only if used effectively)

Eye contact ________
Enthusiasm ________
Voice variation (inflection) ________
Speaker's interest in subject ________
Body movement ________
Speak or identify with audience ________

Hand control ________
Facial expression ________
Use of notes ________
Gesturing ________
Positive humor ________

Comments ____

Section 2: Speech Structure	*Excel-lent*	*Good*	*Accept-able*	*Needs Improvement*
Introduction				
Gained my immediate attention	____	____	____	____
Stated purpose clearly and early	____	____	____	____
Sounded clear, stayed on topic	____	____	____	____
Implementation (body)				
Supported statements with facts	____	____	____	____
Documented facts where necessary	____	____	____	____
Sounded believable	____	____	____	____
Sounded persuasive	____	____	____	____
Conclusion				
Used smooth transition from body	____	____	____	____
Summarized major points	____	____	____	____
Closed smoothly	____	____	____	____
Organization				
Was coherent, easy to follow	____	____	____	____
Was concise	____	____	____	____
Was clear	____	____	____	____
Was correct and appropriate	____	____	____	____

Section 3: Visual Aids (check only if appropriate)

Used appropriate aids ________
Used aids effectively ________

Comments ____

Section 4: Credibility (check only if done effectively)

Content
Extent of coverage ________
Difficulty level of coverage ________
Clarity of coverage ________
Delivery
Diction ________
Semantics (word usage) ________

Overall
Convincing ________
Interesting ________
Positive ________

Comments ____

FIGURE 18-5 Checklist for evaluating oral presentations.

To reduce hostile questioning, try to respond positively to all questions, stressing your purpose and the common goals of the group.

A checklist for evaluating the effectiveness of an oral presentation is shown in Figure 18-5.

GIVING WRITTEN REPORTS ORALLY

Sometimes you may have to convert a written report into an oral presentation. This is what Al Bennett, the controller of a firm that finds executives for companies, has to do. In response to a request by his boss, Al has written a report suggesting how the company's recruiters can decrease their travel expenses, especially the money spent on airline tickets.

In the report, he has suggested (1) revising travel reporting procedures—the forms prepared by field representatives are often inaccurate and incomplete—and (2) taking advantage of the airlines' special triangle fares and bonus programs. Most of the department managers seem unaware of these programs.

To accomplish these goals, Al has recommended that the company hire an administrative assistant to coordinate all travel arrangements. The new assistant would work with department managers on schedules and reservations and would monitor all travel-related expenses.

After reading Al's report, his boss agrees with him that centralizing this function will save money. The next step, she points out, is to put his suggestions into action. In fact, she has already received approval from the firm's president to hire the proposed administrative assistant. But now she and Al have to gain the approval of those affected by the changes, for without them, the proposed plan will not work.

Essentially, this means that two groups of employees must be briefed and prepared: the department managers and the sales representatives, or recruiters. The first group—the managers—are used to a certain degree of independence in making their travel arrangements, whereas the representatives (recruiters) tend to feel that following office procedures and doing paperwork is beneath them.

Al's boss suggests that he speak to each of these groups about the new policy and procedures. Since his report contains all the relevant information and justifications for the change, Al could just distribute it to those involved. However, not all material in the report concerns both audiences, at least not in the way it should be put to them. Some material needs to be summarized; other information criticizes the managers and recruiters for not handling the travel budget efficiently. But, most important, face-to-face discussion will give Al a chance to introduce the changes in a way that can stop negative reaction before it has a chance to begin.

What is the key to success in converting a written to an oral report?

So Al is now faced with converting the information in his written report to an oral form. The key to success in this conversion is flexibility. In other words, a successful oral report derived from one that is written is not a written report that can be read aloud; it is an *adaptation*, a well-planned oral message, designed for a specific occasion, that relies on the information previously presented in written form. To do this requires a flexible approach. By applying the suggestions in the following checklist, you—as well as Al Bennett—should have no difficulty with using written material to create an oral presentation.

CHECKLIST FOR ADAPTING WRITTEN TO ORAL REPORTS

1. *Clarify the assignment.* What is the objective of the presentation? to inform? to persuade? Will the audience be making a decision about whether to act on your report findings? Is your presentation part of a program or a meeting? How much time do you have? Will you be expected to answer questions? Should you coordinate your presentation with those of other speakers? If so, who are they and how do you get in touch with them?
2. *Analyze the audience.* How many people will be present? How familiar are they with your report topic? You may also want to gather further information about the members of the group. If so, do an audience analysis. Besides preknowledge of the topic or situation, consider demographics and psychographics in this analysis. (See Chapter 1 for further information.)
3. *Analyze the information in the written report.* Using the data you gathered in the first two steps as a guide, divide the original report information into three categories: *essential, nonessential,* and *support.* Plan to use all the essential information, none of the nonessential, and as much of the support as you need to reach your objective. Also gather any additional information not found in the original report that might increase the audience's understanding of the topic.

4. *Plan the presentation.* Choose the general format that seems most appropriate for the subject matter and the audience. Also decide whether the speech style will be wholly extemporaneous or will include manuscript material as well.
5. *Consider the location.* Where is your presentation scheduled? What are the advantages or disadvantages of the site? If you have a choice, try to match the size of the room and the size of the group. Avoid the "empty house" feeling of too few people in too large a place.
6. *Consider appropriate audiovisual aids.* Review the material you plan to present. Would audiovisual aids make it easier to understand? If so, which would be best? Find out if the equipment you need is available. Allow enough time to order or prepare the materials you wish, such as handouts, slides, or films.
7. *Prepare a working outline of the presentation.* Organize the major elements of your presentation as you would any other type of speech. Keep it simple and easy to follow.
8. *Anticipate questions.* Be prepared for both positive and negative questions that your audience could ask. Identify different departmental points of view, and include effects on the budget and both short- and long-range effects on your organization. Also consider saving additional supporting information for the question and answer period.
9. *Do a runthrough.* Are you really ready? Practice your presentation at least once before you give it. Check to see that everything you planned is ready. Don't forget the wisdom of Murphy's Law: "Anything that can go wrong probably will."
10. *Make last-minute changes.* Has the situation changed? Check with the program coordinator before the meeting starts. Has anything occurred that you should know about? After the program starts, if you're not the first speaker, listen carefully to whoever precedes you. If necessary, make changes in your material to take advantage of what they present. Then, when it's your turn, do well.

What advantages are there to converting a written to an oral report?

The advantages of converting a written report into an oral presentation rather than revising the original are that it saves time and is more effective. Thus, if you have to get information out quickly, choose an oral presentation over a revision. Further, because of its greater flexibility, the oral report allows you to respond effectively to the audience's verbal and nonverbal responses. For example, if they are restless, you don't have to discuss this paragraph on rising real estate rates or that section on the recent rash of insurance fires in one area of the city—as both are not absolutely essential to your main point. Or, if a question is asked, you can answer it immediately. You can expand on any item that might not be clear by supplying background information, defining terms, or using any of the support material in Checklist point 3. Or, if the audience seems to be familiar with some of the material, you can skip it.

Now, let's return to Al's problem. Consider point 2 in this context. Is he preparing one oral report or two? The answer is two, because he has two different audiences: managers and recruiters. Then what information should he include in each *and* how should he present it?

Obviously, he will have to explain the proposed changes. But, in doing so, he should include only information that is essential to the group to whom he is reporting. For example, in speaking to the managers, Al can focus on their concerns—what are the benefits of having a travel coordinator and how does the new person to be hired fit into the organizational structure? Conversely, in speaking to the recruiters, he can explain how centralized travel coordination will affect them, showing the way the new procedures will assist them. In doing this, Al can concentrate on clarity and the positive aspects of the situation, while ignoring placing any blame for failures on the group.

Both presentations involve persuasion—the new plan is doomed if everyone affected doesn't support it. Therefore, Al must also explain the *specific* benefits each group will receive once the change goes into effect.

These benefits are not necessarily the same for both groups. For example, the managers will probably be pleased that they will no longer have to prepare and justify their department's travel budget. As for the recruiters, they will probably see the advantages of making fewer flights and of not having to prepare the lengthy travel reports that were the bane of their existence, or so they have thought at times.

SUMMARY

1. Oral presentations are a common method of transmitting information in business.
2. The four basic styles of oral presentations are (a) impromptu, (b) extemporaneous, (c) manuscript, and (d) memorized.
3. The first phase in preparing an oral presentation, after topic selection, is to identify the purpose and develop a problem statement.
4. The second phase in preparing an oral

presentation is to gather information and adapt information to the audience.

5. The third phase in preparing an oral presentation is to organize the material. Organization includes (a) selecting a format; (b) developing the parts of the presentation, which include the introduction, body, and conclusion; and (c) drafting an outline using notes or a standard or alternative outline format.
6. The fourth phase of the process is actually making the presentation. This may be divided into three stages: (a) *before,* which includes psychological preparation; (b) *during,* which includes getting started, delivery techniques, handling the jitters, and use of audiovisual aids; and (c) *after,* which involves encouraging and evaluating feedback.
7. Oral presentations are frequently based on information already found in a written report. The key to a successful oral report developed from a written one is in how you adapt the material to the specific situation, which includes (a) selection of material to suit the audience (essential, nonessential, or support) and (b) consideration of the setting where you will make the presentation.

Review Questions

1. What are the four basic steps in preparing written and oral reports? Are they similar to those in written reports?
2. What are the four basic speech styles? Briefly describe each one.
3. Why do you think the extemporaneous presentational style is recommended for most situations?
4. How is technology used to help speakers do a better job?
5. What is the difference between a topic and a purpose in oral presentations? How does a problem statement differ from a topic and a purpose?
6. Does the term "problem statement" sound familiar? Is there a difference in a problem statement in a written report and one in an oral presentation?
7. What are "brights"? Where can you use them in an oral presentation?
8. Can you give an example of a topic in which you would use a "time or date" general format? an inductive or deductive format?
9. What are the three basic parts of an oral presentation? Briefly describe the function of each.
10. What are the advantages and disadvantages of using humor in the introduction to a speech?
11. What functions should a well-prepared conclusion serve in an oral presentation?
12. What is an alternative outline? How does it differ from a standard presentational outline?
13. Given the amount of speaking experience you now have, how can you handle your jitters?
14. When is it appropriate to use an audiovisual aid in an oral presentation? Describe a business situation in which you would make an oral presentation without using an audiovisual aid.
15. Should an oral presentation of information taken from a written report be used in the same way you presented it in the written version? Why or why not? What are the considerations here?

Exercises

1. This exercise will give you practice at impromptu speaking. Your teacher will ask you to speak for two minutes on one of the following subjects:

   Finding bargain merchandise

   The auto repair business

   Money talks

   Mutual funds

   Buying a mobile home

   Health spas for executives

   Women in management

   Investing in stocks

   Starting a part-time business

2. Select three subjects from the list in Exercise 1 and write a topic statement for each one. Also state the purpose for an extemporaneous presentation you will make to a group on each of the subjects. To write the topic statements and identify the purpose, you will need to identify the groups you will speak to and the circumstances of the presentations.
3. Develop *two* introductions for each presentation you chose in Exercise 2. Then select the one you think best for each situation and explain why that is your choice in each case.
4. Prepare and deliver an eight-minute presentation on a business subject of your choice. Use an extemporaneous format and prepare an outline. Examples of topics are "You Should Consider a Small Business Loan" and "Invest Now in Stocks and Bonds."
5. This exercise will give you practice in finding "brights" to use in a presentation. Brights are relevant quotations, anecdotes, or stories used in presentations. Choose a subject from Exercise 1 or another subject of your choice. Then identify an audience to whom you can give an informative extemporaneous presentation. Decide on a topic and the purpose for the presentation and write a problem statement. Then prepare a brief outline. Now go to the library and find a bright that you can use in the introduction of the presentation. Find another one for the body and another for the conclusion.
6. Visit the audiovisual or media center on your campus. Find out what equipment is available and learn to operate it if possible. Then list one way you could use each one in a presentation.
7. For this exercise, choose one of these topics or use one that you identify:

   "How to Start a Mail-Order Business in Your Home"

   "How to Prepare for a Job Interview"

   "The Business of Professional Sports"

   "Choosing a Location for a Fast-Food Retail Outlet"

   "Ways to Get Job Experience Before Starting a Career"

   Now identify an audience to whom you will give a five-minute extemporaneous presentation on the topic you chose. Plan to give an informative presentation. Now, select a general format from among those described in the chapter and explain why you made that choice.
8. Take a written report you've prepared for another class or, if you don't have one suitable, find a feature article in a prominent business journal. Adapt it for a five-minute oral presentation, applying the guidelines for adaptation suggested in the chapter. Give the presentation in class. When you've finished, ask for audience feedback. After considering your

classmates' responses, prepare a one-page written evaluation of this exercise based on your experience.

9. Prepare an outline for a presentation describing the characteristics of a new product that was marketed recently. Examples of appropriate subjects are "Home Computer Graphics," "Telephone Answering Equipment," and "Shampoo for Dogs and Cats."

10. Prepare a presentation designed to sell a product or service with which you are familiar. You may use audiovisual aids, but keep the entire presentation to eight minutes or fewer. Examples of appropriate topics are "You Can Sell Vacuum Cleaners Door to Door" and "You Can Operate an Investment Counseling Service."

CHAPTER 19

FACE-TO-FACE INFORMATION GATHERING: LISTENING AND NONVERBAL COMMUNICATION

For the past two weeks, George Lewis has been trying to develop an ad campaign for a troublesome new account—a Western European country that wants the agency to help turn around a declining tourism industry, which until last year had accounted for a sizable portion of its national capital. Suddenly, pacing back and forth in his office, George has got it: he will ask 30 celebrities to do 15 commercials extolling the glories of travel in the country. The names of the celebrities who would be perfect begin to crowd into his head. But, first, he has to tell the news to his boss, James Wicker. Dashing out of his office, he nearly bumps into the boss. "James," he exclaims, "wait till you hear . . .!".

"Great George," James Wicker says, not breaking his stride, "but I won't be free for another hour."

"James, it will only take a minute. I have the solution to our problem; it'll turn the whole thing around."

In reply, the boss glances at his watch, then at the memo he is clutching, frowns briefly and says, "Sure, why don't you tell me about it while I walk to my meeting with the president."

This exchange illustrates a very basic communication problem. Through verbal and nonverbal messages, James Wicker has tried to communicate to George Lewis that other matters occupy his thoughts just now. However, George has ignored the signals. In doing so, he has ensured the worst possible reception for his "solution."

This unhappy occurrence is all too common in many business offices today. It is the reason why many excellent ideas are never given the time or attention they deserve. Both good listening skills and a knowledge of how to interpret nonverbal communication are necessary to turn this situation around. Each is an essential part of a larger skill—effective face-to-face information gathering. And that skill—the ability to gather valid, reliable information in face-to-face situations—is perhaps the most important ingredient in managerial decision making today.

In this chapter, we will discuss how to listen and how to interpret nonverbal messages. These skills should help you gather accurate information, so that, unlike George Lewis, you will be able to "read" others effectively.

DEVELOPING GOOD LISTENING HABITS

How do hearing and listening differ?

Hearing, or the physical act of recognizing sounds, is the first step in listening. Although listening begins with hearing, it also involves processing sounds and assigning meaning to them. Evidently, this is not so simple. The available research evidence in this area shows that most of us listen with only 25 to 50 percent efficiency. That means that 50 to 75 percent of what we hear is never processed. Such inefficiency results from poor listening habits that range from simply not paying attention to subconscious rejection of certain information for personal reasons. In George Lewis's case, his disregard of James Wicker's signals probably stemmed from a combination of the two: he was simply too excited to notice some of them and those that he did notice, he pushed aside because he wanted to be listened to immediately.

Why do nonlisteners risk professional failure?

In fact, one of the most common complaints in business is "people who don't listen." Consider Lee Ann Kearney, a sales representative for a huge pharmaceutical company. Her job involves visiting doctors' offices, clinics, and hospitals. During these visits, she describes the company's line of products and solicits orders. After ten years in the business, Lee Ann has fallen into the habit of assuming she knows what others are going to say—she then infers what they want to hear from her in reply. Not only does she do this with potential customers, she also talks to people in the office in the same way: first, mentally outlining what she wants to say and, then, regardless of the person's response, saying it.

Thus, most of Lee Ann's dialogues turn into monologues, such as the following:

> Lee Ann begins: "Let me tell you about the new sedative we've developed."
>
> The clinical director to whom she's speaking responds: "I've read your literature on it, Lee Ann. What I'm interested in now is a flu vaccine."
>
> Lee Ann continues, as if she hasn't heard a word: "This sedative seems to be nearly 95 percent effective with virtually no side effects . . .".

The result of such "conversations" is that Lee Ann's sales volume is down dramatically this year. For, not only does the other person give up trying to share information, he or she stops listening—and ordering, too.

What is the cost of poor listening? In this instance, we might say that Lee Ann's functional value is diminished interpersonally and professionally.

On an interpersonal level, communicating with a nonlistener like Lee Ann requires more effort than does communicating with a good listener. Thus, a conscientious speaker—one who wants to get information across—must constantly repeat and question a nonlistener to find out if he or she is receiving the data correctly.

Also, on an interpersonal level, speaking to a nonlistener is an irritating experience. Attentive listening is a compliment. When we make the effort to listen to another carefully, we are conveying a powerful nonverbal message: "You are important" and "I value what you have to say." Listening, then, is a form of respect that if disregarded is often taken as an insult.

On a professional level, the inability to listen can adversely affect job performance. For example, in Lee Ann's case, her customers might not want to deal with her anymore, her co-workers may have a similar response, and her boss, reviewing her record, may begin to question her value to the company.

Finally, on a broader level, most mistakes in business can be traced to miscommunication caused by poor listening. So frequent is such miscommunication that to stem its effects, managers are asked to "put it in writing"; whether *it* is a tentative contract, an idea, or a summation of a meeting does not matter. People dealing with poor listeners know that verifying information is an important way to stem errors.

What are some of the costs of poor listening in business situations?

In addition to the problem just outlined, poor listening wastes time and money. For example, suppose you are employed in a building supply warehouse. By telephone, Milona Rentz, a contractor, orders 20 12″ × 18″ heating registers. You explain that the firm does not take telephone orders for materials. The contractor replies that she has an open account and this is a rush order. You consent to take the order then and send out the requested registers that afternoon. The next day the materials are returned with a note: "I asked for 18 12″ × 20″ registers. Your bungling has put me two days behind schedule."

Checking the receipt you wrote to cover the order, you find "20 12″ × 18″ registers." What should you do? After some hesitation, you ask your supervisor, Ray Tohru, who says, "Well, Milona's a good customer, so send out the new material this afternoon. We'll pay the shipping costs." Then, just as you've turned your back, he adds, "Since this is going to cost us, you won't be getting a commission credit on the sale. Even if it isn't your fault, be more careful next time."

As you can see here, everybody has lost time and money—you, your company, and the contractor who placed the original order. The real cause of the trouble in this example was the lack of feedback. Normally, the order would have been written. Since it wasn't, either you or the contractor should have taken precautions to avoid the possibility of error by saying something like, "Because this is a rush, I want to be sure we've got it right. Twenty 12″ × 18″ registers?" Such a restatement probably would have averted the misunderstanding.

Certainly, the use of telephones compounds the problems of inattentive listening. Experienced listeners will tell you that it is easier to check information in face-to-face encounters than in those that rely on voice only. For this reason, people who conduct much of their business over the phone learn how to listen *and* check information received this way—and then follow up important conversations in writing. Even in face-to-face encounters, this careful procedure is essential.

What role can the telephone play in causing communication problems?

One problem in listening is that people often react to partial messages. For example, in the case of the disputed order, you might have just completed filling out an order for 12″ × 18″ registers when the contractor called to place an order. If so, your thoughts might have jumped to the completed order—*hearing* the numbers and specifications associated with it instead of the contractor's. (For a more detailed discussion of how such "selective perception" works, refer to Chapter 1.) Or you might have been similarly affected by an employee in your own company who had requested 12″ × 20″ registers right after the contractor placed her order. The point here is that it is easy to hear only part of a message in such circumstances. In turn, this becomes a barrier to communication (see Chapter 2) because we often act on the part we've heard as though it were the entire message.

In business, as the example shows, it is necessary to listen as well as hear. In fact, those who listen *to* others are the people most likely to be listened to *by* others. Luckily, listening skills may be *learned.* Through analyzing problems and following guidelines, you can continually grow in your understanding of what is said to you.

To become a good listener, follow these steps:

THE SIX P'S OF LISTENING

1. *Preparing*—setting your mind to the task of being an *active listener.*
2. *Perceiving*—recognizing when *blocking* occurs. Blocking is a barrier that interferes with objective listening.
3. *Participating*—focusing your thoughts on the task of listening well while you are receiving information.
4. *Processing*—thinking about information you hear to try to make sense of it.
5. *Probing*—asking questions to help you understand and process information that you hear.
6. *Personalizing*—fitting information you hear into your own needs and goals framework so that it becomes "yours."

Preparing

Is listening an active or a passive activity? Explain.

Preparing, the first step in good listening, involves setting your mind to the task. Listening is an *active,* not a passive, communication skill. Preparing to listen well means becoming conscious that you are surrounded constantly by sounds and, therefore, that the opportunity to practice listening is always available. Becoming conscious of such sounds can also make you aware that you must be selective in attending to some while ignoring others.

Perceiving

Perceiving, the second step, involves recognizing how sloppy perception can thwart even the best speaker's efforts to communicate. Become aware, then, that people, yourself included, often listen selectively, hearing what they choose to hear. Excuses such as the following can tip you off that the person expressing them is listening poorly:

> "George doesn't know what he's talking about!"
>
> "I can't follow all these figures and junk!"
>
> "Oh, brother, this old gaffer is a real bore!"
>
> "Why did they pick Sally? Nobody likes her!"
>
> "I'll bet I know more about this topic than that 'turkey' up there!"
>
> "I've heard this before . . . wonder what I'll do this weekend?"

How can sloppy perception affect communication?

As the examples show, people often reject a speaker as a source of information. Or they become bored or disinterested. Or they simply refuse to accept information that is counter to their beliefs and attitudes. Referred to as *blocking,* these and similar habits or barriers keep them from listening objectively. Anything—the speaker's personality or choice of words, the ideas that he or she espouses—may trigger blocking. Whatever the cause, however, the result is always the same: poor or selective listening. In contrast, the secret to accurate perception is objective listening. To do this, avoid confusing the message with the source—perhaps the speaker's mannerisms remind you of someone you dislike, for example. Or you may confuse this experience with a related one—perhaps as a child you often had to listen to long lectures from a parent or you heard them from a boss on an old job, one you stayed at too long. Instead, focus on listening for the meaning behind the words, that is, the ideas themselves. Withhold judgment until you have heard the entire message.

Participating

Participating, the third step, is taking part, and it requires that you become actively involved in listening, that you work at it. Your role in this particular communication process is that of receiver of the information, and effective receiving does require concentration—intense concentration at times.

What role do you play when you participate as a listener in communication?

To increase your concentration, react openly (verbally and nonverbally, as appropriate) to provide the speaker with feedback. For example, if a co-worker is describing a departmental reorganization plan, nod your head in agreement as he or she makes each point. In this way, you cue your co-worker that you are listening attentively. Buoyed by this recognition, he or she will then speak even more effectively.

Processing

The fourth step in listening is processing. This involves *thinking*. While someone is speaking to you, think about the message; that is, mentally process the information that you are receiving to make sense of it. If we concentrate, we can all process such information we hear more rapidly than we can speak it. Thus, a normal rate of speech ranges from 125 to 175 words per minute, but you can comprehend two to three times as many words a minute. Although your rate of comprehension (processing) does vary according to how much you know about the topic and how complex it is, nevertheless, you will have time to think as you listen.

In what way or ways can processing information poorly result in poor communication?

While concentrating on your thoughts, you will be able to screen out noise and other distractions. But remember that attention spans are short—after 20 or 30 seconds, most of us tend to lose concentration. Be prepared to refocus your thoughts when these lapses occur.

As it happens, many people misuse the extra thinking time they have when listening. Often, they leap ahead, assuming they are going to hear something that is not then said to them. Sometimes, they simply let their minds wander. At other times, they hear a word or phrase or idea that causes them to think along parallel lines, which makes them lose place with the speech.

Suppose some of these lapses occur when you are listening to a message. What can you do to regain your attention? First, turn inward by focusing your thoughts on the topic. Use the free seconds between ideas to reflect on what the speaker has said so far about the Dow Jones Industrial Average, or short-term interest rates, or whatever. Then, attend to the next point as the speaker makes it. Throughout, think about the direction the speaker is taking at the same time that you follow the ideas to see if you are correct in your assumptions.

Probing

Probing, the fifth step, involves making sense of what the speaker is saying by finding out how the facts fit together by identifying the message's main ideas. Essentially, probing means questioning to help form a complete message from the bits of information given you. When you are unable to understand an idea or how it fits into the larger theme, ask for further information at the appropriate times. In an interpersonal setting—a customer is talking to you, for example—you can usually ask questions immediately. In a group setting—the weekly staff meeting, for example—you may have to wait until a complete segment of information is presented or until the end of the entire presentation is reached.

Effective speakers organize their presentations well and, therefore, make it easier for you to probe. But what about the many people with average or worse speaking abilities? To understand them, you must become a good listener. Ask the speaker on the state of the oil industry today to repeat a point that you couldn't quite hear. Or ask the panelist who is discussing the falling exchange rate of the U.S. dollar to explain something that wasn't quite clear. Or ask a probing question such as, "What was the effect of the lower than expected growth in the world economy on the U.S. dollar?"

Personalizing

How can you direct the information you hear towards your own benefit?

The sixth step in listening—personalizing—requires you to direct the information you are hearing toward your own benefit. Ask yourself, "How do these data help me meet my own wants and needs?" "How do they help me professionally? financially?" In other words, use self-interest to motivate yourself into listening actively. The happy result: The better you listen, the more you come to know.

You can develop a high degree of skill in listening rather quickly just by faithfully following the Six P's. Nonverbal communication is quite another matter, though. Were you to compare all areas of communication skill development to a battle zone in a guerrilla war, surely nonverbal communication would be designated a mine field. But this is one "mine field" we all must traverse to understand one another and, therefore, to conduct our business affairs properly.

EFFECTIVE USE OF NONVERBAL COMMUNICATION

Suppose, as the company's personnel director, you notice something odd about the memos that Grant Estevez, one of your staffers, sends you: some of them, all of which are to be signed or initialed, have Grant's signature at the bottom, whereas others are unsigned. Moreover, those that are unsigned always contain a couple of errors in contrast to the perfect copy of those that are signed. Looking over these memos carefully, you come to a conclusion: when this employee feels that the material is beneath him, he works with less care, and knowing this, perhaps unconsciously, won't sign his name to it, or even initial it. Such an assessment leads you to upgrade the kind of work you send Estevez; in fact, you are quite curious to see the result. Will the next batch of memos from him now be signed or unsigned. Sure enough, they are signed (and so contain no mistakes). Your little experiment has brought a good result: your bored worker's mettle is finally being tested. Morever, it has proved once again the value of *reading* nonverbal communication.

How might you respond when you become fully aware of nonverbal communication?

Most people have two responses when they become fully aware of nonverbal communication: (1) they are surprised that so much is happening, and (2) they cannot believe that everyone is ignoring so many signals. According to Edward T. Hall, author of *The Silent Language,* "Those of us who keep our eyes open can read volumes in what we see going on around us."

Four factors that are important in using nonverbal communication effectively are (1) recognizing the limitations of it, (2) knowing how to classify it, (3) understanding how it works as a process, and (4) dealing with first impressions created by it.

Recognizing Limitations

Can all communication be understood through nonverbal means? Explain.

Although understanding nonverbal communication is useful, we can't understand all communication through this perspective. Some people even consider information gained nonverbally to be unreliable—and often it is. Nonverbal cues are not a substitute for verbal language; you cannot assume, as with verbal language, a direct relationship between observed action and a thought or feeling without encouraging error and confusion. Instead, this silent language, as Hall calls it, is usually, but not always, an extension of your emotions; thus, it can consciously and unconsciously underscore your words. In fact, it can communicate independently of words, written or spoken. In addition, nonverbal behavior differs from culture to culture, among subcultures within a culture, and from region to region and country to country.

Figure 19-1 shows how—based on assumptions—nonverbal and verbal behavior work in relation to motivators to communicate. Note, especially, that nonverbal behavior may *or* may not be limited to verbal language.

Classifying Behaviors

What are the three major divisions of nonverbal communication?

We can divide nonverbal communication into three major divisions: *sign, action,* and *object.* In sign language, specific gestures substitute for words. These signs may communicate complete messages as do the gestures of the American Plains Indians. Or they may be spe-

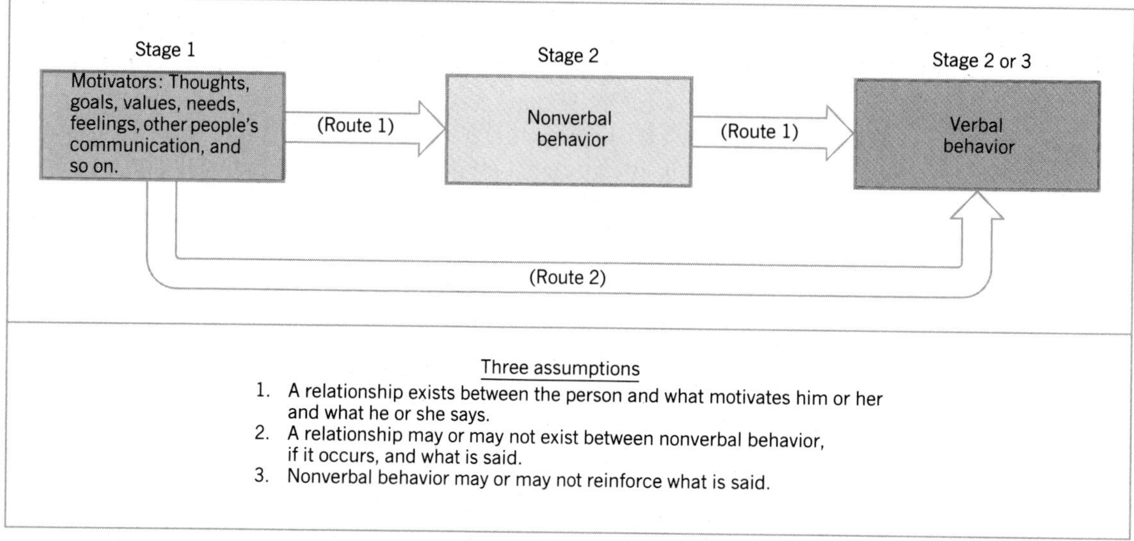

FIGURE 19-1 Relationship between nonverbal and verbal behavior resulting from a motivation to communicate.

cialized, as are the signs used by baseball umpires. Or they may be casual, as "thumbs up" and "thumbs down" gesturing to friends.

In contrast, body movements show an action language—all or parts of the body move—to communicate. Such language supplements or contradicts a spoken message; for example, slumping might reinforce the weariness of your words. Such "body language" also reveals an individual's personality and attitudes.

Finally, the things or artifacts people use can be "read" as an object language. Primarily visuals, these can include clothing, office furnishings, cars, houses, and even the body itself.

Understanding the Process

Is nonverbal behavior simply a series of isolated incidents? Why or why not?

Nonverbal behavior is not simply a series of isolated incidents; it is a *process*. Just as words cluster in a sentence to form larger meanings, so do related actions appear together to perform the same function. For example, suppose you meet a friend who has lost her job. Later, someone back at the office asks, "How did she look?" You say that she looked sad. Could you be more specific? Are her shoulders slumped? walk slowed? head bowed? eyes downcast? clothes untidy? These related behaviors or effects of behavior form the larger meaning: her sad look. Thus, when you see a general sign of a nonverbal behavior, check the specific signs that constitute it to verify your impression. In this way you will treat this behavior as a process and consequently will be able to interpret it more objectively.

Dealing with First Impressions

In a tenth of a second, we can and do judge a person we've just seen for the first time. What we see in this glimpse forms a first impression that we then use to develop a relationship with this person. By looking at this in reverse—the other person forming a first impression of us—it helps to know that what we think others' first impressions are has a powerful effect on our self-image and therefore on our effectiveness.

Are first impressions generalizations? Explain.

Thus, whether accurate or not, first impressions are important, and we should take note that they are generalizations—conclusions drawn from specific bits of information. Without the ability to generalize, we would find ourselves unable to learn anything but basic facts. Yet, as discussed in detail in Chapter 2, there is always the danger of drawing the wrong conclusions. First impressions are particularly subject to this danger: all too often they prove to be wrong once we get to know a person better. Yet they are a necessary part of forming initial relationships, and therefore we should be alert to the dangers involved. To avoid forming the wrong first impression, think of nonverbal cues used to form a first impression as a rough sketch of a person rather than an accurate assessment. That way, you will be less apt to form stereotypes and more willing to change your mind as the facts develop.

An understanding of these four factors that define and limit all types of nonverbal communication will go far in helping us develop skill in gathering information communicated nonverbally.

TYPES OF NONVERBAL COMMUNICATION

What are six types of nonverbal communication?

The types of nonverbal communication are physical characteristics, clothing and accessories, distance and space, body movement, touch, and paralanguage. Figure 19-2 shows clues to follow in observing nonverbal behavior. Use them as guides in learning to recognize and interpret nonverbal signals. One precaution: Begin by thinking, "this might mean"; end by thinking, "but I could be wrong."

Physical Characteristics

Did you know that people associate tallness with power? Studies show that respondents describe tall men as "competitive," whereas short men showing the same behavior are seen as having a "Napoleonic complex." These results are not surprising, for research into body size and shape shows that a direct relationship exists between what we see and how we react. Then, when people have

CLUES TO NONVERBAL COMMUNICATION

Nonverbal behavior

1. May or may not parallel language
2. May or may not be an indication of thoughts, attitudes, needs, feelings, and so on
3. Often as not draws its meaning from the particular situation
4. Is influenced by culture, sex, role, age, and other variables
5. Cannot be relied on as an alternate form of communication
6. May offer hints about unstated responses and reactions in others
7. May or may not be a conscious action
8. Generally is an unreliable *primary* source of information

FIGURE 19-2 Guidelines in observing nonverbal behavior.

been asked to draw conclusions about relationships between physique and temperament, the results have been interesting.

What are the three types of physical characteristics called?

Three types have emerged:

1. *Endomorphs,* who are soft, round, and heavy, are viewed as relaxed, tolerant, warm, generous, and kind.
2. *Ectomorphs,* who are tall and lean, are viewed as tense, serious, introverted, suspicious, and cold.
3. *Mesomorphs,* who are muscular, with athletic builds, are viewed as confident, outgoing, active, enterprising, and optimistic.

Besides body types, the length of people's hair often determines our perception of them. For example, in the 1960s and 1970s some people associated young men who had long hair with independence, freedom, drug use, espousal of liberal political and social causes, immorality, and the antiwar sentiments of the time. In contrast, others viewed young men who had short hair as morally strict, too conservative on social and political issues, warmongers, and resistant to change. Although these distinctions have largely disappeared today, hair length can still be a factor in job interviews and the like.

Finally, we know too little about how race, sex, and physical handicaps affect our perceptions of one another. More research needs to be done about these aspects of nonverbal communication.

Clothing and Accessories

Whereas the way you dress is a primary factor in how others perceive you, these reactions depend greatly on personal values or on the situation itself. Generally, people are more comfortable if you do not look too different from themselves. Through dress guidelines and use of dress accessories, you can get a large part of the "look" you want.

Dress Guidelines

Many people believe there is such a thing as acceptable dress. For such individuals, then, the first dress guideline assumes that every occasion demands a proper way of dress. Thus, those who seek acceptance will normally wear the "correct" dress. For example, men normally will wear a business suit or sport jacket, dress pants, and a tie to a job interview instead of a tuxedo, which is too formal, or a sport shirt and jeans, which are too casual. In this way, they can stay within the confines of "accepted dress."

For school or work, do you normally dress in high, non-, low, or counter fashion?

Another guideline to dress is style or fashion. Four fashion subgroups are

1. *High fashion.* People in this group wear the latest styles. If you wear such clothes, it means that you are willing to spend large sums of money to be fashionable.
2. *Nonfashion.* People in this group wear simple, basic clothes that remain in style. This approach denotes a conservative, functional attitude to dress.
3. *Low fashion.* People in this group wear casual clothes, which perhaps denotes more interest on their part in comfort than in how others perceive them.
4. *Counterfashion.* People in this group wear unstylish clothes, which can indicate a rejection of established guidelines and a desire to be independent.

Other factors affecting dress are practicality, general interest in clothing, exhibitionism, decorativeness, self-image, specific dress codes, climate, basic grooming habits, and the state of the economy. Where a dress code is widely recognized, it can indicate a person's occupation. In banking, for example, the more formal code often calls for executives to wear conservative, tailored suits.

Use of Dress Accessories

How do tangible and intangible dress accessories differ?

Accessories refine and define clothing. Basic tangible accessories include jewelry, handbags, gloves, belt buckles, shoes, and wigs. Intangible accessories include makeup, perfume, cologne, and even tattoos. Intangibles refine basic dress, and in general, you have more freedom to wear or not to wear them than you do with tangibles. Because intangibles are chosen more deliberately than anything else you wear, they communicate more about your interests and self-image than do either clothing or basic accessories. In general, people match accessories to clothing just as they match clothing to the occasion.

In interpreting the communication people send through their dress, don't simply judge them on what they wear on one occasion or on the basis of a single item such as a loud tie or a shirt with frayed cuffs. Look for the usual way they dress. Look for the overall look.

Distance and Space

Suppose you have a boss who never seems to be able to come closer to you than a foot. Because of this one behavior, you have begun to think that he or she is shy or extremely reserved. You also have not tried to violate your boss's sense of space and privacy.

What is territoriality? How is it used in business situations?

Like your boss, most people use space and distance to communicate important information about themselves. The proximity or distance we keep in relation to others in the various situations in which we find ourselves during the course of a business day results from our sense of *territoriality*—ownership of space or territory. For example, two office workers who are unacquainted will be careful not to intrude on each other's space at the lunch counter. Neither will you thrust yourself on your boss—it is far more likely that you will keep a greater distance from him or her than you will from the person who shares your office. Notice too how much closer you stand to a friendly co-worker than to one you don't know too well. By becoming aware of the nonverbal cue of distance, you can learn much about the people you come in contact with in business. Figure 19-3 shows two contrasting uses of distance in business settings.

The way people use space also tells us about them. Everybody uses it differently. Some people are seemingly unconscious of it, others seem to be victims of it, whereas still others manipulate employees or customers with it, and so forth. For example, suppose a conference has been scheduled during the afternoon for members of your department. However, as far as you know, no leader has been named. If you arrive early, you might witness some interesting behavior in regard to seating. Thus, a person who is aggressive or dominating may very well choose to sit at the head of the table. In contrast, a less aggressive person might just sit in whatever place is left after everybody else is seated.

People's relation to space can also tell much about who is whom in the office. Suppose, for example, that your division is currently undergoing two changes: (1) you are moving to another floor, and (2) two executives are in competition for the vice presidency of the division. Like everyone else, you don't know for certain who is going to get the job, but you have an idea. Now that the entire office is relocating, you do have more definitive information about who the frontrunner is by learning that one executive's new office is bigger than his or her rival's, and it has a view. Two weeks later this person is promoted. In this situation, the allotment of office space indicated the new hierarchy.

FIGURE 19-3 Two contrasting uses of distance in business settings.

Body Movement

The study of body movement includes the examination of posture, gesture, facial expression, and eye movement. If we become aware of the nonverbal communication in such movements, we can learn much about fellow employees, clients, and potential customers. For example, suppose you are negotiating with Lee Chavez, a representative of another company, for some disputed timberland. The timberland is worth a fortune, and the negotiations have been dragging on for weeks. However, lately you have noticed that you are most likely to wring concessions from Chavez when he is tired. Moreover, you can always tell when fatigue is about to overtake him—he takes his handkerchief from his breast pocket and wipes his brow slowly, as if trying to erase his tiredness too. Having observed this, you decide to press ahead most firmly when the handkerchief comes out. Two weeks later, you have achieved your goals and the negotiations are over.

What are leaks? What do they reveal in communication?

Generally, people move their bodies in certain ways in response to messages and situations they encounter. Much of the time, they use conscious movement—such as gestures—to add meaning to what they are saying. Also, like Lee Chavez in the example, they employ unconscious movements, called *leaks,* that reveal unstated feelings and attitudes. However, sometimes people alter their movements. An example is the executive who nods his or her head vigorously to conceal boredom during a very long oral report by an overeager staffer on the best use of office supplies.

Posture

What does posture communicate?

People's posture tells us a great deal about them and their lives. Posture includes the way we walk, sit, and stand. Usually, it communicates a degree of alertness, sense of purpose, self-image, and a whole range of emotions. For example, the relaxed set of your assistant's shoulders may indicate that he or she is comfortable with the work load today, just as your own relaxed posture may reflect that you feel at ease working under the new boss.

Some postures are associated with a particular profession, such as those in the military who stand erect with back straight, head up, and arms at the side. Even though no particular posture is inherently right or wrong, we should be aware that everybody's posture communicates something about him or her.

Gestures

Gestures involve communication through movements of the body's extremities. You may gesture using your arms, wrists, hands, fingers, legs, feet, toes, or head. We can divide such gestures into four groups:

Language Substitutes

These gestures are consciously used, and their meanings are defined in the dictionary. For example, you employ such emblems most often to send a single unit message, such as the "V" for victory and the hitchhiker's "thumb." Yet, emblems can also be linked in complex patterns to form complete languages, as in the American Sign Language for the hearing impaired. For such a system to work, those who use an emblem must agree on its meaning. Also, some emblems communicate specific messages only within certain cultures or subcultures. Often, emblems grow naturally out of situations. For example, when you enter an office and the receptionist is on the phone, he or she may flash an emblem (maybe a hand movement) that will tell you to sit down and wait.

Language Additives These gestures emphasize, expand, accent, and otherwise illustrate words. Although not as distinct as emblems, *illustrators,* as language additions are also called, supplement conversation. An example is tapping your fingers on a desk top to underscore important ideas. Or, you might move your hands slowly in the air while searching for the right words to tell an employee that he or she is fired. Or, you might point while giving directions.

What are the four basic types of gestures? How do they differ from one another?

Regulators These gestures direct and control the back-and-forth flow of conversation. A listener uses them to tell a speaker to slow down, continue, speed up, repeat, elaborate, or stop. Regulators also govern turn taking in conversation. For example, raising a single finger while another person is talking indicates that you want to say something. Almost always, regulators are accompanied by facial expressions.

Physical Habits These gestures include pulling, scratching, picking at, squeezing, and pinching yourself. For example, when you are tense, you might bite your fingernails. Also included in this group is the way you use objects while speaking or listening. For example, you may take off your eyeglasses when you speak seriously to a fellow employee, or you might put them on, twiddle them in your hands, and so forth. In a similar way, you can use keys, pencils, paper clips, or whatever is available to communicate nonverbally.

Gestures are more numerous than any form of nonverbal communication, and the meanings we attach to them are diverse. Thus, a single individual may use as many as 700,000 different hand gestures alone, and no one knows how many meanings may be derived from them. Although this may sound awesome, you can learn to recognize and interpret the most obvious.

Facial Expression

Your boss smiles at you and you feel happy; he or she scowls, and you are a little disconcerted, wondering what you might have done wrong. Most facial expressions are more subtle than either of these extremes, however. You can use them too in a variety of ways: to aid or inhibit other people's communication, to complement your own, and to replace spoken messages.

The face rarely sends a single message at a time. Instead, it sends a series (or a blend) of messages. For example, when you meet a customer you may not have seen recently, your facial expression may show anxiety, recognition, hesitation, and pleasure in quick succession.

What is masking in communication? How does it work?

Facial expression is difficult to interpret. In fact, researchers have defined clearly only six basic expressions and 33 blends. Another problem in interpreting them is that people tend to *mask* or hide their meaning. This can be accomplished because we are quite conscious of our facial expressions and so can control them to some extent. For example, we may feel sad and want to cry but do not, or we may not feel sad and still cry.

Eye Movement

We use our eyes to gather information and then to send it. Your eyes can tell a co-worker whether you are listening to his or her complaints about the company's management, where your attention is focused, and even how you feel about what he or she is saying. Your eyes also can assert your authority over others. In fact, only physical force can challenge another person more than a direct gaze or stare can. Thus, such a look from you might reform a lazy worker more quickly than would all the harsh words you could think of.

Can eye movement communicate only a narrow range of meaning? Explain.

Everyone recognizes that eyes can communicate a wide range of meaning, from a fleeting glance to a shifty gaze to a "look that could kill." For example, you might suspect the motives of clients, co-workers, or customers who refuse to look at you directly. Still, even here, the meaning might not be so simple because the facial expression may be combined with another form of communication. For example, a firm handshake accompanied by an indirect gaze is harder to interpret than is a simple glancing away.

You should also note that eye behavior can differ greatly among cultures. For example, most people from the United States will look down when being disciplined to show a sense of shame, guilt, and rejection. But, in certain other cultures, such as Japan, people keep their eyes lowered to show respect. How easy it is to confuse these signals if you are working with Japanese carmakers on a joint project, for example.

Touch

Your boss, Jason Springer, pats you on your back after your presentation on the international monetary situation, and you feel that he must have been pleased with it. Most people would feel the same way when such a touch comes from someone with whom they want to communicate—a friend, professor, or co-worker, for example. Touching is our first nonverbal experience in life. Through it, we learn to relate to people and objects. In fact, touching is critical to our sense of well-being. With it, we feel loved, cared for, and emotionally supported.

Why are some people reluctant to touch others?

However, in the United States, we generally also associate touching with intimacy and sexual relationships. Thus, we are sometimes reluctant to touch publicly, especially strangers or those of the same sex. In fact, the custom is to apologize when we touch someone by mistake.

Remember that each person will respond to touching in a personal way. That response will be based on values affected by age, sex, role, cultural norms, background, and the situation itself. For instance, your touching patterns differ with children and adults, friends and strangers, and co-workers and bosses in the work environment. You should note, too, that with the tremendous increase of women in the workplace, many managers today feel uncertain about whether or not—or how—to touch another person at work. This is especially the case when the other person is of the opposite sex. In interpreting touch, consider the body part being touched, duration of contact, method used, and the strength and frequency of the touch.

Paralanguage

What are the two dimensions of paralanguage? Explain.

Paralanguage is the *how* in language. How people say things is often as important as the words they use. Listen to the tension or "thinness" in your co-workers' voices when they talk. That is paralanguage. Can you remember talking to a customer who was extremely angry? The scream or hurt in his or her voice was paralanguage. Paralanguage is more than the dictionary definition of a word (its denotative meaning), and it is more too than the suggested or implied meaning of a word (the word's connotative meaning).

Paralanguage has two dimensions: *vocal qualities* and *vocalizations.* Vocal qualities are pitch, rate, and volume. Vocalizations include vocal characterizers, qualifiers, and surrogates. Vocal characterizers are the nonlanguage sounds you make while speaking—laughing, wheezing, sighing, panting, sneezing, crying, yawning, for example. Vocal qualifiers show voice intensity, degree of pitch, and extension, which is drawing out or clipping of words associated with accents. Vocal surrogates are sound substitutes for words, such as *ah* and *uh-huh.*

Silence is also paralanguage. Because you cannot *not* communicate, silence can be electric with meaning. For example, suppose two executives are talking together, and one says, "Well, I know you'd tell me if our operating expenses were too high." The other says nothing. After a long pause, the conversation resumes on a different topic. This silence probably means the operating expenses *are* too high. Or suppose, to punctuate a point, a speaker pauses longer than usual. The pause allows the audience to think about what was just said and to anticipate what will be said next. Silence communicates!

Paralanguage influences how people react to messages more than any type of nonverbal communication. Also, it is the most reliable sign of feelings, moods, and stress. Its effect, however, depends on the situation and what else is communicated. Therefore, the meaning in paralanguage lies in the relationship *between* what people say and how they say it, not simply in what they say or how they say it.

SUMMARY

1. Everyday business communication in the workplace relies on oral communication. It is the practical source of immediate information. The process of gathering information effectively in this way involves listening (and speaking), as well as interpreting the nonverbal communication of others.
2. Listening with efficiency requires an understanding of the Six P's: (a) preparing, which is setting your mind to the task of being an active listener; (b) perceiving, which requires alleviating blocking; (c) participating, which is concentrating on the task of listening well; (d) processing, which is reworking new information so that it is similar to other information already available; (e) probing, which requires asking questions to assist in understanding and processing the information; and (f) personalizing, which is fitting the information into your own needs and goals so that it becomes "yours."
3. The effective application of nonverbal communication requires an understanding of its scope and limitations, as well as how it relates to language use in the oral communication process. Four factors important to interpreting nonverbal communication effectively are (a) recognizing its limitations, (b) knowing how to classify it, (c) understanding the process itself, and (d) dealing with first impressions.
4. Physical characteristics, such as body type and hair and skin color, can influence perceptions.
5. Clothing and accessories, or the relationship between dress style and occasion, can be interpreted in a number of ways. Generally, dress is high fashion, nonfashion, low fashion, or counterfashion. Dress accessories are either tangible or intangible.
6. The use of distance and space is based on cultural expectations. It can also underscore status and personality.
7. Body movement can be divided into four basic groups: (a) posture, which includes large movements; (b) gestures, which involves the extremities of the body; (c) facial expressions; and (d) eye movement.
8. Touching is quite culture-bound, and the people of the United States are generally a nontouching society in business situations. At least, touching in these situations is usually done in very defined ways.
9. Paralanguage is the "how" in language—how people say things. The two dimensions of paralanguage are (a) vocal qualities and (b) vocalizations.

Review Questions

1. What is the difference between hearing and listening?
2. How can poor listening habits diminish your effectiveness interpersonally? professionally?
3. How does the use of the telephone compound the problems of inattentive listening? What can be done about it?
4. In your own words, what do you think it means to say that listening is an active, not a passive, skill? How can you be an active listener?
5. What is the result of our tendency to listen selectively? Give an example of this from your work life or school life.
6. What are the differences between participating and processing, the third and fourth steps in the Six P's of good listening?
7. Why is it necessary to probe while listening? What would be the result if you did little probing while listening to an effective speaker? while listening to a poor speaker?
8. What are the four factors that are important in using nonverbal communication effectively? Why are these factors important?
9. Why should we be alert to the dangers of first impressions? Give one example from your work life or school life where a first impression proved to be wrong and one where it proved to be right. What was the difference?
10. What are endomorphs, ectomorphs, and mesomorphs? Into which category do you think you fall? Do you think the description in the text fits you? Why or why not?
11. Are you a high-fashion, nonfashion, low-fashion, or counterfashion dresser at work? at school? Describe one outfit you wear that exhibits this fashion dress guideline you follow.
12. What differences are there between our uses of distance and space to communicate? Give an example of how you have observed distance being used to communicate during the last week—preferably an on-the-job example.
13. Much is said about the meaning of posture as nonverbal communication. For example, slumped shoulders may denote "burdens borne" or a habit of timidity. Can't it be that these people with slumped shoulders are just tired? Briefly discuss your answer.
14. Why are facial expressions difficult to interpret? Do you know anyone who masks his or her facial expression? If so, what emotion or communication is being masked? Can you explain why this person does this?
15. Why is paralanguage called the "how" in language? Give an example at work or school where you recognized paralanguage?

Exercises

1. Make a list of ten common phrases that are related to our attitudes about eyes and eye behavior. Here are two to get you started:

   "He's got shifty eyes!"

   "They see eye to eye on the issue!"

   When you have completed your list, compare your observations with those of others in the class. Discuss what the words mean and what attitudes and assumptions underlie them.
2. Perfumes and after-shave lotions are ac-

cessories. Write a statement about why people wear certain brands. Use specific advertising appeals and familiar brand names to illustrate your points.

3. Pin-striped suits and lace-up shoes are associated with men's business dress, at least in some parts of the country. List three professions and then put down two or three dress items that are associated with women and men in those professions.

4. Based on what you have learned about the relationship between dress and conformity, why does the armed services insist on regulation uniforms? Is the same true of schools and colleges that insist that students wear uniforms? What other occupations require specified clothing as standard dress? Write a short report to your instuctor explaining your ideas.

5. Listen to six people speak, and listen for the use of paralanguage in what they say. What do the people you listen to reveal about themselves through these nonverbals? Write a short report to your instructor explaining your findings.

6. Do an experiment of your own in the use of space and distance by purposely violating the "unwritten" rules. For example, when having coffee with a friend, sit one seat away from her or him. Or move very close when speaking to someone that you have just met. Write a short report about the reactions you observe. In the statement, describe what you did. Also you might want to explain the experiment to your subjects afterward so you can include their reactions in your report as well.

7. This problem on listening involves you as the source of information. Spend a day listening "actively." Take a conversation, speech, or lecture from the day's experience and analyze it according to the Six P's. Write down your analysis and be prepared to share it with the class.

8. This assignment requires making a list of various types of nonverbal behavior you observe: watch various people and see if you can spot examples of

   a. Clothing used to make a personal statement.
   b. Reactions to use of space or distance.
   c. Posture showing attitude or profession.
   d. Gestures used as language substitutes.
   e. Unusual eye behavior.

   Describe briefly the situation and how you interpreted the actions.

9. Review the six examples of poor listening listed earlier in this chapter under "Perceiving." Describe the attitudes each example probably represents in the person. Is there any way to overcome these barriers in others? in yourself? Prepare to discuss your findings in class.

10. Someone has said that "all good human communication begins with good listening." Under what conditions would you disagree with this statement? Write a brief explanation of your attitude toward the need to listen effectively at work. Ask your instructor to point out any possible barriers or inconsistencies in your analysis.

CHAPTER 20

CONDUCTING SUCCESSFUL INTERVIEWS, MEETINGS, AND CONFERENCES

Jill Cassidy is the personnel director of a large publishing company. She has just been asked by her boss to discover why there has been an unusually high turnover rate among employees in the trade paperback division. Naturally, this is a delicate task because Jill will have to interview people in that department, winning their confidence so that they will "open up" and disclose what is really going on. She will need to decide whom to interview first and what questions to ask. For example, she is curious about whether the recent transfer of the president of the division has affected morale or whether various factions are engaged in destructive infighting. (She has heard rumors to this effect.) Still, having written down her goals and a series of questions, Jill knows that the most important asset she will have in these interviews is her ability to listen and then to sort out what she has heard. With this in mind, she picks up the phone and dials the extension of the first person on her list.

In this chapter we will discuss three important types of spoken business communications—interviews, meetings, and conferences—so that you will learn to use them in a way similar to the way Jill Cassidy does.

CONDUCTING INTERVIEWS

Like Jill Cassidy, managers often use interviews to obtain useful or even crucial information. If properly conducted, they can provide a wealth of information about everything from employees' promotability to customer satisfaction with products and services.

But before going any further, what exactly is an interview? Interviews are structured conversations, moderated by the interviewer and conducted to gather and give information to achieve a specific objective. Depending on the purpose or goal, we may divide interviews into four general types:

What are the four types of business interviews? How do they differ from one another?

BASIC TYPES OF BUSINESS INTERVIEWS

1. *Informative*—giving, receiving, or trading information.
2. *Problem Solving*—researching and isolating difficulties, as well as seeking and implementing solutions.
3. *Counseling*—advising employees, including that done in the performance appraisal.
4. *Persuasive*—influencing attitudes, opinions, beliefs, or behavior.

Informative interviews are the ones most commonly used in business. In them information is given, received, or traded. Examples are the interviews conducted by public opinion pollsters, which are used to guide many marketing and advertising campaigns, and the screening and hiring interviews, discussed in greater detail in Chapter 11. As you may remember, an employer conducts a screening interview to narrow the choices for a specific job, and then, having accomplished this, follows with a hiring interview to decide who out of the pared-down list of candidates is most suitable for the job. A third personnel interview that is also informative is the *exit interview*, held when an employee is retiring or leaving the company for some other reason.

How do screening, hiring, and exit interviews related to one another?

Problem-solving interviews are used to find ways to relieve one or more difficulties a company faces. For example, such sessions may be about issues concerning working conditions, production, or employee relations. Employed by both labor and management, they are based on the problem-solving formula described in Chapter 2: (1) identify the problem, (2) discover the cause(s), (3) evaluate alternative solutions, (4) select and apply the best solution, and (5) follow through.

Counseling interviews are held to show employers' continuing interest in employees' problems, job satisfaction, and relations with one another. Because of increasing concern about workers' attitudes and welfare, such interviews are on the increase. The alcohol and drug abuse programs sponsored by many large corporations often include them.

A variation of the counseling interview is the *evaluation interview*. In it the employer assesses job performance so that decisions can be made about promotion, retention, or salary adjustments.

Persuasive interviews are designed to influence interviewees to change their opinions, attitudes, beliefs, or behaviors. Therefore, their emphasis differs from that of the other three types of interviews. For one thing, persuasive interviews stress giving information to interviewees rather than receiving it from them. For another, they rely on the selection and ordering of information to suit the interviewees' needs. Thus, the owner of a messenger service may conduct a persuasive interview with an employee who had more than one accident last year.

During the session, the interviewer might choose—based on his or her knowledge of the employee—to emphasize the negative consequences of unsafe driving more than the positive consequences of safe driving. Such an approach might, the interviewer feels, be more effective in persuading the messenger to drive more carefully. Another example of a persuasive interview is the *sales interview*, in which the interviewer tries to persuade the interviewee to buy a particular newspaper, TV repair service, and so forth.

Suppose you are the production manager of a small manufacturing company. During the last three months, production on the night shift has steadily slipped, and you want to know why. Since you can discover no apparent cause for the slowdown, it is time to obtain more specific information. This information can come from only one source: the workers themselves. But which of the four types of interviews should you use? The answer depends on the approach you take. Perhaps you want to gather information. You could then begin by calling some of the workers into the office and asking them why production is down. What do you think would happen? How useful would the results be? Most probably you would gather a great deal of confusing and conflicting testimony and be no closer to solving your problem than before.

The problem here is that interviews, especially information-gathering ones, appear deceptively simple: you ask a question, you receive an answer. But is this answer valid and useful? That depends on a number of factors related to interviewing techniques. These factors can either create or relieve communication barriers.

As you may remember, the discussion in Chapter 2 focused on intrapersonal, interpersonal, and organizational barriers. Many of these—for example, differences in perception or fear of a supervisor—can crop up during an interview. To eliminate these barriers or decrease their effect, an interviewer needs to be highly skilled.

Does the type of question you ask make a difference in the response you get? Explain.

In conducting interviews to solve your production problem, you will have to be similarly adept. First, you should prepare a series of unthreatening questions, such as "Would you be surprised if I told you production was down?" or "Do you have any suggestions on how we can increase our production?" Those questions are designed to get the workers talking about the situation. Once this is accomplished, you can ask your real questions. In fact, after asking them in a number of interviews, you have assembled information and evaluated it. In this way, you have discovered two problems: the night shift is shorthanded and two of your experienced workers are slowing production with "horseplay." Now, to verify your findings, you can monitor the situation. If the result confirms your perceptions, then you can take appropriate action.

Naturally, the basic format for an interview is question and answer. Normally, the interviewer asks prepared questions and the interviewee responds to them. Unless you have good reason, your questions in an interview should be straightforward, objective, concrete, and not too difficult. As you proceed with the questioning, it is important not to appear to be threatening. If the interviewee feels put on the "hot seat," or believes you are asking trick questions, he or she probably will become defensive. Reaching your objective will then become more difficult.

An interview is dynamic, not static, and the direction it will take is often unpredictable. Knowing this, successful interviewers plan a general strategy; yet, they retain some flexibility to change when needed as the session progresses. So careful planning is crucial to reaching the goal of an interview. Also important are effective gathering and interpretation of information, setting a good interview climate, and evaluation of the interview's success afterward.

Preparing to Conduct an Interview

What are the three stages of the interview process?

The interview process has three stages: (1) *preparation*, or the thought and planning before the interview; (2) *action*, or conducting the interview; and (3) *evaluation*, or interpreting the success of the interview.

Suppose you are preparing for an interview. What should you do first? Begin by deciding what your purpose or goal is. Of course, you won't know exactly what you are going to discover until you hear some responses from the interviewers. However, at this stage, you should be able to state the purpose well enough to establish your informational needs and the criteria you will use in evaluating answers.

After you have defined your goal, you must design questions that will elicit useful responses. Thus, if you are going to interview several people to fill a job vacancy in the stock acquisitions department, your questions should be specific enough so that you will get comparable answers. Yet they should not be so restrictive that interviewees will have little choice about how to respond.

For example, a question such as "What are your qualifications for working?" is too broad. A more appropriate question might be, "In what ways are you qualified for this job?" (When constructing appropriate interview questions, you might find it helpful to review the sections in Chapter 13 on questionnaire development and the section in Chapter 11 on employment interviews.)

The last step in the preparation stage is to select a place to hold the interview. Where an interview is held may have a decided effect on interviewees' responses. For example, in interviewing your night shift workers about the drop in productivity, two places you should *not* have chosen were your office and the production area. Holding the interviews in your office may be intimidating; the production area may be too noisy and too crowded. (The site you finally did choose was an empty conference room, a good natural environment for such a highly charged interview.)

Gathering Information: Listening to Others

Especially for you, the interviewer, listening is an active process. It is active because you cannot assume that interviewees hear you correctly or that you have interpreted their words as they intended. Thus, throughout the session, you should be checking to discover if you and the other person have heard each other correctly.

Which is better, deliberate or empathetic listening? Why?

Two types of listening are *deliberate* and *empathetic*. Deliberate listeners translate information as they hear it. When receiving information during a conversation, they fit it into their own perspective, filtering and prejudging what they hear. In contrast, empathetic listeners focus on the sender's feelings and viewpoint as well as on the information itself. Such listeners try to avoid filtering and prejudging information.

As a result, they listen more thoroughly than deliberate listeners. Also, deliberate listeners hear information within their own context, whereas empathetic listeners hear it from the sender's context. For these reasons, empathetic listeners are more effective in interviewing than deliberate listeners because they receive more and less distorted information.

Besides listening for context, interviewers also actively listen for facts, such as names, dates, places, and other details. To record them, most use a note pad during the session. Some also employ a tape recorder or even a videotape recorder.

An interviewee's nonverbal behavior can also help the interviewer assess attitudes and interpret verbal comments. For example, job seekers often try to hide their nervousness during interviews; however, quivering hands, a high-pitched voice, and so on may communicate these feelings. The most useful application of nonverbal communication in interviewing, though, occurs when the interviewee's words and actions do not agree. Smart interviewers often take this as a cue to explore matters further. (See Chapter 19 for more information on developing listening skills and interpreting nonverbal behavior.)

Giving Meaning to Other People's Words

Every business office you work in will, even on a seemingly slow day, teem with messages; the audible and visible messages often compete with the unspoken or unseen. None of these messages, as noted in Chapter 1, has any meaning independently. They wait for us to assign meaning to them. Thus when you sit at your desk reading the new staffer's memo, you assign meaning to the message, define its importance, and decide if and how you are going to respond.

Whatever interpretation you give a message, this meaning is based on your individual perception. No two people receive messages in the same way. As we have already seen, differing backgrounds and situations create numerous filters through which we process information.

Thus, differences in language skill, views of others, semantics, sense of timing, positions within the company, and so on can affect the meaning we assign to messages that we hear. As for the speakers of these messages, their feelings, listening ability, patterns of thought, and how they deal with others, for example, influence the way they use words. These factors even influence how receivers hear these messages. Because of all these variables, unintentional error is possible in any interpersonal communication—both in speaking and listening.

For these reasons, be especially careful not to interpret messages in interviews from your own perspective alone. Instead, take the entire situation into account, including how interviewees might understand what is being said. For example, when you interviewed your employees about the production problems on the night shift, you had to consider that they might react poorly to a phrase such as, "hiring new employees."

Why do people assign different meanings to words?

Even though you had been thinking of adding more workers to relieve the burden of those on that shift, you were careful. You avoided saying something like, "I'm thinking about hiring some new employees because production is down on your shift." The reason behind your calculated avoidance was relatively simple: you were aware that your current workers might interpret this sentence from the perspective of a fixed number of workers—the present number. In other words, you were afraid they might have interpreted what you said to mean, "We are thinking about *replacing* some of our employees with new workers." If they did, their responses to your questions would have been colored by their fear of being laid off or fired.

Why do interviewers probe for information?

Probing relies on following through on the hints or clues that have been dropped during the interview. When interviewers probe, they temporarily set aside the planned interview structure to investigate a response further. For example, suppose an interviewee answers your question on why he or she left the last job somewhat vaguely. At this point, you might ask for more specific details. Some probe questions you could ask are

"Can you tell me more about that?"

"Can you give me a more specific example?"

"What did you mean when you said . . . ?"

The ability to probe is a measure of the interviewer's skill and flexibility. By probing, he or she reshapes the interview to receive the most accurate responses.

Establishing a Successful Interview Climate

If you can establish the best communication climate possible, you can get the best interview possible. To achieve this, you must first establish a positive and professional rapport with the person(s) you are interviewing. A good climate can be set at the start of the interview with your explaining why you are conducting it and how you plan to use the information you gain. If you are confident, sincere, and objective in your demeanor, the interviewee should respond candidly. If, however, you are unclear or in any way evasive, you might get responses in kind.

Try to act as if the people in your life accept you without being critical or judgmental. If you can create a nonthreatening setting, your interviewees will drop their defenses and talk openly and honestly with you.

Also, remember how you felt when you were being interviewed. If you can draw upon these memories successfully, you can make the interviewee feel both comfortable and valued. Once you set up this supportive atmosphere, you can then use your skills in planning, interpersonal communication, and evaluation.

Evaluating the Interview's Success

What role does evaluation play in interviewing?

You've completed your interview. But have you really? No. You haven't evaluated whether you have reached your goals. For example, if your goal was to gain information about worker satisfaction in your department, did the responses tell you whether your workers were satisfied? You can answer such questions by testing interview information you received against the guidelines laid out in Chapter 11. If you suspect the information you received, you may have to do follow-up interviews.

Another consideration in evaluating an interview is to examine the quality of the decision you make on the basis of the gathered evidence. Remember, any decision is only as good as the data on which it rests. Not only might interviewing permit you to check on whether your decision is working, but it also may help you gain better insight for making future decisions as well. Too, it could help you to head off similar problems when you see them developing.

So far, we have mainly been considering informative interviews. However, the other types of interviews may also be measured in terms of goal achievement. For instance, if you have conducted a sales interview with a new client, has it led to an order for office supplies, or videocassettes, or whatever? If not, what can you do to achieve your purpose? Perhaps you can schedule another interview. Or you might decide to send a sales letter and brochure. The important thing is to work with all the feedback you have after the interview to evaluate your success and plan for appropriate follow-up. To help ensure the success of your interview, consult the interview checklist that follows:

INTERVIEW CHECKLIST

1. Preparing for the interview.
   a. What is the purpose of the interview?
      (1) Informative?
      (2) Problem solving?
      (3) Counseling?
      (4) Persuasive?
   b. What might interfere with communication or the communication climate?
      (1) Intrapersonal barriers?
      (2) Interpersonal barriers?
      (3) Organizational barriers?
   c. What kinds of questions are most appropriate?
   d. What information, if any, should you supply?
   e. What is the best location for the interview?
2. Conducting the interview.
   a. Have you created a positive rapport?
   b. Are you listening with empathy? with an open mind?
   c. What is the interviewee's point of view?
   d. How might your own perceptions differ from those of the interviewee?
   e. Is there any disagreement between the interviewee's words and his or her nonverbal responses?
   f. What specific responses do you want to probe further?
3. Evaluating the interview.
   a. Did the interview fulfill its purpose?
   b. Is the information valid? Is it useful?
   c. Should a follow-up interview be planned?

LEADING GROUPS AND HOLDING MEETINGS

When John Keane looked at his office calendar, he groaned so loudly that his assistant, who was seated outside his office, asked him what was wrong. "Three meetings, today. That's what's wrong. What a waste of time," came the reply.

If a poll were taken among executives, it would without doubt show strong support for John Keane's sentiments. However, the cause of this dissatisfaction is not the meetings themselves; rather, it is the poor planning that goes into them. Or it may be, at least in part, that some leaders do not know how to deal with a group of people. Or it may be that some people do not know when to call a meeting. Some managers, for example, hold weekly meetings even when no one has anything to discuss. Others never hold a meeting, or they wait so long to do so that when one is finally held, everyone reels under the work load.

Or sometimes managers do not know what kind of meeting to have, how to move toward a goal during one, or how to control one without stifling everyone. Or the leader may not know how to resolve conflicts that arise.

In short, so that the John Keanes of the world of work won't groan at the thought of a meeting, modern managers need to know how to lead meetings. To do that, though, they need to know some basics about group communication.

Meetings Mean Group Communication

When people attend a meeting, they usually expect to work in unison to achieve a specific goal. Business meetings, like interviews, are conducted for various reasons:

What are the reasons to hold business meetings?

1. To give and receive information, which may include such ongoing departmental business as reporting, sharing information, and making announcements.
2. To evaluate ongoing projects, such as the next step in a public relations campaign.
3. To solve problems that may arise, such as cost overruns or production shortfalls.
4. To make decisions, such as where to hold an upcoming conference.
5. To implement plans, such as coordinating the efforts of two teams working on different parts of the same project.
6. To respond to special situations, such as raising employee morale after the loss of a key contract bid.

What is group dynamics? What influences it?

Even though a meeting group is composed of individuals, the communication within the group is more complex than is that between individuals. This is true because we are dealing with each person's nature *and* that of the group itself. The group tends to take on its own characteristics and qualities, and they affect communication. Behavior within a group—*group dynamics*—is influenced by three major factors:

1. *The personality of each individual.* Each person's nature affects how he or she acts in a group. Some people are, for example, passive by

nature. In a large group—a meeting of the office staff, for instance—such individuals will tend to hold back and not participate unless they are actively drawn in. Leaders can encourage participation in a number of ways. For example, they can address specific questions to the quieter person, questions they know he or she can answer and feel good about. Or they may ask that person to explain or demonstrate something he or she is expert in.

2. *The role a person plays within the group.* When you attend a business meeting, your function or role is quite different from that when you attend a social event or a lecture. You are the same person, yet your relationship with other members to each of these groups is based on the nature of the gathering and its purpose. For example, in a problem-solving meeting of your department, the vice president may assign you the task of taking minutes. Since you are recording what is said, you will probably be unable to participate in the discussion as readily as other group members. At another meeting, relieved of this responsibility, you may participate more freely.

   People who know what their role is during a meeting will enter into it more fully and usefully than will those who wonder why they are there. One way in which a skilled leader can help those who will attend a meeting he or she has called is to prepare and circulate a clear agenda in advance. Participants will then have some idea of the role they may play. Or the leader may tell key people in advance what their role is.

3. *The activity of the group itself.* As individual members interact, groups assume their own identity. For example, a group that gathered to investigate and give advice about a problem may find its time being taken up by one person. That person may dominate the discussion while offering no assistance in reaching the meeting's goals. If this occurs, it will take a skilled leader to return the group to its mission. In doing so, he or she must understand the interactions that caused members to veer from their original direction. Such interactions influence group communication as much as do individual personalities of the roles each person plays.

Besides these three major influences on group behavior, other factors can affect it also. These include (4) the number of people present at a meeting; (5) their task, goals, or agenda; (6) the structure of the situation, whether formal or informal; (7) how well group members know each other; (8) the status and power of those present; and (9) the setting for the meeting and the occasion of it. Each of these factors can affect perception and attitudes as well as the quality of communication during the meeting. Watch for the ways they make a difference in the examples that follow in the next section.

The Group Leadership Role

What qualities must a leader have? Some people believe a leader is someone who will solve all the problems, foresee all the outcomes, and do all the work for the group. Others see a leader as anyone whom members consent to follow. Yet, a leader is neither all powerful nor a mere figurehead. Perhaps an effective leader can best be described as someone who can help a group reach its goals in the shortest amount of time, using the least amount of energy, and creating the least amount of friction. To achieve the group's goals, the leader may use an endless variety of styles or techniques. Whatever approach the leader of a business group may choose, though, the person who can create and maintain an open, positive climate will get the best results.

What skills must an effective group leader have?

Effective leaders must know what is going on within the group at all times. Thus, they should be able to monitor communication at several levels at the same time. In addition, they should know well the topic under discussion and be sensitive to the group's dynamics. Then, too, the leaders should chart the progress being made, delegate authority when necessary, and deal flexibly with group needs.

Effective leaders also must be able to recognize the positive and negative behaviors of individual group members. If group members begin to behave negatively, skilled leaders should respond quickly. They should either modify the member's course or, if matters become serious, remove the troublemaker from the group. In contrast, most meetings profit from the positive behaviors of group builders or maintainers, just as they are threatened by the negative behaviors of those who block a group's progress.

For example, suppose a meeting has been convened to set the rules for awarding merit pay in your company. During the meeting, a member who can relieve tension might make jokes that help other members keep their tempers, whereas a "playboy" or "playgirl" type might irritate members by showing off. When the showing off begins, the leader should intervene by saying something like, "Thanks for helping us cool down a bit, Annette. Now, Lolita, your point about weights for different tasks deserves more attention . . . ."

Or suppose a member uses the group's time to promote his or her own interests, in this case, expressing a grievance over merit pay. Here the leader might cut off the digression by referring to the meeting's agenda: "Len, that matter falls under Item III-C on the agenda. We'll want to hear your ideas when we reach that point."

Reference to the agenda might also quash a disruption from a member who simply likes to change the subject, especially when the group is making progress.

As for the member who is too aggressive, the leader might say, "Rita Mae, maybe a different approach would better help us advance the discussion. At this point, perhaps we should. . . ." The group may then be asked to take up discussion of another item or to discuss another aspect of the present item.

As you can see, the range of group member behaviors is vast and complex; therefore, leaders must be creative and use different approaches as problems arise. For example, using encouragement and specific questions, members who withdraw and tend not to participate can be brought into the discussion. Of course, others in the group can help the leader deal with problem members. In addition, we should recognize that all members, even the leader, adopt different behaviors at different times, and even do this in the same meeting. An effective group leader, however, can recognize this and deal effectively with situations so they do not disrupt the group's progress toward its goal.

An Ideal: People-on-Task Groups

Business managers traditionally view groups as being either *task oriented* or *people oriented.* This distinction is relevant because the group leader determines the pattern or organization that emerges in a group.

Some people recommend a task-oriented group, saying that company needs come first. Others recommend a people-oriented group, contending that without people, there *is* no organization.

How do task- and people-oriented groups differ?

What are the characteristics of these groups? In task-oriented groups, members tend to play roles that are subordinate to that of the leader whose directions they generally follow. Such groups may be more productive than those that are people oriented because they digress less and concentrate more on the task. However, task-oriented groups have two liabilities: (1) their hierarchical structure discourages members from checking on the quality of the leader's plan and modifying its weaknesses, and (2) new ideas can get ignored or can get a poor reception.

In contrast, because they have no dominant leader, people-oriented groups have the freedom to pursue different ideas and directions if they desire. However, their loose structure causes these groups to waste time reaching their goals. Also, individual members often compete against each other to gain dominance, with the result that people-oriented groups can easily lose their way.

Does a middle ground exist between the two groups? The answer is yes. A *people-on-task group* combines the best of each by offering both efficiency and free inquiry. The leader of such groups encourages members to contribute openly and frankly to the discussion, whereas members understand the need for a leader. Thus each complements the other because they understand the value of their combined contributions.

To form a people-on-task group, first allow some time at the outset to discuss goals and how to reach them. Each member should assist in forming this operational framework. Next, adopt a time schedule and assign or elect a leader. The leader's task is to direct, assist, and keep order during discussions.

Although your leader may challenge a statement to test its merit, he or she does not argue or adopt a particular point of view. Instead, the leader directs the discussion toward the goal. After the members reach a consensus on a particular point, the leader states it and moves on to the next item for discussion. Members assist the process by trying to reach agreement and by not challenging the leader's authority to make decisions and resolve conflicts.

These people-on-task groups have the best chance of arriving at good business decisions. Participants can accomplish a task with speed and ease. Their feelings of accomplishment after reaching goals in this type of group structure add to their self-esteem and sense of importance to the organization. Once begun, the process builds on itself.

When to Hold a Meeting

What goes into making the decision to hold a meeting?

In deciding when to hold a meeting, the first question to ask is, "Do we need it?" If you can reach your goal by selective interviewing, writing a memo, or holding a telephone conference call, you don't need to call a meeting. But you do need to hold a meeting if any of the following six needs is present: (1) to give and receive information, (2) to evaluate continuing projects, (3) to solve problems, (4) to make decisions, (5) to implement plans, or (6) to respond to special situations.

Suppose you do decide to have a meeting. Remember that no particular time of day or day of the week is "best." First, check everyone's schedule to find what is most convenient for most members of the group. Then announce the meeting early enough so that those who have conflicts will have time to resolve them. Stick with holding meetings only when needed but do plan ahead to avoid conflicts in schedules and so on.

You have reserved the conference room for 3:00 P.M. Tuesday. Now the next question is, How much time should you allot to your meeting on production scheduling? The answer depends on how complex you think this problem is and the number of people you have called in to resolve it. Obviously, the more complex the problem, the more time is required to solve it. Moreover, if you have asked ten people to attend the meeting instead of five, then expect the meeting to be longer than if the smaller number were present. When scheduling meeting time, also consider these factors:

1. Has a similar problem been explored by this group before? If so, use the amount of time taken to handle that issue as a guide for setting the time.
2. Is this a new type of problem for this group? If so, allow more time for discussion and clarification.
3. Will the meeting last longer than two hours? If so, allow a break during the proceedings. Group members become less productive when meetings last for long periods of time.

Note too that the amount of time you set aside for a meeting also depends on what type it is.

Types of Meetings

Based on their functions, we may say there are four types of business meetings:

What are the characteristics of the four types of business meetings?

1. *Organizational.* Organizational meetings are held regularly to conduct ongoing business.
2. *Informational.* Informational meetings are held specifically or regularly to present information and gather feedback.
3. *Problem solving.* Problem-solving meetings usually are held specially to seek solutions to specific problems.
4. *Brainstorming.* Brainstorming meetings are a special type of problem-solving meeting held to generate as many solutions to a specific problem as possible. Solutions are evaluated later.

All meetings in business organizations fit one of these categories.

Planning a Meeting Agenda

Of what use is an agenda?

You have been asked to attend a two-hour meeting on the company's cash flow problems. After a few minutes, somebody brings up the subject of office security. Suddenly everyone is actively discussing whether security should be beefed up. Is one guard for the entire company really enough? Should visitors be required to sign in at the desk in the lobby? Should messengers be sent to one place and not be allowed on all floors? By the time the discussion returns to the original subject of the meeting, 30 minutes have elapsed. Planning—making an agenda and sticking to it—could have averted this incident.

An *agenda* lays the basis for a meeting. It is especially critical when, as in the example, conserving time is a factor in the meeting. Agendas show four types of information:

1. Topics to be discussed
2. Relative importance of topics
3. Order in which topics will be discussed
4. Time schedule

As you can see from this list, agendas are guides. Use them to tell yourself where you should be in a meeting, where to go next, and how much time both the individual parts and the whole process should take.

REGULAR MEETING AGENDA*
Athens Valley Board of Realtors

Time: April 7, 7:30 P.M. — Mary Lee Hollyworth, presiding

Old Business:

Approval of the minutes of last meeting	5 min
Treasurer's report	10 min
Vote on tabled motion: "Resolved that the Athens Valley Board of Realtors will endorse no candidate for public office"	5 min

New Business:

Informational items	
Special report by Glenn Miles, analyst, UTI Bank: "Charting Long-Term Interest Rates in Realty"	20 min
Reference material will be distributed for members' personal files.	
Legislative Analysis Committee report by Sam Hall: "The Effect of New Escrow Act SB 410"	10 min
Discussion items	
Carpeting for the board room (report by James and Maria Bacon).	15 min
Action items	
Time and place for annual spring luau	
Elect luau chairperson and committee (four people)	10 min
Authorize treasurer to pay outstanding bills	5 min
Approve new board members: Gerald Manners, DDD Realtors; Sally Gerardo, Smith and Associates	15 min
Bulletin Board—Special Announcements	10 min
Motion to Adjourn	9:15 P.M.

NEXT MEETING: Thursday, April 14, 7:30 P.M.

*All items on this agenda are time certain. Members who wish time on the agenda should call or write Mary Lee Hollyworth at least one week before a regularly scheduled meeting.

FIGURE 20-1 Agenda for regular business meeting.

What are the two types of business meetings?

To prepare an agenda, first consider whether you are holding a *regular* meeting, that is, one that recurs at prescribed intervals, or a *special* meeting. Keeping both the group's size and the meeting's purpose in mind, set reasonable goals and allow time for participants to reach them. Figure 20-1 shows a sample agenda you may follow in planning a regular meeting. When you are planning a special meeting, follow the sample agenda in Figure 20-2.

Both these sample agendas, though, are designed for formal

SPECIAL MEETING AGENDA*
Accounting Department Members, Contrack, Ltd.

8:00–12:00 noon — Presiding: Allan Baker
Wednesday, June 2 — Department Head

PROBLEM: Following our recent merger with Saticoy Industries, problems have emerged because our computer systems are not compatible.

QUESTIONS: Should we change our software to allow interface? If so, what is the best method? How long would it take? How much would it cost? What kinds of difficulties might we expect in the change-over period? And what about our records? How would they be affected?

MEETING TIME

8:00–9:00	Orientation and background (Allan Baker and Geoffrey Richardson). Questions from the floor, general discussion.
9:00–9:30	Technical implications (Jan Ng, field coordinator for Data Processing Company).
9:30–10:00	Informal discussion (coffee and danish in staff dining room).
10:00–10:30	Preliminary recommendations from group.
10:30–11:00	Identification of special problem areas. Assignment of committees to facilitate parts of change-over and special problems. Note all committees will elect their own chairs who will be responsible to present progress reports at end of meeting.
11:00–11:30	Committee work sessions.
11:30–11:45	Committee chairs to present recommendations and estimate of additional time required to complete assignments.
11:45–12:00	Summary of progress (Allan Baker).

* A package of information about our alternatives will be put in your mailbox. *Please read before the meeting!*

FIGURE 20-2 Agenda for a special problem-solving meeting.

meetings. Other occasions, such as an informal meeting among three or four employees of a small company to explain a minor new office procedure, would call for a simpler agenda. It may contain just the time and subject. Thus, the form of the agenda used is determined by circumstances—audience, organization, and purpose of the meeting.

Maintaining Order and Evaluating Feedback

From the first, the meeting on next year's budget is noisy and unruly. Afterward, you vow to maintain order at any future meetings you lead. To do so, you recognize that you need to follow some rules of order, even though your leadership style will vary depending on the formality of the occasion.

How can following rules of order help you run meetings more effectively?

Rules of order are simply a set of procedures that govern the way in which a group will conduct its business. These rules assist progress in much the same way as well-placed traffic signs help to save time and avoid congestion. For example, a motion, the immediate topic for action, is any item that requires a vote of the group. Motions may or may not be discussed—depending on the form they take. How to handle motions, amendments, and other topics of procedure are discussed in books such as *Roberts' Rules of Order*. While these rules have their fullest application in formal meetings, they make useful guidelines in coordinating informal meetings as well.

Such rules of order not only help you keep control of a meeting, but they also save time and allow everyone an equal opportunity to contribute. Although group members should know and abide by them, it is the leader's job to ensure that everyone follow them. Therefore, the group leader should be familiar enough with these rules to use them to conduct a meeting that runs smoothly and is fair too.

During a meeting, group members give both verbal and nonverbal feedback to the leader. He or she should be able to interpret this feedback and thereby keep the meeting on course. Because feedback occurs constantly, the leader has to be quick and accurate in perceiving and interpreting feedback and then in taking appropriate action on the basis of it. (See Chapter 1 for a discussion of the principles of feedback. See Chapter 2 for a description of the communication barriers arising from feedback. And see Chapter 19 to learn how to gather and interpret nonverbal forms of feedback.)

Conflict and Conflict Resolution

Suddenly, during a meeting you are leading on customer complaints about a line of goods, a disagreement between two group members erupts into a shouting match. Although disagreements are inevitable and can result in positive change, here one has reached the *conflict* stage. At this point, its effect on problem solving is negative. Such conflict provokes distrust, aggression, suspicion, and hostility. These, in turn, lead group members to concentrate on winning the argument. In extreme situations, they may even break off communication entirely. The resulting stalemate, unless resolved, will prevent them from reaching the meeting's goal. Can you recognize conflict early and ward it off before it gets out of hand?

Why is it important to control conflict in a meeting?

First, you have to find out what is really going on. Do the people who are fighting disagree about the subject under discussion? Or do they dislike each other? Or is it both? Once you have discovered this, you have to isolate the factors that are creating the conflict. Finally, you need to act to defuse them.

Suppose, for example, you are conducting a departmental meeting with 12 people present. The subject being discussed is when to schedule vacations. One person—someone disliked by the others—selects a date that conflicts with the date chosen by another, more popular person. Ignoring pleas to cooperate, this unpopular person insists that as the most senior employee present, he (or she) has first choice. Quickly, the meeting reaches an impasse.

At first, this may appear to be a conflict over conflicting interests. (Both people gave reasons originally for the dates they preferred.) However, it may also be seen in an entirely different light. The disliked employee is acting as a "blocker," someone who is more interested in himself or herself than in the group's goals or the other members' feelings. Assuming that this person acts like this in other situations as well, the group may (and does) show little support for his (or her) opinions, regardless of the topic discussed.

Whatever its origins, you must solve the immediate problem of the stalled meeting. Your job is to restore order, reinstate communication, and return the meeting to its original course.

One way to achieve this is to move on to the next item on the agenda. Then return to vacation scheduling later when tempers have cooled. Another possible solution is to speak to both employees individually to attempt to resolve the conflict through a compromise. In doing this, you will recognize that decisions should be based on more than popularity, for instance.

Having decided which of these options—or any others you might develop—is best, then move decisively to enact it. The following checklist on conducting meetings should be helpful in guiding you through such encounters. Use it to plan, conduct, and follow them up.

CHECKLIST FOR CONDUCTING MEETINGS

Before *Plan and Anticipate*

1. Is a meeting really needed?
2. Specifically, who should attend? The larger the group, the less the individual participation and usually the less that is accomplished.
3. Where and when should the meeting be held? Location and timing influence both attendance and participation.
4. Has enough time been allowed to prepare and distribute an agenda *before* the meeting is held?
5. Will group members know the meeting goals and what is expected of them *before* the meeting is held?

During *Assist and Guide*

1. Have you assigned someone to keep a record or minutes?
2. Are you using time effectively? Will you start and end as planned? Will the meeting stay on schedule? You might set a time limit for discussing topics, especially those that take more time than necessary.
3. Are you monitoring what is happening? Keep track of both the members and the discussion. Be ready to resolve problems as they develop. Head off digressions and keep order.
4. Are you ready to delegate responsibility? Assign someone to inquire into problems that must be investigated and set a deadline for it.
5. Do you summarize as agreement on topics is reached?

After *Follow-through*

1. Are the records accurate? Check the information carefully.
2. Who will type and distribute the records or minutes?
3. Have you reviewed ongoing items from the meeting to see what steps to take next on them? Make a chart listing (a) unfinished business to continue at the next meeting, (b) names of those assigned special tasks, and (c) deadlines.
4. Were the goals met?
5. Should another meeting be held to complete the business at hand?

HOLDING SUCCESSFUL CONFERENCES

How does a conference differ from a meeting?

The word *conference* is sometimes used as a synonym for the word *meeting*. Yet, actually, a conference is a special type of large meeting in which representatives of various parts of an organization or group discuss a common problem or issue. For example, within a large company, the president might call a conference to be attended by executives from all departments to discuss budget cutbacks or affirmative-action policies.

Sometimes the word is used even more broadly, as when organizations within a similar field send representatives to a conference—or convention—to discuss or share information on common concerns. These kinds of events are usually sponsored by a larger organization of some sort, such as the American Management Association or the Association of Automobile Manufacturers.

Suppose you have to conduct a conference. How would you go about it? Actually, it is done in much the same way as conducting a regular business meeting. If you compare the two, you'll notice that the primary difference is one of *scale*—conferences involving more people and, consequently, a number of support activities. However, conferences also set goals and follow similar procedures as meetings.

What are the four keys to holding successful meetings?

Besides the ever-present need for good communication, the four keys to conference success are

- Planning
- Coordination
- Participation
- Evaluation

Conference Planning

First, you must identify a need and a sponsor. Perhaps a number of steel companies need to discuss their relations to unions. If so, who will coordinate and pay for the event? Whoever does is the sponsor. Sponsors can be as large as an international body or as small as a single manufacturer.

Conference Coordination

What does a conference coordinator do?

After determining a need and finding a sponsor, you have to assign someone to make the necessary arrangements and act as a central source of information. This person, who is in charge of the conference, is the *conference coordinator*. Usually, working in conjunction with a committee, he or she plans and supervises all communications and liaison activities related to the event. The person accepting this job should be reliable, meticulous, decisive, and skilled in working with others.

Conference coordinating is so time consuming because it involves a number of levels of planning. Getting a selected group of people together in a single location for a specific purpose is a complex task. Suppose you have been assigned this job. First, it might be helpful to develop a schedule or time line that will identify each thing you have to do and when. Two basic management tools you might adapt for this purpose are CPM or PERT charts. CPM (critical path method), and PERT (program evaluation review technique) are similar techniques designed to aid in managing complex projects. For example, in planning a conference you can perform some activities at the same time, whereas others must follow one another in some sort of sequence. CPM and PERT charts use networking analysis to show what should be *done* and when it should be done—no matter how many interrelated activities or events are involved.

A conference coordinator's basic checklist might easily include a dozen or more activities where these techniques might be useful, such as

- Program planning
- Site selection
- Housing and reservations
- Air and ground transportation
- Registration and information services
- Meeting facilities
- Exhibit areas and security
- Food and beverages
- Entertainment
- Audiovisual support
- Related tours and activities
- Printed materials
- Promotion and publicity
- Budget, accounting, and gratuities
- Contracts and insurance
- Emergencies and safety
- Postconference evaluation
- Follow-up

Also, if you are coordinating a conference, you might find professional assistance from conference bureaus and services that are sponsored by local hotels, business groups, and government agencies.

Conference Participation

Those people interested in attending your conference should be notified through a series of well-prepared announcements and follow-up messages. A reverse time line, beginning with the date of the event, can show the relationship between your planning and the types of communication it involves. An abbreviated time line might look like this:

Date of conference

Date of third membership mailing: reminder and any recent information.

Date of second membership mailing: final program and registration materials.

Date of first membership mailing: initial announcement and general program description.

Each of your mailings should also include clear deadlines for participants.

Why should conference planners expect the unexpected? Isn't that overly pessimistic?

Finally, when planning a conference, expect the unexpected. Things will rarely work out exactly as you planned. Remember, Murphy's law states, "Whatever can go wrong will go wrong." However, if this happens during the early planning stages, you have time to solve the matter. But, naturally, as the event looms closer, your flexibility in this respect diminishes.

Conference Evaluation

Like meetings, conferences do not end with the last presentation. At least two other tasks remain. The first is to poll attendees for their reactions to the event, including their opinions about fees, publicity, and the program. The second is to submit a final report containing summaries of the program, the participants' reactions, and your own analysis and recommendations as coordinator to the sponsor. This last item is especially critical, for it forms the basis for planning of such similar events in the future.

In summary, as with planning and coordination, communication is required at every stage of a conference. People who are successful at coordinating a conference are skilled in all forms of written and oral communication: able to write memos, letters, and reports; negotiate with a wide variety of individuals and groups; and conduct an equally broad range of meetings. For these reasons, conferences may prove to be a dramatic test of your communicative abilities.

SUMMARY

1. Interviews are structured conversations, moderated by an interviewer, and conducted to gather and give information to achieve a specific objective. The four basic types of interviews are informative, problem solving, counseling, and persuasive.

2. Broadly speaking, the three stages of an interview are preparation, action, and evaluation. Preparation, the first stage, includes defining your goal, designing questions, and selecting a place to hold the interview.
3. Gathering information is part of the action stage of interviewing. It includes listening well and interpreting nonverbal behavior effectively.
4. Interpreting information—giving meaning to words—is also part of the action stage of an interview. Remember that your interpretation is based on individual perception. Sometimes you must probe to get the information you need, and there are effective ways to do it.
5. Establishing a successful interview climate, too, is part of the action stage of an interview. While you should attempt this at the beginning of the interview session, you should maintain a successful climate throughout the session.
6. Evaluation, the third stage of the interviewing process, is one that is too often neglected. Yet, only through effective evaluation can you improve your interviewing skills. In this stage, also, you evaluate the information gotten in the interview and decide whether a follow-up interview is needed.
7. Meetings are very important in business because many decisions—big and small—are made in them. To hold successful meetings, you must be familiar with three aspects of group dynamics: (a) the personality of each individual, (b) the role a person plays within the group, and (c) the activity of the group itself.
8. An effective group leader may best be described as someone who can help a group reach its goals in the shortest time, using the least amount of energy and creating the least amount of friction.
9. The ideal group is neither task nor people oriented to the exclusion of the other. Instead, it is people-on-task oriented.
10. As simple as it may sound, you should hold a meeting when you *need* one. Were this simple rule followed, think how many business meetings would never be held.
11. The types of business meetings are organizational, informational, problem solving, and brainstorming.
12. Whether your meeting is formal or informal, you should prepare an agenda—even if it is only a line or two long. Agendas show topics to be discussed, their relative importance, the order for discussing topics, and a time schedule. Agendas differ somewhat according to whether you're holding a regular or special meeting.
13. No meeting can be successful unless the leader can maintain order. In part, this is done by evaluating feedback.
14. Order is also kept in a meeting by resolving conflict effectively. Once you see that a stage of conflict exists, you may move on to another item on the agenda and return to the present one later, you may attempt a compromise, or you may react in some other appropriate manner. Whatever you decide to do, act decisively.
15. A conference is usually described as a large meeting in which various parts of an organization or group discuss a common problem or issue.
16. Besides the ever-present need for effective communication, the four keys to conference success are planning, coordination, participation, and evaluation.

Review Questions

1. Which of the four basic types of interviews is most common in business? Give an example that is not given in the text.
2. The evaluation interview is a variation of which of the four basic types? Give two examples in which these interviews might take place.
3. What are the three stages in the interview process? Briefly explain what is done in each type.
4. What difference is there between deliberate and empathetic listening in interviews? Which type is more productive? Why?
5. What is probing and how is it useful in interviews?
6. How can you evaluate the success of an interview?
7. Is a business meeting any different from a business interview? If so, what differences are there? If not, why use two terms to describe the same thing?
8. What three major factors influence behavior within a group—group dynamics?
9. What is meant by "people-on-task" groups? Why are they supposedly more effective than either task- or people-oriented groups?
10. What is your response to this statement from a company vice president: "We should hold a meeting every Monday morning to make sure we always keep up with everything"? Explain your answer.
11. Of what value is a meeting agenda? Must they be as elaborate as those shown in Figures 20-1 and 20-2 in the text. Defend your response.
12. Do you see any link between maintaining order in a meeting and evaluating feedback received during the session? Explain your response.
13. When a meeting reaches the conflict stage, does this mean the group leader has failed? Defend your response.
14. Is there any difference between a meeting and a conference, or are they synonyms? What then is a convention? Explain your answers.
15. Besides the ever-present need for effective communication, what are the four keys to holding a successful conference? Briefly explain the meaning of each key.

Exercises

1. Consider the list of communication barriers found in Chapter 2. Which of them could apply to an informative interview? Briefly describe a situation illustrating how each might affect communication? Also state what you would do to alleviate each barrier you find.
2. This exercise is designed to show the relationship between speaking and listening. Review the Six P's of listening described in Chapter 19. Adapt these principles to create Six P's of interviewing. Briefly explain what you mean by each "P."
3. Bring to class a list of the attributes of your class itself that make it a group. Then break up into small groups and compare your list with those of the other members. Discuss each attribute and compile a composite list of class characteristics. Be prepared to compare the list your group prepares with those of the other groups.

4. Assume you work for a company that bottles and sells soft drinks and you have a morale problem with some production line employees: namely, the bottling department workers are not getting along with those in packaging and crating. (Packaging and crating is one department.) Explain how an interview or a meeting might solve the problem. Which type or types of interviews or meetings would you hold? State the purpose for each meeting or interview you suggest.
5. The discussion in the text talks a lot about the need for good leadership and gives quite a few suggestions about how a leader can identify and resolve problems in interviews, meetings, and conferences. Yet, little or nothing is said directly about the qualities of a good leader. Your assignment is to research the qualities of effective leaders, especially in group settings. After gathering the necessary information, write a short informal report in which you explain your findings.
6. Assume you're a member of the conference committee for a professional organization in your academic field. For names, you might consult the *Encyclopedia of Associations* or the *Career Guide to Professional Associations.* The conference coordinator has asked you to prepare three letters to the membership announcing the pending conference. Create supporting details, such as the conference theme and dates, as required.
7. Assume you work in the office of a successful industrial plastics manufacturing company. Your department head comes to you one day and says, "We've got a problem with increased insurance premiums. Our underwriter, Lilly Genrhein of Rushmore Insurance, just telephoned to tell me our employee accident claims last quarter exceeded industry norms. Our insurance premiums have been raised 25 percent. I want to meet with the production supervisors and find out how we can increase worker safety. Call a meeting with them for next Thursday at 11:00." Your assignment is to prepare an agenda for the meeting.
8. This exercise requires four or five class members assuming the roles of employees working for a home appliance manufacturing company. Two others will be needed, one to be the superintendent of the shipping and receiving department and the other to be a police detective.

   The problem is this: Two dozen toaster ovens have been reported missing. Accounting has paperwork that shows they were sent to shipping and receiving last week to be shipped to the Acme Homewares Stores. There is no paperwork indicating that the items were shipped. Yet an exhaustive search has not uncovered the location of the ovens.

   Since this is not the first mysterious loss of merchandise, the supervisor decides to conduct a fact-finding interview with each employee to investigate whether one of them might have stolen the merchandise. After the first round of interviews is completed, the supervisor decides to have a police officer conduct a second round.

   Special instructions: The class members who are going to be the employees should meet outside the classroom—with no one else present—before the first round of interviews. They should agree, among themselves, (a) if there was a theft and (b) if so, who the guilty person(s) is. They should not tell anyone of their decisions but should allow these two factors to govern their answers to any questions that come up during the interviews.

The supervisor should also meet privately with the police officer—between the two interviews—to share impressions.

Conduct both sets of interviews. Have other class members observe the proceedings. After the interviews are completed, those not participating should be ready to vote on two questions: (1) was there a robbery and (2) if so, who is guilty. After the votes are in, conduct an open discussion with everyone about the dynamics of the interviews. Be sure to discuss the information and behaviors that led to forming the opinions that influenced votes.

9. Attend an open meeting of a formal organization, such as the student council on campus or a local business group. Prepare a written evaluation of the effectiveness of the meeting. Consider these points:

   Did participants use an agenda?
   Did they follow any rules of order?
   How well did the leader conduct the session?
   Do you have any recommendation to the group on ways to improve their meetings?

   Give specific examples to illustrate your analysis, such as a revised copy of the agenda or examples of the productive behaviors of meeting participants.

10. Read the following case to prepare for the assignment given in the last paragraph:

    Howard, the oldest member of the department, first heard the news from Irena during their morning coffee break. "While you were out of town, Mr. Gomez was transferred to Accounting. I hear they plan to put Betty Lovell in charge of us while they look for a permanent replacement to head the department." After his initial shock—the move had come quickly and without warning—Howard began to wonder what other changes were in store for him and his coworkers.

    Later that morning, Howard received a memo, signed by Betty, announcing a meeting to be held in two days to reorganize "problem areas" in the department. What did she mean by that? He called a friend, Jimmy Lowery, in Promotion. Jimmy had worked with Betty before. This conversation revealed some discouraging news: Betty Lovell had been assigned to Jimmy's area just before a major layoff and reorganization took place there.

    The morning of the meeting, Howard was still worried. As he sat down at the conference table with half a dozen fellow employees, who'd also heard about "Betty, the Executioner," the atmosphere was grim. Betty entered and called the meeting to order. The agenda, which she then passed out, contained nothing but routine items. But, even though the concerns of Howard and the others seemed unfounded, they were generally sullen and irritable. No one expanded on the items Betty wanted to discuss. It was as if another, more important agenda were on everyone's mind.

    When the meeting was over, Betty commented to her assistant that the staff meeting hadn't accomplished much; everyone had been so unfriendly. "No one mentioned any problems," she mused. "I wonder what's wrong."

    The next day Betty spoke with her boss and asked him what to do. "Well, Betty," he explained, "I can see you're concerned, but don't worry. You're new to that group and you're their superior. This creates a communication barrier, perhaps. You can't expect people to tell you everything right away. But I think you might have a morale problem if the situation keeps up. If it becomes a major problem, the staff probably have been talking among themselves. That would mean you likely could get some answers by conducting a personal interview with each of them. I've found the best way to get people to talk about their concerns is to establish a positive rapport on a one-to-one basis. If you discover you're dealing with individual problems, you can probably handle them immediately and informally; but if you discover a broader conflict, call a special departmental meeting and get everything out in the open."

Assume that the worst did happen: the problem not only continued but grew worse. If you were Betty Lovell, what would you do? Prepare a plan of action that would meet Betty's needs. The plan should provide ways to (a) identify the problems that exist, (b) alleviate them, and (c) assure that similar problems do not reoccur.

CHAPTER 21

COMMUNICATING EFFECTIVELY IN INTERNATIONAL BUSINESS

Your company, a major film producer, is interested in distributing its films and videos in a large Asian country. You are being sent to that country to negotiate the deal. The sales could be astronomical perhaps topping $1 billion, if you are successful.

However, because of the cultural differences between your two countries, some major problems have to be resolved. For example, the Asian country does not have stringent copyright laws that would protect your products against unauthorized duplication and distribution. In addition, the country has in the past only agreed to make transactions on a flat-fee basis, something most U.S. companies—yours included—find unattractive. Now poised on the eve of departure, you are beset by all sorts of worries. Most of them center on your ability to interpret correctly the signals that the public and private officials of this vastly different country will be sending to you. It is on the basis of this ability, you are sure, that the ultimate success of your mission will depend.

Why have many U.S. firms entered the international business market?

In the past 15 years, business agreements such as yours have become increasingly common as international business has grown tremendously. Before the 1970s many foreign countries imposed regulations against the United States that discouraged such transactions. However, since then, many of them have relaxed their regulations and a number of U.S. firms have consequently entered the international business market.

Today, several million U.S. citizens work abroad. Also, several thousand U.S. companies operate entirely outside the country. Because of this growth, management faces new problems. Working abroad for the first time, many managers find themselves in unfamiliar social and cultural environments. To be successful, they must learn to live and work with people with different values, attitudes, and customs.

In this chapter, we will examine a communication perspective that will help you to understand the complexity of international business by analyzing cultural and political differences, language and nonverbal factors, multinational corporate characteristics, and training needs for future international managers.

DIFFERENCES IN CONDUCTING BUSINESS DOMESTICALLY AND INTERNATIONALLY

Do successful business strategies in America always work abroad? Explain.

What symbolizes American business? Among other things, sophisticated marketing plans, elaborate advertising campaigns, and innovative management development programs make it distinctive. However, because these strategies work in America, this does not automatically mean that they will work in other countries.

Differences Between U.S. and International Operations

Factor	U.S. Operations	International Operations
Language	English used almost universally.	Local language must be used in many situations.
Culture	Relatively homogeneous.	Quite diverse, both between countries and within a country.
Politics	Stable and relatively unimportant.	Often volatile and of decisive importance.
Economy	Relatively uniform.	Wide variations among countries and between regions within countries.
Government interference	Minimal and reasonably predictable.	Extensive and subject to rapid change.
Labor	Skilled labor available.	Skilled labor often scarce, requiring training or redesign of production methods.
Financing	Well-developed financial markets.	Poorly developed financial markets. Capital flows subject to government control.
Market research	Data easy to collect.	Data difficult and expensive to collect.
Advertising	Many media available; few restrictions.	Media limited; many restrictions; low literacy rates rule out print media in some countries.
Money	U.S. dollar used universally.	Must change from one currency to another; fluctuating exchange rates and government restrictions are problems.
Transportation/ communication	Well developed and generally efficient.	Varies widely depending on the country and region.
Control	Always a problem. Centralized control will work.	Centralized control won't work. Must walk a tightrope between overcentralizing and losing control through overdecentralizing.
Contracts	Once signed, are binding on both parties.	Are subject to be renegotiated or cancelled if one party becomes dissatisfied.
Labor relations	Collective bargaining; can lay off workers easily.	Often cannot lay off workers; may have mandatory worker participation in management; workers may seek change through political process rather than collective bargaining.
Trade barriers	Nonexistent.	Extensive and very important.

FIGURE 21-1 Differences between U.S. and international operations. [From Robert G. Murdick, Richard H. Eckhouse, R. Carl Moor, and Thomas W. Zimmerer, *Business Policy: A Framework for Analysis*, 4th ed. (Columbus, Ohio: Grid Publishing, Inc., 1984), p. 275.]

In doing business with other countries, the first rule is to recognize that people there may act and react differently from American business managers and workers. Some of these differences are shown in Figure 21-1. As you can see, a number of factors—from language to trade barriers—need to be analyzed when international business is conducted. Differences, especially cultural differences, play a major role.

CULTURAL DIFFERENCES IN INTERNATIONAL BUSINESS

An American businessperson doing business with a Japanese company repeatedly asked its president, Taro Yamada, if he approved of a particular proposed management procedure. In reply, the president seemed vague and elusive. In turn, the American became frustrated and felt that perhaps he was being "toyed" with, that is, until another executive put him straight: the Japanese, he said, simply hate to say no and will do anything to avoid saying it. To find out if they are opposed to an idea, you have to use other methods than the direct yes or no approach so common to American businesses.

What role does cultural differences play in business failures abroad?

As this example shows, having information about cultural differences can provide valuable insight into the actions and behaviors of foreign managers, employees, and customers. Conversely, misinterpretation of these cultural differences can lead to problems. In fact, it is estimated that from 30 to 50 percent of American managers fail to perform adequately abroad because of their poor adjustment to a different culture. (In addition to other losses the company suffers, such failures can cost a firm several thousand dollars per family if a family also has to be relocated.)

But perhaps before going any further, we need to define culture. Culture is a set of social norms acquired by members of a society that affect behavior. Such cultures may be national, regional, or local in scope. Cultural gaps arise because people from different cultures are unable to read each other's values, social mores, and other aspects of interpersonal attitudes and relationships. In particular, American managers often have deep-seated cultural biases that can affect their perceptions of other cultures.

How can ethnocentrism work against you in international trade?

Thus, American managers often try to introduce their own cultural traits to the other country. They also often judge the country by the standards they have developed in America, believing that these standards are superior. This tendency is known as *ethnocentrism,* and, if unchecked, it can limit a manager's effectiveness in assignments abroad, possibly even leading to cross-cultural conflict.

A diagram that will aid you in analyzing such differences is shown in Figure 21-2. This diagram serves as a basis to identify various cultural dimensions necessary for cultural awareness and understanding.

Perhaps the most effective way to gain an insight into the problem of cultural differences is to examine a number of countries and their cultures. In this way you can gain some insight into the complex situations overseas managers face.

Japanese Culture

Of all the countries in the world in recent times, Japan has probably had the most effect on American business. And that influence only promises to grow. What makes the Japanese so dynamic? How have productivity and quality become the trademarks of their business? For the Japanese, commitment to the employer provides a great deal of the source of these trademarks. This close relationship between employer and employee is rooted in a strong, common cultural background.

What are some of the customs and traditions that American managers need to know more about? One is the value put on politeness and formality over the more informal American tradition. For example, the Japanese would rather be vague and ambiguous than convey the blunt truth. We have already seen this in the example of the American manager frustrated by his inability to get a simple "no" from the president of the Japanese company. Thus, in presenting your concerns over a business transaction in Japan, it may be most effective first to develop a personal rapport and then explain why something may be unacceptable or ask if it is. In this way you may get answers to yes and no questions that you are able to interpret correctly.

In Japan, management and employees often view employment as a permanent contract. This commitment is cemented by management's support of employees and their loyalty to the organization. Unlike many American companies, many Japanese firms would rather cut deeply into profits than lay off employees, especially managers. Another Japanese custom is to emphasize the welfare of the group over that of the individual. This results in decisions usually made by groups rather than by individuals. Because of the need for consensus, business decisions in Japan often take longer than they would in America and contrast sharply with our penchant for deadlines, timeliness, and individualism.

What are nemawashi and ringisho?

The Japanese use a two-step technique in their decision making: *nemawashi* and *ringisho.*[1] *Nemawashi* is a search for a solution to a problem through discussions among all individuals involved

[1] Endel-Jakob Kolde, *Environment of International Business,* 2nd ed. (Boston: Kent Publishing Company, 1985), pp. 456–457.

Country A	Culture Dimension	Country B
1. *Pragmatic* Information interpreted in context of practical use or action.	Modes of thinking ⟷	*Universalistic* Information interpreted in context of general principles, ideologies or concepts.
2. *Scientific* Logic and scientific methods used.	Problem solving ⟷	*Traditional* Following precedence or adapting old procedures to new problems.
3. *Explicative* Comprehending subject by relying on facts and logical explanations, making direct statements.	Verbal communication ⟷	*Implicative* Comprehending subject of communication through linkages to its environment or other events, relying on analogies, symbolisms, and indirect statements.
4. *Passive* Personal interaction characterized by avoiding bodily contact and physical expressiveness, gesticulation, "stiff upper lip" syndrome.	Nonverbal communication ⟷	*Active* Personal interaction characterized by touching, gesticulation, facial expressions, and other forms of body language.
5. *Vague* No generally recognized social classes, income and achievement act as main differentiators, social mobility high, individual's social status unrelated to class.	Class structure ⟷	*Distinct* Existence of overt social classes, interclass mobility and interaction restricted, individual's status dependent on class.
6. *Rank dependent* Social standing and esteem linked primarily to managerial position and advancement in organizational rank, class origin nonessential.	Social status of managers ⟷	*Class dependent* Social standing and esteem derive primarily from class origin, organizational rank secondary.
7. *Short* Presumption of hierarchical fluidity; managerial ranks dictated by organizational convenience; equality of superiors and subordinates; emphasis on expertise; unrestrained vertical interaction between organizational layers.	Power distance ⟷	*Long* Presumption of distinct layers of managerial powers and hierarchical inequalities; emphasis on ranks; superior-subordinate interactions formal and restricted; top-down communication dominant.
8. *Low* Uncertainties of life accepted as normal; economic risks judged by potential rewards; deemphasis of rules and procedures, emphasis on flexibility and innovation.	Risk aversion ⟷	*High* Concern about uncertainties of life; economic risk leads to anxiety and psychological stress; drive for security, law and order, consensuses, written rules and procedures; intolerance of deviant behaviors.

FIGURE 21-2 Selected cross-cultural variables. [From Endel-Jakob Kolde, *Environment of International Business,* 2nd ed. (Boston: Kent Publishing Company, 1985), pp. 421–422.] Reprinted with Permission.

Country A	Culture Dimension	Country B
9. *Democratic* Manager is expected to ask inputs from subordinates and others affected before decision is taken; information sharing and informal consultations are accepted procedures.	← Decision-making style →	*Autocratic* Manager is expected to formulate decision either individually or with aid of experts; seeking inputs from subordinates indicates ineptitude; decision is finalized before being announced; informal discussions with subordinates avoided.
10. *Task oriented* Primary attention paid to technological and operational factors; strict enforcement of company rules, legal and contractual commitments, and top-management expectations.	← Leadership style →	*People oriented* Primary attention paid to human factors, organizational morale, and motivation; utilization of group dynamics and intergroup tensions for organizational goals.
11. *Unbalanced* Object of work is wealth-salaries, bonuses, fringe benefits, and other material rewards; need hierarchy downgrade and psychological factors.	← Concepts of achievement →	*Balanced* Object of work is self-actualization; in addition to money employees' needs hierarchy includes recognition, belonging, security, and other non-material rewards.
12. *Weak* Nuclear family structure with husband-wife relationship central; children socialized mainly outside kinship structure and become "autonomous" on reaching adulthood; kinship influence on business slight.	← Kinship bondage →	*Strong* Close identification with family and kin; children socialized mainly in extended family structure; deep commitment to family honor, loyalties, and responsibilities; kinship and business ties coincident.
13. *Individualistic* Reliance on individual initiative, self-assertion, and personal achievement and responsibility.	← Personal orientation →	*Collectivistic* Emphasis on belonging to organizations or clans, acceptance of group decisions, values, and duties.
14. *Masculinity ideal* Identification with machismo attitudes: wealth, power, decisiveness, superiority of males, differentiated sex roles, both at home and at work.	← Sexual stereotyping →	*Femininity ideal* Priority on nurturing attitudes: care of people, interpersonal relations, quality of life, sexual equality, fluid sex roles, and unisex approaches in all spheres of life.
15. *Intense* Correlating time with productivity and progress; time must not be wasted—keep busy; time is money; punctuality is important; preparations for future are essential.	← Time orientation →	*Casual* Time is to be enjoyed; one must not become a slave of time; hurrying and rigorous schedules are to be avoided; understanding and preservation of the past is to be protected against change.
16. *English*	← Language →	*Chinese*

FIGURE 21-2 continued

throughout the organization until a consensus emerges. Top management does not influence this process. Once it is completed, the participants develop a document that contains their solution. This document is known as *ringisho.* Then all participants review the *ringisho;* if they approve, they stamp their *banko* ("seal") on it. Although obviously time consuming, the process ensures that the decision will have the total support and commitment of the individuals involved.

What are quality circles? Have you ever been a member of one?

One extension of *ringisho* has gained a great deal of popularity in the United States. This is the use of quality circles. *Quality circles* are regularly scheduled small-group meetings of employees from all levels who convene on company time to identify and suggest solutions to problems. The purpose is to improve productivity and standards by encouraging dialogue and developing a closer bond between management and employees—both consistently practiced by Japanese businesses.

But what of Japanese companies—such as Sony, Pioneer Electronics, Honda, and Nissan Motors—that have subsidiaries in the United States and employ American managers and workers? Although the companies have attempted to adapt to the American workplace, the same cultural differences still affect relations between the Japanese top command and those who serve under them. So it is hardly surprising that more than one American manager has had to ask a Japanese president or vice president to explain the meaning behind a letter, meeting, or invitation.

Many differences exist between American and Japanese companies. Figure 21-3 is a model that simplifies and identifies some of these differences. Use it to gain some insight into conducting business with the Japanese.

Is business in Mexico conducted more or less leisurely than in the U.S.? Explain.

Mexican and Latin American Culture

The Mexican culture puts greater emphasis on social atmosphere than ours. For Mexicans developing friendships and having a genuine concern for other people is of primary importance. This attitude prevails in many other Latin American countries as well. Thus, business often stops at midday for a siesta and is in general conducted at a more leisurely pace than is American business. Another factor to consider is that Latin American women have not yet achieved the status in business that American women have. This means that U.S. companies have to face the fact that women executives may not be accorded the same respect by Latins as men. Moreover, when their employees express criticisms of the company's policies, Latin American executives are likely to perceive them as a personal attack and may even feel insulted. In these more rigidly stratified cultures em-

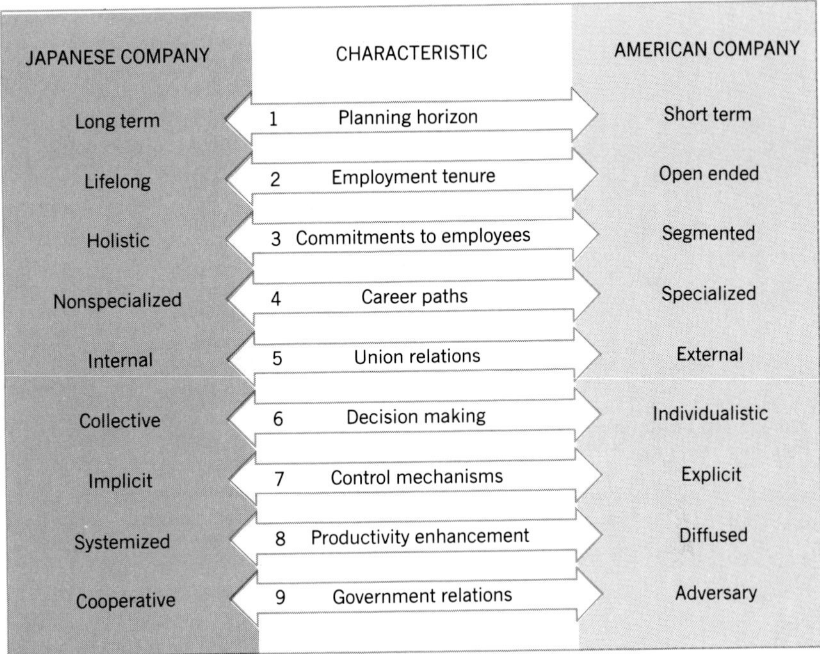

JAPANESE COMPANY
CHARACTERISTIC
AMERICAN COMPANY
Long term
1 Planning horizon
Short term
Lifelong
2 Employment tenure
Open ended
Holistic
3 Commitments to employees
Segmented
Nonspecialized
4 Career paths
Specialized
Internal
5 Union relations
External
Collective
6 Decision making
Individualistic
Implicit
7 Control mechanisms
Explicit
Systemized
8 Productivity enhancement
Diffused
Cooperative
9 Government relations
Adversary

FIGURE 21-3 Differences between Japanese and American companies. [From Endel-Jakob Kolde, *Environment of International Business*, 2nd. ed. (Boston: Kent Publishing Company, 1985), p. 452.] Reprinted with Permission.

ployees are expected to either support their superiors or remain silent.

Middle Eastern Culture

What status do women have in Middle Eastern businesses?

In many Middle Eastern countries women are still not allowed to work in business—and men in business often refuse to work with women, obviously, then, a company thinking of sending a woman to the Middle East to negotiate a contract would be advised to think again. Because of the customs of the culture, her qualifications are likely to be of no importance.

Knowing about such attitudes and the customs and practices that evolve from them can be useful in other ways. For example, some years ago Singer Sewing Machine Company wanted to promote the purchase and use of Singer sewing machines to women in Moslem countries. But how was this to be done when Moslem women wear veils to screen themselves from strangers—such as those who would be teaching the classes? How could the women be encouraged to take the lessons? Singer's solution was to sell the husbands on how much more productive their wives would be after taking such lessons. The strategy worked, and soon, the wives were attending the classes, and Singer's sales rose sharply.

Much change has occurred for women in the Middle East in recent years, largely because of two forces. On the one hand, the influence of Western cultures has led to "Westernization" of the area as demonstrated by the adoption of Western dress and values. On the other hand, the rise of Moslem fundamentalism has led to stricter enforcement of traditional beliefs, such as restrictions on women; Iran is the prime example of this trend.

Asian Culture (Excluding Japan)

Do Indians hold job security or salary more dear? Why?

Hinduism, one of the two great Indian religions, favors hiring and promoting relatives. In America, this would be considered nepotism, a practice frowned on in many or most sectors of business. Also, Indians revere elders and teachers, including their supervisors. They also feel that job security is more important than salary, benefits, and so forth because it alone can ensure happiness with work. In general, other Asian countries seem to follow the same principles. Thus, in doing business with this sector, keep these factors in mind.

Obviously, any glimpse into other cultures can only indicate that an awareness of the differences between American and other cultures is necessary for any success in international business. Mostly, this success is a matter of attitude. A glimpse at how important your attitude can be when you start to work in another country is illustrated in Figure 21-4. As you can see, if you approach your assignment positively, you can develop the necessary rapport and empathy with the people and their culture. If, however, you approach it negatively, you may experience withdrawal and alienation.

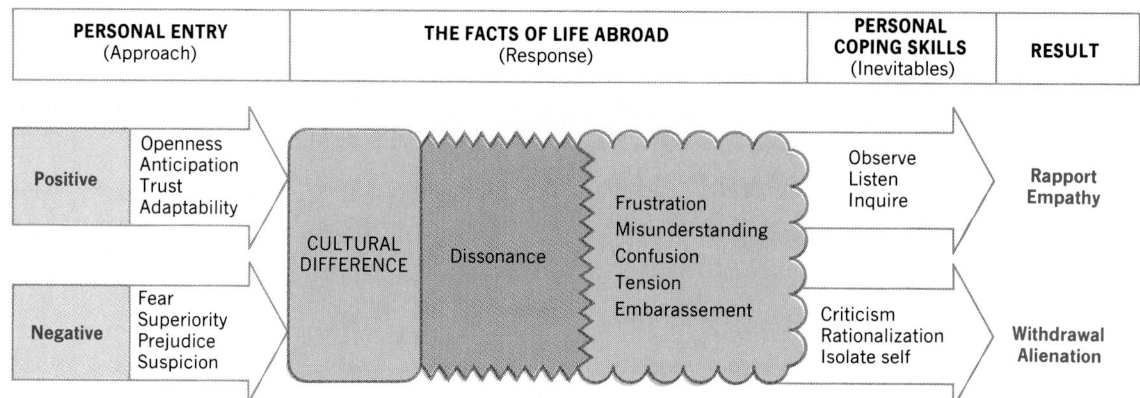

FIGURE 21-4 Role of attitude in coping with cultural differences. [From Chris Lee, "Cross Cultural Training: Don't Leave Home Without It," *Training*, Vol. 20 (July 1983), p. 20.] Reprinted with Permission.

POLITICAL DIFFERENCES IN INTERNATIONAL BUSINESS

Sometimes a country's domestic, economic, and foreign policy goals can interfere with international business. For example, in a famous case, the Indian government requested that Coca-Cola turn over its secret formula to the government. Coca-Cola refused and discontinued operations in India.

How does nationalism affect international business operations?

Sometimes, too, companies may find themselves caught between two governments with contrasting claims or may discover they are victims of nationalism. In this context, *nationalism* means that the allegiance to and promotion of the country should take precedence over any other claim. People in such countries feel a strong identification with the nation and give it their total support and loyalty. This is and will be a problem for international companies: local employees who are more sympathetic to the country's values than to those of the company may resist change, be insecure, and have little initiative; their emotions and sympathies are otherwise engaged. Nationalism can also refer to laws that increasingly protect the host country's resources—as well as demands for nationals to have more responsible managerial positions. Such conditions make the communication process in a foreign country even more complex than it already is. But these conditions also illustrate the importance of becoming aware of another country's politics and policies as you conduct business within its borders.

LANGUAGE DIFFERENCES IN INTERNATIONAL BUSINESS

Perhaps the following letter indicates some of the problems language differences may cause people in international business. The writer is an American manager working in a Spanish-speaking country:

> I had been there two years, and since I spoke the language fluently, I felt that I was getting on very well with the community. On one occasion I was particularly pleased when our top local manager asked me to his home to meet his grandmother, who was the family matriarch and revered by all of the family. When I was introduced to her in rather formal circumstances, without thinking I spoke to her in the familiar form of the verb. Immediately the room turned to ice, and my interview was hastily terminated. I still didn't know what had happened, but on my way home I asked our local manager, and he emotionally told me that this familiarity is not accepted in his culture. It took me weeks to make the proper apologies through necessary intermediaries, and I felt I never did recover socially from this setback.[2]

[2] Keith Davis, *Human Behavior at Work: Organizational Behavior*, 5th ed. (New York: McGraw-Hill Book Company, 1977), p. 362.

Is it enough just to know how to speak the language of the host country? Explain.

As this example shows, different cultures assign different meanings to words. In this case, what is considered a polite verb form in America is reserved only for family and close friends in the other country. Further, although English is spoken worldwide, laws in several foreign countries require that all business contracts and documents be written in the language of the host country. These are only some of the problems that occur when culture interferes with the interpretation of a message.

Translation Problems

Many American businesses have encountered problems caused by the incorrect translation of their advertisements and product names. Sometimes the errors are funny, but they can also be expensive and embarrassing as well. For example, Parker Pen's advertising campaign in Latin America stated that its ink would help prevent unwanted pregnancies. At a Russian trade show in Moscow, Otis Engineering Company's poster promised that its oil well equipment would improve people's sex lives. And an advertisement in Venezuela for an American-made auto battery described it as "highly overrated."

Some other famous (or infamous) translation bloopers are Pepsi Cola's ad theme, "Come Alive with Pepsi," which translated into German as "Coming Alive from the Grave"; the Chevrolet "Nova," which spoken in Spanish as "no va," translated as "it doesn't go" (by the way, the car's name was changed to "Caribe," which means "savage," and it sold well); General Motors car bodies that contained the slogan, "Body by Fisher," which translated to "Corpse by Fisher" in Flemish; a Ford truck sold in developing countries called "Fiera," which translated into Spanish as "ugly old woman"; and, finally, Sunbeam Corporation's hair curling iron called "Mist-Stick," which translated into German as "manure wand."[3]

Why do some companies hire translation firms?

As these examples show, translation is not a simple matter of matching word for word. To translate accurately, you need to understand a country's culture and dialect(s). The importance of accurate and sophisticated translation has increased the demand for translation firms—companies whose sole purpose is to translate terms and concepts accurately across cultures.

International Correspondence

The American approach to correspondence is often too direct for use in other cultures. In fact, if you receive business correspondence from

[3] Richard D. Steade, James R. Lowry, and Raymond E. Glos, *Business: Its Nature and Environment* (Cincinnati: South-Western Publishing Company, 1984), p. 378.

another country, it will probably differ from the formats, plans, and strategies discussed in this textbook. Usually, the style will be more formal, contain different spelling of words—for example, "organisation," "labour," "cheque"—and more punctuation. The tone too may differ, conveying a more reserved or distant level of courtesy than Americans are used to as the following excerpts from a letter from India show:

In what ways does domestic correspondence differ from international correspondence?

"Your kind and sympathetic consideration is respectfully solicited."

"Thank you for your esteemed favour."

"With warm personal regards and the compliments of the season."

Also, in the same letter, the date—November 23, 19XX—is written in military format:

"dt. 23.11. 19XX

In contrast, the Japanese have taken a different tack, preferring to make telephone calls or to visit their clients than to write letters. However, when it is necessary, the Japanese do compose letters. Such letters often begin and end with a formal comment about the season or weather, followed by a remark about the reader's health or an appreciation for past business. Only after such introductory remarks does the writer reveal his or her actual purpose, if the purpose is revealed at all.

The Japanese are especially aware of potential barriers in language. When asked by an American what was the most important language in world trade, a Japanese executive replied, *Okya ku-sama no kotoba,* which means, "My customer's language"![4]

Why must you know the metric system to correspond well in international trade?

Suppose that you have to write a business letter to a customer abroad. First, try to maintain a positive, courteous tone that follows as nearly as possible the sentiments of your reader. Then, if you need to discuss financial matters, you should convert dollar values into the reader's currency. Perhaps indicating the two values side by side may be even more helpful to your reader. Also, use the metric system if possible (and applicable). In most countries, imports and exports are measured in meters, liters, grams, degrees centigrade, and so forth.

International Report Writing

International managers must write reports, especially to corporate headquarters. Usually, such reports are periodic and follow a standardized format. Often, managers feel burdened by having to do these

[4] D. George Harris, *Vital Speeches,* reported in *Quality Circle Digest,* P.O. Box Q, Red Bluff, Calif. 96080.

reports, just as they sometimes do Stateside. Typical types of reports from abroad deal with progress of a corporate plan or with policies and procedures that have been established. Later, these documents may be converted into policy and procedural manuals to be used in a company's international operations.

The following is an outline of a monthly progress report submitted to corporate headquarters from one of its international subsidiaries:

I. Work completed during the report period and work in progress by product category.
II. Products planned for the next three-month period.
III. Problems experienced or anticipated and proposed solutions.
IV. Staff additions, deletions, promotions, and professional achievements of staff.
V. Attachments of work samples.[5]

NONVERBAL COMMUNICATION IN INTERNATIONAL BUSINESS

Did you know that in our culture nonverbal communication can account for as much as 90 percent of a message? If this is so, think about the effect of nonverbal communication in cultures different from America's. In some other cultures, cues are much more difficult to "read" and more necessary to understand, for often, language does not assist them.

What are some common forms of nonverbal communication in foreign countries?

The following are some common forms of nonverbal communication in other cultures. For example, in Latin America, visitors are usually kept waiting at least an hour before a meeting. It is important to know this, because, otherwise, you might get angry because in America lateness is a form of rudeness. Also, once the meeting has begun, you might send the wrong signals if, as in this country, you attempt to do business immediately. Many Latin Americans socialize first. Such behavior is also common in Middle European countries.

Moreover, in both Latin America and the Middle East, people stand closer together than in America while conversing. If you back away during a meeting, you may offend the others who are present. In addition, in the Middle East, it is customary to touch while conversing. Another interesting behavior of Arabs is that they watch the eyes of the other party. This is done because when people are interested in a subject, their pupils dilate. If, however, they hear something they dislike, their pupils contract. As these responses cannot be

[5] Robert F. Roth, *International Marketing Communications* (Chicago: Crain Books, 1982), p. 82.

controlled, many Arabs resort to dark glasses so as to hide their feelings better.

How is time regarded differently in different countries?

Another difference in our nonverbal behavior and that of certain other cultures may be seen in the amount of time taken to answer a communication. In America, a manager would interpret any delay as a signal of lack of interest, whereas in a country like India, the more time that elapses before a reply, the more important the item being discussed. Thus, in India, sending an order "right away" may mean in about two or three months.

What about gift giving? If you plan to give something to a person in another country, consider some of the following customs.[6] When invited to a European home for dinner, send flowers before arriving or take a small gift. In Japan, two days each year are set aside for mandatory business gift giving: *Otoshidama* (January 1) and *Chugen* (July 15). At other times you also may receive small duty or obligation gifts called *giri*. You should also give such gifts, but remember not to outgive your Japanese colleagues so that they are not embarrassed. Remember, too, to bring a gift when invited to a Japanese home; in the past, the Japanese have preferred American brand-name items.

The Arabs are very generous and give lavish gifts. In return, however, they expect similar presents and may even keep a mental tally of who is ahead. Do not, however, present a gift on your first meeting. Also, choose carefully. This translates as do not bring gifts of food or drink to an Arab's home because these signify that you perceive your host to be stingy. Generally, Arabs like American brand-name goods. But avoid giving Arabs company gifts with logos and sculptures or pictures of animals they consider "low," such as grasshoppers or bats. (Always check to see what the bad-luck animals are in any country you visit on a business trip.)

In Latin America, present gifts only in social settings. A good time to give them is during lunch because business is not generally conducted over this meal. If you are invited to dinner, you do, however, need to bring something also. Latins also like American items, but they are sensitive to any implications that any American gift is superior to their own competitive brands. To avoid such a problem, find out what items are scarce or heavily taxed in the area you are visiting and bring such a gift and pay the tax on it. Your Latin American colleagues will appreciate this gesture.

In China, the law forbids people to accept most gifts. Whatever gifts you can give must be presented tactfully so that the receivers are not embarrassed. When entering China, you must declare any gifts you are bringing in at customs. You are expected to take the same gifts home with you. However, if you say that you "lost" an item

[6] Sue Browder, "Handle with Care," *Savvy*, Vol. 4, no. 12 (December 1983), pp. 89–90.

Why is it necessary to be tactful when presenting a gift to a Chinese colleague?

(gave it away), your excuse will be accepted, but you will then have to pay a fee twice what the gift is estimated to be worth. Also, when giving a gift to a Chinese colleague, be sure to present it in private because receiving it in public is impolite.

As you can see from this brief discussion, your greatest need is to be aware that people in other cultures can respond differently and have to be evaluated according to their own frame of reference. To adapt to different systems, then, you have to be empathetic and conscious of the importance of the nonverbal as well as verbal messages being sent.

CHARACTERISTICS OF MULTINATIONAL CORPORATIONS

Can you name several American companies that make more than half their profits from international operations?

Suppose you plan to work in the international business environment. A high probability exists then that you will work for a multinational corporation someday. Such a company sends its resources—goods, services, funds, management, and technological skills—to many different countries. It then often combines these resources with those of the host countries to produce, distribute, and market goods or services. Multinationals are both large and diverse. In fact, several of the 500 largest U.S. corporations make more than half their profits from foreign operations. Some of these well-known corporations are Coca-Cola, Colgate-Palmolive, Exxon, IBM, Mobil, NCR, and Otis Elevator.

As a potential employee of a multinational firm, it may be useful to be aware of the characteristics of such an organization.

Global Influences

Various specialized international trade bodies, such as the International Monetary Fund, influence the global environment within which multinationals operate. These bodies establish operating principles and an atmosphere that promotes international business. Yet the effect of cross-cultural and national interactions on multinationals is hard to determine precisely. Armed with little information, managers of such companies often have to contend with problems arising from too many and sometimes too unknown causes. And confronted with a wide range of alternatives, many of these managers lack experience to resolve their difficulties. Not only this, but some are also unable to relate to the foreign culture and environment, thus compounding their woes. Yet, excellent opportunities for developing additional markets still exist, especially in Central and South America. As these markets continue to open up and grow, the ability to communicate well in a foreign culture will be even more urgently needed.

Performance Evaluation

Why might performance evaluation be more difficult at foreign subsidiaries than at the home office in the U.S.?

Although many managers are experienced in establishing and maintaining performance standards at home, this domestic experience may not relate to foreign operations. Naturally, standards and measurement criteria for evaluating performance under such conditions are far more complex than they would be in the United States. For one thing, each foreign subsidiary is relatively self-contained, and its transactions are usually confined to the local environment.

However, the greater the cultural difference between corporate headquarters and its subsidiaries, the more important it is for the subsidiary to become more autonomous. Of course, greater autonomy requires an increasing degree of trust in the subsidiary's decision-making ability. At the moment, though, this is not the case. Because the foreign subsidiaries of various firms are so unlike one another, any meaningful criteria to evaluate performance are almost impossible to develop. This situation, in turn, leads to managerial frustration. So a *two-way communication channel* between corporate headquarters and a firm's subsidiaries has to be maintained to foster effective and trusting relations and to encourage information sharing.

Distance and the Communication Media

Distance causes both time delays and problems with the smooth flow of information. In contrast, being near lessens the cost of communication and increases the likelihood of personal meetings and telephone calls. Both these observations apply to multinationals.

What role does frame of reference play in communicating internationally?

Remember that even if the information sent is highly reliable, the communication channels perfect—such as telephoning or computer conferencing—and the language clear, the receiver will still interpret the message from his or her own frame of reference. Of course, the other person's frame of reference may be quite different from yours in such situations because of cultural differences. Thus, in the operations of multinationals, problems in understanding messages occur far more often than in organizations that operate only within their own country. For this reason, it is not unusual to follow up a memo or report with a telephone call to explain the initial message.

Multinationals also have to contend with the lack of immediate feedback for written communication. Certainly, such delays hamper decision making. Sometimes, because of the distance involved, these delays are long enough to defeat the very purpose of the communication.

Besides the problem of distance, the communication systems of a number of countries are unreliable or are in the process of being upgraded. Naturally, this, too, compounds communication problems.

TRAINING NEEDS IN INTERNATIONAL BUSINESS

In the quest for opportunities, international businesses face many problems and uncertainties in dealing with political, legal, economic, social, cultural, and governmental constraints. The environments in which these firms operate also change at different rates as do the complex interactions between multinationals and their subsidiaries. For these reasons—and many others—better management training is essential.

Why is training essential for prospective international managers?

Multinational managers need a great depth of understanding about what to expect in a foreign assignment. In fact, several studies have shown such preparation to be highly valuable. Thus, managers who are trained properly are more likely to complete their tours of duty than are those who are not. (Interestingly, the Japanese are strong believers in extensive employee training for overseas assignments.)

But what are some of these training needs? First, potential international employees must be aware of and understand several factors besides the culture and language of the country to which they are going. The following checklist should help you prepare for such an assignment. Remember, too, that if you take your family, their happiness will play an important role in making you a success in your new assignment.

TRAINING NEEDS CHECKLIST FOR INTERNATIONAL ASSIGNMENTS

1. *Managerial styles.* Many cultures are used to different managerial styles than those employed in America. You need to become familiar with the style(s) most effective in the host country.
2. *Cultural awareness.* You need to become sensitive to and tolerant of the differences between cultures. This is necessary if you are to adjust and work successfully in your foreign assignment. You should study specific customs, geography, governmental conditions, health concerns, and social structures.
3. *Technical competence.* Of course, you must have the knowledge and skill to do your job. But because of the other variables, you need not worry too much about technical ability.
4. *Interest in the assignment.* Your motives for accepting an overseas assignment must be positive. You should have a genuine interest in the country and the international affairs of the organization. Lack of motivation can become a problem overseas.

5. *Emotional stability.* You are likely to face a great deal of stress in adjusting to a new environment. You will need to cope with many changes in life style and with personal differences and your physical surroundings.
6. *Job orientation.* Awareness of your specific job responsibilities is a necessity. You must be able to handle the varied demands on you. Becoming aware of the host country's economy, business practices, and legal environment is important during orientation.
7. *Human relations skills.* Having the ability to work with others with dissimilar interests is a key to a successful overseas assignment. Learning and practicing effective group dynamics contributes to this success. Your ability may often have to extend beyond the work environment to interactions and diplomacy with people in government and politics.
8. *Discussions with former international employees.* You can gain valuable personal insight into customs, living conditions, and potential difficulties by discussing your assignment with employees who have worked abroad.
9. *Language training.* You will need to learn how to express yourself in and understand the language of the country in which you will be working.
10. *Change orientation.* Learning strategies for planning and implementing change in a foreign environment is a necessity. You need to adjust to change as well as work toward it in improving overall organizational effectiveness. Remember, however, that change takes time, especially altering something that has been practiced for many years or perhaps many hundreds of years.

CRITERIA FOR COMMUNICATING EFFECTIVELY IN INTERNATIONAL BUSINESS

Perhaps nowhere are experienced communicators—people who know well the subject to be communicated and are skilled in the process itself—so needed as in international business. These international firms must have well-rounded people working for them who are capable of responding intelligently to a rapidly changing world. Further, these people must be conscious of differences in perception and aware too of the relationship among culture, language, and behavior. Remember that one of the most important parts of effective communication is audience analysis, and this is just what a multinational employee does. But in this case, the audience is at first less familiar than usual. The following checklist should help you identify several communication criteria useful for potential international managers and employees.

INTERNATIONAL BUSINESS COMMUNICATION CHECKLIST

1. *Have empathy.* Always try to think of yourself in your foreign colleagues' roles. In other words, try to understand and participate in their feelings, attitudes, and ideas. By having empathy you will begin to see beyond differences and recognize what makes your foreign colleagues unique.
2. *Avoid stereotypes.* Do not be unduly influenced by what you may have read or been told. This can cause you to place your colleagues in categories, even though each is an individual. Avoid letting your biases and prejudices cloud the true personality of foreigners.
3. *Be sensitive.* Develop and maintain sensitivity and personal respect for your foreign colleagues. Understand their orientation and accept their differences. Establish a rapport and trusting attitude. Try to make them feel important.
4. *Be open-minded and perceptive.* When communicating with a foreign colleague, keep an open mind, be perceptive, and remain flexible to ideas that are different from yours. Do not base your expectations on preconceived notions. Recognize the uniqueness of the situation.
5. *Be patient.* Try not to get frustrated when things do not go well for you or follow your plan. Anticipate problems and recognize that time is on your side when dealing with foreign colleagues.
6. *Explain difficult concepts clearly and in simple terms, if possible.* Be aware of the degree of familiarity and frame of reference foreigners have with unfamiliar technical terms and concepts. Use short sentences and many illustrations. By reducing the amount of narrative, you decrease the possibility of translation error. However, be prepared for misunderstanding nonetheless. Your colleagues will often be listening to you in a second language, so do not expect them to pick up every subtle meaning. Remember, your words will be taken literally. In this regard, use words with predictable connotations and avoid slang and figurative cliches, especially. Some examples of phrases to avoid are "hang in

there," "go for it," "what's happening?" or "what are you up to?" These phrases may be meaningless to the people you work with or may be taken the wrong way.

7. *Be courteous.* One key concept in developing effective interpersonal relations is courtesy. Remember that you are a guest in a foreign country and extend the common courtesies expected of you, such as "please" and "thank you." Remember to smile—it's universal.
8. *Have a sense of humor.* Sometimes you have to look at difficulties from a different vantage point and learn to accept them. You can become very frustrated and perplexed if you take everything that happens altogether seriously. Developing a sense of humor will allow you to maintain a well-balanced approach to problems that arise. However, be careful about telling jokes or humorous stories. Although they may be an effective tool to increase better relations, they may not go over well. Remember, your foreign colleagues may not understand or may have a different sense of humor. Usually, it is best to maintain a certain degree of formality.
9. *Learn the language.* You may not need to become proficient in the language of the country you will be working in if your assignment is short, such as a month or two. You do need to learn, however, the basic personal and business language necessary for you to function well. If you are planning to stay longer, you will have to obtain additional proficiency in the language. Your colleagues at work will have a greater respect for you if you speak their language well.
10. *Listen and observe more.* You can find out a lot about another culture by listening carefully to your co-workers and observing their actions and nonverbal cues. Ask questions to clarify your understanding and give those you are communicating with your undivided attention.

SUMMARY

1. In international business, many managers find themselves in unfamiliar social and cultural environments; to be successful in them, they must learn to live with people who have different values, attitudes, and customs.
2. An awareness of cultural differences by Americans engaged in international business will provide an insight into the actions and behaviors of the foreigners with whom they are dealing.

3. Culture is a set of social norms acquired by members of a society that affect behavior.
4. Americans often have strong biases that affect their perceptions of other cultures.
5. Ethnocentrism involves judging other cultures by the values of your own; if unchecked, it can lead to cross-cultural conflict.
6. The political climate of a country often causes the growth of nationalism among its people; some people employed by international companies may be adversely affected by nationalism on the job.
7. Americans working abroad need to be aware of the possible errors that may arise because of differences in language. These problems may occur in understanding both written and spoken language.
8. Many different nonverbal cues provide additional meaning to messages in different cultures.
9. Multinational corporations transmit their resources to many different countries and they combine these resources with those of the hosts' countries to produce, distribute, and market goods and services.
10. Some problems of multinationals occur because of the distance between corporate headquarters and subsidiaries.
11. Well-trained employees and managers are more likely to complete their tour of duty abroad than are untrained or poorly trained personnel.
12. In preparing for an assignment abroad, potential international managers and employees can increase their effectiveness as business communicators by considering other factors besides culture and language.

Review Questions

1. In what ways is conducting business in America different from conducting business in other countries? Are there any similarities?
2. In your own words, what is a good definition of culture? How can culture affect communication?
3. Why does ethnocentrism play a large role in causing cross-cultural conflicts?
4. What are some factors that have contributed to Japan's great success in the world marketplace?
5. How would you compare and contrast the Japanese management style with the typical American style? What roles does communication play in each?
6. Why is a proper attitude important for success in an international assignment? How does communication influence attitude?
7. How can the political climate of a country affect communication?
8. Why do literal translations cause problems in understanding? What criteria should be used to translate a message effectively?
9. What are the main differences between American and foreign correspondence?
10. What is meant by speaking "my customer's language"?
11. Why is it important to be aware of nonverbal cues in international communication? Can a nonverbal message carry more weight than a verbal one? Explain your answer.
12. How do the complexities of multinational corporations affect communications? Give some examples.
13. How important is training an individual

to a successful foreign assignment? Give some examples.

14. What role does audience analysis play in international business communication?
15. Can you identify and explain three additional communication criteria that can be added to the checklist in the chapter? If not, explain the difficulty you had in arriving at an answer.

Exercises

1. Locate a business in your area that is operated by a foreigner. Interview the owner or manager to determine the differences in business practices between the United States and his or her country. Prepare a memorandum for your instructor that describes your findings.
2. Interview two foreign students from two different countries that are attending your school. Ask them about their culture and what changes they have made after coming to the United States. Compare and contrast their responses and report your findings to your class.
3. Pick up Publication 51, "International Postal Rates and Fees," from your post office. Prepare a memorandum for your instructor outlining its key points. Include any implications you draw about methods of communicating internationally—mail, telephone, and so on.
4. Prepare an annotated bibliography of at least ten current articles on any facet of international business communication.
5. Select two of the articles you found in Exercise 4 and prepare an informative speech on their contents. Include at least one visual aid.
6. Review international articles from a local or national newspaper or weekly magazine and locate two that discuss the political climate. What communication implications can you draw from them?
7. Locate an annual report of a multinational corporation. Review its international operations and determine what percentage of the company's sales is attributed to these operations. From the discussion of products or services, what conclusions can you draw about the firm's approach to the international market?
8. Select a multinational corporation and write to its international operations center or a similar division to determine if the corporation has any training program for individuals accepting overseas assignments. Present your findings to your class.
9. Assume you have accepted an overseas position. Prepare an informational report in memorandum format that outlines the areas you need to be aware of before leaving for your assignment.
10. Interview a foreign language instructor at your school. Ask the instructor how much language fluency you should have if you plan to work abroad. Also, ask the instructor to share any particular cultural dimensions of his or her field. Report your findings to your class.

APPENDICES

APPENDIX A

ELEMENTS OF GRAMMAR

Clarity and corrections are two essential elements of communication. Using grammar properly is necessary for being clear and correct in business communication. Follow the guidelines in this appendix when you have questions concerning correct grammatical usage.

PARTS OF SPEECH

Words are the building blocks of communication. These words form the seven basic parts of speech: *nouns, pronouns, verbs, adjectives, adverbs, prepositions,* and *conjunctions.*

Nouns

A noun is the name of a person, place, thing, quality, or concept.

Jane works in *Chicago.*

Money represents *value* in the *economy.*

Classifications

Nouns can be classified in two ways:

1. *Proper nouns:* name of a specific person, place, or thing. Proper nouns are capitalized (see "Capitalization").

    Mary Smith works in *St. Louis* and drives a new *automobile.*

2. *Common nouns:* name used to refer to any one of a number of persons, places, things, qualities, or concepts. Common nouns are not capitalized except when they begin sentences.

    Executives who work in *cities* often keep *pets* for *enjoyment.*

Number

Nouns may be singular or plural in number.

A large *company* often is formed from several small *companies.*

Collective nouns usually name something composed of two or more items. These collective nouns are usually considered singular in number.

The *committee* was chosen from the *staff.*

Our *faculty* is like a *family.*

Note: We generally use *articles* (a, an, the) with singular nouns but not with most plural nouns.

We finally met as *a* committee.

Have you met *the* new sales manager yet?

How many of *the* loans are outstanding?

Concrete/Abstract

A *concrete* noun names something that can be seen (pencil), smelled (flower), tasted (honey), touched (desk), or heard (whistle). Concrete nouns emphasize what they represent more than abstract nouns do.

An *abstract* noun names something that cannot be seen (joy), touched (idea), or heard (religion). Abstract nouns do not emphasize what they represent as much as concrete nouns do.

Pronouns

Pronouns take the place of nouns. Therefore, they serve the same purposes as nouns.

Classifications

Pronouns can be classified in several ways:

1. *Personal pronouns:* refer to specific persons or things.

   You and *I* should meet *them* in the office tomorrow.

2. *Idefinite pronouns:* do not refer to specific persons or things.

   Few or *none* of the employees has *all* the necessary traits.

   Several of them are interested, and *someone* may act soon.

3. *Demonstrative pronouns:* point out or identify.

   This is the file from among *those* in storage *that* Miss Valle requested.

4. *Interrogative pronouns:* introduce a question.

   Which briefcase is yours? *Who* is responsible? *What* time is the meeting? *Whom* should we report to?

5. *Relative pronouns:* join a dependent clause to an antecedent in an independent clause.

   Mr. O'Brien has a daughter *who* is an accountant.

   Mrs. Smith is the one *whose* computer broke down.

   These pronouns may introduce restrictive or nonrestrictive clauses (see "Punctuation—Comma").

6. *Reflexive (intensive) pronouns:* direct action back to antecedent or emphasize an antecedent. Reflexive pronouns are made by adding *self* or *selves* to the pronouns "one" or to *my, our, your, him, them, her,* and *it*.

The administrative assistant is not *himself* today.

Managers often deny *themselves* many privileges.

Person

A *personal pronoun* may have one of three persons; that is, personal pronouns may refer to the person speaking (*first* person), the person spoken to (*second* person), or the person(s) or thing(s) spoken about (*third* person).

I must be *me* to succeed in *my* profession.

You should study for *your* economics examination.

They grabbed *it* quickly. The office belongs to *them*.

Case

A pronoun may take one of three cases: *subjective* (or *nominative*), *objective*, or *possessive*. Case refers to the relationship of a pronoun and other words in the sentence, clause, or phrase. The subjective case is used when the pronoun is a subject or a predicate nominative.

I must see Jack.
The ones remaining were Al and *she*.

The objective case is used when the pronoun is the object of the verb or preposition or the subject or object of an infinitive phrase.

Mary wants *us* to leave with *her* at 5:00 P.M. (*us* is the object of the verb and subject of the infinitive "to leave." The object of the preposition "with" is *her*.)

The possessive case is used when the pronoun shows ownership.

Is this pen *yours, hers, his, theirs, ours,* or *mine*?

Verbs

A verb expresses action, condition, or state of being. Verbs tell what the subject does, what the subject is doing, or what is done to the subject. Without a verb, a group of words cannot be a clause or a sentence.

The boss *walked* to his office.

Classes

The two classes of verbs are *transitive* and *intransitive*. Transitive verbs show physical or mental action between a subject and a direct object.

Miss Ramirez *tacked* the notice on the bulletin board.

Intransitive verbs also show physical or mental action but do not have a direct object.

Jack *was* ill yesterday.

Voice

The way in which a subject and a verb interact in a sentence is termed "voice." The two types of voice—*active* and *passive*—are directly related to the type of verb used.

In active voice, an action verb is used resulting in the subject of the sentence performing the action indicated by the verb.

The board of directors elected a new president.

In this example, the subject (board of directors) is performing the action indicated by the verb (elected).

Passive voice is less direct and less emphatic than active. When a sentence is written with a passive verb, the subject no longer performs the action; rather, the subject now receives the action.

A new president was elected by the board of directors.

Notice that the subject (president) is receiving the action of the verb (was elected).

You can easily determine if a sentence is written in passive voice by answering three questions:

1. Is the subject doing the action indicated by the verb?
2. Does the verb consist of at least two words, one of which is the form of the verb "to be" (*is, being, am, are, was, were, will be, has been, had been, have been,* or *will have been*)?
3. Is the word "by" expressed or implied ("by whom" or "by what")?

Passive voice can be used effectively to emphasize ideas or an action more than the actor. Also, this voice is useful to downplay the harshness of negative information (see Chapter 9).

Mood

The manner in which a verb shows action is termed "mood." The three forms of mood are *indicative, imperative,* and *subjunctive.*

A verb in the indicative mood states a fact or asks a question:

The applicant was hired for the position.

Was the applicant hired for the position?

A verb in the imperative mood expresses a command or makes a request:

Hire the applicant today.

Please call me about the vacancy.

A verb in the subjective mood expresses something contrary to fact, a wish, or a command or request in a "that" clause. The subjunctive verb "were" is used for all three persons to indicate a condition known to be contrary to fact or to indicate a wish.

If he were here, he would know how to handle this complaint.

Sometimes I wish I were head of this company.

The verb "be" is used for all three persons when a command or request is presented in a "that" clause.

The personnel manager recommended that the new clerk be assigned here.

The customer demanded that the clerk be fired for inconsiderate behavior.

Tense

The tense of a verb is the *form taken to express distinctions in time.* Regular verbs form their past tenses and past participles by adding "d" or "ed" to the present tense.

You *manage* the club. You *managed* the club. You have *managed* the club.

Irregular verbs do not follow such a set rule when forming their past tenses and past participles.

You *do* the job. You *did* the job. You have *done* the job.

You *lie* there thinking. You *lay* there thinking yesterday. You have *lain* there thinking may times before.

Adjectives

Adjectives modify, describe, or limit nouns and pronouns. Adjectives answer questions such as which? what kind? how many? whose? how much?

We received a *large* order today.

The skies are *blue* today.

That one did it.

Adjectives may be used to compare persons and things: *comparative degree* compares two persons or things; *superlative degree* compares three or more persons or things. There can be regular forms and irregular forms for these degrees.

Jim is *tall* and Susan is *taller;* but Jo is *tallest.* (regular degree)

Among the operators, Susan is *good,* Jack is *better,* and Steve is *best.* (irregular degree)

Adverbs

Adverbs modify, describe, or limit verbs, adjectives, and other adverbs. Adverbs answer the questions when? where? how? how often? how much?

Mr. Jacoby *rapidly* ate lunch.

Jim is *too* tall for the doorway.

The supervisor spoke *very loudly.* ("Very" modifies the adverb "loudly," and "loudly" modifies the verb "spoke.")

Adverbs may be used to compare persons and things; these forms also may be described as regular and irregular:

The work is *late.* The work is *later* than usual. The work is the *latest* ever. (regular degree)

The sales manager injured himself *badly.* The sales manager injured himself *worse* than last time. The sales manager injured himself the *worst* ever. (irregular form)

For adverbs ending in "ly" the comparative and superlative degrees are made by adding "more" ("less") or "most" ("least"), respectively.

James works *more quickly* than Sam. James works the *most quickly* of anyone in the office.

Prepositions

A preposition relates a noun or pronoun to another word in the sentence. The word related is the object of the preposition in the prepositional phrase.

The head of the department interviewed the applicant. (*of* is the preposition; *department* is the object of the preposition. The prepositional phrase *of the department* serves as a modifier of the noun *head.*)

Conjunctions

Conjunctions join words, phrases, or clauses in a sentence (see "Punctuation—Comma" and "Punctuation—Semicolon").

We will debit accounts today *and* tomorrow.

John went to Acres Manor *and* to the East End.

Neffie joined us when we ate lunch, when we worked on the contract, *and* when we relaxed after work.

Types of conjunctions are the following:

Coordinating Conjunctions

Coordinating conjunctions connect two or more words, phrases, or clauses of equal importance and of equal grammatical construction. The most common coordinating conjunctions are *and, but, or, nor, for,* and *yet.*

Miss Daley *and* Mr. Jones will join us *or* them.

He may go shopping today, *but* he must stay home tomorrow.

Correlative Conjunctions

Correlative conjunctions are coordinating conjunctions used in pairs to connect and relate words, phrases, or clauses. The common pairs of correlative conjunctions are *neither-nor, either-or, not only-but also,* and *both-and.*

Either I will invest in stocks, *or* I will start a savings account.

Both the investment counselor *and* the stockbroker are capable advisors.

Subordinate Conjunctions

Subordinate conjunctions connect a dependent clause with an independent clause. Words that can serve as subordinate conjunctions include *after, although, as, because, when, if, whether, before, since, though, while, whenever,* and *unless.*

After completing the Apex project, we should begin work on the master files.

We will take a vacation this month *although* we took one earlier this year.

Conjunctive Adverbs

Conjunctive adverbs connect two independent thoughts of equal importance and grammatical construction in a sentence. In addition, since these words are adverbs, they show a relationship between the clauses. The common conjunctive adverbs include *however, moreover, therefore, furthermore, then, consequently, besides, accordingly, also, nevertheless,* and *thus.*

The economy will improve this year; consequently, sales will improve this year as well.

Mrs. Thomas said she would like to attend both meetings; however, she can afford to attend only one of them.

PUNCTUATION

Whenever you use a mark of punctuation, your sole purpose should be to achieve clarity. Omitting needed punctuation often results in ambiguity.

Period

1. Use a period at the end of a statement or command.

   The personnel office is on the third floor.

   Sign all letters before mailing them.

2. Use a period at the end of a courteous request for action.

   Won't you please let us know your decision soon.

3. Use a period in various abbreviations (see "Abbreviations").

Question Mark

Use a question mark after a direct question where the intent is to obtain a direct answer.

Do you market your product through a retailer or do you sell directly to the consumer?

Exclamation Mark

Place an exclamation mark after an interjection or an exclamation.

Yes! Sell the stock immediately!

Comma

1. Use a comma to set off a parenthetical expression. Parenthetical expressions are words or groups of words that may be removed from a sentence without affecting the meaning or clarity of the sentence. When such an expression comes at the end of a sentence, only one comma is necessary, whereas two commas are needed when the expression is in the middle of a sentence.

The report, however, is not complete.

The applicant is not qualified for the position, in my opinion.

2. Use a comma to set off an appositive. An appositive is a word or group of words immediately following another word or expression that explains or modifies the first expression. Some appositives are essential for clarity; no commas are used. Other appositives are not essential and should be set off by commas before and after the appositive. Only one comma is needed when the appositive ends a sentence.

    My sister Claire was hired for the position of chief accountant. (Claire is the essential appositive; no comma is used.)

    John Jenkins, our sales manager, will be happy to meet with you.

    Please send your order to Miss Mary Cummings, our order manager.

   The following are additional expressions in apposition:

   a. State when city precedes it.

      Our transportation center has been moved from Springfield, Missouri, to Kansas City, Missouri.

   b. Year when month or month and date precede it.

      He was elected president of Exmore Company on January 3, 1986, and promoted to Chairman of the Board on July 7, 1987.

   c. Titles and degrees following a person's name.

      Please send all correspondence to John James, Jr., in care of this office.

   d. Inc. (but not Ltd.) in company names.

      Our parent corporation, Mitchell, Inc., changed its name to Mitchell Ltd.

3. Use a comma to set off an introductory expression, series of prepositional phrases, participial phrase, or dependent clause at the beginning of a sentence.

    However, your order is being processed at this time.

    To be of better service to you, we have just installed a toll-free "800" line.

    Knowing that you would need the goods now, we immediately shipped them to you.

    When it is necessary to place a last-minute order, simply use our toll-free service.

4. When three or more items are listed in a series with the last item separated from the others by a conjunction, place a comma after all items except the last.

   You are assured of quick, efficient, and courteous service.

   Note: Some business writers suggest omitting the comma before the conjunction. If you choose to omit it in one series in a document, omit it in all series in that document. If a conjunction is placed between all items in a series, no commas are used.

   Our itinerary takes us to Chicago and Phoenix and Los Angeles.

   If "etc." is used in a series, the word "and" does not precede it, but a comma does follow the "etc."

   Include direct costs, equipment, personnel, etc., in your proposal.

5. Use a comma to join two independent clauses of a compound sentence when a comma does not appear elsewhere in either of the two clauses (see "Sentence Structure—Compound Sentences").

   Will you attend the sales meeting, or will you send a substitute?

   Note: Some business writers place a comma between independent clauses even though a comma appears elsewhere in the compound sentence.

6. Use a comma to set off a nonrestrictive clause or phrase. A nonrestrictive clause is not essential to the completeness of the sentence. A restrictive clause, however, is essential to the clarity of the sentence.

   Send your questions to Mary Adams, who is director of public relations, for a quick reply. (nonrestrictive clause)

   Companies that develop employee training programs have reported excellent results. (restrictive clause)

7. Use a comma in numbers containing four or more digits. The comma separates thousands, millions, and so on.

   We have in stock *7,193* widgets, *342,961* bolts, and *4,805,977* nuts.

   Note: Some business writers omit using a comma with four-digit numbers (for example, $1200).

Commas are not used in the following numbers: serial numbers, house numbers, policy numbers, page numbers, volume numbers, zip codes, telephone numbers, and digits of a year.

Semicolon

1. Use a semicolon to join two closely related independent clauses when no conjunction has been used.

    The ability to communicate is essential; the ability to communicate on the job is critical.

2. Use a semicolon before a conjunctive adverb that joins two closely related independent clauses.

    Expenses have increased drastically; consequently, next year's budget has been prepared carefully.

    Note: A comma follows the parenthetical conjunctive adverb (see "Punctuation—Comma," rule 1).

3. Use a semicolon before a coordinating conjunction in a compound sentence when one or both of the independent clauses contain a comma (see Comma rule 5 note).

    Our order was for paper, ribbons, and envelopes; but you sent only paper and envelopes.

4. Use a semicolon instead of a comma in a series when commas appear within the various elements of the series.

    Our offices are located in Atlanta, Georgia; Des Moines, Iowa; Birmingham, Alabama; and Portland, Oregon.

5. Use a semicolon before expressions such as *for example* and *namely* when the words that follow these expressions seem to have been added as an explanation.

    When greeting callers on the telephone, always identify your department and give your name; for example, Accounting, Miss Smith.

Colon

1. Use a colon before expressions (such as for example, namely, and thus) that connect ideas when they introduce ideas alluded to earlier in the sentence.

    There are three requirements for the job: namely, speaking knowledge of the German language, five years' working experience, and a bachelor's degree in business administration.

2. Use a colon to introduce a list, either in sentence form or on separate lines.

    Three persons were suggested for Sales Representative of the Year: Gladys Ortiz, Samuel Bigelow, and Joanne Strait.

3. Use a colon to separate hours and minutes when expressing time.

   Our hours are from 8:30 A.M. to 4:30 P.M.

Quotation Marks

1. Use quotation marks to
   a. Set off a direct quotation.

      The personnel manager stated, "We hire only persons with an M.B.A. degree for that type of position."

   b. Set off a slang expression, coined expression, or technical term.

      When questioned about a client's behavior, the consultant replied that the person appeared to be "uptight."

   c. Set off titles of songs, magazines and newspaper articles, chapters in published works, and unpublished works.

      The research report, "Sexual Harassment in the Office," is due for distribution next month.

2. When combined with quotation marks,
   a. Always place a period or comma inside the ending quotation mark.

      The accountant stated, "Our taxable income is at an all-time high."

      He labeled the report on our hiring practices as "garbage," and I must agree.

      Note: When a quoted statement begins a sentence, place a comma inside the ending quotation mark and a period at the end of the sentence.

      "We provide our new employees with a two-week paid vacation after twelve months," replied the interviewer.

   b. Place question and exclamation marks outside the ending quotation mark if the question or exclamation is the entire sentence. Place these marks inside the ending quotation mark if the quoted material is the question or exclamation.

      Did she say, "I can go"?

      "What type of vacation policy does your company have?" she asked.

      He exclaimed, "I accept the offer!"

      Note: When the question mark or exclamation mark is placed inside the ending quotation mark, no additional punctuation is necessary immediately outside the ending quotation mark (see second and third examples just presented).

c. Always place semicolons and colons outside the ending quotation mark.

> You stated, "I'll pay the bill by the end of the week"; however, we still haven't received payment.

Apostrophe

1. Show omission of letters in contractions by inserting an apostrophe at the exact point of omission.

   It's time for the appointment; he'll represent me.

2. An apostrophe is used to show possession in
   a. Singular nouns not ending in "s." Add an 's at the end of the noun: *manager's report.*
   b. Singular nouns ending in "s." Add an 's at the end if a new syllable is formed: *boss's remarks.*
   c. Singular nouns ending in "s." Add only an apostrophe if pronunciation would be difficult if the 's rule were applied:

      Did you hear President *Hastings'* speech?

   d. Regular plural nouns (those ending in "s"). Add an apostrophe:

      We received the committee *members'* reports.

   e. Irregular plural nouns (where the form of the word changes—*man-men, child-children*). Add an 's:

      Sears sells *men's* hats.

3. Do not include an apostrophe with possessive pronouns:

   This brochure is *ours,* but that one is *yours.*

Hyphen

1. Use a hyphen when dividing a word at the end of a typewritten line (see "Word Division").
2. When two or more adjectives precede a noun, the adjectives may jointly modify the noun. In this instance, the adjectives should be hyphenated.

   The well-placed barrier stopped all traffic.

   The up-to-the-minute news is that the stock will be sold.

Note: If the compound expression follows the noun it is modifying, the expression is not hyphenated.

The consultant they hired is well known.

3. If the first word in a compound expression ends in "ly," do not hyphenate the expression even if it precedes the noun.

   He edits a widely read magazine.

CAPITALIZATION

Some business writers differ on some of the rules of capitalization. The rules that follow apply to most situations where you might have a question.

Abbreviations

Capitalize abbreviations as you would normally capitalize the words for which the abbreviations stand.

First Words

Capitalize

1. The first word of a sentence.
2. The first word of a direct quotation regardless of its location in the sentence.

   The recently posted sign read, "Unauthorized persons are prohibited."

3. The first word of each item in a listing.

   1. Storage disks
   2. Continuous-feed paper

4. The first word of a complete statement following a colon if such a statement is a formal rule, a direct quotation, or a statement introduced by a single word.

   Note: All visitors must register with the receptionist.

   Murphy's law states as follows: "If anything can go wrong, it will."

5. The first word of a complimentary closing.

   Sincerely yours   Very truly yours

Proper Nouns

Always capitalize proper nouns. Several specific rules relate to particular categories of proper nouns.

1. Titles.

   a. Capitalize a title that precedes a name, but do not capitalize a title that follows a name.

      President Reagan visited farms in Iowa recently.

      The man standing beside her is Beauregard Butler, *president* of the P.T.A.

   b. Unless it is a title of a high-ranking government official, foreign dignitary, or international figure, do not capitalize a title that is used as a substitute for a specific person's name.

      The Pope will visit your country this month.

      The president of the corporation will speak to the stockholders.

   c. When used as substitutes for names, capitalize words showing family relationships or when the title precedes the name.

      Please call Father when you get home. (used as a name)

      Please call your father when you get home. (used to designate family relationship)

      Your Uncle Phillip and your two cousins will be visiting next month.

   d. Capitalize all words in the titles of books, magazines, and other publications, except articles (a, an, the), prepositions of four or fewer letters, and conjunctions, unless these are the first or last word in the title.

      Have you read *Management of Organizational Theory?*

      Yes, and I just finished reading *In Search of Excellence.*

2. Place names.

   a. Capitalize the official names of cities and their "coined" or imagined names.

      New York City is the *Big Apple.*

      Philadelphia is the *City of Brotherly Love.*

   b. Capitalize "city" when it follows the name of the city; do not capitalize "city" when it precedes the name of the city unless it is part of the corporate name of the city.

New York City is a major financial center of the world.

Wall Street is in the city of New York.

c. Capitalize "state" when it follows the name of the state; do not capitalize "state" when it precedes the name of the state.

The Grand Ole Opry is in the state of Tennessee; however, Carnegie Hall is in New York State.

d. Capitalize the names of streets, buildings, rivers, and mountains. Also capitalize the words "street" or "river" when they are part of the proper name. Do not capitalize the generic term when it stands alone or plural generic terms when used with the proper nouns.

Maymont Park is located off Byrd Avenue.

The Mississippi River is the largest river in the United States; however, the Missouri and Ohio rivers are also very large.

3. Organizations.

a. When referring to a specific organization, such as a business, capitalize the major words in the name.

We completed a major sale of computer software to Glasgow Controls Company last week.

The Wharton School of Finance is a part of the University of Pennsylvania.

The annual blood drive will be conducted by the American Red Cross.

b. Generally, only capitalize terms such as personnel department, maintenance division, and board of directors when they are actual units within your own organization. When referring to someone else's organization, do not capitalize these terms.

c. Do not capitalize generic terms that are used in place of the full name of an organization unless special emphasis is intended.

When you enroll in the M.B.A. program at our university, you will study a comprehensive, up-to-date curriculum.

4. Brand names. Capitalize the brand name or trademark associated with a product; however, do not capitalize the generic product following the brand name.

Orion International purchased only Ford automobiles for its sales fleet.

5. Days of the week, months of the year, events, and holidays.
   a. Capitalize the names of days, months, holidays, events, and religious holidays.

      On the first Monday in September, we celebrate Labor Day; other days we celebrate include Thanksgiving, Christmas, and Memorial Day.

   b. Do not capitalize the names of the seasons unless personified or used to designate a special event.

      The annual fall stockholders' meeting will be held in San Francisco.

      As the Spring Fling will be sponsored by our organization, all employees are encouraged to attend.

Derivatives of Proper Nouns

1. Capitalize a word derived from a proper noun.

   The Spanish Ambassador visited our company to discuss our products.

2. Capitalize all names derived from races, people, tribes, religions, and languages.

   The Afro-American League has requested it be allowed to use our auditorium.

Miscellaneous

Do not capitalize

1. Points of the compass unless they designate a definite region or are part of a proper noun.

   Several major companies have moved their headquarters to the South because of favorable labor laws and climate.

   The West Coast has become known for its electronics industry; many of these electronics companies moved west early in the 1950s.

2. Names of subject areas except for proper nouns or specific course titles.

   She completed several courses in accounting, for example, Tax Accounting I and II and Auditing I.

   A business English course is very beneficial to students majoring in business administration.

3. First words in indirect quotations or interrupted quotations.

   The personnel manager said he could attend the meeting.

   "Let's come to order," exclaimed the president, "so that we can quickly finish this meeting!"

ABBREVIATIONS

Generally, avoid abbreviations in your writing as they may not be clear to the reader. When you find you must abbreviate, there are several widely accepted rules to follow:

1. If a term has a common abbreviation that will be used throughout the document, write out the word in full the first time and place the abbreviation in parentheses.

   Ms. Mary Constantine will head the Word Processing (WP) Department.

2. Always abbreviate courtesy titles when used with a person's name. The regular courtesy titles are Dr., Mr., Mrs., and Ms. Always abbreviate Jr., Sr., and Esq. when they follow a full name. No courtesy title precedes a name when Esq. is used.

   Dr. Sarah Barnard, *Mr.* Sam Simpson, *Mrs.* Lillian Heilman, and *Ms.* Kate Jurardo attended the conference.

   The letters are addressed to *Dr.* Nathan Patten, *Jr.; Mr.* Matt Billingsley, *Sr.;* and Lewis Swiller, *Esq.*

3. In general, do not abbreviate military, political, or religious titles.

   Governor McCormick, *General* Pate, and *Reverend* Tutu attended the plant opening ceremonies.

4. Generally, do not abbreviate the points of the compass when used with street names.

   Please address the letter to me at *134 South Main Street* rather than *134 S. Main Street.*

5. Generally, do not abbreviate Incorporated, Company, Corporation, Manufacturing, and other similar terms in business names unless the company does so in its letterhead.
6. In general, do not abbreviate the names of the days of the week and months of the year.
7. Write the following without periods.

   a. Acronyms:

      Are you studying *COBOL* and *JCL* this semester?

b. Widely known names of businesses or other organizations.

Representatives from *IBM, AT&T,* and the *NAACP* attended the meeting.

c. Radio and television stations and television networks.

WQXR, the local radio station, is owned by *CBS.*

d. Names of well-known government agencies and international organizations.

Our interests in the matter are being represented by the *FCC,* the *IRS,* and the *UN.*

e. Time zones.

On which date do we change from *EST* to *EDT?*

8. Write the following with periods.

a. Academic degrees.

Linda Berkeley holds these degrees: *B.A., M.Ed., Ph.D.,* and *D.D.S.*

Note: CPA, CPS, CAM, and so on have no periods when they stand alone but have periods when used with academic degrees.

b. Expression of time.

The time is 6 *A.M.* here and 2 *P.M.* there.

c. Geographic abbreviations consisting of single initials.

Plant managers from the *U.S.* and the *U.S.S.R.* will meet to exchange ideas.

d. A.D. ("in the year of our Lord") and B.C. ("before Christ"). These two abbreviations should always be written in all capitals. A.D. should be written in front of the year, B.C. after the year.

The events you inquired about took place in *A.D.* 7 and 231 *B.C.*

NUMBERS

The following rules will assist you in writing numbers:

1. Generally, spell out numbers from one to nine and use figures to express numbers of 10 and above.

The manager interviewed three candidates for the position.

Please order 75 reams of letterhead paper.

2. Avoid starting a sentence with a number. If you must, spell out the number in words.

   Twenty-three employees are on vacation this week.

3. When one number immediately precedes another number, express the smaller of the two in words.

   He made six 10-minute phone calls to close the sale.

4. Use figures with A.M. and P.M. Use figures with o'clock in informal writing (such as business writing).

   Our hours are from 9:00 A.M. to 5:30 P.M.

   The accountant left for the meeting at 10 o'clock.

   Note: If all times are on the hour, the colon and zeroes are not necessary when using A.M. or P.M.

   We left for the board of directors meeting at 10 A.M.

5. Use figures to express exact or appropriate amounts of money, but spell out indefinite amounts of money.

   The invoice amounted to $1,200, but we were allowed nearly a $7 discount.

   Current starting salaries for persons with M.B.A. degrees are several thousand dollars over those of beginning teachers.

   Note: Use a "$" (with figures) instead of writing out dollars. Express whole dollar amounts without a decimal point and two zeros.

6. Use figures and the word "cents" for expressing amounts under a dollar except when related amounts require a dollar sign.

   Photocopies on this machine cost only 3 cents each.

   These audio/tapes are on sale for $1.25 each or $.75 each if bought in quantity.

7. Use cardinal numbers (1, 2, 3) when the day follows the month; use ordinal numbers (1st, 2nd, 3rd), either as words or figures, when the day precedes the month.

   The data processing convention will begin on the 21st of September.

   She was hired as the personnel manager on July 7.

8. Use figures and the word "percent" spelled out when expressing percentages in sentences.

    The interest rate was quoted at 15 percent on the bond issue.

9. When the street name is a number, spell out the name if nine or below. Use figures for street names of 10 and above. Cardinal numbers may be used if preceded by a point of the compass; for clarity, use ordinal numbers if no word precedes the street name.

    Send the order to 231 Fifth Street; however, send the invoice to our office at 147 East 52 Street.

    All applications can be mailed to our personnel department at 749 65th Street.

WORD DIVISION

As a general rule, avoid dividing words at the end of typewritten lines. However, when you must divide, follow these simple rules.

1. Divide words only between syllables. Thus, no matter how long a word, if it has only one syllable, it cannot be divided:

    through chrome

2. Divide only words of six letters or more regardless of the number of syllables:

    let-ter order prior

3. Do not separate a one-letter syllable at the beginning of a word. Do not separate a two-letter syllable at the end of a word. Do not separate a syllable that does not contain a vowel:

    enough (not e-nough) poorly (not poor-ly) wouldn't (not would-n't)

4. Hyphenated compound words should be divided only at the point of the hyphen:

    self-control (not self-con-trol)

5. Avoid dividing proper names. If necessary, place the person's first name at the end of one line and surname at the beginning of the next:

    Sandra Smith (not San-dra Smith)

6. Do not use a hyphen when placing part of a date on the next line. Attempt to put month and day together on the same line.
7. Do not divide the last word on a page.

SENTENCE STRUCTURE

Four types of sentences are simple, compound, complex, and compound-complex. The advantage of using various sentence structures are discussed in Chapter 3.

Simple Sentences

A simple sentence contains one complete thought. The sentence may contain a compound subject or a compound predicate, but the result is one thought.

> The committee approved the report.

Compound Sentences

A compound sentence contains two complete but related thoughts. Each thought could stand by itself as a separate sentence.

> The sales department accepted the report, but the collection department rejected it.

The two independent clauses in a compound sentence can be joined with a coordinating conjunction, a conjunctive adverb, or a semicolon (see "Parts of Speech—Conjunctions" and "Punctuation—Comma and Semicolon").

Complex Sentences

A complex sentence contains an independent clause (a complete thought) and a dependent clause (a thought that cannot stand by itself).

> Because you already have an account with our bank, the procedure for authorizing us to handle your payroll deposit is simple.

In complex sentences, the dependent clause starts with a subordinate conjunction (see "Parts of Speech—Conjunctions"). The dependent clause may be at the beginning or at the end of the sentence.

Compound-Complex Sentences

A compound-complex sentence contains at least two independent clauses and one dependent clause.

> Although sales have increased, our company's profits have continued to decline; but management has developed a new marketing strategy.

Common Sentence Errors

Six common errors are committed when constructing sentences: sentence fragment, run-on sentence, comma splice, misplaced phrase, subject/verb agreement, and pronoun/noun antecedent agreement.

A sentence fragment is a group of words that does not form a complete thought.

> After he delivered his speech

A run-on sentence usually contains two or more complete thoughts that have not been joined with a conjunction or appropriate punctuation mark.

> The employee evaluations arrived the follow-up interviews were held.

A comma splice occurs when two independent clauses are joined by a comma without an accompanying conjunction.

> The ability to communicate clearly is essential, the ability to communicate on the job is critical.

A misplaced modifying phrase results in a phrase being separated from the idea it modifies.

> We can sell you this desk at a very reasonable price, which has a leather top.

The number of the subject and verb must agree—singular subjects take singular verbs; plural subjects, plural verbs. This type of error can result from many situations, the most common of which is intervening phrases.

> The sales manager, as well as her three assistants, are attending the meeting in St. Paul.
>
> The evaluations of the employment procedure is on your desk.

Since pronouns take the place of nouns, they should agree in number with the nouns they are replacing.

> The salesmen should take care in the preparation of his report.

Another problem with pronoun/noun antecedent is the ambiguity that exists when there is not a clear indication of what the pronoun refers to.

> The sales manager and his assistant finished the report, but he made several errors in it.

APPENDIX B

CORRESPONDENCE PARTS AND FORMAT

You should use standard parts and layout for letters mailed outside the company and for memos routed within the company. Using these standard parts and layout helps in two ways. First, the reader will recognize them and will be able to follow along easily and quickly. Second, employers can hold down costs by standardizing their systems for handling correspondence. This section covers letter parts, salutations and complimentary closes, letter styles, punctuation styles, margins, and addressing procedures. The section on memos covers memo parts, styles, margins, and addressing procedures.

LETTERS

Letters have both *major* and *minor* parts. Major parts are those you would normally include in any letter. Minor parts are those you include as needed or preferred.

Major Letter Parts

The major parts of letters described in the order that they appear in the typewritten copies are as follows:

Letterhead (Writer's Return Address)

The letterhead includes the company name, address, and zip code. It may contain the company logo, slogan, or telephone number as well.

Dateline

Type the complete date in one of these three ways: June 19, 1987; 19 June 1987; or 1987 06 19. The third method is called the *international standard.*

Inside Address (Receiver's Address)

Include the name and title; department, branch, or division; company name; street number and name; city; state or province abbreviation; and zip code.

Salutation

Use a greeting such as "Dear Mr. Jax" to introduce the message, except when using the simplified letter style, where the salutation is omitted.

Message

Include the entire text or body of the letter. (If you include a post-script, then that too is part of the message even though a postscript is a minor letter part.)

Complimentary Close

Close the message with a statement such as "Sincerely yours," except when using the simplified letter style, where this closing is omitted.

Signature Block

Include both signed and typed signatures and the writer's position or department in the company.

Reference Initials

Include the typist's initials. You may also include a file code when a letter is typed on word processing equipment.

The major letter parts appear in Figures B-1, B-2, B-3, and B-4. Notice that both the salutation and complimentary close are omitted in Figure B-4.

Minor Letter Parts

Minor letter parts appear in some letters but not in others. Use them *when needed.* For example, if you enclose materials with a letter, include an enclosure notation in the letter. You may sometimes use minor parts *when preferred* or *for clarity or emphasis.* An example of all three is the use of a subject line. The minor parts of a letter in the order in which they should appear are as follows:

Attention Line

Use an attention line to name the person (or perhaps the position) to whose attention you are calling the message. Do this in cases where the letter itself is addressed to a company or a division or department within a company.

Subject Line

The subject line names the letter topic. If you prefer, you may place the subject line before the salutation rather than after it for a more personal tone. (A subject line is a major letter part in the simplified letter style, shown in Figure B-4.)

Company Name

Use the company name in the signature block whenever the writer prefers to sign the letter directly under the company name or it is in keeping with the company's correspondence style.

Enclosure Notation

Use an enclosure notation to denote that you included some other material with a letter. Whenever more than one enclosure is included, write either the number or names of the enclosures.

Copy Distribution Notation

Use a copy distribution notation to name those people who will receive a copy of the letter. Use one of these three methods: "c: Julia Jones" or "cc: Julia Jones" or "pc: Julia Jones." (Use of the colon is optional.) The letter "c" represents copy; the letters "cc," carbon copy; and the letters "pc," photocopy. Do not denote file copies.

Blind Copy Distribution Notation

Use the blind copy notation instead of the copy distribution notation whenever copies are sent to others without the knowledge of the person receiving the original letter. Now and then, you may send both copies and blind copies. Remember not to put the blind copy notation on the original. As with the copy distribution notations, choose one of these methods: "bc: Julia Jones" or "bcc: Julia Jones" or "bpc: Julia Jones." (Use of the colon is optional.)

Postscript

Use a postscript to add comments at the end of the letter. A postscript might contain an idea you wish to emphasize by placing it last on the page.

Additional Page Notation

Use an additional page notation at the top of each page other than the first page of the letter. Include the name of the person receiving the letter, the page number, and the date.

Examples of all minor letter parts appear in Figures B-1, B-2, B-3, and B-4.

Salutations and Complimentary Closes

You may choose your own salutations and complimentary closes based on how formal the situation is or use those designated by your employer. When addressing a firm, you may use the terms *Ladies and Gentlemen, Gentlemen and Ladies, Dear Madam or Sir,* or *Dear Sir or Madam.* When using the simplified letter style shown in Figure B-4, omit both the salutation and the complimentary close.

Here is a list of commonly used salutations arranged in order of decreasing formality:

Sir (or Madam)
My dear Sir (or My dear Madam)
Dear Sir (or Dear Madam)

My dear Mr. Victors
My dear George
Dear George

The formality of the complimentary close in a letter should agree generally with that of the salutation. Here is a list of commonly used complimentary closes arranged in order of decreasing formality:

Yours respectfully
Very respectfully yours
Respectfully yours
Yours truly
Very truly yours
Yours very truly
Sincerely yours
Sincerely
Cordially yours
Cordially

Letter and Punctuation Styles

The major standard letter styles are *block, modified block with blocked paragraphs, modified block with indented paragraphs,* and *simplified.* Punctuation styles are *open* and *mixed.* Descriptions of these letter and punctuation styles follow.

Block Style

When using block style, begin all lines of the letter on the left margin. A letter arranged in this format is balanced visually toward the left side of the page. Block format letters can be typed in less time than either of the modified block styles. A sample block letter style with vertical spacing cues is shown in Figure B-1.

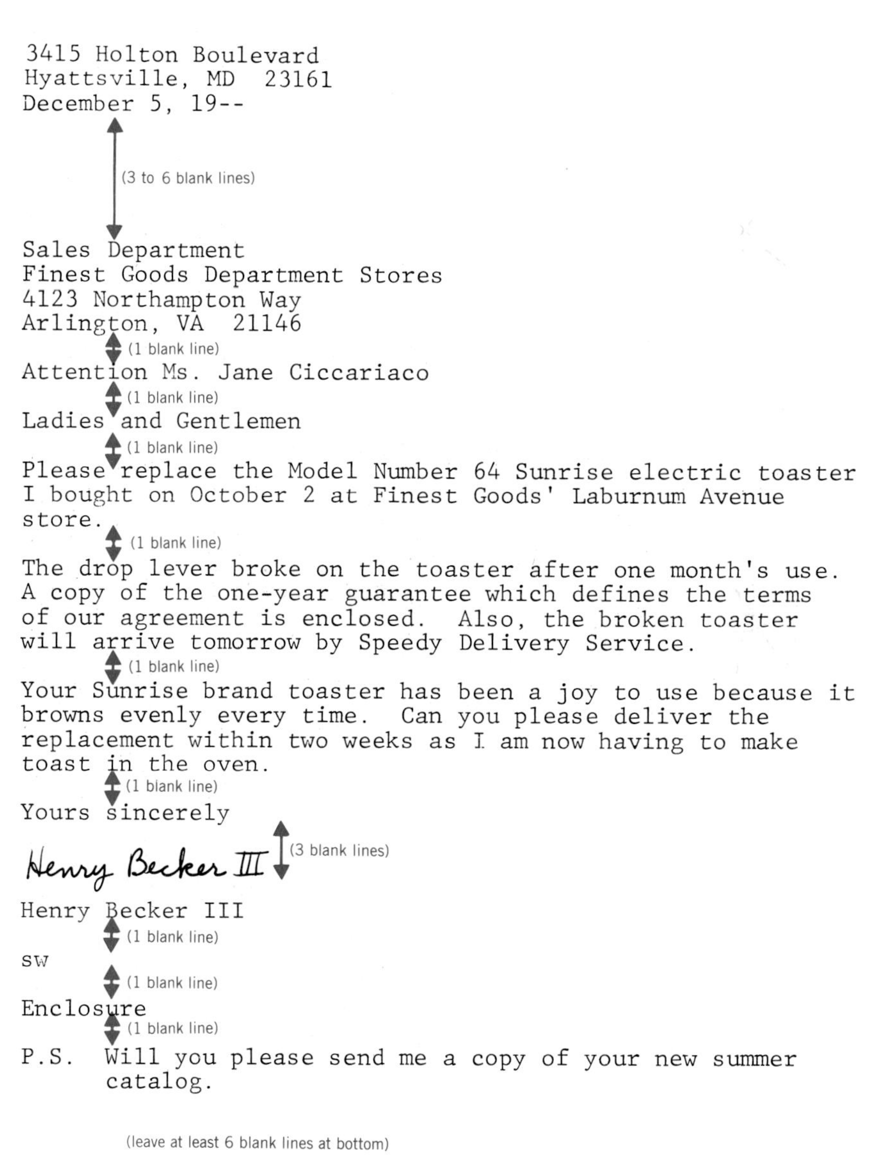

3415 Holton Boulevard
Hyattsville, MD 23161
December 5, 19--

(3 to 6 blank lines)

Sales Department
Finest Goods Department Stores
4123 Northampton Way
Arlington, VA 21146

(1 blank line)

Attention Ms. Jane Ciccariaco

(1 blank line)

Ladies and Gentlemen

(1 blank line)

Please replace the Model Number 64 Sunrise electric toaster I bought on October 2 at Finest Goods' Laburnum Avenue store.

(1 blank line)

The drop lever broke on the toaster after one month's use. A copy of the one-year guarantee which defines the terms of our agreement is enclosed. Also, the broken toaster will arrive tomorrow by Speedy Delivery Service.

(1 blank line)

Your Sunrise brand toaster has been a joy to use because it browns evenly every time. Can you please deliver the replacement within two weeks as I am now having to make toast in the oven.

(1 blank line)

Yours sincerely

(3 blank lines)

Henry Becker III

Henry Becker III

(1 blank line)

sw

(1 blank line)

Enclosure

(1 blank line)

P.S. Will you please send me a copy of your new summer catalog.

(leave at least 6 blank lines at bottom)

FIGURE B-1 Letter typed in block style with open punctuation. (Includes these minor letter parts: attention line, enclosure notation, and postscript).

BETA SPORTSWEAR COMPANY
1891 RAINBOW CIRCLE / PHILADELPHIA, PA 10245
Telephone: (215) 542-6125

15 March 19--

Miss Celia Bonevac
Credit Supervisor
Ace Wholesale Sporting Goods
11897 Lackawanna Avenue
Erie, PA 11302

Dear Miss Bonevac:

Subject: Request for Credit Information

Please send us credit information on Alpine Sporting Goods Company. The firm applied for credit with us and gave your company as a credit reference.

Mr. Jose F. Rodriguez of Alpine asked that the company be allowed to charge $1,000 monthly on open account for goods purchased from us. Because this is their first such application with us, we shall appreciate as much information as you can give us.

Alpine requested that the first order be shipped by April 10. So that this request can be met, can you complete and return the attached credit information form to us by April 5?

Yours truly,

BETA SPORTSWEAR COMPANY

John M. Bentley, Jr.

John M. Bentley, Jr.
Credit Supervisor

som
(1 blank line)
bc: Janice Loxley, Sales Department

FIGURE B-2 Letter typed in modified block style with blocked paragraphs and mixed punctuation. (Includes these minor letter parts: subject line, company name, and blind copy distribution notation). (Note: The blind copy distribution notation does not appear on the original.)

WEYGANDT HOME FOR CHILDREN
52888 BROADWAY STREET
LUBBOCK, TX 77523

December 5, 19--

Mrs. Joyce Xavier
888 Madison Street
Lubbock, TX 77532

Dear Mrs. Xavier:

Helping children grow up happily can be a joyful experience.

When a young child smiles at you or calls your name, it makes you feel special.

Feeling special to someone else is something that all of us can appreciate, especially when that someone is a child.

How many times have you thrown away your children's clothing thinking it a waste that they outgrew them before they wore them out? Here at the Weygandt Home, our children's needs are basically provided for through generous donations by the citizens of Lubbock. But right now, some of them do need warm clothes for the winter.

You can help in a special way by donating some of the used clothing (sizes 3-12) that your children have outgrown. We especially need overcoats, gloves or mittens, and pants and skirts. The clothes that your children outgrew last year would serve our children well this year.

Donations to the home are tax deductible and receipts will be provided. But these donations will provide more than tax deductions. They provide an opportunity to feel the warmth that comes from being special in a child's world.

We will gladly pick up your donations any weekday between 9 a.m. and 5 p.m. If you prefer, you are welcome

FIGURE B-3 Modified block letter style with indented paragraphs and mixed punctuation. (Includes an additional page notation. If you prefer, block the additional page notation on three lines flush with the left margin. Also includes a filing code number with the reference initials.)

(6 blank lines)

Mrs. Joyce Xavier 2 December 5, 19--

(2 blank lines)

to bring them to the home at 18 Cross Lane and meet the children while you're here. Please call us at 732-6570 before November 5, the closing date of the appeal.

Sincerely yours,

Robert E. Carter

Robert E. Carter
Director

pjs: S1/Z03

FIGURE B-3 (continued)

Modified Block Letter Style with Blocked Paragraphs

When using the modified block style with blocked paragraphs, begin the dateline, complimentary close, and each line of the signature block at the horizontal center of the page. Begin all other lines on the left margin. A letter arranged in this format is balanced visually toward the center of the page. A sample modified block style letter with blocked paragraphs and with an additional vertical spacing cue is shown in Figure B-2.

Modified Block Letter Style with Indented Paragraphs

When using the modified block style with indented paragraphs, begin the dateline, complimentary close, and each line of the signature block at the horizontal center of the page. Indent the first line of each paragraph in the message (usually five spaces). Begin all other lines of the letter on the left margin. A letter arranged in this format is balanced visually toward the center of the page. A sample modified block style letter with indented paragraphs and with additional vertical spacing cues is shown in Figure B-3.

Simplified Letter Style

When using the simplified style, begin all lines on the left margin. This style contains no salutation or complimentary close. A subject line is placed in capital letters where the salutation is placed in the other letter styles. Place the writer's name and position in capital letters below the last line of the body. A letter typed in this style is balanced visually toward the left side of the page. A sample simplified letter style with additional vertical spacing cues is shown in Figure B-4.

Open Punctuation Style

The open punctuation style includes no punctuation after the salutation and complimentary close. A sample of open punctuation style is shown in Figure B-1.

Mixed Punctuation Style

The mixed punctuation style includes a colon after the salutation and a comma after the complimentary close. Samples of the use of mixed punctuation style are shown in Figures B-2 and B-3.

Letter Margins

For eye appeal, you should frame letters in white space (margins). The letterhead appears in the top margin of most business letters. However, when typing a letter on a blank page, leave a 1″ to 1½″ top

ACE WHOLESALE SPORTING GOODS
11897 Lackawanna Avenue
Erie, PA 11302

THE "ACE" IN SPORTING GOODS SINCE 1928

December 5, 19--

Mr. John M. Bentley, Jr.
Credit Supervisor
Beta Sportswear Company
1891 Rainbow Circle
Philadelphia, PA 10245

(2 blank lines)

CREDIT INFORMATION ON ALPINE SPORTING GOODS

(2 blank lines)

As the enclosed credit information form shows, Alpine Sporting Goods has our highest recommendation for credit purchases with your firm.

Alpine always pays us on time. Also, they seem eager to maintain a sound business relationship with us. Therefore, we think you will enjoy doing business with them.

Just write or call us at 843-0098 when we can supply you with credit information again.

Celia Bonevac (3 to 4 blank lines)

MISS CELIA BONEVAC, CREDIT SUPERVISOR

tsm

Enclosures: Credit information form
Business card

(1 blank line)

pc Prince Hawley, Sales Department

FIGURE B-4 Simplified letter style. (Includes these minor letter parts: multiple enclosures notation and copy distribution notation.)

Correspondence Format and Layout

Two-Letter Mailing Abbreviations for the United States and Canada

United States			
State	Abbreviation	State	Abbreviation
Alabama	AL	Montana	MT
Alaska	AK	Nebraska	NE
Arizona	AZ	Nevada	NV
Arkansas	AR	New Hampshire	NH
California	CA	New Jersey	NJ
Colorado	CO	New Mexico	NM
Connecticut	CT	New York	NY
Delaware	DE	North Carolina	NC
District of Columbia	DC	North Dakota	ND
Florida	FL	Ohio	OH
Georgia	GA	Oklahoma	OK
Guam	GU	Oregon	OR
Hawaii	HI	Pennsylvania	PA
Idaho	ID	Puerto Rico	PR
Illinois	IL	Rhode Island	RI
Indiana	IN	South Carolina	SC
Iowa	IA	South Dakota	SD
Kansas	KS	Tennessee	TN
Kentucky	KY	Texas	TX
Louisiana	LA	Utah	UT
Maine	ME	Vermont	VT
Maryland	MD	Virginia	VA
Massachusetts	MA	Virgin Islands	VI
Michigan	MI	Washington	WA
Minnesota	MN	West Virginia	WV
Mississippi	MS	Wisconsin	WI
Missouri	MO	Wyoming	WY

Canada			
Province	Abbreviation	Province	Abbreviation
British Columbia	BC	Nova Scotia	NS
Labrador	LB	Ontario	ON
Manitoba	MB	Prince Edward Island	PE
New Brunswick	NB	Quebec	PQ
Newfoundland	NF	Saskatchewan	SK
Northwest Territories	NT	Yukon Territory	YT

FIGURE B-5 Two-letter mailing abbreviations for United States and Canada.

margin. The width of the side margins depends on the length of the letter, but they should be at least 1″ on the left side. On the right, they should be at least 1″ if the margin is justified (even) or average at least 1″ if ragged (uneven). The bottom margin should be at least 1″.

Many companies use a standard length horizontal writing line for all letters. When this is done, the side margins are predetermined. This practice has increased with the increased use of word processing equipment to produce letters.

HOW ZIP CODE® WORKS

ZIP Code is a 5-digit geographic code that identifies areas within the United States and its territories for purposes of simplifying the distribution of mail by the U.S. Postal Service. It should appear on the last line of both the destination and return addresses of mail, following the name of the city and State. The ZIP Code alignments do not necessarily adhere to boundaries of cities, counties, States, or other jurisdictions. The following example illustrates how 5-digit ZIP Codes are formulated and what the significance of each digit is:

ZIP CODE NATIONAL AREAS

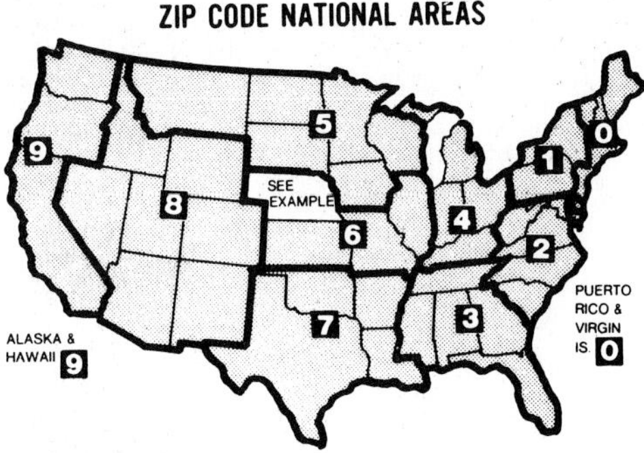

The first digit of a ZIP Code divides the country into 10 large groups of States numbered from 0 in the Northeast to 9 in the Far West.

EXAMPLE

693 ■ 692 ■ 687 ■ 691 ■ 688 ■ 686 ■ 680 ■ 681 ● 683 ■ 684 685 ● 690 ■ 689 ■

■ SCF
● LARGE CITY
○ POST OFFICE

Within these areas, each State is divided into an average of 10 smaller geographic areas, identified by the 2nd and 3rd digits of the ZIP Code.

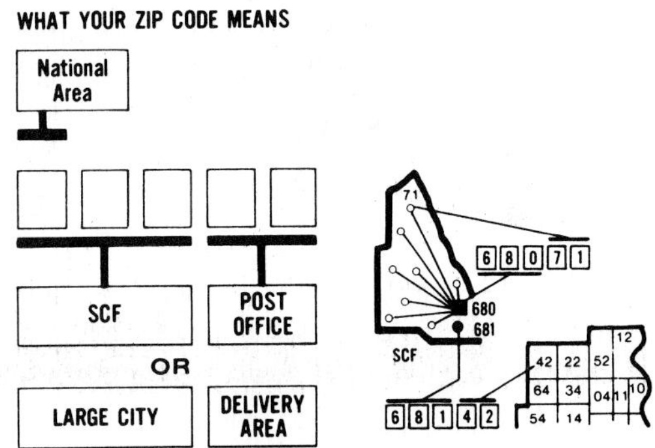

The last 2 digits identify a local delivery area.

FIGURE B-6 Explanation of five-digit Zip Codes.

Letter and Envelope Addressing Procedures

You should typewrite business envelopes to get the fastest delivery service for mail sent through the federal government's postal service. The postal services of some industrialized countries use machines called optical character recognition readers to "read" addresses on envelopes automatically. The mail then is sorted automatically for routing. Use a two-letter state or province abbreviation and a zip code in both the mailing address and the return address on an envelope. (A list of two-letter abbreviations for the United States and Canada is

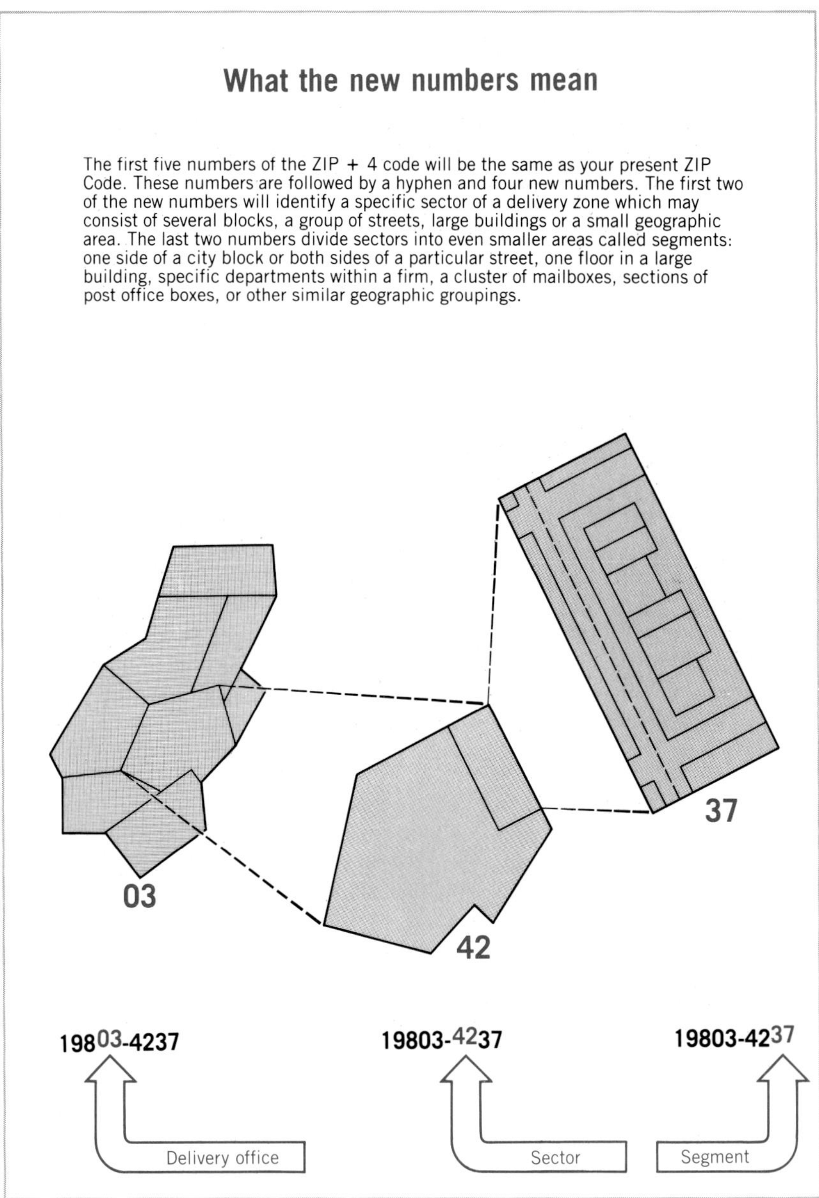

FIGURE B-7 Explanation of nine-digit Zip Codes (Zip + 4).

given in Figure B-5. An explanation of the standard five-digit zip codes used in the United States is shown in Figure B-6, and the new nine-digit zip codes—zip + 4—are explained in Figure B-7.) Use the same information in the letter address that you use on the envelope.

Letter Addresses

The return address in a letter usually is printed on a letterhead. This address probably will contain a two-letter state or province abbreviation and a zip code. Examples of how these letterhead addresses look are shown in Figures B-2, B-3, and B-4. Examples of return addresses as typed on a blank page (without letterhead) are shown in Figure B-1 and as follows:

Scott Swallenberg
4213 Massen Lane
Springfield, MO 60112

Examples of how to typewrite the address (inside or reader's address) in a letter are shown in Figures B-1, B-2, B-3, and B-4.

Envelope Addresses

The two standard types of business envelopes are Number $6\frac{3}{4}$ (small envelope) and Number 10 (large envelope). The United States Postal Service suggests that the mailing address on an envelope be typed in

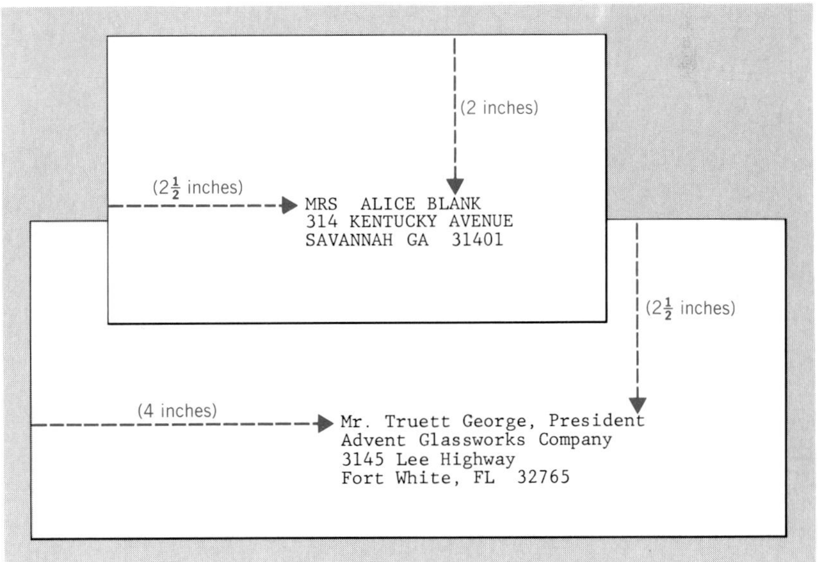

FIGURE B-8 Mailing addresses on small (above) and large (below) envelopes.

capital letters and without punctuation, but this practice is not yet widely used. Examples of how to address both small and large envelopes are shown in Figure B-8. Notice that the mailing address on the small envelope is shown as recommended by the Postal Service. Also, note that placement notations are given in both examples.

MEMOS

Typewritten memos have standard parts just as letters do. In fact, some memo parts serve the same function as they do in letters. Addressing memos is somewhat different from addressing letters, though.

Memo Parts

Memos have both *major* and *minor* parts. Major parts are those you would normally include in any memo. Minor parts are those you include as needed or preferred. Memos also have a *heading* section and a *body* section.

Memo Heading Section

The following are the parts of the heading section of a memo in their usual order of appearance. All those listed are major parts in a typewritten memo.

Memo Heading The memo heading includes the company name and may include the company logo and slogan as well.

To Type the name and position of the person who is to receive the memo after the word *To.*

From Type the name and position of the writer after the word *From.*

Date Type the complete date after the word *Date* in one of these three ways: December 5, 1987 or 5 December 1987 or 1987 12 05. The third method is called the *international standard.*

File or Reference Number Type a file or reference number whenever you assign a number for filing or cross referencing.

Subject Type the title of the topic discussed in the message of the memo after the word *Subject.*

Memo Body Section

The following are the parts of the body section of a memo in their usual order of appearance. Major and minor parts are noted.

Message (major part) The message is the discussion of the subject of the memo.

Signature Block (minor part) Include a signature block only if you wish to sign the memo and do not wish to sign or initial it beside the writer's typed name in the heading section.

Reference Initials (major part) Include the typist's initials. You may also include a code number when typing a memo on word processing equipment; when doing this, do not include a file or reference number in the heading section.

Enclosure Notation (minor part) Use the enclosure notation to show that you included some other material with the memo. Whenever you include more than one enclosure, type either the number or the names of the enclosures after the word *Enclosures.*

Copy Distribution Notation (minor part) Use the copy distribution notation to name those people who will receive a copy of the memo. As in letters, you may use the notations *c* (copy), *cc* (carbon copy), or *pc* (photocopy). You may also use the word *Distribution.*

Postscript (minor part) Use a postscript to add comments at the end of the memo. A postscript might contain an idea that you want to emphasize.

Additional Page Notation (minor part) Use an additional page notation at the top of each page of a memo other than the first page. Include the name of the person receiving the memo, the page number, and the date.

Examples of all memo heading and body section parts except the additional page notation are shown either in Figure B-9 or B-10. The additional page notation is typed like the one in the letter shown in Figure B-3.

Memo Styles

Memo styles are not as standardized in business practice today as are letter styles. However, to improve efficiency and cut costs, adopt a style and use it consistently. Two popular styles that are easy to use are *block* and *modified block.*

To: J. Stuart Laws
Corporate Legal Counselor

(1 blank line)

From: Amanda R. Loos *arl*
Personnel Assistant

(1 blank line)

Date: August 4, 19--

(1 blank line)

Subject: Preparation of Equal Employment Opportunity Report

(2 blank lines)

Will you please help me prepare the state requirements section of our annual equal employment opportunity report?

(1 blank line)

As a result of changes in the state legal code this year, we must meet additional requirements. Therefore, I need your legal assistance in preparing Section 6 of the report.

This will take only about 15 minutes of your time. I can meet you any day this week or next, whatever suits you best. The report must be mailed to the Equal Employment Opportunity Commission within three weeks.

(1 blank line)

st

(1 blank line)

Enclosure: Copy of Section 6 of EEO Guidelines

(1 blank line)

cc Tibbet Arns, Legal Assistant

FIGURE B-9 Memorandum in block style. (Includes these minor parts: enclosure notation and copy distribution notation.)

To: Amanda R. Loos
Personnel Assistant

From: J. Stuart Laws
Legal Counselor

Date: August 5, 19--
(1 blank line)
File: CX 11.21
(1 blank line)
Subject: Meeting for Equal Employment Opportunity Report Preparation

Let's meet in my office (Suite 245) this Friday at 10:30 a.m. to complete Section 6 of your annual equal employment opportunity report.

This year, you will need to report how you advertised available jobs to minority races. Also, you will need to report the procedure you followed to assure that an applicant's place of residency was disregarded in hiring practices. Please bring this information with you to the meeting in addition to information that you normally include in this section of the report.

I look forward to meeting with you on Friday, Amanda.

(3 to 4 blank lines)

J. Stuart Laws

tc
(1 blank line)
P.S. Thanks for sending the copy of Section 6 of the EEO Guidelines.

FIGURE B-10 Memorandum in modified block style. (Includes these minor parts: signature block and postscript.)

Block Memo Style

When using the block style, align all parts of the heading section on the left margin except the memo heading. The memo heading usually is printed on the page, and often the names of the other heading section parts are too (*To, From, Date, File, Subject*). All lines of the body section begin at the left margin. A sample block style memo is shown in Figure B-9, including vertical spacing cues.

Modified Block Memo Style

When using the modified block style, align the *To* and *From* entries of the heading section on the left margin. Then, begin the *Date, File* (if included), and *Subject* entries at the horizontal center. The memo heading usually is printed on the page, and often the names of the other heading section parts are too. All lines of the body section begin at the left margin except the signature block, which begins at the horizontal center. A sample modified block style memo is shown in Figure B-10.

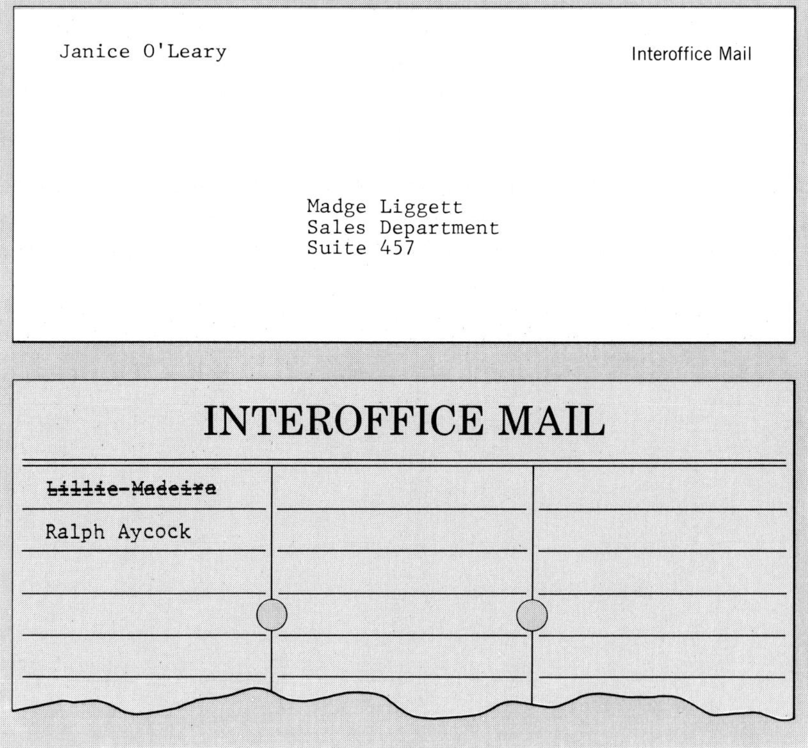

FIGURE B-11 Letter envelope (upper) and reusable envelope (lower) for routing memorandums.

Memo Margins

Often the memo heading will be printed at the top of the page. When this is done, the top margin is fixed before you begin to type the memo. When typing a memo on a blank page, however, type the word *memo* in capital letters centered horizontally 1″ to $1\frac{1}{2}$″ from the top of the page. When a standard writing line length is used throughout a company, the side margins are predetermined. Be sure to leave at least 1″ margins on both sides if the right margin is justified (even). If the right margin is ragged (uneven), leave at least a 1″ average margin on that side. The use of standard writing lines for memos has increased with the increased use of word processing equipment to produce memos.

Leave at least a 1″ bottom margin for memos. When a memo is short and several inches of blank space arc left at the bottom of the page, just leave the space blank.

Addressing Memos

The two most common ways to package memos for routing are to place them in either a letter envelope or a reusable manila or paper envelope. When using a letter envelope, type the words *Interoffice Correspondence* or *Interoffice Mail* across the space where a stamp is usually placed. Type the sender's name in the upper left corner and the receiver's name and location where the letter address normally is placed.

When routing a memo in a reusable envelope, draw a line through the last name on the envelope and type or write the name of the receiver on the next available line. Sample letter and reusable envelopes are shown in Figure B-11.

APPENDIX C

BUSINESS RESEARCH REFERENCE SOURCES

Because information is the basis for decision making, knowing the types of published materials that are available is important. Many reference sources exist for the business student to use in researching problems, preparing cases, and writing reports. This appendix contains names and descriptions of the basic business reference sources. Remember that public, academic, and corporate libraries often have a variety of materials. Whenever you are unable to locate the materials you need, ask your librarian for help.

PERIODICALS AND FINANCIAL NEWSPAPERS

Periodicals and newspapers offer both current information and specialized studies. The following is an annotated list of the most important ones.

Accounting Review. American Accounting Association, Sarasota, Florida (quarterly).

Advertising Age. Crain Communications, Chicago (weekly). Major source of advertising statistics and current news on market strategies, product lines and brands, and advertising firms.

Barron's. Dow Jones & Company, New York (weekly). National business and financial weekly with articles on investment companies, industries, trends, companies, and other business topics. Stock and bond prices are given.

Business Week. McGraw-Hill Publications Company, New York (weekly). Essential reading for business students regardless of particular area of interest. Gives important business indicators, surveys of corporate performance, investment outlook and articles on new business developments and trends in all aspects of business, government, environment, management, marketing, and foreign affairs.

Dun's Business Month. Dun & Bradstreet Corporation, New York (monthly).

Forbes. Forbes, Inc., New York (semimonthly). First issue each year contains "Annual Report on American Industry."

Fortune. Time, Inc., New York (biweekly). Articles on various companies and company executives, new products, and discoveries. Also contains the famous *Fortune* list of 500 largest corporations.

Harvard Business Review. Graduate School of Business Administration, Harvard University, Boston (bimonthly). Business management journal. Articles written for the practitioner.

Investor's Daily. Investor's Daily, Inc., Los Angeles, Calif. (daily, Monday–Friday).

Journal of Business. University of Chicago Press, Chicago (quarterly). Scholarly articles on business, economic methodology.

Journal of Marketing. American Marketing Association, Chicago (quarterly). Scholarly articles on themes and practices in marketing.

Management Review. AMACOM (American Management Association), New York (monthly). Articles on current management literature.

Monthly Labor Review. U.S. Department of Labor, Washington, D.C. (monthly). Articles providing current statistics on unemployment, employment consumer prices, wholesale prices, earnings.

Nation's Business. Chamber of Commerce of the United States, Washington, D.C. (monthly). Popular articles on business, economics, and politics.

Personnel Journal. A. C. Croft, Inc., Costa Mesa, Calif. (monthly). Short articles on various issues in personnel management and industrial relations.

Sales & Marketing Management. Bill Communications, Inc., New York (monthly, with special issues in February, April, July, and October). Trade journal that publishes annual statistical issues: survey of buying power, survey of industrial purchasing power, and survey of selling costs.

The Wall Street Journal. Dow Jones & Company, New York (daily, Monday–Friday). Contains business and financial news and articles on mergers and other corporate strategies. Also contains stock and bond prices.

Washington Post. The Washington Post Company, Washington, D.C. (Monday edition). Monday edition has section on business that provides an overview of the week's activities and features on companies and business issues.

ABSTRACTS AND INDEXES

Abstracts are short, concise summaries of articles provided to give readers a clear indication of the contents of the articles. Indexes give the access points for articles. Some indexes are general (such as *Reader's Guide to Periodical Literature*); others are specialized (such as *Accountants' Index*). A number of general business and economic indexes are listed here. You may wish also to consult abstracts and indexes in other fields, for example, psychology, education, and engineering.

Abstracting and Indexing Services Directory. John Schmittroth, ed., Gale Research Company, Detroit, Mich., 1982 to present (three times a year). New publication giving detailed information on about 1500 abstracts, indexes, digests, serial bibliographies, and catalogs. Title announcement bulletins in all subject areas. Title, publisher, and key word indexes.

Area Business Databank. Information Access Corporation, Belmont, Calif., 1983 to present (monthly, with quarterly cumulation). Provides indexing for more than 100 local and regional business newspapers and journals. Also includes abstracts and microfiche copies of the articles.

Business Index. Information Access Corporation, 1979 to present (monthly, with monthly cumulation). Coverage includes 800 journals, The *Wall Street Journal,* and *The New York Times* Business Section. Arranged by Library of Congress Subject Heading, with some modification. Microfilm, easy-to-read indexing, preloaded.

Business Periodicals Index. H. W. Wilson Company, New York, 1958 to present (monthly, except July, with annual cumulation). Cumulative subject index covering accounting, marketing, taxation, industries, trade, finance, and all aspects of business. The primary business periodicals index.

Business Publications Index and Abstracts. Gale Research Company, Detroit, Mich., 1983 to present (monthly, with annual cumulations). Print form of Management Contents on-line data base. Covers more than 700 periodicals in management, accounting, finance, and other areas and includes abstracts of each article.

Journal of Economic Literature (formerly *Journal of Economic Abstracts*). American Economic Association, Nashville, Tenn., 1963 present (quarterly). Contains review articles, book reviews, annotations of new books, and abstracts of selected journal articles.

Predicasts F & S Index Europe. Predicasts, Inc., Cleveland, Ohio, 1978 to present (monthly, with quarterly and annual cumulations). Indexes articles on business developments and operations in Europe and the Soviet Union. Arranged by Standard Industrial Classification (SIC) number or product, region and country, and company.

Predicasts F & S Index United States. Predicasts, Inc., Cleveland, Ohio, 1960 to present (weekly, with monthly and annual cumulations). Covers U.S. company, industry, and product information included in journals, business-oriented newspapers, trade magazines, and special reports. Arranged by industry, product, and corporate name.

Predicasts F & S Index International. Predicasts, Inc., Cleveland, Ohio, 1967 to present. U.S. companies with foreign offices and industry and product information. Arranged by SIC number, region and country, and company.

PROMT (Predicasts Overview of Markets and Technologies). Predicasts, Inc., Cleveland, Ohio, 1977 to present (monthly, with quarterly and annual cumulations of the index). Indexes periodicals dealing with products, industries, and new technologies. Extensive abstracts often include statistical information.

Public Affairs Information Service. Public Affairs Information Service, Inc., New York, 1915 to present (biweekly with quarterly and annual cumulations). An index to economic, social, and political affairs covering all types of materials published internationally in English.

Social Sciences Citation Index. Institute for Scientific Information, Philadelphia, 1973 to present (triannually, with annual cumulations). A citation index with author, corporate, permuterm subjects (key word index), and source indexes. Allows user to see the assocation of ideas between author and those that the author cites. Covers over 1000 journals in the social sciences. Useful for studies in economics, organization, and behavioral management.

The Wall Street Journal Index. Dow Jones & Company, New York, 1957 to present (monthly, with annual cumulations). After 1981, the annual cumulation includes *Barron's Index.* Index to *The Wall Street Journal.*

BUSINESS AND FINANCIAL SERVICES

Business and financial (subscription) services give the latest information on stock prices, developments in industries, current evaluations of companies, and changes in laws and/or their interpretations. Some are published in looseleaf format to allow for constant updating. Many times the same information is covered by two or more services.

Directory of Business and Financial Services, edited by Mary M. Grant and Norma Coté, 8th ed. Special Libraries Association, New York, 1984. Describes business, economic and financial services issued on a regular basis. Title arrangement with subject and publisher indexes.

Federal Taxes. Prentice-Hall, Englewood Cliffs, N.J. (looseleaf, with weekly supplements). Gives complete information about all federal tax laws, regulations, court decisions, and administrative rulings. Also covers tax planning. Comes with supplemental guides.

Industry Surveys. New York: Standard & Poor's Corporation. Gives summaries of industry activities (number of shipments, and so forth), trends, and outlook for future. Useful in case analyses.

Investment Companies. Wiesenberger Services, New York (annual with supplements). Provides information on mutual funds and investment companies. Covers United States and Canada.

Labor Relations Reporter. Bureau of National Affairs, Washington, D.C. (looseleaf, with weekly supplements). Very comprehensive. Covers current labor relations, state laws, fair employment practices, wages and hours, and labor arbitration.

Moody's Handbook of Common Stocks. Moody's Investors Service, New York (quarterly). Contains price charts and financial data for over 1000 common stocks.

Moody's Manuals. Moody's Investors Service, New York (seven volumes, published annually with semiweekly supplements). Manuals cover United States and Canada and foreign companies listed on U.S. exchanges. Information about major foreign companies is contained in the International Manual. Gives company information, including brief history, financial statements and ratios, products, officers, and subsidiaries. Similar to Standard & Poor's *Standard Corporation Records.* Individual titles are as follows:

Moody's Bank and Finance Manual

Moody's Industrial Manual

Moody's International Manual

Moody's Municipal and Government Manual

Moody's OTC Industrial Manual

Moody's Public Utilities Manual

Moody's Transportation Manual

Standard Corporation Records. Standard & Poor's Corporation, New York (looseleaf, with bimonthly supplements). Similar to *Moody's Manuals,* but company names are listed alphabetically rather than by type. Covers companies having listed and unlisted securities.

Standard Federal Tax Reports. Commerce Clearing House, Chicago (looseleaf, with weekly supplements). Gives complete information about federal tax laws, regulations, court decisions, and administrative rulings. Covers tax planning. Includes supplemental guides.

Value Line Investment Survey. A. Bernhard and Company, New York (looseleaf, with weekly supplements). Excellent investment service giving information about stocks. Describes trends in industries as they relate to investors. Gives statistical data on individual companies, such as price-earnings ratios, profit margins, and quarterly sales. Also gives betas, stock price averages, and ratings.

DIRECTORIES

Directories are systematic listings of companies, associations, agencies, organizations, products, or individuals. They may have alphabetical, geographical, or subject arrangements.

America's Corporate Families: The Billion Dollar Directory. Dun's Marketing Services, Parsippany, N.J. (annually). Includes listings of ultimate parent companies in the United States. Lists divisions, subsidiaries, and other information similar to listings in the *Million Dollar Directory.*

Directory of Corporate Affiliations. National Register Publishing Company, Inc., Skokie, Ill. (annually). Contains listings of parent companies and their divisions and subsidiaries. Includes name and geographical indexes.

Directory of Directories. Gale Research Company, Detroit, Mich., 3rd ed., 1985. Detailed listing of all types of directories, including company and industry directories. A good source to use when trying to locate a specific directory.

Encyclopedia of Associations. Gale Research Company, Detroit, Mich. (annually, with periodic supplements). Covers labor unions; public affairs organizations; chambers of commerce; trade, business, and commercial organizations; and scientific, engineering, and technical organizations. Includes name, address, divisions, purpose, publications, and trade associations.

Kelly's Manufacturers and Merchants Directory. IPC Business Press Ltd., East Grinistead, West Sussex, England (annually). Lists British and European companies by classified trade, company name, and exporting service.

Million Dollar Directory. Dun's Marketing Services, Parsippany, N.J. (annually). Directory of over 120,000 companies with net worth over $500,000. Gives officers, product line, SIC number, approximate sales, and number of employees. Has division index, alphabetical listing of officers, and geographical and industrial indexes.

National Trade and Professional Associations of the United States and Canada and Labor Unions. Columbia Books, Washington, D.C. (annually). Lists 5800 trade and professional associations; has geographic, association, and subject index.

Principal International Businesses. Dun & Bradstreet International, New York (annually). Covers over 50,000 businesses in 133 countries. Lists country, product lines, sales volume, number of employees, chief officers, and address. Has geographical, product classification, and alphabetical access.

Reference Book. Dun & Bradstreet Corporation, New York (bimonthly). Very comprehensive geographical listing of U.S. and Canadian firms for which estimated financial strength and credit appraisal are given. Also given are SIC number and product line (not widely available in libraries).

Standard & Poor's Register of Corporations, Directors and Executives. Standard & Poor's Corporation, New York (annually). This national "directory of directors" lists corporations, officers, directors, and trustees. Has SIC, geographical, and corporate family indexes.

Standard Directory of Advertisers. National Register Publishing Company, Skokie, Ill. (annually). Guide to over 17,000 corporations that advertise nationally. Has geographical and classified indexes. Gives number of employees, basic product line, approximate sales, advertising agency, and type of media and distribution.

Thomas' Register of American Manufacturers and Thomas Register Catalog File. Thomas Publishing Company, New York (annually). Comprehensive listing of American manufacturing firms. Lists arranged by specific product and alphabetical name with index to product classification. Also has list of trade names and catalogs of some companies.

Trade Names Dictionary. Gale Research Company, Detroit, Mich., 4th ed., 1985–86. Identifies manufacturers by product trade names. Includes company names and addresses.

United States Government Manual. Office of the Federal Register, General Services Administration, Washington, D.C. (annually). Directory of governmental agencies and key personnel with addresses and telephone numbers.

Industrial and manufacturers' directories for states are published by *McRae's Blue Book Company* and by state chambers of commerce.

BIBLIOGRAPHIES

Bibliographies are publications designed to bring together all material that has been published on a topic or at least the most significant works. They include descriptions and attributes of the publications arranged by subject or author. Some are comprehensive recurring bibliographies, retrospectives, or literature guides. Literature guides include source lists and describe the characteristics of the literature of the field as well; they also include explanations of differences among the types of sources and the information provided.

Brownstone, David M., and Gorton Carruth. *Where to Find Business Information: A Worldwide Guide for Everyone Who Needs the Answers to Business Questions.* New York: Wiley-Interscience, 1982. Describes major sources.

Daniells, Lorna. *Business Information Sources,* rev. ed., Berkeley: University of California Press, 1985. Describes major sources in broad areas of business—finance, personnel, and so forth.

Directory of Industry Data Sources, 2nd ed. Cambridge, Mass.: Ballinger, 1982. Bibliography of sources of marketing and financial information published since 1979 on key industries in the United States and Canada.

Economics Information Guide. Detroit, Mich.: Gale Research. Specific volumes are as follows:

Vol. 1 *East Asian Economies: A Guide to Information Sources,* edited by Molly K. Lee, 1979.

Vol. 2 *Economics of Minorities: A Guide to Information Sources,* edited by Kenneth L. Gagala, 1975.

Vol. 3 *History of Economic Analysis,* edited by William K. Hutchinson, 1976.

Vol. 4 *Russian Economic History: A Guide to Information Sources,* edited by Daniel R. Kazmer and Vera Kazmer, 1976.

Vol. 5 *Transportation Economics: A Guide to Information Sources,* edited by James P. Rakowski, 1976.

Vol. 6 *Economic Education: A Guide to Information Sources,* edited by Catherine A. Hughes, 1977.

Vol. 7 *Health and Medical Economics: A Guide to Information Sources,* edited by Ted J. Ackroyd, 1977.

Vol. 8 *Labor Economics: A Guide to Information Sources,* edited by Ross Azevedo, 1977.

Vol. 9 *Economic History of Canada: A Guide to Information Sources,* edited by Trevor J. Dick, 1978.

Vol. 10 *Mathematical Economics and Operations Research: A Guide to Information Sources,* edited by Joseph Zaremba, 1977.

Vol. 11 *Money, Banking and Macroeconomics: A Guide to Information Sources,* edited by James M. Rock, 1977.

Vol. 12 *Regional Statistics: A Guide to Information Sources,* edited by M. Balachandran, 1980.

Vol. 13 *Urban and Regional Economics: A Guide to Information Sources,* edited by Jean A. Shackelford, 1980.

Vol. 14 *Statistics and Econometrics: A Guide to Information Sources,* edited by Joseph Zaremba, 1980.

Vol. 15 *American Economic History: A Guide to Information Sources,* edited by William Kenneth Hutchinson, 1980.

Fletcher, John, ed. *The Use of Economics Literature.* Hamden, Conn.: Archon Books, 1971. Information source for research and development.

Harvard University, Graduate School of Business Administration, Baker Library. *Business Reference Sources: An Annotated Guide for Harvard Business School Students,* rev. ed. Compiled by Lorna Daniells. Boston: Baker Library, Graduate School of Business Administration, Harvard University, 1979.

Hills, William G., André W. Van Rest, Richard C. Kearney, and Stephen T. Smith. *Administration of Management: A Selected and Annotated Bibliography.* Norman: University of Oklahoma Press, 1975.

How to Find Information About Companies. Washington, D.C.: Washington Researchers, 1983. Excellent guide designed for the practitioner.

International Bibliography of Economics—Bibliographie International de Science Economique. New York: International Committee for Social Sciences Documentation, UNESCO, 1959 to present.

Management Information Exchange Business Services and Information: The Guide to the Federal Government. New York: John Wiley, 1978.

Management Information Guide. Detroit, Mich.: Gale Research. Specific guides are as follows:

1. *Real Estate Information Sources,* edited by Janice B. Babb and B. F. Dordick, 1963.
2. *Building Construction Information Sources,* edited by Howard B. Bentley, 1964.
3. *Public Finance Information Sources,* edited by Vera H. Knox, 1964.
4. *Textile Industry Information Sources,* edited by Joseph V. Kopycinski, 1964.
5. *Developing Nations: A Guide to Information Sources,* edited by Eloise Re Qua and Jane Statham, 1965.
6. *Standards and Specifications Information Sources,* edited by Erasmus J. Struglia, 1965.
7. *Public Utilities Information Sources,* edited by Florine E. Hunt, 1965.
8. *Transportation Information Sources,* edited by Kenneth M. Metcalf, 1965.
9. *Business Trends and Forecasting Information Sources,* edited by James B. Woy, 1965.
10. *Packaging Information Sources,* edited by Gwendolyn Jones, 1967.
11. *Government Regulation of Business Including Antitrust Information Sources,* edited by Beatrice S. McDermott and Freada A. Coleman, 1967.
12. *Systems and Procedures Including Office Management Information Sources,* edited by Chester Morrill, Jr., 1967.
13. *Electronic Industries Information Sources,* edited by Gretchen R. Randle, 1968.
14. *International Business and Foreign Trade,* edited by Lora J. Wheeler, 1968.
15. *Computers and Data Processing Information Sources,* edited by Chester Morrill, Jr., 1969.
16. *Food and Beverage Industries: A Bibliography and Guidebook,* edited by Albert C. Vara, 1970.
17. *Commercial Law Information Sources,* edited by Julius J. Marke and Edward J. Bander, 1970.

18. *Accounting Information Sources,* Rosemary Demarest, 1970.
19. *Investment Information: A Detailed Guide to Selected Sources,* edited by James B. Woy, 1970.
20. *Research in Transportation: Legal, Legislative and Economic Sources and Procedures,* edited by Kenneth U. Flood, 1970.
21. *Ethics in Business Conduct: Selected References from the Record: Problems, Attempted Solutions, Ethics in Business Education,* edited by Portia Christian and Richard Hicks, 1970.
22. *Public Relations Information Sources,* edited by Alice Norton, 1970.
23. *American Economic and Business History Information Sources,* edited by Robert W. Lovett, 1971.
24. *Insurance Information Sources,* edited by Roy Thomas, 1971.
25. *Communication in Organizations: An Annotated Bibliography and Sourcebook,* edited by Robert M. Carter, 1972.
26. *Public and Business Planning in the United States: A Bibliography,* edited by Martha B. Lightwood, 1972.
27. *National Security Affairs: A Guide to Information Sources,* edited by Arthur D. Larson, 1973.
28. *Occupational Safety & Health: A Guide to Information Sources,* edited by Theodore P. Peck, 1974.
29. *Chemical Industries: A Guide to Information Sources,* edited by Theodore P. Peck, 1976.
30. *Purchasing: A Guide to Information Sources,* edited by Douglas C. Basil and others, 1977.
31. *Executive and Management Development for Business and Government: A Source Book,* edited by Agnes O. Hanson, 1976.
32. *Management Principles and Practice: A Guide to Information Sources,* edited by K. G. Bakewell, 1977.
33. *Management and Economics Journals: A Guide to Information Sources,* edited by Vasile Tega, 1977.
34. *Agricultural Enterprises Management in an Urban-Industrial Society: A Guide to Information Sources,* Portia Christian, 1977.
35. *Developing Organizations: A Guide to Information Sources,* Jerome L. Franklin, 1977.
36. *Health Sciences & Services: A Guide to Information Sources,* edited by Lois F. Lunin, 1979.
37. *Employee Counseling in Industry and Government: A Guide to Information Sources,* Theodore P. Peck, 1979.
38. *New Product Planning: A Guide to Information Sources,* Sarojini Balachandran, 1980.

Small Business Bibliographies. Washington, D.C.: U.S. Small Business Administration, 1963 to present (irregular). A series of annotated bibliographies on various aspects of small business management.

The Source Directory. Cleveland, Ohio: Predicasts, Inc., 1973 to present (annually, with quarterly supplements).

Wasserman, Paul, and others. *Encyclopedia of Business Information Sources: A Detailed Listing of Primary Subjects of Interest to Managerial Personnel, with a Record of Sourcebooks, Periodicals, Organizations, Directories, Handbooks, Bibliographies, On-Line Data Bases, and Other Sources of Information on Each Topic,* 5th ed. Detroit, Mich.: Gale Research, 1983.

Woy, James B. *Investment Methods: A Bibliographic Guide.* New York: R. R. Bowker, 1973.

Woy, James B. *Commodity Futures Trading: A Bibliographic Guide.* New York: R. R. Bowker, 1976.

GOVERNMENT DOCUMENTS AND STATISTICS

The federal government is one of the world's largest publishers, spending over $800 million yearly to gather and publish statistical data. Governmental publications range from pamphlets on child care to specialized research treatises. Most libraries have selected governmental publications. However, certain libraries throughout the United States are full or partial depositories for these publications. State, provincial, and local governmental publications also are data sources.

American Statistics Index: A Comprehensive Guide and Index to the Statistical Publications of the United States Government. Bethesda, Md.: Congressional Information Service, 1973 to present (annually with supplements).

Andriott, John L. *Guide to United States Government Publications.* McLean, Va.: Documents Index, 1973 to present.

Andriott, John L. *Guide to United States Government Statistics,* 4th ed. McLean, Va.: Documents Index, 1973 to present.

Bureau of the Census Catalog. Washington, D.C.: U.S. Bureau of the Census (annually). The Census Bureau is the largest publisher of federal statistical data. Its catalogs give descriptive lists of publications. The Bureau publishes both census data and projections based on sampling. The following is a partial list of these catalogs:

Census of Agriculture

Census of Construction Industries

Census of Governments

Census of Housing

Census of Manufacturers

Census of Mineral Industries

Census of Population

Census of Population and Housing (contains "Census Tract Reports" for each Standard Metropolitan Statistical Area)

Census of Retail Trade

Census of Selected Service Industries

Census of Transportation

Census of Wholesale Trade

County Business Patterns, annually (good source for local data)

Enterprise Statistics

Congressional Information Service. Washington, D.C.: Congressional Information Service, 1970 to present (annually with supplements).

Economic Report of the President. Washington, D.C.: United States Office of the President (annually). Included with *Annual Report of the Council of Economic Advisers.* Gives state of economy and outlook for future as seen by the president of the United States.

Economics Sourcebook of Government Statistics, compiled by Hoel, Arline Alchian, Kenneth W. Clarkson, and Roger LeRoy Miller. Lexington, Mass.: D. C. Heath, 1983. Provides a description of numerous statistics gathered by the government and cites publications where these statistics may be found.

Handbook of Basic Economic Statistics. Washington, D.C.: Economic Statistics Bureau (monthly since 1947). Issues by a private research organization. Contains compact compilation of more than 1800 statistical series about all aspects of national economy. Material is selected and condensed from federal governmental sources. Often publishes information before federal government publishes it.

Handbook of Labor Statistics. Washington, D.C.: U.S. Department of Labor (biennially). Compiles major series produced by the Bureau of Labor Statistics into one volume. Covers labor force, employment, unemployment, productivity, compensation, prices and living conditions, earnings/employment by industrial relations, occupational injuries and illnesses, and selected foreign labor statistics.

Index to U.S. Government Periodicals. Chicago: Infordata International, Inc., 1970 to present (quarterly). Contains many lay and research-oriented periodicals not indexed in major abstracts and indexes.

Monthly Catalog of United States Government Publications. Washington, D.C.: U.S. Superintendent of Documents, 1896 to present (monthly). Index to all governmental publications. Arranged alphabetically by agency with subject and title indexes.

Monthly Checklist of State Publications. Washington, D.C.: Library of Congress, 1910 to present.

Standard Industrial Classification Manual (SIC). Washington, D.C.: Office of the President, Office of Management and Budget, 1972, updated in 1977. The SIC defines industries according to the composition and structure of the economy and covers entire field of economic activity. Used by businesses to classify customers and suppliers. Helps make easier comparison of statistics describing the economy.

Statistical Abstract of the United States. Washington, D.C.: U.S. Bureau of the Census, 1878 to present (annually). Standard summary of statistics on social, political, and economic organization of the United States. Appendix IV has the *Guide to Sources of Statistics* and the *Guide to State Statistical Abstracts.*

Statistical Reference Index. Bethesda, Md.: Congressional Information Service, 1980 to present (annually with supplements). Indexes nongovernmental statistics such as those from trade associations.

Survey of Current Business. Washington, D.C.: U.S. Department of Commerce (monthly). Most comprehensive source for current business statistics. Contains business indicators and information on employment and earnings, labor force, finance, foreign trade, commodities, products, and industries. Also contains articles and special statistical reports such as "Corporate Profits" and "Balance of Payments." *Business Statistics* is biennial supplement to this publication; it contains statistics recorded in the monthly issues.

United States Industrial Outlook. Washington, D.C.: U.S.Department of Commerce (annually). Provides economic outlook for five years for over 200 industries. Based on state of economy at time of writing and likely future directions.

Wasserman, Paul. *Statistical Sources,* 9th ed. Detroit, Mich.: Gale Research, 1984.

SUBJECT HANDBOOKS, SUBJECT DICTIONARIES, AND ATLASES

Some other helpful sources for business references are subject handbooks, subject dictionaries, and atlases. Examples of useful subject handbooks are *Handbook of Financial Management* and *Handbook of Marketing Research.* The *Dictionary of Economics and Business* is an excellent subject dictionary. An outstanding atlas is Rand McNally's *Commercial Atlas and Marketing Guide.*

COMPUTER-ASSISTED INFORMATION SERVICES

Much useful information is available today through machine-readable data bases. Some of these data bases are primarily bibliographical, but others contain actual data that can be analyzed for specific purposes. Libraries, companies, information brokers, and some individuals use these services. A fee is usually charged for these services, and they can be expensive.

ABI/Inform. Data Courier, Inc., Louisville, Ky. A bibliographical data base service for management, marketing, finance, personnel and other business-related journals.

Bibliographic Retrieval Services (BRS). Latham, New York. BRS After Dark is available from 6 P.M. to 4 A.M. Eastern time. Covers *Harvard Business Review* and more than 50 other files in business, education, environment, science, and general reference.

CompuServe. CompuServe Information Services, Columbus, Ohio. Offers news, financial reports, and stock quotations. Electronic mail and home shopping also is offered.

Compustat. Investors' Management Service, Standard & Poor's Corporation, Denver, Colo. A statistical data base of financial information. Many business schools have these files for use in conducting research projects.

Dow Jones News Retrieval System. Dow Jones, Inc., Princeton, N.J. Provides financial news and market data. Also contains summaries of stories and columns from *The Wall Street Journal* and *Barron's.*

Management Contents. Information Access Company, Belmont, Calif. (biweekly). Covers 200 business and economics journals. Offers an "on-line" computerized database service that many libraries use in searches. Also published in paper format.

Microcomputer Index. Contains abstracts from over 30 microcomputer periodical sources.

NewsNet. Bryn Mawr, Pa. Provides information from more than 100 newsletters, including such areas as telecommunications, computers, publishing, and broadcasting.

Orbit. SDC Information Services, Santa Monica, Calif. Contains more than 80 data bases, including such areas as business and economics, government and legislation, patents, and technology.

Predicasts Terminal System. Predicasts, Inc., Cleveland, Ohio. Combined bibliographical and statistical data base covering many Predicast publications, such as the *Predicasts F & S Index to Corporations and Industries* and PROMPT. Excellent for searching current articles and statistics on a particular industry.

PsychInfo. Covers periodicals, books, technical reports, and monographs in psychology and related behavioral science areas.

Social Sciences Citation Index. Institute of Scientific Information, Philadelphia. A bibliographical data base. Also available in paper format.

The Source. McLean, Va. Includes UPI wire reports, stock quotes, as well as electronic mail and home shopping.

APPENDIX D

STANDARD DOCUMENTATION METHODS

Preparing documentation is a part of both primary and secondary research. In primary research, you generate your own data. In secondary research, you gather data prepared elsewhere. Presenting documentation of primary research includes discussing the primary research procedures you used to gather your data. Presenting documentation of secondary research procedures involves giving credit to those who originated the data.

Three standard types of reference citations are *footnotes, full citations within the report text,* and *references to a list of sources.* You should select one procedure and use it consistently throughout a report. Also, you might include a bibliography to give documentation and to cite sources for further study.

FOOTNOTES

The main purpose of footnotes is to give credit to the source that has supplied data for your report. The data may be ideas, concepts, opinions, or direct quotations, for example. A footnote of this type is called a *source footnote.* A second purpose for using footnotes is to give details about ideas that might be related indirectly to the topic being discussed. Such a footnote is called a *discussion footnote.* You also can use footnotes to refer to related sources or to cross-reference other report parts. Here, you would use a *reference footnote.*

Numbering and Indenting

Number each footnote consecutively with arabic numerals. Generally, the number is raised slightly above the writing line. This raised number is called a *superscript.* The superscript numbers in the footnotes correspond to those in the report text. Indent the first line of each footnote five spaces, and then start any other lines flush against the left margin. Single space the footnote lines.

Sometimes, rather than using a superscript, you can place the number in parentheses ( ) on the line where the cited material appears. This format makes it much easier when typing or printing, but it can be confusing if you have numeric listings in your report.

Content and Arrangement—Source Footnotes

For source footnotes, usually the footnote includes the name(s) of the author(s) or editor(s), publication title, publication facts, publication date, and page number(s). The publication facts and date are placed in parentheses. Because first-time reference is complete, later references to the source can be shortened. The examples that follow are common types of source footnotes for references made the first time you cite the source in a report.

1. *Book with one author:*

   [1] Bruce A. Artwick, *Applied Concepts in Microcomputer Graphics* (Englewood Cliffs, N.J.: Prentice-Hall, Inc., 1984), p. 334.

   The author's name, book title, publication facts (city of publisher, publisher's name, and publication date), and page number are given in book citations. Do the same thing for handbooks and pamphlets. Also, you may type the book title in all capital letters rather than underline it.

2. *Book with two authors:*

   [2] Larry R. Smeltzer and John L. Waltman, *Managerial Communication: A Strategic Approach* (New York: John Wiley & Sons, Inc., 1984), pp. 188–189.

3. *Book with three authors:*

   [3] C. Glenn Pearce, Ross Figgins, and Steven P. Golen, *Business Communication: Principles and Applications*, 2nd ed. (New York: John Wiley & Sons, Inc., 1988), pp. 212–231.

   When a book is an edition other than the first, you should include the edition number. Also, when the city of the publisher might not be known by the reader, then include the state, which is abbreviated.

4. *Book with four or more authors:*

   [4] Craig E. Aronoff and others, *Getting Your Message Across: A Practical Guide to Business Communication* (St. Paul, Minn.: West Publishing Company, 1981), p. 214.

   When a book has a subtitle, you should include it in the footnote. Use a colon or a dash to separate the title from the subtitle. This colon or dash might or might not appear in the actual title of the book. Also, you could use the Latin form "et al." instead of "and others."

5. *Book with no author but with an editor or editors:*

   [5] Steven P. Golen, Ross Figgins, and Larry R. Smeltzer, eds., *Readings and Cases in Business Communication* (New York: John Wiley & Sons, Inc., 1984), pp. 3–4.

   Note that this book is a collection of works by various authors but that the reference is to pages not written by one of the authors.

6. *Book with one author identified in a collection of works but with an editor or editors:*

   [6] Thomas H. Inman, "Effective Management Needs Upward and Downward Communication," in *Readings and Cases in Business Communication*, Steven P. Golen, Ross Figgins, and Larry R. Smeltzer, eds. (New York: John Wiley & Sons, Inc., 1984), pp. 22–29.

   Notice that the author's work is placed within quotation marks.

7. *Article in a magazine or journal with author given:*

[7] Joseph A. Boyd, "A Manager's Guide to Specialized Networks," *Administrative Management,* Vol. 43, no. 5 (May 1982), p. 27.

The author's name, article title placed within quotation marks, magazine name, issue volume and number, publication date, and page number are given. Instead of underlining the magazine name, you could type it in all capital letters.

8. *Article in a magazine or journal with no author given:*

[8] "Computers Create Picture-Perfect Graphics," *Modern Office Procedures,* Vol. 27, no. 4 (April 1982), pp. 56–57.

9. *Article in a newspaper:*

[9] Thomas Petzinger, Jr., "Double Talk Grips Business Reports as Firms Try to Sugarcoat Bad News," *The Wall Street Journal,* March 31, 1982, p. 25.

If you footnote a newspaper that your report audience may not know, then you could put the newspaper's city in parentheses after the title.

10. *Government publication:*

[10] United States Department of Commerce, *Graphics Compatibility System* (Springfield, Va.: National Technical Information Service, 1983), p. 4.

Notice that the name of the governmental body is placed in the author's position.

11. *Unpublished material:*

[11] Alan C. Morse, "Using Computer Graphics as an Aid to Understanding Simulation Data," unpublished Ph.D. dissertation, University of Massachusetts, 1981, pp. 51–52.

12. *Interview:*

[12] Personal interview with John Sampson, Controller, Babon Manufacturing Company, Las Vegas, Nevada, June 21, 1987.

An interview is the only primary research source that you would include in a footnote.

As an alternative to using the superscript number in the footnote itself, you can type the number on the first line of the footnote. An example follows:

1. Bruce A. Artwick, *Applied Concepts in Microcomputer Graphics* (Englewood Cliffs, N.J.: Prentice-Hall, Inc., 1984), p. 334.

Content and Arrangement— Discussion and Reference Footnotes

A discussion footnote explains an idea in complete sentences. The following is an example:

[1] Although the LIFO and FIFO methods of inventory evaluation are used in this analysis, other methods, such as weighted average and specific invoice, could be used as well.

A reference footnote can refer to related sources or cross-reference another report part. A related source reference footnote follows:

[2] For an additional discussion of inventory procedures, see William W. Pyle and Kermit D. Larson, *Financial Accounting,* rev. ed. (Homewood, Ill.: Richard D. Irwin, Inc., 1983), pp. 265–267.

A cross-reference footnote is the following:

[3] See Table 5, "Perceptions of Real Estate Brokers About the Effect of High Interest Rates in the Housing Market," p. 15.

Short Forms of Source Footnotes

You might need to footnote a particular source more than once in a report. After you present the complete citation in the first footnote, you can shorten later references. Two ways to do this are to use the author's name and page number or to use the traditional Latin abbreviations. The latter method is not commonly used in business writing and can be confusing, but you should at least be aware of what the abbreviations mean in case you see them used.

An example using the author's last name and page number(s) is as follows:

[1] Uma Sekaran, *Research Methods for Managers: A Skill-Building Approach* (New York: John Wiley & Sons, Inc., 1984), p. 49.

[2] Sekaran, p. 49.

[3] Sekaran, pp. 53–54.

[4] William G. Zikmund, *Business Research Methods* (Chicago: The Dryden Press, 1984), p. 206.

[5] Sekaran, p. 52.

[6] Sekaran, p. 52.

If you're using this system and you happen to cite a second source from the same author(s), include a shortened title of the source (e.g., book title, magazine or journal article title) and place it between the author's name and page number. This format will help the reader differentiate between the two sources.

Here is an example of Latin abbreviations using the same six citations that were used to illustrate the author's last name and page number(s) format:

[1] Uma Sekaran, *Research Methods for Managers: A Skill-Building Approach* (New York: John Wiley & Sons, Inc., 1984), p. 49.

[2] Ibid. (Ibid. is an abbreviation for *ibidem,* meaning "in the same place.")

[3] Ibid., pp. 53–54. (same source but different pages)

[4] William G. Zikmund, *Business Research Methods* (Chicago: The Dryden Press, 1984), p. 206.

[5] Sekaran, op. cit., p. 52. (Op. cit. is an abbreviation for *opere citato,* which means "in the work cited.")

[6] Sekaran, loc. cit. (Loc. cit. is an abbreviation for *loco citato,* which means "in the place cited." Here, this source is on page 52 as well. If it were a page other than page 52, you would use op. cit. again.)

As you can see from comparing the two methods, the first method is much easier to use.

Placement of Footnotes

You may place footnotes at the bottom of the same page where the superscript numbers appear in the report text. Once the reader sees the superscript number in the report, he or she can look at the bottom of the page for the source citation. Use a $1\frac{1}{2}''$ horizontal line begun at the left margin to separate the footnote entries from the report text. Indent the first line of each footnote five spaces and type the remaining lines flush against the left margin. Use single spacing but leave one blank line between footnotes. The following excerpt from a report shows the placement of the footnotes:

> Developing and maintaining an effective employee relations program is extremely important for companies today. Geib remarked that companies should "give employees a maximum amount of information concerning the status of business, competition, new developments, finances, goals, and anything else that will further their knowledge of the company."[3] Geib went on to say that "changes in policy, procedure, or equipment should be made with advance notice and sufficient explanation of why they were necessary."[4]

---

[3] Dennis M. Geib, "F.Y.I.: Good Communication Makes for Good Employee Relations," *Management World,* Vol. 12, no. 9, October 1983, p. 39.

[4] Geib, p. 39.

Some report writers place the footnotes on one or more pages at the end of the report. Type these footnotes in the same order as they appear in the report text and entitle them *endnotes.* Also, note that when typing endnotes, you can either type superscript numbers or type the numbers on the first line of each footnote.

Placement of Long, Direct Quotations

Short, direct quotations, paraphrases, and summaries are placed directly in the text of the report without using any special indentions. However, when a direct quotation is four or more lines long, the quotation should be set out from the text, indented five spaces on both sides, and single spaced. The following report excerpt is an example of this situation:

> . . . define what it is expected to do. Thompson stated,
>
> > A business should buy equipment that can be expanded easily with new programming features as they become available. Any equipment purchased must be compatible with other manufacturers' equipment already owned.[1]
>
> In addition, the servicing of the equipment should be considered . . .

FULL CITATIONS WITHIN REPORT TEXT

Another procedure for acknowledging a source is to enclose the complete citation within parentheses (or brackets) at the point at which you make reference to the source in your report. For example, consider the following illustrations of this procedure:

> One objective of office systems planning, according to Mark A. Lieberman, Gad J. Selig, and John J. Walsh [*Office Automation: A Manager's Guide for Improved Productivity* (New York: John Wiley & Sons, Inc., 1982), p. 37], is "to integrate the functional areas of information systems, telecommunications, and office technology within the organization."
>
> Lou Pilla ["New Directions in Telecommunications," *Management World,* Vol. 11, no. 3 (March 1982), p. 12] noted that "advances in communications technologies now allow computer systems to transmit greater quantities of information, faster, to more locations."

REFERENCES TO A LIST OF SOURCES

A third procedure for acknowledging a source is to insert a key number and page number(s) in parentheses where the reference to the source appears in the report text. The key number will refer the reader to a numbered list of sources at the end of the report. Arrange this list in alphabetical order by author's last name or in the order the references appear in the report text. The page number(s) identifies the specific page(s) location of the original source. A colon generally separates the key number and page number(s). An example of this procedure follows:

> One objective of office systems planning, according to Lieberman, Selig, and Walsh, is "to integrate the functional areas of information systems, telecommunications, and office technology within the organization" (1:37).

> Pilla noted that "advances in communications technologies now allow computer systems to transmit greater quantities of information, faster, to more locations" (2:12).
>
> **List of Sources (at end of report)**
>
> 1. Mark A. Lieberman, Gad J. Selig, and John J. Walsh, *Office Automation: A Manager's Guide for Improved Productivity* (New York: John Wiley & Sons, Inc., 1982).
> 2. Lou Pilla, "New Directions in Telecommunications," *Management World,* Vol. 11, no. 3 (March 1982), pp. 11–12.

Sometimes you can modify this procedure another way by indicating the author, date, and page number of the source within the report text. You alphabetize the list by author's last name, but you would not number each entry. Also, you could use "References" as the title of your sources. Here is an example of this style:

> One objective of office systems planning is "to integrate the functional areas of information systems, telecommunications, and office technology within the organization." (Lieberman et al., 1982, p. 37)
>
> Pilla (1982, p. 12) noted that "advances in communications techologies now allow computer systems to transmit greater quantities of information, faster, to more locations."
>
> **References (at end of report)**
>
> Lieberman, Mark A., Selig, Gad J., and Walsh, John J. *Office Automation: A Manager's Guide for Improved Productivity.* New York: John Wiley & Sons, Inc., 1982.
>
> Pilla, Lou. "New Directions in Telecommunications." *Management World,* Vol. 11, no. 3 (March 1982), pp. 11–12.

COMMON REFERENCE ABBREVIATIONS

As you might have noticed in the actual citations of the sources presented not only in this chapter but also throughout this book, various abbreviations were used. In addition to the Latin abbreviations discussed earlier, the following are some abbreviations and the words they refer to as they might appear in any type of reference:

Abbreviations	*Terms*
anon.	anonymous
bk., bks.	book, books
c	copyright
cf.	confer or compare
ch., chs.	chapter, chapters

Abbreviations	*Terms*
col., cols.	column, columns
cont.	continued
ed., eds.	editor, editors; edition, editions; edited
e.g.	for example (exempli gratia)
et al.	and others
f., ff.	page, pages following
fig., figs.	figure, figures
fn., fns.	footnote, footnotes
i.e.	that is (id est)
illus.	illustration, illustrated, illustrator
incl.	including
l., ll.	line, lines
ms., mss.	manuscript, manuscripts
n.b.	note well (nota bene)
no., nos.	number, numbers
p., pp.	page, pages
pseud.	pseudonym
rev.	revised
sec., secs.	section, sections
tr.	translation, translator
vol., vols.	volume, volumes

BIBLIOGRAPHY

The bibliography lists the sources you used or consulted during the entire report process. Very often, you might compile a tentative bibliography of sources about a particular topic during the report planning phase. Then you might add sources as you gather additional data.

Placement and Indention

The bibliography is a supplemental part of the report that is placed at the end. Place the first line of each bibliographical entry flush against the left margin. Indent the second and other lines five spaces. Remember to single space the lines and leave one blank line between entries.

BIBLIOGRAPHY

Aronoff, Craig E., Otis W. Baskin, Robert W. Hays, and Harold E. Davis. Getting Your Message Across: A Practical Guide to Business Communication. St. Paul, Minn.: West Publishing Company, 1981.

Artwick, Bruce A. Applied Concepts in Microcomputer Graphics. Englewood Cliffs, N. J.: Prentice-Hall, Inc., 1984.

Boyd, Joseph A. "A Manager's Guide to Specialized Networks." Administrative Management, Vol. 43, No. 5, May 1982, pp. 26-28, 50, 54, 56.

"Computers Create Picture-Perfect Graphics." Modern Office Procedures, Vol. 27, No. 4, April 1982, pp. 56-58.

Golen, Steven P., Ross Figgins, and Larry R. Smeltzer, eds. Readings and Cases in Business Communication. New York: John Wiley & Sons, Inc., 1984.

Inman, Thomas H. "Effective Management Needs Upward and Downward Communication." In Readings and Cases in Business Communication. Steven P. Golen, Ross Figgins, and Larry R. Smeltzer, eds. New York: John Wiley & Sons, Inc., 1984, pp. 22-29.

Morse, Alan C. "Using Computer Graphics as an Aid to Understanding Simulation Data." Unpublished Ph.D. dissertation, University of Massachusetts, 1981.

Pearce, C. Glenn, Ross Figgins, and Steven P. Golen. Business Communication: Principles and Applications, 2nd edition. New York: John Wiley & Sons, Inc., 1988.

Petzinger, Thomas, Jr. "Double Talk Grips Business Reports As Firms Try to Sugarcoat Bad News." The Wall Street Journal, March 31, 1982, p. 25.

Sampson, John, controller. Babon Manufacturing Company, Las Vegas, Nevada. Personal interview, June 21, 1987.

Smeltzer, Larry R., and John L. Waltman. Managerial Communication: A Strategic Approach. New York: John Wiley & Sons, Inc., 1984.

United States Department of Commerce. Graphics Compatibility System. Springfield, Va.: National Technical Information Service, 1983.

FIGURE D-1 A bibliography.

Content and Arrangement

The content of the bibliography is similar to that of footnotes and other references. The last name is presented first, followed by the first and middle names or initials. Periods instead of commas separate the various sections of the entry. Also include the total number of pages in the periodical citations rather than the specific page number(s) cited in footnotes.

You could type the word *bibliography* in all capital letters as the main heading of this list. The sources that follow the heading could be organized in one of two ways. First, the entire bibliography could be presented in alphabetical order based on the author's last name. Second, the bibliography could be organized into categories of books, periodicals, and miscellaneous sources. Within each category, however, the sources should be alphabetized. An example of an entire bibliography in alphabetical order is shown in Figure D-1. The 12 sources used in this example are the same sources shown as source footnotes earlier in the appendix.

Annotated Bibliography

An annotated bibliography includes a brief summary of each entry. The purpose of this format is to provide the reader with a summary of the primary contents and perhaps value (i.e., critical analysis of the source's content) of a book, article, or report. The reader can then decide whether to read the entire publication. At the beginning of a research assignment, your instructor may ask you to prepare an annotated bibliography on a particular topic to determine whether there is enough material on the topic.

Here is an example of an annotated bibliographical entry (for other examples, see Appendix C):

Golen, Steven P., Ross Figgins, and Larry R. Smeltzer, eds. *Readings & Cases in Business Communication.* New York: John Wiley & Sons, Inc., 1984.

This book contains 32 articles and 19 cases dealing with various business communication areas, such as communication principles, correspondence and report writing, technology, oral presentations, nonverbal communication, listening, and employment communication.

APPENDIX E

READING SKILLS IN BUSINESS COMMUNICATION

Throughout this book, continuing emphasis is placed on your responsibility as a writer to establish a *specific purpose* whenever you prepare a business communication of any kind. For example, see the comment in Chapter 3 that step 1 in organizing a writing plan is to identify the purpose for writing. Another example is the observation in Chapter 7 that before writing, you should know your objectives, both general and specific. When you shift roles from writer to reader of business messages, you will still need to think about *purpose.* But now, in addition to recognizing the writer's objective, you will need to be very much aware of your own purposes as a reader.

Sometimes the two purposes clash. For example, in Chapter 10 you learned (or will learn) that a persuasive letter or memo should open with a statement designed to attract the reader's attention. But sometimes such a statement can backfire. The editors of *The New Yorker* have a feature that they call "Letters We Never Finished Reading" or, sometimes, "The Ho-Hum Department." If, as the overworked senior partner of a CPA firm, you received the following letter (from the Institute for Business Planning, Englewood Cliffs, N.J.), would you react as *The New Yorker* editors did? They put it in their "Ho-Hum Department," which is their way of dismissing it:

> Dear Accountant: It's not easy to excite the accounting profession—but the staff of the Institute for Business Planning has done it with their expanded Fourth Edition of the *Accounting Desk Book.* Rarely does something come along to warrant the adjective "apocalyptic." We use the word to describe the manual and we use it without apology.[1]

Probably you would discard the letter, too, as soon as you came to the ridiculous word *apocalyptic*—especially if you had on your desk four or five memos to react to, six or seven important letters to answer, and three lengthy reports to go through as well as three or four letters on the order of this one that your assistant had somehow let slip through. Your correspondent's purpose of luring you with exaggerated claims for a product would be no match for your purpose of clearing your desk of all but the essentials.

LEARNING TO COPE WITH THE COPIOUS: BEGINNING WITH SQ3R

If your working life becomes like that of most men and women in business, you will face daily a formidable stack of printed pages on your desk, even after you have cast aside obviously irrelevant items (like the letter). To solve the perennial problem of "getting through the material," many businesspeople take speed reading courses, and

[1] *The New Yorker,* January 16, 1978.

you may want to consider doing that sometime, too. But another way you can begin right now to cope with the problem when it comes is to master a *study skills* technique that you will find helpful in your present and future course work and that you can then adapt to other kinds of reading, including the reading of business communications. The technique works as well as it does because it encourages you to read *purposefully*—with continuing attention to both the writer's purpose and your own.

The method is called SQ3R for *survey* (or *skim*), *question, read, review,* and *recite.* It was designed by Francis Robinson of Ohio State University, after he had examined the study habits of hundreds of successful and unsuccessful students. It consists of five simple steps:

S: *Survey* the entire chapter to get an idea of its scope and direction (its purpose). Instead of reading through any portion completely, look only for signals the writer has provided to focus your attention on especially important ideas and information. Pay particular attention to the title, the first paragraph or two, the subheadings, and a summary or review section if there is one.

Q: Ask a *question* that you expect the first section of the chapter to answer (use the first subheading as the source for your question; that is, turn it into a question).

R: *Read* the first section, looking for an answer to your question.

R: *Recite* the various parts of the answer to the question. (Steps 2, 3, and 4 are then repeated on all sections of the chapter.)

R: *Review* the entire chapter, making certain that you understand how the various parts go together.

The method works especially well for textbooks that are set up as this one is. Notice that each chapter in this book is divided into major sections and subsections, that the headings for the major sections are listed in an outline at the beginning of the chapter, and that the last section is a summary of the entire chapter. That kind of organization makes both *surveying* or *skimming* and *studying by sections* easy to do.

LEARNING TO SKIM

If you are like most readers, you will have to learn to skim, and that will take some practice. You probably find it "natural" to read right through a work from the first word to the last, be it a business letter or a textbook chapter. And you may find it just as "natural" to let your mind drift away from the subject of the communication several times before you finish. The main purpose of the "skim-first" approach is to lessen the chances of that happening by pointing you in the direction the work is taking, that is, by giving you a sense of the writer's purpose.

Consider, for example, how a survey or skim-first approach can help you to stay on the track as you study Chapter 1 of this book. (If you have already read the chapter, go back to it again and try approaching it this new way. Remember, if you can, how you went about studying the chapter before and how much difficulty you had understanding it.)

First turn to the page that outlines Chapter 1. Checking the chapter title and the headings of the four major sections, ask yourself, What does this chapter emphasize? What theme or idea or purpose (sometimes one of these words will work better for you than another) do all these subsections appear to be developing?" Then read the first paragraph (in this case, the introduction to the chapter), looking particularly for generalizations about the chapter's scope and purpose. Finally, turn to the chapter summary and read the outline. Noting how often the words *communication, theory, language,* and *meaning* occur, it won't take you long to conclude that the chapter emphasis is on *theories* about ways language is used to communicate meaning. And once you know this, you will be able to think along with the writers. For example, you won't be asking yourself, "Why isn't there anything here on writing business letters?" or "What has this material on using feedback got to do with business writing?" You will be able to sense how the topics covered relate to one another.

SKIMMING IN READING BUSINESS COMMUNICATIONS

With much practice and continuing resistance to your urge to always "read right through," you will find that you can adapt the surveying or skimming-first approach (also sometimes called "previewing") to much of your college, work, or recreational reading. The approach works regardless of whether you are reading reports, essays, articles, or textbooks, for example.

In your previewing you will learn to recognize more subtle directional signals than subheadings. For example, words that are underlined or are in boldface print and words that are repeated in key places such as titles, introductions, and concluding statements, are directional signals. You will become very conscious of direct statements of the main ideas of pieces of writing. (One such direct statement of a main idea is in the second paragraph of Chapter 1: "language is *words (or other symbols) communicated in a meaningful order*.") Also, you will learn to pick up implied main ideas where these are not stated directly.

As you develop the habit of at least briefly skimming or previewing everything you pick up to read, you will be developing a skill that will become very useful to you in business—the skill of making quick decisions about how each of the items in the pile of printed material on your desk fits *your purposes*, if it fits them at all. That is, you will learn how to spot quickly the writer's main idea or purpose and then to determine whether to read the work carefully yourself, to delegate responsibility for it to someone else, or to discard it altogether. As you probably know, the ability to make decisions of this kind efficiently is one that people in the business world value highly.

LEARNING THE Q AND THE R's IN SQ3R

But there will be times in your business career when you will need to study material closely, noting details and remembering them. For that kind of reading, the study-by-sections part of SQ3R can be excellent preparation. It also can be adapted to the kind of reading you probably will do every day on the job, going through an article, memo, or letter quickly to find the main idea and the principal points that are made in developing that idea. First, though, it will be helpful to learn the method in its "pure" form (or nearly that) to apply to textbook study.

To get started, turn back to Chapter 1 and review briefly the subheadings that are listed on the outline page. Then take a few minutes to skim through the chapter again, section by section, framing a specific question for each major subheading as you note the ground that the section following that subheading appears to cover. This time in your skimming, pay particular attention to opening and closing sentences of sections and to secondary subheadings. Sometimes these signals will provide clues that will help you find a more focused question than simply "What is ____________?" (although sometimes that will be the obvious question to ask).

Then compare your questions with those listed at the end of this appendix. Those questions listed are not the only appropriate ones by any means, but they do illustrate specific, focused questioning.

When you have a set of appropriate questions for the chapter headings, you will be ready to go through the chapter a section at a time, applying the three "R" steps. (You may want to revise your original questions or use some of those at the end of this appendix.)

As you *read* through a section for the first time, you will be looking for a *general* answer to the question you have formed. You will probably find that you can concentrate better than you usually do because you will be reading purposefully. How many times in your study or other reading have you had the experience of suddenly realizing that you have been reading far too many paragraphs or pages without having any idea what the writer is saying? That is much less likely to happen when you are reading to answer a basic question.

When you move to step 4—*reciting*—you simply carry purposeful reading one step farther. At this point, you are concerned not only with the main idea of the chapter section but also with the way important details support any generalizations that are made—the kind of information you need to know for tests, for example. Robinson found that the easiest way to keep this kind of information in mind is to outline the material briefly in the margins of the pages. Outlining is particularly easy to do when you are studying a text such as this one because you can often use secondary headings or words in boldface print as major headings of your outline.

The point of *reviewing* is to determine to yourself how much you remember of what you have studied and how much you understand about how the parts of the chapter fit together. In this last step of SQ3R, you will work through the chapter one last time, section by section, asking yourself the questions you raised in the first place and seeing how specifically and in how well organized a fashion you can answer those questions.

As you review Chapter 1, if you find that you do understand the principles treated and you do recall much of the specific information covered, you should realize that you have discovered a useful study tool. If most of the material in Chapter 1 was new to you, then it was probably not an easy chapter to read. Another problem particular to the chapter is that many of the ideas presented are abstract. But by thoroughly applying SQ3R, that is by *purposeful studying,* the material becomes easier to master.

APPLYING SQ3R TO READING BUSINESS COMMUNICATIONS

In one important way, your purpose in reading professional materials will differ from your objective in studying a textbook. You will no longer be concerned with demonstrating to *someone else* how much you know about the subject you have been reading about. You will be *making your own use* of what you read. And since the study method you have been learning was designed primarily to help students do well on college tests, you should not expect to be able to apply it directly and literally to reading all the items in that stack of papers on your desk. But what you can and will do in this reading is to apply the *questioning attitude* that you, as a reader, will have acquired by this time. Developing this questioning attitude is a by-product of working with SQ3R.

Even a very casual and general (and perhaps almost unconsciously asked) question can be useful as a way to begin to "think along" with the writer of a business message. Examples of such questions are "Why did Joe think he needed to write this memo, anyway?" or "Is Jones complaining about trivia again in this letter?"

Sometimes, however, particularly when you are reading formal reports or articles in professional magazines, you will question the writer's purpose in a more direct and specific way. (This happens also when the material you read is especially important to you.) Sometimes the title of a report or an article can be converted to a question that will lead you to the writer's main idea, the principal points that support this idea, and the details that back up these points—as they did in your textbook study. And don't be surprised if you find yourself occasionally taking out a pencil and preparing a brief outline of sorts, much in the SQ3R fashion, to get a sense of the relationships of the parts of an article or report.

But whether your questioning and follow-up reading of professional materials is casual or systematic, if it follows years of consistent use of SQ3R for study purposes, it will always be inspired and directed by a sense of purpose. Such a sense is the result of a search for the writer's purpose and method of accomplishing it and a matching of the writer's purpose with your own.

Suggested Questions for Major Headings in Chapter 1

1. What is the nature of language? (The obvious question will work here.) What are the characteristics of language? (The minor subheadings will be particularly useful clues in answering this question.)
2. What human factors affect communication? (And how is it that these factors have an effect?)
3. How are messages sent, received, and processed? (A quick look at the minor headings will quickly show how this question will be answered.)
4. How is communication used to inform and persuade? (Sub-questions are: What is the difference between informing and persuading? and When is it appropriate to do the one, the other, or both?

Note: You may want to go on to form questions for other levels of headings—at least secondary headings—within each major section as well. The more thorough your questioning as you read, the more thorough your understanding of the material will be.

APPENDIX F

LEGAL AND ETHICAL ISSUES IN BUSINESS COMMUNICATION

The constant challenge of meeting the demands of the firm and its clients often requires different approaches to achieving the hoped-for or expected business results. Experience shows that organizations sometimes seek to achieve these results through unlawful or unethical practices. This approach affects not only the customers and related business contacts but also the people within the organization. In response to these difficulties, laws have been enacted to protect the consumer, employee, and others from unscrupulous behavior. Additionally, self-regulatory codes of ethical standards have been developed and adopted by many organizations to work toward maintaining the integrity of these groups. This appendix provides a brief overview of legal and ethical concerns for you to be aware of when working in the business world.

LEGAL ISSUES

Consumers, employees, and even managers are becoming more aware of and vocal about their rights under the law. As a consumer and as a manager, you need to know about the legal concerns you may face in the workplace. The five most relevant are (1) privacy, (2) defamation, (3) employment laws, (4) credit and collections, and (5) copyright.

Privacy

The right of privacy is a right of any individual, and the invasion of this privacy is unlawful. The need for legislation protecting individual privacy has become even more pronounced with the increased use of technology in personal data collection. For example, records from your use of credit cards, to your tax return, to your insurance coverage are recorded on computers. Should others gain access to these records for purposes unknown to you, that then infringes on your right to privacy. Computer system safeguards and other legal means are being developed constantly to ensure our protection from any abuse in these circumstances.

In addition to the use of technology, let's consider some other areas in which privacy can be invaded. For example, you cannot legally use another person's name or his or her picture for promotional purposes without obtaining that person's permission. Also at issue is the public disclosure of private information about another person, even if it is true. For example, a creditor cannot publish your debt record in a newspaper. One exception to this is that the media, under the protection of the First Amendment to the U.S. Constitution, can print information—including that of debt—about public figures. The final privacy issue considered here is that of intrusion by illegally searching a person's possessions, illegally wiretapping or eavesdropping, or persistently telephoning someone. Companies that monitor telephone calls to protect the rights of those involved need to develop a monitoring policy. Such a policy can protect the rights of both employer and employee. Whenever such a policy is to be put into effect, all employees should be told in writing what the monitoring policy entails. Failing to do so provides grounds for legal action.

Many federal government agencies have information on individuals. The Privacy Act of 1974 gives these individuals some control over what information is collected as well as how it can be used. You have a right to see your files and to sue the government if it releases the information without your permission or knowledge. Also, if you find any incorrect information in your file, you can amend the record by asking the person who released the record to you to make the necessary corrections. However, certain exemptions allow an agency to withhold information from you. For example, information on national security or criminal investigations are two such exemptions.

Where the Privacy Act deals with the access rights of those who are the subject of the records being sought, the Freedom on Information Act of 1966 deals with your right to review all records of federal agencies of the executive branch. But you should know that some records are specifically exempted by the act. These exemptions range from defense and foreign relations classified records to records involving your personal privacy. This act does not apply to records of the U.S. Congress, federal courts, state and local governments, or private organizations. Although not required by law, many companies are adopting a policy to allow access to employee files. Additional privacy issues under consumer credit protection are discussed later in the "Credit and Collections" section.

Defamation

Defamation occurs when someone makes false statements that injure or discredit another's reputation. Defamation is not limited just to individuals; corporations can be defamed as well. If a statement of defamation made in writing injures another person's character or good reputation, it is referred to as *libel;* if it is made orally, it is called *slander*.

To sue for libel, the injurious information must be (1) false, (2) communicated in writing or pictures, and (3) read by a third person. To collect damages for libel, a desire to inflict injury and damage your reputation must be proven. A person commits slander through spoken words or with gestures that are false and are heard or seen by a third person. To guard against committing slander as a manager, be very careful when giving statements to the press about the status of an employee.

When writing or speaking about an employee, remember to avoid making statements about mental incapacity; insolvency or bankruptcy; or immorality, disloyalty to his or her country, or any other fault that would incite public hatred or contempt."[1] In addition, juries look for proof of defamation made in firing an employee as represented by the answers to these questions:

- Did the manager invent any reasons to justify the firing?
- Did the manager tell people who did not need to know about the firing?
- Was the employee somehow treated unfairly before being fired?
- Did the manager or others conspire to get the employee fired?
- Did the manager make the employee a scapegoat for problems in the company that the employee had nothing to do with?[2]

Employment Laws

Several federal laws have been enacted setting standards for equal employment opportunity that affect the employer's recruiting, hiring, testing, promoting, and firing practices.

The *Civil Rights Act of 1964* prohibits job discrimination in any way on the basis of race, color, religion, sex, or national origin. This act created the Equal Employment Opportunity Commission (EEOC) to oversee the enforcement of the act. *Executive Order 11246* of the Civil Rights Act requires businesses to employ certain proportions of minorities and women. This order established the *Affirmative Action Compliance Program,* which requires that goals be established for hiring minorities and women. The *Equal Pay Act of 1963* prohibits pay differences on the basis of sex, and the *Age Discrimination Act of 1967* bans discriminating against potential employees ages 45 and older.

With all these laws, no effective provisions for enforcing the antidiscrimination clauses were available. Therefore, the *Equal Employment Opportunity Act of 1972* was passed. This act amended the Civil Rights Act by prohibiting any discrimination by employers with 15 or more employees, by employment agencies, or by labor unions. Various EEO guidelines were established to govern actions from recruitment through termination. For example, during an interview, the law prohibits questions about race, color, age, marital status, religion, national origin, physical or mental handicaps, criminal convictions, home ownership, military discharge, membership in organi-

[1] Richard L. Cassin, Jr., "Careless Whispers: When Communication Is Defamation," *Management World,* Vol. 14, no. 11 (December 1985), p. 31.
[2] Ibid., p. 31.

zations, child care arrangements, and questions about a spouse. These questions are prohibited unless knowledge of these factors are necessary for job performance.

In a related area, the EEOC in 1981 issued guidelines on sexual harassment. As a result, lawsuits seeking compensation for sexual harassment have grown rapidly since that time. According to these guidelines, sexual harassment includes "unwelcomed sexual advances, requests for sexual favors, and other verbal or physical conduct of a sexual nature." As a manager, you should tell your subordinates about the dangers of such behavior. Any behavior that fits the description of sexual harassment is considered offensive and humiliating. It interferes with job performance and is illegal under both state and federal laws.

Credit and Collections

Several laws have been enacted to protect consumers in the consumer credit area. As a credit customer and a manager in areas that involve credit, you need to be aware of some of these laws. First, the *Truth in Lending Act* requires lenders to provide borrowers with clear credit cost information in writing that discloses the annual percentage rate and the total finance charge. Any creditor who fails to disclose this information or gives false or inaccurate information is liable.

Second, the *Fair Credit Reporting Act* provides consumers access to information contained in a lender's credit report. The FCRA deals with the privacy issue as well. For example, you may sue a creditor or credit reporting agency that violates the rules about who may have access to your credit records. When potential employers, lenders, or insurers request an investigative report on you, they must tell you about it. If you wish, you can end the business transaction that warrants the investigative report and thereby prevent the report from being obtained.

Third, the *Equal Credit Opportunity Act* prohibits discrimination against any applicant for credit because of that person's age, sex, marital status, race, color, religion, national origin, receipt of income from any public assistance programs, or exercise rights under consumer credit laws. This act imposes certain restrictions on the questions you may ask consumers in completing a credit application form and the way you evaluate the information. Also, the creditor must disclose the reason(s) why a consumer was denied credit. Thus, a consumer has the opportunity to dispute the reason(s) for his or her denial of credit.

Fourth, the *Fair Credit Billing Act* requires the prompt correction of billing mistakes. Any creditor who receives a written notice from a debtor indicating a billing error must respond in writing about the status of the error. The consumer must be notified that the error was corrected or receive reasons supporting the correctness of the billing statement.

Fifth, the *Fair Debt Collection Practices Act* protects the personal privacy of consumers by prohibiting debt collectors from publicizing debts in newspapers or harassing consumers by calling at an inconvenient or unusual time or place. This act also precludes using other unfair practices to collect debts such as the use or threat of violence or harm to consumers, to their reputation, or to their property.

Copyright

A *copyright* is issued by offices of the United States Register of Copyrights to protect the publications rights of those who own original written material. If granted before 1978, a copyright lasts 28 years and is renewable for 47 years. If granted during or after 1978, it lasts for the owner's life plus 50 years. However, anonymous works and those created under pseudonyms are protected for 75 years from publication or 100 years from creation, whichever is shorter. When two or more people hold a copyright together, protection lasts for 50 years after the death of the last survivor.

According to the Copyright Act, the owner(s) of a copyright has the exclusive right to do and to authorize others to do the following:

- To reproduce the copyrighted work in copies or phonorecords.
- To prepare derivative works based upon the copyrighted work.
- To distribute copies or phonorecords of the copyrighted work to the public by sale or other transfer of ownership or by rental, lease, or lending.
- To perform the copyrighted work publicly, in the case of literary, musical, dramatic, and choreographic works; pantomimes; and motion pictures and other audiovisual works.
- To display the copyrighted work publicly, in the case of literary, musical, dramatic, and choreographic works; pantomimes; and pictorial, graphic, or sculptural works, including the individual images of a motion picture or other audiovisual work.[3]

Any violation of these rights is plagiarism and is unlawful; however, you may make *fair use* of copyrighted material, which usually means that you can make one copy for noncommercial use. The factors involved are the following:

1. Purpose and character of use, including whether it is commercial or for nonprofit educational purposes.
2. Nature of the work.

[3] *Copyright Basics,* Circular R1 (Washington, D.C.: U.S. Government Printing Office, 1981), p. 3.

3. Amount and substantiality of the portion used in relation to the whole work.
4. Effect of use on potential market for or value of the work.

When you are duplicating copyrighted material, consider the following guidelines:

1. Single copies of material may be made for personal files or posting on a bulletin board.
2. Multiple copies of material may be made if a notice of copyright permission is included on the material, the timing renders it unreasonable to wait for permission, or it is to be used one time for classroom use.
3. Unlimited use may be made of U.S. government works and "fair use" items such as tables, slogans, formulas, and so on.
4. Publishing an original work, table, or illustration requires formal permission from the copyright holder. The simple acknowledgment of the source in the manuscript cannot substitute for formal permission when (a) prose of 400 words or more from a full-length book is used or (b) a table, diagram, or illustration (including cartoons, photographs, or maps) is reproduced exactly or adapted only slightly.[4]

One area of copyright violation now hotly debated is the unauthorized copying of computer software. This growing problem now affects the entire computer software industry. As a result, the Copyright Act was amended in 1980 to protect owners of computer programs. This amendment prevents others from unauthorized copying or adaptation of an original work. Therefore, software developers now have the same rights as authors of other types of copyrighted works. In addition, this amendment gives software developers exclusive rights to authorize (or refuse to authorize) the making of an archival or backup copy. In fact, software purchasers must get permission to make such a copy. To see how one computer software developer protects itself, consider the following statement that appears in MicroPro software programs:

> This software has been provided pursuant to a License Agreement containing restrictions on its use. The software contains valuable trade secrets and proprietary information of MicroPro International Corporation and is protected by federal copyright law. It may not be copied or distributed in any form or medium, disclosed to third parties, or used in any manner not provided for in said License Agreement except with prior written authorization from MicroPro.

[4] Larry R. Smeltzer and John L. Waltman, *Managerial Communication: A Strategic Approach* (New York: John Wiley & Sons, Inc., 1984), pp. 513–514.

ETHICAL ISSUES

In recent years, the issue of ethics in business has provoked renewed controversy. With an increasing number of watchdogs (the media and government, for example), businesses have had to change their practices to maintain a positive public image. This image is often promoted through social programs that work to enhance the consumers' and general public's perception of the company or industry.

But how do employers deal with the ethical questions facing them in their daily operations with customers, company personnel, and external associates, such as suppliers and creditors? Where do the loyalties lie? What personal and organizational standards are appropriate? And what role does communication have in fostering a sense of ethical standards throughout a company? Answers to these questions do not come easily, but the questions themselves do serve as a basis for evaluating the ethical decisions that employers must make.

Business ethics is a system of moral principles or standards that influence your behavior or conduct in a business situation. Ethical behavior is merely the practice of ethics in your daily business life. In practice, what we "ought" to do sometimes is not what we wind up doing. The reasons for this type of behavior vary, but they often stem from a belief that the profit motive is the major organizational objective of a firm. Meeting the profit objective at the expense of what is considered to be responsible ethical behavior is a fact of life in business practice today. There exists a conflict between what is said about ethical standards and what is actually practiced in many organizations.

Sometimes, the business attitude that "if it works, it's okay" pervades an organization. Of course, such an attitude compromises ethical standards. The honesty and integrity of those who are affected may be taxed, and guilt feelings may result. Because loyalty to the company is a basic tenet of ethical conduct, an "anything that makes it okay" philosophy can have very harmful effects. Once formed, the philosophy may be carried outside the organization and may even be conveyed to family, friends, and society in general.

What can companies do to develop and implement a strong sense of ethics? A first step is to develop a set of standards that defines what behavior or conduct is expected of each employee. These standards should be written as policy and should be communicated to all employees. Openness, trust, and good interpersonal relations help to foster this communication. However, written policies do not ensure ethical behavior.

Leadership for appropriate ethical behavior should come from top management; it will then filter down to the employees. Managers should demonstrate the behavior that the policy dictates, and they should encourage feedback. Following this procedure is especially important because of the special influence that supervisors have on their employees. As discussed earlier in the text, reference groups have a strong influence on the behavior of the groups' members, on those who aspire to become members, and on those who are loyal to the group. As a group, those who work for a company need a mechanism that enforces and regulates its standards. This mechanism should include appropriate disciplinary action for violations of these standards. As with any corporate policy, companies need to monitor their ethics policies to maintain their integrity.

Many organizations today have developed ethical standards that every member must follow. One example is that of the National Association of Acountants "Standards of Ethical Conduct for Management Accountants," as shown in Figure F-1.

STANDARDS OF ETHICAL CONDUCT FOR MANAGEMENT ACCOUNTANTS

Management accountants have an obligation to the organizations they serve, their profession, the public, and themselves to maintain the highest standards of ethical conduct. In recognition of this obligation, the National Association of Accountants has promulgated the following standards of ethical conduct for management accountants. Adherence to these standards is integral to achieving the objectives of management accounting. Management accountants shall not commit acts contrary to these standards nor shall they condone the commission of such acts by others within their organizations.

Competence

Management accountants have a responsibility to:

- Maintain an appropriate level of professional competence by ongoing development of their knowledge and skills.
- Perform their professional duties in accordance with relevant laws, regulations, and technical standards.
- Prepare complete and clear reports and recommendations after appropriate analyses of relevant and reliable information.

FIGURE F-1 A set of ethical standards. Used with Permission of the National Association of Accountants.

Confidentiality

Management accountants have a responsiblity to:

- Refrain from disclosing confidential information acquired in the course of their work except when authorized, unless legally obligated to do so.
- Inform subordinates as appropriate regarding the confidentiality of information acquired in the course of their work and monitor their activities to assure the maintenance of that confidentiality.
- Refrain from using or appearing to use confidential information acquired in the course of their work for unethical or illegal advantage either personally or through third parties.

Integrity

Management accountants have a responsibility to:

- Avoid actual or apparent conflicts of interest and advise all appropriate parties of any potential conflict.
- Refrain from engaging in any activity that would prejudice their ability to carry out their duties ethically.
- Refuse any gift, favor, or hospitality that would influence or would appear to influence their actions.
- Refrain from either actively or passively subverting the attainment of the organization's legitimate and ethical objectives.
- Recognize and communicate professional limitations or other constraints that would preclude responsible judgment or successful performance of an activity.
- Communicate unfavorable as well as favorable information and professional judgments or opinions.
- Refrain from engaging in or supporting any activity that would discredit the profession.

Objectivity

Management accountants have a responsibility to:

- Communicate information fairly and objectively.
- Disclose fully all relevant information that could reasonably be expected to influence an intended user's understanding of the reports, comments, and recommendations presented.

FIGURE F-1 (continued)

INDEX

Page numbers in *italics* refer to figures.